HISTORICAL ENCYCLOPEDIA OF AMERICAN LABOR

HISTORICAL ENCYCLOPEDIA OF AMERICAN LABOR

VOLUME 1
A–O

Edited by
Robert E. Weir and James P. Hanlan

GREENWOOD PRESS
Westport, Connecticut • London

Library of Congress Cataloging-in-Publication Data

Historical encyclopedia of American labor / edited by Robert Weir and James P. Hanlan.
p. cm.
Includes bibliographical references and index.
ISBN 0-313-31840-9 (set : alk. paper)—ISBN 0-313-32863-3 (vol. 1 : alk. paper)—ISBN 0-313-32864-1 (vol. 2 : alk. paper)
1. Labor—United States—History—Encyclopedias. 2. Labor movement—United States—History—Encyclopedias. 3. Industrial relations—United States—History—Encyclopedias. 4. Labor laws and legislation—United States—History—Encyclopedias. I. Title: Encyclopedia of American labor. II. Weir, Robert E., 1952– III. Hanlan, James P.
HD8066.H57 2004
331.88'0973'03—dc21 2003052847

British Library Cataloguing in Publication Data is available.

Library of Congress Catalog Card Number: 2003052847

ISBN: 0-313-31840-9 (set)
0-313-32863-3 (vol. 1)
0-313-32864-1 (vol. 2)

First published in 2004

Greenwood Press, 88 Post Road West, Westport, CT 06881
An imprint of Greenwood Publishing Group, Inc.
www.greenwood.com

Printed in the United States of America

The paper used in this book complies with the Permanent Paper Standard issued by the National Information Standards Organization (Z39.48–1984).

10 9 8 7 6 5 4 3 2 1

Every reasonable effort has been made to track down the owners of copyright materials in this book, but in some instances this has proven impossible. The editors and publisher will be glad to receive information leading to more complete acknowledgments in subsequent printings of the book and in the meantime extend their apologies for any omissions.

Contents

Acknowledgments

The magnitude of this project makes it inevitable that small errors will occur. We take full responsibility for such slip-ups, although we have taken pains to ensure that the overall integrity of the historical record has not been compromised.

Our codicils aside, we are very proud of this work. That is in no small part due to the outstanding support we got from the labor history community and from Greenwood Press. When we put out a call for contributors to the H-Labor LISTSERV discussion group, we were overwhelmed by the number of those who responded, as well as by their generosity, knowledge, and desire to help. There are too many to list individually, but their names are listed with their entries and in the front matter, and we encourage readers to seek out their work. We thank each and every contributor.

Several individuals went above and beyond the call of duty in helping bring this project to fruition. Professor Weir's undergraduate labor history class at Bay Path College helped with some of the initial research in the fall of 2000. He wishes to thank Lisa Barber, Michele Bernier, Cheryl Conley, Yasmin Correa, Pauline Gladstone, Heather Hite, Shalynn Hunt, Leslie Juntunen, Maria Medina, Sara Pleva, Carina Reid, Maria Ruotolo, Aryu Sunyoto, and Teri Voight for their invaluable assistance. Professor Hanlan also drew upon the hard work of the students at Worcester Polytechnic Institute enrolled in his labor history seminar. They served as a sounding board and an inspiration. His colleagues Kent Ljungquist, Robert W. Thompson, Edmund Hayes, and Penny Rock provided companionship, counsel, and the best of friendship that any college faculty member could hope for. They showed me the joys of interdisciplinary and interdepartmental collegiality. I owe them much. Likewise I thank Provost John F. Carney for providing release time.

Our friend Scott Molloy, who directs the labor center at the University of Rhode Island, toiled long and hard on behalf of the project. Scott not only served on the advisory board, but he also enlisted his graduate students in the project and wrote numerous entries. A special thanks goes to another good friend and colleague, Bruce Cohen of Worcester State College. Other than our own names, Bruce's name appears more than any other in these volumes. Whenever we were stuck for coverage, we contacted Bruce and he took over our troublesome topics, to say nothing of the dozens of entries for which he actually volunteered. Bruce inspired both of us through his dedication to teaching and scholarship and especially through his genuine and heartfelt commitment to the well-being of the men and women who work and struggle to earn their livings.

The staff at the George Meany Memorial Archives at the National Labor College in Silver Spring, Maryland, were extremely generous in helping track down images and in providing support materials for the project. A special thank you goes to Lynda DeLoach at the archives and to Bob Reynolds, who edits the wonderful *Labor's Heritage* from the same location. They helped make Professor Weir's research and visit to the archives an absolute delight.

Greenwood Press could not have been more accommodating. Barbara Rader, the executive editor of the School and Public Library Reference division, got the ball rolling and showed great confidence in the editors' ability to get the job done. She then turned the editors over to the capable hands of Kevin Ohe and John Wagner, who shepherded the project to completion. Elizabeth Kincaid did a fine job of tracking down photos. The editors are indebted to Greenwood for their faith in them and for making this a quality work.

* * *

I would like to thank my wife, Emily, for her ongoing love and support. She is also the most affable research partner that one could hope to have. I am truly blessed to be able to share life's road with her.

In the middle of this project, I was fortunate enough to be a Fulbright scholar in New Zealand. I want to thank Jim Hanlan for taking up the slack while I was on the adventure of a lifetime. I had endless hours of fascinating discussions with Kiwi colleagues like Melanie Nolan and Pat Moloney at Victoria University, Jim McAloon at Lincoln University, Kerry Taylor at Massey University, Miles Fairburn and Graeme Dunstan at the University of Canterbury, and Tom Brooking and Erik Olssen at the University of Otago. My conversations with these individuals helped shape my words and thoughts in more ways than I can count. So too did my time at the Alexander Turnbull Library in Wellington, where I learned so much more not only about New Zealand labor history but also about American history. Many thanks to Frank Rogers, who came to one of my Turnbull talks and proceeded to share his wisdom with me, and to John Martin, the senior historian with the historical branch of the Department of the Interior and one of the most careful researchers I've ever met. A special thank you to Janet Horncy and Margaret Calder at the Turnbull Library, who gave me the freedom to pursue various research interests, but also made me feel like part of their extended families. And finally, a thank you to Jenny Gill and her staff at Fulbright New Zealand. You folks are simply the best!

I would like to dedicate my part of this work to my father, Archie Weir, a longtime union member, who died on April 11, 2002. His loss is deeply felt, but his fighting spirit lives on.

Robert E. Weir

I am indebted more than I can express to my wife, Gaye D. (Francis) Hanlan. She tolerated my distractions and absences and eased my burdens through this long project. Likewise, my children, George, Janet, and Jamo, served as promise for what the future can hold. I would like to express my thanks to the Lowell Central Labor Council, which, many years ago, provided a scholarship for my undergraduate education.

I dedicate my part of this work to the memory of my father and mother, George J. and Cecilia G. (Tynan) Hanlan. They knew what it was to endure a long and painful strike and to persevere. My father's pride in craftsmanship was exemplary. Together my parents inspired my life.

James P. Hanlan

Preface

Compiling the *Historical Encyclopedia of American Labor* has been a daunting task, to say the least. Like most historians, each of us is trained in a narrow specialty. Our long years of teaching experience have broadened us, but there were, invariably, gaps in our knowledge. Luckily, the labor history community is stocked with numerous bright and affable individuals who were ready to lend their expertise to the project. We thank them profusely and without them could not have finished these volumes.

The project was imposing because we knew from the outset that some professional labor educators were going to take umbrage with how we covered certain topics, what we covered, and what we left out. Our only defense is to say that this is *not* a collection for experts in the field. Ours is a guide for those starting research projects, writing school reports, or familiarizing themselves with hitherto unknown people, ideas, events, and organizations. It is designed primarily for public libraries, college and university library reference sections, high school libraries, and general repositories. Although we certainly hope that labor research centers, unions, and graduate schools find our efforts useful, we would be the last to say that the *Historical Encyclopedia* is the final word on *any* of the subjects it contains.

The *Historical Encyclopedia* offers almost 400 entries covering unions, union leaders, labor-related events, important statutes and court cases, and labor terminology. The entries are thoroughly cross-referenced, with mentions of other related entries highlighted upon their first appearance in the text of any particular entry. Entries conclude with a listing of suggested readings for those wishing to read in more detail on a particular subject. The *Historical Encyclopedia* is also illustrated with numerous photographs and includes an appendix containing excerpts from fifty-eight labor-related primary documents, including items such as statutes, interviews with workers, passages from the autobiographies of labor leaders, union documents, congressional testimony, and newspaper and magazine articles on labor topics and events. Finally, as a quick reference supplement to the entry readings, the *Historical Encyclopedia* offers a bibliography of important books and Web sites on labor-related topics and also includes a detailed subject index to provide quick, in-depth access to the information in the entries.

It is easy for experts immersed in the intricacies of research to forget that the general public knows little or nothing about American labor history. Most high school textbooks give scant attention to labor history, and our recent perusal of a half dozen popular college U.S. history survey texts reveals that among labor leaders only Terence Powderly, Samuel Gompers, A. Philip Randolph, Mary Jones, John L. Lewis, and Cesar Chavez are mentioned with any degree of regularity. Likewise, the only labor actions to warrant much coverage are the eight-hour-movement, the railroad strikes of 1877, the Pullman and Homestead strikes in the 1890s, the sit-down strikes of the 1930s, and the Professional Air Traffic Controllers Organization (PATCO) walkout of 1981. And even then, the operative word is "mentioned." Thorough discussions of the arc of labor history are noticeably absent. It has been more than four decades since the new social history admonished historians to consider race, class, and gender when writing history. Our observations reveal that class largely remains a junior partner within the troika.

When we began this project, we met with many people, scoured the indexes of numerous labor history textbooks, put out calls on the World Wide Web, and endlessly brainstormed. Our question was a basic one: *What would individuals with little or no background in labor history need to learn if they wished to begin studying the subject?* We tried to remember our own initial forays into the subject and Professor Weir recalled his high school teaching days. Experts may be dismayed to discover that cherished topics they've been researching for years are absent from this work. Our exclusion of topics is in no way a value judgment of their relative importance. Neither of us holds to elitist views of history that privilege some topics and individuals as more important than others. Our main criterion for choosing topics was simply the likelihood of a researcher to encounter it in the initial stages of a bigger project. We also endeavored to be as inclusive as possible on matters pertaining to race, gender, and ethnicity, but the fact is—and we decry it in numerous entries—the organized labor movement in the United States has been distressingly dominated by white males. Numerous entries on nonorganized labor made their way into the work as a way of partially addressing this imbalance.

Throughout the project, we remained cognizant that we were writing an encyclopedia. In that spirit, we opted to present general knowledge rather than specialized research, though we apologize in advance for what will seem to experts gross simplifications. We also opted, whenever possible, to avoid technical language, jargon, and arcane terminology. The staff at Greenwood continually reminded us that our target audience is a general one, and we tried our best to serve that readership. Those seeking to expand their understanding of American labor leaders not covered in these volumes are directed to another Greenwood publication, Gary Fink's superb *Biographical Dictionary of American*

Labor Leaders. We had to be very selective in choosing specific unions to include, but most labor unions past and present can be researched further on the World Wide Web, and several have outstanding Web sites that surpass any efforts on our part. The same is true for most of the events and terms we present. Good public, college, and university libraries are also filled with fine works from professional historians—many of whom we are proud to name as friends and colleagues—and we hope readers will consult them. Like all encyclopedias, this one is designed to make readers want to learn more. If it inspires novices to plumb depths we could not, our job will have been well done.

Robert E. Weir
Florence, Massachusetts

James P. Hanlan
Worcester, Massachusetts

Entry List

A

Adair v. The United States. *Adair v. The United States* 208 U.S. 161 (1908), addressed the legitimacy of **yellow-dog contracts**, agreements whereby workers were compelled to pledge, as a condition of their employment, that they would not join a union. The *Adair* case tested the constitutionality of a provision of the **Erdman Act** (1898), which prohibited employers from discriminating against workers on interstate railways because of their union membership. The Supreme Court majority in the *Adair* case found these provisions of the Erdman Act unconstitutional as a violation both of personal liberty and property rights. Following Adair, the court ruled, in *Coppage v. Kansas*, 236 U.S. I (1915), that similar state laws were likewise unconstitutional. Justice Oliver Wendell Holmes, Jr. dissented, writing in *Coppage* that, "a workman not unnaturally may believe that only by belonging to a union can he secure a contract that shall be fair to him." Holmes went on to argue that, under the social circumstances of the time, if reasonable men held that only by joining a union could a worker hope for a fair contract, then the outlawing of yellow-dog contracts could be a necessity to establish the equality of position that genuine liberty of contracts requires. However, Holmes's eloquent dissent did not sway his brethren on the court, and yellow-dog contracts remained legal until the **Norris-LaGuardia Act** of 1932.

Suggested Reading: Alfred H. Kelly and Winfred Harbison, *The American Constitution: Its Origin and Development*, 1976.

James P. Hanlan

Adamson Act (1916). The Adamson Act established an eight-hour day for railroad workers engaged in interstate commerce, stipulated that railroads could not dock their pay to reflect the reduction in hours, and mandated that companies had to pay railroad employees time and a half for **overtime**. President Woodrow Wilson signed the bill largely because he feared that a planned strike by railroad brotherhoods would disrupt the defense industry, but the Adamson Act proved to be influential in the **eight-hour movement**'s long struggle to reduce the work week. The Adamson Act also marked the first measure by Congress to regulate hours of private workers.

Although some federal employees won an eight-hour day as early as 1868, it was not strictly enforced, nor did it expand to the private sphere as quickly as activists hoped. Neither Congress nor the courts was inclined to enforce the eight-hour day; it was not until 1908 that the Supreme Court upheld the validity of various state eight-hour bills. Hours were notoriously long in the railroad industry and the industry was wracked by numerous bitter and dramatic strikes in the late-nineteenth and early-twentieth centuries. These included the **Great Labor Uprising** of 1877, various strikes during the **Great Upheaval** of the 1880s, the Great Burlington strike of 1888, the New York Central strike of 1890, the **Pullman** boycott of 1894, and a strike against the Illinois Central that lasted from 1911 into 1914. By 1916, nearly all railroad employees worked at least nine hours and many worked more. Various labor organizations, including the **Knights of Labor**, the **American Railway Union**, and several railroad brotherhoods called upon the government to either seize or tightly regulate railroads. Although much rail traffic was subject to the provisions of the Interstate Commerce Act of 1887 and the Elkins Act of 1903, Congress and various presidents remained aloof until four brotherhoods threatened a strike in 1916.

The Adamson Act was hailed by most railway brotherhoods and, in 1918, the government actually seized control of the railroads for the duration of World War I. After the war, railroads began to decline as automobile traffic increased. The greatest impact of the Adamson Act lay in the precedent it set for government intervention in defining a fair day's toil. The 1938 **Fair Labor Standards Act** reduced the work week to forty-four hours. A 1940 amendment to the act lowered it to forty hours, thereby establishing the long-sought eight-hour work day.

Suggested Readings: R. Alton Lee, ed., *The Encyclopedia of the United States of America, Past and Present*, 1997; Walter Licht, *Working for the Railroad*, 1983; Paul Taylor, *The ABC-CLIO Companion to the American Labor Movement*, 1993.

Robert E. Weir

Bruce Cohen

Adkins v. Children's Hospital. *Adkins v. Children's Hospital* 261 U.S. 525 (1923) involved the issue of **protective labor legislation**. Protective legislation was originally designed only for women and children. The Supreme Court upheld the constitutionality of such legislation in its 1908 decision in ***Muller v. Oregon***, 208 U.S. 412. *Muller* dealt with restrictions on the maximum hours of work per day. In its decision, the Court maintained that women, just as children, constitute a special category of workers in need of protection. In the aftermath of *Muller*, supporters of social welfare legislation, in particular the National Consumers' League, lobbied to expand restrictions of work hours to include male workers. This strategy proved to be effective. In *Bunting v. Oregon*, 243 U.S. 426 (1917), the court upheld a ten-hour-day statute for male workers, but granted that these hours might be exceeded if employers provided financial compensation for overtime work.

In contrast to *Muller*, *Adkins* was concerned with earnings rather than hours. In the spirit of protective legislation, some states had adopted **minimum-wage** laws for women and children. Endorsement of these statutes, however, was slower than maximum-hours legislation and, in 1923, only seventeen states possessed a minimum-wage law. After a wage board in the District of Columbia had established and enforced a minimum salary, the Congress Hall Hotel in Washington, D.C., fired their female elevator operator, Willie Lyons. According to the new law, the hotel would have to pay Lyons a monthly wage of $71.50 instead of the $35 they already paid her, which was the market rate. As a consequence, Lyons lost her job to a man. Disgruntled, and fearing that she would never find another job in D.C. as long as the minimum-wage law existed, she joined female employees at the local Children's Hospital to contest the constitutionality of the statute. In arguing before the Supreme Court, proponents of the minimum-wage law focused on the special situation of female workers. They argued that, as women were paid only about 50–65 percent of men's wages, their health as well as their morals were endangered. This argument failed to convince the majority of judges. They decided that a minimum-wage statute interfered with the freedom of contract. As women had gained full citizenship rights in 1920, when the Nineteenth Amendment granted them the vote, they no longer required the special protection of the law, as they were just as able to negotiate a fair-labor contract as were male workers.

Adkins constituted a strong departure from the spirit of protective legislation that had, undoubtedly, not always been beneficial to female workers. Protective laws oftentimes narrowed their job choices and restrictions on working hours limited women's earnings, which they otherwise could have increased through **overtime**. The latter option the court had held explicitly open to men. As a back door to social welfare legislation, protective laws could be used to improve the situation of all workers regardless of their gender. But, while the Supreme Court had gone along with this strategy in regard to hours laws, it did not support the regulation of wages. Although only concerned with women and minors, the *Adkins* decision had, in the long run, a negative impact on male workers as well. The judges also came to a rather unrealistic conclusion regarding female workers' ability to negotiate labor conditions. Because of sex discrimination, only a limited number of jobs in a few industries were open to women. Here, they congregated in positions that required a minimum of training. As employers assumed that women would only work for a few years and then drop out of the labor force to get married, they saw no need to provide training or promote female workers into better paying jobs. All working women, therefore, had to compete for a small number of low-paying positions. In a discriminatory and highly competitive labor market, female employees possessed little bargaining power.

Men, of course, also faced a competitive labor market. But their interests were aggressively defended by labor unions. Union representatives frequently held the same assumptions about women workers as did employers. They did not regard women as permanent and autonomous members of the labor force. Rather, they saw them either as dependents who labored to supplement the family income or as frivolous creatures who needed "pin money" for trinkets and amusements. Most unions assumed that women's interests would be sufficiently represented by fighting for a wage for the male breadwinner that was high enough to allow his female dependents to stay at home. Labor unions therefore assumed that all women workers were protected members of a family unit. This assessment, however, was frequently untrue. Many female workers were either single or had to take care of their own dependents. Only under the influence of the Great Depression and New Deal legislation would the Supreme Court depart from its freedom-of-contract doctrine. In *West Coast Hotel v. Parish*, 300 U.S. 379 (1937), it overruled *Adkins* and granted minimum wages to women and minors. Here, the court acknowledged that the special situation of these underprivileged employees made it almost impossible for them to bargain for a living wage. Social welfare proponents soon tried to extend minimum wage laws to men. This success finally materialized with the Supreme Court's 1941 ruling in *United States v. Darby*, 312 U.S. 100 (1941).

Suggested Readings: Joan Biskupic and Elder Witt, *The Supreme Court and the Powers of the American Government*, 1997; Joan Hoff, *Law, Gender, and Injustice: A Legal History of U.S. Women*, 1991; Alice Kessler-Harris, *Out to Work: A History of Wage-Earning Women in the United States*, 1982.

Babette Faehmel

Affirmative Action. Affirmative Action is a term that means taking positive steps to compensate for past injustices that have left some members of society at a competitive economic and social disadvantage. It originated in the field of labor relations, having been coined by National Labor Relations Board (NLRB) officials to direct employers to stop unfair labor practices and to comply with the 1935 **National Labor Relations Act (NLRA)**. Ironically, union compliance was not mandated by the NLRA, thus some segments of the organized labor movement have been among those least compliant with affirmative action principles. Affirmative action became associated with equal employment opportunities after 1941, when President Franklin D. Roosevelt created the **Fair Employment Practices Committee (FEPC)**, which was eventually led by two ex-NLRB officials, Father Francis J. Haas and Malcolm Ross. When Ross became FEPC chairman, "affirmative action" began to appear in FEPC directives to employers that discriminated against workers because of their race, creed, color, or national origin. Although it never fully defined what affirmative action meant, the FEPC expected that employers would take positive steps to end discrimination and ensure full participation of minority workers in the war effort.

The concept of affirmative action was transformed after 1961, when President John F. Kennedy issued an executive order requiring federal contractors to take affirmative action when hiring workers. Affirmative action was also a centerpiece of Title VII of the 1964 Civil Rights Act. As the Office of Federal Contract Compliance (OFCC) began to define the ambiguous term in the 1960s and 1970s, affirmative action in the federal contracting system became synonymous with goals and timetables, though critics called them "quotas." Conservatives frequently repeat charges of quotas, asserting that they produce "reverse discrimination" against whites by undermining supposedly color-blind principles in the U.S. Constitution. The 1978 Supreme Court case *University of California Regents v. Bakke* greatly curtailed all quota plans, and there have been many affirmative action challenges since then. The court routinely takes the view that the central goal of affirmative action is correcting past patterns of discrimination, but the legal future of affirmative action is cloudy.

Until the mid-1980s, the Equal Employment Opportunity Commission (EEOC) was instrumental in advancing affirmative action. Created in 1964 and strengthened in 1972, the EEOC has been in charge of enforcing the fair employment provisions of the 1964 Civil Rights Act. Both the EEOC and the OFCC linked job bias to the concept of "disparate impact" (i.e., group-specific impact) and argued that affirmative action is a necessary corrective to disparate impact. In recent years the EEOC—partly staffed by political appointees—has been less aggressive in advancing such ideas as the agency has fallen victim to ideological and partisan differences.

Affirmative action remains a hotly contested issue in American politics. Both business and labor have had mixed reactions to the concept. Some employers have adopted affirmative action plans without much protest. A few labor unions such as the **United Auto Workers** and the **United Steelworkers of America** have been strong backers of affirmative action programs. Other unions—including firefighters' unions—view affirmative action as antithetical to the **seniority** system and have mounted legal challenges. Some unions, most notably those in the building trades, have even been plagued by **rank-and-file** violence from members opposed to affirmative action. The intense nature of the debate surrounding affirmative action suggests that it will remain a potent political issue for some time.

Suggested Readings: Herman Belz, *Equality Transformed: A Quarter-Century of Affirmative Action*, 1991; Hugh Davis Graham, *The Civil Rights Era: Origin and Development of National Policy*, 1990; Paul Moreno, *From Direct Action to Affirmative Action: Fair Employment Law and Policy in America, 1933–1972*, 1997.

Andrew E. Kersten

AFL-CIO. *See individual entries for the American Federation of Labor and the Congress of Industrial Organizations.*

African American Labor. *See Minority Labor and also entries on specific individuals and organizations.*

Agency Fee. An agency fee is a sum paid by employees in a **union shop** who do not want to join the union that represents that shop. That payment is usually slightly less than the dues paid by union members.

Some employees object to their dues being used for political lobbying for causes they do not support, while others are philosophically opposed to unionism. In addition, organized **right-to-work** groups oppose coerced paying of union dues under any circumstances, claiming that paying or not paying dues is a matter of individual choice. Appeals to personal liberty notwithstanding, paying or withholding dues is more complicated than opponents claim. Unions claim, with some justification, that the very act of **collective bargaining** brings benefits to all who work in a particular establishment, irrespective of their desires to belong or not belong to a union. Employers sign a union contract that covers all workers, hence, the workplace is collective, not individual, by nature. By this reckoning, employees who refuse to pay dues are "free riders" attempting to reap the benefits of union bargaining without paying for them.

The agency fee has emerged in many workplaces as an attempted compromise. Employees choosing not to join a union pay the union what is essentially a fee for negotiating their contract. That amount is usually somewhat lower than regular union dues, the deduction based on calculations of how much a union spends on matters not directly related to representing workers within the specific workplace. Agency fees are most common among public employees, many of whom are barred from specific political activity, thus making it easier for them to object to union money being spent for political purposes.

Not surprisingly, there is great debate over the percentage of union dues that goes directly to serving local unions. In 2000, the U.S. Court of Appeals ruled in *Penrod v. the* ***International Brotherhood of Teamsters*** that the Teamsters had to reveal to members how much money was spent on political campaigns. The *Chicago Teachers Union v. Hudson* Supreme Court ruling further stipulated that unions must submit to independent audits to justify expenses. Much of this legal activity has been funded by virulently anti-union groups like the National Right to Work Legal Defense Foundation, which objects even to agency fees. Agency fees are likely to be a point of future contention and Supreme Court challenges, by both unions and their opponents, are probable.

Suggested Reading: National Right to Work, http://www.nrtw.org.

Robert E. Weir

Agency Shop. *See Union Shop.*

Agent Provocateur. The term *agent provocateur* refers to a company-hired infiltrator who poses as a unionist to discredit the union. They seek to intensify factional strife within an organization, create friction between labor groups, or incite unionists to make rash statements or take violent action. The ultimate goal is to make worker organizations liable to criminal prosecution or discredit them before public opinion. Agent provocateurs aim at developing an atmosphere of hysteria against labor unions, placing the blame for violence on organizers. They prepare the ground for the arrest of key activists, the prohibition of union publications, and campaigns of general repression. Their tactics include defamation, starting incidents at union meetings and demonstrations, encouraging reckless acts, bombings, sabotage, and arson. A favored tactic is spreading rumors that key union members are spies for employers or the police. This both creates tension within the union and helps conceal the agent provocateur's identity.

Agent provocateurs often create the conditions they wish to have suppressed. Many historians believe that **Pinkerton** detective, agent James McParland, was responsible for much of the violence that occurred during his investigation of the **Molly Maguires** in the 1870s. An agent provocateur may also have thrown the bomb that precipitated the **Haymarket** tragedy in 1886, and they are certainly responsible for a variety of mine bombings and train derailments in labor disputes that engulfed those industries in the nineteenth and twentieth centuries. The 1937 **La Follette Senate Committee** investigation of labor relations and civil liberties revealed widespread use of agent provocateurs. Although the use of such individuals is illegal, allegations circulate of continued use by employers.

This World War I poster equates labor agitation with aiding the enemy. © George Meany Memorial Archives.

Suggested Readings: Anthony Bimba, *The Molly Maguires*, 1950; Gary Fink, *Fulton Bag and Cotton Mills Strike of 1914–1915: Espionage, Labor Conflict, and New South Industrial Relations*, 1993; Leo Huberman, *The Labor Spy Racket*, 1971.

Evan Daniel

Agricultural Labor Relations Act (ALRA). The Agricultural Labor Relations Act became law in California on June 5, 1975. The ALRA is designed to protect the rights of farmworkers, secure stability in labor relations, and prevent both employers and unions from interfering with farmworkers' rights.

The ALRA was born out of the organizing efforts of **Cesar Chavez, Dolores Huerta**, and others associated with efforts to unionize field and migrant workers. The ALRA allows agricultural workers to make their own decisions about whether they wish a union to negotiate working conditions, hours, and wages. In locales where workers select a union, employers are required to bargain in good faith. It is also unlawful to discharge, punish, discriminate against, or refuse to rehire an employee because he or she supports a union or seeks better working conditions. The Agricultural Labor Relations Board oversees, interprets, and enforces the ALRA. Its members are appointed by the governor and confirmed by the California state senate. There is also a general counsel, appointed by the governor, whose purpose is to investigate unfair labor practice allegations and determine whether or not an official complaint should be filed. The counsel also presents the case to an administrative law judge whose decision may be appealed to the Board.

Advocates hoped that the ALRA would become a model for agreements elsewhere. Thus far, its impact beyond California has been minimal. Critics complain that the ALRA has become politicized and its overall effectiveness dependent upon the ideology and attitudes of elected officials making appointments to the Board.

Suggested Readings: Maralyn Edid, *Farm Labor Organizing: Trends and Prospects*, 1994; Susan Ferriss and Ricardo Sandoval, *The Fight in the Fields: Cesar Chavez and the Farmworkers Movement*, 1997.

T. Jason Soderstrum

Agricultural Workers Organizing Committee. The Agricultural Workers Organizing Committee merged with the National Farm Workers Association (NFWA) during the Delano grape strike in 1965 to form the **United Farm Workers of America (UFW)**. The roots of the union can be traced back to 1958, when **Dolores Huerta** and Father Thomas McCullough complained to directors of the American Federation of Labor-Congress of Industrial Organizations (AFL-CIO) about conditions and wages in California fields. When the federation declined to assist field workers, McCullough and the Catholic Church formed the Agricultural Workers Association (AWA). One year later, the AFL-CIO decided to provide McCullough with seed money and several professional organizers. The newly christened Agricultural Workers Organizing Committee (AWOC) chose Huerta as its secretary-treasurer and she recruited Larry Itliong, an effective advocate for Filipino workers.

The AWOC negotiated some pay raises, but had trouble recruiting Mexican and Chicano workers, who were a majority of the state of California's field workers. Many of the AWOC's top organizers were Anglos who had never worked with Mexican workers before. Huerta resigned in 1959, after an unsuccessful attempt to convince AWOC leaders to invite **Cesar Chavez** to train organizers to work with Spanish-speaking workers. Yet, the AWOC was effective with other groups, particularly Filipinos and Hindus. On September 8, 1965, Filipino workers in nine work camps surrounding Delano went on strike. Workers discovered that the nine growers who had raised their wages to $1.40 were only willing to pay them $1.00. The workers consulted with Larry Itliong, who got no response from the growers. A strike vote was taken, but Itliong realized that the support of Mexican and Chicano workers was crucial for any hope of success. He consulted with Chavez and on September 16, Chicano and Mexican workers agreed to join the AWOC in their strike. With the Mexicans joining the Filipinos, 48 ranches were to be picketed. Working out of Filipino Hall in Delano, Itliong and other officials invited Mexicans and other strikers to dine with them and used other means to strengthen the ties between the two unions. AWOC leaders also called upon the AFL-CIO to enlist the support of other unions and politicians in America. In 1966, NFWA and AWOC formed the United Farm Workers Organizing Committee, later renamed the United Farm Workers.

Suggested Readings: Joan London and Henry Anderson, *So Shall Ye Reap*, 1970; Eugene Nelson, *Huelga: The First Hundred Days of the Great Delano Grape Strike*, 1966; Craig Scharlin and Lilia V. Villanueva, *Philip Vera Cruz: A Personal History of Filipino Immigrants and the Farmworkers Movement*, 1992.

T. Jason Soderstrum

Amalgamated Association of Iron, Steel, and Tin Workers (AAISTW). The Amalgamated Association of Iron, Steel, and Tin Workers was an early attempt to organize the iron and steel industry, which was among the most union-resistant of all American industries prior to the 1930s. Its story illustrates the challenges facing American steel workers seeking to improve their lives. The AAISTW was formed in 1876 when the Sons of Vulcan; the Associated Brotherhood of Iron and Steel Heaters, Rollers, and Roughers; and the Iron and Steel Roll Hands of the United States merged. Shortly thereafter, the Nailers' union also joined. At the time of the merger, the union had 3,775 members.

The Amalgamated was a conservative **craft union** that was noted for its co-operation with management and its distaste for **strikes**. In the 1880s, AAISTW president William Weihe did not even oppose the twelve-hour/seven-day workweek imposed by many employers. Nonetheless, the union often found itself embroiled in strikes against concerns owned by steel magnate Andrew Carnegie, despite the latter's hollow brag that he favored working people. The AAISTW lost strikes against Carnegie concerns in 1881, 1884, and 1885. In the 1884 strike in Beaver Falls, Pennsylvania, and the 1885 action against the Edgar Thompson works in Pittsburgh, Carnegie imported **scabs** to break the strike. In 1887, the AAISTW joined the newly formed **American Federation of Labor (AFL)**. The Amalgamated lost members after strikes in the 1880s, but rebuilt its strength to represent about 24,000 workers by the early 1890s.

The Amalgamated, a conservative union that represented only skilled and (for the most part) English-speaking workers, was willing to discuss concessions. Nevertheless, Carnegie and Henry Clay Frick, who managed Carnegie's giant Homestead works near Pittsburgh, decided to break the union. In 1892, although business and profits had been robust, Carnegie and Frick instituted large wage cuts and announced their intent to run the works as a non-union **open shop**. This precipitated the **Homestead steel strike**, one of the most dramatic and bitter clashes in American labor history. The AAISTW coordinated strike efforts, though it represented only about 800 of the 3,800 employees at the works. The strike ended in a rout of the workers; some wages were cut by as much as 60 percent and only about 400 workers—most of whom were not AAISTW members—got their jobs back. By the late 1890s, Homestead was known as one of the poorest communities in the country and its social problems were legion.

The AAISTW was eviscerated by the Homestead strike and was reduced to representing a handful of steel mills, mostly in the West. In 1901, and again in 1910, it attempted to organize U.S. Steel, a corporate conglomerate which formed when J. P. Morgan purchased Carnegie assets in 1901. Both attempts failed and by the 1910s, low pay and six twelve-hour days were the standard feature of most steel mills. The AAISTW also took part in the nation-wide **Steel Strike of 1919** led by **William Z. Foster**, which also failed. The union was so weakened that by the early 1930s it was a **federal labor union** within the AFL. In 1935, the Amalgamated had only 8,600 members. That year, **Phillip Murray** and the Steel Workers' Organizing Committee began to make inroads into the steel industry, and the AAISTW cast its lot with the **Congress of Industrial Organizations (CIO)**. When the **United Steelworkers of America** joined the CIO, the AAISTW ceased to exist as an independent entity.

Suggested Readings: David Brody, *Steelworkers in America: The Non-Union Era*, 1960; Sidney Lens, *The Labor Wars*, 1974; William Serrin, *Homestead*, 1993.

Bruce Cohen
Robert E. Weir

Amalgamated Clothing Workers of America (ACWA). The Amalgamated Clothing Workers of America was one of several garment workers unions formed to combat the exploitation of needle trades workers in the Progressive Era, and one of the nation's first successful **industrial unions** in that trade. It was officially formed on December 26, 1914, to address perceived weaknesses in its predecessor union, the United Garment Workers (UGW). The UGW was badly weakened by garment worker strikes in 1909–10, and it did not organize immigrant tailors involved in the production of men's suits and coats. The newly formed ACWA contained numerous Lithuanian, Italian, and Jewish members. **Sidney Hillman**, a Lithuanian Jew, was elected first president of the ACWA, and held the post until his death in 1946.

Unlike the UGW, the ACWA stayed outside of the **American Federation of Labor (AFL)** except for a brief time in 1933. Hillman and other ACWA members found the AFL structure too confining to accommodate industrial unionism and the militant tactics of the ACWA. It was one of the first unions to affiliate with the **Congress of Industrial Organizations (CIO)** in 1935. The ACWA also pioneered in delivering union-operated benefits for members, and developed such programs as unemployment insurance, free checking accounts, cooperative apartments, employer-paid health and life insurance schemes, and union daycare centers.

The ACWA engaged in numerous bitter strikes. A 1919 job action against Hart, Schaffner, and Marx established an industry standard of a forty-four-hour workweek. In 1934, the ACWA took part in a nation-wide **general strike** of textile workers and added 50,000 workers to its rolls. Although the strike was largely a failure, the ACWA continued to grow and Hillman became a key advisor to Roosevelt. In 1937, the CIO set up the Textile Workers Organizing Committee to expand membership and the ACWA often coordinated efforts with the newly formed Textile Workers Union of America (TWUA). Despite setbacks while attempting to organize Southern workers in **Operation Dixie**, by 1952, the ACWA was able to negotiate the first **master contract** (master agreement) in the menswear industry. The ACWA joined the AFL-CIO when the federations merged in 1955.

In 1963, the TWUA and ACWA tried to organize J. P. Stevens workers. Although the Supreme Court upheld a ruling in favor of the unions in 1967, it took a boycott and seventeen years before a contract was finally signed in 1980. (The Hollywood film *Norma Rae* depicts this struggle.) Other bitter battles included a strike and boycott against Oneita Knitting Mills in 1973, and a twenty-two-month campaign against Farrah that ended in 1974; both led to ACWA contracts. It also championed investigations into "brown lung" disease, a respiratory ailment associated with textile dust.

In the 1976, the ACWA and TWUA merged to form the American Clothing and Textile Workers Union (ACTWU). In the 1990s, ACTWU campaigned for national health insurance, reform of labor laws, and investigations into capital flight. It was unsuccessful in its opposition to the **North American Free Trade Agreement**. By the 1980s, however, the clothing industry was in severe decline. In 1995, various remaining unions, including ACTWU, merged to form the **Union of Needletrades, Industrial, and Textile Employees**.

Suggested Readings: Sue Davidson and Joan Jensen, eds., *A Needle, a Bobbin, a Strike*, 1984; Foster Dulles and Melvyn Dubofsky, *Labor in America*, 1993; Union of Needletrades, Industrial, and Textile Employees, http://www.uniteunion.org/research/history.html.

Michele Bernier

Robert E. Weir

Amalgamated Meat Cutters and Butcher Workmen of North America. The Amalgamated Meat Cutters and Butcher Workmen of North America was originally sanctioned by the **American Federation of Labor (AFL)** in 1897. It was an unusual AFL union because it attempted to organize both skilled and unskilled workers, although skilled butchers provided the early leadership. There had been earlier attempts to organize meat cutters, notably by the **Knights of Labor**, but those efforts faltered after the collapse of the 1886 Chicago stockyards strike.

The need for unionization was clear. During the last decade of the nineteenth century, the whole business of meat processing was dramatically transformed by new technology—such as refrigerated railroad boxcars—and by centralized production methods that concentrated butchering in large factory-like settings. The introduction of mass production butchering, the use of railroads to ship meat, and a burgeoning urban population dramatically transformed meat production from small, local producers to mass production. Meatcutting was dominated from the turn of the century to the 1970s by "the Big Four": Armour, Cudahy, Swift, and Wilson. Together these firms controlled 78 percent of national meat production in 1937.

In many ways, the meat industry foreshadowed what was soon to come in the automobile industry. Large-scale production was aided by the use of hoists, conveyors, endless chains, chutes, and moving benches. The assembly line of auto production was preceded by the *dis*assembly line of meat production, along with the attendant de-skilling of many butchering operations. The meat industry was labor intensive, like early auto production, and attracted European immigrant workers, women, and African Americans.

The conversion of living animals on the hoof to their constituent parts for human use was at best a messy and brutal business. In the meatpacking industry, as in the early auto industry, jobs were assigned according to national origin, gender, and race. This practice was a conscious decision by management to fight labor organization. The horrors of the meatpacking industry are chronicled in Upton Sinclair's 1906 novel *The Jungle*.

The Amalgamated grew slowly until the 1898 election of Michael Donnelly, a South Omaha sheep butcher. By the middle of 1900, the Amalgamated had 4,000 members. Rather than organize workers by particular skill, as had been the practice in nineteenth-century labor organizing, he chose to organize the union's workers by department and vowed to eliminate a labor aristocracy. Although this method worked, at least for the short term, the Amalgamated was never able to overcome the tension between skilled and unskilled workers in the same union locals. Nevertheless, by 1904 the Amalgamated was able to call out 28,000 Chicago packinghouse workers to strike for shorter working hours and better conditions. They were joined by thousands of packinghouse workers across the country.

Unfortunately for the Amalgamated, the 1904 strike and a similar action in 1921–22 were dismal failures. The packinghouses were simply too strong and used the tactic of pitting workers against one another. In both strikes, African Americans from the deep South were brought in by the trainload as **scabs**. Although the scabs were let go and the union workers returned to work after the strikes were settled, the fragmentation, racial mistrust, and hatred created by the packinghouses lingered. The Amalgamated retreated from the packinghouses but continued to organize skilled butchers in commercial and retail enterprises, behaving more like a typical AFL craft union.

During the great labor organizing surge of the 1930s, a rival union, the **United Packinghouse Workers of America (UPWA)** was organized by the **Congress of Industrial Organizations (CIO)** which focused on unskilled and industrial workers. The UPWA was able to create more solidarity among its immigrant, African American, and women workers than the Amalgamated had. Although the two unions competed for workers to a certain extent, they were able to cooperate in some labor actions in the late 1940s.

In the post–World War II era, the Amalgamated continued to organize retail butcher shops and chain stores, some meat packing plants, food processing plants, fur and leather workers, some migratory agricultural workers, and sheep shearers. By 1964, it boasted 350,000 members and was one of the AFL's larger unions. It was hardly radical, however, and its president, Pat Gorman, subscribed to AFL president **George Meany**'s particular brand of conservative **business unionism**, avoiding strikes and supporting, for example, American actions in the Vietnam War through 1973. In the late 1970s some high-ranking officials of the Amalgamated were convicted of crimes including federal charges of racketeering, conspiracy, extortion, illegal labor payments, tax evasion, and perjury.

By the late 1970s new competition in the industry, decentralization, and considerable anti-union pressure resulted in the consolidation of meatpacking unions. In 1979, the **United Food and Commercial Workers Union (UFCW)** was formed by a merger of the Retail Clerks International Union, the **Boot and Shoe Workers' Union**, and the Amalgamated. The Amalgamated thus ceased to exist as an independent union.

Suggested Readings: James Barrett, *Work and Community in the Jungle: Chicago's Packinghouse Workers, 1894–1922*, 1987; David Brody, *The Butcher Workmen: A Study of Unionization*, 1964; Rick Halpern, *Down on the Killing Floor: Black and White Workers in Chicago's Packinghouses, 1904–1954*, 1997.

Frank Koscielski

American Federation of Government Employees (AFGE). The American Federation of Government Employees is the nation's largest union representing federal civil-service employees. It is affiliated with the American Federation of Labor-Congress of Industrial Organizations (AFL-CIO) and its diverse membership includes airport screeners, correction officers, diplomats, lawyers, mine inspectors, scientists, and clerks. AFGE membership spreads across the United States and into several foreign lands where U.S. government personnel are posted. The bulk of its more than 1,750,000 members work in the greater Washington, D.C. area, and AFGE maintains its highest levels of representation among white-collar workers in the Department of Veterans Affairs, the Social Security Administration, and the Department of Justice.

Organizing public employees has been an especially difficult challenge. Local and state government often took a dim view of union efforts among taxpayer-supported employees, and many federal agencies have their budgets set by the U.S. Congress, a restraint that limits their power of **collective bargaining**. Moreover, the applicability of existing labor laws for public employees is not always clear. It was not until the 1912 Lloyd-La Follette Act that federal employees had any official right to organize—and that bill expressively forbade **strikes**. Many government workers are deemed "essential personnel," a designation that limits on-the-job action. In the past, public employee unions often fared poorly during strikes. During the **Boston police strike of 1919**, the government of the Commonwealth of Massachusetts fired most of the striking officers. Congress responded by making it illegal for police and firefighters in the District of Columbia to unionize, a law not repealed until 1939. More recently, more than three-quarters of the nation's air traffic controllers was fired by President Ronald Reagan during the 1983 **Professional Air Traffic Controllers Organization (PATCO)** strike.

Nonetheless, federal civil service workers have long felt the need to organize. In the nineteenth century, the civil service bureaucracy was small, but federal workers were notoriously overworked and underpaid. Navy yard employees struck for shorter hours in 1835 and 1836. In 1840, President Martin Van Buren signed a ten-hour bill for federal employees, and the **eight-hour-movement** found a receptive audience among federal workers. An eight-hour day was granted in 1868, but federal laborers and mechanics struggled for four years to restore the 20 percent wage cuts that came with it. Government employees periodically complained that the eight-hour rule was widely violated. Government workers achieved a small victory when Congress passed the Pendleton Act in 1883, which set up the Civil Service Commission to fill some federal jobs through examinations and qualifications rather than political patronage.

Both the **Knights of Labor** and the **American Federation of Labor** represented small numbers of federal workers, but progress was modest until the establishment of the National Federation of Federal Employees (NFFE), which received an AFL charter in 1917. The Great Depression ravaged the civil service, with layoffs, wage cuts, and supervisor favoritism as the order of the day. The AFGE formed when the NFFE disaffiliated with the AFL in 1931; those who wished to remain in the AFL formed AFGE in 1932. John Shaw was elected first AFGE president, but the work of chief organizer Helen McCarthy stands out as especially impressive. Within three years, McCarthy increased AFGE membership to over 20,000 organized into thirteen districts and more than 200 locals. The union's first major campaign was to restore wage cuts, an audacious undertaking during the depression. Wages did slowly rise, though this may have been due to an improving economy rather than AFGE pressure.

The union won the right for workers to determine their own beneficiaries for their retirement funds, and it increased the amount of sick leave an employee could accumulate. The 1935 **National Labor Relations Act (NLRA)** included government workers, but upheld the 1912 ban on strikes.

Both World War II and the Korean War led AFGE to curtail some union activities to meet national emergencies. The Federal Pay Act of 1945 gave government workers a nearly 16 percent pay increase, but the union's political voice was muted. The 1940 Hatch Act made political campaigning by federal employees illegal and forbade membership in ill-defined "subversive organizations." The 1947 **Taft-Hartley Act** reiterated Hatch Act political restrictions, imposed a **no-strike** clause on federal workers, and reversed perceived gains under the NLRA by defining government employee groups as "associations" rather than unions. Anti-communist hysteria in the late 1940s and early 1950s hampered union efforts, with the accusations of communist infiltration of the State Department, leveled by Senator Joseph McCarthy, making the AFGE susceptible to red-baiting.

AFGE won concessions on wages, **overtime** pay, and work transfers, but made only modest gains until the 1960 presidential election. President John Kennedy showed greater sensitivity for federal employees, and his Executive Order 10988 established relaxed rules for federal unions. It established three tiers of representation for federal employees, with those at the highest level enjoying full bargaining rights. Workers also gained wage increases, better **pensions**, and improved benefits. AFGE membership jumped from 61,000 in 1942 to over 108,000 in 1962. The AFGE enjoyed even greater membership surges after 1964, when President Lyndon Johnson's Great Society programs increased the size of the federal bureaucracy.

The **postal strike of 1970** altered the landscape for public employees. Although workers committed felonies by walking out, they ignored both government threats and the orders of union leadership to raise the strike. Neither NFFE nor AFGE members went on strike, but both organizations struggled to keep members from doing so. AFGE leaders appealed to the need to remain on the job while the United States was fighting in Vietnam, a call that resonated with some employees but alienated others. All government employees gained a 6 percent pay increase when the postal strike was settled but, more importantly, the nation's first successful government employees strike pointed to the potential strength of concerted power.

After 1972, federal employees struggled against changing public opinion and political adversity. Taxpayer revolts were exploited by conservatives, who often used civil-service employees as rhetorical whipping posts to rail against wasteful government expenditures. President Richard Nixon clashed with the AFGE and his successor, Gerald Ford, vetoed reform of the Hatch Act. Federal employees cheered the election of Jimmy Carter in 1976, and Carter's 1978 Civil Service Reform Act is a milestone for federal workers. It created a Federal Labor Relations Authority (FLRA) for federal workers that was modeled after the NLRA's board for private sector employees, and also established the Merit Systems Relations Board to protect workers not covered by the FLRA.

Government/employee relations deteriorated significantly with the election of Ronald Reagan in 1980. Reagan's anti-big-government rhetoric was matched by actions found objectionable by the AFGE and the NFFE. Reagan subcontracted (see **subcontracting**) government work to private sector employers, threatened to trim the federal bureaucracy, imposed a federal worker pay freeze, fought the union over extending **Occupational Safety and Health Administration** safety and health rules for federal workers, opposed comparable worth legislation, and supported decertification votes among Internal Revenue Service employees. The AFGE responded by supporting the massive 1983 Solidarity Day rally against Reagan policies, and by launching successful organizing drives in the Veterans Administration and Social Security Administration. The union also set up a political action committee to raise money for political campaigns. Relations were equally testy between the AFGE and President George H. Bush.

In 1993, President William Clinton signed a reform of the hated Hatch Act, and federal employees finally won full protection of their political rights. Clinton's Executive Order 12871 created a National Partnership Council with presidential cabinet members and representatives of the AFGE, the NFFE, and several smaller federal unions. The Council seeks to derail problems and complaints arising among federal employees before they become serious. The AFGE was stung by the 1994 Congressional elections that brought a Republican majority to Congress, but lobbied against implementation of House Speaker Newt Gingrich's "Contract With America," which contained anti-union pledges. The GOP shut down the government several times in late 1995 and early 1996, thereby denying paychecks to federal employees. AFGE worked hard to reelect Clinton in 1996 and reduce GOP strength.

Shaky relations between the AFGE and Republican Party arose anew when George W. Bush entered the White House in 2001. The AFGE opposed Bush's attempt to streamline the Equal Employment Opportunity Commission's complaint-processing guidelines because employees felt the proposed streamlining would eliminate due process protections. The Homeland Security Act passed in the wake of the September 11, 2001, terrorist attacks on New York and Washington has also proved contentious. Bush originally wanted to hire private sector security firms for airports and public buildings, largely because he did not want to create new unionized workers. He has also sought the right to hire and fire civil servants in designated security-sensitive positions without going through normal civil service procedures, a move opposed by the AFGE and blocked by the Senate in 2002. The AFGE is currently attempting to organize airport security screeners.

The AFGE has an admirable record on civil rights and gender equity, holds periodic civil rights conventions, and maintains a Women's and Fair Practices Department, whose current head is Andrea Bruce. As of 2002, the president of the AFGE was Bobby Harnage. It enjoys good relations with the NFFE, which is again affiliated with the AFL-CIO as Federal District 1 of the **International Association of Machinists and Aerospace Workers**.

Suggested Readings: Kate Bronfenbrenner and Tom Juravich, *Union Organizing in the Public Sector: An Analysis of State and Local Elections*, 1995; Jack Stieber, *Public Employee Unionism*, 1972; "History of the AFGE," http://www.afge.org/Documents/History.pdf.

Robert E. Weir

American Federation of Labor (AFL). The American Federation of Labor was the one of the forerunners of the American Federation of Labor-Congress of Industrial Organizations (AFL-CIO), the nation's largest labor federation. The AFL-CIO currently represents the interests of some sixty-four constituent unions, fifty-one state federations (including Puerto Rico), and 590 central labor unions. Of the 16 million union members in the United States, 13 million belong to the AFL-CIO. The federation also acts as a lobby group and is a powerful force in American politics. Although in theory each affiliated union has great independence from the umbrella-like organization, in practice AFL and AFL-CIO leaders set much of the policy that governs how contemporary unions conduct themselves.

During the upheavals of the late nineteenth century, leaders of two secret labor societies, the Knights of Industry and the Amalgamated Labor Union, convened trade union representatives in Pittsburgh, Pennsylvania. On November 15, 1881, over 100 delegates from various trades and several local assemblies of the **Knights of Labor (KOL)** founded the Federation of Organized Trade and Labor Unions (FOTLU). It was chaired by John Jarrett, president of the **Amalgamated Association of Iron, Steel, and Tin Workers**, and **Samuel Gompers** headed the Committee on Organization. Like the KOL, the FOTLU called for an end to convict and **child labor**, advocated immigration restriction laws, and lobbied for the creation of a **bureau of labor statistics**, but it rejected more radical KOL proposals like government ownership of railroads and the formation of producer and consumer **cooperatives**. The FOTLU also restricted membership to skilled workers, unlike the more inclusive KOL.

The FOTLU was largely a paper organization, but shortly after the **Haymarket bombing** in May 1886, leaders called for a December conference in Columbus, Ohio. There, labor representatives created the American Federation of Labor (AFL). Even more than its predecessor, the AFL patterned itself after British models that emphasized member benefits, high dues, centralized control over local unions, and collective bargaining. Gompers was elected AFL president and held that post, except for one year, until his death in 1924. Gompers, whose own Cigarmakers International Union feuded with the KOL, launched an aggressive campaign to convince skilled workers to quit the Knights in favor of the AFL. Gompers fervently believed that occupational commonality was the only true basis of labor solidarity, and he criticized the KOL's practice of mixing trades in its locals. He was dedicated to a model of **pure and simple**

unionism that focused on short-term objectives, relied on economic power rather than politics, limited membership to workers, and organized strictly on occupational lines. Unlike the KOL, the AFL saw **strikes** as labor's primary weapon against intransigent employers.

Some AFL practices were considerably less enlightened than those of the KOL. Autonomy of constituent unions was a central principle, thus the AFL allowed each to set its own racial and gender guidelines. In practice, many AFL unions excluded African Americans and women. Despite Gompers's ridicule of the Knights for allowing employers to join the KOL, the AFL proved more comfortable working closely with employers. Gompers even joined the **National Civic Federation** to promote peaceful meditation of labor disputes. By 1900, the AFL was dominant and the KOL moribund. By 1932, 85 percent of all union workers was under its aegis.

The AFL's pure-and-simple unionism worked best during the first two decades of the twentieth century. In cities like San Francisco, it had stunning success not only in organizing businesses such as construction but also in controlling politics. Although the AFL was officially non-partisan, it worked closely with pro-labor politicians and their parties, a transparent subterfuge that persists to the present. Political leverage paid off in the early twentieth century. Despite the constant attacks by the anti-union **National Association of Manufacturers (NAM)**, the Federation's membership grew from over 1.6 million in 1904, to 2.6 million by 1914. During World War I, the Federation made gains, but the number of both nonunion workers and those in independent unions also grew. In part, the problem lay with the racist, sexist, and nativist mindset of the union's leadership and **rank-and-file**. When the AFL granted charters to unions with **minority** workers, it did so begrudgingly as in the case of the **Brotherhood of Sleeping Car Porters**. Additionally, the union's conservative leadership stifled those of a more radical bent, encouraging new unions like the **Amalgamated Clothing Workers** to stay outside the AFL fold. More significant problems arose in the 1920s, with new president **William Green** proving a less forceful leader than Gompers. Challenges like the NAM-led **open shop** movement, violence against unionists, the Supreme Court's anti-labor decisions, challenges by more radical unions, and the onset of the Great Depression led to a decline in membership. By 1933, membership sank to pre–World War I levels.

Fortunes reversed with the advent of the New Deal and its support for organizing and collective bargaining. By 1934, the Federation had added almost a million new members. The dramatic resurgence of the labor movement in the 1930s was a mixed blessing for the AFL. Many newly organized workers were located in large industrial concerns that were ill-adapted to the **craft union** models. Although the AFL reorganized itself in the 1910s and 1920s to make some concessions to **industrial unionism**, it did not adapt quickly enough and some of its more staid members resisted such overtures. In 1935, an internal cadre—backed by automotive, mine, and rubber workers and led by the **United Mine Workers' John L. Lewis**—created the Committee on Industrial Organizations to pursue industrial unionism. The AFL hastily denounced the Committee and, in 1936, suspended CIO unions. Those unions bolted the AFL and, as the **Congress of Industrial Organizations (CIO)**, expanded membership to the detriment of the AFL and obtained political access far greater than that of the AFL.

Despite losses in mass production industries, the AFL made other gains from the 1930s through 1950s, especially in construction, transportation, communication, and service industries. In the post–World War II period, the differences between the AFL and CIO narrowed, especially after the latter purged its left-wing radicals and embraced the Cold War patriotism that pervaded AFL leadership ranks. The two signed non-raiding pacts and cooperated in their opposition to the **Taft-Hartley Act**. The larger AFL also signaled its willingness to compromise on key CIO concerns like racial equality, industrial unionism, and grassroots organizing. In December 1955, the AFL and CIO merged to create a 15.5 million–member organization it hoped would be powerful enough to counter conservative assaults on organized labor. AFL president **George Meany** became the first AFL-CIO president.

Those hopes have gone largely unrealized. More anti-labor legislation followed in the wake of Taft-Hartley and promised grassroots organizing programs largely remained in the planning stage. At the beginning of the 1960s, AFL-CIO leaders were perceived as unresponsive to a new generation of workers who had not participated in the struggles of the 1930s and 1940s. To many critics, the organization only grew more conservative as time passed. The AFL-CIO fully embraced the Cold War objectives of U.S. foreign aid policy. It failed to stifle corruption and instead clamped down on rank-and-file militancy. More importantly, it was slow to react to anti-Vietnam, civil rights, and feminist movements. In fact, some AFL-CIO–affiliated unions sought to impede social reform, opposing programs like **affirmative action**. By the 1970s, the AFL-CIO was administratively top-heavy and under the control of cautious **business unionists**. Although AFL-CIO membership grew in the 1960s, it proved unable to maintain its members, and several more progressive unions, like the **United Auto Workers**, quit the organization.

From the 1970s through the 1990s, **deindustrialization**, capital flight, and **globalization** of trade have further sapped the AFL-CIO's political and economic influence. This became clear in its failure to prevent the passage of the 1993 **North American Free Trade Agreement**. The old alliance between the federation and the Democratic Party has weakened, as has the AFL-CIO's public stature. No new significant labor legislation has been passed since the 1970s, and current AFL-CIO membership is near the level at the time of the merger. It remains a potentially powerful player in U.S. labor relations and politics, but the federation's future role is uncertain. Recently elected president **John Sweeney** has vowed to place renewed emphasis on recruiting unorganized workers, expanding in Latin America and overseas, and improving the organization's racial and gender record. In short, the AFL-CIO remains committed to proving that traditional labor unions can play an important role in a global economy.

Suggested Readings: Paul Buhle, *Taking Care of Business*, 1999; Philip Taft, *The A.F. of L. from the Death of Gompers to the Merger*, 1959; Robert Zieger, *American Workers, American Unions*, 1986.

Andrew E. Kersten

American Federation of State, County, and Municipal Employees (AFSCME). The American Federation of State, County, and Municipal Employees grew out of efforts taken by Wisconsin state employees to protect civil service jobs during the Great Depression. In 1932, they formed the Wisconsin State Administrative, Clerical, Fiscal, and Technical Employees Association and fended off an attempt to destroy the state's civil service system in favor of one that would have reintroduced the spoils system. In 1933, the union—then known as the Wisconsin State Employees Association (WSEA)—was granted a charter by the **American Federation of Labor**. The WSEA was led by state examiner Arnold Zander, who helped expand organizing efforts to other states. By 1935, the organization was known as AFSCME, though it was officially a department within the AFL's **American Federation of Government Employees** until Zander negotiated separate status in 1936, and became the first AFSCME president.

AFSCME had only about 10,000 members in 1936, and most states refused to grant collective bargaining rights to civil service employees. Despite harsh post–World War II anti-labor legislation, ASFSCME continued to grow, largely because of the expansion of public service jobs after 1945. AFSCME had 61,000 members by 1945, and over 104,000 in 1955, when the AFL and the **Congress of Industrial Organizations** merged. Still, no state recognized AFSCME's right to bargain until New York state did so in 1958, and it was not until President John Kennedy signed **Executive Order 10988** in 1962, that said right was conferred on federal employees.

Most states continued to resist. Then in 1964, **Jerry Wurf** became AFSCME president. Wurf used militant tactics, common in the 1960s, to expand AFSCME's clout and, by 1977, twenty states granted bargaining rights to civil servants. In 1965, AFSCME issued a Bill of Rights for union employees, the first large union to do so. It also took part in the civil rights movement; the Reverend Martin Luther King, Jr. was in Memphis, Tennessee, assisting striking AFSCME sanitation workers when he was assassinated in 1968.

AFSCME set up a political action committee in the 1970s, its membership soared to over 684,000 by 1975, and it absorbed smaller unions throughout the 1970s and 1980s. Wurf died in 1981, but his successor, Gerald McEntee, continued the union's militant stance. In 1981, AFSCME sent the nation's largest union contingent to the **Solidarity** Day rally that protested President Ronald

Reagan's perceived assault on American workers. It also opposed President Clinton on the **North American Free Trade Agreement**.

By the turn of the twenty-first century, AFSCME had over 1.3 million members, making it the largest single union in the AFL-CIO. It represents not only civil service employees, but also workers in public and private hospitals, nonprofit organizations, school districts, and universities. There are over 3,500 locals across the United States, Puerto Rico, and Panama. As of 2002, McEntee remains president, Linda Chavez-Thompson is executive vice president, and William Lucy the secretary-treasurer.

Suggested Readings: Ellen Applebaum and Rosemary Batt, *The New American Workplace*, 1994; *AFSCME Steward Handbook*, 2000; American Federation of State, County, and Municipal Employees, AFL-CIO, http://www.afscme.org/about/history.htm.

Cheryl Conley
Robert E. Weir

American Federation of Teachers (AFT). The American Federation of Teachers was founded in 1916, an outgrowth of unionization efforts commencing in Chicago in 1897. Teaching was predominately a female profession in the nineteenth and early twentieth centuries, with teachers working for low pay and subject to strict moral and personal codes of conduct. Schools, especially in rural areas, were often quite primitive, with rudimentary conditions and heavy demands on teachers. Although the **National Educational Association (NEA)** was formed in 1857, it functioned more as a professional guild than as a teacher advocacy group. Margaret Haley, whose father had been active in the **Knights of Labor**, and Catharine Goggin formed the Chicago Teachers Federation (CFT) in 1897, with Goggin serving as president. In 1902, the CFT affiliated with the citywide Chicago Federation of Labor.

The CFT moved cautiously and slowly, but it attracted the attention of several Progressive Era reformers, most notably philosopher John Dewey. In 1916, the CFT changed its name to the American Federation of Teachers and secured a charter within the **American Federation of Labor (AFL)**. Goggin died in a traffic accident, and the new AFT chose Charles Stillman as its first president. The AFT quickly established itself in other cities, despite the fact that many states and municipalities, including Chicago, had laws preventing teachers from unionizing. In many cities, women led the charge to organize, with Florence Rood directing efforts in St. Paul, Minnesota, and Mary Barker leading in Atlanta.

Despite these pioneering efforts, the AFT remained a small organization of modest success until the 1960s. Teachers were not protected by the 1935 **National Labor Relations Act**, and most states forbade teacher strikes. The AFT-led **New York City teachers strike** of 1960 was a landmark in changing perceptions of teachers as workers entitled to collective bargaining rights. In the next decade and a half, over 800,000 teachers took part in over 1,000 strikes. Of all the teacher unions, the AFT, then led by **Albert Shanker**, was the most militant. The union grew from 59,000 members in 1960 to over 200,000 in 1970. By 1980, over 70 percent of all public school teachers were covered by collective bargaining agreements and the AFT was strong in every section of the United States except the South.

As part of the AFL-CIO, the AFT is usually more partisan than the NEA, and Shanker advised both presidents Carter and Clinton. The AFT has over 2,200 locals today and it represents custodians, guidance counselors, bus drivers, and university faculty as well as public school teachers. It also represents a smattering of nurses and state employees. Membership estimates for the year 2000 vary from a low of 580,000 to over 900,000.

Suggested Readings: Marjorie Murphy, *Blackboard Unions*, 1990; Paula O'Connor, "Grade School Teachers Become Union Leaders," *Labor's Heritage* 7:2 (Fall 1995); American Federation of Teachers, AFl-CIO, http://www. aft.org/history.htm.

Leslie Juntunen
Robert E. Weir

American Labor Party (ALP). The American Labor Party was a third-party movement based in New York between 1936 and 1956. The efforts of the ALP offer insights into the perceived need for an independent **labor party**, the difficulties involved in sustaining one, and the tendencies toward factionalism that often subdivide the political left.

David Dubinsky (with cigar), the president of the International Ladies' Garment Workers' Union, was one of the founders of the American Labor Party. © George Meany Memorial Archives.

By the 1930s, numerous European industrial democracies had labor parties, as did Australia, Canada, and New Zealand. The United States, however, lacks the proportional representation mechanisms associated with most parliamentary democracies. Its winner-takes-all electoral system has been dominated by the Democratic and Republican Parties since the latter's emergence in 1856. Third parties have often enjoyed local or fleeting electoral success but, to date, none has broken the national dominance of the current two-party system.

The ALP was something of a hybrid in that it mostly endorsed other candidates, but occasionally put forth its own. In essence, it was as much of a political education group as a political party. The ALP sought to educate the working class about which candidates best promoted its interest. It formed as a splinter group among New York Socialist Party (SP) members. Many felt that the SP's presidential candidate, **Norman Thomas**, was ineffectual and served only to advance the fortunes of GOP candidate Alf Landon. ALP founders, which included David Dubinsky of the **International Ladies' Garment Workers' Union**, felt that President Franklin Roosevelt's New Deal advanced **socialist** programs better than Thomas. The ALP sought to get out the vote for Roosevelt and for U.S. Senator Herbert Lehman. Voters in New York could vote for Roosevelt or Lehman on either the ALP or Democratic ticket. ALP votes were largely responsible for Roosevelt carrying New York in 1936, 1940, and 1944. It also aided Lehman's victories in two close Senate races.

The ALP appeared shortly after the formation of the **Popular Front**. Like the latter, it contained an amalgam of radicals and progressives, including **communists**. It even contained a smattering of conservatives, including (briefly) **George Meany**. ALP fortunes frequently mirrored those of the Popular Front, peaking when it was closest to the mainstream and dipping during the brief Hitler-Stalin pact in 1940, and again after 1948. The ALP was twice instrumental in helping reelect New York City's Republican pro-labor mayor Fiorello LaGuardia; in 1937, over 21 percent of all LaGuardia voters were from the ALP. It also aided Adam Clayton Powell's election to Congress in 1942, and the election of Oscar García Rivera to the New York state assembly in 1937, the first Puerto Rican officeholder in the mainland United States.

The ALP also fielded its own candidates. For the most part, these did not fare well, though it did elect several members of the New York City Council and, in 1948, elected Leo Issacson to Congress to represent the South Bronx. Its most successful high-profile candidate was Vito Marcantonio, a radical and communist, who served seven terms in the U.S. Congress between 1934 and 1950. Marcantonio was popular among his East Harlem constituents, whom he constantly reminded that they were ignored by Democrats and Republicans.

The early promise of the ALP began to unravel during and after World War II. Marcantonio's outspoken defense of the Communist Party caused some—especially old-line social democrats—to leave the ALP in 1944, and create still another third party, the Liberal Party, which remains active in New York politics. In 1948, the ALP declined to endorse Harry Truman and threw its support to the presidential bid of Henry Wallace. Wallace's Progressive Party was not on the New York state ballot, but he nonetheless polled over half a million votes in New York as an ALP candidate and cost Truman the state's electorals.

Postwar red-baiting made association with communism problematic and ALP votes fell dramatically after 1948. Marcantonio lost his reelection bid in 1950, and the ALP's 1954 gubernatorial candidate, John McManus, polled only 47,000 votes. The latter election pointed to another ALP problem: its strength was largely confined to the New York City metropolitan area and was quite weak in upstate New York. Even the communists deserted the ALP in 1953, concluding that working within existing political structures was cooperation with fascism. Under New York law, a party polling under 50,000 votes could not be registered as an official party. In 1956, the ALP officially folded.

Despite the ALP's mixed record, its innovative mix of political endorsements and third-party candidacies suggests an alternative to traditional labor parties. It also highlights the pitfalls of factionalism.

Suggested Readings: Gerald Meyer, "American Labor Party," *Encyclopedia of the American Left*, eds. Mari Jo Buhle, et al., 1992; Gerald Meyer, *Vito Marcantonio: Radical Politician*, 1989.

Robert E. Weir

American Plan. American Plan was the name given to an employer-led drive toward the **open-shop** movement after 1921. In that year, representatives from various chambers of congress, manufacturer associations, and organizations like the **National Association of Manufacturers** and the League for Industrial Rights gathered in Chicago to announce the American Plan. Open shops were defended under the rubric of American individualism. Coming four years after the Russian Revolution, the very term was politically charged, playing off the fears of international Bolshevism that fueled the post–World War I Red Scare. Unions were tainted as forms of collective behavior more at home in Soviet Russia than in the United States. Patriotic appeals, red-baiting, and an economic downturn in 1921 and 1922 combined to weaken organized labor in the 1920s. Manufacturers adhering to the American Plan openly discriminated against union members, maintained a blacklist of union activists, and required employees to sign **yellow-dog contracts**. Employers also made extensive use of injunctions to stymie collective action.

The American Plan fostered an extensive network of open-shop organizations and greatly crippled unions even in traditional hotbeds like Detroit and San Francisco. Although the American Plan failed to survive the New Deal era under that name, it found renewed strength in the 1947 **Taft-Hartley Act** and in the post–World War II **right-to-work** movement.

Suggested Readings: Irving Bernstein, *The Lean Years*, 1960; Foster R. Dulles and Melvyn Dubofsky, *Labor in America*, 1993.

Yasmin Correa
Robert E. Weir

American Railway Union (ARU). The American Railway Union was the culmination of several attempts to unite separate railway organizations into a single union to tackle powerful rail corporations. Its early promise was largely shattered by the lost **Pullman strike** of 1894, an event that delayed the onset of **industrial unionism**.

Beginning with locomotive engineers in 1860, railway workers organized craft-specific "brotherhoods." Conductors, firemen, repairmen, brakemen, and switchmen each had their own organizations that operated independently of one another. Most of the brotherhoods were more like fraternal organizations than labor advocacy groups. None, with the exception of the cash-rich **Broth-**

erhood of Locomotive Engineers (BLE), was powerful enough to combat Gilded Age railroad magnates. Coordinated efforts proved difficult, with rail workers scabbing on each other as often as they cooperated. The **Great Labor Uprising** of 1877, precipitated by a series of spontaneous railroad strikes, revealed the weaknesses of the brotherhoods. The lost strikes and brutal repression that ensued retarded efforts to unite rail workers, and the potentially powerful BLE fell into the hands of cautious leaders who distanced themselves from other workers and cooperated with management.

In the 1880s, the **Knights of Labor (KOL)** proved successful in organizing rail workers in the West and Southwest, with Union Pacific workers enrolled in a prototypical industrial union. The KOL's 1885 victory over Jay Gould's Southwestern Railway conglomerate inspired many rail workers, despite well-publicized jurisdictional disputes with the BLE. **Eugene V. Debs**, the secretary of the Brotherhood of Locomotive Firemen (BLF) and editor of its magazine, forged a temporary alliance between his organization and the BLE, but the latter turned out to be a self-serving ally. The BLE, led by P. J. Arthur, scabbed on the KOL during its 1887 dispute with the Reading railroad, and some Knights retaliated in kind during the 1888 Chicago, Burlington, and Quincy strike. But the BLE also left the BLF high and dry by obeying a court **injunction** and crossing picket lines.

In 1889, Debs formed the Supreme Council of the United Order of Railway Employees to cement ties between firemen, switchmen, and brakemen. It managed to negotiate with several lines, but the BLE's refusal to endorse the Council limited its effectiveness. When disputes broke out between brakemen and switchmen, the Council disintegrated and, in 1892, was abandoned. Debs, however, remained convinced that only united action would bring success and he resigned from the BLF. He and several others formed the ARU in June 1893. Unlike the brotherhoods, the ARU opened its ranks to unskilled workers, not just craft unionists. The ARU also forbade black members, a practice that hindered efforts to recruit former KOL members in the West, who had a tradition of biracial unionism.

Despite a raging economic depression, the ARU grew quickly. Within a year, the ARU represented 150,000 rail workers. Like the KOL in 1885, ARU growth was linked to successful job actions. The union restored wage cuts to Union Pacific workers and won a strike against James Hill's Great Northern line. Unfortunately, it also attracted enmity from both the old brotherhoods and the **American Federation of Labor**, the latter seeing the ARU as a threat to **craft unionism**.

The ARU might have weathered this opposition had not the Pullman boycott and strike intervened. Pullman workers, bludgeoned by layoffs and wage cuts, struck in May 1894, against the advice of the ARU. Although he personally opposed involving the union in the Pullman dispute, Debs threw himself and ARU resources into the battle when the organization endorsed the Pullman workers in June. The strike was a disaster that pitted the power of the court system, the federal government, the BLE, and the AFL against the nascent ARU. (Only the moribund KOL supported the ARU.) Debs and seven other ARU leaders were jailed as a result of the strike. At the 1897 ARU convention, only two dozen delegates attended and the ARU was dissolved.

Suggested Readings: Stanley Buder, *Pullman*, 1967; Ray Ginger, *The Bending Cross*, 1949; Sidney Lens, *The Labor Wars*, 1974.

Ralph Shaffer

Anarchism. Anarchism is a loosely defined political philosophy that took root in the United States in the late nineteenth century. At its core, anarchism postulates that government control is the enemy of true liberty and freedom, and that humans can live harmoniously without external controls. In a labor context, the term often implies the right of every worker to negotiate freely for available productive labor. For anarchists, a tension always exists between individual freedom and the oppressiveness of all organizations and hierarchies, especially government. Anarchism exists in variant forms, variously labeled as individualist, mutualist, collectivist, communist, and **anarcho-syndicalism**.

Anarchy derives from ancient Greek ideals, but most forms of American anarchism were brought by European immigrants arriving after the 1870s. The only indigenous American variety of anarchism was its individualist strain, which holds that radically free individuals can exist independently of external constraints. Individualist anarchism stems from the writings of Thomas Paine, who inspired nineteenth-century practitioners like Henry David Thoreau, Benjamin Tucker, and Joseph Labadie. To some degree, 1960s counterculture movements derived inspiration from individualist anarchism. Libertarianism is a modern offshoot of individualist principles.

Nineteenth-century labor movements were largely influenced by mutualist and collectivist anarchism, though anarchism of any variety was embraced by a very small minority of American workers. Immigrant anarchists brought with them simmering tensions over definitions and tactics. Those drawing inspiration from Karl Marx and Mikhail Bakunin called for revolutionary upheaval as a precondition for establishing a future collectivist society where the means of production and distribution rested in the hands of workers. Even those lines were unclear. Followers of Bakunin—who came to be called "collectivists"—charged that Marx's "communist" version of anarchism depended on a revolutionary vanguard that was prone to authoritarianism and which relied too heavily on reactionary trade unions. Complicating matters further was the presence of mutualist anarchists who followed the lead of French writer Pierre-Joseph Proudhon and espoused a peaceful, evolutionary road to anarchism in which the machinery of an oppressive state would be gradually dismantled.

Although many involved with anarchism and trade unionism movements rejected violence, as espoused by radicals like the German-born anarchist Johann Most in his New York–based journal *Die Freiheit*, violence became equated with both movements. Much of this was due to the fear generated worldwide by the Paris Commune (1870–71) and the stage of European anarchism in 1880s known as "propaganda of the deed," which was marked by assassination attempts. From the 1870s on, whenever there was a strike in America, the specter of anarchism was raised to discredit it.

The **eight-hour-movement** and its associated strikes nationwide during 1886 had significant consequences for both labor and anarchism. Chicago's **Haymarket** riot erupted when a bomb thrown at the end of an eight-hour meeting left seven police and four workers dead. Five leaders of the movement, all avowed anarchists, were arrested, tried, convicted, and executed, while two others were sentenced to life in prison; another committed suicide before he went to trial. Although the **Knights of Labor** attempted to distance itself from Haymarket, the nationwide hysteria that ensued linked radical labor with anarchism. The so-called "Black International," an anarchist labor group, drifted apart after the Chicago events. Subsequently, labor anarchism was mostly followed by Jewish, Italian, and Russian workers in large urban areas.

This cartoon from the July 21, 1894, issue of *Harper's Weekly* identifies unionism as part of the "vanguard of anarchy." © George Meany Memorial Archives.

In 1892, at the height of the **Homestead steel** lockout, Alexander Berkman, a young anarchist acting on his own volition, attempted to assassinate plant manager Henry Clay Frick. Berkman's rash act harmed the labor movement as it was once again tarred with the brush of revolutionary anarchism. The violence associated with the late nineteenth century also aroused middle-class fears of anarchism, even though much of that violence was precipitated by **Pinkerton** agents, **scabs**, and government militias. Although some workers embraced anarchism, the majority tried to distance labor from the politics of violence.

In the twentieth century, the labor organization most associated with anarchism was the **Industrial Workers of the World (IWW)**. Formed in 1905, the IWW sought to organize workers shunned by the **American Federation of Labor**. Thomas Hagerty, a defrocked Catholic priest, fashioned a model loosely based on the precepts of anarcho-syndicalism, although overall IWW ideology tended to be somewhat vague. Nonetheless, the IWW's attachment to the class struggle, antagonism to government and employers, hostility to professional leaders, and belief in the **general strike** as the mechanism to bring on a workers' revolution, were traits compatible with anarchism. A majority of U.S.-based anarchists sympathized with the IWW, but the organization never embraced anarchism officially.

Prior to and during World War I, anarchists led protests against the draft and American involvement with the war. The IWW followed their lead. When the United States entered the war in 1917, most unions participated in the war effort. Those that did not, like the IWW, were viewed as disloyal and were suppressed. When the leading figures of the anarchist movement, **Emma Goldman** and Alexander Berkman, were deported after the war, the movement languished.

By 1921, anarchists no longer provided a meaningful political alternative and many union members associated with anarcho-syndicalism drifted in and out of the **Communist Party** during the following decades. Several became partisans of the labor upsurge of the 1930s that resulted in the formation of the **Congress of Industrial Organizations**. A few old-style anarchists remained, like Rose Pesotta, who rose to become vice president of the **International Ladies' Garment Workers' Union**, but she was an exception among labor leaders.

In the aftermath of World War II and the ensuing political repression of the late 1940s and 1950s, anarchists involved with the labor movement kept a low profile. After the amalgamation of the AFL-CIO in 1955, anarchists found it even harder to make inroads in the labor movement. In recent years, anarchists have been associated with radical environmental groups, struggles against the **globalization** of capital, and various civil liberties campaigns, but they remain on the fringes of political expression in contemporary America.

Suggested Readings: Carlotta Anderson, *All-American Anarchist*, 1998; David DeLeon, *The American as Anarchist: Reflections on Indigenous Radicalism*, 1978; Philip Foner, *History of the Labor Movement in the United States*, vol. 4: *The Industrial Workers of the World*, 1976.

Linnea Goodwin Burwood

Anarcho-Syndicalism. Anarcho-syndicalism is an ideology and movement that advocates workers' ownership of their workplaces and production, with no state or government authority to control their lives. It usually has revolutionary implications. The terms "syndicalism" and "revolutionary syndicalism" can be used interchangeably with anarcho-syndicalism, as mostly the terms reflect local preference or linguistic nuance rather than actual substance.

Anarcho-syndicalism sets itself apart from radical ideologies and movements through its emphasis on **direct action**, sabotage, and the **general strike**. Pure anarcho-syndicalism denounces existing political structures as corrupt and incapable of substantial change. Instead of customary, legal, or political channels, anarcho-syndicalists strive for change through immediate and direct intervention tactics that increase workers' control and initiative. An example of such tactics, sabotage, has two dimensions. In the short run, it warns capitalists to stop the further exploitation of workers. In the long run, it weakens **capitalism** and prepares the stage for the ultimate weapon of anarcho-syndicalism: the general strike. Anarcho-syndicalists believe that a properly conducted general strike paralyzes the system and enables the shift to workers' control of all production. Once this happens, the state and government will be discarded in favor of productive and distributive networks coordinated by democratic departments designed to meet the needs of all of society rather than maximizing the profits of a few.

Anarcho-syndicalism became a visible and growing movement in the first decade of the twentieth century, especially in Europe and the Americas. In the United States, the most significant anarcho-syndicalist movement was the **Industrial Workers of the World (IWW)**, founded in 1905. The IWW envisioned dismantling capitalism and replacing it with seven "departments" (building, manufacturing, public service, distribution, food stuffs, mining, and transportation). Each department (or "syndicate") was subdivided into specific crafts and tasks, while coordination between the departments would be directed by a democratically chosen "general administration." Both private profit and private property would disappear as all goods and services would be directed towards the common good. It's doubtful that many IWW members grasped the overall intricacies of the organization's anarcho-syndicalist vision, but aspects of those ideals surfaced during strikes like that in **Lawrence**, Massachusetts (1912) and in **Paterson**, New Jersey (1913). Anarcho-syndicalist speeches and tracts also appeared during several general strikes during the late 1910s and 1920s, including the one in Seattle (1919).

There are a variety of anarcho-syndicalist organizations in the world today, including the IWW in the United States but their strength is relatively weak compared to the heyday of anarcho-syndicalism in the first few decades of the twentieth century. However, in the late 1990s, anarcho-syndicalists played a significant part in the formation of worldwide protests against **globalization**.

Suggested Readings: Rudolf Rucker, *Anarcho Syndicalism*, 1989; Marcel van der Linden and Wayne Thorpe, *Revolutionary Syndicalism: An International Perspective*, 1990; Anarcho-Syndicalism 101, http://www.anarchosyndicalism.org/.

Alex Corlu

Anthracite Coal Strike of 1902. The Anthracite Coal Strike of 1902 was an important victory for the nascent **United Mine Workers of America (UMWA)**. It occurred in central and eastern Pennsylvania between May and October, and was essentially a continuation of a 1900 strike in which miners struck in protest of low wages, high company store prices, arbitrary work rules, and irregularities in weighing coal. In 1900, mine owners were pressured to compromise by Republican national chairman Marcus Hanna, who worried that a prolonged strike would jeopardize President William McKinley's reelection chances. Owners agreed to wage increases and made other concessions, but refused to grant union recognition to the UMWA.

By 1902, eroding conditions threatened to scuttle the tenuous peace achieved two years earlier. UMWA president **John Mitchell** was a cautious man who disliked strikes and believed that miners needed public support to win concessions. His calm and responsible leadership paid dividends during the ensuing work stoppage. Union delegates met in March 1902 and issued demands including: union recognition, a 20 percent wage increase, an eight-hour day, standardization of weighing procedures, and fixed work rules. Mitchell offered to mediate disputes as he believed a strike would be lengthy and costly for both sides. Several months of meetings and attempted negotiation through the **National Civic Federation** produced few results and, on May 12, Mitchell called for a "temporary" strike. Two days later he told UMWA delegates that a permanent strike would be disastrous and cautioned against it, but most locals ignored his advice.

More than 125,000 miners left their posts during the strike. Solidarity was bolstered through strong links to ethnic communities and there were very few incidents of workers breaking ranks. The strike was relatively peaceful, though there were isolated incidents of abuse against imported **scabs** and in some locales police beat strikers. Mine owners employed private police forces and pressured the Pennsylvania government to send national guardsmen to the region.

By fall, public sympathy was on the side of the miners. Mitchell continually called for mediation and stated the UMWA would abide by an arbitrator's decision. By contrast, mine operators intransigently refused what seemed to the public to be modest proposals. Rising anthracite prices and the impending heating season served to elevate public concerns. Theodore Roosevelt—who ascended to the presidency when McKinley was assassinated in 1901—met with operators and UMWA representatives on October 3. Mitchell repeated his offer to submit to binding **arbitration** whilst operators refused to discuss matters, accused Mitchell of precipitating violence, and harangued Roosevelt to send in troops to force miners to return to work.

Roosevelt was offended by the operators' arrogance, whereas Mitchell impressed him with his respect. He instructed Secretary of War Elihu Root to meet with financier J. P. Morgan. Morgan, who had considerable influence with mine owners, worked out a plan whereby operators would choose representatives to a presidential commission that would investigate the disputes. Most of the owners agreed to this, fearing that Roosevelt might nationalize the mines. The UMWA agreed to return to work on October 23, 1902.

The Anthracite Coal Strike Commission met for three months, called over 500 witnesses, and rendered its decision on March 23, 1903. Miners gained a 10 percent pay increase and reduced hours. Standard weighing and UMWA recognition were left unresolved, but an Anthracite Board of Conciliation was created to handle future disputes. Although the UMWA achieved only partial success, it claimed victory and began to make steady gains in its organizing efforts. The dispute also marked the first time in American industrial history in which the federal government did not side with employers in a major industrial dispute.

Suggested Readings: Perry Blatz, *Democratic Miners: Work and Labor Relations in the Anthracite Coal Industry*, 1994; Robert Cornell, *The Anthracite Coal Strike of 1902*, 1957; Robert Weibe, "The Anthracite Coal Strike of 1902," *Mississippi Valley Historical Review* 48 (September 1961): 229–51.

Stephen Micelli

Apprentice. An apprentice is a person who works as a trainee under the supervision of a more skilled person. The use of such training can be traced back to the medieval guild societies. Crafts such as blacksmithing, metal work, and printing often used apprentices. Originally, apprentices were usually children who boarded with a **master craftsman**. The apprentice did not receive remuneration beyond board and training. Today the term refers simply to the lowest tier of a training program.

The modern concept of apprenticeship is found most often in the construction trades. Building trade unions often use apprenticeship programs to ensure proper instruction in skilled work. Unions can also manipulate the number of trained members by limiting apprenticeships and therefore controlling the supply of labor in a particular craft.

Apprenticeship programs may be jointly administered by the employer and the union, or done in conjunction with vocational schools. Many combine technical instruction with work experience. The duration of training can vary between crafts. A barber serves at this first tier for two years before graduating to **journeyman**; meat-cutters three years; electrical workers, three to four years; and printers five years. Successful completion of an apprenticeship signals a mastery of the trade.

Suggested Readings: Robert Glen, *Urban Workers in the Early Industrial Revolution*, 1984; Bruce Laurie, *Artisans into Workers*, 1989; Ronald Schultz, *The Republic of Labor: Philadelphia Artisans and the Politics of Class, 1720–1830*, 1993.

Carolyn Anderson

Arbitration/Conciliation/Mediation. *Arbitration*, *conciliation*, and *mediation* are terms that represent ways of resolving capital/labor disputes through a third party. Arbitration is the final step to dispute resolution. Prior to arbitration there are other forms of dispute settlement that can be used, two of which are conciliation and mediation. Mediation is a process by which a neutral third party is sought as a discussion facilitator and a presenter of ideas to move the parties toward a mutually agreeable result. Mediation, in some instances, can be mandated prior to sending a dispute to arbitration. This practice is often seen in disputes within the public sector. Conciliation is the continuing of discussions between parties without a third party present. Compromise is the essence of mediation and conciliation. During arbitration, a final judgment—called an award—is rendered and both sides are expected to abide by it. The goal is to avoid **strikes**, **boycotts**, **lockouts**, and other forms of work stoppage.

In the nineteenth century, labor organizations like the **National Labor Union** and the **Knights of Labor** called for mandatory and binding arbitration of labor conflicts in the belief that neither employer nor employees recouped losses incurred during prolonged battles. Numerous states set up arbitration boards, but the United States never followed the path of nations like Australia and New Zealand, where government laws made arbiters' decisions binding. Most arbitration boards remained weak.

The modern concept of arbitration came to the forefront with the enactment of the **National Labor Relations Act** in 1935. This legislation promoted the idea of **collective bargaining** and **contract** arrangements between labor and management. During World War II, the government became concerned that labor disputes would interrupt vital industrial production necessary for the military. In an effort to head off problems, President Franklin Roosevelt established the **National War Labor Board** to safeguard essential manufacturing related to the war effort. When labor disputes erupted, the Board could compel the parties to argue the dispute before a neutral third party. The arbitrator listened to both arguments before issuing a binding decision. The War Labor Board also encouraged the voluntary use of an arbitration process within collective bargaining agreements.

In this 1886 cartoon both labor and management are urged to quit their high horses, labeled, respectively, "socialism" and "monopoly," and submit their differences to arbitration. © George Meany Memorial Archives.

After World War II, arbitration was touted as part of a national policy to encourage industrial peace. The 1947 **Taft-Hartley Act** established the Federal Mediation and Conciliation Service (FMCS), which promoted the use of arbitration, conciliation, and mediation as methods of dispute resolution. A series of court cases fine-tuned the obligation of labor and management to work things out. Arbitration is a substitute for court action. It is done in an informal proceeding, usually outside the court setting. In its simplest form, a neutral party is chosen by mutual agreement. Both sides have the opportunity to present evidence and witnesses. The neutral party will then make a decision which is binding on both parties. Professional sports unions, like the **Major League Baseball Players Association**, have made effective use of arbitration to win lucrative contracts for its members.

Suggested Readings: Walter Baer, *Arbitration for the Practitioner*, 1998; Frank and Edna Elkouri, *How Arbitration Works*, 5th ed., 1985; Julius Steiner, *The Arbitration Handbook*, 1989.

Carolyn Anderson

Aristocrats of Labor. Aristocrats of Labor is a controversial term used to describe an upper tier of wage earners whose wages, skills, working conditions, and aspirations set them apart from other members of the **working class**. They are often considered to be more "respectable" and more politically conservative than other laborers. Though they share the social reality of drawing wages and of being dependent upon an employer class, such workers tend not to identify with the toiling masses. The term has been applied to highly skilled craft and trades workers whose wage rates placed them well above the average of fellow workers, as well as to lower-level "white-collar" workers whose salaries are comparable to those of wage-earners even though they don't work with their hands.

The term holds currency in Marxist historical analysis and is customarily used in an unflattering fashion. To most Marxists, an aristocrat of labor is one who has been seduced by (largely unattainable) materialist dreams and has identified with bourgeois values in hopes of realizing them. Extreme critics denounce such individuals as class traitors and enemies of labor **solidarity**. Other historians find the Marxist critique simplistic and decry mechanistic stereotypes of assumed working-class values. To these individuals, "genteel" aspirations are sometimes culturally mediated strains of "working-class respectability" rather than simple endorsement of bourgeois values. Although the term is disputable and imprecise, it serves to warn against monolithic views of what is, in reality, a divided working class.

Suggested Readings: Martin Burke, *The Conundrum of Class*, 1995; Robert Gray, *The Aristocracy of Labour in Nineteenth Century Britain*, 1981.

Robert E. Weir

Assembly Line. *See Fordism.*

Association for Union Democracy. The Association for Union Democracy was founded in 1969 by Herman Benson, a skilled toolmaker and part-time labor journalist, and a group of civil libertarians outraged at the murder of two California painters' union reformers in 1966. As a nonprofit, pro-labor organization (Benson hoped to reestablish the link between intellectuals and the labor movement that existed in the 1930s), its roots lay in *Union Democracy in Action* (renamed *Union Democracy Review* in 1972), a newsletter Benson began publishing in 1959 to bring public attention to members fighting corruption and undemocratic leadership within their unions. He used the newsletter not only to publicize the struggles of reformers within the machinists, seamen, painters, paperworkers, and other unions, but also to solicit legal and financial support for litigation brought under the newly passed **Labor-Management Reporting and Disclosure Act (Landrum-Griffin Act)**.

In the years since its founding, AUD has monitored contested elections in the **United Mine Workers**, the **United Steelworkers**, and the **International**

Brotherhood of Teamsters unions. It has also initiated projects to include representation of the concerns of women and minorities in union decision-making, and has established itself as the premier information clearinghouse and educational resource for members seeking **rank-and-file** control of their unions. The Association for Union Democracy, under current executive director Carl Biers, has a dues-paying membership of about 4,000 and is headquartered in Brooklyn, New York. Herman Benson, who served as executive director during the organization's first twenty years, continues to edit *Union Democracy Review*.

Suggested Readings: Herman W. Benson, *Democratic Rights for Union Members: a Guide to Internal Union Democracy*, 1979; Alice H. Cook, *Union Democracy: Practice and Ideal*, 1963; Association for Union Democracy, http://www.uniondemocracy.org/.

Margaret Raucher

Association of Catholic Trade Unionists (ACTU). The Association of Catholic Trade Unionists was formed in the winter of 1937 in New York City by a small group of Catholics who had gathered to study the social encyclicals of Pope Leo XIII (***Rerum Novarum***, 1891) and Pope Pius XI (*Quadregisimo Anno*, 1931). While studying the encyclicals, the small group, which included John Cort, George Donohue, Edward Squitieri, and Martin Wersing, created ACTU to put the teachings of the encyclicals into practice. From this modest start ACTU grew into a highly influential Catholic labor organization having chapters in over twenty cities and over 10,000 members when it was at its peak in the 1940s.

From its founding in 1937 to its demise in 1950, ACTU was a Catholic lay organization that operated with explicit Catholic Church approval. Each ACTU chapter had a supervising pastor and was under the authority of the bishop in its own diocese. Membership in ACTU was restricted to practicing Catholics as determined by the supervising pastor. ACTU sought to bring the teachings of the Catholic Church into trade unions and to educate Catholic workers about the importance of supporting trade unions as explained in the papal encyclicals and in the Bishops' Program of 1919. These Catholic Church teachings supported class harmony between labor and management and looked to the guild system as a model where management and labor would settle differences through reasoned cooperation instead of hostile confrontations. The encyclicals also warned that the failure to support workers' organizations and to create a fair and more organized capitalism allowed socialists and communists to gain support in the **working class**.

Although it always operated under these primary tenets, the activities of ACTU changed over time. Initially it focused heavily on supporting striking unions and organizing drives, particularly among the unions in the emerging **Congress of Industrial Organizations (CIO)**. At the beginning, its activities were concentrated on building the CIO in a non-sectarian manner. But, as the organization grew, between 1937 and its first national convention in 1940, it focused less on strikes and organizing support and more on educational activities. ACTU chapters throughout the country formed an impressive number of labor schools that taught Catholic trade unionists parliamentary procedure, labor history, Catholic social doctrine, ethics, public speaking, and union leadership. They were training Catholic **rank-and-file** activists for leadership positions in their local unions. ACTU chapters became involved in other education-related activities, such as publishing labor newspapers and coordinating speaking engagements.

The focus on educational activities coincided with an increase in a strong anti-communist impulse in ACTU. ACTU members, many trained in its labor schools, and some of the ACTU allied priests, like **Monsignor Charles Owen Rice** in Pittsburgh, became increasingly involved in the intra-union factional battles between the left and the right that emerged in many of the CIO unions. ACTU's uncompromising anti-communist position found few allies during World War II as the left and the right cooperated to support the war. After the war ended, however, ACTU was well situated to create and support alliances in unions in opposition to communist leadership. In fact, in the post-World War II period, the battle against communists in CIO unions dominated ACTU's activities. It supported, encouraged, and created anti-communist factions in many unions, including the **United Electrical, Radio, and Machine Workers of America (UE)**, Transport Workers Union (TWU), **United Auto Workers (UAW)**, the **Newspaper Guild**, and others. It had a great deal of influence in some of these unions, like the UAW, where the Detroit ACTU was an important component of an anti-communist coalition that elected Walter Reuther president in 1946. But ACTU's attempts to rid the union movement of communist leadership through the electoral process was only partially successful. Consequently, ACTU vigorously supported the CIO's decision to expel eleven unions in 1949 and 1950 because they were communist-dominated. For example, although ACTU had helped the anti-communist rank-and-file movement in the UE gain strength and elect its allies to positions in some of the UE's most important locals, they were unable to unseat the popular national leaders that had alleged Communist Party ties. Unable to change the leadership of the national UE through electoral process, the ACTU supported the CIO's decision to expel the UE in 1949, and then establish the **International Union of Electrical Workers** as an alternate national union. The CIO's expulsion of the communist-dominated unions in 1949 and 1950, however, eliminated what had become ACTU's primary reason for existing. Consequently, ACTU ceased to be a functioning entity in the labor movement soon after the expulsions. ACTU faded away from the labor scene almost as rapidly as it had emerged. But its support of anti-communism in the labor movement had a long-term impact on the development of trade unionism in the United States. Many feel that ACTU's contribution to the anti-communism of the period is one of the reasons that the labor movement developed such a conservative political posture in the 1950s and onward.

Suggested Readings: John C. Cort, "The Association of Catholic Trade Unionists and the Auto Workers," *U.S. Catholic Historian* 9:4 (Fall 1990): 335–53; Dennis Deslippe, "'A Revolution of Its Own': The Social Doctrine of the Association of Catholic Trade Unionists in Detroit, 1939–1950," *Records of the American Catholic Historical Society of Philadelphia* 102:4 (Winter 1991): 19–36; Douglas P. Seaton, *Catholics and Radicals: The Association of Catholic Trade Unionists and the American Labor Movement, from Depression to Cold War*, 1981.

Joseph Turrini

Auto-Lite Strike (1934). *See Depression-Era Strikes.*

Automation. The term *automation* generally refers to manufacturing processes in which machines perform much of the labor and human interaction is minimal. Labor unions often resist automation as it usually increases production output but supplants human workers.

Labor historians do not employ a common definition of automation, but they are in accord about its far-reaching effects on industrial relations in the United States, particularly in the twenty years following the end of World War II. The term was first coined by Ford Motor Company vice president Del Harder in 1947, to describe the mechanical work-feeding and material-handling devices coming into factories. Automation also referred to 1950s-era computer electronic feedback devices which made machines self-setting and self-connecting. The first of these phenomena appeared in the nineteenth century, and by the 1920s, labor-saving machinery was commonplace in textiles, rubber, and shoe industries. The second development caused great alarm among unionists and intellectuals when electronic devices began replacing human judgment in processing plants in the 1950s.

Assembly-line workers polish auto bodies in a Ford Motor Company plant in Minnesota. March 1, 1935. © Minnesota Historical Society/Corbis.

Although the "automation hysteria" predictions of robot factories did not materialize in the immediate post–World War II period, automation succeeded in strengthening the hand of employers. In basic industries, automation reduced the need for workers and curtailed their bargaining power in dramatic fashion. **Rank-and-file** workers struggled against its effects to no avail: on docks containerization transformed longshoremen's work; in the pressroom, linotype gave way to cold-type composition; and in machine shops, engineers and machinists battled for control of the programming function on the first generation of automated tools. Labor leaders, committed to an increasingly circumscribed **collective bargaining** framework, did not effectively challenge work reorganization. Attempts to hold onto jobs opened unions to charges of **featherbedding** and made them appear inefficient. Unions did win the creation of "automation funds" to protect some senior workers, but failed to affect the shape and character of automation overall.

By the 1960s, automation was commonplace and its pace has accelerated unabated since. Its impact can be seen most dramatically in auto, electronics, machine tools, and steel, where robots now perform handling, welding, grinding, and assembly tasks once performed by humans. Automation also renewed charges that assembly line work was dehumanizing. Once machines took over judgment tasks, those workers who remained on the job complained their labor was monotonous. This was an issue in the 1972 **Lordstown**, Ohio strike against Chevrolet, and has been an ongoing dispute for aircraft machinists and postal workers since the 1980s.

Automation empowered women workers in indirect but significant ways by removing many elements previously used to justify job typing by sex. This broke down the old rationale for gender inequality in the workplace. As industrial engineers made "heavy" or "male" jobs obsolete, support for **protective legislation** for women no longer seemed compelling. The rise of working-class feminism in the late 1960s was rooted, in part, in this transformation a decade earlier. A new type of automation, however, has roused women and men alike. Advances in computers and communications now allow employers to electronically monitor employees and set demanding production quotas. In the past decade, this has led to worker-management conflict with keypunch and telephone operators.

Suggested Readings: Barbara Garson, *The Electronic Sweatshop*, 1989; David Noble, *Forces of Production: A Social History of Industrial Automation*, 1984; Harley Shaiken, *Work Transformed: Automation and Labor in the Computer Age*, 1984.

Dennis A. Deslippe

B

Back Pay. The term *back pay* refers to paying wages that were earned but withheld for one reason or another. One concept of back pay involves an award issued to an employee as a result of a process of dispute resolution. This is called a "make whole" award. In this situation, an employee is denied the right to work by a management action that is later deemed an inappropriate application of a **contract**. An example would be laying off the wrong employee. The employee and/or union could file a grievance and would ask to be "made whole" for any monetary losses. If the complaint is upheld in **arbitration**, the grievant is awarded back pay. Settlements for back pay can be calculated to include wages and any lost benefits such as vacation time, overtime, and bonuses. Back pay calculation can also include any out-of-pocket monies spent on things like health insurance that would have normally been covered by the employer. The arbitrator determines the extent of the back pay calculation. Back pay can also encompass any retroactive wages owed to employees after ratification of a contract.

Suggested Readings: Terry Leap, ed., *Collective Bargaining and Labor Relations*, 1995; Harold Roberts, *Roberts' Dictionary of Industrial Relations*, 1994.

Carolyn Anderson

Bagley, Sarah (April 19, 1806–?). Sarah Bagley was president of the Lowell Female Labor Reform Association (LFLRA) and the first female labor leader to exert influence beyond her local area. Bagley was born in Candia, New Hampshire. Little is known of her life before she arrived in Lowell, Massachusetts in 1836, although she obtained enough formal education to become a highly articulate writer and speaker.

In 1836, Lowell was considered the ideal factory city and was a popular tourist destination, as well as a thriving industrial concern. Bagley originally took part in Improvement Circles, designed to enrich the educational and cultural lives of mill workers, and she wrote for the *Lowell Offering,* a paper sponsored by the Boston Associates, the consortium that owned Lowell's textile mills. Conditions in Lowell worsened even before Bagley arrived, however, with a short walkout occurring in 1834. The Panic of 1837 caused more wage cuts, **speed-ups** in the factory, and high turnover rates. Another wage cut and strike in 1840 apparently radicalized Bagley. She became an advocate of the theories of Charles Fourier (1772–1837), a French utopian advocate of **cooperative** production and communal living.

In December 1844, Bagley became the cofounder and first president of the LFLRA, widely hailed as America's first union of factory women. Within six months it had over 500 members, and Bagley left her mill job to expand the association's reach to other cities. Eventually Female Labor Reform groups met in Waltham and Fall River, Massachusetts; Dover, Nashua, and Manchester, New Hampshire; and across western Pennsylvania. Central to the LFLRA platform was the call for a ten-hour work day. Bagley immersed herself in the ten-hour struggle and testified before a Massachusetts legislative committee on behalf of the cause in 1845. She also affiliated the LFLRA with the New England Working Men's Association and served as the editor of its newspaper, *The Voice of Industry*. Her attacks on the *Lowell Offering* hastened that paper's demise, and her organization the Industrial Reform Lyceum, brought a steady stream of radical speakers to Lowell.

Despite Bagley's tireless efforts, the ten-hour plea was rejected by the Massachusetts legislature and a call for a **general strike** on July 4, 1846, fizzled. *The Voice of Industry* foundered and Bagley resigned after a dispute with a sexist editor. In 1846, Bagley became the first female telegraph operator in the city of Lowell, a trade she also plied in Springfield, Massachusetts in 1847, before returning to Lowell as a millhand. She later moved to Philadelphia and became a Quaker. Sometime in the 1850s she married James Durno, an Albany, New York homeopathic doctor and patent medicine manufacturer. They moved to Brooklyn Heights, New York, where Durno died in 1872. Bagley disappears from the historical record after 1883.

Suggested Readings: Eleanor Flexner, *Century of Struggle: The Woman's Rights Movement in the United States*, 1972; Philip Foner, *Women and the American Labor Movement: From the First Trade Unions to the Present*, 1982.

Robert E. Weir

Bargaining Unit. Employees with common interests or skills will organize into a single entity called a bargaining unit. The National Labor Relations Board (NLRB) defines a bargaining unit through a certification process. Employees within a defined bargaining unit have the right to hold an election to determine who will represent them as a union.

The common goal of a bargaining unit is to work towards securing a union **contract** through the process of **collective bargaining**. Once an agreement is obtained the unit will vote to accept or reject it. If accepted, the contract will determine the wages, hours, and conditions of work for the particular group. If rejected, the bargaining unit may enter into concerted activities such as **picketing** or **strikes** to persuade management to change its position.

Suggested Reading: Terry Leap, ed., *Collective Bargaining and Labor Relations*, 1995.

Carolyn Anderson

Barry, Leonora Marie (August 13, 1849–July 15, 1930). Leonora Marie Barry was the general investigator for women's work for the **Knights of Labor (KOL)**, and a pioneer in organizing women into labor unions. She was one of the first to compile accurate statistics and reports on women laborers, to bring women into the union fold, and to insist that women's organizing models should reflect their interests, not those of men. Partly due to Barry's efforts, the KOL contained as many as 60,000 female members at a time in which very few unions even tried to organize women.

She was born Lenora Marie Kearney on August 13, 1849, in County Cork, Ireland, the daughter of John and Honor (Brown) Kearney. The family emigrated to upstate New York in 1851. Leonora's mother died in 1864, and her father remarried. She quarreled with her stepmother and left home at age sixteen. She studied at a girls' school in Colton, New York, and did well enough to obtain a certificate and begin teaching before she was seventeen. Leonora taught until 1871, when she married William E. Barry, a Potsdam, New York painter. Their first child, Marion Frances, was born in 1873, followed by William Standish in 1875, and Charles Joseph in 1880. The family moved several times before settling in Amsterdam, New York.

In 1881, both Leonora's daughter and husband died of lung disease. She was forced to seek employment to support her sons and settled into an Amsterdam hosiery mill after an unsuccessful attempt at being a seamstress. In 1884, she joined the Knights of Labor's Victory Assembly in Amsterdam, the KOL having begun organizing women in 1880. Barry rose quickly in the KOL. By 1886, she headed Victory Assembly's 900 women and led them during a successful mill strike. That same year, she helped the national order resolve a dispute with retail magnate John Wannamaker, and at the KOL's fall convention she was designated the KOL's first general investigator for women's work.

Barry put her sons in boarding school and spent nearly four years traveling, lecturing, organizing, and compiling reports on behalf of the Knights. In 1888 alone, Barry visited over 100 cities. Her reports detailed low wages, shocking conditions, and abuses against women workers. Barry routinely chided male Knights for not living up to the organization's platform plank on gender equality, and women workers for their apathy towards organized labor. She was one of the first to insist that organizing women required different methods than unionizing male workers.

Barry also got embroiled in the KOL's internal politics and earned the antipathy of General Secretary John Hayes, who plotted to remove much of Barry's power. In 1888, the Women's Department was placed under Hayes's control and he harassed Barry. In April 1890 Barry shocked the KOL by announcing she was resigning from the order because of her recent remarriage to Obadiah Reed Lake, a St. Louis editor and printer. In her resignation, Barry opined that a woman's proper place was in the home.

Barry returned to public life to campaign for women's suffrage and to lecture on behalf of the Women's Christian Temperance Union and the Catholic Total Abstinence Society. She retired to Minooka, Illinois, where she died of mouth cancer on July 15, 1930.

Suggested Readings: Philip Foner, *Women and the American Labor Movement*, 1982; Robert Weir, *Knights Unhorsed: Internal Conflict in a Gilded Age Social Movement*, 2000.

Robert E. Weir

Battle of Blair Mountain. The Battle of Blair Mountain was an armed encounter between miners and deputy sheriffs, state police, state militia, and Baldwin-Felts detectives. It took place in West Virginia during August 1921, and ended when President Warren Harding sent federal troops to the area, as well as ordering the aerial bombing of entrenched miner positions. It came near the end of the West Virginia-Kentucky coal strike of 1920–23, a struggle that included the infamous **Matewan** massacre. Some sources maintain that Blair Mountain was the largest armed struggle on American soil since the Civil War.

Blair Mountain was in direct response to events in Matewan, West Virginia. Matewan police chief Sid Hatfield was on trial for the murder of detective Albert Felts when, on August 1, 1921, Baldwin agents murdered him as he was on his way to his trial. Miners planned a march from Kanawha County to the Logan County courthouse to protest Hatfield's murder, as well as the ongoing refusal of coal operators to bargain with the **United Mine Workers of America (UMWA)**. Inflamed miners announced their intention to hang the local sheriff, burn the courthouse, and then proceed to Mingo County and free imprisoned miners. The march commenced on August 24, 1921, and was dubbed "Mother Jones's will," even though **Mary Harris Jones** counseled against it.

The march never made it to the courthouse. It was met by an armed resistance force at a mountain ridge near Lens Creek. The two groups took up positions in the ridges and the full-scale Battle of Blair Mountain ensued. No one knows for certain how many miners were involved; estimates vary from 7,000 to over 20,000, as miners from nearby counties flocked to give assistance. They faced a foe armed with machine guns and bombing planes, but nonetheless routed a force of deputy sheriffs. Miners briefly controlled much of the area south of the state capitol in Charleston, plundering stores, waylaying trains, posting sentries, and causing many politicians to flee.

On August 30, President Harding placed all of West Virginia under martial law and on September 1, 2,500 federal troops arrived with more machine guns, percussion and gas bombs, and fourteen airplanes. Bombs were dropped on miner positions, though accuracy in the early days of flight was problematic. The insurrection soon collapsed, many miners refusing to take up arms against their government.

An estimated twenty-five miners died during the ten-day confrontation, and more than 1,500 men were charged with treason, murder, and conspiracy, though none was convicted. The Battle of Blair Mountain broke the spirit of the miners, though the UMWA did not officially call off the strike until 1923. Its membership plummeted in the aftermath of Blair Mountain, but the harsh conditions of American mines guaranteed that the union's presence would remain. By the 1930s, the UMWA began to reverse its fortunes and its national president, **John L. Lewis**, became a commanding force in capital-labor relations.

Suggested Readings: David Corbin, *Life, Work, and Rebellion in the Coal Fields: The Southern West Virginia Miners, 1880–1922*, 1981; Howard Lee, *Bloodletting in Appalachia*, 1969; Lon Savage, *Thunder in the Mountain: The West Virginia Mine War*, 1990.

Robert E. Weir

Bellamyite Nationalism. Bellamyite Nationalism was a short-lived but influential movement that emerged in reaction to the publication of Edward Bellamy's utopian novel, *Looking Backward*, in 1888. The narrative centers on Julian West, a member of the nineteenth-century bourgeoisie, who is placed in a hypnotic trance and awakes in the year 2000. West finds that the strike-plagued, poverty-ridden Boston of his youth has been supplanted by an egalitarian utopia in which all members of society serve in an industrial army from age twenty-one until their retirement at forty-five. Competitive capitalism has been replaced by a network of state-owned production and distribution centers. Also banished are class conflict, money, accumulated wealth, taxes, nonproductive labor, domestic toil, gender inequality (as Bellamy understood it), and virtually every other social problem. This remarkable transformation occurred peacefully; Americans used the ballot box to apply political solutions to the social and economic problems that had troubled West's world.

Although a novel, Bellamy's book fired the public imagination to the point where it was selling a thousand copies per day. It brought fame to the otherwise unassuming western Massachusetts novelist and reporter for the *Springfield Daily Union*. Much to Bellamy's surprise, *Looking Backward* was taken by some as a blueprint for the future, and it inspired a movement dedicated to making Bellamy's fictive evolutionary socialism a reality. In 1889, Bostonians set up the first Bellamy Club and within a decade, over 165 groups had sprung into existence. The movement became known as Nationalism because of the state-directed nature of Bellamy's utopian enterprise. Appeal for both the book and Nationalism was strongest among the middle class; Bellamy's peaceful road to reform appealed to genteel citizens weary of economic depression and social conflict. But the working classes also embraced Bellamy's book, with both the **American Federation of Labor** and the **Knights of Labor** endorsing it. Many Knights joined Nationalist clubs and several clubs, in turn, formed labor unions.

Bellamy came to take a more active role in the Nationalist movement. In 1897, he published a sequel, *Equality*, that addressed criticisms leveled by opponents of his utopia. The book lacked the conventional Victorian romance of its predecessor and languished; Bellamy died the following year. Today, certain aspects of *Looking Backward* seem quaint, and others naïve. The book's critique of Gilded Age problems remains incisive, however. He attracted a host of thinkers and leaders who gleaned inspiration and ideas that they applied in their own quests for social justice. Bellamy's admirers included: **Eugene V. Debs**, **Daniel DeLeon**, **Elizabeth Gurley Flynn**, Charlotte Perkins Gilman, and Upton Sinclair. Many leaders of the Populist party cited Bellamy as a mentor. The work was also widely read, quoted, and modified among reformers in both the Progressive Era and New Deal. Nationalism also proved a powerful force in Australia and New Zealand, where social legislation was modeled on Bellamyite precepts.

Suggested Readings: Edward Bellamy, *Looking Backward*, 1888; Peter Coleman, *Progressivism and the World of Reform*, 1987; Franklin Rosemont, *Apparitions of Things to Come*, 1990.

Robert E. Weir

Blackleg. *See Scab.*

Black Lung Strike. The Black Lung Strike was a short coal strike in West Virginia during 1969. As a result of the strike, miners' pneumoconiosis ("black lung" disease) was officially recognized as an occupationally induced illness for which **workman's compensation** was entitled.

The strike was called by the **United Mine Workers of America (UMWA)**, and it began on February 18, 1969, as part of a larger dispute with Westmoreland Coal's East Gulf Mine in Rhodell, West Virginia. Within days it spread and more than 40,000 miners went out. A key strike leader was Arnold Miller, a reformer within what was then an autocratic union. The strike lasted twenty-three days and saw the miners muster a mass demonstration at the state capitol in Charleston. At the time, black lung was not recognized as an official ailment, despite mounting scientific evidence to the contrary. In 1968, miners set up the Black Lung Association and engaged in several **wildcat strikes** to publicize the dangers of black lung. Although West Virginia Governor Arch Moore was angered by the wildcats and the 1969 UMWA protest in Charleston, he eventually signed legislation making black lung eligible for compensation. The strike ended on March 11, 1969.

Later in 1969, Congress passed the Coal Mine Health and Safety Act and placed enforcement of the bill under the auspices of the Mine Safety and

Health Administration. Not surprisingly, many miners filed for compensation after the bill's passage. Congress established the Black Lung Trust Fund at the prompting of West Virginia congressmen. In 1986, Senator Jay Rockefeller led a successful fight against the Reagan administration's efforts to raise the tax on coal, an action he claimed would have led to a decline in production that would imperil the fund.

Miners' pneumoconiosis is now recognized by all credible scientists as an occupational hazard associated with coal mining. Awareness of black lung and related diseases—like "brown lung" and "white lung" among textile workers and stone cutters—have led to dramatic improvement of factory ventilation and dust control systems to control the ingestion of airborne particulates. The successful fight also led to changes inside the UMWA. Miller led the Miners For Democracy (MFD) **rank-and-file** insurgency group that protested union corruption. In the wake of the dramatic murder of **Joseph Yablonski**, for which opponent Tony Boyle was convicted, the MFD gained control of the UMWA. In 1972, Arnold Miller was elected UMWA president.

Suggested Reading: Kim Moody, *An Injury to All: The Decline of American Unionism*, 1989.

Robert E. Weir

Blue-Collar Workers. Blue-collar worker is an increasingly out-of-fashion term that refers to those who do manual labor. They are often juxtaposed against "white-" or "pink-" collar workers, white referring to office workers and professionals, and pink to clerical workers who, beginning in the twentieth century, were often women. The inference is that manual workers get dirty in their jobs and would soon ruin a white collar. It also generally implies male workers, thus its contrast to pink-collar labor. It is said that blue-collar workers toil with their hands, while white- and pink-collar workers work with their minds. As a group, blue-collar workers tend to have less formal education. One should approach these generalizations with caution, however, as individual cases prove them to be over-simplifications.

The first coinage of the phrase is unknown, but it was in wide circulation by the 1940s, and was a commonly used category in sociological studies in the 1950s. Blue-collar work is most associated with factory labor, though other manual laborers, especially construction workers—some times also called "hard hats"—also fit the bill. By the 1960s, social analysts spoke of the "blue-collar blues," a growing disillusionment among manual laborers that employers and society at large undervalued their work, their concerns, and their well-being. Work itself was often viewed as demeaning, especially on assembly lines. (See **Fordism**.) Numerous young workers found factory discipline distasteful and many engaged in **rank-and-file** rebellions during the 1960s, and took part in **wildcat strikes** and social protests during the decade. Other, often older, workers complained that Baby Boomer children claimed privileges denied to hard-working "average" Americans. Some were deeply troubled by social unrest in the 1960s. In 1970, an incident dubbed the "hard-hat-riot" saw several hundred New York City construction workers attack anti–Vietnam War protestors on Wall Street. Some observers began to speak of "working-class conservatism."

Politicians like Richard Nixon began to fashion appeals to supposed working-class conservatives. Although their numbers were exaggerated by the media, the Democratic Party largely underestimated worker resentment. Since the New Deal, blue-collar voters had been a core Democratic constituency, but many blue-collar voters cast ballots for former segregationist George Wallace in 1968, and for Nixon in 1968 and 1972. A majority of blue-collar voters opted for Ronald Reagan in 1980 and 1984.

By the 1970s, the "blue-collar blues" were compounded by rising unemployment, inflation, and factory closings. A wave of **deindustrialization** struck once-vaunted American industries like steel, rubber, mining, and electronics, making it appear that blue-collar workers were an endangered species. This, coupled with lingering ideological clashes from the 1960s, contributed to the blue-collar voter shift toward the Republican Party. The trend continued, despite the fact that Republican policies in the 1980s exacerbated the decline in blue-collar work. By the 1990s, commentators spoke of the "betrayal" of manual workers, though the term blue collar was out of vogue. From this line of reasoning, workers—especially men—found that the ideals and implied promises of American society were no longer attainable. Hard work alone did not guarantee that a worker could support his family and live in material comfort. Between 1973 and 1995, real wages—those adjusted for inflation—tumbled in most construction and manufacturing jobs.

The fate of semiskilled and unskilled workers is uncertain in the age of **globalization**, **runaway shops**, and movable capital. Although manufacturing remains an important part of the American economy, it is clearly in decline. In 1960, manufacturing employed about 28 percent of the workforce; by 2000, that figure had declined to around 16 percent. Economists now speak of a "postindustrial" economy in which service sector and retail jobs proliferate while blue-collar work continues to decline. On average, the new postindustrial jobs pay 25 percent less than most manufacturing jobs and only about half of those available in construction. If such trends continue, "blue-collar" will likely become a historical term referencing bygone work patterns.

Suggested Readings: Barbara Ehrenreich, *Fear of Falling*, 1990; Susan Faludi, *Stiffed: The Betrayal of the American Man*, 2000; Studs Terkel, *Working*, 1974.

Robert E. Weir

Bonus. A bonus is usually an amount of money that is given over and above an employee's base wage. For example, an employee who completes a training program might be awarded a $200 bonus as a one-time achievement payment. Contract signing, longevity, recruitment, and retention can all trigger similar awards. Employees covered under a **collective bargaining** agreement must negotiate the amount, duration, and end point of all bonus money. Such awards can be negotiated to become part of the base wage, however, it is not the norm.

Employees under a merit system or non-collective bargaining system may also receive increments as bonuses. The amount may depend upon the success of the employee over a set time period. This money often becomes a part of the employee's base wage. In this respect, it is synonymous with a **merit raise**.

Suggested Reading: Harold Roberts, *Roberts' Dictionary of Industrial Relations*, 1994.

Carolyn Anderson

The Boot and Shoe Workers' Union. This union was organized in Boston in 1895 and was part of a long and largely unsuccessful effort to organize shoemakers. Shoemaking has been a notoriously poorly paid profession, even in Colonial times. Disgruntled shoemakers were among the earliest craft workers to embrace the cause of the American Revolution, though it did little to improve their lot. **Journeymen** shoemakers meeting in Philadelphia beginning in 1792 are often credited as being the first union to collect **dues** and organize for the purpose of **collective bargaining**. It was also the first union to be deemed an illegal criminal conspiracy. The group reorganized as the **Federal Society of Journeymen Cordwainers** in 1794, but faded from existence after 1806.

Conspiracy laws were used against most shoe and boot makers seeking to organize in the antebellum period. In 1842, a Boston association was broken by the use of conspiracy laws. Organization efforts were also hampered by the transformation of work. Technological innovations like the McKay stitching machine displaced **master** craftsmen and subdivided the profession into various semiskilled tasks like cutters, heelers, lasters, and stitchers. Like the textile industry, many of these positions were filled by women and the industry often bristled with gender conflict. Still, the proliferation of shoe factories, especially in New England, New York, and Pennsylvania, made it ripe for organization. The **Shoemakers Strike of 1860** in Lynn, Massachusetts, was, at the time, the largest mass walkout in American history. In all, some 20,000 New England shoemakers went on strike.

After the Civil War, the Lasters' Protective Union (LPU) and the **Knights of St. Crispin (KOSC)** attempted to fill the organizational needs of shoe and boot makers. The KOSC was badly crippled by lost strikes in 1870 and the economic ravages of 1873. Numerous KOSC leaders made their way into the **Knights of Labor (KOL)** and, in 1878, most KOSC locals were absorbed into the KOL. The KOL and LPU enjoyed good relations until a devastating 1887 shoe strike that engulfed New England drove the two apart. KOL shoemakers pressed for a national trade district to represent their craft within the Knights. Such a group was formed in 1888 but, in 1889, many KOL shoemakers quit the organization and, along with some LPU locals, formed the Boot and Shoe Workers' International Union (BSWIU) and affiliated with the **American Federation of Labor (AFL)**.

The period between 1890 and 1910 was a militant one in shoemaker union history, with key leadership roles being played by dynamic women like Mary Nason, Emma Steghagen, and Mary Anderson, the last of whom became a key figure in the **Women's Trade Union League** and in the **Department of Labor**. The BSWIU expanded from its base in the Northeast to other shoemaking centers like Chicago, Cincinnati, Detroit, and St. Louis. Massachusetts saw several strikes in the 1890s, again with women taking the lead. Most of these ended in defeat and by 1900, the BSWIU membership sank to around 5,000. It was rejuvenated in the early twentieth century through an aggressive **union label** campaign that linked union fortunes to consumer buying habits.

The BSWIU never successfully unified all shoemakers into a single **industrial union**, however. Even as it enjoyed growth in the early twentieth century, it fought **jurisdictional** battles with the LPU, the upstart Shoe Workers' Protective Union, and remnant KOL assemblies. Members also complained of heavy-handed union tactics, and stitchers, who were disproportionately female, felt especially aggrieved. Rivals to the BSWIU stood ready to take their place during a 1903 strike in New England that became a referendum on the BSWIU that greatly weakened it in its home base. By strike's end, still another rival, the Federation of Shoe and Leather Workers, sprang into existence. The **Industrial Workers of the World** siphoned off still more. By 1920, women especially had bolted the BSWIU.

Organization within the shoe and boot industry was further hindered by the displacement of workers by technology, by the influx of cheaper immigrant labor, by industry consolidation, and by corporate decisions to move operations to the antiunion, lower-wage South. Various shoemaking unions experienced modest growth spurts in the 1930s and several new organizations appeared, but the heyday of organizational efforts came before 1920. For the most part, shoemaking remained a poorly paid occupation into the early 1960s, by which time production increasingly took place outside the United States. Today, almost all shoe production takes place overseas. BSWIU locals continued to operate into the late 1970s, but most either passed out of existence or were absorbed by other unions.

Suggested Readings: Mary Blewett, *Men, Women, and Work: Class, Gender, and Protest in the New England Shoe Industry, 1780–1910*, 1990; John R. Commons, "American Shoemakers, 1648–1895: A Sketch of Industrial Evolution," *American Journal of Economics*, 24 (1909), 39–84; Norman Ware, *The Labor Movement in the United States 1860–1895*, 1929.

Bruce Cohen
Robert E. Weir

Boston Police Strike of 1919. The Boston Police Strike of 1919 was one of a series of industrial conflicts that erupted after World War I. In 1919 alone, over three thousand work stoppages occurred, idling about four million workers. Some Americans feared that these uprisings were precursors to a working-class revolution similar to the one that toppled the Russian government in 1917. Others worried that the unionization of public employees endangered civic order and the protection of private property. Officials in Boston and elsewhere were especially loath to sanction the affiliation of police unions with larger labor federations, asserting that **dual unionism** threatened justice and undermined loyalty to the state. The **American Federation of Labor (AFL)** countered that public employees were trade workers and thus entitled to union protection. The Boston Police Strike became the battleground between these competing ideals.

Boston police turned to the AFL for relief from low wages and poor working conditions. Police had received only two raises since 1898, and postwar inflation eroded their purchasing power. Police routinely worked between seventy and 100 hours per week. The Boston Social Club, ostensibly a channel for airing grievances, was controlled by administrators and proved an inadequate bargaining agent. In August 1919, Boston police formed an independent union, but within weeks it received an AFL charter.

Governor of Massachusetts (John) Calvin Coolidge (1872–1933) inspecting troops that he brought in to quell a police strike and riots in Boston. Hulton/Archive.

When police rebuffed pressure to abandon their union from new police commissioner Edward Curtis, he issued Order 110 on August 11. This document forbade police from joining extradepartmental organizations except for approved veterans' groups. On September 7, Curtis suspended nineteen suspected union leaders. The next day, the Boston Police Union voted to strike by a vote of 1,134 to 2. On Tuesday, September 9, 1,117 of Boston's 1,544 police officers walked out.

The strike was severely compromised when, that very night, Bostonians engaged in an orgy of open gambling, destruction of property, store looting, and assaults on bystanders, volunteers, and non-striking police. Mayor Andrew Peters called out the Massachusetts National Guard the next day and personally assumed control of the police department. Peters, a Democrat, probably hoped to embarrass Republican political rivals, including Commissioner Curtis and Governor Calvin Coolidge. By Thursday, September 11, calm was restored—with most of the property damage and casualties having been inflicted by the Guard rather than rioters.

Public outrage erupted over the strike, fueled by newspapers heralding it as the vanguard of a "Bolshevik" revolution. This provided Curtis and Coolidge with pretext for smashing the strike. Coolidge removed Peters as emergency head of the police department and restored control to Curtis, who announced a plan to fire striking police and replace them with new recruits. Coolidge also rejected an appeal to withhold action from AFL president Samuel Gompers, who volunteered to mediate. Coolidge tartly replied, "There is no right to strike against public safety by anybody, anywhere, anytime." His hard-line stance frightened the Boston Central Labor Union, which voted against a **sympathy strike**.

By September 13, the strike was effectively broken, though some actions continued into October. Most strikers lost their jobs. The defeat of the strike destroyed a nascent movement for public-sector unionization, and it catapulted Coolidge into national politics. Public-sector workers subsequently were excluded from protection under the **National Labor Relations Act**, and it would not be until the 1960s that the federal government would provide for some protection. Many states still lack laws granting collective bargaining rights to public employees.

Suggested Readings: Robert Murray, *Red Scare: A Study in National Hysteria, 1919–1920*, 1955; Francis Russell, *A City in Terror: 1919, The Boston Police Strike*, 1975; Joseph Slater, "Public Workers: Labor and the Boston Police Strike of 1919," *Labor History* 38:1 (1997): 7–27.

John McKerley

Boulwarism. Boulwarism is named for Lemeul Boulware, General Electric's chief labor negotiator after World War II. It refers to a "take-it-or-leave-it" bargaining posture by management. Following a 1946 strike victory led by the leftist **United Electrical, Radio, and Machine Workers of America (UE)**, General Electric applied marketing principles to collective bargaining designed to keep the UE on the defensive. These included studying and correcting selected employee concerns, and improving communications with employees. During bargaining sessions, GE placed a single and "final" offer on the table, challenging the UE to accept it or reject it. Changes in GE's offer were made solely on the basis of new research or information, not in response to union demands or pressure. Boulware also took advantage of the UE's expulsion from the **Congress of Industrial Organizations** in 1949, and the creation of the rival **International Union of Electrical, Radio, and Machine Workers** to force the UE into an unfavorable settlement.

In 1964, the National Labor Relations Board ruled that Boulwarism constituted bargaining in bad faith and that efforts to negotiate with individual workers violated collective bargaining rights. Nonetheless, some union activists cite Boulwarism as a model for future corporate intransigence.

Suggested Readings: Lemuel Boulware, *The Truth About Boulwarism*, 1969; James Matles and James Higgins, *Them and Us*, 1975.

Albert V. Lannon

Boycott. A boycott occurs when a supporter of organized labor refuses to purchase a product or service from a concern deemed unfair to its employees. The term is borrowed from Irish nationalists. In the mid-1800s, Captain Charles Cunningham Boycott managed lands in Ireland for an absentee English landlord. When tenants requested rent deductions, Captain Boycott refused and tenants launched a protest that included refusing to work and ostracizing him in the community. By 1880, Charles Stuart Parnell and the Irish Land League were using the term boycott as a general term to mean non-patronage of a hated rival.

Among nineteenth-century American workers, boycotts were often preferred to strikes, as the latter incurred economic hardship on workers as well as employers. Groups like the **Knights of Labor** were officially opposed to strikes and ordered untold numbers of boycotts. The Knights sought to publicize boycotts, encourage widespread compliance, and apply such economic pressure on employers that they would be forced to bargain with unions in exchange for raising the boycott. Although boycotts never lived up to the exalted expectations of the Knights, they did indeed pressure some employers to settle labor disputes.

There are two types of boycotts: primary and secondary. Primary boycotts involve direct refusal to patronize a single employer or corporation, whereas the secondary boycott targets distributors and others who do business with the concern in dispute. In a struggle against a newspaper, for example, a secondary boycott would discourage purchasing any product from a store carrying the boycotted newspaper. This was the approach employed by the **American Railway Union** during the 1894 **Pullman strike/lockout** and strike. Rail workers across the country refused to make up trains that included Pullman cars.

Secondary boycotts often proved more successful than primary boycotts, but they have been more difficult to launch since the 1947 **Taft-Hartley Act** banned most types of them. In recent labor history, one of the most successful uses of the boycott was led by the **United Farm Workers (UFW)** with its five-year boycott of table grapes from 1965 to 1970. Since farm workers are exempt from most national labor laws, the UFW found it easier to launch a secondary boycott. Aspects of the secondary boycott also endure in so-called **corporate campaigns**, particularly when labor disputes involve union pension funds invested in banks that also deal with recalcitrant employers.

Suggested Readings: Philip Foner, *History of the Labor Movement in the United States, Vol. II*, 1955; Daniel Jacoby, *Laboring for Freedom*, 1998; Robert E. Weir, *Beyond Labor's Veil*, 1996.

Cheryl Conley
Robert E. Weir

Bread and Roses Strike. *See Lawrence Textile Strike.*

Brewery Workers. Brewery workers were seldom unionized in Germany, and this situation continued when many of them emigrated to the United States. Numerous mutual aid societies were founded by German-American New York City in 1867—but attempts to unionize came relatively late. Breweries were exceptionally resilient to unionization, though brewery workers endured deplorable working conditions and worked long hours.

Failed attempts to organize were made in St. Louis in 1850, in New York City in 1860, and in August 1866, when brewery workers convened in Baltimore to demand the **eight-hour** day. Many Eight-Hour Leagues were formed across the country and a nascent organization was already in place when a strike of building trades broke out in New York City in May 1872. Brewery workers demanded a shorter workday and higher wages, and workers went from one brewery to another presenting their demands. Refusals led to strikes and clashes between police and strikers. The strike was quickly lost, and many workers were blacklisted.

Conditions in the breweries worsened during a series of depressions after 1873. Many workers wrote letters to the German-language *New Yorker Volkszeitung* (NYVZ) detailing their deteriorating conditions. In the wake of the railroad strikes during the **Great Labor Uprising** of 1877, brewery workers in Cincinnati began organizing and, after several failures, organized the Brauer Gesellen Union (BGU) in December 1879. This union quickly allied with the Central Trades Assembly. In 1881, the BGU presented a series of demands to brewery owners asking for a shortened workday, a minimum-wage agreement, freedom to procure board and lodging of their own choosing, and a reduction of working hours on Sunday. Four breweries granted these demands, but nineteen others refused. A strike was called, but it failed and the unions lost membership. Breweries finally did reduce working hours, but the unions were weakened.

In 1881, workers in the St. Louis breweries tried and failed to organize, but that same year, New York City workers were mobilized by a fire at the Peter Doelger Brewery that resulted in several deaths. The foreman at the brewery was accused of physically striking workers and making them perform hazardous tasks. In February 1881 an appeal was sent out by an anonymous group of brewery workers that called for a union. Workers at the Henry Elias Brewery circulated the appeal to a number of other establishments, and workers held a general meeting on March 6, 1881. *NYVZ* journalist and union organizer George Block, a German-speaking immigrant, attended the meeting and helped organize the Brewery Workmen's Union of New York and Vicinity. Initial membership consisted of 121, but soon grew to include brewery workers from Manhattan, Brooklyn, Union Hill, Newark, New Jersey, Staten Island, and other nearby locales.

As the union spread through the city, the J. Ruppert, Ringler, and Schaefer Breweries dismissed a number of union members. After this was reported in the *NYVZ*, the Cigar Makers International Union, the Piano Maker's Union, and the **United Brotherhood of Carpenters and Joiners** all called for a **boycott** of the above breweries' beer. While this boycott was successful, the strike of 1881 was not. A demand for shorter working hours and higher wages was refused by the smaller breweries, and a strike was called on June 6, 1881. Some brewery workers refused to join in the strike, and non-union teamsters from non-striking breweries were called in to substitute for the strikers. Despite the boycott led by the **Central Labor Union** and the Socialist Labor Party, the strike was over in five weeks. Union membership declined and blacklists were enforced. But, as in St. Louis, the larger New York breweries implemented some of the demands. The Brewery Workmen's Union, however, was destroyed.

Although workers in one New York City brewery formed a union under the aegis of the **Knights of Labor (KOL)**, no widespread organization took place until 1884. On August 10, the Central Labor Union assisted the workers in organizing the Brewers' Union #1, out of which developed the Union of United Brewery Workmen of America. Originally comprised of only twelve members, Brewers' Union #1 steadily grew in the intervening years, and affiliated itself with the KOL. The 1885 boycott of the Peter Doelger Brewery was a particular success, and by 1886 the Brewers' Union decided to withdraw from the Knights and attempt a national organization. Brewery workers in Baltimore, Detroit, Newark, Philadelphia, San Francisco, and St. Louis also joined the KOL, which chartered the Brewery Workers International Union in 1884. The KOL also organized brewery workers in Chicago, Cincinnati, and Milwaukee. By 1889, nearly all brewery unions had quit the Knights, largely over the order's temperance policies. Several subsequently affiliated with the **American Federation of Labor (AFL)**.

In 1886, the brewery workers of Cincinnati, Baltimore, Chicago, Newark, St. Louis, Philadelphia, Detroit, and Buffalo organized unions, and in 1887 Albany, San Francisco, Cleveland, Milwaukee, New Haven, Boston, and other places followed suit. On August 29, 1886, the first national convention of brewery workers was held in Baltimore. The name chosen for the national union was the National Union of the Brewers of the United States, and the seat of the national executive committee was located in New York City. It originally counted 2,700 members, and grew to over 4,000 by January 1887. Union membership was overwhelmingly German in origin, therefore the first journal of the organization, published beginning in October 1886, was the *Brauer Zeitung*. This publication—whose name was changed to *Brauerei Arbeiter Zeitung* in 1910—continued to be published in German until 1917.

At the 1887 convention in Detroit several new locals were recognized, and the name of the organization was changed to the National Union of United Brewery Workmen of the United States. At this convention the membership debated whether to admit coopers, teamsters, maltsters, and firemen, but the decision of whether to include these crafts or to give them their own union was left up to the locals. In addition, the union executive passed resolutions condemning the Knights of Labor's president, **Terence V. Powderly**, for recent statements he had made in support of prohibition. The growing prohibitionist sentiment provided a major irritation for the union in the years to come.

The new union was mainly German in origin, and it evinced little desire to include the Irish and other groups working in the ale and porter breweries. In addition, Local #1 in New York City was closed to new immigrants in 1887.

This protectionist stance and ethnic isolation had grievous consequences in the 1887–88 strikes. In the past, the union depended on community support for boycotts, but the new isolation cut the union off from its potential support. First the Milwaukee local went on strike in the fall of 1887, resulting in a nationwide boycott of beer produced in Milwaukee. Brewers across the nation were incensed, and in early 1888, breweries began refusing to renew previous union **contracts**. In the ensuing summertime strikes, Eastern European and Italian **scabs** were recruited, the boycott proved ineffective, and the saloonkeepers who had initially supported the unions were brought to heel by the breweries. As a result, the union began losing members; support outside of the German community was almost nil, and the strikes failed. New York lost its status as the center of the Brewers' Union, and the city's unions did not recoup until 1902. Matters were no better in other locales. The union was only kept alive due to its affiliation with the AFL in 1887, which ended the socialist and German ethnic character of the union and integrated it into the wider labor movement. Under the AFL, the union began to rebuild, starting in the 1890s with organization drives and boycotts in the larger breweries like Pabst and Anheuser-Busch.

The union changed its name to the United Brewery Workmen of the United States in 1899, the United Brewery Workmen of America in 1903, the United Brewery and Soft Drink Workers of America in 1918, and later that year was amalgamated into the International Union of United Brewery, Flour, Cereal, and Soft Drink Workers of America (1918–47). By 1917, integration into the AFL was more or less complete. The next year the union began publication of its first English-language publication, the *Brewery and Soft Drink Workers' Journal*. Like the union itself, the publication changed names numerous times between 1917 and 1973.

Between 1919 and 1933, the brewing industry fell upon hard times due to Prohibition. The Eighteenth Amendment to the Constitution outlawed the manufacture, sale, and transportation of alcoholic beverages. Thus brewery unions concentrated their efforts on soft drink bottlers and other non-alcoholic drinks. Prohibition was repealed by the Twenty-first Amendment in 1933, and brewers' unions attempted to organize workers in what was essentially a start-up industry. From 1947 through 1962, the primary union organizing bottlers and distillers was the International Union of United Brewery, Flour, Cereal, Soft Drink, and Distillery Workers of America. From 1963 to 1973 it was known as the International Union of United Brewery, Flour, Cereal, Malt, Yeast, Soft Drink, and Distillery Workers of America.

Changes after World War II have made it difficult to sustain a separate international union among brewery workers, especially in the beer industry. As early as the 1950s, regional breweries began to close and industry giants like Anheuser-Busch, Coors, and Miller were increasing their dominance. For example, northern New Jersey alone once sported over two dozen brewing companies; by 1983, only the Anheuser-Busch plant in Newark remained. Many workers turned to other unions for help, especially the **International Brother-**

hood of Teamsters (IBT), which has been chartering brewery workers since 1953. Moreover, like many other **industrial unions**, brewers' unions consolidated. In 1973, the IBT and the United Brewery Workers merged to form the Teamsters' Brewery and Soft Drink Workers Conference, which is still actively organizing workers. Today, most national brands of beer in the United States are produced by union workers, and about 80 percent of these workers are Teamsters.

For brewery workers, the highest profile fight in recent years was the campaign against Coors, a notoriously right-wing and anti-union corporation. In one span of twenty years, Coors defeated union drives nineteen times. In the 1960s, Coors even offered its trucks to California grape growers trying to break the **United Farm Workers** boycott, and the company gave money to such right-wing groups as the John Birch Society and the Heritage Foundation. A series of strikes in the 1970s mostly ended in defeat. In 1974, workers walked out over wage issues and a company policy of administering lie-detector tests to employees in which, among other things, they were asked about their sexual preferences. The American Federation of Labor–Congress of Industrial Organizations (AFL-CIO) launched a boycott of Coors, and was joined by numerous gay rights organizations. The strike failed, though Coors took back about three-quarters of the strikers.

The boycott, however, had an effect on Coors. Although the company maintained ties to right-wing groups into the 1990s, company policies began to change. In 1987, Coors struck a deal with the AFL-CIO. In exchange for lifting the boycott, Coors agreed to not interfere with future union drives at Coors. Eventually, workers at the Golden, Colorado, plant affiliated with the Operating Engineers Union, and those at its Memphis brewery signed with theTeamsters. (Some gay and Chicano groups maintain a boycott against Coors, though the company has instituted a domestic partnership benefits system and has been cited by some gay groups for its progressive policies.)

The future of independent brewery worker unions is uncertain. Most organized workers currently belong to the IBT, with smaller numbers spread across a handful of unions, including the United Automobile Workers. To date, little organizing has taken place in the "microbrew" industry, which began to grow in the 1980s. Many of these concerns are probably too small to warrant organizing drives, but several have been acquired by larger corporations and may be ripe for unionization.

Suggested Readings: Russ Bellent, *The Coors Connection: How Coors Family Philanthropy Undermines Democratic Pluralism*, 1991; Norman Ware, *The Labor Movement in the United States 1860–1895*, 1929; International Brotherhood of Teamsters, http://www.teamster.org/divisions/brew/brew.asp.

Jeff McFadden

Bridges, Harry (July 28, 1901–March 30, 1990). Born Alfred Renton Bridges, son of a prosperous real estate dealer, in Melbourne, Australia, Harry

Bridges became a merchant seaman and emigrated to the United States in 1920. He joined the **Industrial Workers of the World (IWW)** and began organizing longshoremen on the docks of San Francisco. In 1934, Bridges led the San Francisco longshoremen in a strike that led directly to the infamous San Francisco General Strike, which resulted in pitched battles being waged up and down the west coast. It became the largest **general strike** in American history. The longshoremen won control of their own hiring halls and the popular image of longshore workers evolved from "wharf rats" to "lords of the docks." Harry Bridges would lead the International Loreshoremen's and Warehousemen's Union (ILWU) for the next forty years. Bridges saw the strength that the **National Industrial Recovery Act (NIRA)** and later the **National Labor Relations Act** gave to unions and became the west coast director of the **Congress of Industrial Organizations (CIO)**. His outspoken and radical views led to the initiation of proceedings to deport him in 1939 under charges that he was a **communist**. The U.S. House of Representatives passed a bill calling for his deportation in 1940, but the Supreme Court ruled the act unconstitutional in 1945. Thereafter Bridges became an American citizen. Bridges's aggressive tactics, such as those used in the organization of Hawaiian pineapple workers in 1944–46, caused him to be anathema to many conservatives. His involvement with the presidential campaign of Henry Wallace in 1948 led to his loss of the west coast directorship of the CIO. The CIO expelled the ILWU in 1950 as part of its purge of allegedly communist-dominated unions. In 1950, Harry Bridges was convicted of perjury for testifying at his naturalization hearing that he had never been a member of the Communist Party. In 1953, the Supreme Court again came to Bridges's defense and set aside the indictment, thus voiding his five-year prison sentence. By 1955, the Justice Department announced that it would give up its effort to deport Bridges and, in 1958, he was issued his first U.S. passport. Bridges never backed away from controversy, often embracing views and positions that placed him at the center of a maelstrom. In 1961, the ILWU signed a mechanization and modernization agreement that provided workers some protection from the unavoidable loss of jobs that would result from the introduction of mechanical and computer innovations on the docks. Bridges saw the inevitability of job reductions on the waterfront and sought to minimize the impact of labor-saving technology on the economic well-being of his members. In return for a reduced work force on the docks, employers created a multi-million dollar trust fund for workers' pen-

Harry Bridges. © George Meany Memorial Archives.

sions and guaranteed a no layoff agreement for registered workers. In 1971 and 1972, Bridges led a strike that tied up the west coast waterfront for 135 days, thus driving home the economic impact of ILWU actions. Bridges was respected by waterfront workers who saw him as a leader who put **rank-and-file** concerns foremost. Harry Bridges outspokenly led the way on issues of workplace safety, holidays and holiday pay, pensions, healthcare, and racial equality. Bridges retired in 1979 and died in 1990.

Suggested Readings: Charles P. Larrow, *Harry Bridges: The Rise and Fall of Radical Labor in the U.S.*, 1972; Nelson Lichtenstein, *Labor's War at Home: The CIO in World War II*, 1982.

James P. Hanlan

Bridgestone-Firestone Strike, 1994–95. On December 12, 1996, members of the **United Steelworkers of America (USWA)** ended a bitter twenty-eight-month labor dispute by over 4,000 workers when they ratified a contract with Bridgestone-Firestone, Inc. The strike had begun in July 1994, when the company demanded concessions from the **United Rubber Workers (URW)**. In 1995, the URW offered to return to work and the company declared victory, but the return to work set the stage for the URW merger into USWA. USWA initiated a worldwide campaign to force the company to negotiate a new contract.

In 1988, Japan-based Bridgestone bought its way into the American market by acquiring Firestone Tire and Rubber Company in a bidding war which cost Bridgestone $2.6 billion, more than the fair market value of the acquisition. When time came to negotiate a new contract with URW in 1994, Bridgestone demanded huge wage and benefit concessions, the elimination of union protections such as **arbitration**, and the elimination of American national holidays. On July 12, 4,000 workers walked out of five Bridgestone-Firestone plants. The URW launched a national **boycott**, but lacked the funds to effectively promote it. In October, the company began the first of numerous illegal actions. Secretary of Labor Charles Reich requested a meeting with company executives, but was rebuffed. It was the first time in his administration that a company had refused to meet with him. On March 8, President William Jefferson Clinton issued an executive order terminating federal contracts with employers that permanently replaced legally striking workers. The company stubbornly refused to cooperate either with the government or the union.

URW members who returned to work found themselves working alongside **scabs** who had taken their jobs, and returning workers were assigned the worst jobs in the plants, constantly harassed and intimidated, and constantly monitored by in-plant security cameras. The USWA launched a worldwide campaign against Bridgestone-Firestone. Demonstrations against the company were held in the United States, Japan, and Europe. Leaflet distribution and demonstrations were conducted at retail outlets and at automobile trade shows and car races. AFL-CIO executives lent support to the USWA, focusing on the dispute because it involved one of the largest uses of permanent replacement workers in the nation's history. In its international campaign, the USWA tirelessly publicized the company's environmental pollution record, its workplace safety and health violations, and its lack of civic responsibility. The campaign was the largest worldwide campaign against a single company in American labor history.

Suggested Reading: United Steelworkers of America, http://www.uswa.org.

James P. Hanlan

Brookwood Labor College. Brookwood Labor College was located in Katonah, New York. It was launched in 1921 as an experimental college by **socialist** and pacifist opponents of World War I. Creating an alternative to traditional colleges, Brookwood (1921–37) was the second of a mere three major American labor colleges to prepare union leaders, the others being Work People's College (1904–41) in Duluth, Minnesota; and Commonwealth College (1923–41) near Mena, Arkansas.

In 1921, **A. J. Muste** (1885–1967), a former clergyman turned socialist, joined other progressives to organize Brookwood, with Muste becoming its educational director. Unlike the formal educational system, labor colleges stressed working-class culture and provided adult worker/students with the knowledge and skills necessary to serve the labor movement. Some forty to fifty liberal unionists, mostly in their twenties and thirties, paid $500 a year for a two-year course in history, English, sociology, economics, theories of labor organizing, speech and rhetoric, and labor history. Its graduates included celebrated organizer **Rose Pesotta**; Victor and Roy Reuther; Merlin Bishop, the educational director of the **United Auto Workers (UAW)**; and Frank Winn, the UAW's publicity director.

A class at the Brookwood Labor College. © George Meany Memorial Archives.

Brookwood's student body was small, but its conferences drew activists from around the country and provided a forum that helped legitimize the labor movement. Many labor leaders lectured there, and Brookwood graduates became leaders in various unions, particularly the new **Congress of Industrial Organizations (CIO)**. Although Brookwood was originally supported by the **American Federation of Labor (AFL)**, its conservatism conflicted with the militancy of the CIO activists and the AFL withdrew its aid. Scarce funds during the Depression forced its closing.

In 1971, the AFL-CIO purchased a former junior college campus in Silver Spring, Maryland, and opened the National Labor College. Like Brookwood, it operates labor conferences, trains union leaders, and offers academic courses. Through a cooperative program with the University of Baltimore, it offers both bachelor's and master's degrees in labor studies.

Suggested Readings: Richard J. Altenbaugh, *Education for Struggle*, 1990; *Brookwood Review*, vols. 1–14 (Haverford College, PA, 1923–36), microfilm.

Don Binkowski

Brophy, John (November 6, 1883–February 19, 1963). John Brophy was born into a coal mining family in St. Helens, Lancashire, England, on November 6, 1883. His father, Patrick Brophy, labored in coal mines in England. His grandfather on his mother's (Mary Dagnall) side of the family was also a coal miner in England. Patrick Brophy moved the family to the United States in 1892 when John was just nine years old. They settled initially in Philipsburg, Pennsylvania, and his father continued to work as a coal miner. After the family moved to Urey, Pennsylvania, in 1895, John, who had just celebrated his twelfth birthday, began working in the mines with his father. The family moved regularly as Patrick and John Brophy sought steady work in mines throughout Pennsylvania.

John Brophy joined the **United Mine Workers of America (UMWA)** in 1899 and quickly became a **rank-and-file** activist. Trusted by his fellow miners as an honest and bright man who stood up to the employers when treated unfairly, he was elected to a number of local positions in the UMWA beginning in 1904. Brophy's formal schooling had ended when he entered the mines at age twelve. But he always had an active and thoughtful mind and was a self-educated man. As a local leader in the UMWA he was exposed to, and studied, economics and politics. He read many of the **socialist** tracts and newspapers and agreed with socialists on many issues—such as government ownership of the mining industry—but never fully embraced the socialist movement. Brophy also studied ***Rerum Novarum***, Pope Leo XIII's 1891 papal encyclical that encouraged Catholic worker and clergy support for trade unions. This allowed Brophy, a devout Catholic, to mesh the two most important aspects of his life: support for working people through democratic trade unions and Catholicism. These tenets would guide his actions for the rest of his life.

By 1916 Brophy had established a solid reputation among his fellow miners and was elected president of UMWA District #2 (central Pennsylvania). He argued for government ownership of the mines through his position on the UMWA's Nationalization Research Committee in the early 1920s. Like most unions in the United States, the UMWA lost significant membership in the years following World War I. An assortment of radicals, Communist Party members, and rank-and-file activists disgruntled with the decline of the UMWA formed the "Save Our Union Committee" to help revitalize the union in the mid-1920s. The group supported Brophy's challenge to UMWA President John L. Lewis in the 1926 union election. Brophy lost to Lewis in an election filled with alleged voting irregularities. The autocratic Lewis did not appreciate Brophy's challenge to his undisputed rule of the union and, in 1927, expelled Brophy from the union on false charges of **dual unionism**.

Brophy worked a number of odd jobs between 1927 and 1933 to support his family, which now included his wife Anita (Anstead), whom he married on August 13, 1918, and his two young children, Philip Noel (b. July 30, 1919) and Jacqueline (b. March 11, 1923). He worked as a laborer, real estate salesmen, and at the Columbia Conserve Cooperative, a collective owned by the father of fellow UMWA activist, Powers Hapgood.

Brophy maintained close ties to the labor movement after being expelled from the UMWA. He continued to support the nationalization of the mines and UMWA strikes. Brophy also taught in a labor school in Pittsburgh, visited the Soviet Union as part of a trade union delegation in 1927, and conducted extensive historical research on mining in the United States. (He later completed a short unpublished manuscript, *The American Coal Miner*, on the history of coal mining in the United States.)

In late 1933, John L. Lewis brought Brophy back into the labor movement. He hired Brophy to work in the national offices of the UMWA for a brief period and then made him a central figure in the newly formed **Congress of Industrial Organizations (CIO)**. As the CIO's first director of organization, Brophy worked tirelessly creating and coordinating the central office of the CIO in Washington, D.C. His primary responsibility was to establish a coherent national office, and he coordinated local and state affiliated organizations in the CIO. He helped establish and charter local and state industrial union councils and local industrial unions throughout the country. Brophy was also sent to the battle lines in many of the early CIO labor struggles in the steel, auto, and rubber industries, including the **United Auto Workers (UAW)** historic Flint **Sit-Down Strikes** of 1936–37. Although his responsibilities and official position in the national CIO office changed as the organization grew and as his relationship with Lewis ebbed and flowed, Brophy was an important component in the national CIO office during its entire twenty years as an independent labor federation (1935–55). CIO Presidents John L. Lewis (1935–40), and later **Philip Murray** (1940–52) and **Walter Reuther** (1952–55), were well known throughout the country because of the enormous national press coverage they garnered as heads of the CIO, but it was Brophy who did much of the daily work necessary for the CIO's success. When local CIO leaders had problems that needed fixing, they usually talked with Brophy.

In 1955, the CIO merged with the **American Federation of Labor (AFL)**, creating the American Federation of Labor–Congress of Industrial Organizations (AFL-CIO). Brophy worked in the Industrial Union Department of the AFL-CIO, primarily in the Community Services Department, but also as a highly respected elder statesman trouble-shooter until he retired in 1961. After he retired from the AFL-CIO, Brophy continued to research and write until he died on February 19, 1963. He was seventy-nine years old.

Suggested Readings: John Brophy, with John O. P. Hall, *John Brophy: A Miner's Life*, 1964; Alan Singer, "John Brophy's 'Miner's Program': Workers' Education in UMWA District 2 During the 1920s," *Labor Studies Journal* 13, no. 4 (1988): 50–64.

Joseph Turrini

Brotherhood of Locomotive Engineers (BLE). Brotherhood of Locomotive Engineers is the oldest railway union in North America and represents the interests of about 55,000 engineers and train dispatchers in the United States and Canada. Today it operates much as other trade unions do, but for much of its history scholars invoke it as an example of conservative unionism. BLE members are often grouped, by some, as "**aristocrats of labor**." Progressive unions frequently vilified the BLE, and its own refusal to cooperate with other groups did little to discourage this.

The first major railway strike occurred on the Baltimore and Ohio line in 1854. This led engineers to form a short-lived organization that was sidetracked by the onset of the Civil War. Representatives meeting in Marshall, Michigan created the BLE on May 3, 1863, and chose William Robinson as "grand chief engineer." The BLE sought to create favorable relations with management and insisted in the mutuality of capital/labor interests. In 1864, however, Robinson was ousted when the BLE lost a strike against the Michigan Southern and Indiana Railroad. His successor, Charles Wilson, shifted the BLE's emphasis to one of "moral uplift," and great power was placed in the hands of the BLE chief. Power was centralized and a majority of affiliates had to approve of a strike before any local could take action. Wilson cooperated with the American Railway Association, an employers' consortium. In 1873, he refused to endorse the BLE's strike against the St. Louis, Kansas City, and Northern, an act that led to his replacement by Peter M. Arthur the next year.

Arthur was a dynamic and powerful leader, but also one of the century's most controversial. He began the process of converting the BLE from a guild-like society into a modern trade union, but did not complete the process. In 1875, Arthur negotiated a contract with William Vanderbilt's New York Central System, the nation's first union railroad contract and the first to contain provisions for a guaranteed daily wage. The lost Boston and Maine strike of 1876, it and the **Great Labor Uprising** of 1877 shook the BLE. During the latter struggle, the BLE briefly cooperated with attempts by the Trainmen's Union to unite railroad workers, and even struck an alliance with the **socialist** Workingmen's Party of the United States. After 1877, however, the BLE grew even more insular. Only literate whites over the age of twenty-one with at least one year's experience could join the BLE. Most strikes were discouraged and, in 1885, a BLE bylaw forbade members from belonging to other labor organizations.

Arthur shepherded steady growth and, by 1887, the BLE represented over 25,000 engineers. The BLE negotiated contracts with over 100 employers in the 1880s, helped define **seniority** rules, and set up model insurance and employee benefit schemes. But the Brotherhood's relationship to the labor movement was tense, especially with the **Knights of Labor (KOL)** and the Brotherhood of Locomotive Firemen (BLF), which saw BLE exclusivity as a way of preventing its own members from rising to an engineer's rank. Arthur's refusal to endorse or honor the strikes of the KOL or other railroad brotherhoods had severe consequences. When the BLE crossed picket lines during the 1887 Philadelphia and Reading strike, the KOL and BLF returned the favor during the BLE's disastrous 1888 action against the Chicago, Burlington, and Quincy. Arthur retaliated by refusing to support the KOL's 1890 strike against the New York Central and by sandbagging the efforts of **Eugene V. Debs** and the **American Railway Union** in 1893–94. By the early twentieth century, the BLE's stock was so low among other labor organizations that **Industrial Workers of the World** songwriter **Joe Hill** even lampooned BLE martyr John Luther "Casey" Jones as a union **scab**.

A poster promoting the Brotherhood of Locomotive Engineers (BLE). © George Meany Memorial Archives/Library of Congress.

Arthur died in 1903, and new BLE chief Warren Stone invested BLE resources in real estate and bank holdings that made the brotherhood wealthy, but struck some observers as inappropriate. In 1915, the BLE finally cooperated with other railroad brotherhoods to secure passage of the 1916 **Adamson Act** that granted rail workers an eight-hour day. Railroads were controlled by the government during World War I but thereafter, the BLE engaged in a short progressive burst in which it supported Robert La Follette's quixotic bid for the presidency and divested many of its holdings to make union insurance funds solvent.

The advent of automobiles, the consolidation (and overall decline) of railroading, and changing government roles led to upheaval in the rail industry and changes for the BLE. The 1934 Railway Labor Act set up government boards to mediate grievances, settle disputes, and facilitate contract negotiations, but it also thrust the federal government into the collective bargaining process. When the BLE called a 1946 strike, it had to weather President Truman's threat to draft strikers before it won wage concessions. By the 1950s, the BLE was fighting a rearguard action to salvage jobs in the wake of closing rail lines and management charges of **featherbedding**. Nor did it dramatically improve its relationship with the BLF, with whom it rejected amalgamation in 1964, and from whom it turned back a court challenge for a BLE **apprenticeship** program that BLF officials insisted was an attempt to monopolize engineer training. The BLE also battled the rival United Transportation Union in the 1980s.

In 1971, the bulk of the nation's passenger intercity rail service was reorganized under Amtrak and, in 1976, many of its freight carriers were placed in the ConRail system. These government-run carriers further complicated BLE relations with federal authorities, as did the passage of the 1980 Staggers Rail Act which deregulated the rail industry. BLE officials complained that vital safety issues were being ignored. A 1982 BLE strike ended after only five days when President Ronald Reagan imposed an agreement forcing employees to abide by a commission report that took three years to issue. Many BLE members were infuriated by provisions for a two-tier wage system for new hires and for mandatory drug tests they felt were demeaning. A 1987 train collision that killed sixteen and injured 170 served to verify BLE safety concerns.

In 1988, U.S. chapters of the BLE affiliated with the American Federation of Labor–Congress of Industrial Organizations. It sanctioned a 1991 strike when a government mediation board failed to resolve wage and safety disputes, but President George H. Bush ordered workers back within twenty-four hours. In the mid-1990s, the BLE enjoyed some success with "dual-track bargaining" in which wages, hours, and benefits are negotiated on a national level, while locals bargained for more parochial concerns. The future of the BLE, however, is an uncertain one that likely depends more on what transpires in the national transportation grid than on BLE tactics.

Suggested Readings: Walter Licht, *Working for the Railroad*, 1983; Shelton Stromquist, *A Generation of Boomers*, 1987; Brotherhood of Locomotive Engineers, http://www.ble.org/pr/history.html.

Robert E. Weir

Brotherhood of Sleeping Car Porters (BSCP). The Brotherhood of Sleeping Car Porters was the first African American labor organization to affiliate with the **American Federation of Labor (AFL)**. African-American porters began serving on Pullman Palace cars in 1870, and by the turn of the century, nearly all porters were black. Within the black community the Pullman uniform conferred great status, though porters worked long hours, were at the beck and call of railroad patrons, and suffered abuse from racist passengers.

By the 1920s, Pullman porters complained of long travel times, low pay, and company practices such as not paying porters for work performed when trains were not in motion. **A. Phillip Randolph** created the BSCP in 1925, after two earlier unionization attempts failed, and he served as union president until his retirement in 1968. Randolph functioned as the spokesperson for the BSCP and often relegated administrative details to capable leaders like Milton Webster, Ashley Totten, and C. L. Dellums. Pullman refused to recognize the BSCP, but the passage of the **Railway Labor Act of 1926 (RLA)**—which set up a National Mediation Board (NMB) to arbitrate railroad disputes—gave the union needed breathing room. Randolph bluffed calling a strike in 1928, using the threat of NMB intervention to stave off Pullman attempts to crush the BSCP.

The BSCP petitioned the AFL for membership in 1928. Although president **William Green** rejected the application due to low BSCP membership, the union gained access to Green's inner council. The RLA was amended in 1934, allowing sleeping car employees to organize legally. The BSCP won collective-bargaining rights in June 1935 and, one year later, gained a long-sought-after charter from the AFL. In 1937, the BSCP wrung a contract from Pullman that brought improved work conditions and wage increases.

The BSCP began to decline after World War II as rail passenger service dwindled and other rail unions removed racial barriers. In 1978, the BSCP merged with a larger AFL-CIO union, the Brotherhood of Railway and Airline Clerks.

Suggested Readings: William Harris, *Keeping the Faith*, 1977; David Perata, *Those Pullman Blues: An Oral History of the African American Railroad Attendant*, 1996; William Harris and Martin Schipper, *Records of the Sleeping Car Porters*, 1990.

Robert E. Weir

Browder, Earl Russell (May 20, 1891–June 27, 1973). Earl Russell Browder, a **Communist** Party and labor leader, was born in Wichita, Kansas, to William and Martha (Hankins) Browder. One of eight children, Browder grew up in poverty and was forced to leave school at the age of ten when his father, an elementary school teacher, suffered a nervous breakdown. To help support the family, Browder worked as an errand boy. He eventually completed a correspondence course in law. His father tutored him in politics, often lecturing him on the virtues of the Populist Party. In 1906, Browder joined the Socialist Party. In 1911, he married the former Gladys Grooves.

Browder quit the **socialists** in 1913, and, one year later, became the president of his local Bookkeepers and Stenographers Union. By 1916, he was living in Kansas City, where he worked in a **cooperative** store. He opposed U.S. involvement in World War I and was twice jailed for antiwar activism. While in jail, he studied Marxist theory and became enamored with the Russian Revolution.

Upon his release in 1920, he deserted his wife and child, moved to New York City, and joined the nascent American Communist Party. The next year, Browder became an organizer for the American Trade Union, a Communist Party front organization. He also began editing the party's journal, the *Labor Herald*. He made several trips to the Soviet Union and, during a 1926 visit, began a long affair with legal scholar Raissa Luganovskaya, with whom he had two children. His Russian divorce from his first wife and subsequent marriage to Luganovskaya were of doubtful legality.

In 1930, Browder became general secretary of the U.S. Communist Party (CPUSA), a post he held until 1944. Under Browder's leadership the CPUSA took an active role in creating unemployed councils and leading rent strikes. Communists also played a crucial role in labor organizing during the Great Depression. The CPUSA officially dissolved in 1944, and Browder headed the Communist Political Association, which endorsed President Franklin Roosevelt's reelection to hasten the defeat of fascism. Two years later, Browder was expelled from the reconstituted Communist Party. In 1949, the Communist Party declared the policy of strategic cooperation with capitalism a forbidden form of revisionism and labeled it "Browderism."

Browder remained defiant, despite his fall from grace. He accused his former communist allies of degenerating into a sect that had little to offer American workers. Before his death in 1973, Browder authored some sixty-five pamphlets. His stewardship of the CPUSA remains the most vital in party history.

Suggested Readings: Mari Jo Buhle, Paul Buhle, and Dan Georgakas, *Encyclopedia of the American Left*, 1990; Maurice Isserman, *Which Side Were You On?*, 1982; Harvey Klehr, *The Heyday of American Communism*, 1984.

Shalynn Hunt

Buck's Stove & Range Co. vs. American Federation of Labor et al. *Buck's Stove & Range Co. vs. American Federation of Labor et al.* was an extensive and expensive court battle that drained the energies and resources of the **American Federation of Labor (AFL)** between 1907 and 1914. It involved attempts to limit labor's **boycott** power through the use of injunctions and a broad reading of the 1890 **Sherman Antitrust Act**. The Supreme Court's ambiguous resolution of the dispute left the door open for future capital/labor struggles over the boycott. The *Buck's* case, plus that of ***Loewe v. Lawler*** (1908) threatened to make illegal virtually any action on the part of labor unions that harmed a company financially. It also raised serious questions over fundamental issues like the right to free speech.

The Buck's Stove and Range Company was centered in St. Louis and had long been known for its anti-union bias. In the 1880s and 1890s, the **Knights of Labor** battled with the company. Its president, James Van Cleave, was a leading member of the American Anti-Boycott Association, as well as president of the **National Association of Manufacturers**, which called for **open shops**. He was known for his use of labor spies and for seeking any pretext to void union contracts. In 1907, Van Cleave increased the workday from nine to ten hours for nickel plating workers in St. Louis, which led to a showdown between the company and unions like the Founders' Association and the Iron Moulders and Metal Polishers' Union, both of which were AFL affiliates. Van Cleave fired protesting workers, precipitating a strike.

Van Cleave rebuffed an offer from AFL President **Samuel Gompers** to mediate the dispute, which led the AFL to call for a boycott of Buck's products. Accordingly, the AFL placed the company in the "We Don't Patronize" columns of its official journal, the *American Federationist*, and encouraged all of its locals and affiliates to honor the boycott. On August 19, 1907, the Buck's Company asked the Supreme Court of the District of Columbia for an injunction against the boycott, claiming that its activities were an illegal restraint of trade under the provisions of the Sherman Act. On December 18, the D.C. court issued a temporary injunction; it was made permanent on March 23, 1908.

The court's injunction was stunning in its broadness. Coming on the heels of the *Loewe* decision, it forbade the AFL, its leaders, and its members from in any way restricting Buck's business through writing or speech. The union was not even allowed to denounce the company within its own journal. Gompers declared the decision a violation of fundamental constitutional rights, and the AFL appealed the decision to the Court of Appeals of the District of Columbia. On July 20, 1908, before the appeals court could hear the case, the Buck's Company asked the original court to find the AFL in contempt of the original injunction. On December 23, AFL leaders Gompers, **John Mitchell**, and Frank Morrison were each convicted and were sentenced to jail terms of one year, six months, and three months respectively. These convictions were also appealed.

On March 11, 1909, the appeals courts modified the original injunction slightly, making it illegal to conspire or combine to boycott, but removing individuals from the injunction. Both the Buck's Company and the AFL appealed to the Supreme Court. On November 2, the appeals court also upheld the convictions of Gompers, Mitchell, and Morrison. That too was appealed to the Supreme Court. During these bitter court battles the AFL had to undertake numerous fund-raising efforts. Attempts to pressure Congress and elicit political aid fell largely upon deaf ears. The AFL received some succor in 1910, when Van Cleave died and the Buck's Company settled with its striking employees.

On February 20, 1911, the Supreme Court dismissed both company and union appeals over the injunction on the grounds that the recent settlement rendered the question moot. This left open the entire question of whether or not it had been legitimate in the first place. Likewise, the conviction of AFL officials was reversed on a technicality; the court ruled that only the courts, not the company, could initiate contempt charges. The Supreme Court of the District of Columbia proceeded to do exactly that and, on June 16, 1911, filed new charges against Gompers, Mitchell, and Morrison. They were convicted anew on June 24, 1912, and again appealed. The district appeals court again upheld the convictions, though it drastically reduced the penalties, and the AFL again appealed to the federal Supreme Court.

The *Buck's* case came to an inglorious and ill-defined end on May 11, 1914, when the court overturned the convictions. Once again the court dodged the essential legality questions by ruling, simply, that the new charges against AFL officials were lodged after the three-year statute of limitations expired. The repercussions of the *Buck's* case reverberated for quite some time, however. The case and others like it have led labor historians to reinterpret the period of American history known as the Progressive Era (c. 1901–17). Although the period ushered in many needed reforms, it also saw many attacks on personal liberties and was largely a difficult time for organized labor.

Suggested Readings: Daniel Ernst, *Lawyers Against Labor: From Individual Rights to Corporate Liberalism*, 2002; Philip Foner, *History of the Labor Movement in the United States, Vol. 3: The Policies and Practices of the American Federation of Labor 1900–1909*, 1964; Benjamin Taylor and Fred Witney, *U.S. Labor Relations Law: Historical Development*, 1992.

Bruce Cohen
Robert E. Weir

Bumping. Bumping is a procedure wherein a laid-off worker can displace a worker in another job who has less **seniority**. Bumping clauses are usually outlined in job security clauses of negotiated contracts and, therefore, nonunion employers who do not recognize seniority rights may not follow the practice. Seniority is usually the determining factor, though seniority can be calculated by overall company service, time within a department, or time on the job, depending on contract language.

Force reductions are routinely done in inverse seniority order within a given job classification. Workers subject to force reduction are usually given timely written notice and may elect to exercise their seniority right to displace a worker in the same, equal, or lower-level classification; take a force reduction furlough for a specified period of time, with recall rights when the same or equal job becomes available; accept severance pay; or receive a pension if eligible. The worker who is bumped may then exercise his own seniority to displace another with less seniority or to accept the various options outlined above. Both employers and their unions tend to prefer these arrangements as they bring stability to the workplace and assure that the most-qualified workers remain on the job when job cuts are made.

Bumping was routine practice among nineteenth-century railroad workers, even when such clauses were not written into formal contracts, and was an established principle among skilled workers even before trade unions were officially recognized. It was also common practice in non-union workplaces as it was easy to administer, rewarded seasoned employees, and improved morale by assuring job security. Customary practices were formalized in contracts during the upsurge of mass production unionism in the 1930s and 1940s. The **United Auto Workers** secured bumping rights in 1934, and the Commercial Telegraphers Union in 1946. Today, bumping rights are standard operating procedure in many businesses, though the past several decades have seen conflict between seniority and those of recently hired minorities who have asserted **affirmative action** rights.

Suggested Readings: David Brody, "Workplace Contractualism," in *Industrial Democracy in America*, eds. Nelson Lichtenstein and Howell Harris, 1993; L. Dulude, *Seniority and Employment Equity for Women*, 1995.

Anthony Silva

Bureau of Labor Statistics (BLS). The Bureau of Labor Statistics is the division of the **Department of Labor (DOL)** that collects economic data on unemployment, wages, consumer spending, labor productivity, and the cost of living. This data is broken down and categorized in various ways. For example, within the national unemployment rate, separate tabulations are made for geographic region, seasons of the year, work sectors, gender, age, and race.

Although the federal government had collected economic statistics since the 1880s, under the auspices of the Department of the Interior, labor statistics were not central to governmental planning until 1913, when the DOL was born and absorbed the BLS. (The BLS is the last remaining division of the four bureaus that originally formed the DOL.) Because the BLS exists as a wing of the DOL, it receives cabinet-level representation in the person of the secretary of labor. Labor statistics became a central part of the Labor Department's work.

Labor unions played an integral role in establishing the BLS. Many nineteenth-century advocates believed that the scientific collection of employment statistics and data on working-class life were necessary precursors to reform. Publicizing the data was viewed as an important public relations step in convincing the general public to support labor unions. The information could also be used to lobby local, state, and federal governments to pass pro-labor legislation. In 1871, Massachusetts became the first state to setup a BLS. In 1874, a federal BLS was set up, with Massachusetts BLS head Carroll Wright stepping up to direct its efforts. The federal BLS failed to live up to the hopes invested in it by advocates like the **Knights of Labor** and the **American Federation of Labor (AFL)**, which regarded the BLS as a possible source of pressure for reform. Before 1913, the staff of labor statisticians was drawn more from the business sector than from labor unions. Business leaders found that the BLS provided data useful for business planning and economic development issues dominated labor concerns. The AFL pressed for many of the changes that were incorporated when the DOL formed in 1913.

After 1913, the configuration of the DOL and BLS reflected increasing participation from labor unions. William Wilson, the first secretary of labor, had been an administrator for the **United Mine Workers of America**. With his appointment the sentiments of labor gained access to the top echelons of federal administration. Nonetheless, the BLS became and remains more of an accounting and bureaucratic tool than a vehicle for social change.

Since its formation, the BLS has developed and refined statistical methods to track both the national economy and its workers. The bureau depends on different measurements to give varied accounts of the economic lives of America's workers. For example, the economic disruptions of World War I led to the creation of the Cost of Living Index to show how much people pay for basic items like food, housing, and clothing, and to compare those costs over time. In 1919, the bureau launched the Consumer Price Index to chart industrial growth in various sectors.

Despite the apparently neutral quality of statistical methods, the BLS has often been the site of political contention. During the Great Depression, the bureau came under fire when the accuracy of its methods and measures was called into question. In particular, unemployment numbers were based on estimates that many thought undercounted the number of people without work. In response, President Franklin Roosevelt ordered a revamping of BLS data collection methods. During World War II, the BLS provided important information to the War Labor Board and the Office of Price Administration that helped steer the volatile war economy. Over the last fifty years the BLS has sought to mediate tension between corporate and union economists, whose calculations on cost-of-living and the rate of inflation often differ. During the economic plateau of the 1960s, for example, labor statisticians maintained that the BLS was underreporting unemployment, while business statisticians claimed that workers refused to consider many of the jobs that were available.

Such tensions are not likely to disappear because BLS indices and data impact, either directly or indirectly, all Americans. Bureau data influences interest rates, wages, cost-of-living allowances, and investment. Though the methods and ideology of the BLS have been contested, the importance of its work has not. Its annual market-basket report on the cost of key goods and services is a central feature of union collective bargaining strategy, just as the business sector often relies on BLS inflation calculations to frame employee raises.

Suggested Readings: Ewan Clague, *The Bureau of Labor Statistics*, 1968; Donald Whitnah, ed., *Government Agencies*, 1983; U.S. Department of Labor, Bureau of Labor Statistics, http://www.bls.gov.

Simon Holtzapfel

Business Agent. A business agent is a person employed by a **union local** to negotiate with employers, help settle grievances, and see that both parties observe the terms of the **collective bargaining** agreement. The business agent is a paid, full-time officer elected by the members of the local, or is appointed by a higher union official. The business agent is independent of any workplace covered by the union agreement, but has knowledge of the industry through previous employment.

Business agents usually run craft union locals. Since members frequently move from one job site to another, the business agent keeps stability between the worker and the job. Some of the business agent's duties include: organizing non-union craft workers within their territory, administering employee benefit programs, political lobbying, administering **grievance** hearings and, in some unions, maintaining the union's hiring hall. Unlike union officers in **industrial unions**, the business agent is likely to deal with multi-employer contracts or multiple contracts with several companies. Basically, a business agent floats from one union job site to another, depending on where services are needed.

Suggested Readings: Terry L. Leap, *Collective Bargaining & Labor Relations*, 1995; Florence Peterson, *American Labor Unions: What They Are and How They Work*, 1963.

Walter Hourahan

Business Roundtable (BR). The Business Roundtable is an anti-union consortium of over a thousand corporations whose chief executive officers (CEOs) attempt to influence government policy on civil rights, education, labor, tax policies, and numerous other issues. It is a deeply conservative organization whose attacks on organized labor are as virulent as those of the **National Association of Manufacturers (NAM)**. It enjoyed its greatest successes to date in the late 1970s and into the 1980s, where it exercised tremendous influence during the presidencies of Jimmy Carter, Ronald Reagan, and George H. Bush, and it retains great influence.

The BR is headed by a chairperson who serves up to two one-year terms. The chairperson reports to a policy committee made up of CEOs, which meets four times per year. Both the chairperson and the policy committee are elected at a yearly conference. The BR also has numerous task forces that develop policies and strategies on specific topics. Its day-to-day activities are supported by a full-time staff of lawyers, specialists, and policy analysts.

Although the BR did not form officially until 1972, its genesis lay in the business community's desire to derail union-led efforts to pass labor law reform. Since the passage of the **Taft-Hartley Act** in 1946, much labor legislation has favored business over unions. The **American Federation of Labor (AFL)** and the **Congress of Industrial Organizations (CIO)** merged in 1955, in part, because the two organizations hoped their combined strengths could pressure Congress into repealing Taft-Hartley. That did not happen, but AFL-CIO political action committees (PACs) did succeed in raising money to support pro-labor candidates.

Corporations, by contrast, complained that labor laws handcuffed the business community with needless regulations. In 1965, CEOs from AT&T, Bechtel, Exxon, General Dynamics, General Electric, General Motors, Union Carbide, U.S. Steel, and others formed the Labor Law Study Group (LLSG) to put forth the business community's positions. It spawned two spinoff groups, one of which represented building contractors whose opposition to **prevailing wage** laws led them to call for repeal of the **Davis-Bacon Act**. In 1972, the three groups merged to create the Business Roundtable.

BR leaders felt that existing groups like the Chamber of Commerce and NAM were not doing enough to influence public policy. Publicly, the BR stated its goals were to help CEOs coordinate efforts to stimulate the economy, and to provide government and the public with statistics and information germane to keeping American business strong. Privately, the BR's agenda also involved an assault on organized labor and on labor laws. It especially desired repeal of Davis-Bacon and the **National Labor Relations Act (NLRA)**. The BR also launched a massive public relations campaign to sell the idea that organized labor was out of touch with mainstream citizens, and was an outmoded idea that no longer had a place in American society. By the 1980s, it had succeeded so well that the media and many high-school textbooks regularly put forth that proposition.

Reforms in the early 1970s made it easier for business to form PACs of its own, a move the BR heartily supported. Corporate PACs began handing out financial support to both political parties, a strategy that bore success beginning in the late 1970s. The BR met regularly with President Carter, and his presidency did little to advance legislation favored by unions. An attempt to increase the **minimum wage** failed in 1977, and a 1978 tax code reform greatly reduced corporate taxes. Despite this, the BR joined many other business groups to support Ronald Reagan's successful bid to unseat Carter in 1980.

Reagan proved an even better ally for the BR than Carter. A centerpiece of the BR agenda was winning support for business **deregulation**. Reagan-era tax cuts dwarfed those of the Carter years and made it easier for businesses to write off expenses. It paved the way for a speedup of **deindustrialization**, as numerous corporations closed plants, shifted assets, and invested in the stock market rather than replace aging machinery. Efforts to overturn the NLRA directly were rebuffed, but the BR helped hand pick several Reagan appointees who indirectly subverted it. Under Reagan, appointees to the National Labor Relations Board often had anti-union track records. The BR also exerted influence more directly; for example, former Bechtel executive George Schultz became Reagan's secretary of state, and most unions opposed all three individuals who served as secretary of labor under Reagan. The BR also applauded Reagan's handling of the **Professional Air Traffic Controllers Organization strike**, an act many analysts believe emboldened CEOs to undertake the numerous **downsizing, decertification, and concessions strikes** of the decade. The BR also aided numerous campaigns to repeal prevailing wage laws, as well as efforts to increase the number of **right-to-work** states.

The Democratic Party's response to BR influence on GOP policy in the 1980s disappointed many labor activists. The Democrats actively courted BR CEOs and, by the mid-1980s, BR PACs doled out massive amounts of money to both parties. Thus, while President William Clinton did raise the minimum wage and slow the assault against organized labor, he also supported programs favorable to the BR and opposed by labor, most notably the **North American Free Trade Agreement** and American participation in the World Trade Organization. Some voices within the labor movement call for unions to sever their relations with the Democrats and argue that it has been co-opted by the BR and like-minded groups.

The BR is also opposed by civil rights and women's organizations, as part of its agenda calls for easing workplace rules pertaining to **affirmative action**. Consumer groups also decry to BR's push to limit consumer liability suits, change **workman's compensation** laws, and place caps on punitive damage awards. It has drawn the ire of the **American Federation of Teachers** and the **National Education Association** for its support of teacher and student testing and other conservative educational reforms.

BR-affiliated corporations had revenues in excess of $3.5 trillion in 2002. This assures that it will maintain political clout in the future. Labor unions rightly view it as a powerful foe against which they will struggle.

Suggested Readings: Kim Moody, *An Injury to All: The Decline of American Unionism*, 1989; Business Roundtable, http://www.brtable.org/.

Robert E. Weir

Business Unionism. Business unionism is associated with the emphasis on practical goals and organizational strength as begun by **Samuel Gompers** in the early days of the **American Federation of Labor**. He believed that **collective bargaining** was the best way to achieve fair wages and working conditions. Despite an early flirtation with **socialism**, that and other radical ideas for transforming the capitalist system had no place in Gompers's AFL. He and business unionists that followed believed that workers and management could come to recognize their mutual interests. Strikes should be held as a last resort and should be carefully managed by the central organization. To that end, the union needed to be a businesslike operation with enough financial reserves to sustain it through hard times. High initiation fees and dues provided funds to help keep strikes going. They also allowed for sick and death benefits, helping ensure loyalty while doing the good work of aiding members. Most large labor unions of the twentieth century followed this model.

Most analysts juxtapose business unionism against **social reform unionism**. Business unionism is predicated on the assumption that the structure of modern unions must parallel that of the very corporate interests from which they seek to win **concessions**. In many ways it was one of the driving forces behind the merger between the **American Federation of Labor** and the **Congress of Industrial Organizations**. Its critics complain that business unionism is more bureaucratic than democratic, and that it fosters career-path administrators who are insulated from the concerns of the **rank-and-file**. Because most business unions are highly centralized, they are often less responsive to the concerns of **locals**. In the long term, this blunts rank-and-file participation in the union. Some opponents even place part of the blame for the decline of organized labor on business unionism. As they see it, unions can gain more by maintaining high levels of militancy than through rigid adherence to procedures, drawn-out negotiations, or funneling **grievances** through a set chain-of-command.

Suggested Readings: Paul Buhl, *Taking Care of Business: Samuel Gompers, George Meany, Lane Kirkland, and the Tragedy of American Labor*, 1999; Foster Rhea Dulles and Melvyn Dubofsky, *Labor in America: A History*, 1993.

Elizabeth Jozwiak

C

Capitalism. Capitalism is the dominant economic system in the United States and many other industrial and postindustrial societies. It is also known as the "free enterprise system" and the "free market economy." Unlike **socialism**, **communism**, or **anarcho-syndicalism**, which emphasize planned economies whose decision making is dictated by collective need, proponents of capitalism uphold the liberty of individual producers, distributors, and consumers to make economic decisions. In classical theory, **wages** and prices are determined by what the market will bear, thus the proper role of government should be one of noninterference in economic matters, aside from guaranteeing access to free markets. In most capitalist economies, the right to private property is a sacrosanct ideal. Property is construed broadly to include such public forms of wealth as land, natural resources, businesses, stock, and money (capital), as well as items of personal property. Thus pursuit of personal profit is another key concept underlying capitalist thought. In capitalist economies, most goods, services, financial systems, and production units lie in private hands.

The roots of capitalism can be traced to medieval Europe where urban guilds, merchant traders, and a small band of commercial lenders articulated a money-based economy that rivaled traditional land-based wealth systems. As a full-blown practice, however, capitalism is of more recent vintage. In 1776, Scottish thinker Adam Smith published *Inquiry into the Nature and Causes of the Wealth of Nations*, a book considered seminal in defining capitalism. Smith's ideas gained currency as revolutions engulfed the North American colonies and France. Although many aspects of capitalism were already in place by the eighteenth century, the American colonies were subject to an economic system known as mercantilism. In this mercantilist economy, national power, a positive balance of trade, and global competition took precedence over individual pursuits of wealth. Access to raw materials, colonies, and precious metals were linked to national might, and regulations governed numerous economic transactions. Some American historians cite the desire of prototypical capitalist merchants to break free from colonial constraints as among the causes of the American Revolution.

The spread of American capitalism largely coincided with its industrial revolution, but it did not enjoy an unchallenged rise. In capitalism, labor is a commodity like any other and it is in the best interest of those who pay workers or answer to profit-seeking stockholders to keep wages low. Moreover, the very idea of lifelong wage earning was in conflict with older American ideals of independence and self-reliance. For much of the nineteenth century, agrarian production outstripped that of industrial goods and services, and even traditional elites were somewhat suspicious of unbridled capitalism. Labor unions emerged to try to strike better wage bargains for laborers, and every nineteenth-century labor federation except the **American Federation of Labor** called for an end to the wage system. Many groups equated wage labor with slavery and accused capitalists of profiting from chattel labor. The rise of amoral robber barons after the Civil War did much to advance capitalist principles, but that group also engendered fierce opposition. Various anarchist, communist, and socialist groups formed to challenge an emerging capitalist class, as did trade unions and the **Knights of Labor**. Most upheld alternatives to capitalism, especially **cooperatives**. By the end of the nineteenth century, however, capitalism had largely driven out its challengers, and the twentieth century was one of capitalist dominance.

It is important to note, however, that American capitalism in practice seldom resembled Smith's classical model. Despite investor calls for a complete laissez-faire approach, some degree of regulation has been a feature of American capitalism since larger national trade goals, development schemes, wartime exigencies, and demands to reform pernicious business practices took priority over individual profit-seekers. During the Progressive Era (roughly 1901–17), numerous restraints were placed on business, and capitalism suffered a near-crippling blow during the Great Depression (1929–41). New Deal programs during the 1930s and early 1940s further curtailed laissez-faire practices. In some cases, the federal government set up enterprises in direct competition to private concerns. Since the 1940s, unions, reformers, and progressives have pushed agendas that circumscribe the free market in a number of ways, ranging from curtailing discriminatory hiring practices to ensuring consumer safety.

Although most now accept capitalism as a permanent feature of the American economy, labor unions have been at the fore of lobby efforts to regulate business and practices such as the eight-hour workday, workplace safety standards, **child labor** laws, the **minimum wage**, **workman's compensation**, unemployment benefits, vacation pay, and product safety codes are directly attributable to union efforts. Currently many unions are battling international capitalism and seek to frustrate efforts of groups like the World Trade Organization to break down trade barriers that unions fear will erode needed regulations on capital.

Capitalism dominates the American economy today, but like most nations America maintains a *mixed* economy. Monetary and military policy owe much to a mercantilist worldview, while programs like public education, Social Security, Medicare, and agricultural subsidies are (mildly) socialist in nature. The United States does, however, allow individual investors, entrepreneurs, and merchants far more economic freedom than is common in European and Asian capitalist economies. Conservative efforts at **deregulation** since the 1970s have both broadened capitalist opportunities and intensified calls for more control.

Suggested Readings: Robert Asher, *Concepts in American History*, 1996; Robert Heilbroner, *The Making of Economic Society*, 1985; Adam Smith, *An Inquiry into the Nature and Causes of the Wealth of Nations*, 1776.

Robert E. Weir

Captive Mines/Shops. Captive mines or captive shops are general terms referring to a form of vertical combination in which a manufacturer owns and/or controls parts of the production process that are integral to making the finished product but are customarily separate operations. This practice was especially widespread in the steel and auto industries. Steel manufacturers often owned captive mines that supplied the coal and coke necessary for steel manufacturing, while some auto firms set up their own tool-and-die shops rather than subcontract said work.

Organized labor opposed captive mines and shops. Coal and ore workers in captive mines usually drew lower pay than those employed in independent pits and conditions were frequently worse. Especially contentious were issues like weight checking for those miners whose pay rate was tied to tonnage. Until the 1930s, most steel and iron firms resisted unionization efforts and kept a tight rein on miners, lest organizing drives in the coal fields spread to steel mills. A series of 1933 strikes led by the **United Mine Workers of America (UMWA)** failed to organize captive mines, but the UMWA conducted strikes throughout the 1930s and 1940s that eventually brought most captive mines into the UMWA fold.

Laborers resisted closed shops because they tended to reduce skilled work to a mere component of the mass-production process. Craft workers accustomed to owning their own tools, hiring their own **apprentices**, working at their own pace, and setting their own prices found themselves subject to assembly line discipline and lower rates. Skilled tool-and-die workers resisted attempts by the auto industry to set up captive tool rooms, but they, like those resisting other closed shops, generally had less success than miners.

Suggested Readings: Steve Babson, *Building the Union: Skilled Workers and Anglo-Gaelic Immigrants in the Rise of the UAW*, 1991; David Brody, *In Labor's Cause: Main Themes on the History of the American Worker*, 1993.

Robert E. Weir

Carey, James Barron (August 12, 1911–September 1, 1973). James Barron Carey was the president of several electrical workers' unions, an anticommunism crusader, and an architect of the merger between the **American Federation of Labor (AFL)** and the **Congress of Industrial Organizations (CIO)**. He was born in Philadelphia, the son of John, a paymaster for the U.S. Mint, and Margaret (Loughery) Carey. He attended public schools in Glassboro, New Jersey, before going to work at Philco Radio, where he developed his stance on **industrial unionism**. From 1921 to 1931, Carey also attended Drexel Institute and studied electrical engineering. In 1931 and 1932, Carey studied finance at the Wharton School of the University of Pennsylvania. Carey received guidance from the values instilled during his early upbringing by his Catholic, liberal, Democratic parents and in later years from **socialist** (anticommunist) hosiery workers in the Philadelphia area. He was strongly influenced by the prounion, antisocialist stance in the papal encyclicals ***Rerum Novarum*** and *Quadregisimo Anno*.

As the leader of a group of manufacturing inspectors, Carey played a key role in the formation of a Philco Radio union local in 1933. This local became a major building block for the **United Electrical, Radio, and Machine Workers of America (UE)**. Carey led a successful strike for union recognition at RCA's Camden, New Jersey, plant in 1936. His arrest during the strike vaulted him into prominence in the labor movement and helped to earn him the title of "boy wonder." During the formation of the UE in 1936, the twenty-five-year-old Carey was elected as the first president of the union.

From the UE's earliest beginnings, it was accused of being dominated by **communists**. Carey flatly denied communist control of the UE in 1936, but by 1941 the UE general executive board and Carey had split. At the 1941 UE convention, Albert Fitzgerald defeated Carey for international president. At the same convention, the UE recommended Carey's candidacy as the CIO's secretary-treasurer, and he was duly elected in 1942. Carey served on several government boards during World War II and as a CIO delegate to the 1945 World Trade Union Conference. Carey divided his time between the CIO and several governmental committees. He was an outspoken member of President Harry Truman's Committee on Civil Rights, supported progressive civil rights legislation, and served as the CIO's chief spokesman on civil rights.

With the passage of the **Taft-Hartley Act** in 1947, the UE came under attack for harboring communists, and other unions began to raid its members. Leaders of the CIO, including influential CIO President Philip Murray, grew preoccupied by allegations of communist control of their affiliates. The 1949 CIO convention approved a charter creating the **International Union of Electrical, Radio, and Machine Workers of America (IUE)**, and Carey was named the IUE's first international president. Carey and the IUE were devoted to purging all communist influence in the electrical manufacturing industry and the CIO. To that end, Carey made frequent use of radical-hunting congressional committees, raids on UE locals, decertification elections, and the

National Labor Relations Board to weaken the UE's influence. Carey was a key member of the unity committee that negotiated the merger of the **American Federation of Labor** and the **Congress of Industrial Organizations (AFL-CIO)** in 1955, and he served as a vice president and an executive board member of the AFL-CIO. The lifelong advocate of industrial unionism also served in the federation's Industrial Union Department, a committee devoted to advancing the industry-wide model of organizing.

Carey's ardent anticommunism earned him enemies as well as friends. The civil war between the UE and the IUE wounded both sides, rendering them ineffective representatives of the factory workers they claimed to defend. Some of the allies he made while attacking the UE became his staunchest opponents. Paul Jennings, Carey's protégé, ran against Carey in 1964, and Carey limped to a slim victory. In 1965, however, the Labor Department ruled that Carey's supporters had stolen the election. Carey was never prosecuted, but the presidency was passed to Jennings in 1966. After leaving the IUE, Carey served as a labor representative to the United Nations and did work for the Democratic Party but quickly passed out of the public eye. He died in Silver Spring, Maryland, in 1973.

Suggested Readings: R. L. Filippelli and M. D. McColloch, *Cold War in the Working Class: The Rise and Decline of the United Electrical Workers*, 1995; Ron Schatz, *The Electrical Workers: A History of Labor at General Electric and Westinghouse, 1923–1960*, 1983; Robert Zieger, *The CIO, 1935–1955*, 1995.

Mike Bonislawski

Caterpillar Strike. The Caterpillar Strike was a disastrous struggle between the **United Auto Workers (UAW)** and Caterpillar, the world's largest manufacturer of earth-moving equipment, which took place between 1991 and 1995. It ended in complete victory for the corporation, dealt a blow to the prestige of the UAW, and led to great dissatisfaction among the union's **rank-and-file** members.

The UAW's failure at Caterpillar is a dramatic chapter in a series of **downsizing, decertification, and concession strikes** that have marked capital/labor relations since the 1970s. It is also emblematic of the challenges that globalism poses for the American labor movement. Caterpillar is based in Illinois and has large plants in Decatur, East Peoria, and other Midwestern cities. The UAW and Caterpillar enjoyed relatively good relations in the 1970s and 1980s. At its 1983 convention, the UAW unveiled its "Blueprint for a Working America: A Proposal for an Industrial Policy" that created union-management committees to resolve potentially thorny issues like production quotas, layoff decisions, and work rules. While UAW President Owen Bieber hailed the plan as giving labor a say in the production process, it also cast the union into a managerial role and tended to distance it from the rank and file. The UAW was silent as Caterpillar expanded operations to Indonesia, Mexico, and Scotland that reduced its U.S. workforce by nearly 30 percent. Few UAW workers knew of strikes that took place in Scotland in 1987 or in Canada in 1991. This made them ill prepared to call upon workers outside the United States when their own troubles began in 1991.

When the Caterpillar/UAW contract expired in 1991, Caterpillar demanded **concessions** from its U.S. workforce, the core of which were the introduction of a two-tier wage system under which new hires would receive lower wages, changes to health-care coverage, and a redefinition of **overtime**. When workers balked, Caterpillar instituted a **lockout**. In November, the UAW voted to strike against several Caterpillar plants in Illinois and Tennessee. The strike held for five months, but in April 1992, Caterpillar announced its intention to hire permanent replacement workers. The UAW called off the strike and workers returned without a contract. The union banked partly on hopes of a political solution, and it campaigned for William Clinton in the U.S. presidential election.

Workers continued to labor for two and a half years without a contract; Caterpillar simply imposed concessions despite the fact that its stock was soaring. The period saw numerous acts of rank-and-file militancy, however, with several **wildcat strikes** breaking out that UAW officials worked hard to suppress. Local militants also maintained levels of **solidarity** by wearing provocative shirts, emblems, and badges that lampooned the company and vilified **scabs**.

Conditions at Caterpillar deteriorated so badly that the UAW authorized a new strike in June 1994. The union, however, made numerous tactical errors. It refused to authorize mass **picketing**, partly out of fear that militants would commit acts of **sabotage** and violence and partly due to an incorrect belief that Caterpillar would not be able to assemble enough skilled workers to maintain production. Rather than call out all 13,000 Caterpillar workers, it ordered engine assemblers and parts workers not directly involved in the disputes to remain working. Only about 4,000 workers actually left their posts.

President Clinton did not push for the passage of antireplacement worker legislation, and this ultimately doomed the hopes of Caterpillar workers. The company hired **replacement workers** and quickly increased production, though the National Labor Relations Board determined that the more than 150 **unfair labor practices** pending against Caterpillar barred it from firing strikers. After seventeen months, the UAW accepted Caterpillar's offer and, on December 3, 1995, called off the strike. Leadership was badly shaken when more than 80 percent of the strikers rejected Caterpillar's offer. The UAW ordered workers back to the job and told them that no more strike benefits would be paid.

The UAW and its new president, Stephen Yokich, tried to save face. Officially, the strike was placed in recess, and the rank and file was told that the strike was broken by UAW members crossing picket lines, but there was little it could do to sugarcoat the harsh conditions imposed by Caterpillar. After more than three years of struggle, workers faced a settlement that was worse than what they could have accepted in 1991. Caterpillar's six-year contract called for a pay scale for new hires that was 30 percent lower, the right to hire more part-time workers, and changes in **grievance**, medical insurance, sick leave, and layoff policies. Caterpillar also demanded that workers divest themselves of anti-Caterpillar and anti-scab clothing and paraphernalia, and it reserved the right to assign more than eight hours of work without paying overtime until a worker logged more than forty hours for the week. It also refused to pay overtime for weekend work.

Since 1995, the UAW has managed to modify some of Caterpillar's conditions, but the fact that one of the richest unions in the United States could be so thoroughly routed does not bode well for the future of **industrial unionism**. The city of Decatur, the center of the maelstrom, was also engulfed by the **Staley lockout** and the **Bridgestone-Firestone strike** during the Caterpillar struggle, and only the latter ended on a note of hope. Ideological radicals tend to blame leaders' betrayal, **business unionism**, and misguided political alliances for the loss; many have used it to call for a separate **labor party** to represent workers. Those charges notwithstanding, the Caterpillar debacle was due as much to pressures of **globalism** as UAW errors or misalliances. Caterpillar remained profitable throughout the fight, largely by decentralizing production, outsourcing, and diversifying its assets.

The Caterpillar strike is an important reminder that American organized labor is not likely to win consistently using strategies that worked in the 1930s. It suggests a need to organize globally and across decentralized production lines, perhaps even to outsourcers and subsidiaries.

Suggested Readings: Jeremy Brecher, "World Crisis and Workers Response," http://depts.Washington.edu/pels/workingpapers.breacher.pdf; Stephen Franklin, *Three Strikes*, 2001; Sharon Jones and Barry Grey, "UAW Debacle at Caterpillar: The Political Lessons"; Chicago-Kent College of Law, Illinois Institute of Technology, http://www.kentlaw.edu/ilhis/cat.htm.

Robert E. Weir

Central Labor Union (CLU). A Central Labor Union is a coordinating body for various unions within a given geographic area. The term was popular in the nineteenth and early twentieth centuries; today it is usually called a central labor council. It usually constitutes an intermediary level between a **union local** and the federation with which it is affiliated.

The idea behind a CLU is that there occasionally arise issues that involve workers generally, irrespective of their individual unions. A CLU brings together leaders from various unions to plan regionwide strategy for issues that do not necessarily involve workers outside the area. This can be something as noncontroversial as coordinating parade plans or as controversial as publicizing a **boycott**, organizing a picket line, calling a **sympathy strike**, or launching a **general strike**. Building local coalitions assures that unions respect each other's issues and do not work at cross-purposes.

Larger cities tend to foster the most powerful CLUs. The New York City CLU planned what is considered to be the first **Labor Day** in 1882, and

Chicago's CLU aided in the **May Day** events of 1886 that led to the Haymarket fiasco. In the 1960s, New York City's Central Labor Council played a key role in helping to organize hospital and health care workers and exerted an important political role within the city. More recently, councils in Los Angeles, Boston, and elsewhere have given important logistical support to the "Justice for Janitors" movement.

In general, nineteenth-century CLUs had more autonomy than modern labor councils, which must have their actions approved by the federations of constituent unions. They remain an important sounding board for discussing issues of mutual importance, as well as fostering ties across the labor movement.

Suggested Readings: Stanley Aronowitz, *From the Ashes of the Old*, 1998; R. Emmett Murray, *The Lexicon of Labor*, 1998.

Robert E. Weir

***Charles River Bridge v. Warren Bridge*.** The case of *Charles River Bridge v. Warren Bridge*, 11 Peters 420 (1837) seriously challenged former Chief Justice John Marshall's reverence for the sanctity of contractual law. In the *Charles River Bridge* case, Chief Justice Roger Taney applied Jacksonian social philosophy to modify the absolute property rights that Marshall favored. In 1785, the Commonwealth of Massachusetts incorporated the Charles River Bridge Company for a forty-year period and gave the company the right to erect a bridge over the Charles River and collect tolls. In 1792, the state extended the life of the company to seventy years. When the state authorized the construction of a competing bridge, the Warren Bridge, less than 300 yards from the Charles River Bridge, the Charles River Bridge Company, in 1829, sought an injunction against the construction of the new bridge. The new bridge would revert to the state as soon as the expenses of its construction were paid for by tolls. Thus, the potentially toll-free bridge would destroy the value of the earlier bridge. The Charles River Bridge Company argued that, by implication, it had been given sole and exclusive rights in the lifetime of its charter to bridge the Charles River. The Warren Bridge charter thus constituted an impairment of the obligation of contracts. John Marshall's defense of vested rights suggested that contracts would be regarded by the court as sacred and inviolable. Taney, though, responded to the growth of corporations, especially in banking and transportation, with suspicion. Taney, believing that corporations required close state vigilance to "promote the happiness and prosperity of the [entire] community," refused to go along with the implication of exclusive monopoly argued by the Charles River Bridge Company. Taney believed that a rapidly expanding country could easily be hobbled if older turnpike and canal companies were empowered by presumptive or ambiguous clauses in their charter to forestall competitors. Taney's decision did not reverse Marshall's doctrine that a state-granted charter was a valid contract protected under the contract clause of the Constitution, but it more narrowly restricted such contracts to the actual, as opposed to the implicit, provisions of the charter. Taney's decision sought to balance the rights of property with the state's obligation to provide for the larger public good. Conservative justices Story, Webster, and Kent dissented, but the Taney position soon was reflected in most state charters, which preserved the state's right to modify or terminate charters in the interest of public welfare.

Suggested Reading: Oyez: U.S. Supreme Court Multimedia, http://www.oyez.org/oyez/Resource/Case/70/.

James P. Hanlan

Chavez, Cesar Estrada (March 31, 1927–April 23, 1993). Cesar Estrada Chavez was the cofounder of the **United Farm Workers of America (UFW)** and an influential Hispanic leader. Chavez was born near Yuma, Arizona, the son of migrant farm workers. He attended countless elementary schools and obtained an eighth-grade education before he turned to full-time agricultural labor. He served in the U.S. Navy during World War II. He married Helen Fabela, with whom he had eight children.

In 1946, Chavez joined the National Agricultural Workers Union, an organization associated with radical grassroots organizer Saul Alinsky's Community Service Organization (CSO). He was the CSO organizer for California from 1952 to 1962 and its national director from 1960 to 1962. Although a devoted Roman Catholic, Chavez was much influenced by Mahatma Gandhi's principles of passive resistance. Under Chavez, the CSO and UFW parlayed nonviolent protest—including marches, hunger strikes, and rallies—into pressure tactics that garnered nationwide attention.

Cesar Chavez addressing a rally. © George Meany Memorial Archives/Sam Reiss.

In 1962, Chavez moved to Delano, California, set up the National Farm Workers Association, and led several **strikes** against growers. A 1965 strike and **boycott** against Coachella Valley grape producers united Hispanic and Filipino workers and gained national attention. It also attracted support from influential labor and political leaders like **Walter Reuther** and Senator Robert Kennedy. Chavez faced stiff competition and **raiding** from the **International Brotherhood** of **Teamsters**. In 1966, Chavez won contracts from several corporate farms, including Schenley and DiGiorgio. This promoted AFL-CIO support, and the Chavez-led **Agricultural Workers Organizing Committee**'s successful nationwide grape boycott in 1967 resulted in **wage** increases, union hiring halls, improved field conditions, and agreements over the use of pesticides. In 1968, the AFL-CIO charted the UFW, although the union struggled with Teamsters raiding until 1977. In 1970, most grape growers capitulated and signed agreements based on the 1967 model.

Chavez subsequently led a campaign against vegetable growers when they signed an agreement with the Teamsters. When grape producers tried to wring concessions from the UFW in 1973, Chavez, **Dolores Huerta**, and the UFW renewed their call for a nationwide boycott. In 1975, growers agreed to recognize farm worker **collective bargaining** rights under California's **Agricultural Labor Relations Act**. The UFW won most of the subsequent contract votes and negotiated health, pension, and wage benefits for its members. In the 1980s, Chavez switched his attention to pesticide poisoning and, in 1986, he fasted for thirty-six days in support of a new boycott against grapes.

Chavez's control over the UFW was not without controversy. Some complained of autocratic rule and self-aggrandizement, though Chavez's salary never exceeded $5,000 per year. His unexpected death shocked the UFW and more than 40,000 people attended his funeral. In 1994, he was posthumously awarded the Presidential Medal of Freedom, only the second Mexican American to be so honored. In 1998, he was elected to the Labor Hall of Fame.

Suggested Readings: Juan Gonzalez, *Harvest of Empire*, 2000; David Goodwin, *Great Lives: Cesar Chavez*, 1991; Jacques Levy, *Cesar Chavez*, 1975.

Yasmin Correa

Robert E. Weir

Checkoff. Checkoff is the policy whereby an employer automatically deducts union **dues** from an employee's paycheck. When a worker is hired, an authorization form allows the employer to deduct a specified amount of money from **wages**. This money goes into the union account. If the worker chooses not to use checkoff, he may be able to pay the union dues on his own. Most workers prefer the checkoff method since it is convenient, and ensures that the dues will be paid in a timely manner. Those who opt to pay on their own and neglect to do so could be expelled from the union and/or dismissed from their job.

Some agreements between employers and unions provided for automatic checkoff for all union members, but the 1947 **Taft-Hartley Act** permits checkoff only for those employees who individually authorize the employer to make such withholdings. If there is no agreement for checkoff, then the **shop steward** or another union official must collect dues from each member. Union officials view this as time-consuming, and it is irritating to some union members because it casts officials as bill collectors. However, some unions see it as a chance to visit members and solicit opinions on issues.

Employers see the checkoff as a good idea because allowing union officials to collect dues on company property during work hours can be disruptive. Automatic checkoff, in the eyes of most critics, has led to push-button unionism and the rise of a labor bureaucracy. Checkoffs were quite rare until the twentieth century. Several unions, including the **Industrial Workers of the World**, oppose them on principle.

Suggested Readings: Terry L. Leap, *Collective Bargaining and Labor Relations*, 1995; Florence Peterson, *American Labor Unions: What They Are and How They Work*, 1963.

Walter Hourahan

This cartoon criticizes the 1922 Supreme Court decision that declared the second national child labor law unconstitutional. © George Meany Memorial Archives.

Child Labor. Child labor, one of the oldest social problems in American history, has also sometimes been the most controversial. Even the definition, particularly concerning what kind of work performed by children constitutes child labor, has been debated. From the Colonial era, children have worked in many capacities, from agriculture to domestic work. Following in part the Puritan ethic, it was believed that work kept children from idleness and mischief and taught them trades and good work habits. By the end of the nineteenth century, however, with the growth in industrialization and the increasing incidence of children performing repetitive, menial tasks that impaired their health and opportunities for education, these arguments became increasingly difficult to sustain.

This boy is a bobbin tender, a position requiring little skill, and thus an entry-level job for children in New England textile mills. © George Meany Memorial Archives/Public Affairs Press.

The Progressive Era brought increased public concern for child welfare and, with it, a nationally organized effort to regulate, if not eradicate, child labor. The National Child Labor Committee (NCLC) was founded in 1904, first to document child labor and then to advocate national legislation to control it. The NCLC's task was not easy, thanks to opposition from business leaders, who used child labor in part to keep costs down, and from the Southern states, who viewed national legislation as an infringement of states' rights. The first successful national child labor law, the Keating-Owen Act, was passed in 1916, only to be struck down by the Supreme Court in 1918. A second child labor law, passed the following year, was struck down in 1922. A subsequently proposed child labor amendment to the Constitution failed to achieve ratification. Finally, in 1938, the **Fair Labor Standards Act** successfully established minimum ages and maximum hours for most forms of work, with more lenient standards for agricultural work. Although child labor has been largely eliminated, problems remain, especially among migrant agricultural workers.

Shorpy Higginbotham, "greaser" on the tipple at Bessie Mine, of the Sloss-Sheffield Steel and Iron Co., said he was fourteen years old, but it is doubtful. © Library of Congress.

Suggested Readings: Sandy Hobbs, Jim McKechnie, and Michael Lavalette, *Child Labor: A World History Companion*, 1999; Walter I. Trattner, *Crusade for the Children: A History of the National Child Labor Committee and Child Labor Reform in America*, 1970; Stephen B. Wood, *Constitutional Politics in the Progressive Era: Child Labor and the Law*, 1968.

Susan Roth Breitzer

Chinese Exclusion Act. The Chinese Exclusion Act curtailed the number of Chinese immigrants entering the United States. Congress passed the bill in 1882, and President Chester Arthur signed it into law. It came in the wake of more than a decade of intense lobbying on the part of organized labor in protest against the importation of Chinese labor. Labor's support for the act is an example of the popular racism that infected many workers in the late nineteenth century. The act was the first legislation to ban immigration from a specific country and lent legitimacy to later immigration restrictions.

Following the news of the gold rush in 1849, large numbers of Chinese entered California to pan for gold and provide services like cooking, laundering, and retail activity to other miners. Although their numbers were never as large as propagandists claimed, the overall population of Chinese increased dramatically, especially in California and the Pacific Northwest. By 1870, nearly 50,000 Chinese lived in California alone. In addition to mining, Chinese laborers entered factories, laundries, restaurants, shops, and increasingly worked for the railroads. Caucasian labor organizations accused Chinese workers of undermining local **wage** structures and of diverting jobs from white workers. Many Chinese workers were restricted to menial positions and were subjected to other forms of discrimination like special taxes that applied only to Chinese miners.

Despite early discrimination, Caucasians tolerated the Chinese until the economic downturn in the West after the Civil War. During the Panic of 1873, whites proved unable to protect their jobs from the Chinese, thus galvanizing organized labor in California against Chinese labor. By 1877, the Workingmen's Party rose to prominence in California. While advocating general labor reform, banning Chinese immigration became the group's banner goal. Led by Denis Kearney, himself an Irish immigrant, the Workingmen's Party made anti-Chinese agitation a national issue. Kearney took a national tour in 1878 to promote Chinese exclusion, though he received a mixed response in the East. Some Eastern labor organizations, while opposed to the importation to all forms of gang or coolie contract labor, argued that individual Chinese workers should be accorded the same rights as native workers or European immigrants. This was the position of shoemakers organized as the Knights of St. Crispin, even though a North Adams, Massachusetts, manufacturer imported Chinese **scabs** during an 1870 strike.

Eventually, however, anti-Chinese hysteria became widespread in the organized labor movement. In 1864, President Abraham Lincoln signed into law "An Act to Encourage Immigration," which required enforcement of labor contracts drawn abroad. The **National Labor Union** opposed this and all forms of contract gang labor. Anti-Chinese propagandists succeeded in spreading rumors that Chinese workers were contracted as low-wage coolie gangs, though the vast majority of Chinese immigrants had little contact with that system. National politicians took up the issue to promote themselves and their parties in the tight electoral climate of the period. Support from national politicians led to the passage of the Fifteen Passenger Bill in 1879, which limited the number of Chinese passengers entering the United States on any ship. While President Rutherford B. Hayes vetoed the bill, anti-Chinese agitation continued nationally, with Eastern labor eventually joining with West Coast labor groups in favor of Chinese exclusion. Increased fear of Chinese migration to the eastern United States and pressure from Western locals led the **Knights of Labor (KOL)**, the nineteenth century's largest labor federation, to endorse Chinese exclusion. Although some Knights, especially in New York City, denounced the anti-Chinese hysteria and organized Chinese workers, the KOL as a whole was rabidly anti-Chinese and lobbied Congress for an exclusion act. They were joined in their efforts by numerous national trade unions.

Both major political parties supported restricting Chinese immigration in the election of 1880, thus paving the way for the passage of the Exclusion Act in 1882. The bill banned new Chinese immigration for ten years and required Chinese living in the United States to secure a residency permit. The bill's passage did little to curtail short-term hysteria, with some groups calling for the expulsion of all Chinese already in the United States. Vicious racist propaganda proliferated from the 1870s on, and the 1880s were marked by numerous assaults on Chinese workers. The worst of these occurred in Rock Springs, Wyoming Territory, in 1885, when gangs of white workers rioted and killed as many as forty Chinese. Partly in hopes of quelling such incidents and partly as a result of political pressure, Congress passed the **Foran Act** in 1885, which repealed the 1864 bill allowing the recruitment of foreign contract labor.

Congress extended the Chinese Exclusion Act in 1892 and again in 1902, the latter bill continuing the ban indefinitely. Congress did not repeal the Chinese Exclusion Act until 1943, by which time China was an ally in the war against Japan. Many West Coast labor groups turned to anti-Japanese sentiment to keep their organizations strong as the threat of Chinese immigration dissipated. Those efforts may have swayed some politicians to support the internment of Japanese Americans during World War II.

Suggested Readings: Andrew Gyory, *Closing the Gate: Race, Politics, and the Chinese Exclusion Act*, 1998; Alexander Saxton, *The Indispensable Enemy: Labor and the Anti-Chinese Movement in California*, 1971; Craig Storti, *Incident at Bitter Creek: The Story of the Rock Springs Chinese Massacre*, 1991.

Erik Loomis

Clayton Antitrust Act. The Clayton Antitrust Act was signed into law by President Woodrow Wilson in 1914. In theory, it was an important bill protecting the rights of organized labor, though, in practice, it was not widely respected. The Clayton Act revised the 1890 **Sherman Antitrust Act**. The latter bill was designed to outlaw monopolies and curtail the power of trusts. It proved ineffective in doing so and was a disaster for organized labor. Unions were frequently cited for illegal restraints against trade, and businesses used the Sherman Act to get **injunctions** against **strikes** and **boycotts**.

The Clayton Antitrust Act closed many of the loopholes in the Sherman Act, set up the Federal Trade Commission, and reformed numerous business practices. From the standpoint of organized labor, its most important provision was Section 17, which stated that human labor was "not a commodity or article of commerce." It went on to argue that, therefore, antitrust laws were not applicable to labor unions, mutual-aid societies, or other groups engaged in lawful activity, and that such organizations were not "illegal combinations or conspiracies in restraint of trade." In essence, the section legitimized such time-honored union tactics as strikes, boycotts, and **picket-**

ing. It was also the first clear statement of the right of labor unions to exist as lawful enterprises.

Samuel Gompers, president of the **American Federation of Labor**, hailed the Clayton Act as "Labor's Magna Carta." His reaction was understandable given the assault on labor unions during the Progressive Era (c. 1901–17), which culminated in antiunion court cases like *Buck's Stove and Range Company v. American Federation of Labor* and *Loewe v. Lawlor*, the persecution of the **Industrial Workers of the World** et al. and the business community's push for **open shops**. Gompers's optimism proved to be misplaced, however. The business community decried Section 17, condemned Congress for drafting it, and pressured courts to ignore it. The 1921 Supreme Court decision in *Duplex Printing v. Deering* outlawed secondary boycotts and allowed the use of certain types of injunctions.

Although the Clayton Act was an important symbolic victory for labor, it was largely ineffective until the passage of the **Norris-LaGuardia Act** in 1932. Both acts remain controversial in many segments of the business community, which call for its repeal.

Suggested Readings: Anthony D. Becker, St. Olaf College, www.stolaf.edu/people/becker/antitrust/statutes/clayton.html; Daniel Ernst, *Lawyers Against Labor: From Individual Rights to Corporate Liberalism*, 2002; Benjamin Taylor and Fred Witney, *U.S. Labor Relations Law: Historical Development*, 1992; "The Clayton Anti-Trust Act."

Bruce Cohen
Robert E. Weir

Coalition of Labor Union Women (CLUW). The Coalition of Labor Union Women (CLUW) is a nonprofit organization of American and international trade union women dedicated to promoting the interests of working women within unions and advancing social justice for women within society. It was founded in 1974 when Olga Madar of the **United Auto Workers** and Addie Wyatt of the **United Food and Commercial Workers Union** convened a conference in Chicago that, among other things, addressed issues of sexism within the organized labor movement. When delegate Myra Wolfgang told AFL-CIO leaders "we did not come here to swap recipes," the phrase quickly became an identifiable CLUW slogan.

Part union reform movement and part political pressure group, the CLUW has fought for a variety of issues, including an increase in the minimum wage, comparable-worth legislation, preservation of existing Social Security laws, daycare programs for working women, enforcement of **affirmative action** laws, aggressive identification of workplace sexual harassment, women's reproductive rights, women's health issues, workplace safety, elimination of gender wage differentials, and overall gender equality. The CLUW was very active in the unsuccessful attempt to add an Equal Rights Amendment to the U.S. Constitution. At its annual conferences, CLUW women discuss workplace and union issues that affect all working women.

In 1978, the CLUW established a national Center for Education and Research to train women for leadership roles within their unions. Its summer institutes have been especially effective leadership training forums. In 1980, CLUW President Joyce Miller was elected to the AFL-CIO executive council and helped convene its first conference to discuss strategies for recruiting unorganized workers.

CLUW filed a brief to the Supreme Court on sexual harassment that figured prominently in the 1986 *Vinson v. Meritor Savings Bank* case. It also filed a brief in the 1989 *UAW v. Johnson Controls* case dealing with hazardous chemicals and reproductive health. In 1993, Miller resigned as CLUW president and was replaced by Gloria Johnson, the current head. Johnson also heads the AFL-CIO's Standing Committee on Women's Issues, and holds offices within her own International Union of Electronic, Electrical, Salaried, Machine, and Furniture Workers. In the 1990s, the CLUW took up issues like the **North American Free Trade Agreement**, international trade, **sweatshop** production, **child labor**, human rights, and women's health.

The CLUW has a national executive board that meets three times a year and has numerous standing committees on issues as diverse as affirmative action, violence against women, and issues germane to older workers. Its relationship to the AFL-CIO varies and ranges from purely advisory roles to official sponsorship of summer institutes.

Suggested Readings: *Coalition of Labor Union Women Newsletter*, March/April 2000; Coalition of Labor Union Women, http://www.cluw.org.

Pauline Gladstone
Robert E. Weir

Coal Miners Strike of 1943. The Coal Miners Strike of 1943 actually began in December 1942, when thousands of members of the **United Mine Workers of America (UMWA)** walked off of their jobs. The UMWA was one of the only unions to defy labor's **no-strike pledge** in the midst of World War II, and it exposed weaknesses in capital/labor/government boards established to safeguard wartime production. To some critics, the strikes were also acts of folly on the part of union president **John L. Lewis** and the UMWA.

The strike started because **rank-and-file** members were upset about a 50 percent increase in union dues. Although UMWA leader Lewis helped end the December 1942 rank-and-file rebellion, he did not denounce the strikers. Instead, months after the grass-roots strike began, Lewis reclaimed the respect of union members by demanding **wage** increases for all members of the UMWA and by staging official strikes. Throughout much of 1943, Lewis sponsored a series of massive unionwide uprisings involving tens of thousands of coal miners.

The national coal miners' strikes are significant largely because they occurred despite the federal government's central role in managing the national economy. Shortly after Pearl Harbor, President Franklin Roosevelt called on business and labor leaders to maintain high levels of production and resolve capital/labor conflicts peacefully. Significantly, Roosevelt convinced labor leaders, including Lewis, to support a no-strike pledge, insuring that workers would not disrupt wartime manufacturing. Union and political leaders told employees that it was their patriotic duty to support the war, and most workers concurred.

In January 1942, Roosevelt established the **National War Labor Board (NWLB)**, an organization designed to deal with industrial conflicts. Made up of labor, business, and government representatives, the NWLB established wage ceilings for industrial workers and heard workplace grievances. To coal miners, the NWLB was infamously known for the **Little Steel Formula**, a wage scale imposed after the government intervened in a workplace settlement involving 500,000 steelworkers. According to the Little Steel Formula, wage increases for industrial workers could not exceed the inflation rate between January 1941 and March 1942. The rate was about 15 percent.

Mineworkers believed that wartime regulatory policies were deeply unfair, particularly the NWLB's wage caps. Insisting that such policies only benefited employers, John Lewis negotiated for a unionwide raise of $2 a day, a pay increase that exceeded 15 percent. The NWLB refused the union's requests, which precipitated a series of illegal strikes. The NWLB eventually made concessions to the miners, offering them a wage increase of $1.50 a day in November 1943.

Although Lewis won the respect of his members by breaking the Little Steel Formula, the year's dramatic strikes elicited disapproval from politicians and most members of the press, even though the walkouts did not threaten the country's coal supply. Frustrated with the persistent walkouts, Congress passed the Smith-Connally Act to penalize wartime strikers. The act also gave the federal government greater power over strike-threatened industries, which it used in late 1943. For a brief period in November of 1943, the government nationalized the country's mines.

These coal strikes demonstrated the limitations of the NWLB. Praised by miners for being more responsive to the demands of his members than to the pressure of politicians, Lewis infuriated powerful elements in government. In 1940, Lewis publicly split with Roosevelt, opposed his reelection, and resigned as **Congress of Industrial Organizations** president when Roosevelt won a third term. The UMWA's wartime strikes gave further ammunition to the foes of organized labor and cooled the ardor of erstwhile Democratic Party supporters. Some commentators see a link between the strikes, negative public opinion, and the 1947 **Taft-Hartley Act**.

Suggested Readings: James Atleson, *Labor and the Wartime State: Labor Relations and Law During World War II*, 1998; Nelson Lichtenstein, *Labor's War at Home: The CIO in World War II*, 1982; Alan Singer, "'Something of a Man': John L. Lewis, the UMWA, and the CIO, 1919–1943," in *The United Mineworkers of America: A Model of Industrial Solidarity?*, ed. John H. M. Laslett, 1996.

Chad Pearson

Cold War and Unions. The Cold War posed distinctive challenges to labor's advances during the New Deal and World War II, both domestically and abroad. America's successful military intervention against fascism gave way to a less certain struggle against international communism that dominated foreign policy, internal security concerns, and economic development schemes from 1946 into the 1990s.

One result of World War II was to convince Americans of the necessity of taking an active international role. For the **Congress of Industrial Organizations (CIO)** descent into the Cold War posed a dilemma. The **Popular Front**—a broad alliance of liberals and leftists that included the Communist Party—played a pivotal role in CIO organizing drives of the 1930s and 1940s and helped articulate key international initiatives like the formation of the United Nations and the World Federation of Trade Unions (WFTU). In the face of growing hostility and intransigence, CIO leaders feared the fallout from the CIO's ties to leftist groups. Unresolved until 1948, the CIO attempted to balance the increasingly conflicting forces.

No such dilemma troubled the unremittingly anticommunist **American Federation of Labor (AFL)**, which had always refused to cooperate with its political foes. Beginning with the 1944 formation of the semiautonomous Free Trade Union Committee, the AFL labored to turn Western European labor activists against communism. It cooperated with the State Department and security services throughout Western Europe in subsidizing noncommunist labor leaders. Where it could not garner sufficient popular support, the AFL split national labor movements as it did in France and Italy.

The deepening Cold War forced the CIO to choose sides. Several actions reduced the differences between the CIO and the AFL. The CIO embraced the Marshall Plan to rebuild Europe in 1948 and withdrew from the WFTU in 1949. CIO leadership made opposition to Progressive Party candidate Henry Wallace's 1948 bid for the presidency a test of loyalty to the organization, a slap in the face of many Popular Front allies. Despite rank-and-file protests, the CIO complied with **Taft-Hartley Act** bans on communists holding union office. In 1949 and 1950, it expelled unions it considered communist-led, thus disenfranchising one-third of its members. These actions paved the way for the AFL and CIO to merge in 1955.

During the 1950s, American organized labor's international activism was largely funded by U.S. government agencies. The budget for these global ventures was greater than all domestic AFL-CIO expenditure. This tended, however, to subsume AFL-CIO objectives to government Cold War policies. In the 1960s, the American Institute for Free Labor Development caused havoc in Latin America and operated as a tool of American multinational corporations and the government, most notably as a funded arm of the Agency for International Development. Similarly, in Africa and Asia, American labor set up institutes to further U.S. Cold War objectives and was especially active in Kenya, Nigeria, Vietnam, and Indonesia. In the 1980s, it played an important role in supporting the Polish labor group Solidarity in an effort to destabilize communism in Eastern Europe.

In all of this, rank-and-file union members played no active role. When they considered Cold War policies at all, union members largely supported American actions abroad, including the Korean War (1950–53), overt and covert military interventions in the Caribbean and Central America, and even early phases of the Vietnam War (1961–75). Vietnam, however, proved a watershed as criticisms grew that AFL-CIO and individual union leaderships were acting without discussion and input from the rank-and-file. Yet it was not until 1984 that an open debate on foreign policy was allowed at an AFL-CIO annual convention.

Domestically, American labor faced a related but broader dilemma. Government tolerance of labor unions led not only to an overall political strengthening of unions but also to its envelopment in a system of labor relations that produced skilled labor managers rather than militant organizers, some of whom willingly signed iron-clad, penalty-laden contracts with employers as a way to discipline the own rank and file. Moreover, organized labor grew dependent on the **paternal** benevolence of government. These arrangements yielded benefits, but these benefits came at a cost.

The conservative political backlash after World War II was strengthened immeasurably by the Cold War. It provided impetus to employer campaigns to reassert their right to manage, a prerogative many were forced to compromise during the New Deal industrial order. An assault on labor's newly gained rights led to passage of the Taft-Hartley Act. In addition, Cold War–inspired loyalty boards, the House Un-American Activities Committee, various federal and state investigation committees, and the non-communist affidavits required of union officials by the Taft-Hartley Act forced labor to make some harsh choices. Political assaults on labor by conservative politicians put unions on the defensive. So too did the elevation of Dwight Eisenhower to the presidency in 1953.

Both the CIO and the AFL were forced to recognize that much of their success depended on the government, and they could not afford to alienate or defy it. The Popular Front alliance had already been abandoned. To survive the unsympathetic Eisenhower years (1953–61), further concessions were made. Some critics argue that the post-1955 AFL-CIO became a junior adjunct of the corporate state, an action that tended to distance further union leaders from members. During the 1960s, numerous leaders showed little understanding of rank-and-file civil rights and antiwar activism, and they clamped down hard on **wildcat strikes**. Such rigidity led to stagnation of membership, followed by decline. The AFL-CIO's tepid response to civil rights and its unwavering support for Cold War foreign objectives led the United Auto Workers to disaffiliate in 1967.

Close cooperation with Democratic administrations during the 1960s led to positive gain on some fronts. The **Occupational Health and Safety Act**, Medicare, increases in the **minimum wage**, worker training programs, and other advances for labor testified to the worth of political influence. On the other hand, Democrats failed to overturn the repressive Taft-Hartley Act or the unpopular 1959 Landrum-Griffin Act. Nor was help forthcoming on issues like **automation**, containerized cargo, the rise of nonunion service industries, **right-to-work** legislation, or **deindustrialization**.

After 1970, labor had even less influence in government. As mass production industries declined along with union membership, the blatantly antiunion policies of Republican presidents Richard Nixon, Ronald Reagan, George H. and George W. Bush and the failed promises of Democratic administrations headed by Jimmy Carter and Bill Clinton signaled to many the bankruptcy of Cold War unionism. To the harshest critics within labor's ranks, there was little essential difference between the two parties.

The collapse of European communism between 1988 and 1991 led to a drive for a new world order signaled by bipartisan political support for the **North American Free Trade Agreement**, a measure deeply unpopular with union leaders and members. During the Cold War, Republicans and Democrats largely agreed on foreign policy but differed on domestic issues. The end of the Cold War suggests an emergent new consensus on economic strategy that omits labor's voice.

The Cold War shaped many of organized labor's assumptions and alliances from 1948 into the 1990s. Organized labor enters the twenty-first century grappling with changed realities. Much of the debate surrounds the question of what, if any, benefits resulted from Cold War alliances between unions and government. Overall, historians and labor studies scholars are deeply critical of labor's decisions after World War II and deem them unwise steps that have contributed to labor's decline in the past four decades. Even so, some scholars argue that labor leaders had few other choices.

Suggested Readings: Stephen Burwood, *American Labor, France, and the Politics of Intervention, 1945–1952*, 1999; Mike Davis, *Prisoners of the American Dream*, 1989; Nelson Lichtenstein, *Walter Reuther: The Most Dangerous Man in Detroit*, 1997.

Stephen Burwood

Collective Bargaining. Collective bargaining is the method of determining terms and conditions of employment by negotiation between representatives of an employer and employees, usually a labor union. The results of the bargaining are set forth in an agreement or **contract**. A union's elected representatives bargain for all workers as a group instead of individually. Coinage of the term is often credited to British Fabian **socialists** Sidney and Beatrice Webb in the 1890s.

In the United States, the practice of collective bargaining can be traced back to 1799, when a group of Philadelphia cordwainers (leather craftsmen) met with master shoemakers and brokered a trade agreement.

For much of the nineteenth century, however, labor unions struggled to win collective bargaining rights and often encountered legal barriers that declared them illegal combinations. The fate of collective bargaining waxed and waned according to union strength and individual state laws. Many states had anti-conspiracy laws that were applied to labor unions. Generally, these were weakened after the Civil War, but they received an unintended boost from the 1890 **Sherman Antitrust Act**, which some courts interpreted broadly to encompass labor unions as well. It was not until the 1914 **Clayton Antitrust Act** that unions were fully exempt from antitrust laws, and labor's absolute right to bargain collectively was not established until the 1935 passage of the **National Labor Relations Act (NLRA)**. The NLRA currently governs procedures for collective bargaining.

In case of an impasse, both employers and unions have weapons that they use to achieve their objectives. Unions establish leverage through work slowdowns, **boycotts**, **strikes**, **picketing**, and political lobbying. Management has injunctions, **lockouts**, strikebreakers, and the threat of relocation at their disposal. A major purpose of the NLRA, however, is to establish collective bargaining procedures that lead to mutually acceptable agreements between an employer and a union. The advent of these processes has resulted in a certain degree of stability in the labor-management field after World War II.

Suggested Readings: Walter Licht, *Industrializing America*, 1995; Adrian A. Paradis, *Labor in Action: The Story of the American Labor Movement*, 1963; Florence Peterson, *American Labor Unions: What They Are and How They Work*, 1963.

Walter Hourahan

TRIAL
OF TWENTY-FOUR
JOURNEYMEN TAILORS,
CHARGED WITH A
CONSPIRACY:
THE MAYOR'S COURT
OF THE CITY OF
PHILADELPHIA,
September Sessions, 1827.
REPORTED BY
MARCUS T. C. GOULD,
Stenographer.

For much of the nineteenth century, most states had anti-conspiracy laws that viewed labor unions as illegal conspiracies in restraint of trade. The tailors mentioned in this 1827 legal report were tried under such a law. © George Meany Memorial Archives/Public Affairs Press.

Colorado Coalfield Troubles. Colorado's coalfield, in southern Colorado, is on the east side of the Rockies in the counties of Las Animas and Huerfano. It has historically supplied high-grade bituminous coal that was made into coke for the steel industry and was dominated by a few large corporations. The largest was the Colorado Fuel and Iron Company (CF&I), founded in 1880 by John Osgood. By 1892, CF&I produced 75 percent of Colorado's coal. In 1903, the company was acquired by the Rockefeller and Gould interests. **Strikes** broke out throughout the southern coalfield, including a bitter dispute at Cripple Creek in 1904, which saw **Mary "Mother" Jones** come to Colorado in support of the miners. The commander of the National Guard was a Denver ophthalmologist, General Chase, whose natural sympathies were with the mine owners. Chase declared martial law in the strike zone and used the military power of the state to suspend habeas corpus, hold miners in bull pens, torture and beat prisoners, and organize mass jailings. In one incident, Chase, a poor natural horseman, was humiliated when his horse was spooked, and he ordered the troops to ride down the miners' wives. Colorado miners lived in **company towns** located in canyons, bought their goods at company stores, and were paid in scrip, privately printed money good only at the company store. The companies controlled every aspect of life in the mining towns, while the mines themselves were among the least safe in the nation. From 1884 through 1912, Colorado miners died at over twice the national average and coroner's juries found the miners themselves responsible for their own deaths. The miners were largely immigrants from Southern and Eastern Europe. The **United Mine Workers of America (UMWA)** was successful in the northern field but not in the south. The UMWA secretly organized the southern field and, by September 1913, announced a set of demands that included the right to trade at noncompany stores, payment for so-called dead work (work such as shoring, timbering, and laying track for which miners were not paid), and a union check-weightman.

The resulting 1913–14 Colorado Coal Strike was one of the most violent in American history. It went on for fourteen months, with miners camped out in makeshift tent colonies at the entries to the canyons. Mine owners used, in addition to the National Guard, the Baldwin-Felts Detective Agency, which specialized in brutal strikebreaking. The Baldwin-Felts detectives utilized, among other weapons, the Death Special, an improvised armored car that sprayed the miners' tents with machine gun fire. On April 20, 1914, the infamous **Ludlow Massacre** took place, drawing national attention to the situation in the Colorado coalfields. Colorado's governor sought federal intervention, and the strike ended in defeat for the UMWA seven months later. After the strike, 408 miners were arrested, with 332 being charged with murder. The trials dragged on until 1920, but there were no convictions. Similarly, of the ten officers and twelve enlisted men court-martialed, all were acquitted. The troubles in the Colorado coalfields led John D. Rockefeller, Jr., whose injudicious comments during the strike caused him to become a figure of national scorn, to engage Ivy L. Lee and former Canadian Labor Minister William L. McKenzie-King to rehabilitate his family's image. The resultant Colorado Plan of Industrial Representation amounted to a **company union** but was effective in introducing benefits and improved conditions and in quelling disturbances in Rockefeller-owned enterprises.

Suggested Readings: Howard M. Gitelman, *Legacy of the Ludlow Massacre: A Chapter in American Industrial Relations*, 1988; Zeese Papanikolas, *Buried Unsung: Louis Tikas and the Ludlow Massacre*, 1982.

James P. Hanlan

Colored National Labor Union (CNLU). The Colored National Labor Union was an attempt to create a coordinating body to direct African American unions between 1869 and 1871. It was the brainchild of Issac Myers, a black ship caulker, who fostered relations with the **National Labor Union (NLU)**. Alas, neither the NLU nor the CNLU survived.

Black laborers were especially vulnerable in the immediate aftermath of emancipation. Although slavery itself was ended, whites remained deeply divided as to what role African Americans should play in post–Civil War society. The majority of whites, in both the North and the South, held racist views, even if they had supported abolitionism. This was true also of labor unions, many of which excluded black workers. A series of labor congresses was held in the 1860s that took up various issues, including forming a labor federation and how white workers should view black laborers. When the NLU was formed in 1866, delegates at the founding convention split over whether or not to admit African Americans and the issue was tabled. The NLU's guiding spirit, **William Sylvis**, supported admitting African Americans, however, and the 1867 convention appointed a Committee on Colored Labor to explore the possibilities, though it was headed by A. W. Phelps, a carpenter whose union excluded blacks. The committee's 1868 report recommended against admitting African Americans to the NLU.

Nonetheless, Sylvis pushed for admission and nine black delegates attended the 1869 NLU convention, including Issac Myers of the Colored Caulkers Trade Union Society. In the end, the NLU voted to allow black members. This was due in part to the fact that African Americans had already begun organizing without the NLU's sanction, having held their own labor congresses in 1868 and prior to the NLU's 1869 meeting. In addition, many black workers were organized into trade unions, though they often maintained secrecy to protect against retaliation.

In December 1869, Myers convened 214 Negro Labor Congress members in Washington, D.C., and those assembled formed the CNLU. Most of the delegates represented trades, though there were also smatterings of ministers, reformers, and Prince Hall Freemasons. Its structure mirrored that of the NLU, with which it voted to affiliate, as did much of its agenda. The CNLU echoed the NLU's call for an eight-hour day, the establishment of **cooperatives**, free public education, abolishing **child labor**, and women's suffrage. It even followed the NLU's lead in holding yearly labor congresses, in calling for a **Chinese Exclusion Act**, and in renouncing **strikes** in favor of mandatory **arbitration**. Myers was appointed to organize workers in the South, while Sella Martin was sent to Paris to represent the CNLU at the Marxist First International. Only in politics did the CLNU's agenda differ substantively with that of the NLU. Given that the Republican Party supported abolition and authored the Thirteenth, Fourteenth, and Fifteenth Amendments ending slavery and extending civil rights to African Americans, its members remained loyal to the GOP and eschewed the third-party call of the NLU.

The CNLU's alliance with the NLU unraveled over racism and politics. African Americans complained bitterly that NLU unions retained racial barriers. One 1870 delegate, J. M. Langston, introduced a resolution to ban white members from the CNLU, an act that led to his exclusion from the NLU's convention in the fall. When that same NLU convention decided to form a third party, Myers led the CNLU move to disaffiliate with the NLU. That same year, however, Frederick Douglass replaced Myers as CNLU president and was charged with smoothing relations with the NLU. Douglass proved just as incapable of getting the NLU to reverse racist policies; his own son was denied entrance into an NLU-affiliated typographers' union.

Ironically, the CNLU's refusal to support third-party efforts came at a time in which some of its members had begun to criticize the Republican Party's commitment to African American equality. As Reconstruction efforts dwindled, the Democratic Party regained strength in the South, opportunities for black farm laborers declined, and groups like the Ku Klux Klan began terrorizing African Americans, the Republicans seemed little inclined to do anything about it. Douglass's efforts to pressure the GOP came under scrutiny at the 1871 CNLU convention, but by then the organization was a spent force.

So too was the NLU, which faded quickly after an ill-fated 1872 presidential campaign in which the federation attempted to transform itself into a political party. Several labor congresses were held between 1873 and 1875, but none were under NLU auspices and no African American delegates attended. Economic depression associated with the Panic of 1873 doomed hopes of reviving either the NLU or CNLU.

The CNLU's track record as an independent organization was not particularly noteworthy. Its major achievement was the rhetorical force with which it supported African American rights. Both its congresses and its official paper, *New National Era*, exposed the hypocrisy of white workers espousing views of **solidarity** and universal brotherhood while continuing to discriminate against black workers. The CNLU deserves credit for paving the way for more successful groups that came after it. In particular, the **Knights of Labor** learned from CNLU mistakes and went on to organize about 90,000 African American workers.

Suggested Readings: Philip Foner and Ronald Lewis, eds., *Black Workers: A Documentary History from Colonial Times to the Present*, 1989; Peter Rachleff, *Black Labor in Richmond, 1865–1890*, 1989; Robert E. Weir, "Colored National Labor Union," in *Organizing Black America*, ed. Nina Mjagkij, 2001.

Robert E. Weir

Commercial Telegraphers Union (CTU). The Commercial Telegraphers Union is an international union formed by the merger of the International Union of Commercial Telegraphers (IUCT) and the Order of Commercial Telegraphers (OCT). The CTU received a charter from the **American Federation of Labor (AFL)** in 1903, twenty years after a failed **strike** in 1883.

The powerful Western Union Telegraph Company, founded in 1851, dominated the early days of telegraphy. It faced little competition until the Postal

Telegraph Company began operations in 1881. Telegraphy was a notoriously low-paying profession in which operators faced exacting standards, long hours, and dictatorial supervisors. Early efforts at unionization came to little as the job market was overcrowded and employers fired agitators. Members of the secret Telegraphers' Protective League struck in 1870, but they were easily defeated. A more substantial effort was made by the Brotherhood of Telegraphers, who formed in 1882 under the auspices of the **Knights of Labor**. The Brotherhood struck Western Union in July 1883, seeking an eight-hour day, an increase in wages, and equal pay for female telegraphers. The so-called "Great Strike" failed, and on August 17, workers returned to their posts to face layoffs, firings, blacklists, and **yellow-dog contracts**. Telegraphy remained largely unorganized until the CTU emerged in 1903. By then, the business was diversifying, with new competitors arising.

The CTU's first strike occurred in November 1903, when Canadian workers won the reinstatement of discharged union members after a four-hour walkout. By 1904, it represented nearly 10,500 members and was strong enough to wrangle wage concessions from Canadian Pacific Telegraph, Hearst News Services, Scripps-McRae Press Association, and several brokers, though negotiations with the Associated Press (AP) failed. In 1906, it won an agreement with Postal Telegraph, raising hopes. In 1907, however, a CTU strike against Western Union again ended disastrously. The company pulled out all the stops to defeat the CTU, including hiring **Pinkerton** agents, at least one of whom was an **agent provocateur**.

The CTU slowly rebuilt its power base, winning wage increases from Great Northwestern Telegraph in 1911, renewing its contract with Canadian Pacific in 1912, and negotiating a contract with United Press International in 1913. The union's 1917 agreement with the Marconi Wireless Telegraph Company set the industry standard for telegraphers sailing from U.S. ports. AP, however, granted its telegraphers wage increases without bargaining with the CTU.

The CTU hoped that the **National War Labor Board** would help it win collective bargaining rights without reprisal, but its hopes vanished when Western Union and several other companies defied the board's directives. President Woodrow Wilson did place the nation's telegraphs and telephones under the control of Postmaster General Albert Burleson, but his inability to win reinstatement for fired workers resulted in a June 1919 strike against American Telephone and Telegraph, Postal Telegraph, and Western Union. This strike was also lost and Western Union set up a **company union** for its employees.

The 1920s were hard years for the telegraphers. Like many unions, the CTU's position was altered by the New Deal. In 1939, the National Labor Relations Board ordered Western Union to dismantle its company union and workers began to drift into more legitimate bargaining units. On May 13, 1945, the CTU won the right to represent Western Union workers and on April 1, 1946, signed its first contract with the company. In 1952, the CTU endured a fifty-three-day strike against the company to establish an eight-hour day. Relations with Western Union remained problematic, however, with a strike taking place in 1972 to save the union pension fund and another in 1985.

Technological change reduced the importance of telegraphy as a stand-alone profession. In 1971, the CTU changed its name to the United Telegraph Workers and, in 1986, merged with the Communications Workers of America, which today represents telegraphers' interests.

Suggested Readings: Edwin Gabler, *The American Telegrapher*, 1988; Robert Thompson, *Wiring a Continent*, 1974; *Telegraph Workers Journal*, 1971–85.

Anthony Silva

***Commonwealth v. Hunt*.** In March 1842, in the case of *Commonwealth v. Hunt* (45 Mass. {4 Met.} 11, 38 Am. Dec. 346), Chief Justice Lemuel Shaw, of the Massachusetts Supreme Court, set aside an indictment of the boot makers union for conspiracy to restrain competition. Employers had argued that unions' striking for concessions from their employers restrained competition, thus damaging the economy. Shaw agreed that competition was vital to the economy but concluded that unions were a way of stimulating, rather than restraining, competition. Shaw argued that it was not inherently illegal for workers to organize a union or to try to compel recognition of that union by means of a **strike**. As long as the methods employed by unions were within the law, Shaw argued, unions were free to seek recognition and concessions from their employers. Shaw's decision was in advance of its time: by the end of the nineteenth century, courts generally held that strikes for higher **wages** or shorter hours were legal.

Suggested Reading: Alfred H. Kelly and Winfred Harbison, *The American Constitution: Its Origin and Development*, 1976.

James P. Hanlan

Communism and Unions. Many kinds of **socialists** and radicals played important roles in the labor movement, but since World War I, perhaps none were so important or controversial as communists who were affiliated with the Communist Party of the United States of America (CPUSA). The relationship between communism and unions has (at least) two main characteristics. On the one hand, the actions of communists and the Communist Party (CP) influenced the formation and direction of many modern trade unions. On the other hand, anticommunist reactions from within and outside the trade unions proved important for the trajectory taken by twentieth-century unionism. The key decades of this complex relationship span the Great Depression, World War II, and the early–post-war era (1930–60). However, this period left a legacy that continues to inform U.S. labor unions and politics.

Left-Socialist Party members, in solidarity with the Third International and the Russian Revolution, founded the CPUSA in 1919. During its first decade, the CPUSA related to the official trade-union movement, mostly represented by the **American Federation of Labor**'s craft unions through their own association known as the Trade Union Educational League (TUEL). The primary goal of TUEL was to convince the existing union movement to amalgamate by industry rather than craft. In **William Z. Foster**, the man who led the militant but failed **Steel Strike of 1919**, TUEL had a famous and able unionist as its architect and leader. In **Samuel Gompers**, however, TUEL had a bitter antagonist; during his lifetime (to 1924) and in his footsteps, the AFL did all in its power to limit or destroy any communist presence and influence in its unions. The probusiness, antiunion, and anticommunist climate of the 1920s militated against the CP's success.

However, at the end of the decade, the CP changed tactics and began forming their own red unions. These were united in a new organization called the Trade Union Unity League. Though, again, the actual goals of the communists went unrealized—most unions were destroyed before being recognized—the experience of the TUEL period proved decisive for the history of the trade-union movement in a few respects. Over the five years it spent failing to create **dual unions**, the CP had succeeded in creating hundreds of field-tested organizers of the unorganized who were deeply committed to the project of industrial unionism. The CP had also formed networks with thousands of militant workers. By 1933–34, with the passage of the **National Industrial Recovery Act (NIRA)** and a slight economic recovery, the tide against unionism in the United States had turned. **John L. Lewis**, **United Mine Workers of America** president and cofounder of the **Congress of Industrial Organizations (CIO)**, saw the CP's skills, networks, and tactics as remarkable resources for the project of industrial unionism and encouraged the hiring of hundreds of CP members to help organize steel and other industries.

Members of the CP were therefore in CIO leadership positions at its inception: from the shop floor to the organizing campaigns to the central offices. **Leonard De Caux** (CIO press secretary), Lee Pressman (CIO counsel), Wyndham Mortimer (**United Auto Workers [UAW]** vice president), **Harry Bridges** (International Longshoremen's and Warehousemen's Union [ILWU] president), and Ben Gold (Furriers president) were some of the more famous Communists in leadership positions, though it is significant that only one, Gold, was publicly identified as a member of the CPUSA. More than individuals, it was communist unions and CPUSA units (small groups inside workplaces) that started organizing drives and CPUSA papers that provided strategies for action. CP members outside the trade unions helped bring public attention and solidarity to scores of trade-union issues and actions in the latter half of the1930s. Some of the labor organizations formed by the CP or sustained with crucial CP support include the following: the Steel Workers Organizing Committee; the United Auto Workers; the Share Croppers Union; the Transport Workers Union; the **United Electrical Workers**; the National Maritime Union; the United Office and Professional Workers of America; Local 1999 (then the Retail Drug Employees Union); the United Canning, Agricultural, Packing and Allied Workers; the International

Longshoremen and Warehousemen Union; and perhaps most glamorous, the Screen Writers Guild, the Screen Actors Guild, and the Screen Directors Guild. In many of these and others, the CP became the leadership of the organization: during World War II, communist-controlled unions accounted for about 25 percent of CIO membership.

But, what of the influence of communism as an ideology in U.S. unions? In many respects, there was very little. At the height of CP influence in the trade unions (c. 1935–45), no more than a few thousand workers were members of the party at any given time. During most of this period known as the **Popular Front**, the CPUSA placed its revolutionary politics on the back burner, supporting Roosevelt, the New Deal, and after Germany's invasion of the Soviet Union, avidly supporting war efforts. For the most part, party organizers and shop papers argued good trade-union politics, and by 1939, the party had dissolved its units in the unions, further removing specific communist politics from the shop floor and making it difficult if not impossible for fellow workers to know who was a communist and who was not. Their admiration and support for the Soviet Union was not a large liability for much of this period: Depression-era realities made the ideas of a planned economy and state supports attractive to many, and the USSR was allied with the United States.

One manner in which the CP's politics did play a role in the trade unions was as the left end of the left-liberal spectrum that characterized much of the New Deal. The CPUSA consistently fought for racial equality in unions, workplaces, and government policy. Its support for immigrants won it a large immigrant base. The CPUSA generally supported **rank-and-file** democracy within unions. It popularized international causes and initiated solidarity efforts, as with Ethiopia against Mussolini and Spanish Republicans against Franco.

Yet there was another way in which communism functioned in the unions. CP unionists were subject to changes in the perspective of the CPUSA. To various unionists, CP support for the USSR during the period of the Hitler-Stalin pact seemed a cynical position for antifascist fighters to take; support for the **no-strike pledge** during WWII contradicted typical CP support for rank-and-file militancy; and after the war, CP support for Henry Wallace's third-party presidential campaign threatened to isolate labor from the Democratic Party during a period of antilabor reaction.

Anticommunism was present throughout this period, within the government, the business community, and the unions themselves. Much of the resistance to the New Deal took the form of antisocialism, with Roosevelt and the Democratic Party being accused of "leading us towards Moscow." The CPUSA quickly became the main, but not the only, target of anti–New Dealers. In 1939, the Hatch Act barred suspected communists from federal jobs, and in 1940, the Smith Act made belonging to an organization that advocated the overthrow of the U.S. government a criminal offense (in addition to instituting other civil-liberty restrictions). Starting in 1938, the House Special Committee on Un-American Activities (HUAC) began investigating the CIO and New Deal agencies for communist infiltration. (HUAC would later conduct postwar anticommunist investigations and blacklisting under the infamous leadership of Joseph McCarthy.)

During the Cold War, the government's need to gain support for its foreign policy dovetailed with the antilabor backlash that had begun prior to the war, culminating in the red scare of the 1940s and 1950s. The unions were attacked in the name of anticommunism, and the labor movement became fiercely divided. In the **Taft-Hartley** legislation of 1947, restrictions placed on labor unions were combined with a requirement that all union officials sign a non-communist loyalty oath to use the National Labor Relations Board (NLRB). Though most unions resisted at first, by 1950 eleven communist-led unions were expelled from the CIO. Much of the non-communist leadership of the trade unions had only worked with the CP for reasons of expedience, and after the war CIO President **Philip Murray** and UAW President **Walter Reuther** (among others) actively worked to purge Communists from their organizations. Catholic organizations such as the **Association of Catholic Trade Unionists** helped lead the fight against the communists. Among much of the trade union rank and file, the CP's secrecy, support for the World War II anti-strike pledge, and association with the Soviet Union worked against it (though as good unionists, CP members were also often defended, and in the case of the expelled unions, remained in leadership). In general, where the choice was patriotism or communism, most American workers identified with their country.

The toll of the scare was enormous. From 1945 to 1952, congressional committees conducted eighty-four hearings concerning subversive activities. Thirteen million five hundred thousand Americans fell under purview of the investigations; one in five workers were forced to take loyalty oaths; 15,000 federal employees and thousands more in many industries and professions lost their jobs or were blacklisted. But the effects of the anticommunist backlash in the unions went beyond individual hardship and communists per se. Anticommunism was used—and continues to be used—as a weapon by employers against trade unionists of every stripe, who are red-baited when taking militant action or making demands deemed threatening.

Further, the red scare succeeded in purging the unions of labor-left people and politics. The labor movement had historically been open to a host of different ideologies, but in the aftermath of the Cold War, its social vision was dimmed and its political spectrum narrowed considerably. Fights for shorter hours, national health insurance, racial equality, or political independence through a labor party have at various times been linked to communist ideas and therefore held suspect. Though by the 1960s labor regained some of its ideological roots and is today associated with liberal viewpoints and policies, anticommunism has contributed to weakening labor's ability and willingness to fight against employer offensives and for more radical government policies, a legacy keenly felt in the movement today.

Suggested Readings: Bert Cochran, *Labor and Communism: The Conflict That Shaped American Unions*, 1977; Roger Keeran, *The Communist Party and the Auto Workers Unions*, 1980; Tricia Cayo Sexton, *The War on Labor and the Left*, 1991.

Penny Lewis

Company Town. A company town is a village, town, or section of a municipality where a significant number, if not all, essential housing units, utilities, and services are owned by the region's dominant business. The term is also applied rather imprecisely to situations in which a single corporation exerts undue political influence due to its economic dominance within the region.

Company towns are largely the product of nineteenth-century **paternalism** and are rare in contemporary America. In theory, company towns stood to fatten company coffers as workers returned part of their pay in the form of rent, utility costs, and the purchase of goods and services. Company towns also frequently made moral demands upon workers, like sobriety or mandatory church attendance, on the theory that a moral workforce would be more pliable and stable. In practice, few company towns lived up to the expectations of founders or investors.

In company towns, such as the one pictured here, all housing, utilities, and services were company-owned. © George Meany Memorial Archives/U.S. Department of the Interior.

Samuel Slater was one of the first entrepreneurs to attempt company towns. Flush with success at Pawtucket, Rhode Island, where workers lived in company-owned dormitories adjacent to his textile mill, Slater and his partners expanded northward along the Blackstone River valley towards Worcester, Massachusetts. Several factory villages emerged in what are now the towns of Dudley, Oxford, and Webster, Massachusetts. When disputes arose with workers over issues like water rights or wages, Slater simply opened a new village. The Slater family continued to operate these factory villages into the 1870s, but over time these small-scale operations grew antiquated, and absolute control dwindled. From the start, profits were realized on textiles, but seldom on the towns.

More famed, and for a time, more successful experiments in textile-based company towns were those undertaken by a group of investors known as the Boston Associates. Building from their success in Waltham, Massachusetts, in 1815, the Associates expanded on a grand scale. In 1821, they began construction in Lowell, Massachusetts, and in less than a decade operated a company town of more than twenty thousand employees. Lowell was designed to be the antithesis of English factory towns, which were infamous for their harsh working conditions and the squalor in which people lived. By contrast, Lowell featured sturdy boarding houses, tree-lined streets, public gardens, and other amenities amidst its red brick factory buildings. Virtually every institution from the schools and churches to the lyceum and literary journal was controlled by the company. The targeted workforce was composed of single farm women rendered available by a slump in New England agrarian revenues. To that end, the Boston Associates also attempted to build a moral environment. By the 1830s, Lowell was so successful that the industrial city was actually a tourist destination.

As was the case in most factory towns, however, the aspirations of workers were often ignored and corporate profit took precedence over employee livelihoods. Some workers chafed under what they saw as excessive company control and the long hours required, but more grumbled over wage cuts that ensued during economic downturns. Since wage cuts were seldom accompanied by reductions in rent or services, industrial conflicts ensued. A series of strikes rocked Lowell in the 1830s and 1840s, and the Lowell Female Labor Reform Association (LFLRA), led by **Sarah Bagley**, is regarded by many scholars as the first women's trade union in the United States. The LFLRA forged broader bonds with the Workingmen's Movement as well as 10-hour leagues. Conflict plus an influx of Irish immigration led to the steady decline of Lowell as a utopian experiment. Nonetheless, the Associates transplanted the Lowell model to Chicopee, Holyoke, and Lawrence in Massachusetts; Dover, Manchester, Nashua, and Somersworth in New Hampshire; and Biddeford and Saco in Maine.

Lowell was merely the most famous antebellum company town. Iron workers in Troy, New York, and textile workers in nearby Cohoes lived in company towns, though their proximity to Albany made total control more difficult than Boston Associate communities that arose in the midst of agricultural regions. Rockdale, Pennsylvania, was also a company-owned textile town.

One of the most common models for company towns, as well as perhaps its harshest application, were those that emerged in mining regions across the United States. Mining operations were often mere villages—called patches in some regions—many miles from a major city. Mine operators thus exercised a level of control that only the operators of lumber camps rivaled. Housing was controlled by the company and the local company store was often the only retail establishment and pedaled goods at inflated prices. In extreme cases, workers were not even paid in legal tender, rather they received scrip, redeemable only at the company store. Most patch towns were mere villages, extensive social services were rare, and upkeep was spotty. Northeast Pennsylvania sported numerous such villages, and it is hardly surprising that labor agitation was intense there, including the **Molly Maguires** troubles of the 1870s. Company mine towns were often the site of bloody labor strife, including the **Colorado coalfield troubles** from 1881 through 1905, the **Lattimer Massacre** of 1897, the 1914 **Ludlow Mas-**

sacre, and conflict among Kentucky and West Virginia coal miners that included the famed shootout at **Matewan**, West Virginia, in 1920.

Some company-town efforts were born out of nineteenth-century utopian impulses. Robert Owen's New Lanarck community in Scotland inspired imitators. Owen managed to both make a profit and operate an industrial community whose humane quality of life stood in marked contrast to working-class life in the rest of Britain. His son, **Robert Dale Owen**, came to the United States in 1925 to operate his father's **cooperative** community in New Harmony, Indiana. It failed within four years. Like other utopian industrial schemes—including the Brook Farm experiments of the 1840s that built upon cooperative schemes developed by French intellectual Charles Fourier—New Harmony was undercapitalized, relied too much on intellectuals, and was not productive. A more successful utopian industrial community was the Oneida community, founded in 1836 as a religious experiment and involved in industrial production as a means of becoming self-supporting. In 1881, the religious community was dissolved and Oneida became a joint-stock company producing high-quality tableware.

Utopian communities blur the definition of company towns, as communalism was built into their structures rather than corporate profit. The maturation of **capitalism** after the Civil War increasingly rendered the logic of company towns archaic. By the 1880s, most capitalists found greater profit opportunity in industrial production, stock investment, and selling goods and services than in operating entire towns. Once such towns grew beyond the size of mine patches, the cost of operating and maintaining them was enormous. Moreover, the hegemonic philosophy of **Social Darwinism**—which applied the evolutionary principle of survival of the fittest to society and the economy—made American entrepreneurs more comfortable with the cold-blooded logic of their English counterparts. Fewer investors cared about how workers lived or their moral development so long as profits were healthy. Thus, fewer were interested in the paternalistic motives that fueled Lowell, and even fewer in cooperative or communal principles.

That skepticism was no doubt reinforced by the spectacular failure of Pullman, Illinois. The **Homestead Steel Strike** of 1892 had already dampened enthusiasm; the 1894 **Pullman Strike/Lockout** seemed to confirm that company towns were seldom profitable or stable. George Pullman constructed an industrial city near Chicago to produce his railroad sleeping cars. Pullman was, in many ways, even more impressive than Lowell. In addition to factories and worker housing, Pullman also featured a splendid community center, a luxury hotel, an ornate library, and an artificial lake. It was meticulously landscaped. In 1881, the first residents moved in and almost immediately resented Pullman's paternalistic control. Rents in Pullman were higher than working-class neighborhoods of Chicago, as were utilities, retail prices, and fares on the one rail line that serviced the town. Workers joked that they lived in Pullman's houses, worshiped in his church, were buried in his cemetery, and would undoubtedly spend eternity in Pullman hell.

Tensions were already high when the Panic of 1893 caused Pullman to slash wages. He did not, however, reduce rents or other costs associated with living in Pullman. The bitter lockout and strike of 1894 was the death knell to Pullman's experiment. By 1899, the factory town was decrepit; in 1904, the land and houses were sold to the city of Chicago.

By the twentieth century, the majority of classic company towns were owned by mining firms. (A rare company town startup was Hershey, Pennsylvania, where chocolate magnate Milton Hershey opened his namesake town in 1903. Until the late 1950s, there were company-written covenants that all citizens had to follow.) Instead of ownership of most or all city assets, many twentieth-century corporations chose instead to flex their economic and political muscle. Numerous towns and cities dominated by a single employer became de facto company towns, even when owning little or no real estate beyond that upon which their factories stood. For all practical purposes, Gary, Indiana, was a U.S. Steel company town, and Flint, Michigan, was the preserve of General Motors. Few city jobs did not somehow rely upon the health of these corporate giants. The same patterns were true of textile towns in the Southern Piedmont, one-industry New England mill towns, Arizona mining towns dominated by **Phelps-Dodge**, and in many other places across America.

The Great Depression challenged but did not destroy this new type of company town. Many held sway until **deindustrialization**, globalism, and **deregulation** altered the economic landscape in the 1970s. Most towns and cities have sought to diversify their economies since the economic crises of the 1970s and the recession of the late 1980s. In places where older corporations remain dominant, a subtle type of company-town mentality persists, but few of these can claim the sort of control of nineteenth-century paternalist towns or mid-twentieth-century one-industry regions. Where the ideal remains strongest is in those locales where military bases or Defense Department contracting command disproportionate numbers of local employment opportunities. Thus, for all intents and purposes, a place like Parris Island, South Carolina—home to the Marine Corps' training base—is a modern company town. Economists are nearly unanimous in their assertion that company towns past and present are less economically stable than municipalities with diversified economies.

Suggested Readings: Stanley Buder, *Pullman: An Experiment in Industrial Order and Community Planning*, 1967; David Corbin, *Life, Work, and Rebellion in the Coal Fields*, 1981; Stephen Hahn and Jonathan Prude, eds., *The Countryside in the Age of Capitalist Transformation*, 1985; Daniel Walkowitz, *Worker City, Company Town: Iron and Cotton Worker Protest in Troy and Cohoes, New York, 1855–84*, 1978.

Robert E. Weir

Company Union. Company union refers to a **bargaining unit** set up by the employers on behalf of their own employees. Also known as employee representation plans, company unions thrived in the 1920s but were outlawed as unfair labor practices under the 1935 **National Labor Relations Act (NLRA)**.

Although employers experimented with employee shop committees and worker councils in the nineteenth century, most scholars see a 1915 structure put in place at the Colorado Fuel and Iron Company as the prototypical company union. It, like those that followed, allowed employees to negotiate **wages**, layoffs, benefits, and hours with the company. Company unions were often implemented at the same time as generous benefit packages **(welfare capitalism)** were put into place. By 1933, as many as 2.5 million workers were represented by company unions.

Many observers found company unions problematic. Since the company in effect bargained with itself, company unions could not hope to compete as equals, nor could their negotiators operate free from potential reprisals. Moreover, there was little to compel employers to maintain welfare capitalism systems during times of economic distress like the Great Depression (1929–41). Company unions were expressly eliminated by Section 8 (a) (2) of the NLRA.

Most scholars and union activists interpret the company union ideal as an employer dodge to stifle legitimate unionization efforts. A small group of scholars argues that many company unions operated in more liberal firms and that a few delivered superior benefits than those won by noncompany labor unions. Company unions have proven easier to ban in theory than in reality. Many firms operate staff councils, advisory groups, and ad hoc committees that operate much like 1920s-style company unions. In the 1990s, Republican members of Congress proposed amending the NLRA to allow new company unions under the guise of what they dubbed the TEAM (Teamwork for Employees and Managers) Act. It has been bitterly opposed by the AFL-CIO, and President William Clinton refused to sign such a measure.

Suggested Readings: Irving Bernstein, *The Lean Years*, 1960; Stuart Brandes, *American Welfare Capitalism, 1880–1940*, 1995; Bruce Kaufman, "The Case for the Company Union," *Labor History* 41, no. 3 (August 2000): 321–50.

Robert E. Weir

Concessions. Concession is the general term for a regressive contract whose terms are less advantageous than the contract it replaces. Sometimes called givebacks, concessions are wrung from employees bargaining from a position of weakness. In essence, unions bargain away power, conceding to management the right to invest, determine production, organize work, and make financial decisions. During negotiations, concessions are often offered as an ultimatum and can involve significant cuts in **wages** and benefits.

Concessions have long been a staple of the **collective bargaining** process, with employers seeking to regain advantages yielded in previous contracts. They are standard management bargaining tactics during economic downturns and in highly competitive industries, with management threatening to lay off workers or cease operations if unions fail to grant economic concessions. Until the 1970s, however, concessions were usually negotiated within individual firms or within a particularly vulnerable industry. More common was **pattern**

bargaining, in which unions targeted an industry leader and used its contract as the basis for others within that industry.

By the late 1970s, however, employers argued that stagflation and the pressures of globalism placed U.S. firms at a competitive disadvantage. They demanded employee givebacks to reduce company operating costs and make them more profitable. Typical of this sort of reverse pattern bargaining was what happened in the auto industry. By 1979, Chrysler Corporation was in deep financial distress and eventually declared bankruptcy. To prevent the loss of tens of thousands of jobs, the federal government devised a bailout plan to rescue the ailing firm. As part of its restructuring plan, Chrysler got the **United Auto Workers (UAW)** union to agree to $673 million in employee concessions, ranging from pay cuts to reductions in benefits. Ford and General Motors quickly demanded similar cuts, which the beleaguered UAW was forced to grant.

Unlike earlier versions of concessions, those unleashed in the 1970s were not isolated or confined to a single industry, rather they were part of an overall cross-business management strategy to reduce the power of unions. Many firms relocated outside of the United States, thereby demonstrating their willingness to eliminate jobs if concessions were not granted. The decline and near disappearance of American basic industries in steel, rubber, glass, and electronics made blue-collar workers especially vulnerable.

These trends accelerated in the 1980s. The Reagan and Bush administrations were largely hostile to organized labor, thereby emboldening employers. In addition, the Supreme Court ruled that employers need not negotiate with unions to close plants, relocate, or transfer work from one site to another. Reagan-Bush tax policies also accelerated capital flight. In 1981, new union contracts averaged a nearly 10 percent wage increase for members; by 1986, this was down to a mere 1.2 percent increase, a figure that failed to keep up with inflation. Wage concessions were often coupled with deep cuts in **fringe benefits**, with employees being forced to reduce their number of paid holidays, pay higher premiums for healthcare coverage, agree to mandatory **overtime**, give up **cost-of-living adjustments**, and give firms more discretion in investing employee **pension** funds.

Most unions were ill-prepared for concessions battles and fought rearguard campaigns in which success was measured by how little they were forced to concede rather than how much they won. By the late 1980s, some union leaders spoke of concession bargaining and argued that their choice was between concessions and unemployment. Many unions opted to protect older members by accepting two-tier contracts, wherein new employees began work at lower pay rates and benefit packages than those already working. The UAW accepted such a contract in 1996.

By the mid-1990s, however, unions began to hold a firmer line on concessions. Studies revealed that employers often squandered employee pension funds in reckless stock market speculation and that there was precious little link between granting concessions and saving jobs. Manufacturing jobs continued to evaporate as firms moved their operations outside U.S. borders or invested their savings in the stock market rather than rebuilding aging plants. The overall contraction of manufacturing meant that unions were left strongest in those businesses least susceptible to capital flight such as the professions, government work, education, and service industries. **Rank-and-file** rebellion against concessions-minded labor leaders also played a part, as did a new generation of leadership more committed to fighting concessions. **John Sweeney** made an end to concession bargaining a centerpiece of his successful 1995 bid for the presidency of the American Federation of Labor-Congress of Industrial Organizations.

As of 2003, union efforts to end concessions remain an unfinished task. The tidal wave of the 1980s has been stemmed, but many workers remain vulnerable to concessions drives, a reality made more palpable by the rise in part-time workers, professional adjuncts, and temporary workers. Soaring health-care costs are the source of numerous contemporary employer demands for concessions.

Suggested Readings: Stanley Aronowitz, *From the Ashes of the Old: American Labor and America's Future*, 1998; Martin Jay Leavitt, *Confessions of a Union Buster*, 1993; Kim Moody, *An Injury to All*, 1988.

Robert E. Weir

Conciliation. *See Arbitration/Conciliation/Mediation*.

Congress of Industrial Organizations (CIO). The Congress of Industrial Organizations was the most vibrant force in American labor relations in the twentieth century. During its twenty-year existence from 1935 to 1955, the CIO brought unionization to the nation's central industries. It dramatically expanded the scope of collective bargaining, helping millions of working people to win economic security and fair treatment on the job. The CIO made organized labor a major force in American public life.

The CIO was founded in 1935 to extend the labor movement into the mass-production industries—like the steel, auto, and electrical appliance industries—that dominated the American economy. Union leaders had long wanted to organize workers in those industries. But, the leading labor organization of the day, the **American Federation of Labor (AFL)**, was slow to do so as its **craft-union** leaders were suspicious of **industrial unionism**. Frustrated by the AFL's inaction, eight union presidents broke with the federation in October 1935. Led by **John L. Lewis**, the combative president of the **United Mine Workers of America**, the rebels formed a new labor federation dedicated to organizing workers into industrial unions.

The CIO's leaders began cautiously, quietly sending organizers into the factory towns of the East and Midwest to spread the union message. They discovered that industrial workers did not need to be converted to labor's cause. They desperately wanted unions and leapt at the opportunity the CIO offered them. Throughout 1936 and 1937, working people created a massive wave of **strikes** that rolled across the industrial heartland. In February and March 1936, for example, workers at the Goodyear Tire plant in Akron, Ohio, struck to demand that the company recognize their union, the **United Rubber Workers of America**. A year later, workers at the General Motors plants of Flint, Michigan, seized control of their factories to demand recognition of their union, the **United Auto Workers (UAW)**. The strike wave quickly spread to Detroit, where workers at Chrysler and other auto manufacturers likewise insisted on UAW representation. In the spring of 1937, workers in the steel industry struck to win recognition of their union, the Steel Workers Organizing Committee. A few months later, workers at Radio Corporation of America (RCA) struck to gain recognition of their union, the **United Electrical, Radio, and Machine Workers' Union (UE)**. A few corporations—most notably in steel—beat back the union tide. But, most corporate officials were overwhelmed by their workers' sudden militancy. By the close of 1937, the CIO had three million members organized into 6,000 **union locals**. Just two years after its founding, the CIO had achieved its central goal of bringing unionization to the masses of industrial workers.

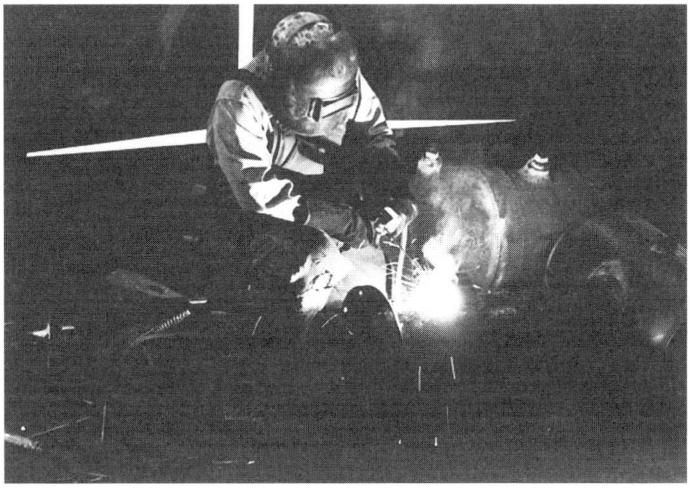

The CIO brought unionization to mass-production industries, such as the steel and auto industries, making the benefits of union membership available to industrial workers, such as this welder. © George Meany Memorial Archives/M.E. Warren Photo.

No labor organization could sustain such fierce activism for long. In the late 1930s and early 1940s, the CIO traded its militancy for the slower, less spectacular work of building a stable organization. It continued to organize workers, sometimes by staging strikes, other times by using legal challenges to force employers to recognize workers' rights. By the U.S. entry into World War II in December 1941, the CIO had organized workers at some of America's most viciously anti-union companies, including the Ford Motor Company and Bethlehem Steel. The breakthroughs at such companies proved vitally important, since they gave the CIO representation at most of the major mass industrial corporations in the country. When employment at those corporations skyrocketed during the war, the CIO's membership shot up as well. By 1945, the CIO, four million members strong, had won a seemingly permanent place in the American economy.

CIO unions used the organization's power to secure significant gains for their members. Union officials pushed workers' wages higher than they had ever been. They forced corporations to concede benefits—healthcare coverage, pension plans, paid vacations—that had previously been reserved for middle-class Americans. The most creative CIO unions demanded even more. The UAW, for instance, forced the auto companies to pay workers a portion of their wages even when they were laid off, an unprecedented benefit to workers for whom unemployment once meant destitution. The CIO also brought a measure of justice to the factory floor by insisting that its members deserved the protection of **grievance** procedures, **seniority** systems, and clearly defined job descriptions. Together, these mechanisms assured workers that their bosses could not exercise arbitrary power over them.

CIO leaders were not satisfied with improving conditions for their members. From the beginning, they were also committed to expanding labor's role in national politics. In 1936, Lewis forged an intimate relationship with the Democratic Party. Lewis's successors as CIO president, **Philip Murray** and **Walter Reuther**, nurtured that relationship, weaving the CIO's political operations together with those of the Democrats. The CIO then used its position within the party's councils to promote a greatly expanded welfare state, vigorous government management of the economy, civil rights for African Americans and other minority groups, and other progressive causes. In the 1940s and early 1950s, in fact, the CIO became the driving force of the Democrats' liberal faction.

The CIO's aggressive promotion of workers' rights and political change also made it a lightning rod for conservative forces. As early as 1938, right-wing politicians attacked the CIO as a radical threat to the American way of life. Those attacks grew more serious in the immediate aftermath of World War II, as the nation slipped into the Cold War. Thrown on the defensive, CIO officials forced some of the more radical affiliates out of the organization in 1948 and 1949. All told, the CIO lost 900,000 members in the purge. What's more, it lost much of its vibrancy. As rabid anticommunism gripped the nation in the early 1950s, the CIO found it difficult to maintain the militancy that had been its hallmark, both on the shop floor and in politics. Torn by internal dissension and weakened by external attack, the CIO sought security by turning back to the labor center it had left two decades before. After prolonged negotiations, the leaders of the CIO and the AFL agreed to merge their organizations in December 1955. The new federation, the American Federation of Labor-Congress of Industrial Organizations, gave the CIO unions the security they needed. But it lacked the vigor, imagination, and courage that had made the CIO so extraordinary.

Suggested Readings: Irving Bernstein, *Turbulent Years: A History of the American Worker, 1933–41*, 1971; Nelson Lichtenstein, *Labor's War at Home: The CIO in World War II*, 1982; Robert Zieger, *The CIO, 1935–55*, 1995.

Kevin Boyle

Contingency Labor. Contingency labor is an increasingly controversial form of work in contemporary American society where as many as one-quarter of all workers are **part-time** workers. In common parlance, the term has come to mean any part-time worker, though technically contingency labor is work taken for a limited period of time with no promise or expectation that it will be permanent. Critics refer to it as disposable labor and charge that contingent workers are exploited by unscrupulous employers seeking to maximize profits. Issues concerning both contingency and part-time workers were given higher public profile by the 1997 **UPS Strike**, in which the **International Brotherhood of Teamsters** wrangled promises to convert part-time jobs into full-time employment.

According to the **Bureau of Labor Statistics**, those who work fewer than thirty-five hours per week are considered part-time workers. How many of these workers are coerced and/or contingent is a matter of some debate. Defenders of current hiring programs claim that only the 20 percent of current part-time employees who wish full-time work should be considered contingency labor. They accuse unions and social activists of being alarmist, claiming that the total percentage of part-time workers has remained constant at 18 percent since the 1970s. Moreover, only one in five is a head of household, many have health insurance through other family members, and most part-time workers are students, retirees, or women seeking flexible hours. They also point out that of those who are involuntarily working part-time, only one out of five remains so after a year. From this point of view, the number of true contingency workers appears quite small, about 5 percent of the total workforce.

Although there is truth in the above logic, it also contains flaws. Unions claim that the number of part-timers seeking full-time work is much higher than 20 percent. Even if one accepts the lowest estimates, more than one-half million workers seeking full-time employment cannot secure it. Contingency work tends to be concentrated in the retail and service sector, but it is also found in large firms that could afford to hire more full-time workers. For example, software giant Microsoft employs about 6,000 contingency workers at any given time, and a large number of Wal-Mart employees are contingency or part-time workers, even though it is the world's richest corporation. An especially egregious employer of contingency labor is higher education; more than half of all classes in many colleges and universities are taught by graduate students and adjuncts, the bulk of the latter seeking full-time work. Moreover, women make up a disproportionate percentage of contingency workers. Wages for contingency workers tend to be lower and benefits are few.

Organized labor has begun to pay more attention to contingency and part-time workers, groups it has historically ignored. The battle over contingency labor is likely to intensify in the coming decades.

Suggested Readings: Kathleen Barker and Kathleen Christensen, eds., *Contingent Work: American Employment Relations in Transition*, 1998; Employment Policy Foundation, "Part-Time Work: Not a Problem Requiring a Solution," http://www.epf.org/polpartwork.htm.

Robert E. Weir

Contract. A contract is an agreement between two or more parties in which each is bound to fulfill enumerated obligations. Labor contracts are customarily written and enforceable by law. Both parties agree to the terms and conditions contained within. Union membership usually needs to ratify a contract before it goes into effect.

North American labor contracts date to the early 1600s. The earliest forms involved laborers and skilled craftsmen working as **indentured servants** for a specified period of time, usually five to seven years. In exchange, they received passage across the Atlantic Ocean from Europe. At the end of the agreed upon term of work, the workers were free to leave. Sometimes they received land, money, or goods at the end of their contracts. Later, contracts were set up between **master craftsmen** and their **journeymen** and **apprentices**. Some of these contracts were oral agreements, though many were written. With the advent of labor unions, contracts were more likely to be written, and they grew more complex. It was not unusual, however, for late-nineteenth-century contracts to be rather straightforward and short.

Contracts grew more complex as labor law increased in complexity. A modern contract between a union and an employer has many parts to it. Standard items like **wages**, hours of employment, and benefits are spelled out. Other work conditions and grievance procedures are frequently quite detailed; it is commonplace to have lawyers review the minutiae of contract language that is carefully crafted during labor negotiations. Both labor and management view the contract as a temporary truce; the average contract is in effect for three years. Contract violations by either side can result in **grievance**, **arbitration**, or the filing of an **unfair labor practice** charge.

Suggested Readings: Terry L. Leap, *Collective Bargaining and Labor Relations*, 1995; R. Emmett Murray, *The Lexicon of Labor*, 1998.

Walter Hourahan

Contract Labor Act (1864). An Act to Encourage Immigration, also known as the Contract Labor Act, was passed by Congress in 1864 in direct response to the labor shortage in the northern states caused by the Civil War draft. The act allowed the advancement of passage money to prospective immigrants in return for a lien upon their wages. Encouraged by the Act, influential Americans—including Secretary of the Navy Gideon Welles, Senator Charles Sumner of Massachusetts, and the Reverend Henry Ward Beecher—invested in the American Emigrant Company, capitalized at $1 million. The company's announced intention was to import laborers, especially skilled workers, from England, Belgium, France, and other northern European countries and provide workers to employers requiring miners, puddlers, mechanics, machinists, and other skilled workers. The workers were required by law to repay the cost of their passage and whatever expense moneys were "advanced" on their behalf. During the repayment period, the workers received no wages, thus they were effectively indentured servants. The time of their **indenture** frequently had to be extended in order to cover their living costs. Contract workers were often used as strikebreakers. Opposition to contract labor came from unions which saw the encouragement of contract labor as an effort by elites to create a labor surplus that artificially depressed wages, discouraged unionization, and caused unemployment. Various national craft unions as well as the **National Labor Union (NLU)** made repeal of the Contract Labor Act a key goal of the labor movement. The Act was repealed in 1868; however, the repeal did not ban the practice of contract labor, but merely ended official government support for the importation of contract labor. The **Foran Act**, passed in 1885, finally prohibited such practices as the importing of contract labor.

Suggested Readings: Joseph G. Rayback, *A History of American Labor*, 1966; Paul R. Taylor, *The ABC-CLIO Companion to the American Labor Movement*, 1993.

James P. Hanlan
Bruce Cohen

Cooperatives. A cooperative is an enterprise owned and operated for the benefit of those individuals who consume its products or use its services. Cooperation is often touted as an alternative to the systems of individual ownership and private profit that are the hallmarks of **capitalism**. Cooperatives usually maintain open, voluntary membership and make decisions democratically. They espouse community ideals, but tend to operate autonomously, as the United States has never developed extensive syndicalist structures within its economy.

Although cooperation is rooted in ancient communal ideals, the inspiration for much of the movement came from progressive factory owner Robert Owen (1771–1858). He established a cooperative store as part of his model factory in New Lanarck, Scotland, and encouraged the growth of a wider cooperative movement that resulted in five cooperative conferences between 1831 and 1833. Many of the town's 2,000 people were recruited from Edinburgh and Glasgow slums. New Lanarck's 500 children attended school, stores sold items at cost, laborers worked an eight-hour day, and **profit-sharing** plans helped maintain high productivity levels. Owen's lectures and writings on cooperation attracted widespread attention, even after New Lanarck converted to more conventional business methods.

Owen's ideas came to the United States in 1825, when he purchased land from a religious group and announced the creation of New Harmony, Indiana. His son, **Robert Dale Owen**, was involved in New Harmony, as was **Frances Wright** and other members of the **Workingmen's movement**. American cooperation experiments were also inspired by the writings of French social theorist Charles Fourier, whose ideas were introduced into the United States by Albert Brisbane. Their views on self-sufficient agricultural communities led to several short-lived Brook Farm communities in Massachusetts (1841–46) and another community in Red Bank, New Jersey.

The present cooperative movement began with the establishment of the Rochdale Society of Equitable Pioneers. The first Rochdale cooperative in the United States was established in 1863 and was located at Lawrence, Kansas. It sought to pool the capital of members to buy and sell goods and return part of the profits back to members in the form of a dividend. However, the cooperatives differed from simple profit sharing in that they sought to radically modify, and ultimately abolish, the **wage** system.

There are three primary types of cooperatives: consumption cooperatives, production cooperatives, and credit or financial cooperatives. A consumption cooperative is an association that seeks to benefit members as consumers by eliminating the merchant's profits and selling goods at or near wholesale cost. Production cooperatives are those in which workers themselves own the facilities and control manufacturing processes. All the profit accrues to producers instead of being siphoned off by an intermediary employer. Credit or financial cooperatives are associations of persons who desire to benefit themselves by combining their capital and their credit.

The first consumer-cooperative movement in the United States was the New England Workingmen's Association, organized in Boston in 1844. A store was started in 1845, and by 1847, twelve groups of people banded together to form the Workingmen's Protective Union (later named the New England Protective Union). The **Knights of Labor** started at least 185 production cooperatives and many assemblies operated cooperative stores that provided discounts to members of the organization. The profits were used for **strike** funds and to establish mutual-aid programs.

For much of the nineteenth century, cooperatives were viewed as alternatives to capitalism. The movement reached its apex in the 1890s, when various groups allied with Farmers' Alliances and the Populist Party formed cooperatives. The idea proved especially attractive to farmers whose thin operating margins were squeezed by exorbitant grain elevator operators, wholesalers, and assorted middlemen. Farmers banded together to set up their own elevators, milling centers, and collective-distribution networks. Many even operated their own retail outlets. Farmer co-ops persist as the most enduring example of the production cooperative. In recent times, they have proven one of the few ways in which small farmers can resist competition from corporate farming conglomerates.

Most cooperatives have not fared well as they have lacked the resources to compete with large-scale capital concerns. Few cooperatives have large enough capital reserves to weather economic downturns, and business practices like advertising and marketing are inimical to cooperative principles. Ideological attacks have also sapped the cooperative movement, with advocates often enduring charges of **socialism** and **communism**. Cooperation experienced a small renaissance during the 1960s, and several employee-owned retail stores remain in business. Perhaps the most visible of consumption cooperatives are food co-ops, grocery outlets that are often staffed by volunteer members. Shareholders band together to purchase goods in bulk and resell these goods to their members at lower prices than for-profit stores. However, the most successful remnant of the cooperative movement are credit unions, quasi-cooperative financial institutions that deliver banking services to members at more favorable rates than stockholder-controlled commercial banks. Numerous unions operate credit unions. Cooperative housing—often called co-housing—has gained in popularity recently. In 1996, the International Co-operative Alliance drafted a statement of identity to facilitate the spread of cooperation.

Suggested Readings: Edward Bemis, *Cooperation*, 1888; John Curl, *History of Work Cooperation in the United States*, 1980; Robert Jackall and Henry Levin, eds., *Worker Cooperatives in America*, 1984.

Evan Daniel

Protestors take part in the 1970s corporate campaign directed against the antiunion policies of the textile giant J. P. Stevens, maker of the Farah line of menswear. © George Meany Memorial Archives/Irv King Photo.

Corporate Campaign. A corporate campaign is an attempt to force employers to bargain with their workers by applying pressure across the corporate structure rather than concentrating solely on an individual workplace. In traditional disputes and **strikes**, most union activity takes place at the site of the alleged **grievance**, and the bulk of negotiations (if there are any) takes place between local management and union officials. Corporate campaigns extend the battle lines and may include such things as: protesting at stockholder meetings, waging public-relations campaigns against companies, investigating the holdings and activities of corporate officials, applying pressure to a corporation's subsidiary holdings, filing multiple lawsuits, threatening to withdraw union funds from banks that lend money to a corporation, and blowing the whistle on unpopular or illegal corporate behavior that is generally hidden from view (like violation of pollution laws). The goal is to isolate a company by bringing pressure to bear from so many sources that is so expensive and/or damaging to the corporate image that management will be forced to the bargaining table.

Corporate campaigns are largely the brainchild of Ray Rogers, who heads Corporate Campaign, Inc. (CCI) in New York City, although many of its tactics evoke those pioneered by the **United Farm Workers of America**. Rogers felt that traditional union strategies no longer worked given that local shops were often owned by corporations that were headquartered many miles away. Mergers, **globalization**, **deregulation**, and **runaway shops** rendered old tactics problematic. Unions no longer faced local firms with limited resources, rather multinational companies with stuffed coffers. Rogers first applied a corporate campaign against J. P. Stevens, a Southern textile manufacturer that had resisted unionization efforts by the Textile Workers Union of America since 1963, and was infamous for its practices of blacklisting, harassing organizers, and threatening employees. Even after Stevens was cited for more than 1,200 violations of the **National Labor Relations Act** in 1976, it continued its aggressive antiunion campaign. Beginning in the 1970s, Rogers and CCI began to largely bypass Stevens management. Instead, more lawsuits were filed against Stevens, a national consumer **boycott** of Farah—a Stevens line of menswear—was launched, protesters picketed stockholders and union officials, and various unions threatened to pull their considerable funds out of a bank that provided Stevens's major credit line. The CCI also proved adroit at building alliances against Stevens, arraying local churches against the firm and organizing a consumer boycott of Avon products, as its chair was a Stevens board member. Stevens finally settled in 1983.

The overall record of corporate campaigns has been mixed. Corporate campaigns also helped American Airlines flight attendants, Boston hotel workers, and **Watsonville** (California) cannery workers in the 1980s. There have been equally dramatic failures, most notably those involving **Phelps-Dodge** workers in 1983 and **Hormel** workers in Austin, Minnesota, whose 1985–87 corporate campaign was undermined by the parent **United Food and Commercial Workers Union**. Perhaps the most spectacular recent victory occurred during the 1992 **Ravenswood Steel Lockout**, when a corporate campaign succeeded in building multinational alliances and linking financier Marc Rich, an international fugitive from justice living in Switzerland, to the dispute in faraway West Virginia.

The future of corporate campaigns is uncertain. They seem to some an innovative alternative to increasingly outmoded tactics from the past and more realistically address the complex structure of global business. They usually require a long-term commitment, however, and some critics feel they are too expensive and merely pit the financial resource of unions against those of deep-pocketed corporations. Moreover, conservative union leaders have been reluctant to embrace CCI methods, while progressives feel that some corporate campaigns alone are too inflexible and do not pay enough attention to local concerns and issues. Most strategists favor using corporate campaigns in combination with community organizing, traditional bargaining methods, and solidarity building, as was done at Ravenswood.

Suggested Readings: Tom Juravich and Kate Bronfenbrenner, *Ravenswood*, 1999; Kim Moody, *An Injury to All*, 1989; CorpWatch: Holding Corporations Accountable, www.corpwatch.org/trac/research/labor.html.

Robert E. Weir

Cost-of-Living Adjustment (COLA). A cost-of-living adjustment is a negotiated **contract** clause that automatically adjusts **wages** to compensate for inflation. The cost of living is the amount of money needed to purchase the goods and services necessary to maintain a certain standard of living. Shortly after World War I, the **Bureau of Labor Statistics** of the **Department of**

Labor began collecting statistics as to what this amount of money would be. The consumer price index (CPI) measures monthly prices for various goods and services, including food, shelter, transportation, fuels, utilities, household furnishings and operations, medical care, entertainment, and personal care.

A cost-of-living adjustment (COLA) was created by negotiators of labor contracts who were looking for a way to automatically adjust wages and salaries during the life of a contract. It was popularized by the post–World War II negotiations between the **United Auto Workers (UAW)** and General Motors. Since many contracts are for three or more years, union officials wanted to insure that contract gains were not eviscerated by inflation. Many UAW contracts contained escalator clauses that automatically raised wages and salaries without opening up the contract for further negotiations. COLAs are usually tied to the CPI and may contain certain components such as adjustments at certain intervals, usually quarterly, semiannually, or annually. They may contain formulas for a percentage of the actual CPI. They may also provide floors or ceilings to limit any potential change, or they may trigger increases in benefits like retirement, vacation pay, or medical benefits.

Suggested Readings: Terry Leap, *Collective Bargaining and Labor Relations*, 1995; Lawrence Mishel, Jared Bernstein, and John Schmitt, *The State of Working America, 1998–99*, 2000.

Michael Bailey

Coxey's Army. Coxey's Army was a dramatic response to the national depression that began in 1893 and was the first time that unemployed citizens marched on Washington, D.C. Jacob Sechler Coxey (1854–1951) hoped to amass vast industrial armies to converge on the Capitol to petition Congress and President Grover Cleveland for relief in the form of government sponsored public-works projects. Coxey was also an ardent advocate of monetary reform and called upon the government to print more money to stimulate the economy.

Ultimately, Coxey hoped to entice both the state and federal governments to employ idle workers on improvement projects. The flamboyant Carl Browne agreed with many of Coxey's economic ideas, and it was he who conceived of the idea to march to Washington. Coxey and Browne envisioned an army of over 400,000 that would rendezvous in Washington on **May Day**, 1894. National unemployment stood at nearly 20 percent by 1894, as the economy foundered in the worst depression the United States had experienced to date. Desperation and Browne's public-relations acumen created support for the Coxey movement. Groups as far away as Los Angeles and Seattle began trekking toward Washington. In all, eight armies massed, each headed by a general. Coxey led the most famous of these ragtag assemblies and dubbed his group the "Commonweal of Christ." Coxey was hardly representative of those he commanded. He was the owner of three ranches and a stable of thoroughbred horses and had amassed over a quarter of a million dollars as his personal fortune. He and Browne often slept at local rooming houses and hotels instead of with their army.

There was no central coordination of efforts and each army used any available means to reach Washington. Some tramped their way along the rail lines or rafted down dangerous rivers, while others commandeered wagons and horses; one group actually stole a locomotive. Only Coxey's Army reached Washington intact. It marched from Massillon, Ohio, with great fanfare and encountered spectator-lined streets and masses of supporters en route. Each stop added new recruits to Coxey's Army. As they crossed the Pennsylvania border, Coxey's Army was greeted by 30,000 spectators and given five tons of food. Enthusiasm proved greater than commitment, however, and only about 500 marchers actually reached the Capitol.

On May 1, 1894, Coxey and Browne entered Washington, but Coxey was dragged away before he could speak and mounted police clubbed demonstrators. Coxey was arrested for trespassing on the Capitol lawn, and by May 2, police had chased most of his army out of the District of Columbia. Despite its failure as a reform movement, the Coxey movement illuminated the economic ills plaguing America from 1893 to 1897. Coupled with the government's equally heavy-handed response to the **Pullman lockout** in 1894, it soured industrial workers on the Democratic Party, stimulated interest in **farmer-labor alliances**, and focused public attention on the plight of the unemployed. Many historians place Coxey's Army among the crises of the 1890s that inspired Progressive Era reforms from 1901 to 1914.

Suggested Readings: Melvyn Dubofsky and Foster Rhea Dulles, *Labor in America: A History*, 1999; Udo Sautter, *Three Cheers for the Unemployed: Government and Unemployment Before the New Deal*, 1991; Carlos Schwantes, *Coxey's Army: An American Odyssey*, 1985.

Mike Bonislawski

Craft Unionism. Craft unionism is the principle that holds that **solidarity** is best maintained in an organization in which members share a common trade and level of skill. Members customarily perfect their skill by serving an **apprenticeship**. Craft unions are exclusionist and seek to maintain common rates of **wages** and conditions of labor within a trade.

Craft unions are organized on the basis of craft or occupation distinctions, rather than along the lines of the actual structure of industry. They tend to be more moderate ideologically and are often suspicious of radical theories within the labor movement. Colonial benevolent societies and guilds were customarily organized by craft. Craft mentality was reinforced by a production system based on imported European traditions in which clear distinctions were made between **apprentices**, **journeymen**, and **master craftsmen**. Since most goods from the seventeenth through the first half of the nineteenth centuries were custom-made (bespoken), most workers identified strongly with their craft.

Nineteenth-century unions were stimulated in part by the breakdown of customary relations between journeymen and masters, but craft identity remained integral to both groups. During the first half of the nineteenth century, labor unions grew and developed among skilled artisans in East Coast cities, especially in Philadelphia, New York, Boston, and Newark. Craft unions waxed and waned before the Civil War, their fortunes often mirroring national economic conditions. With the exception of select industries, most notably shoes and textiles, however, most early-nineteenth-century factories remained small and resembled a collection of workshops. Craft workers often owned their own tools and most possessed irreplaceable skills that enhanced their bargaining power.

Depression and repression decimated craft unions in the 1870s, but they renewed themselves with great vigor in the 1880s. In 1886, several craft unions federated under the aegis of the **American Federation of Labor (AFL)**, and it quickly became the voice for skilled workers throughout the United States. Started in 1886, the AFL shied away from the broad reform agenda and political involvement of its main rival, the **Knights of Labor (KOL)**, in favor of "pure-and-simple" issues like wages and working conditions. The AFL supplanted the KOL and dominated the union movement from the 1890s into the 1930s. The spread of mass-production techniques proved craft unionism's biggest challenge, with technology serving to reduce the need for craft workers. Advocates of **industrial unionism** charged that craft unions were outmoded as well as exclusionary. In the 1930s, the **Congress of Industrial Organizations** challenged the AFL's views on craft unionism. The rivals merged in 1955, but technological and economic change have further eroded the vitality of craft unionism. It remains an important ideal in industries like engineering, the building trades, and printing, but it is often little more than a convenient label in traditional blue-collar trades. Ironically, those with the greatest levels of craft identity today are found in professions like teaching, the law, medicine, and journalism, though many remain unorganized. The most successful craft unions today are those found in the entertainment industry and in professional sports, like the **Major League Baseball Players Association**.

Suggested Readings: American Federation of Labor, *American Federation of Labor History Encyclopedia Reference Book*, 1919; United Federation of Teachers, *Organized Labor: Source Materials for the Study of Labor in America*, 1974.

Evan Daniel

D

Davis-Bacon Act. The Davis-Bacon Act is the first federal law controlling **wages** for nongovernmental employees, and it requires contractors working on federally funded construction projects to pay local **prevailing wages** to their workers. It became law on March 31, 1931, and with several minor amendments, continues in effect into the twenty-first century.

The Davis-Bacon Act began to take shape in 1927. Although it was two years before the Great Depression began, the construction industry long struggled to find new projects, and wages plummeted. When an Alabama contractor won a bid to build a Veteran's Bureau hospital on Long Island in 1927, New York Congressman Robert Bacon filed a bill to prevent poorly paid workers from migrating north with the contractor, thus undercutting Bacon's more highly paid constituents. His "A Bill to Require Contractors and Subcontractors Engaged on Public Works of the United States to Comply with State Laws Relating to Hours of Labor and Wages of Employees on State Public Works" was the kernel of the Davis-Bacon Act. Although the original bill failed, Bacon filed thirteen additional bills over the following four years, all seeking to protect local workers from what he termed "irresponsible contractors, with itinerant, cheap, bootleg labor." A draft cosponsored with Senator James J. Davis was signed into law by President Herbert Hoover in 1931.

The act was important in the early years of the depression, as half of all money spent on construction in the United States went toward federal projects. Because the Act covered all federal contracts exceeding $5,000, very few federal projects avoided Davis-Bacon. The law did not, as many critics charge, force contractors to hire union labor. However, since many urban labor markets held a large percentage of unionized workers, relatively well-paid union rates raised local prevailing wages to higher levels.

The Davis-Bacon Act has been amended at various times, particularly concerning complex formulas used by the U.S. Department of Labor to determine the prevailing wage for dozens of individual job classifications in various cities and regions. The most important amendment affecting workers was added in 1964, when Congress determined that **fringe benefits,** like medical insurance, **pensions,** vacations, and sick pay, should be factored into determining the prevailing wage. During the 1980s and 1990s, the Davis-Bacon Act repeatedly came under fire from critics seeking to alter or eliminate the law. Business opponents rail against extravagant wages paid to workers on federal construction jobs that they charge drive up costs and taxes. Repeated attempts at legislative repeal have failed, thus critics have attempted to overturn the act on constitutional grounds. They argue that the Davis-Bacon act violates the civil rights of minority workers, and insist that the original bill was motivated by a desire to support white Northern workers and punish Southern migrant laborers. In spite of this claim, the Davis-Bacon Act continues to receive support from African American groups like the National Association for the Advancement of Colored People. The Davis-Bacon Act continues to ensure wage stability on federal projects. It has also generated imitators, with many states and cities passing their own versions of the act to cover construction funded by state and local tax money.

Suggested Readings: John Gould and George Bittlingmayer, *The Economics of the Davis-Bacon Act: An Analysis of Prevailing Wage Laws*, 1980; Armand Thieblot, Jr., *The Davis-Bacon Act*, 1975; Armand Thieblot, Jr., *Prevailing Wage Legislation: The Davis-Bacon Act, "Little Davis-Bacon" Acts, The Walsh Healey Act, and The Service Contract Act*, 1986.

John Cashman

Davis, Richard L. (December 24, 1864–January 24, 1900). Richard L. Davis was an African American organizer for the **Knights of Labor (KOL)** and the **United Mine Workers of America (UMWA).** Although Davis is not particularly well known, his brief career illustrates the promises and limits of organizing black workers at the end of the nineteenth century.

Biographical details of Davis's life are sketchy and are mostly inferred from clues left behind in his voluminous speeches and writings on behalf of the UMWA. He was born in Roanoke, Virginia, at a time when Union armies controlled most of the region around the city and just months before they captured Richmond. He received some formal education, though he began working in a Roanoke tobacco factory at age eight and continued doing so until he began mining in nearby West Virginia at age seventeen. In 1882, he moved to Rendville, Ohio, where he also worked as a miner.

Davis arrived in Ohio's Hocking Valley at a time when the KOL was organizing area miners and was embroiled in numerous **strikes** against operators. The KOL pioneered in interracial unionism, and Davis joined the Knights. He was thought to have taken part in KOL campaigns in the region, though details of this (as well as his marriage and family life) are unknown. The KOL met with fierce resistance from coal-mine operators and was so thoroughly eviscerated in the region that miners began discussing the formation of a new union as early as 1885.

In 1890, Davis took part in the convention that fashioned the UMWA from KOL miner organizations and several smaller unions. Davis devoted the remainder of his brief career to advancing the UMWA and the principles of interracial unionism. He warned white miners that failure to treat African Americans as equals would ensure the influx of black **scabs** during strikes, and he upheld the morality of treating all men as brothers. He denounced the **American Railway Union** when it chose to exclude black members, and was critical of many unions involved with the **American Federation of Labor (AFL),** even though the UMWA affiliated with the AFL.

Davis was a devout Christian who peppered his speeches and writings for the UMWA journal with scriptural references. He organized black and white workers in Ohio, West Virginia, and Alabama and was elected to the executive board of UMWA District 6 in 1892 and again in 1894. In 1896, he joined the UMWA's national executive board and was reelected in 1897. At the time, this was the highest post any African American held in a white-dominated union.

In 1897, the UMWA dispatched Davis, **John Mitchell**, and others to West Virginia to try to convince miners there to join a nationwide coal strike. This effort bore little fruit except in McDowell County, a former KOL stronghold, where Davis convinced black workers to maintain solidarity. The UMWA's campaign in the state faltered and Davis's life was in danger. So too was his financial well-being. He was blacklisted for most of 1896, worked infrequently in 1897, and was permanently blacklisted in 1898, the year he lost his bid for reelection to the UMWA's national board. He called upon white friends and UMWA leaders for help in securing work, but none was forthcoming. He died impoverished of lung fever in 1900, most of his work on behalf of the UMWA received posthumous praise.

Davis's brief life was heroic, but his frustrations clearly define the limits of black union efforts at the turn of the century. The decline of the KOL left a void for **minority labor** that the AFL did little to fill. The UMWA was easily the AFL's most progressive union on race, and the AFL's overall record was abysmal. Davis did much to advance interracial unionism. By 1900, more than 20,000 UMWA members were black, nearly 25 percent of the union's total. The UMWA and a handful of other unions upheld tenuous equality principles that awaited more enlightened times before penetrating the union mainstream.

Suggested Readings: Gary Fink, ed., *Biographical Dictionary of American Labor Leaders*, 1974; Philip Foner and Ronald Lewis, eds., *Black Workers*, 1989; Herbert Gutman, *Work, Culture and Society*, 1976.

Robert E. Weir

Day, Dorothy (November 8, 1897–November 29, 1980). Dorothy Day was the founder of the Catholic Worker Movement. Day was born in Brooklyn, New York, the daughter of John and Grace (Satterlee) Day. She entered the University of Illinois at age sixteen, completed two years, joined the Socialist Party, and moved to New York to become a journalist. She was active in the bohemian lifestyle and radical politics of Greenwich Village, illegally aborted a pregnancy, and wrote articles for left-wing journals like the *New York Call* and the *Masses*. In 1917, Day was jailed for **picketing** the White House in support of women's suffrage. Upon her release, she protested U.S. involvement in World War I, worked as a nurse in a Brooklyn hospital, and moved to Europe for a year. During the postwar Red Scare, Day was falsely arrested as a prostitute while visiting a friend at a boarding house run by the **Industrial Workers of the World**.

In 1924, Day published *The Eleventh Hour,* a book loosely based on her own life, and managed to sell the movie rights. The following year she became romantically involved with an anarchist fisherman, Forster Batterham, with whom she had a daughter, Tamar Teresa, in 1927. Tamar's birth induced a religious crisis and Day converted to Catholicism in December 1928. She severed relations with Batterham, moved to Hollywood, and took employment as a scriptwriter for Pathé Studios.

Day moved back to New York in 1932. There she met Catholic activist Peter Maurin, with whom she discussed the plight of working people during the lingering depression. In 1933, the two founded the Catholic Worker Movement (CWM) to empower laborers and alleviate their economic distress. She also began writing and editing *Catholic Worker,* the official CWM journal. Day took vows of pacifism and voluntary poverty and dedicated herself to the task of providing food and shelter to the destitute. She founded St. Joseph House of Hospitality in New York to shelter the poor. By the late 1930s, Catholic hospitality houses had spread across the country and to Europe and Australia. She and Maurin also set up short-lived cooperative farms for the needy.

Long a champion of labor rights and an outspoken critic of government intrusion into personal liberties, Day was often found on picket and protest lines. In 1937, she helped form the **Association of Catholic Trade Unionists**, the first official Catholic labor group. During World War II, she organized the Association of Catholic Conscientious Objectors, a group that helped arrange alternate service for pacifists. By then, she was the most famous Catholic laywoman in America.

Day remained an activist for her entire life, was arrested at least a dozen times, and used her pen in support of various radical causes in the 1960s and 1970s. She did, however, remain faithful to Catholic doctrine and refused to join those demanding the church alter its stand on birth control and abortion. Her writing won several awards. Shortly after her death in 1980, Day's name surfaced for possible sainthood, though New York's conservative Cardinal

O'Connor opposed it. In the year 2000, her name resurfaced and the Catholic church is investigating her worthiness for said status.

Suggested Readings: Dorothy Day, *From Union Square to Rome*, 1938; Judith Neis, *Seven Women: Portraits from the American Radical Tradition*, 1977; Garry Willis, *Certain Trumpets*, 1994.

Sara Pleva
Robert E. Weir

Deadheading. Deadheading is a term that derives from nineteenth-century passengers traveling without a ticket, particularly preachers and politicians returning to their constituencies. It was also applied to those admitted or smuggled into theaters free of charge. Deadheading came to mean railroad engines pulling empty cars (or none at all), and by the 1930s, was frequently used when referring to taxicabs and trucks without passengers or cargo. By the late twentieth century, deadheading was applied most often to the trucking industry and continues to be an important labor issue for truckers.

Until deregulation of the trucking industry in the early 1980s, union drivers usually hauled empty trucks back to their originating terminal, a practice deemed wasteful and unproductive by industry leaders. Deregulation removed controls on freight delivery, a move that led to consolidation of the trucking industry. Freight rates dropped, but **wages** and the number of employed drivers fell more drastically. Many trucking companies, particularly unionized companies with higher wages and benefit structures, went out of business. Independent owner-operators were even more vulnerable; many were forced to accept return cargoes at rates barely able to meet fuel costs. By the beginning of the twenty-first century, the desire to avoid deadheading and acquire backhauls has forced many truckers to depend upon cell phones, laptops, and the Internet in search of work.

Suggested Reading: Michael Agar, *Independents Declared: The Dilemmas of Independent Trucking*, 1986.

John Cashman

Dead Time. Dead time refers to lost time for which an employee is not responsible and for which he or she may or may not be paid. For example, a delivery person might arrive at a location to find that an office is closed for lunch, or bricklayers might be idled as they await a delivery of more bricks. Dead time can be controversial when employers and employees disagree over why dead time exists, or if an employer refuses to pay workers for dead time. It may also involve disputes over the very nature of work. The construction industry has seen battles over dead time. On most projects built by union labor, strict **jurisdiction** rules exist as to who is allowed to do what. A mason, for example, would not be permitted to do carpentry work. This enrages some employers who see this as a form of **featherbedding** and argue that dead time simply drives up costs. Such employers argue that a work crew should be able to perform multiple jobs. In some states this has led to attempts to deny **wages** for dead time as well as lobbying efforts to change regulations regarding the awarding of construction contracts. Unions counter that these employers are merely seeking to keep workers at their beck-and-call without paying for that service, and that they seek to assign complex tasks to those lacking the expertise to do them properly. Dead time is especially a problem in the trucking industry. In the past, the **Teamsters** have been successful in winning dead-time pay for drivers forced to sit at terminals waiting to load or unload. The union has recently cooperated with the longshoremen's unions on the West coast to try to win dead-time pay for harbor drivers.

Suggested Readings: Florence Peterson, *American Labor Unions*, 1945, 1963; "Glossary of Labor Terms," http:// www labor-studies.org/glossary.htm; Bill Mongelluzzo, "Port Unions, Teamsters in Labor Push," http://groups.yahoo. com/group/ILWU,message/17.

Bruce Cohen

Robert E. Weir

Suffragettes show their support for Eugene Debs during his 1920 presidential campaign. © Library of Congress.

Debs, Eugene Victor (November 5, 1855–October 20, 1926). Eugene V. Debs was a socialist, labor leader, and five-time presidential candidate. Debs was born in Terre Haute, Indiana, the son of Jean Daniel and Marguerite Marie Debs, French immigrants who operated a grocery store. At age fifteen, he left school to work as a locomotive paint scraper but within two years became a locomotive fireman. At age twenty, he helped organize a Terre Haute local of the Brotherhood of Locomotive Firemen (BLF) and served as its secretary. In 1878, he became an associate editor of the *Locomotive Firemen's Journal* and became its editor-in-chief two years later. He also became active in local Democratic Party politics and was elected city clerk in 1879, followed by election to the Indiana legislature in 1884.

Debs continued his rise within the BLF, becoming national secretary, then vice president. He became increasingly dissatisfied with the BLF, however, as it continued to operate more as a fraternal organization than as a labor union. Debs was an ardent supporter of emergent **industrial unionism** and wished to merge separate railroad brotherhoods into a single union. He resigned his BLF offices in 1892, to assume the presidency of the newly created **American Railway Union (ARU).** The ARU's successful 1893 strike against James Hill's Great Northern line catapulted Debs and the ARU to fame. Nonetheless, Debs opposed the 1894 **Pullman strike** as he felt the ARU was not ready to tackle such a formidable foe as the Pullman Palace Car Corporation. When his counsel was rejected, Debs assumed leadership of the ensuing **boycott** of Pullman Palace cars. He was arrested for violating a federal injunction prohibiting interference with delivery of the U.S. mail and was sentenced to six months in the federal penitentiary in Woodstock, Illinois.

Legend holds that Debs converted to **socialism** while in jail, though his political thought was evolving long before this. In 1898, Debs founded the Social Democratic Party. Two years later he garnered 96,000 votes in his first bid to become president of the United States. In 1901, Debs merged his party with another to create the Socialist Party of America (SP). Debs went on to become the nation's most prominent socialist spokesperson, crisscrossing the country to make speeches and authoring numerous pamphlets. He was present at the 1905 founding convention of the **Industrial Workers of the World (IWW)** and helped draft its preamble, though he resigned in 1908, when the organization rejected ballot-box politics.

Eugene V. Debs speaking in Chicago in 1910. © Bettmann/Corbis.

Debs ran for president in 1904, 1908, and 1912, increasing his vote total in each election. As the United States moved toward involvement in World War I, Debs denounced the hostilities as a **capitalist** war and urged workers to avoid it. He was convicted of violating the wartime Espionage Act and, in 1918, entered a federal prison in Atlanta to begin a ten-year sentence. He conducted his final presidential bid from his cell and gathered more than 915,000 votes in the 1920 presidential election. He was pardoned by President Warren G. Harding and left prison on Christmas Day, 1921. By then he was in frail health and he spent much of the rest of his life working on his prison memoir, *Walls and Bars*, published posthumously in 1927. Debs is credited with removing much of the stigma that socialism was a foreign import. To the degree that socialist ideals took any root in American soil, Debs played an influential part.

Suggested Readings: Ray Ginger, *The Bending Cross*, 1949; Ronald Radosh, ed., *Debs*, 1971; Nick Salvatore, *Eugene V. Debs*, 1982.

Lisa Barber
Robert E. Weir

De Caux, Leonard Howard (October 14, 1899–May 24, 1991). Leonard Howard De Caux was a leading figure in militant labor movements in the first half of the twentieth century. He was born in Westport, New Zealand. His father, Howard, was a minister employed by the Church Missionary Society, and his mother, Helen (Hammond) De Caux, was the beneficiary of a small inheritance that afforded the luxury of sending "Len" to the prestigious Harrow School. He enlisted in the Royal Field Artillery during World War I and spent a year touring France after the conflict ended.

De Caux's observations of war-torn France helped shape his radical politics. He blamed the war's carnage on greedy **capitalists**, a view that deepened after he moved to England in 1919. He attended Hertford College at Oxford University from 1919 to 1921 before immigrating to the United States. De Caux traveled frequently and became an astute observer of U.S. society. His various occupations included busing tables at the YWCA, clerking in a hosiery company, and building railroads. During a period as an itinerant laborer in the West, De Caux joined the **Industrial Workers of the World (IWW)**. The IWW had barely survived government persecution during World War I, and De Caux was only peripherally involved in the rapidly dissolving organization. He moved to Chicago in 1923, where he continued his nomadic employment as a laborer, printer, reporter, and editor. Chicago's mainstream news business blacklisted him for his radical beliefs, so he became assistant editor of the union-published *Illinois Miner* in 1925.

Throughout his life he eagerly joined organizations dedicated to improving workers' lives, and it was not unusual for him to simultaneously carry membership cards from two or more unions representing the same craft. During his wanderings in the 1920s, De Caux briefly returned to England, where he joined the Communist Party of Great Britain; he joined the Communist Party of the United States of America (CPUSA) after his return to the United States. De Caux found major differences between British and U.S. communists, and felt that the CPUSA lacked the pragmatism of its British comrades, a romanticism that blinded them to **communism**'s limitations. De Caux returned to New York City, briefly attended **Brookwood Labor College**, and worked at various occupations. Once again moving to Chicago, De Caux continued his journalism career, writing several articles for the IWW's *Industrial Solidarity*.

After his 1928 marriage to Caroline Abrams (with whom he had one child, Shirley), De Caux traveled less frequently. He was the assistant editor of the *Locomotive Engineers Journal* from 1926 to 1934, followed by a stint as the Washington correspondent for the *Federated Press* later in 1934. His background in labor and journalism led **John L. Lewis** to select him as the national publicity director of the fledgling **Congress of Industrial Organizations (CIO)** when it was organized in 1937. De Caux was also the first editor for the *CIO News*. Through the CIO's formative years he was one of the organization's few full-time employees.

De Caux also became one of labor's first casualties in the post–World War II red scare, when CIO President **Philip Murray** fired him in 1947. De Caux found union work difficult to secure as organized labor waged an internal struggle to purge unions of suspected communist influence. De Caux spent the years from 1947 through 1949 wandering through the West and working on Henry Wallace's 1948 presidential campaign, before settling in California. There he became a reporter for the *March of Labor,* a leftist newspaper that was a voice for individuals and organizations expelled from postwar unions.

In 1952, De Caux was summoned before the House Un-American Activities Committee (HUAC), where he refused to answer questions and invoked the First and Fifth Amendments. As a result of HUAC, De Caux was again blacklisted and the prevailing political climate relegated De Caux to a renewed cycle of itinerant work. De Caux fabricated his work history and references to find temporary employment. He finally found steady work as a proofreader with a nonunion printer in Chicago, but was fired when he was called before HUAC again in 1954. He was kept under FBI surveillance for most of his life, and agents often appeared wherever he found work. De Caux eventually found regular employment in the linotypers' union and wrote two autobiographical accounts of his life. The first, *Labor Radical: From the Wobblies to the CIO*, was published in 1970, and *The Living Spirit of the Wobblies* appeared in 1978. De Caux died in 1991.

Suggested Readings: Len De Caux, *Labor Radical: From the Wobblies to the CIO, A Personal History*, 1970; Len De Caux, *The Living Spirit of the Wobblies*, 1978; Harvey Levenstein, *Communism, Anticommunism, and the CIO*, 1981.

John Cashman

Decertification. Decertification is the process by which an employee-approved union can be stripped of its right to represent workers. Procedures for decertifying a union are outlined in the 1935 **National Labor Relations Act (NLRA)**. Under the NLRA, a decertification vote is held if 30 percent of those workers legally defined as a bargaining unit petition the National Labor Relations Board to hold such a vote. Just as in the certification process, however, a majority must agree before a union is decertified. The 1947 **Taft-Hartley Act** also facilitates decertification. In particular, it guarantees an employer's right to free speech, including antiunion opinions. It also makes so-called **right-to-work** laws easier to pass, which have made decertification easier than certification in some states. In addition, the union members "bill of rights" in the 1959 **Labor-Management Reporting and Disclosure Act** has made it easier for workers to vote out unpopular unions.

Workers may decide to decertify their unions for a number of reasons. After World War II, some quit unions that members felt were too radical. In the late 1940s, for example, some locals of the **United Electrical, Radio, and Machine Workers of America (UE)** disbanded in light of charges that the UE was dominated by communists. Many UE members joined the more conservative **International Union of Electrical, Radio and Machine Workers of America**. In rare cases, workers decertify unions because they feel leadership is too conservative. Some Canadian locals of the **United Food and Commercial Workers**

Union (UFCW) have recently discussed bolting the union in rejection of perceived **business unionism** practices within the UFCW.

Union **raiding** has also led to decertification votes. For example, the Hollywood-based International Alliance of Theatrical Stage Employees and Moving Picture Machine Operators (IATSE) routinely used decertification votes to raid members of the Conference of Studio Unions (CSU) during the 1940s. IATSE often resorted to red-baiting to convince former CSU members to change allegiance. In the 1960s, the **International Brotherhood of Teamsters** tried to use decertification votes to raid members of the **United Farm Workers of America**.

Some unions have been decertified because of union corruption, as in the case of some dockworkers locals in the 1950s. Still another reason is strategic: sometimes workers feel their current union is too weak and seek stronger representation. This was the case of Union Pacific rail workers in 2000 when they sought to leave the United Transportation Union and join the **Brotherhood of Locomotive Engineers**.

In recent years, most decertification drives have been employer instigated and (often) employer financed. Decertification votes have been part of an overall strategy to put unions on the defensive and give management the right to conduct business affairs like mergers without union interference. This trend has been noticeable in the newspaper industry where mergers have threatened the existence of the **Newspaper Guild**. Newspaper unions in the South were largely broken in the 1950s, a harbinger of things to come. In the 1980s and 1990s, media conglomerates like Gannett and the Hearst Corporation sought to destroy the Newspaper Guild in cities such as Cincinnati, Detroit, Tacoma, San Antonio, and Santa Barbara. At the *New York Daily News*, management precipitated a **strike**, hired **scabs**, and then encouraged its new employees to decertify the Newspaper Guild.

Many law firms have partners who specialize in assisting firms to achieve decertification votes. Employers resort to a variety of tactics, ranging from **paternalistic** promises to threats of job elimination. They have been quite successful at portraying contemporary unions as outmoded and/or corrupt. By the 1980s, for every three new members unions gained, one member was lost in a decertification drive. This trend slowed somewhat in the 1990s, though unions continue to lose more votes than they win. In 1998, 475 decertification votes were held, with unions losing 71.1 percent of the time and suffering a net loss of 12,879 members. In 1999, there were 373 decertification votes, with unions winning only 35.7 percent of the time and hemorrhaging an additional 9,400 members. In recent years, unions have taken a more proactive approach to avoiding decertification votes, but the practice remains a potent challenge to organized labor's future.

Suggested Readings: Patricia Sexton, *The War on Labor and the Left*, 1991; Steve Simurda, "Sticking with the Union?" *Columbia Journalism Review* (March/April 1993); Labor Research Association, www.laborresearch.org.

Robert E. Weir

Deindustrialization. Deindustrialization refers to the processes in which investment in basic production declined, resulting in plant closings, mass layoffs, and the loss of U.S. manufacturing dominance in the global market. Many locate its genesis in the 1973 Organization of Petroleum Exporting Countries (OPEC) oil boycott, the hyperinflation of the late 1970s, and the economic policies of Ronald Reagan in the 1980s. All played a significant part, but so too did the post–World War II recovery of European and Asian economies as they became manifest in the 1960s.

From the early twentieth century through the 1960s, the United States dominated the global economy in the production of industrial goods like automobiles, electronics, steel, and textiles. This changed dramatically beginning in the 1970s. In 1946, American firms provided 60 percent of the world's steel; by the late 1970s, this fell to 16 percent. In 1963, the United States imported only about 2 percent of the clothing sold by retailers; by 1980, U.S. imports of clothing rose to 50 percent. Even the venerable automobile industry suffered, with imports capturing more than 30 percent of the U.S. market by 1987. The loss of market shares led to a decline in blue-collar jobs. Overall, employment within the manufacturing sector fell from 25.1 percent of the workforce in 1959 to 18.5 percent in 1984.

Unions have been dramatically affected as historically their members have been concentrated within the very industries most hurt by deindustrialization. Union membership fell from 31.4 percent of the workforce in 1960, to 16.1 percent in 1990. Real **wages** fell for American workers from 1975 until 1992.

Inflation in the 1970s badly crippled the ability of U.S. manufacturers to compete in the global market. American factories were older than those in emergent economies like West Germany and Japan. Faced with soaring labor costs and the high costs of retooling, many American manufacturers decreased their investments, thereby conceding much of the domestic market to higher-quality, cheaper imported goods.

Labor critics also blame the financial policies of presidents Ronald Reagan and George H. W. Bush for exacerbating the problem. They particularly blame **deregulation** policies that encouraged **downsizing**, mergers, investment abroad, **runaway shops**, and stock speculation rather than direct investment in manufacturing. There is much truth in such a critique, though factors such as technological change, increased demand in the economy's service sector, and advances made by developing nations also played a part. As of 2000, American manufacturers were globally dominant only in military hardware and pharmaceutical production, though the United States continued to lead in fields like information technology, education, and entertainment.

Deindustrialization has changed many aspects of American life. For good or ill, many American workers find themselves part of a global economy. Employers increasingly demand high skills, exacting work, and longer hours from employees under the rubric of maintaining global competitiveness. Organized labor often fears that lower global standards of worker safety, environmental protection, wages, and working conditions will lead to erosion of hard-won rights within the United States. Many union workers participated in protests outside of the World Trade Organization meeting in Seattle in 2000. Deindustrialization and **globalization** have also convinced many of the urgency to take unionization efforts worldwide.

Suggested Readings: Donald Bartlett and James Steele, *America: What Went Wrong?* 1993; Barry Bluestone and Bennett Harrison, *The Deindustrializing of the United States*, 1982; Michael Dertouzos, et al., *Made in America*, 1989.

Robert E. Weir

DeLeon, Daniel (December 14, 1852–May 11, 1914). Daniel DeLeon, a radical labor leader and theorist, was born on the island of Curaçao off the coast of Venezuela. He was the son of Salomon and Sarah DeLeon, Dutch Jews. DeLeon left Curaçao to pursue a European education. He studied medicine and languages before immigrating to the United States in early 1874. He worked as a schoolteacher in Westchester County, New York, and also studied law at Columbia University, where he became a lecturer after a brief law practice in Texas. In 1882, he married Sara Lobo. Upon her death, he married Bertha Canary in 1892, with whom he had one child.

While at Columbia, DeLeon grew interested in reformers like **Henry George**, Edward Bellamy, and the **Knights of Labor (KOL)**, which he joined in 1888. His burgeoning **socialism** was a major factor in being denied tenure at Columbia. In 1890, DeLeon joined the Socialist Labor Party (SLP). He quickly assumed leadership roles in the SLP, became editor of its English-language journal *People*, and ran for governor of New York on the SLP ticket in 1891 and again in 1902. He also translated Karl Marx and the works of other European radicals into English. Under his tutelage, the SLP became a doctrinaire Marxist organization.

His involvement with the KOL likewise coincided with a shift among New York Knights from **Lassalleanism** toward Marxism. DeLeon and like-minded individuals such as Lucien Sanial failed to transform either the KOL or the SLP into sufficiently revolutionary organizations. In 1895, DeLeon split from the KOL and led his followers and the rump of the SLP into the newly formed Socialist Trades and Labor Alliance (STLA). The STLA was never able to compete with the mainstream **American Federation of Labor**, and its brief history was marked by intense internal doctrinal conflicts.

DeLeon made many enemies. Critics accused him of being an unyielding ideologue whose dogmatism weakened the labor movement. Among his detractors was **Eugene V. Debs** of the Socialist Party of America, who admired DeLeon's dedication but felt his purist attitudes did little to advance the socialist cause. By 1904, both the SLP and the STLA were on the verge of collapse. For a brief moment, DeLeon appeared to reevaluate the wisdom of combining political action and labor reform. In 1905, DeLeon attended the founding convention of the **Industrial Workers of the World (IWW).** DeLeon embraced its vision of overthrowing **capitalism**, though he doubted that unions would be the fulcrum by which this would be accomplished, and he continued to lobby for an IWW political agenda.

DeLeon soon proved fractious again, however, and many felt he was only using the IWW to recruit more SLP members. Many members of the IWW were suspicious of politics, and in 1908, this faction expelled DeLeon. He, however, formed a rival group known as the Detroit IWW. He led the splinter group but began to succumb to poor health. There was periodic discussion of uniting various socialist factions, but they came to no avail by the time DeLeon died of heart disease in 1914. The SLP continues to the present day and remains an ideologically driven, but small, third party.

Historians are split over DeLeon's overall contribution. He advanced socialism among English speakers at a time when it was seen as a foreign import. De Leon was also a dogged advocate for the cause and a clear thinker, as expressed in three books and numerous pamphlets. Yet he was also argumentative and split from every organization to which he belonged.

Suggested Readings: Stephen Coleman, *Daniel DeLeon*, 1990; L. Gene Seretan, *Daniel DeLeon: The Odyssey of an American Marxist*, 1979; Socialist Labor Party of America, www.slp.org.

Jim Riordan

Department of Labor (DOL). The Department of Labor (DOL) is part of the executive branch of the federal government and was created to promote and develop policies to benefit working Americans. It also seeks to improve working conditions and mediate between the interests of capital and labor. Thoughts of creating a labor department first emerged in the 1860s, with **William Sylvis** often given credit for the idea, although the modern DOL dates only to 1913. Groups like the **National Labor Union** and the **Knights of Labor** supported the formation of a national **Bureau of Labor Statistics (BLS)**, patterned on a body founded in Massachusetts in 1871, that would gather information on wages and working conditions. Many activists felt that educating the public would be the first step to labor reform. A national BLS was founded in 1874 and is today a division of the DOL.

In 1884, Congress created the Bureau of Labor as part of the Department of the Interior. It operated independently of the Department of the Interior from 1888 until 1903, when it was placed under the jurisdiction of the Department of Commerce and Labor. Immigration policy consumed much of the DOL's work in its early days. President William Taft signed legislation in 1913 that created the modern DOL, elevating it to a Cabinet-level position. William B. Wilson served as the first secretary of labor and he began the process by which agencies such as the BLS, the Bureau of Immigration, and the Children's Bureau were consolidated by the DOL. Wilson also appealed to labor unions to allow the DOL to mediate disputes, but **arbitration** was not made mandatory, and it was not until 1916 that Congress allocated money to assist DOL mediation efforts. Wilson also used DOL resources to set up employment bureaus, and during World War I, to maintain wartime production codes that included the eight-hour day for some workers.

Between 1921 and 1933, the DOL largely concerned itself with regulating labor, especially curtailing child labor. A special Women's Bureau was set up to address child care and maternity leave and to expand work opportunities for women, though the latter effort stalled at the onset of the Great Depression. The DOL expanded its role during the period from 1933 to 1945, when **Frances Perkins** held the position of secretary of labor. The DOL was directly involved in establishing New Deal programs such as the Works Progress Administration, Social Security, and **minimum-wage** legislation. Under Perkins's tenure, the eight-hour day became standard for many American workers. The DOL also directed wartime production efforts during World War II.

The political nature of the DOL hampered many of its efforts after World War II. The **Taft-Hartley Act** curtailed labor rights and a Republican-controlled Congress rejected all modifications to the act, causing President Eisenhower's Labor Secretary, Martin Durkin, to resign. Aside from directing production during the Korean War, the DOL was relatively quiescent until 1961, when it was called upon to administer parts of the Area Redevelopment Act. In 1962, the DOL began overseeing the Manpower Development and Training Act, a retraining program for long-term unemployed workers. This dovetailed into the Economic Opportunities Act of 1964, in which the DOL oversaw a program designed to train disadvantaged youth. The DOL also played a central role in President Lyndon Johnson's "war on poverty."

Administering the 1970 **Occupational Safety and Health Act (OSHA)** is perhaps the DOL's most important post–World War II initiative. Each year, the DOL is called upon to set safety and health standards in American workplaces and to use the power of the executive branch to enforce said standards and seek penalties against violators. Another important program was the 1983 Job and Training Partnership Act, which sought to build alliances among government, workers, and the private sector to promote job training. But critics charged that the DOL was weakened by an antilabor political climate in the 1980s and early 1990s. Alexis Herman, secretary of labor under President Clinton, is credited with restoring morale to a beleaguered DOL, though unions maintain that they were kept in low profile.

Today the DOL administers twenty-two separate sections, ranging in responsibility from law enforcement to international labor standards. A key issue in the latter sphere is the DOL's campaign to curtail child labor globally.

Suggested Readings: Donald Whitnah, ed., *Government Agencies*, 1983; United States Department of Labor, http://www. dol.gov.

Lisa Barber
Robert E. Weir

Depression-Era Strikes. The stock market collapsed in October 1929 and triggered the onset of the Great Depression. President Herbert Hoover's initial response to the deepening crisis was timid, as he and his advisors believed the downturn would be short-lived. By 1932, however, approximately fifteen million people were unemployed. The number of hoboes and homeless people increased and desperation soared. Midwestern farmers destroyed crops and animals to protest low commodity prices, Harlan County coal miners struck rather than accept starvation-level **wages**, and unemployment demonstrations convulsed numerous cities. When World War I veterans marched on Washington, D.C., to lobby Congress for early payment of bonuses due in 1945, they were routed by the standing U.S. Army. Anger levels and Hoover's unpopularity rose.

Many workers fortunate enough to retain their jobs had to endure repeated wage cuts and periodic layoffs. Conditions for working people were dire and they overwhelmingly voted for Democratic candidate Franklin Roosevelt in November 1932. In June 1933, President Roosevelt signed the **National Industrial Recovery Act (NIRA)**, which gave workers the right to form, join, or assist unions of their choosing. Continuing harsh economic conditions led thousands to respond to **William Green**'s call to join the **American Federation of Labor (AFL),** and independent unions such as the **Mechanics Educational Society of America**. The Automotive Industrial Workers Association grew as well.

This famous photo of the so-called Memorial Day Massacre, which occurred during the Republic Steel strike in 1937, was later made public by the La Follette Subcommittee on civil liberties. © George Meany Memorial Archives/Press Association.

In 1933 alone, more than 1.2 million workers went on strike, a six-fold increase from 1930. Typical of these struggles was that involving West Coast dockworkers. By August 1933, nearly 95 percent of San Francisco's longshoremen joined the International Longshoremen's Association (ILA), the first successful organizing drive since the **Industrial Workers of the World** enrolled waterside workers in the 1910s. Anger had long simmered among dock workers, riggers, and longshoremen. Many were tired of the dehumanizing morning **shape-up,** in which men stood on the docks while foremen decided whom to hire. On May 9, 1934, some 12,000 dock workers from British Columbia to San Diego stayed away. Coordination of strike policy fell largely to the ILA's **Harry Bridges**. Within two weeks, an additional 10,000 workers were on strike. In July, the city of San Francisco was virtually closed by a four-day general strike that idled more than 125,000 workers from a variety of trades. The strike fizzled out, due in part to brutal repression, but mainly because a Longshoremen's Board was established to arbitrate long-standing disputes. Dock workers made gains, including the right of unions to help operate hiring halls, but the situation remained tense with more than 350 additional strikes breaking out by mid-1938.

Another violent strike broke out at the Auto-Lite Plant in Toledo, Ohio, in April 1934. This strike was unusual because it was the first time unemployed workers came to the aid of employed workers. National Guardsmen were dispatched to break the strike, and they battled those who had gathered at the plant. The troops killed two workers and wounded fifteen. Even though the demonstrators were dispersed, the Auto-Lite owners could not operate the plant and agreed to worker demands. Renewed demonstrations forced the company to rehire all of the former strikers.

Almost simultaneously, coal haulers struck Minneapolis coal yards. Early in 1934, members of **Teamster** Local 574 who were fed up with low wages, long hours, and being cheated at the scales closed nearly all the coal yards. After three days, the owners recognized the union and the strike ended. While negotiating their first contract, the owners refused to agree to issues raised by the union, thereby precipitating a second strike. Many Minneapolis citizens joined the strikers and one rally marshaled more than 25,000 people in support of the union. During the strike, police killed two and wounded sixty-seven. After a month of intense confrontation, the strike was settled with workers winning their demands, including union recognition.

The remains of the encampment of World War I veterans at Anacostia Flats after U.S. troops, acting on orders of President Herbert Hoover, drove the members of the so-called Bonus Army out of Washington, D.C. © George Meany Memorial Archives/U.S. Signal Corps.

Textile workers conducted their own strike in 1934. Harsh working conditions and low wages were a way of life for textile workers, with **speedups**, **stretch-outs**, and layoffs commonplace. In July, Alabama mill hands walked off. By September, their actions spawned a **general strike** involving more than 400,000 textile workers in twenty states. The strike reached an ambiguous end when President Roosevelt appointed a board to mediate the dispute, but efforts paved the way for greater organizing success under the aegis of the **Congress of Industrial Organizations (CIO)** in 1936 and 1937. In all there were 1,856 separate strikes involving nearly 1.5 million workers in 1934.

The passage of the **National Labor Relations Act (NLRA)** in 1935 gave labor an additional boost when it restored and expanded labor rights which had been struck down by the Supreme Court's invalidation of the National Industrial Recovery Act (NIRA). NIRA's Section 7A had guaranteed a union's right to exist as part of industry agreed-upon "codes of fair competition." With NLRA, the right of workers to organize unions was made a matter of law. Still reeling from the Great Depression, thousands of workers took advantage of the NLRA and joined unions. By 1936, workers faced the challenge of transforming legal rights into formal recognition from owners. The method of choice to gain union recognition was the **sit-down strike**. In the six-month period between September 1936 and June 1937, more than half a million workers engaged in sit-downs. The most dramatic of these occurred in early 1937 when the **United Auto Workers (UAW)** won a monumental strike in Flint, Michigan, by barricading themselves inside a General Motors plant for forty-four days. Many historians believe this strike made the UAW and gave credibility to the fledgling CIO. It certainly sent shock waves through the ranks of working Americans. Production workers in rubber, textile, and glass engaged in sit-downs, as did waitresses, newspaper delivery boys, truck drivers, sewer workers, teachers, and numerous others.

Organized labor kept up the pressure throughout the 1930s. The **United Steelworkers** organized U.S. Steel in early 1937, though it proved less successful among smaller firms and lost the so-called Little Steel strike in 1937, when intransigent management used strong-arm tactics and violence to resist unionization, including the famed Memorial Day Massacre in which Chicago police murdered ten picnicking steelworkers and wounded over 100 others. Little Steel was not organized until 1941. Rubber and textile workers fared better, with a series of short strikes resulting in union contracts in various locales. The UAW successfully organized Chrysler Motors, but Ford resisted. Its **goons**, labor spies, and hardball tactics prevailed until a series of sit-downs and conventional strikes led to UAW recognition in 1941.

Reeling from the **open shop** drives of the 1920s, organized labor hit back during the Great Depression. Between 1933 and 1938, workers engaged in an average of 2,541 strikes each year. The most strike-prone year was 1937, in which 4,740 work stoppages took place. Despite the many problems organized labor faced in the future, Depression-era strikes established the CIO, the AFL, and other unions as forces to be reckoned with in American society.

Suggested Readings: Irving Bernstein, *Turbulent Years: A History of the American Worker, 1933–1941*, 1969; Jeremy Brecher, *Strike*, 1997; Sidney Lens, *The Labor Wars*, 1973; David Selvin, *A Terrible Anger*, 1996.

Mike Bonislawski

Deregulation. Deregulation is the elimination of state and federal laws that place restrictions on how a company is able to do business. Companies that operate in regulated industries may have the prices they charge for goods and services set by the government. Federal agencies also mandate safety standards to which companies have to adhere. Laws may also restrict access to markets. One advantage of regulation is that it controls cutthroat competition in a free market that may destabilize the national economy.

American industries were largely unregulated until after the Civil War, and most business leaders sang the virtues of a laissez-faire approach in which the government remained aloof from economic decisions made in the private sector. In classic economic theory, the system of supply and demand within free markets provides natural regulations. In practice, however, the abuses and excesses of nineteenth-century robber barons led to demands for business regulations, the breakup of trusts, protections for consumers, public health bills, labor laws to protect workers, and a host of other restrictions on how business was conducted. Opposition to regulation has always been shrill, but by the 1960s, the business community and conservative political allies complained that regulations handcuffed American business and made it less competitive globally.

Government-directed deregulation from the 1970s on eliminated some of these restrictions and has had a major impact on unionization. In newly deregulated industries such as trucking (1976), airlines (1976), railroads (1980), and communications industries (1981), the effect of deregulation was to allow firms to operate more like nineteenth-century oligarchies. Many deregulated enterprises were nonunion and undercut **prevailing wage** structures. This forced the unionized companies to shut down or sell inefficient production units, thereby reducing the number of organized workers.

Nonunion firms increased profits through lower labor costs and often required employees to make partial payments for medical benefits. Flexible personnel policies and practices, job assignments, promotions, and transfers became **concessionary** items that affected **collective bargaining** for unionized firms. This led to tension within unions and demands from the rank and file for better protection. In some cases, it also awakened nonunionized workers to realizing the benefits of union representation, job security, a voice in workplace issues, and a **grievance** process.

In the airline industry, for example, deregulation created both opportunities and problems. Under regulation, the government provided a bottom line for airline fares. Deregulation led to lower fares that benefited the consumer but also forced many airlines into mergers or bankruptcy. Also, previously designated market sectors were opened to any provider. Eastern Airlines, Braniff International, and Pan American World Airways were casualties of the lower fares. Some also charge that fleet maintenance and safety standards have declined in the deregulated airline industry.

Critics have pummeled the federal government for the poor labor-management relations that ensued after deregulation, with some charging that conditions have reverted to those paralleling the late nineteenth century. The labor movement has struggled to cope with the loss of members, benefits, and safety regulations undermined by deregulation.

Suggested Readings: Harry Katz and Thomas Kochan, *An Introduction to Collective Bargaining and Industrial Relations*, 2000; Terry Leap, *Collective Bargaining and Labor Relations*, 1991; "Air Transport Industry," Microsoft Encarta Online Encyclopedia 2001, http://encarta.msn.com.

Michael Bailey

Detroit Newspaper Strike. The Detroit Newspaper Strike was an unsuccessful job action called by six unions against the *Detroit News*, owned by the Gannett Corporation, and the *Detroit Free Press*, part of the Knight-Ridder chain. The **strike** began on July 13, 1995, and involved more than 2,500 reporters, printers, circulation workers, and support staff; it ended in defeat five and half years later. It has been seen by some analysts as a textbook case of contemporary union busting and as part and parcel of modern management's commitment to the **open shop** movement. The strike certainly illustrates that **solidarity** alone cannot sustain a strike under current labor law. It also raises disturbing questions about media control in contemporary America.

The roots of the Detroit strike lay in the media merger wave that engulfed the nation from the 1970s on. City after city saw competition dwindle to the point where most had only one daily newspaper, and it was usually owned by one of the corporate chains such as Gannett, Hearst, or Knight-Ridder. By 1988, Detroit was one of the few metropolitan areas that still had viable competing papers. In that year, the *News* and the *Free Press* set up the Joint Operating Agreement (JOA) to fuse the advertising and circulation departments of the two papers, even though said plan was opposed by the mayor's office and the Justice Department's antitrust division, which denied the JOA petition. Both corporations vigorously lobbied Attorney General Edward Meese III, who headed President Ronald Reagan's Justice Department. Meese ultimately overturned the Justice Department's decision, allowing the JOA to go into effect. The newly christened Detroit Newspaper Association (DNA) began publishing both papers.

As critics warned, once the papers were no longer in direct competition, advertising rates soared, staff was laid off, and harsh **concessions** were demanded from remaining workers, including wage cuts and higher medical insurance co-payments. These demands were made despite the fact that both chains posted record profits. Gannett was charged with attempting to wring concessions from its profitable papers to underwrite its money hemorrhaging and critically panned *USA Today* venture.

Reporters and newsroom personnel associated with the **Newspaper Guild** voted to strike after the implementation of a merit pay system, which came after six years of pay freezes. Circulation department employees joined after further layoffs of what management deemed **featherbedding** jobs, a transparent claim in light of the fact that nearly all of those let go were union workers. Workers represented by the Communication Workers of America and the International Brotherhood of **Teamsters (IBT)** also took part in the strike and

boycott. Once workers walked out, both companies hired **scabs** and announced their intentions to operate as union-free papers. It was later revealed that the DNA had contacted Alternative Work Force (AWF) months before the strike, thus preparations to replace workers were readied before the strike was called.

The strike was marked by acrimony and violence from the start, nearly all of it precipitated by management. Private security guards contracted from Huffmaster Security clashed with picketers and beat them. In another 1996 incident, two Gannett delivery trucks rammed picketers. Huffmaster was later replaced by Vance International, a firm that specializes in security during labor disputes and which has been charged by labor unions with inciting violence through the use of **agent provocateurs**. Very little news of the strike made its way into the mainstream media, leading media critics to charge that corporate control of newspapers causes a de facto censoring of information in accordance with corporate principles. On the local level, striker resolve remained high during the strike's early days. Union networks also spread information to such degree as was possible. Boycotts dramatically reduced revenues for both papers, and several unions aided strikers in underwriting the *Sunday Detroit Journal*, an alternative to the *News* and *Free Press*. Deprived of a broader public platform, however, the strike began to fizzle and about half of the Newspaper Guild's strikers drifted back to work. On February 14, 1997, more than a year and a half after the initial walkout, the strike was called off and unions unconditionally offered to return to work. The DNA responded by placing a small number of workers on a preferential hiring list for future openings, but declaring that the vast majority had forfeited their jobs. Merit pay, wage cuts, open shop policies, and other concessions remained in effect.

Although the strike was officially over, the boycott remained in effect. In June 1997, Detroit hosted a huge solidarity march in which unions such as the **United Farm Workers**, the **United Auto Workers**, and the **Industrial Workers of the World** pledged support, as did international officers of the American Federation of Labor–Congress of Industrial Organizations (AFL-CIO). Weeks earlier, the National Labor Relations Board (NLRB) ruled that Gannett and Knight-Ridder were guilty of **unfair labor practices**; both appealed the ruling and then ignored it. In September 1998, the NLRB again found unfair labor practices and ordered that former strikers be rehired. That decision was also appealed.

Many labor activists were critical of strike tactics. Strikers did not stop production for a single issue, causing some activists to question the wisdom of relying too much on boycotts and not enough on militancy. Others charged that AFL-CIO president **John Sweeney** placed too much faith in political pressure. He met several times with President William Clinton, but little came of those meetings. Sweeney also drew criticism for being too slow to organize rallies in support of the original job action. Strikers also were criticized. A significant number of AWF scabs were African Americans, and picketers occasionally hurled racist epithets, a political as well as social faux pas in a city that is predominately black.

Remaining hope dissipated in July 2000, when the U.S. Court of Appeals reversed NLRB findings against the DNA. Judge Laurence Silberman ruled that since the strike was over economic issues, the DNA had not engaged in unfair labor practices by hiring replacement workers. In December 2000, the last remaining strikers settled when IBT drivers and mailers ratified an agreement. Teamster President James P. Hoffa ruffled feathers when he asserted it was time for labor to cut its losses. With the IBT settling, the last remaining boycott call was removed.

The Detroit newspaper strike was a disaster for organized labor. The IBT alone spent over $30 million in the unsuccessful fight against Gannett and Knight-Ridder. There is no question that both companies suffered losses as well; most estimates place revenue losses at more than $100 million, in addition to the $650 million spent to combat the strike and boycott. Paper circulation dropped dramatically. In 2002, the combined circulation of the daily papers was around 604,000, down from 900,000 before the 1995 strike. Sunday sales plummeted from 1.1 million to 750,000. Nonetheless, the Detroit newspaper strike is a poignant reminder that corporations generally have far deeper pockets than labor, and it is hard to defeat employers who are determined to implement long-term programs to crush unions. Especially distressing is the fact that the loss occurred in an industry whose production isn't easily moved to another locale. From this perspective, the Detroit battles are a late example of the concessions and **downsizing** strikes of the 1980s.

The failed efforts in Detroit have fueled the call for increased militancy. Activists point once again to the inability (or unwillingness) of the Democratic Party to intervene on behalf of unions; some radicals have called for the repeal of *all* existing labor laws, charging that alleged legal protections are chimeras that lead to false hopes and provide management with delaying tactics. In their view, workers would be better served fighting management *mano e mano*. Cautious observers counsel that assessment of the Detroit losses must be balanced by recent victories like those of Ravenswood steelworkers and United Parcel Service employees. At the very least, though, the Detroit strike and boycott raise anew questions of the efficacy of traditional tactics.

Suggested Readings: David Bacon, "The New Face of Unionbusting, Part 3: The Blood and Guts Strikebreakers," http:// www.igc.org/dbacon/Unions/02bust3.htm, (December 1996); "Business as Usual Lost the Newspaper Strike," *Labor Notes* (February 2001); "One Love, Too Little Too Late for Detroit Newspaper Strikers," *Love and Rage, Vol. 8, #4* (August/September 1997), Radio 4 All, http://www.radio4all.org/anarchy/detroit.html.

Robert E. Weir

Direct Action. Direct action is a loosely defined but basic concept associated with the **Industrial Workers of the World (IWW)**. Direct action entails an assertion of ongoing worker power in the workplace. Slowdowns and **strikes** of every kind were part of the IWW's direct-action campaign. Its position on violence remained ambiguous, as did the meaning of sabotage, a term used often in conjunction with direct action. In general, direct action was associated with militant and immediate actions taken to assert labor's rights. Rhetorically the IWW claimed that direct action would be a mechanism in the destabilization and destruction of capitalism.

Direct action was the main mechanism by which individual workers were to be empowered. Decision to take direct action would be made by workers on the job, not by absentee union officials. The IWW took steps to empower workers at the point of production and deemed conventional union practices contrary to direct-action principles. Power was concentrated as much as possible in individual members and their locals rather than in national organizations. As such, automatic dues **checkoffs** were rejected, union fees were kept low, and health and life insurance deductions were banned. Most structural impediments to spontaneous militant action were barred, including signing written **contracts** with employers. Contracts were avoided, lest workers be hemmed in by stipulations that would prevent direct action to redress **grievances**.

The IWW lost much of its influence after 1917, but direct action continued to be a powerful concept, if not always by that name. Perhaps the most notable example was that of the **sit-down strike**, an IWW tactic revived by the General Motors workers at Flint, Michigan, in 1936.

Suggested Readings: Melvyn Dubofsky, *We Shall Be All: A History of the Industrial Workers of the World*, 1969; Joyce L. Kornbluh, *Rebel Voice: An IWW Anthology*, 1972.

Linnea Goodwin Burwood

Dodge Revolutionary Union Movement (DRUM). The Dodge Revolutionary Union Movement (DRUM) was the prototype for a series of Marxist labor action groups formed in the late 1960s. DRUM inspired a series of Revolutionary Union Movements (RUMs) that galvanized African American, Asian, Latino, and Native American workers into the 1970s.

DRUM came to public light on May 2, 1968, when 4,000 workers at Chrysler Corporation's Dodge Main plant in Hamtramck, Michigan, held a five-day **wildcat strike** that caught both the company and the **United Auto Workers (UAW)** by surprise. Although the immediate cause of the strike was worker complaints about assembly line **speedups**, its roots lay in the rising tide of black militancy that peaked in the 1960s. During the 1960s, civil rights groups, students, and antiwar activists transformed American political and social dialogue. By the middle of the decade, some African American leaders and organizations came to question the pacifist tactics that had hitherto governed civil rights protests. Black organizations like the Student Non-Violent Coordinating Committee (SNCC) and the Black Panther Party began to discuss militant Black Power as the antidote to what they saw as the implicit accommodationism of passive-resistance tactics.

As whites fled to the suburbs, urban areas became a powder keg of racial tension. Beginning with Harlem (New York) in 1964, and Watts (Los Angeles) in 1965, a series of riots, many of which were racial in nature, engulfed American cities. One of the worst occurred in Detroit in July 1967, where large sections of the city were burned, snipers fired from vacant buildings and highway overpasses, and near anarchy reigned for over a week before more than 4,700 U.S. Army paratroopers and 8,000 National Guardsmen imposed heavy-handed order. At least forty-three people died in the riots, hundreds were injured, and nearly 4,000 were arrested.

The Detroit riots reflected the city's changing face. The city had long been the preserve of native-born whites and European immigrants. By the 1960s, however, it was a predominately black city with an entrenched white power structure. This extended to Detroit's auto industry and unions. In the suburb of Hamtramck, 85 percent of all Dodge workers were black, but only 2 percent of its foremen were people of color. Unions were no better; black autoworkers complained that UAW stood for "U Ain't White." The Hamtramck wildcat strike of May 1968 was as much a critique of the UAW as Chrysler.

It was also an indictment of liberalism, as the UAW had long fancied itself to be one of the more progressive labor unions in the United States. UAW President **Walter Reuther** supported black rights, and the UAW frequently gave money to assist civil-rights groups. In 1967, the UAW ceased paying dues to the American Federation of Labor–Congress of Industrial Organizations (AFL-CIO), in part because Reuther felt it was too slow to embrace civil rights and the antiwar movement. DRUM activists such as General Gordon Baker, Luke Tripp, and John Watson, in turn, complained that white UAW leaders were paternalistic and that its economic assumptions were unsound. Many DRUM leaders schooled themselves in the theories of Karl Marx, V. I. Lenin, and other radical theorists. Instead of the UAW's program of higher wages and behind-the-scenes political lobbying, DRUM called for a revolution to cast off both white oppression and **capitalism**.

How much of this revolutionary fervor extended to the rank and file is difficult to determine, but DRUM did inspire copycat organizations. Ford workers in Detroit and Mahwah, New Jersey, created the Ford Revolutionary Union Movement (FRUM), African American Cadillac assemblers formed the Cadillac Revolutionary Union Movement (CADRUM), and Revolutionary Union Movements (RUMs) appeared at United Parcel Service, the *Detroit News*, and among autoworkers in California and Maryland. Black steelworkers at Sparrow's Point, Maryland; Birmingham, Alabama; and elsewhere formed RUM-like groups of their own. Many of these groups cultivated ties with other black militant groups such as SNCC and the Black Panthers.

In 1971, Detroit-area RUMs created the League of Revolutionary Black Workers (LRBW), a loose federation that attempted to coordinate efforts. Its membership was closed to whites, though Asians, Latinos, and Native Americans were represented. The LRBW issued fiery rhetoric, but its achievements were modest. The bulk of its activities took place in Detroit. John Watson took over editorship of Wayne State University's paper, *South End*, and converted it into a socialist daily with links to the Black Panthers, much to the chagrin of university officials. Copies were distributed to autoworkers. The LRBW's most dramatic action was to underwrite the defense of James Johnson, who slayed two foremen and a coworker in 1971. Johnson's defense team admitted that he had committed the killings but pointed to race relations at Chrysler to argue that racism had driven Johnson crazy. Johnson was judged criminally insane and Chrysler was ordered to pay workers' compensation to help defray his mental-health-care costs.

By the mid-1970s, though, RUMs and the LRBW were spent forces. Some radicals argue that decline occurred because the movements rested too much on past laurels, others blame oppression, and a handful claim that by gaining an official voice RUMs attracted students and professionals but abandoned their revolutionary worker base. Dispassionate observation suggests that social and structural changes doomed the RUMs. African American workers were unquestionably angry over the everyday racism they encountered on their jobs and in society, and the heightened social tensions of the 1960s and early 1970s created opportunities and organizations in which to express that fury. It is doubtful, however, that the rank and file were as devoted to revolutionary praxis as leaders. In this regard, the RUMs parallel the experience of the **Industrial Workers of the World**.

Structural changes also explain the passing of DRUM and the LRBW. On the positive side, by the early 1970s, the Equal Employment Opportunity Commission finally began to have the impact that those who created it in 1964 had hoped. Detroit's power structure changed dramatically, with African Americans winning control of the mayor's office and city council. Unions responded as well; the UAW elevated African Americans to leadership roles, and even the stodgy AFL-CIO followed suit. In general, the mid-1970s saw a cooling of the activist fervor of the previous ten years.

On a less sanguine note, fervor wavered in part because of economic challenges after 1973. When DRUM was at its height, one of six jobs in Detroit was linked to the auto industry. By the 1970s, however, the auto industry was troubled and the overall American economy was in deep decline. Soaring gasoline prices, inflation, and imported vehicles challenged Detroit's near-monopoly of auto sales. Lagging sales led to layoffs and plant closures; by the 1980s, **deindustrialization** ravaged Detroit. For thousands, immediate needs for economic survival took precedence over a revolutionary future.

Suggested Readings: Dan Georgakas and Marvin Surkin, *Detroit: I Do Mind Dying*, 1998; Heather Thompson, *Whose Detroit? Politics, Labor, and Race in a Modern American City*, 2001.

Robert E. Weir

Downsizing. Downsizing refers to a deliberate company strategy to reduce its workforce, usually to cut costs and increase profits. A wave of downsizing occurred in the 1980s and took the form of plant shutdowns, worldwide consolidations, outsourcing, and technological updating of manufacturing facilities. Unlike a traditional layoff where workers are asked to leave a company temporarily during periods of weak demand, downsizing permanently eliminates positions, displacing many workers and forcing them to seek unemployment benefits.

This caused many unions in the 1990s to bargain for explicit employment security clauses as part of their **collective bargaining** agreements. **Seniority** of employees became an increasingly important subject as layoffs usually start with the least senior worker. Downsizing also led to joint management–labor partnerships as unions, fearing the increased loss of members, worked with employers to reduce inefficiencies and retain as many workers as possible.

Downsizing became a controversial practice by the 1990s as it began to take place within profitable firms. What began as a survival strategy for companies experiencing weak demand for products and services turned into a way for thriving companies to boost shareholder values of company stock. At a time when executive salaries consisted of stock options, day-to-day decisions were based on how to increase the value of the stock. Many companies, however, never reached profit goals anticipated from the layoffs, produced a lower-quality product, experienced poor employee morale, and eventually rehired laid-off laborers or searched for new workers. Many union activists want stricter controls on the conditions under which a profitable firm can downsize.

Suggested Readings: Terry Leap, *Collective Bargaining and Labor Relations*, 1995; David Hornestay, "Reconsidering Downsizing," http://www.govexec.com./reinvent/downsize/0796view.htm.

Michael Bailey

Downsizing, Decertification, and Concessions Strikes. "Downsizing, decertification, and concessions strikes" is a phrase that refers to a series of actions that peaked in the 1980s and 1990s, in which businesses launched an assault against organized labor. Most of the associated **strikes** and **lockouts** were initiated by the business community to increase corporate profits and/or weaken unions. To a large extent, the corporate strategy was successful; by the mid-1990s, union workers represented just 15.5 percent of the American workforce.

The American economy sputtered after 1973, falling into a condition economists labeled stagflation that was marked by flat growth, yet high inflation. Some companies—particularly in the **blue-collar** manufacturing sector—found themselves saddled with outmoded equipment and high-waged workers that made it difficult for them to compete with cheaper foreign imports. Between 1969 and 1976 alone, some twenty-two million jobs were lost due to plant closures. Most of the new jobs created during the period paid lower **wages.** Employers who stayed in business demanded **concessions** from workers in the form of wage freezes (or cuts), reduced benefits, and/or increased production rates. Unemployment rose to its highest levels since the Great Depression. In 1979, the Chrysler Corporation declared bankruptcy, and only a huge taxpayer-funded bailout saved the company. The **United Auto Workers** agreed to a concessions package to help keep the company afloat. The net effect, however, was for other employers to jump on the concessions bandwagon and make similar demands from their employees.

By the 1980s, buzz words like "competitiveness," "becoming lean," and "downsizing" (or the more euphemistic "rightsizing") were translated into corporate policy. Workforces were trimmed, concessions imposed, and productivity quotas increased as employers sought to cut costs and compete in the global economy. Economists continue to debate how much cost cutting was legitimate and how much simply padded the bottom line of already profitable companies, but trends begun in the 1970s accelerated in the 1980s. No sector of the economy was spared. Even states and municipalities were forced to cut budgets in the wake of taxpayer revolts like Proposition 13 in California and Proposition 2½ in Massachusetts. That situation was worsened by Reagan-era cutbacks on social spending.

In 1980, Ronald Reagan was elected president, and politics moved sharply rightward. A sizable part of the American business community has always opposed labor unions and it found an ally in the White House. When Reagan fired striking **Professional Air Traffic Controllers Organization (PATCO)** workers in 1981, he emboldened antiunion forces across the nation. The decade was marked by bitter strikes and lockouts, almost all of which were initiated by management. Southwestern copper miners—many of whom were Hispanic—were routed by Phelps-Dodge during 1983 and 1984, as were Midwestern meatpackers during a 1985–86 confrontation with **Hormel**. The Hormel strike was marked by ugly internecine struggles between local unions and the parent **United Food and Commercial Workers Union (UFCW)**, with Austin, Minnesota, workers attempting to decertify the UFCW. Workers also suffered stinging defeats in battles against Eastern Airlines, Greyhound, International Paper, **Pittston Coal**, and USX (the former United States Steel Corporation), to name just a few.

In all, the 1980s saw the largest assault against labor unions since the **open shop** drives of the 1920s. The situation in the 1980s was, in many ways, more dire. The American Federation of Labor–Congress of Industrial Organizations (AFL-CIO) failed in its attempts to get labor law reforms passed during the presidency of Jimmy Carter (1977–81), opening the door for the aggressive antiunion tactics of the Reagan and Bush administrations (1981–93). Openings on the National Labor Relations Board often went to individuals more sympathetic to management than to labor and, in a few cases, to those with track records of opposing unions. Law firms sprouted that specialized in helping employers launch **decertification** drives against unions, while numerous consultant agencies counseled corporations on how to keep their workplaces free of unions. The Chamber of Commerce set up a National Right-to-Work Committee that churned out negative publicity about unions, and the **National Association of Manufacturers** unveiled its Committee on a Union Free Environment. More damaging still was the use of replacement workers, **scabs** hired on a permanent basis to take the jobs of strikers. These came to the fore during the PATCO walkout, and courts have upheld the right of corporations to hire replacement workers during economic strikes in which there are no findings of **unfair labor practices**. With the rightward shift of the NLRB, fewer such findings were made, but even when they were, a favored corporate tactic was simply to tie up cases in lengthy appeals that few workers could weather and even well-heeled unions found expensive.

Corporations received a further boost from Reagan tax reforms in 1981 that dramatically slashed taxes for corporations and high-income individuals. In 1977, 8.1 percent of corporate profits were taxed; by 1985 that figure was nearly halved (4.2 percent). Generous tax write-offs allowed companies to shield profits, and they also benefited from **deregulation**. The cornerstone of Reagan-Bush economics was adherence to the supply-side economic ideas of Arthur Laffer and George Gilder. In theory, tax cuts and laissez-faire policies encourage corporations and wealthy individuals to invest in the economy. This, in turn, creates opportunity for all Americans. That was not, however, the reality. Many companies used tax loopholes to close factories, sell the assets, and invest in the stock market. By the mid-1980s, economists spoke of the **deindustrialization** of America; America's share of the world's industrial output slipped from 50 percent in 1960 to under 25 percent by 1985. Fully three-quarters of *Fortune Magazine*'s top 100 new companies of the 1980s were, in fact, the product of mergers; U.S. Steel, for example, reemerged as the USX Corporation and derived more income from shopping malls, real estate, and insurance than from steel. Some 57 percent of the jobs that were created in the 1980s paid wages that sank a family of four below the poverty line. A substantial number were **part-time** jobs. Adjusted for inflation, real wages fell by 9 percent from 1980 to 1989.

Globalism posed the biggest challenge of all. A 1976 tax revision encouraged American companies to set up subsidiaries in U.S. possessions. By the 1980s, many went a step further and simply moved their operations overseas to take advantage of lower wage structures, lax environmental laws, and union-free workplaces. Between 1980 and 1995, more than 2,200 factories employing some 800,000 workers were built in Mexico, the vast majority of them by American-based firms. President William Clinton earned the enmity of many union workers for signing the 1993 **North American Free Trade Agreement (NAFTA)** with Canada and Mexico, a bill that has hastened relocation of manufacturing plants to Mexico.

In fact, organized labor fared only slightly better during the Democratic administration of the Clinton years (1993–2001) than under Republicans Reagan and Bush. The 1990s saw bitter battles like the **Staley lockout**, and strikes against **Bridgestone/Firestone**, **Caterpillar**, **General Motors**, and newspapers in **Detroit** and Seattle. Organized labor has won a few battles in recent years. Favorable settlements for workers at Bridgestone/Firestone, **Fieldcrest**, **United Parcel Service (UPS)**, NYNEX operators, and **Ravenswood** during the 1990s have slowed the decline of unions and have given rise to new hope. AFL-CIO President **John Sweeney** pledged to renew union militancy and reverse patterns of downsizing, decertification votes, and concessionary give-backs. To date, results have been mixed.

To many observers, the troubles of the 1980s and beyond signal the need to rethink how organized labor conducts itself. Prevailing labor law is slanted toward employers, and the threats of globalism and movable capital render old union tactics obsolete. The most successful work stoppages of recent years have come from service and public sector workers who are not threatened by capital flight. Deindustrialization, outsourcing, and the rise of a service economy have led to structural changes to which old-style unions have not yet adapted. Unions remain optimistic that global organizing, new tactics, and political pressure will revitalize the labor movement. Less sanguine observers feel that unions should abandon organizing production industries and concentrate on the service sector, white-collar workers, and professionals.

Suggested Readings: Stanley Aronowitz, *From the Ashes of the Old: American Labor's Future*, 1998; Donald Bartlett and James Steele, *America: What Went Wrong?* 1993; Thomas Geoghegan, *Which Side Are You On?* 1992.

Robert E. Weir

Downtime. Downtime refers to shutting down a machine or factory for the purpose of maintenance, cleaning, or repair. Although this is a standard and necessary practice in American industry, at times it entails controversy. One issue is whether or not workers not directly involved with downtime procedures should remain on the clock and thus draw their pay. If they are off the clock for an extended period, a question arises as to whether or not they should be eligible to receive unemployment compensation. There is no national standard for downtime and unions generally negotiate this on a case-by-case basis.

Equally contentious are the questions of when downtime is needed and how much maintenance is needed. In classic **Taylorism**, downtime is the sole prerogative of management and an essential principle of business is to avoid it whenever possible. This has led to clashes with unionized workers who have charged that businesses sometimes skip maintenance cycles necessary for safety or consumer protection. In 1999, for example, the **United Food and Commercial Workers Union** accused the Tyson Corporation of **speedups** and failure to schedule downtime for processing machines, thus causing unclean and diseased chickens to be packaged for public consumption.

Repairs are generally not within management's power to dictate, but they sometimes exert pressure on the one area of downtime over which they have some control: the speed at which workers complete downtime tasks. There have been clashes over this in the auto industry, especially in changeovers, wherein a machine or operation producing a particular pattern or part is converted to a new task. Historically, the **United Auto Workers** has filed **grievances** on behalf of members harried by management, though in recent years there has been much more union/management cooperation.

The recent proliferation of **subcontracting** arrangements has led to new downtime problems. Repairs and maintenance procedures are now often performed by workers not directly employed by the firm, sometimes at the cost of eliminating jobs once held by union workers. Not all firms have profited from subcontracting deadtime functions. In some cases, allegations of false billings arise, with subcontracting firms allegedly falsifying hours, services delivered, and/or materials used. Quality is also under scrutiny, with some workers complaining that supervisors blame them for problems that are actually due to poor subcontracted maintenance.

Suggested Readings: R. Emmett Murray, *The Lexicon of Labor*, 1998; Florence Peterson, *American Labor Unions*, 1945, 1963; Frederick W. Taylor, *The Principles of Scientific Management*, 1911.

Bruce Cohen
Robert E. Weir

Dual Unionism. Dual unionism refers to a situation in which an individual worker (or group) belongs to more than one labor federation or **international union**. In most cases, unions frown on dual unionism and many have specific constitutional bylaws forbidding it. It is seen as dividing workers' loyalty and, in some cases, forcing them to choose among competing ideals or **jurisdiction** disputes.

Numerous dual unionism disputes have marked American labor history. During the late nineteenth century, many workers were simultaneously members of the **Knights of Labor (KOL)** and of specific **craft unions**. This proved problematic in situations in which a local or international union authorized a **strike**, **boycott**, or decision with which the KOL disapproved. This led to several bitter clashes that forced members to choose sides. For example, the KOL sided with a renegade faction of the Cigar Makers International Union (CMIU) in New York City in 1884, which led the CMIU to disaffiliate two years later. This experience had a profound influence on CMIU officials **Samuel Gompers** and **Adolph Strasser**. When they helped found the **American Federation of Labor (AFL)** in 1886, many of its constituent unions expressly forbade dual membership in the KOL. Later in the century, **Daniel DeLeon** set up the Socialist Trade and Labor Alliance, seen by both the KOL and AFL as a dual union. In the twentieth century, the AFL urged members to avoid the **Industrial Workers of the World (IWW)**, which sometimes had overlapping members. Although the IWW was contemptuous of the AFL, it did not impose restrictions against dual unions on its members.

Sometimes dual unionism is a deliberate tactic used by movements seeking to alter existing organizations, protect themselves, or both. This was the strategy of the American Communist Party of the United States of America (CPUSA) on several occasions. The Red Scare after World War I made it difficult for communists to openly espouse their views. The CPUSA set up the Trade Union Educational League to bore within existing AFL unions. Skilled leaders such as **William Z. Foster** demonstrated some success in leading AFL workers to a more militant stance. In 1929, the CPUSA abandoned boring within, set up its own **Trade Union Unity League (TUUL)**, and moved away from dual unionism. Nonetheless, the experience left the AFL so shaken that many of its more conservative leaders viewed advocates of **industrial unionism** as supporters of dual unions. The inability to resolve that clash led to the establishment of the **Congress of Industrial Organizations (CIO)**. Ironically, the CPUSA later dismantled the TUUL and returned to working within existing unions. Until a renewed Red Scare after World War II led the CIO to purge communists, some of its best organizers had ties to the CPUSA.

Most analysts assumed that serious dual unionism disputes would disappear after the 1955 AFL-CIO merger. That was not the case. Occasionally, **wildcat strikes** were denounced by international unions as a form of dual unionism, as were reform groups like the Teamsters for a Democratic Union, which sought to democratize the International Brotherhood of **Teamsters**. More recently, dual unionism charges have been leveled against **rank-and-file** militants who battle against what they see as entrenched **business union** bureaucrats. The decline of labor unions since the 1970s has led some to lead **decertification** drives against their own unions to establish independent militant organizations or join another they deem better able to represent them. For example, in 2002, the Transport Workers Union leveled charges of dual unionism against American Airline mechanics contemplating affiliation with the **International Association of Machinists and Aerospace Workers**.

In an age of union mergers, overlapping jurisdictions, and broader worker representation, jurisdictional and dual unionism debates are likely to continue.

Suggested Readings: Harvey Klehr, *The Heyday of American Communism*, 1984; AFL-CIO, http://www.aflcio.org.

Robert E. Weir

Dues. Dues consist of the money paid by a union member to a labor organization to generate income and defray the costs of the organization. Dues are periodic payments, usually on a weekly or monthly basis, and are often deducted from members' paychecks through the system known as **checkoff**. This automatic deduction eliminates the need for the union to collect individually from each member. Historically, **shop stewards** collected dues individually, creating a personal relationship with their fellow workers. It also provided officials with the opportunity to visit members and solicit opinions on job-related matters. Some charge that the transition to push-button unionism fosters an impersonal relationship between the rank and file and labor officials. Unions without the checkoff system, however, often experience great difficulty in collecting member fees.

In the American Federation of Labor–Congress of Industrial Organizations (AFL-CIO), local unions are responsible for collecting dues. Approximately 40 percent of all dues go to the parent organization. Each level within the labor movement receives a portion of dues money to pay for staff salaries, administrative and educational expenses, publication of the union's journal, and other membership benefits. Smaller portions of the dues go to intermediate bodies like citywide labor councils and state federations. Usually, local leaders and shop stewards do much of the work necessary for union operations voluntarily or for minimal compensation.

Some portion of the dues may be deposited in special strike funds when tough negotiations are anticipated. These funds are subject to rapid depletion during those times, so long-term investment of this money is usually inappropriate. With only a trickle of walkouts by the end of the twentieth century, many strike funds have been redirected to education and organizing.

Suggested Readings: Harry Katz and Thomas Kochan, *An Introduction to Collective Bargaining and Industrial Relations*, 2000; Terry Leap, *Collective Bargaining and Labor Relations*, 1991.

Michael Bailey

E

Efficiency. *See Taylorism.*

Eight-Hour Movement. The Eight-Hour Movement and earlier attempts to trim the number of hours in a workday stood as the Holy Grail of American and European workers for nearly a century. A popular poem turned into a song and chant proclaimed, "Eight hours for work; eight hours for rest; eight hours for what we will!" Not until the passage of the **Fair Labor Standards Act** in 1935 did the dream become a reality for all American workers, although some skilled operatives and government employees obtained the desired standard in the nineteenth century. Ten hours a day, however, remained the norm into the twentieth century. Some employees, like streetcar employees, worked a sunup-to-sundown schedule that paralleled agricultural work until the industry itself disappeared.

Significant ten-hour day struggles appear throughout the first blush of factory employment. Young female weavers at Slater's Mill in Pawtucket, Rhode Island, birthplace of the American industrial revolution, went on **strike** in 1824, partially against an increase in hours. Several years later, local citizens there actually subscribed funds to erect a public clock in the city to compete with the suspected time rigging of the mill owners. Significant attempts to lower the workday to ten hours flared during the 1830s with the emergence of the **Workingmen's** parties. Skilled craftsmen, such as mechanics, carpenters, and iron molders who shouldered the industrial revolution with their mechanical abilities, were able to seize the time literally but sporadically before and after the Civil War.

The post–Civil War era witnessed ten- and eight-hour petition drives by factory operatives who tried to influence state legislatures to pass such laws. On the few occasions when such bills saw the light of day, even at the federal level, the rules were compromised by provisions that allowed individual workers to contract for as many hours as they or their employer chose. Mill workers also engaged in many spontaneous strikes during the 1870s, but without the leadership of labor unions.

The victory of industrial time over an agricultural way of life governed by the sun and moon gave way for good in factory towns by the 1880s, when mass production appeared with an ever-greater reliance on mechanized time and industrial discipline. The acceleration of time, at home and in the workplace, helped embolden and popularize an obscure labor organization known as the Noble and Holy Order of the **Knights of Labor**, which embraced the eight-hour day as one of its main tenets. Despite a fracture between some leaders and the **rank and file**, an unusual but fragile alliance was forged in the mid-1880s between the Knights, the nascent **American Federation of Labor (AFL)**, and various left-wing groups, especially among German American immigrants.

Banner promoting passage of a national law establishing an eight-hour workday. © George Meany Memorial Archives/Public Affairs Press.

These disparate parties orchestrated a national walkout for an eight-hour workday on May 1, 1886. Despite predictions of violence and mayhem, the day came and went in a militant but peaceful manner. Many employers retreated before the union show of force and caved in to a shorter workday. Unrelated labor strife in Chicago a few days after the great walkout turned violent when a bomb injured and killed protestors and police alike in Chicago's **Haymarket** Square. Chicago had been the center of eight-hour agitation and that meant the bloodshed at Haymarket would be inextricably tied to efforts for the shorter workday. The ensuing prosecutions set back the movement for some time.

The struggle for shorter working hours waxed and waned and also served as a unifying theme for employee **solidarity**. Shorter hours in one trade usually influenced others to seek a similar accord and helped open the job market to the unemployed. Immigrants with strong ties to cultural and religious holidays also chipped away at the longer workday. Some nineteenth-century successes grew out of an effort to reduce hours, especially for women and children. Although designed to be **protective labor legislation**, the eight-hour-day principle could be expanded to the male workforce. Some labor theorists even linked the question of how long to work to job conditions and how to work.

The consolidation of the AFL in the 1890s assisted skilled trades in obtaining the eight-hour day through **collective bargaining** contracts and increased legislative pressure, especially in states with a high union density. The onset of the Great Depression boosted arguments for shorter hours to decrease rampant unemployment. The culmination came under the provisions of the New Deal's **Fair Labor Standards Act** in 1935 which, with some exceptions, enshrined the eight-hour day as the standard in the United States. For a while, serious talk in this era even centered around a thirty-hour work week.

In the ensuing years, organized labor and the American worker increasingly traded productivity increases for higher **wages** and benefits, not reduced work time, shorter days, or more vacations. The ideology of a consumer society trumped that of working-class leisure time. With the advent of globalism by the 1970s, hours of work, especially in the nonunion sector, crept higher while unionized assembly workers gobbled up **overtime** opportunities. Employers acquiesced in **salaries** and **premium pay** over the expensive proposition of hiring and training new workers with added benefit packages. By the beginning of the twenty-first century, however, a hurried society began to examine the ailments caused by work that no longer ended when one left the job. The computer, cell phones, and faxes fostered labor as a full-time endeavor. The efforts for a shorter workday, trumpeted as finally realized in the 1930s, is returning as a union and social concern.

Suggested Readings: David R. Roediger and Philip S. Foner, *Our Own Time: A History of American Labor and the Working Day*, 1989; Juliet B. Schor, *The Overworked American: The Unexpected Decline of Leisure*, 1991.

Scott Molloy

Equal Pay Act (1963). The Equal Pay Act is only 150 words long, but it established an important principle for the workers of the United States. It prohibits employers from discriminating among workers on the basis of sex when tasks require equal skill, effort, and responsibility under similar working conditions. In short, the law demands equal pay for equal work.

In 1963, women earned fewer than sixty cents for every dollar earned by men. The social consequences of this inequity grew in the 1960s as women participated in greater numbers in the workforce, and rising divorce rates meant more children were dependent on the income of a single parent, usually a mother. Part of President Lyndon Johnson's Great Society legislative initiative, the Equal Pay Act aimed to redress pay inequalities and earning differentials that had plagued women workers since the establishment of **wage** labor in the United States. In addition to bringing justice to women workers, the law also sought to protect the jobs and wages of men. In theory, the law prevents companies from competing with each other to hire the traditionally cheap labor of women, thus removing a danger to traditionally higher male wage scales.

Twenty years after the act was put in place, women's earning rates had improved only very slightly, leaving many pondering what had gone wrong. Supporters and detractors of the law agreed that its language was imprecise. Many feminists also noted that enforcement of the law was apathetic and halfhearted. Beyond these problems, a well-entrenched dimension of the labor market operated outside the act's purview: job segregation. Most jobs had been formally or informally branded as "men's work" or "women's work." Those jobs in which women dominated—nursing, teaching, and clerical work, for example—consistently paid lower wages than those in which men were paramount.

To address continuing pay inequity some analysts advocate comparable worth scales that would reclassify work based on skill, demand, and responsibility levels rather than job titles. Others argue that the only way to honor the spirit of the Equal Pay Act is to raise pay levels in traditionally female occupations.

Suggested Readings: Walter Fogel, *The Equal Pay Act*, 1984; Catherine Selden, *Equal Pay for Work of Comparable Worth: An Annotated Bibliography*, 1984.

Simon Holzapfel

Erdman Act. The Erdman Act was passed in 1898 in response to the Pullman Strike of 1894 and the findings of the United States Strike Commission. It prohibited interstate railroads from imposing **yellow-dog contracts** on their employees. In 1908, the U.S. Supreme Court invalidated this provision of the Erdman Act in ***Adair v. The United States*** (1908) on the grounds that it violated freedom of contract and Fifth Amendment program rights. In effect, the court reinstated the yellow-dog contract.

Suggested Readings: R. Emmett Murray, *The Lexicon of Labor*, 1998; Paul R. Taylor, *The ABC-CLIO Companion to the American Labor Movement*, 1993.

Bruce Cohen

Escalator Clause. *See Cost-of-Living Adjustment (COLA).*

Escape Clause. An escape clause is a provision in a **contract** that establishes conditions by which one or both parties can void an agreed-upon obligation without liability. Escape clauses were first widely applied during World War II, when many unions secured **maintenance of membership** rights under which union membership was a condition of employment. Escape clauses provided employees an opportunity to resign from the union after advising both the union and the company of their intent. Escape clauses generally stipulate a period of time in which the employee can "escape" from membership obligation. Members who fail to give the appropriate notification are required to maintain union status until the next escape period. In practice, social pressure caused most workers to retain union membership.

The escape clause was developed because of union security concerns during the **National War Labor Board**'s existence. Unions wanted to establish closed shops and employers wanted **open shops** in cases that went before the board. Special elections provided evidence that employees overwhelmingly favored union security. Maintenance of membership was a compromise solution, and the escape period was added due to ongoing opposition from employers who were members of the board. A fifteen-day period became standard for the escape clause. Escape clauses are still in some union contracts, but are no longer as common because they benefit the company more than the union's security of membership.

Suggested Readings: Henry C. Black, *Black's Law Dictionary*, 1999; Harold Roberts, *Roberts' Dictionary of Industrial Relations*, 1994.

Danielle McMullen

Executive Order 10988. Executive Order 10988 was issued by President Kennedy in January 1962. It established a procedure for **collective bargaining** for unions representing employees of the federal government, employees who had been denied collective-bargaining rights under the **National Labor Relations Act** (1935). While many federal employees, especially in the postal service, had been union members prior to this executive order, their unions were primarily lobbying associations. (The Tennessee Valley Authority, under special legislation, had previously recognized and bargained with unions.)

During the 1950s, the AFL-CIO and some congressional Democrats pressed for the extension of bargaining rights to federal employee unions. In the late 1950s, Philadelphia, New York City, and Wisconsin began to recognize municipal or state employee unions. These actions paved the way for Kennedy's executive order.

E.O. 10988 allowed unions, after winning a representation election, to bargain with a federal agency as "the exclusive representative of the employees." E.O. 10988 also provided that an association, regardless of membership levels, could present its views to management, and that agencies must "consult" with an association with 10 percent membership in a unit. It prohibited closed or **union shops**, continued the ban on **strikes** by federal employees, and prohibited recognition of unions that advocated the right to strike. It also mandated that federal employee unions not discriminate by race.

Unlike the NLRA, E.O. 10988 did not allow formal bargaining over **wages**, as Congress set wage rates for federal workers. Among the issues subject to bargaining were job descriptions, working conditions, subcontracting, and **grievance** policies.

Despite its limitations, E.O. 10988 led to a rapid expansion of membership in federal unions and of **contracts** between federal agencies and unions. By 1963, the number of federal employees covered by bargaining agreements had increased from 19,000 to 670,000, and this number doubled by 1968. The National Federation of Government Employees quickly became the largest federal union, with almost a half million members by 1970. E.O. 10988 also stimulated legislative changes and organizing drives in local government. By 1969, eighteen additional states provided for collective bargaining for state or local employees. Public employee unionization was the major growth sector of the union movement in the 1960s.

President Nixon's E.O. 11491, in 1969, superseded E.O. 10988. E.O. 11491 ended informal consultation with employee associations, altered the ways bargaining units would be determined, and expanded the range of negotiable issues. While retaining other restrictions on unions, it strengthened them by providing for third-party arbitration when negotiations stalled.

Suggested Readings: Irving Bernstein, *Promises Kept: John F. Kennedy's New Frontier,* 1991; Michael Moskow, J. Joseph Loewenberg, and Edward Koziara, *Collective Bargaining in Public Employment,* 1970; Jack Steiber, "Executive Order 10988," in Herbert Marx, Jr., ed., *Collective Bargaining for Government Employees;* Department of Labor, "Recommended Changes in Executive Order 10988," in Herbert Marx, Jr., ed., *Collective Bargaining for Government Employees.*

Robert Shaffer

F

Fair Employment Practices Committee (FEPC). The Fair Employment Practices Committee was created in 1941 to deal with complaints of racial discrimination in hiring practices. Although FEPC originally lacked enforcement power, its creation signaled the federal government's willingness to revisit civil rights issues largely abandoned with the collapse of Reconstruction in the 1870s.

As American factories, stimulated by defense preparations, began to shake off the Great Depression, African Americans and other minorities found that a disproportionate number of new jobs went to white workers. **A. Philip Randolph** pressured President Franklin Roosevelt to address racial inequity by threatening a march on Washington, D.C. Randolph claimed he would rally over 100,000 African Americans, and he garnered support from the National Association for the Advancement of Colored People (NAACP). Randolph perhaps exaggerated his strength, but widespread coverage in both the white and black press embarrassed Roosevelt and made a mockery of preparations to fight fascism in the name of democracy.

Roosevelt met with NAACP President Walter White and, in June 1941, agreed to meet certain demands if the planned march was canceled. Roosevelt's Executive Order 8802 established the FEPC, which had the power to hold hearings and issue directives to combat discrimination in defense industries and federal agencies. It quickly became apparent, however, that the FEPC's reach was limited. Executive Order 8802 did not desegregate the military, forbid **contracts** with discriminatory employers, or grant the FEPC power to compel compliance with its directives. Moreover, its first chair, white Louisville publisher Mark Etheridge, took moderate positions on racial issues that pacified some white Southerners, but disappointed most African American leaders.

Etheridge resigned after only a few months on the job and was replaced by Malcolm MacLean, who held widely publicized hearings into employment discrimination in Birmingham, Alabama. In July 1942, however, the FEPC was placed under the aegis of the War Manpower Commission headed by Paul McNutt. McNutt, no friend of civil rights, shackled the FEPC by supervising field personnel and dictating which industries it could investigate. MacLean resigned in protest.

A. Philip Randolph was instrumental in the 1941 creation, by executive order, of the Fair Employment Practices Committee (FEPC). © National Archives.

Roosevelt reorganized the FEPC and increased its powers when he issued Executive Order 9346 on May 27, 1943. The newly independent agency began to take on life after Malcolm Ross ascended to its chair in October 1943. Ross pressed cases that included complaints against Washington and Philadelphia transit companies, Southern railroad firms, and Midwestern defense plants. In all, the FEPC processed over 12,000 cases and settled nearly 5,000 to its satisfaction.

An invigorated FEPC raised the hackles of conservatives and racists. Mississippi Representative John Rankin attacked it as a group of "crackpots" attempting to "force whites to accept" African Americans as equals, while Congressman Howard Smith hauled Ross before Congress to defend charges that the FEPC was riddled with communists. When attacks failed to slow the commission, congressional opponents succeeded in halving its funding, a move supported by the **American Federation of Labor**, but opposed by the **Congress of Industrial Organizations**. In June 1946, Congress cut off funds altogether, and the FEPC passed out of existence.

Despite the FEPC's exceedingly modest achievements and checkered history, it nonetheless stands as an important landmark in the federal government's willingness to support the employment and civil rights of minorities. It was the role model for several subsequent reforms, including the 1948 Fair Employment Practices Act and the 1964 creation of the Equal Employment Opportunity Commission.

Suggested Readings: Herbert Garfinkel, *When Negroes March*, 1959; Andrew Kersten, *Race, Jobs, and the War*, 2000; Merl Reed, *Seedtime for the Modern Civil Rights Movement*, 1991.

James Wolfinger

Fair Labor Standards Act (FLSA). The Fair Labor Standards Act was enacted in 1938 and is considered the last major piece of New Deal legislation to address the concerns of working people. The FLSA set the forty-hour workweek as the national standard and required employers to pay time and a half for **overtime** work. It also established a federal **minimum wage** and placed restrictions on **child labor**. Subsequent rises in the minimum wage have entailed congressional amendments to the FLSA. Among those exempted from the act are farmworkers, journalists, personal companions, babysitters, and employees in amusement parks and camps. Since 1938, the FLSA has expanded to include state and local hospitals, educational institutions, and most federal and public employees.

The 1963 **Equal Pay Act** amended the FLSA to require equal pay for men and women performing tasks of equal skill and provides standards for compensatory time in lieu of overtime pay. Enforcement of the FLSA is through the U.S. **Department of Labor**'s Wage and Hour Division, but many observers claim that it is the single-most violated labor law by employers.

Suggested Reading: Barbara Repa, *Your Rights in the Workplace*, 2000.

Albert V. Lannon

Family and Medical Leave Act (FMLA). The Family and Medical Leave Act, a bill supported by most labor unions, was passed by Congress and signed by President William Clinton in 1993. It allows some employees to take up to twelve weeks of unpaid leave per year to address family needs. Those employees in firms of fifty or more employees are legally entitled to said leave to attend to their own "serious health conditions," or those of a spouse, parent, or child. Leave is also granted for the birth, adoption, or establishment of foster care for a child. Employers must allow employees to return to their old jobs when their leave expires. The FMLA sets a minimum base and does not override existing employer parental or personal leave policies that go beyond its scope.

The FMLA was bitterly opposed by the business community, which complained that the FMLA would lead to serious declines of productivity, and that it is needless government regulation of the private sector's affairs. Their fears have proved alarmist. If anything, the small number of labor and social activists who complained that the FMLA was too weak have proved more accurate.

The FMLA is very limited when compared with family legislation in other industrialized nations. Some New Zealand employees, for example, are entitled to a full year's leave at partial pay to attend to newborns, and nearly every European democracy grants more liberal leave. Moreover, the FMLA has numerous restrictions. To be eligible, an employee must have worked at least 1,250 hours during the course of twelve months with the employer from which leave is requested.

While on leave, employees might be required to pick up their own health-care premiums and are not entitled to **seniority** rights. Under some conditions, employers can actually terminate a position while an employee is on leave. The law also allows employers to require periodic reports of their employees' leave status. Some employees have complained they were pressured to return early.

Most critics contend, however, that the biggest shortfall of the FMLA is that leave is unpaid. They contend that most employees cannot sustain three months of **wage** losses and are thus forced to substitute vacation leave, sick days, and personal days for the FMLA. In addition, the FMLA applies only to larger firms of more than fifty employees, thereby leaving millions of Americans beyond the law's reach.

Despite its limitations, most labor unions hailed the FMLA as an important first step in making American work policies more profamily. The FMLA is administered by the Wage and Hour Division of the U.S. **Department of Labor**.

Suggested Reading: American Federation of State, County, and Municipal Employees, AFL-CIO, http://www.afscme.org/wrkplace/fmla.htm.

Robert E. Weir

Family Wage. Family wage is a concept that developed in response to the rise of industrialization in the early decades of the nineteenth century. It is the idea that the wages earned by a male breadwinner should be sufficient to support a workingman and his family. As early as the 1830s, labor organizations championed the family wage. Initially seen as the just reward for a man's labor in the evolving industrial economy, the family wage was also viewed as a way to ensure that the wives and children of working-class men would not be forced into industrial labor, and was in keeping with then-current ideologies regarding middle-class women and their relegation to the domestic sphere. By the end of the nineteenth century, the **American Federation of Labor** became a vocal champion of the family wage, primarily in response to the argument that the lower-paid labor of women and children drove down the wages of male workers. In reaction to high unemployment during the Great Depression, the federal government passed legislation limiting the employment of married women during the 1930s. More recently, "living wage" campaigns continue the argument for a family wage but not necessarily one that is earned by a male worker.

Suggested Readings: Martha May, "Bread before Roses: American Workingmen, Labor Unions, and the Family Wage," in *Women, Work and Protest: A Century of U.S. Women's Labor History*, ed. Ruth Milkman, 1987; Robert Pollin and Stephanie Luce, *The Living Wage: Building a Fair Economy*, 1998.

Kathleen Banks Nutter

Farmer-Labor Alliances. Farmer-labor alliances are attempts to bring workers who till the soil into cooperative political action with **wage** earners to advance common working-class interests. These alliances have been numerous and problematic, in part because of the United States' winner-take-all electoral system that mitigates against the formation of third parties. In addition, the interests of producer farmers and consumer wage earners are often antithetical.

One of the first attempts to bring the groups together was associated with the **Workingmen's Movement** of the 1830s. In Massachusetts, several local campaigns organized under the rubric of the Association of Farmers, Mechanics, and Other Workingmen. Candidates supported a host of reforms like free public education, the abolition of debtor prisons, land reform, currency reform, and restrictions on monopolies. Although the groups enjoyed some success, they did not survive the decade's economic downturns.

After the Civil War, farmers faced heavy debt and falling commodity prices, while craft workers were confronted by a rising entrepreneurial class intent on driving down wages and resisting unionization. The **National Labor Union** sought to redress these inequities through the country's first nationwide farmer-labor organization, the Labor Reform Party, but it failed to attract a strong power base. Simultaneously, the major farmer organization, the Patrons of Husbandry (Grange), advocated regulations on railroads and other monopolies, often seeking support from urban workers.

Farmer and labor interests also unified over the issue of currency reform, both groups favoring the issuance of government **greenbacks** to ease prevailing hard-money policies that favored lenders. Labor hoped that easing credit would encourage business growth and lead to rising wages, while farmers longed for lower interest rates and an inflationary rise in commodity prices. This led to the creation of the Greenback-Labor Party (GLP). The GLP fared poorly in national elections, but did surprisingly well in local and state elections during the late 1870s, spurred on by a sagging economy and industrial unrest exemplified by the railroad strikes during the **Great Labor Uprising**. In 1878, GLP candidates got over a million votes. Future **Knights of Labor (KOL)** President **Terence Powderly** became the GLP mayor of Scranton, Pennsylvania, and fifteen GLP candidates won seats in Congress.

The GLP waned as the economy recovered in the 1880s, with the greenback cause mutating into the "free silver" movement. In addition, urban workers abandoned the GLP in the early 1880s, seeking relief through unions rather than politics. The KOL and several other unions launched rural organizing efforts, but farmer-labor coalitions were weak outside of agrarian states.

When the economy faltered again in the 1890s, discontent mounted anew, especially in the South and West. High tariffs, tumbling grain prices, and crop lien systems in the south led Grangers, members of Farmers Alliances, and numerous labor activists to descend on Omaha, Nebraska, in 1892, and fashion a national People's Party (Populists) from the various state third parties in circulation since the late 1880s. The Populist platform declared that farmer-labor interests were identical, as were their enemies. Its platform included items cherished by labor—like government ownership of railroads and the eight-hour day—but rural concerns dominated. Many within the KOL endorsed Populism, but those in the **American Federation of Labor** avoided third-party agitation. Eighteen ninety-two Populist presidential candidate James Weaver garnered over a million votes and won twenty-two electoral votes, but the bulk of his support came from farm-state voters.

Workers looked more to the Populists in the immediate aftermath of the Pullman **boycott** in which President Grover Cleveland called out federal troops against railroad workers. In 1896, however, the Democrats nominated William Jennings Bryan, who co-opted enough of the Populist platform to win its endorsement. When he lost to William McKinley in both 1896 and 1900, the Populist movement dissipated.

Farmer-labor alliances reemerged during World War I, especially in northern plains states where the Nonpartisan League promoted farmer interests. The league enjoyed its greatest success in North Dakota, where it captured the governor's chair and enough seats in the legislature to enact laws making farm foreclosure tougher. Labor unrest after World War I factored into the 1920 formation of the Farmer-Labor Party which included progressive labor platform planks. Like its predecessors, however, its strength lay in farm states, particularly those in the West and upper Midwest.

Farmer-labor politics reached their zenith in 1924, when representatives from railroad unions, the Nonpartisan League, socialists, progressive reformers, and the Minnesota Farmer-Labor Party created the Progressive Party. Even the AFL endorsed its 1924 presidential candidate, Robert La Follette, who polled over five million votes, but carried only Wisconsin. Partly because the party did not enter state or local races, it failed to attract wide attention. Various local groups, especially in the Midwest, survived, and Minnesota spawned an active Farmer-Labor Party that controlled the governorship during much of the 1930s. The New Deal succeeded in recruiting many farm-labor advocates to the Democratic Party.

The last serious attempt to unite farmers and laborers occurred in 1948, when a new Progressive Party formed. Its candidate, Henry Wallace, had served President Roosevelt as secretary of agriculture and as vice president. Wallace, however, was perceived to be a radical and his campaign faltered due to a red-baiting campaign that foreshadowed Cold War anticommunist hysteria looming on the political horizon. He got a million votes and the Progressives soon disbanded.

Although politicians have attempted to assume a "populist" mantle since 1948, this has been largely a rhetorical device. Moreover, the decline of family farming and the rise of agribusiness renders problematic the future of farmer-labor alliances. In some cases, however, powerful coalitions have emerged. The **United Farm Workers** have relied upon labor union support in several of its campaigns and is affiliated with the AFL. Some union leaders also envisioned organizing farmworkers on an international scale.

Suggested Readings: Nathan Fine, *Labor and Farmer Parties in the United States*, 1961; Elizabeth Sanders, *Roots and Reform: Farmers, Workers, and the American State, 1877–1917*, 1999.

Ralph Shaffer

Fasanella, Ralph (September 2, 1914–December 16, 1997). America's leading labor folk artist, Ralph Fasanella was born in New York City on **Labor Day**, September 2, 1914, to Joseph Fasanella, an iceman, and Ginevra (Spanoeletti), a buttonhole maker, both from the Apulia region of Italy. His boyhood was spent in immigrant neighborhoods in Greenwich Village and the Bronx and in reformatories where he was sent for truancy. He dropped out of school in 1914 when his father left the family to return to Italy. Fasanella's social consciousness came from his mother, a literate woman and a **socialist**, with whom he marched in demonstrations and helped produce a small, Italian-language antifascist newspaper. During the 1930s, he got involved with radical politics and the labor movement, including a stint driving a truck for the Abraham Lincoln Brigade during the Spanish Civil War. In 1940, he joined the **United Electrical Workers (UE)** staff, successfully organizing a number of electrical equipment and machine plants in and around New York City.

Fasanella started painting in 1944, after an artist friend suggested drawing as therapy for arthritis-like pains in his hands. He eventually quit his job as an organizer—he'd already become disillusioned with labor's turn toward business unionism—occasionally pumping gas at his brothers' service stations to help support himself and, after marriage to schoolteacher Eva Lazorek in 1950, a family. He painted in relative obscurity until a 1972 cover article in *New York* magazine hailing him as the "best primitive painter since Grandma Moses" made him famous.

Fasanella's cityscapes of street festivals and stickball games, Yankee Stadium and Coney Island, union meetings and political rallies are richly detailed, boisterous, and colorful, proclaiming the beauty and hopefulness he saw in ordinary working-class culture. True to his ethnic, working-class roots, he didn't want his paintings to "hang in some rich guy's living room," preferring to place them in public spaces and museums where workers and their families would see them, like the Ellis Island Immigration Museum ("Family Supper"), the Heritage Park Visitor's Center in Lawrence, Massachusetts, birthplace of America's industrial revolution ("Lawrence 1912: The Bread and Roses Strike"), the 53rd Street and 5th Avenue subway station in New York City ("Subway Riders"), and the Baseball Hall of Fame ("May Day"). Ralph Fasanella died December 16, 1997, at his home in Ardsley, New York.

Suggested Readings: Peter Carroll, "Ralph Fasanella Limns the Story of the Workingman," *Smithsonian* 24, no. 5 (August 1993): 58–69; Patrick Watson, *Fasanella's City*, 1973; "Don't Mourn, Organize," Developing Arts and Humanities Curricula Through Technology, http://miculturelink.h-net.msu.edu/curricula/painting.htm.

Margaret Raucher

Featherbedding. Featherbedding is a derogatory term used to describe having more workers than is necessary to complete a job. It is customarily used by management to complain about labor unions, or to justify **downsizing** to save on payroll costs. The term is wordplay and implies that workers engaged in featherbedding have cushy jobs in which the labor of one is being casually performed by two or more. The term was apparently first used during World War II when railroad carriers complained of provisions requiring firemen on trains no longer powered by steam. (Rail workers retorted that firemen served as **apprentice** and emergency engineers.) The term gained wider currency in railroading, dock work, and offices where technological change altered the nature of work. For example, electronic advances reduced exigencies for railway signalmen and conductors, containerization lessened demand for stevedores, and office computerization reduced the need for switchboard operators, receptionists, and secretaries.

Featherbedding was curtailed somewhat by the 1946 Lea Act, but has been addressed mostly by aggressive employer action. Unions and employees charge that some touted technological "advances" have been veiled excuses to fire workers rather than increase efficiency. They also charge that what some see as featherbedding practices are actually needed relief and backup crews. Long-distance truckers, telephone operators, and flight crews have been among the workers complaining of modern-day **stretch-outs** that require them to work faster, harder, and longer. Featherbedding remains a widely perceived practice, though studies indicate that Americans put in more hours than workers of any other industrialized nation, and that many perform the equivalent of one-and-a-half jobs.

Suggested Reading: Juliet Schor, *The Overworked American*, 1993.

Robert E. Weir

Federal Emergency Relief Administration (FERA). For most of American history, poor relief was regarded as the province of states, localities, and private charities. Following on the Puritan belief that the plight of the poor was their own fault, the relief administered was more often than not designed to be as unpleasant and demeaning as possible. Sharp distinctions were also made between the "deserving" and "undeserving" poor, the former including those considered "unemployable," such as the old, blind, and mothers with young children. The disbursement of relief was never regarded as the responsibility of the federal government, even during the periods of economic depression that occurred from the late nineteenth century through the early 1920s, even though statewide poor relief was often inadequate at best.

When the Great Depression of the 1930s proved to be so pervasive that it largely erased the old distinctions between "deserving" and "undeserving," President Herbert Hoover clung to the old view, which was that the federal government should not get involved in relief for the poor and unemployed because it would necessitate massive tax increases, and that direct handouts, in particular, would discourage self-reliance. By early 1933, the depression had worsened to the point that, on a national scale, 25 percent of Americans were unemployed, and, in some places, unemployment was upward of 50 percent. Shortly after President Franklin Delano Roosevelt was elected, therefore, he used the model of the New York State Temporary Emergency Relief Association (TERA) to craft a national agency for disbursing emergency relief. Roosevelt appointed Harry Hopkins, who had previously headed the TERA, to direct this new federal agency.

The resulting agency, the Federal Emergency Relief Administration (FERA) was passed by Congress on May 12, 1933. The FERA, was granted $500 million in funds, half of which was given to the states as matching grants, at a rate of $1 to every $3 each state provided. The other half was administered on the basis of need, on a discretionary basis, by Hopkins, although some historians have argued that politics played a role in Hopkins's decision making. Due to the comparatively small size of the federal government at that time, actual use of the funds was dictated by the states and localities that received them. Therefore, although the intention of the FERA was to provide work relief rather than handouts, the federal government was largely unable to control the decisions of many states to give handouts rather than to provide work. Nor could the FERA, created in response to the new realities, eliminate the older attitudes that prevailed in many localities. Thus, many recipients often obtained FERA aid with difficulty, and only after humiliating and invasive means testing. Other problems included inefficiency and discrimination against minorities and immigrants. The FERA was most successful in assisting transient and migrant workers, of which there were many during the early years of the depression.

Because President Herbert Hoover held the traditional belief that the federal government should not involve itself in poor relief, the shanty towns of distressed poor that sprang up during the Great Depression, such as this one in Seattle, were called Hoovervilles. Franklin Roosevelts's Federal Emergency Relief Administration (FERA) constituted a reversal of the Hoover policy. © George Meany Memorial Archives.

The FERA, subject to widespread criticism, was dismantled in 1935, as the emphasis of the New Deal shifted to "putting people to work." Even before, Hopkins, who had fairly quickly become frustrated and discouraged by the limits of the FERA, was made head of the Civil Works Administration (CWA). The CWA, and later the Works Progress Administration (WPA), subsequently provided work for millions of needy working Americans. The FERA nonetheless served its purpose as a stopgap measure, providing relief that states, localities, and private charities could not during this period of sustained and deepening economic hardship. The willingness of the Roosevelt administration to immediately implement this unprecedented program, then replace it when it became clear that it was less than ideal, made it a prime example of the "bold, persistent experimentation" that characterized the New Deal. It also had some lasting effects on American society. First, it completely changed the relationship between the government and society, allowing for the creation of the welfare state, and specifically making the idea of direct federal relief more acceptable. More profoundly, however, it introduced the idea that the public welfare is ultimately the responsibility of all Americans, through their government. This idea still prevails in spite of recent challenges to the American welfare state.

Suggested Readings: Lorena A. Hickok, *One-Third of a Nation: Lorena Hickok Reports on the Great Depression*, 1981; Harry L. Hopkins, *Spending to Save: The Complete Story of Relief*, 1936; Fiona Venn, *The New Deal*, 1998.

Susan Roth Breitzer

Federal Labor Union. A federal labor union was a local union affiliated directly with the **American Federation of Labor (AFL)**. Federal labor unions usually consisted of the sort of workers that the **Congress of Industrial Organizations (CIO)** organized into industrial unions.

Federal labor unions were often found in isolated areas in which there were not enough workers in a particular craft to form a separate local, or in areas where no national or international union had jurisdiction. The expectation was that the members of a federal labor union would eventually join the appropriate national or international craft union. The AFL used these unions as a building device for new national organizations and granted nearly 1,800 federal charters between 1932 and 1934. However, many federal unions were formed in mass production industries whose unskilled and semiskilled workforces did not easily fit into the AFL's structure, and were thus marginalized by the AFL's conservative craft union advocates. Many federal unions bolted the AFL for the CIO and became such union mainstays as the **United Auto Workers**, the **United Steel Workers**, and the **United Rubber Workers**. The 1955 AFL-CIO merger established an industrial union department, thereby obviating the need for federal unions.

Suggested Readings: Steve Babson, *Building the Union*, 1991; Foster Dulles and Melvyn Dubofsky, *Labor in America*, 1984; Harold Roberts, *Roberts' Dictionary of Industrial Relations*, 1994.

Danielle McMullen

Federal Society of Journeymen Cordwainers (FSJC). The Federal Society of Journeymen Cordwainers is considered to be the first permanent labor union in the United States. Although earlier workers formed short-term alliances, in 1794, Philadelphia **journeymen** boot- and shoemakers seem to be the first to contemplate an ongoing organization to protect **wages** and pressure **master craftsmen** for better working conditions.

At the time, American industry was in its infancy, and its work structure mirrored the guild system. Most production was done in small shops owned by masters, who hired journeymen for wages, and maintained unpaid **apprentices**. Journeymen cordwainers were among the poorest craftsmen in pre-Revolutionary America and had hoped their overwhelming support for independence would result in better conditions. On the contrary, the American Revolution disrupted trade, and its aftermath threw the economy into a temporary tailspin. Work was irregular, wages declined, and markets contracted. The economy recovered somewhat in the early 1790s, but opportunities were rare for journeymen; by 1794, fewer than one-tenth of them were able to obtain master status. To some, the power of master shoemakers seemed as arbitrary as that of the British government. Threatened with lifelong status as a wage earner—a degraded status by the ideological standards of the day—cordwainers formed the FSJC.

The FSJC struck several Philadelphia masters in 1799 and is credited with launching one of the first successful **boycotts** in post-Revolutionary America. It passed out of existence in 1806, when the organization ran afoul of the legal system. Labor unions were illegal in most locales, and the FSJC's attempts at betterment resulted in criminal conspiracy convictions for the FSJC and several members. (The right to form unions was not guaranteed in total until the passage of the **Clayton Antitrust Act** in 1914, and even it had numerous loopholes that were addressed by the 1935 **National Labor Relations Act**.)

The FSJC ceased operations at a time in which the shoemaking industry was on the cusp of great change. Shoemaking and textile manufacturing (and, to a lesser extent, iron production) were the first American industries to move toward large-scale factory production, with masters becoming owners and journeymen becoming factory hands. The spirit of the FSJC lived on within the trade; by 1815, most cities had similar cordwainer associations, though they too suffered legal setbacks that destroyed them. However, later shoemaker organizations like the **Knights of St. Crispin** and the **Boot and Shoe Workers' Union** were the ideological offspring of the FSJC. In the 1830s, journeymen papers like *The Awl* drew upon FSJC experiences, and **strikes** like that of Lynn shoe workers in 1860 can be viewed in the context of a pattern of strained employer/employee relations within the industry.

The FSJC was also important because it was part of a broader pattern of discontent among journeymen in the early American republic. New York printers set up a lasting typographical society later in 1794, while others created organizations that led to the ten-hour movement. While most early groups were destroyed by a combination of legal impediments, employer intransigence, and severe economic downturns in the 1820s, their pioneering efforts were the foundation upon which the American union movement was built.

Suggested Readings: Foster Dulles and Melvyn Dubofsky, *Labor in America*, 1984; Theodore Hershberg, ed., *Work, Space, Family, and Group Experience in Nineteenth-Century Philadelphia*,

1980; Billy Smith, "The Vicissitudes of Fortune: The Careers of Laboring Men in Philadelphia, 1750–1800," in *Work and Labor in Early America*, ed. Stephen Innes, 1988.

Robert E. Weir

Fieldcrest Settlement. In June 1999, the **Union of Needletrades, Industrial, and Textile Employees (UNITE)** won union recognition for 5,200 Pillowtex workers at the Fieldcrest Cannon plant in Kannapolis, North Carolina. On February 10, 2000, more than 90 percent of UNITE's membership voted to approve a **contract** calling for a 9 percent raise in hourly and **piecework** rates, increased retirement benefits, and the company's first-ever sick-pay policy. This culminated more than a decade of union struggle and has been hailed by activists as an important victory for future organization of the South. North Carolina has the lowest percentage of unionized employees in the nation, and UNITE hopes to use the Fieldcrest settlement as the basis for expansion.

Fieldcrest is the remnant of the once-powerful Cannon Mills, a family-owned enterprise that controlled workers through **paternalism** and political influence. Kannapolis was largely a **company town**. By the 1930s, Cannon Mills was the nation's largest textile manufactory, with more than 18,000 employees. After World War II, the **Congress of Industrial Organizations** attempted to organize Cannon Mills as part of its **Operation Dixie** drive in the South, but was rebuffed by a combination of red-baiting, racism, and strong-arm tactics.

Although the Cannon family maintained a façade of paternalist concern for its workers, conditions at Kannapolis were notoriously poor, and **wages** low even by Piedmont standards. In 1982, the Cannon family sold the firm to a California financier, who eliminated jobs, implemented a stretch-out, and failed to make capital improvements. The **Amalgamated Clothing and Textile Workers Union (ACTWU)** attempted to organize Cannon workers, but a 1985 recognition vote lost by nearly a 2:1 margin of its 9,512 factory hands. That same year, Cannon was sold again, this time to Fieldcrest.

Conditions deteriorated further, and more jobs were lost. In August 1991, the ACTWU again forced a union recognition vote. Fieldcrest Cannon used a variety of scare tactics to dissuade prounion votes, including threats to hire replacement workers or to close Kannapolis operations. The latter threat was made more palpable by the fact that Fieldcrest Cannon had recently closed two other operations organized by the ACTWU. Even with such threats looming, the union failed by the scant margin of 3,233 to 3,094.

The ACTWU charged that its loss was the result of illegal votes from clerical workers and petitioned the National Labor Relations Board to require a revote. That request came to naught, but in 1995, the ACTWU and the **International Ladies' Garment Workers Union** merged to form UNITE and launched a new campaign against Fieldcrest Cannon. That campaign succeeded in 1999 when employees accepted UNITE by a wide margin, though the 5,200 votes cast also denote the continuing hemorrhaging of textile jobs in the Piedmont region.

The union victory ended a ninety-three-year, antiunion epoch in the Southern textile industry and has heartened UNITE activists. Some industry analysts are less sanguine of UNITE's prospects of finally organizing the South. The problem, according to pessimists, is no longer paternalism and hardball antiunion tactics, but rather **deindustrialization**. At 5,200 employees, the Kannapolis Fieldcrest Cannon operation is easily the nation's largest, but is only one-third its pre–World War II size. More than half a million manufacturing jobs have been lost since the passage of the **North American Free Trade Agreement** and many observers see little future in American textiles. Whether the Fieldcrest settlement is a harbinger of change or a Pyrrhic victory remains to be determined.

Suggested Readings: Clete Daniel, *Culture of Misfortune*, 2001; Robert Weissman, "Labor Organizing the South," in Multinational Monitor, http://multinationalmonitor.org/hyperissues/1991/09/mm0991_07.html.

Bruce Cohen
Robert E. Weir

Film and Labor. One of world's earliest films, the Lumiere brothers' *Workers Leaving the Factory* (1895), put the **working class** on the silver screen. But this was a chance debut—the Lumieres filmed employees because they were handy, not for any political purpose. Throughout the first century of American film, viewers had to look hard for depictions of unionization or working-class life. Feature films addressing these themes have been scarce, leaving documentarians, unions, and radical organizations to fund and produce most labor images on the screen.

A film still from *On the Waterfront*. © Columbia/The Kobol Collection.

When workers are on film, they are typically caricatured as wild-eyed, uncontrollably violent mobs stirred up by outside agitators and foreign radicals. Organized labor is generally seen as comprising mindless factory drones and corrupt officials eager to sell out the **rank and file**. Rarely does one see the underlying causes of labor/capital conflict or the legitimacy of workers' concerns.

The early years of American film were the heyday of labor cinema. Costs were low, so films could be made by anyone with a story to tell. Some 600 films were created by labor unions, workers, and radicals before 1917. Few have survived and most are known only from written accounts, but they represent a parallel cinema to the mass-market pictures created by the emerging film industry. Worker-owned film companies made class central and featured **strikes**, union organizing, and even radical challenges to dominant American values and institutions. As early as D. W. Griffith's 1908 *The Song of the Shirt*, audiences were asked to contrast heartless business owners with exploited workers. Others included the pro-socialist *From Dusk to Dawn* (1913); the meatpacking industry exposé *The Jungle* (1914); *Why?* (1913), which questioned the humanity of **child labor**; and *The Blacklist* (1916), which featured violent strikebreaking thugs.

A film still from *Norma Rae*. © 20th Century Fox/The Kobol Collection.

Until the 1920s, film audiences were overwhelmingly working class. Many were immigrants who learned both English and American values from those flickering images. Censors and government figures rallied to keep viewers away from "radical" notions. While leftist organizations tried to inspire class consciousness by showing films about labor/capital conflict, mainstream features that used working-class characters largely ignored class issues or promoted harmony between the classes.

By the 1920s, the Hollywood film industry was coalescing, with studios flocking to California in part to avoid unionized workforces back east. Studios controlled what was produced and how it was distributed. Censors feared that showing labor unrest on the screen encouraged it offscreen. Together they blocked worker-made films from reaching mass audiences. Grandiose film palaces built in the 1920s convinced middle-class audiences that films were respectable, and a change in content followed. Filmmakers less often featured working-class characters, assuming that middle-class patrons would rather see people like themselves on the screen.

By the 1930s, films had sound and sometimes they addressed labor. During the Great Depression, ignoring labor was problematic, and a wave of "social-problem" films took a liberal or radical perspective. Independent filmmakers and union-sponsored productions, now pushed firmly to the fringes, still tried to educate and organize mainly by way of documentaries and docudramas such as *Native Land* (1942) and *The Wave* (1937), in which Mexican fishermen strike for a living **wage**. Conservatives fought back, gutting the pro-labor screenplay of 1935's *Black Fury* (which criticized mine owners) and turning it politically conservative. A few films made it to the screen with a pro-labor slant. Among them are the Charlie Chaplin blistering anti-industrial classic *Modern Times* (1936) and King Vidor's vision of a communal workers' utopia *Our Daily Bread* (1934), though the latter was attacked bitterly by conservatives.

The 1940s brought more labor-themed features. Pro-labor sensibilities were obvious in *The Grapes of Wrath* (1940), which showed the gritty determination of displaced farm workers, and in *How Green Was My Valley* (1941), which chronicled the family devastation caused by conditions in Welsh coal mining towns. Even in the commercial *The Devil and Miss Jones* (1941), a boss works undercover in his own department store and learns a lesson about workers' lives. But labor-oriented films became scarcer as the decade progressed, especially as World War II brought a wave of feature films supporting the war effort.

Postwar fears of communism further decimated the number of pro-labor productions. In 1947, the House Un-American Activities Committee (HUAC) began investigating alleged communist subversion in the film industry. HUAC's efforts were aided by internal battles between the conservative International Alliance of Theatrical Stage Employees and Moving Picture Machine Operators (IATSE) and the Conference of Studio Unions (CSU), whose ranks included communists. IATSE exploited anticommunist sentiments to win **contracts** for its members at the CSU's expense. In so doing, it also brought the entire industry under closer scrutiny. In 1947, the "Hollywood Ten," a mix of writers and directors, was hauled before HUAC, convicted of contempt of Congress, and served jail terms.

The HUAC hearings caused a ripple effect through the industry. Studios blacklisted actors, writers, technicians, directors, and anyone else whose political views rendered them controversial. Numerous individuals, including Screen Actors Guild President Ronald Reagan, cooperated with government attempts to ferret out left-wingers in Hollywood. Widespread prosperity in the 1950s led Hollywood to disingenuously portray a nation where harmony reigned. It also avoided controversial content. When workers appeared onscreen, individual heroism, rather than collective action, was championed. *On the Waterfront*, a 1954 classic about New York City dockworkers and their corrupt union, bears this out. Although set in a unionized world, problems are solved by Karl Malden's tough-kind clergyman and Marlon Brando's loner longshoreman.

One outstanding exception to this generally conservative period in film is one of the most progressive, pro-labor films ever made, *Salt of the Earth* (1954), which showed how a strike changed individuals and their community. It also interwove class and gender more effectively than most films of any age. Director Herbert Biberman faced stiff opposition at every stage of production and distribution, and despite the film's cinematic merits, it largely went unseen by the public.

Labor was seldom seen on American screens for the next decade and a half. Among the very few films of the late 1960s and early 1970s to feature working-class people were *The Pawnbroker* (1965), with its elements of working-class despair; *Joe* (1970), about a hard-drinking, working-class bigot and vigilante justice; and *The Molly Maguires* (1970), which depicted the nineteenth-century rebellion of Pennsylvania coal miners.

In the late 1970s and 1980s, workers had a comeback. Even apolitical films such as *Saturday Night Fever* (1977), *Blue Collar* (1978), *An Officer and a Gentleman* (1982), and *Flashdance* (1983) had working-class settings, characters, or subplots. Though studio features often exploited or trivialized their labor themes—unions are in cahoots with the Mob in *Blue Collar,* for example—their very presence stands in contrast to most films of the preceding decades. Several features actually made working-class life central. *Breaking Away* (1979) follows a bicycle-racing enthusiast whose working-class roots set him apart in a university town. *Twice in a Lifetime* (1985) gives a full and realistic portrait of a steelworker's life. *Bound for Glory* (1976) is a biopic of folk singer and labor organizer Woody Guthrie; *Silkwood* (1983) shows a working-class heroine battling corporate lies; and Woody Allen's *The Front* (1976) dramatizes the blacklisting of Hollywood leftists during McCarthyism. *Reds* (1981) went even further, following the triumph of Soviet **socialism** and sympathetically portraying American communists. *Norma Rae* (1979) was a rare commercial feature that sympathetically showcased union organizing.

More radical than the features was a string of superb documentaries focusing on labor unions and workers' lives: *Union Maids* (1976), *Harlan County, USA* (1977), *With Babies and Banners* (1978), *The Wobblies* (1979), *The Life and Times of Rosie the Riveter* (1980), *You Got to Move* (1985), *American Dream* (1989), and *Roger and Me* (1989). Equal in power and scope to *Norma Rae,* a decade later, is John Sayles's 1987 *Matewan,* which follows a bitter strike in the West Virginia coalfields. Sayles's stark portrayal of unionists, miners, and socialists against the evil corporate bosses nonetheless used classic Hollywood entertainment structure. But Sayles is one of the few contemporary filmmakers openly favorable to workers, as seen also in his *Eight Men Out* (1988).

Labor-themed films largely faded from view again during the 1990s. A lone example of a major studio film about labor is the 1992 Jack Nicholson vehicle *Hoffa.* This biopic of the International Brotherhood of **Teamsters** boss is union-centered, but focuses on the drama of Hoffa's life rather than on the workers he leads or the causes of the strikes they undergo. At the turn of the millennium, labor-themed films are still rarely seen other than in documentaries like Michael Moore's anticorporate *The Big One* (1998).

Suggested Readings: Geoffrey Nowell-Smith, ed., *The Oxford History of World Cinema,* 1996; Steven Ross, *Working-Class Hollywood: Silent Film and the Shaping of Class in America,* 1998; Peter Stead, *Film and the Working Class,* 1991.

Emily Harrison Weir

Flint Sit-Down Strike. *See General Motors Sit-Down Strike.*

Flynn, Elizabeth Gurley (August 7, 1890–September 5, 1964). Elizabeth Gurley Flynn was born on August 7, 1890, in Concord, New Hampshire, as one of three daughters of Irish Americans Tom and Annie Flynn. When Elizabeth was in her teens, her parents moved to New York's South Bronx. There, the Flynns introduced their daughters to radical ideas. Tom Flynn, a frequently unemployed civil engineer, was actively involved in **socialist** circles and the labor movement. Elizabeth's mother, a tailoress and main breadwinner of the family, was well-read in feminist and socialist literature and encouraged all her daughters to strive for achievements beyond the stereotypical female roles of mother and wife. When Elizabeth first showed her extraordinary talent as a public speaker, she met strong encouragement from both her parents to cultivate her gift and to use it to support the cause of the labor movement. Flynn made her first public speech at the age of fifteen and, only a year later in 1907, she dropped out of high school to become an organizer for the **Industrial Workers of the World (IWW)**. The IWW was a revolutionary labor union devoted to the overthrow of the capitalist system by means of the general **strike**. While the more conservative **American Federation of Labor (AFL)** was organized along craft lines, the IWW targeted all unskilled workers. These workers came from various ethnic backgrounds, and were often recent immigrants who barely spoke English. Further, most female industrial workers held unskilled jobs. The AFL considered both groups extremely difficult to organize and, hence, rarely made an effort. The success with which Elizabeth Gurley Flynn drew ethnic workers as well as women into the IWW proved the AFL wrong. Flynn's greatest organizing successes occurred during the textile strikes in the mill towns of **Lawrence**, Massachusetts, in 1912, and **Paterson**, New Jersey, in 1913. She further played an important role in free speech fights in the mining regions of the West. Because of her lively speaking style, her straightforward language, and her captivating personality, Flynn won many workers to the cause of the IWW. The misery she often encountered in her contacts with working-class families also made her a strong proponent of birth control and economic independence for women. Flynn saw the urgent need to secure the support of women for the labor movement and realized that female workers had needs different from males. But she did not see herself as a feminist.

Flynn devoted her time primarily to the fight against economic inequality, and her allegiances lay with fellow members of her class rather than her gender. Nevertheless, she cultivated friendships with middle-class suffragists and frequently secured the support of these women for the politics of the IWW. Because of rising tensions between her and other leaders of the IWW, Flynn left the organization around 1919. Her energies were soon consumed by other causes. The late 1910s were a particularly bad time for American radicals. The government reacted with antiradical hysteria to the Bolshevik Revolution in the Soviet Union, widespread labor unrest in the United States, and the founding of two American communist parties in 1919. Agents of Attorney General A. Mitchell Palmer raided labor organizations and sought to deport those activists who had not yet become naturalized citizens. In reaction to the mass indictments, Flynn cofounded the Workers Defense Union (WDU) to provide legal and financial aid to victims of the Red Scare. Physical exhaustion forced her to withdraw from public life in 1926. Flynn returned to political activism in 1936. In the America of the Great Depression, she saw the end of **capitalism** close at hand. Flynn now considered the Communist Party (CPUSA) the best representative of working-class interests. She became an official member in 1937. The CPUSA was eager to embrace Flynn as a new member as she was still a well-known figure with considerable public appeal. In the same year, Flynn participated in the founding of the American Civil Liberties Union (ACLU). From the late 1930s on, her energies were again consumed mainly by efforts to combat government harassment of radicals. In 1938, Texas Democrat Martin Dies founded the House Un-American Activities Committee to investigate the alleged infiltration of New Deal programs by **communists**. The antiradical climate of this second Red Scare culminated in the infamous witch-hunts of the McCarthy era. Many liberal organizations cracked under pressure from government agencies and rid themselves of members with suspected or known communist leanings. The ACLU ousted their founding-member Flynn in 1941. In 1951, Flynn was arrested under the Smith Act, a 1940 statute that made it unlawful to advocate in theory the overthrow of the U.S. government by force or violence. Because of the deliberate vagueness of the statute, it was possible to indict radicals for their membership in the CPUSA alone. Flynn spent twenty-eight months in the Federal Reformatory at Alderson, West Virginia. Here, she wrote her autobiography, *The Rebel Girl*. After release from prison, Flynn continued her work for the Communist Party. From 1961 to 1964 she served as its chairperson. The party honored Flynn's wish to see communism in practice and to have time for her own writing. As a representative of the CPUSA, Flynn traveled repeatedly to Eastern Europe and the Soviet Union. On September 5, 1964, she died in Moscow.

Elizabeth Gurley Flynn's contributions to the labor movement are those of an activist rather than a thinker or ideologue. Although she was well-read and familiar with the theoretical foundations of the labor movement as well as communism, she preferred to address her audiences in simple and straightforward terms. Her ability to breach lines of ethnicity, gender, and class was highly important. She managed to organize strikers of widely divergent backgrounds and also gained the support of members of the middle or upper class for the cause of organized labor. These abilities were first cherished and cultivated by the IWW and later by the Communist Party. In her work for political prisoners and as a member of the WDU and ACLU, Flynn further devoted herself to the defense of the constitutional right of free speech.

Suggested Readings: Rosalyn Fraad Baxandall, *Words on Fire: The Life and Writing of Elizabeth Gurley Flynn*, 1987; Helen C. Camp, *Iron in Her Soul: Elizabeth Gurley Flynn and the American Left*, 1995; Elizabeth Gurley Flynn, *The Rebel Girl, An Autobiography, My First Life (1906–26)*, 1955.

Babette Faehmel

Foran Act. Passed by Congress in 1885 and amended in 1887 and 1888, the Foran Act made illegal the importation of foreign contract labor. It is named after its sponsor, Representative Martin A. Foran, a popular prolabor Ohio Democrat who had once been president of the Coopers International Union. Its passage capped more than a decade of intense labor lobbying for its passage by the **Knights of Labor (KOL)** and various trade unions.

The earliest European workforce in North America was comprised of **indentured servants**, who labored under a set **contract** in exchange for room, board, and overseas passage. By the time of the American Revolution, however, this labor system was in decline. Slave labor was widespread in the South, but was slowly dying in the North. With the articulation of the early factory system and a building boom in canals and railroads, the United States experienced a labor shortage. By the early nineteenth century, many employers actively recruited immigrant labor, and Congress passed bills easing naturalization procedures. Large numbers of German and Irish workers arrived in the 1840s, followed by Chinese in the 1850s.

Individual immigrants negotiating **wage** bargains met little opposition from organized labor, though immigrants often suffered discrimination at the hands of nativist bigots. Contract labor, however, was another matter. By the mid-nineteenth century, two types of contract labor systems were in place, one reviving the concept of indenturedom, the other a gang-labor agreement usually negotiated with a third party. Entire crews of Irish canal diggers and rail workers were hired at set rates through agents, who usually siphoned a hefty percentage of their wages. Native-born workers complained that contract labor undercut their own wages.

Even more controversial was the coolie system involving Chinese workers. Although the practice was relatively rare in the United States, Chinese and Indian labor gangs had been used since the eighteenth century in British colonies. Still, Congress attempted to outlaw the practice in 1862. Congressional action proved inadequate, in part because the laws were vague, but also because employment agents in China were willing to recruit laborers under the fiction that they were individually contracted. American employers were quite willing to accept Chinese employment gangs; some readily saw them as a hedge against paying high wages. The use of Chinese as **scabs** during labor disputes, like one involving North Adams, Massachusetts, shoemakers in 1870, heightened fears of coolie labor.

Contract labor became a burning concern for organized labor when Congress passed "An Act to Encourage Immigration" in 1864. This bill revived indentured servitude, by promising that Congress would enforce labor contracts made overseas. The bill also provided that up to one year's labor could be required of immigrants in exchange for transport to America. President Lincoln signed the bill, perhaps anticipating labor shortages once slavery was abolished or perhaps yielding to pressures from Northern entrepreneurs. (The stated purpose was to replenish factories undermanned due to the Civil War.) Organized labor resented this act from the beginning. Both the **National Labor Union** and the KOL lobbied for its repeal and both had anticontract labor planks in their organizational platforms. The success of American Emigrant Aid Society agents in recruiting cheap labor served to intensify resentment against the act.

The Foran Act came in response to the fervor and anger with which union members and workers responded. Foreign contract work was expressly forbidden under the bill, and most of the provisions of the 1864 act were eviscerated. Despite passage and subsequent amendments of the Foran Act, it proved difficult to enforce and not much effort was made to do so. Only the Chinese, who were banned by the 1882 **Chinese Exclusion Act**, were greatly affected by the Foran Act. The KOL and trade unions complained bitterly about the lack of enforcement, but the business community's desire for cheap labor and its ties to political figures proved more powerful than labor's efforts. By the 1880s and 1890s, labor gangs from southern and eastern Europe were more prevalent than coolie labor had ever been. Numerous Italian workers toiled under the *padrone* system in which their wages were doled out by a foreman who held the pay for his entire crew. In the twentieth century, Mexican *braceros* agricultural workers' worked under similar arrangements. As recently as 2001, reports surfaced of African and Chinese workers being held in veritable bondage whilst their "employers" extracted money allegedly used to "sponsor" their passage to America.

Suggested Readings: Andrew Gyory, *Closing the Gate*, 1998; Norman Ware, *The Labor Movement in the United States, 1860–95*, 1929.

Robert E. Weir

Fordism. *Fordism* refers to assembly-line production methods and management techniques associated with the Ford Motor Company. Marxist and radical critics also use the term as a synonym for industrial exploitation. Central to assembly line production is a machine-driven, continuous flow of parts and material to individual workstations where unskilled or semiskilled laborers fit together single pieces of the total product.

Contrary to popular belief, Henry Ford did not invent assembly-line production. Flour mills were the first American businesses to use the assembly line, adapting methods pioneered by Oliver Evans around 1784. In the nineteenth century, meatpackers and gun manufacturers adopted the assembly line. In 1914, Henry Ford converted his Dearborn, Michigan, Model-T plant to assembly-line production, and the price of automobiles dropped dramatically. The assembly line also deskilled the workforce. By 1926, a Ford automobile required

7,782 separate operations for completion, but more than three-quarters of all plant jobs required less than a week's training to master.

Assembly-line production found very few advocates among working people. Many complained it distanced workers from the final product, was mind-numbing, and robbed workers of control over tools and the pace of work. To get workers to accept the machine-driven pace and monotony of the line, Ford offered higher **wages** than other manufacturers, but nonetheless often experienced yearly turnover in excess of 300 percent. Subsequent employers often sought to make the assembly line more efficient through the application of scientific management principles and time-and-motion studies **(Taylorism)**.

By the 1950s, many industrial sociologists equated assembly-line production with worker alienation, and in the 1960s and 1970s, younger autoworkers resorted to **stints** and sabotage to resist the tedium of the line. General Motors was particularly hard hit by resistance from Chevrolet Vega workers at **Lordstown**, Ohio.

Despite resistance, by the 1930s assembly-line production was the norm in many American factories until the full effect of **automation** began to transform manufacturing in the 1970s. By the 1980s, some manufacturers began to abandon the assembly line in favor of a more varied workplace, like **quality circles**. However, the line remains in widespread use in the United States and is the method of choice in many developing nations to which **runaway shops** have relocated. Among radical critics, the assembly line is part and parcel of an exploitative labor system called "Fordism," that encompasses managerial systems designed to maintain a compliant workforce.

Suggested Readings: Harry Braveman, *Labor and Monopoly Capitalism: The Degradation of Work in the Twentieth Century*, 1974; Mike Davis, *Prisoners of the American Dream*, 1988.

Robert E. Weir

Foster, Frank Keyes (December 18, 1855–June 27, 1909). Frank Keyes Foster was a leading trade-union journalist of the late nineteenth and twentieth centuries and an opponent of Marxist ideals within the union movement. He was born in Palmer, Massachusetts, the son of Charles Dwight and Jane Elizabeth (Burgess) Foster, was educated at Monson Academy, and learned the printer's trade in Hartford, Connecticut, while working for the publication, *Churchman*. Foster began his activities in the labor movement in Hartford, when he joined the Hartford Typographical Union and was elected secretary of the organization.

He married Lucretia Ella Ladd on May 22, 1879, and within a year the couple moved to Boston. Foster was then elected president of the Cambridge Typographical Union, serving as delegate to its international union. He was also active with the Boston Central Trades and Labor Union, serving as secretary and delegate for the organization. In 1883, he joined the **Knights of Labor (KOL)** and served in executive positions on the local, state, and national levels. In 1886, he made an unsuccessful bid to become the Democratic lieutenant governor of Massachusetts.

Foster's experience in the labor movement served him well as he ventured into his career as a labor journalist. His activities with the labor press intensified in 1884, when he took over the editorship of the *Haverhill* (Massachusetts) *Daily and Weekly Laborer,* the KOL's official journal in Massachusetts. In 1886, he was the editor and the publisher of the *Liberator.* His most noted venture in the labor press came in 1887, when he began working with **George E. McNeill** on the official paper of the Massachusetts Federation of Labor, the *Labor Leader.* At about this time, McNeill was editing a book, *The Labor Movement: The Problem of Today* (1887), and Foster contributed a chapter on shoemakers.

McNeill retired within a year of Foster's arrival at the *Labor Leader,* and Foster continued to comment on Boston-area labor. In a fashion typical of the personal journalism of the period, the paper featured Foster's editorials, short stories, and news articles. He guided the *Labor Leader* until 1897, offering one of the period's rare examples of a successful labor paper.

Foster was a **socialist** in his youth, but he became increasingly opposed to Marxist collectivism. Foster derided Marx's emphasis on revolution and argued for evolutionary change. He was enamored with the philosophy of Herbert Spencer, particularly his Law of Equal Freedom, which emphasized complete individual freedom, so long as one did not infringe on the self-expression of others. He also espoused pragmatic, pure and simple trade unionism, often echoing the ideology of **Samuel Gompers** and the **American Federation of Labor (AFL).** Foster split with the KOL when he determined it to be hostile to trade unions, and was editorially critical of it. Gompers was a regular reader of the *Labor Leader* and frequently corresponded with its editor. Foster asserted that one could believe in both individualism and working-class association, and outlined his theory of "collective-individualism" in his autobiographical novel, *The Evolution of a Trade Unionist* (1903). Later in his life, Foster penned a volume of poetry, *The Karma of Labor* (1903). His reputation as a commentator on labor issues often put him in demand as a **Labor Day** speaker. As an orator, he gave addresses in twenty-three states.

Suggested Readings: Joseph DePlasco, "The University of Labor vs. the University of Letters in 1904: Frank K. Foster Confronts Harvard University President Charles W. Eliot," *Labor's Heritage* 1, no. 2 (April 1989): 52–65; Arthur Mann, *Yankee Reformers in the Urban Age: Social Reform in Boston, 1880–1900,* 1966.

Mark Noon

Foster, William Zebulon (February 25, 1881–December 1, 1961). William Zebulon Foster was a prominent, American-born leader of the **Communist** Party. He was born in Taunton, Massachusetts, the son of James, an Irish immigrant rail-yard worker and Elizabeth (McLaughlin) Foster. His poverty-stricken youth was spent in a Philadelphia Irish slum known as "Skittereen." He was apprenticed to an artist in 1891 and learned rudimentary stonecutting, but held a variety of odd jobs and received little formal schooling. During the first decade of the 1900s, Foster frequently traveled as a hobo in search of work. In 1918, he married Ester Abramovitch.

He joined the Socialist Party (SP) in 1900 and immersed himself in Marxist literature. Foster grew critical of the SP and, in 1909, the party expelled him. In that year he joined the **Industrial Workers of the World (IWW)**, as he was attracted to its program of revolutionary syndicalism. When a 1910 conference in Budapest refused to seat Foster as an official IWW delegate, he toured Europe and studied syndicalism instead. These experiences soured him on the IWW, and he quit the organization in 1912, convinced that a policy of radicals "boring within" existing trade unions was the surest path to syndicalism. To that end he authored the pamphlet *Syndicalism* that outlined the goals of the newly formed Syndicalist League of North America (SLNA), a propaganda organization aimed at converting the **rank and file** of the **American Federation of Labor (AFL)** to SLNA principles.

Foster proved an effective AFL organizer. He was the business agent of a Chicago railroad union and led both a 1917 meatpackers **strike** and the **Steel Strike of 1919**. Both strikes saw Foster maintain levels of racial solidarity between white and African American workers that were rare during the period. The steel strike deepened his radicalism and, in 1920, he founded the Trade Union Educational League (TUEL), a group that largely supplanted the SLNA. He was an open admirer of the 1917 Russian Revolution, visited the Soviet Union in 1921, and joined the Communist Party of the United States (CPUSA).

From this point on, Foster's fate was tied to party fortunes. He became national chairman of the CPUSA in 1932, a time in which it and the TUEL received money and directions from Moscow. He was arrested for criminal syndicalism in 1922 but was acquitted. He was also the CPUSA presidential candidate in 1924, 1928, and 1932, achieving his greatest success in the last year, though he suffered an emotional and physical breakdown during the campaign from which he did not recover until 1935.

Foster embraced Stalinism in the 1930s, but during his convalescence, control of the CPUSA shifted to **Earl Browder**, with whom Foster frequently clashed ideologically and tactically. When Browder was discredited in 1945, Foster regained control of the party and served as its chair until 1957. He encountered intense Cold War anticommunist hysteria, and, despite his voluminous newspaper writings and pamphleteering, the CPUSA declined precipitously. Premier Nikita Khruschev's 1956 denunciation of Stalinism further weakened the party, though Foster continued to defend Stalin. Foster died during a 1961 visit to the USSR.

Foster's long association with the CPUSA and Stalinism have obscured his overall contributions to the labor movement. His racial organizing models during 1919 remain admirable efforts, and his commitment to working people was sincere. Foster should be considered as a revolutionary labor activist rather than an ideologue.

Suggested Readings: James Barrett, *William Z. Foster and the Tragedy of American Radicalism*, 1999; William Z. Foster, *Pages from a Worker's Life*, 1939; Edward Johanningsmeier, *Forging American Communism*, 1998.

Jay Miller

Fraser, Douglas Andrew (December 16, 1916–). Douglas Andrew Fraser is the former head of **United Auto Workers (UAW)** union and was among the last of the "pioneer generation" to head the union. Fraser was born in Glasgow, Scotland, but his family moved to Detroit in 1922, before he was six. The Great Depression interrupted his education; in 1934, he dropped out of high school to obtain work at a Dearborn machine shop. Fraser was soon fired for union organizing. In 1936, he was hired as metal finisher at Chrysler's Dodge Main assembly plant in Hamtramck, Michigan. A year later, Fraser moved to the De Soto assembly plant where he started his career in the UAW. He joined UAW Local 227, became its president in 1943, and served through 1946. Four years later, he joined the UAW's international staff.

In 1950, he distinguished himself as a tough negotiator during the historic 104-day **strike** against Chrysler, attracting the attention of UAW President **Walter Reuther**, who made Fraser his administrative assistant. In 1959, Fraser won election to become UAW Region 1A codirector and, in 1962, was selected to the UAW executive board. Fraser became a UAW vice president in 1970. His tenacity and integrity at the bargaining table won the respect of management as well as the admiration of the UAW **rank and file**. When Reuther died in an airplane crash in 1970, it was thought that Fraser would succeed Reuther, but Fraser lost to Leonard Woodcock (1911–2001) by one vote. Upon Woodcock's retirement in 1977, Fraser finally succeeded to the presidency of the UAW.

Although some critics took Fraser to task for not doing enough to form new **locals** or encourage member militancy, he was a hardworking executive who cultivated rank-and-file support. Fraser often paid visits to factory workers and was a familiar face on picket lines, civil rights marches, and at meetings with international leaders. He also advised several presidents, though he did not hesitate to lambaste politicians he perceived to be antilabor. In 1978, Fraser resigned from the Labor-Management Group when Congress failed to enact labor-law reform. He accused business leaders of waging class war against workers and charged that there was little difference between the labor policies of Republicans and Democrats.

Fraser's toughest challenges as UAW president came during downturns in the auto industry in the late 1970s. Tough competition from Japanese autoworkers and an oil shortage necessitated a government bailout of Chrysler Corporation in 1978. Gas prices skyrocketed and fuel-efficient imported cars captured a growing slice of domestic sales. The smallest of the "Big Three" automakers—which includes Ford and General Motors (GM)—Chrysler was saddled with a gas-guzzling fleet in desperate need of retooling and restyling. The firm was in such desperate condition that its workers agreed to **concessions**, unheard of in the auto industry. Had it not been for these concessions, coupled with the lobbying of Chrysler President Lee Iacocca, the political strength of the UAW and its allies, like Detroit Mayor Coleman A. Young, Chrysler would not have survived. Fraser helped negotiate a bailout that included over $1.2 billion in federally guaranteed loans and tax concessions. In 1980, Fraser became the first American labor leader to sit on the board of directors of an American corporation when he joined the Chrysler board. Under Iacocca's leadership, the board redesigned Chrysler products and returned the firm to profitability. (A 1998 merger with Germany's Daimler-Benz has been problematic, and the newly christened Daimler-Chrysler is currently struggling.)

Nonetheless, troubles at Chrysler were emblematic of difficulties elsewhere. By the 1970s, employers routinely demanded concessions and givebacks from their employees. The UAW resisted concessions at General Motors and Ford. The situation at Chrysler led the UAW to seek early negotiations at Ford and GM before economic conditions became worse and bargaining strength weakened. These negotiations resulted in providing the so-called Guaranteed Income Stream (GIS) that provided income for long-term employees in the event of layoffs. At International Harvester, however, the UAW endured an inconclusive 172-day strike. In 1981, Fraser presided over negotiations that led the UAW to reaffiliate with the American Federation of Labor–Congress of Industrial Organizations. Fraser hoped that this alliance would bolster UAW efforts to resist the concessions movement, a trend accelerated by Ronald Reagan's election in 1980, and the antiunion policies of his administration. Those efforts bore mixed results.

In 1983, Fraser retired after over forty years of union leadership at the local, national, and international levels. He continued to speak out in the interests of labor and civil rights. Both he and his wife, Winnie, have taught labor studies courses at Detroit's Wayne State University. The university's Center for Workplace Issues now bears Fraser's name.

Suggested Readings: Kevin Boyle, *The UAW and the Heyday of American Liberalism, 1945–68*, 1995; Lee Iacocca, *Talking Straight*, 1988.

Don Binkowski

Free Labor. Free labor is a term that implies the ability of American workers to bargain **wages** and conditions within an open and competitive labor market. It first gained currency in the early nineteenth century and was tied to the ability of **journeymen** to make wage deals with masters. As the century progressed, however, free-labor ideology emerged as an attack on slavery. According to its articulators, Northern free labor's freedom of **contract** and freedom of movement created an overall economic system that was incentive-driven and thus more efficient and profitable than that of the South. In theory, it also afforded workers the possibility of upward mobility. Southern critics countered that free labor was a myth that masked an overall degradation of Northern labor that was worse than that of chattel slaves. Nonetheless, a substantial number of labor reformers embraced free-labor ideology.

Some aspects of the Southern critique proved accurate. After the Civil War, free labor mutated into a defense of individual wage bargaining. Many employers used this logic to attack **collective bargaining** and oppose the recognition of labor unions. In the twentieth century, free labor was often used by management to defend the **open-shop** movement, **right-to-work** laws, the hiring of **scabs**, and the calling of **decertification** votes. Free-labor precepts mesh well with cherished notions of individualism and have proven especially attractive to the middle class, a factor that has undoubtedly retarded the growth of white-collar unionism.

Suggested Readings: Mike Davis, *Prisoners of the American Dream*, 1986; Eric Foner, *Politics and Ideology in the Age of the Civil War*, 1980.

Robert E. Weir

Frey, John Phillip (February 24, 1871–November 29, 1957). John Phillip Frey was an important leader of the iron molders union in the early twentieth century. Frey was so committed to the ideals of **craft unionism** that he is often invoked as an example of outmoded thinking that retarded the organizing efforts of the **American Federation of Labor (AFL)**.

He was born in Mankato, Minnesota, the son of Leopold, a former army officer and manufacturer and Julia (Beaudry) Frey. He attended public school until 1885, when he went to Canada to work in a lumber camp. In 1886, Frey departed for Worcester, Massachusetts, where he trained as an **apprentice** iron molder after a brief stint as a grocery clerk. He got his first molding job in 1891, the same year he married Nellie Josephine Higgins, with whom he would have three children.

In 1893, Frey joined Local 5 of the International Molders and Foundry Workers Union of North America (IMFWU) and became its president just two months later. In 1898, he became treasurer of the New England Conference of Molders and, the following year, was chosen as vice president of the Massachusetts Federation of Labor. In 1900, Frey became vice president of the IMFWU, a post he held for the next fifty years. He quickly befriended AFL President **Samuel Gompers** and gained a reputation of being an "enforcer" who could bend AFL conventions to do Gompers's bidding. Frey served on three labor missions to Europe during and after World War I, faithfully supporting AFL policy on each.

In 1921, Frey moved to Norwood, Ohio, and became president of the Ohio Federation of Labor. Gompers died in 1924, but his successor, **William Green**, continued to call upon Frey. In 1927, Frey was appointed to the AFL's Metal Trades Department and, in 1934, he was elevated to the presidency of that powerful AFL coordinating body. Frey also served on numerous government boards. In 1950, he retired from all labor activities.

Four themes run through Frey's career. First, he vehemently opposed labor radicals, especially communists and socialists. Second, his devotion to craft-union principles made him a stubborn and outspoken opponent of **industrial unionism**. Most scholars place Frey at the center of those who insisted that craft ideals were the only legitimate principle by which workers could be organized. Many credit Frey with forcing the decision of industrial unions to form the **Congress of Industrial Organizations (CIO)**. Predictably, Frey denounced the CIO as a communist front organization. He opposed an AFL-CIO merger, and it did not take place until five years after he retired. Third, Frey was a proponent of **pure and simple unionism**, and thus shied away from all forms of political activism. He was suspicious of all government-induced labor reforms and was against most of the New Deal's social and labor reforms.

Finally, Frey was an active writer on behalf of craft unionists. He edited the *Iron Molders' Journal* from 1903 to 1927, and authored three books on labor subjects. At the time of his death in 1957, Frey was hailed an exemplar of conservative, "respectable" trade-union policies, and a stalwart patriot. Many historians subsequently came to view him as an uncompromising hindrance to the labor movement who rallied support for outmoded ideals.

Suggested Readings: Melvyn Dubofsky and Warren Van Tine, *John L. Lewis: A Biography*, 1977; John Frey, Obituary, *New York Times*, November 30, 1957; Philip Taft, *The A.F. of L. From the Death of Gompers to the Merger*, 1959.

Andrew E. Kersten

Fringe Benefits. Fringe benefits are advantageous provisions in addition to an employee's regular **salary** or **wage**. These are typically important negotiated items in a union **contract**. Examples include health insurance, profit-sharing plans, paid holidays and vacations, paid sick leave, **pensions**, and unemployment insurance. In the last two decades of the twentieth century, some contracts provided for a "cafeteria" style of benefit options, including dental care for employees' children, legal insurance, or finance-based extras like a 401(k) savings option.

Fringe benefits increase an employee's overall compensation and are considered mandatory negotiating items during **collective bargaining**. In general, union workers receive both a greater variety and a higher level of fringe benefits than nonunion workers do. Although workers have always negotiated for fringe benefits, they became standard during the 1940s. During World War II, the **National War Labor Board** encouraged bargaining over fringe benefits to hold down basic wage increases that would otherwise jeopardize agreed-upon wage scales. Thereafter, unions fought to broaden the scope of fringe benefits included among the mandatory subjects of bargaining. In a 1948 National Labor Relations Board decision, it was ruled that pensions and retirement funds belonged under such a heading. In the 1950s, supplemental unemployment benefits, vacations, and holidays became standard provisions in almost all union contracts. By the year 2000, the rising cost of benefits, especially medical, created negotiating conflicts between companies who wanted employees to contribute a copayment for such "perks" and unions trying to hold the line against eroding benefit packages.

Suggested Readings: Henry C. Black, *Black's Law Dictionary*, 1999, Harry Katz and Thomas Kochan, *An Introduction to Collective Bargaining and Industrial Relations*, 2000.

Danielle McMullen

G

Gastonia Strike. The Gastonia Strike was part of a wave of labor struggles that hit the cotton textile industry in North and South Carolina in the spring of 1929. The most famous of these occurred at the Loray Mill in Gastonia, North Carolina, which featured the active involvement of youthful members of the Communist Party of the United States.

Events at Gastonia were set in motion by the formation of the National Textile Workers Union (NTWU) in September 1928, an organization that hoped to supplant the United Textile Union (UTW) affiliated with the **American Federation of Labor**. The major goals of the NTWU included solidarity with the Soviet Union and the organization of textile workers in the American South. Southern textile towns developed a reputation as a refuge from unionism. Mill operators also exploited adolescents willing to work in low-wage textile factories to flee tenant farms and mountain cabins. In early 1929, Fred Beal, a young communist who had organized textile workers in Massachusetts, worked to rally Loray workers. On April 1, approximately 1,800 workers walked out of the mills, demanding higher **wages**, a reduction in their fifty-five hour workweek, an end to the stretch-out system, and union recognition.

Mill owners responded to the walkout by obtaining a court injunction to end **strike** activity. Governor Max Gardner ordered the National Guard to break up worker **picketing**. The local press played a significant role in the strike by successfully inciting the general public to violence through red-baiting. About two weeks into the strike, the NTWU union hall in Gastonia was destroyed by masked members of a mob. Strikers, mostly women and children, were beaten and jailed. By the third week of April, the strike was virtually over as workers drifted back to work, took work in other mills, or went back home to the Carolina hills. Violence, however, did not end when the strike collapsed. In May, the families of workers who did not return to work were evicted from company housing. On June 7, a union-sponsored tent colony set up for evicted strikers was attacked by local officers. In a shootout, the chief of police was killed. Beal and other organizers were convicted of murder and sentenced to lengthy prison terms. Through the efforts of the American Civil Liberties Union, the strike leaders were able to post bail and they fled to the Soviet Union. On September 14, Ella Mae Wiggins, a popular organizer who was known as the "Bard of Gastonia" because of her ballads addressing the plight of the workers, was shot and killed by armed men who ambushed a truck full of strikers headed for a union rally. Wiggans's killers were never convicted despite dozens of witnesses to the crime.

The Gastonia Strike led to a slight reduction in the workweek for Loray Mill workers and elimination of night work for women and children. However, it did little to bring about the organization of textile workers in the South. Defeat at Gastonia was mirrored throughout the Piedmont region. The NTWU disappeared and the UTW went into decline. Because of the key role of women in the strike, Gastonia is now cited in studies of gender and labor militancy. In addition, the strike contributed greatly to a revival of proletarian literature in the 1930s. Writers from the literary left found inspiration in the drama of Gastonia, and several traveled there to collect firsthand accounts and enhance the realism of their novels. The Gastonia Strike was fictionalized in works by **Mary Heaton Vorse**, Sherwood Anderson, Grace Lumpkin, Dorothy Myra Page, William Rollins, and Olive Tilford Dargan.

Suggested Readings: Fred Beal, *Proletarian Journey: New England, Gastonia, Moscow*, 1947; Bert Cochran, *Labor and Communism: The Conflict That Shaped American Unions*, 1977; Cletus E. Daniel, *Culture of Misfortune: An Interpretive History of Textile Unionism in the United States (Cornell Studies in Industrial and Labor Relations, Vol. 34)*, 2001; Liston Pope, *Millhands and Preachers: A Study of Gastonia*, 1942.

Mark Noon

General Agreement on Tariffs and Trade (GATT). The General Agreement on Tariffs and Trade (GATT) is a no-longer-operative trade agreement that reduced trade barriers between signatory countries. It was effected in 1947, with twenty-three member nations. The ambitious mission of the GATT was to raise global standards of living, implement full-employment policies, create a rise in income, regulate demand, develop global resources, and expand international trade. GATT signatories believed that lower tariffs and dedication to free-trade principles were key to achieving their goals. While the success of GATT's mission is open to debate, the agreement substantially lowered tariffs and stimulated trade. Historically, many labor unions opposed the GATT, and are skeptical of its successor, the World Trade Organization (WTO).

A key GATT principle was to undermine tariffs by eliminating quotas. This tactic encouraged overall economic growth because tariffs tax each individual unit sold overseas without regard to quantity. Tariffs allow trade in a particular good to increase without any quantitative limit, yet offer each nation's economy some protection. Quotas, by contrast, set fixed ceilings on the quantity of goods that can be sold.

Another central principle of the GATT was nondiscrimination between signatory nations. When a nation joined the GATT, it was obliged to open its markets to other signatory nations equally. Thus, a tariff reduction that was negotiated between two nations ("most-favored nation status") was automatically extended to every other GATT member. This reciprocity made **protectionism** more difficult and discouraged favoritism between select GATT signatories. The GATT also instituted uniform customs regulations among members, although it was equipped with an escape clause that theoretically allowed nations to change trade terms if **concessions** seriously damaged production within their country. Finally, nations were obliged to negotiate tariff reductions if requested to do so by another member nation.

The GATT was born out of the economic and political aftermath of World War II. It sought to restore stability to an international economic system wracked by nearly two decades of economic depression and warfare. Its mission statement reflected concern for the provision of jobs and a basic level of material well-being. It also tried to put forth a positive, progressive vision of global **capitalism**. The GATT was revised and expanded numerous times before it was scrapped in 1994.

Though the primary focus of the GATT was on narrowly defined trade issues, occasional GATT meetings—dubbed "rounds"—produced multilateral trade agreements and confronted broad trade issues. Since its inception, the GATT went through seven different major rounds of negotiation. The 1986–94 Uruguay Round was the most sweeping of the rounds, both for its impact on trade and on the nature of economic **globalization**. Negotiators aggressively pursued worldwide expansion of free-trade aims and began to address the booming trade within the service sector of the global economy. The GATT was dissolved during the Uruguay Round to set up a new mechanism to regulate and monitor global trade.

In 1995, the WTO formed. By that time, one-hundred-twenty-five nations had joined the movement for global trade regulation. The GATT and the WTO differed in some important ways. One key difference is that the GATT was a set of rules applied on a provisional basis, while the WTO is a durable institution to which member nations commit fully and permanently. Second, the GATT applied to trade in merchandise goods, while the WTO also covers trade in services and trade-related realms of intellectual property.

Since the WTO's creation, an increasingly mobile and vocal opposition movement has challenged its authority to dictate national behavior and the effects that authority claims on workforce and environmental standards. These critics span a broad spectrum, including environmentalists, labor unionists, human-rights groups, economic-justice groups, and anarchists. Many American labor unions have been especially outspoken in their opposition to the WTO. As they see it, hard-fought union campaigns to raise **wages**, establish safety standards, and create humane working environments will be undermined if the United States agrees to trade agreements with nations whose labor laws are less stringent. Moreover, the lack of global environmental accords threatens to undercut American wages by flooding the market with goods produced by manufacturers unencumbered by pollution controls. Many unions believe this will also encourage capital flight out of the United States and into low-wage nations. (Historically most unions have supported some form of protectionism to promote domestic production.) Most unions demand international labor and environmental bills of rights as a minimal precondition for supporting the WTO.

Other critics charge that the WTO violates national sovereignty and is inherently undemocratic, with nonelected leaders negotiating agreements that are beyond public scrutiny. Beginning with highly organized and publicized protests in Seattle, Washington, in late 1999, anti-WTO groups have publicized the case against the WTO and its aims. Since then, protesters have surfaced at all WTO meetings to voice their concerns, including a 2001 protest in Genoa, Italy, that resulted in a demonstrator's death.

Suggested Readings: Susan Aaronson, *Trade and The American Dream: A Social History of Postwar Trade Policy*, 1996; Carolyn Rhodes, *Reciprocity, U.S. Trade Policy, and the GATT Regime*, 1993; Thomas Zeiler, *Free Trade Free World: The Advent of GATT*, 1999.

Simon Holzapfel

General Motors Sit-Down Strike. The General Motors Sit-Down Strike, also called the "Great Flint Sit-Down Strike," was a successful tactic used against General Motors (GM) in Flint, Michigan, from December 30, 1936, to February 11, 1937. It is perhaps the most famous **strike** in American labor history and is often credited as establishing the legitimacy of both the **United Auto Workers (UAW)** union and the **Congress of Industrial Organizations (CIO)**. The UAW's victory at Flint buoyed the spirits of workers across the United States, spawned numerous imitators, and led to a resurgence of union-organizing activity.

During the 1920s, the auto industry boomed, and Americans began in earnest their desire for and dependence upon cars. Nonetheless, the industry was badly hurt by the Great Depression that began in 1929. Numerous strikes took place as workers tried to stem **wage** cuts and job losses, but the traditional **craft unionism** of the **American Federation of Labor (AFL)** proved inadequate. Some groups, like the **Mechanics Educational Society of America (MESA)** espoused **industrial unionism** as a better alternative for autoworkers, a sentiment shared by **communist** organizers and radical **socialists** associated with the labor movement. This was precisely the position taken by CIO rebels inside the AFL who eventually bolted and formed a new labor federation. By the mid-1930s, most autoworkers drew about one-third less pay than they had before 1929, and overall employment in the industry (about 244,000) was down by nearly half from 1929 (435,000). Manufacturers also took steps to minimize unionization of the auto industry and riddled their ranks with **stool pigeons**, **agent provocateurs**, and labor spies. According to a 1937 **La Follette Committee** report on labor strife, GM spent nearly a million dollars on labor spies between 1934 and 1936.

The UAW-CIO was relatively weak when the Flint strike began. Key leaders like Wyndham Mortimer, **Walter Reuther**, and Homer Martin discussed the possibility of shutting down GM's Fisher Body plants in Cleveland and Flint, as they produced the body and chassis needed for every GM car. There was conflict among UAW leaders, however, especially between UAW president Martin and vice president Mortimer, who had ties to the Communist Party and decried Martin's cautious policies. In addition, Flint workers were deeply divided. Most belonged to a **company union** hostile to the UAW, and an organization known as the Black Legion attracted many white Protestant workers with its antipathy toward African Americans, Catholics, and Jews.

The UAW made some inroads through left-wing organizers. Bud Simons was sympathetic to the communists, while Bob Travis was a veteran of the 1934 Auto-Lite Strike in Akron, Ohio, that was led by MESA. Travis, like the Reuther brothers—Walter, Victor, and Roy—was a socialist, and Flint also had a smattering of **Trotskyites**. The radicals were heartened by an incident in Flint in November 1936. When Fisher Body Number One reduced its three-man crews to two, one team refused to work. When they were fired, 700 workers sat down at their machines. GM was forced to rehire the three men, and Travis began enrolling workers in the UAW.

Contrary to popular belief, the **sit-down strike** was not a new tactic. European workers used it in the nineteenth century, and members of the **Industrial Workers of the World** used sit-downs against General Electric in Schenectady, New York, in 1919. There had been numerous sit-down strikes during 1935 and 1936 that predated actions in Flint, including several in which the Reuthers had participated. While UAW officials debated their next move, Fisher Body workers in Cleveland spontaneously sat down on December 28, 1936, to protest a delayed meeting with GM management. Two days later, Flint workers also took matters into their own hands. In all, Flint workers at Fisher Number One and Two would spend forty-four days inside the plant.

The UAW proved adroit at organizing the spontaneous strike. At any one time, there were between 500 and 1,000 men inside Fisher One. Simons and other UAW leaders molded the strikers into a disciplined industrial army. Women were sent home to avoid any hint of impropriety, alcohol was banned, and destruction of property was prohibited, lest it be used as pretext for forcibly evicting strikers. The UAW also organized the workers into fifteen-member "families," each headed by a "captain." Work groups, recreation committees, labor-history classes, and food details were established, and a sentry rotation schedule was put in place. When GM sent alcohol and prostitutes to the plant on New Year's Eve for the pleasure of GM foremen and police still inside the plant, the UAW expelled all GM management personnel. Absolutely vital to the UAW's success was the creation of the Women's Emergency Brigade (WEB), spearheaded by Genora Johnson. Most of the approximately 350 WEB members—identified by their red berets—had family members inside the plant, and they took charge of getting food to workers (often through smuggling and subterfuge), coordinating protests, launching public-relations campaigns, and relaying vital information between UAW leaders and the sit-down strikers.

The UAW also benefited from a change in government when, on January 1, 1937, Frank Murphy took office as governor of Michigan. Murphy was a New Deal Democrat who owed his election to the state's **working classes** and was loath to side with GM. Attempts to serve an injunction to key leaders failed when they were tipped off, and revelations that the issuing judge was a major GM stockholder quelled Murphy's incentive to assist GM in enforcing the injunction. Appeals to President Franklin Roosevelt and CIO President **John L. Lewis** also fell upon deaf ears, and the UAW steadfastly refused to cave in to GM's negative publicity campaign or take the bait of its offer to negotiate once the plant was evacuated.

A key moment of the strike occurred on January 11, 1937, when GM foolishly attempted to retake Fisher Number Two, which was not essential to production. Heat and power to the plant were cut off, and GM guards stopped food deliveries. A squad of **goons** went into the plant and fought with workers; tear gas was fired into the building, and armed sheriff's deputies stood ready to charge the factory. Outside, Victor Reuther manned a sound truck. As tear gas was launched, Genora Johnson went to the microphone and exhorted the women of Flint to protect their husbands, brothers, and fathers. Women surged toward the plant, smashed windows to ventilate the factory, and tossed tear-gas canisters back at the deputies. Inside the plant, workers rained down a fusillade of car-door hinges using makeshift slingshots and turned high-pressure water hoses against their attackers. The goons and deputies retreated, and the so-called "Battle of the Running bulls" ended in victory for the strikers and the WEB. (*Bull* was a slang term for policeman.)

As a result of the incident, Murphy authorized stationing 1,500 National Guard troops around the plant, but refused GM's calls to have them evict strikers. GM was beginning to feel the pinch, as weekly production fell from over 6,100 cars to just 3,800. Yet it continued to play hardball; UAW workers were beaten in Anderson, Indiana, and several other locales, and Travis, the Reuthers, and several others were charged with inciting a riot. All the while, UAW sign-ups soared. On January 16, it looked as if an agreement had been reached, but, at the last minute, GM reneged on its promise to recognize the UAW.

Flint workers once again forced GM to act. The UAW decided to occupy Chevrolet Number 4 on February 1, as it was essential in Chevy production. Knowing their ranks were filled with stool pigeons, Walter Reuther, Travis, and a few others discussed taking Chevrolet Number 9 instead. As expected, GM guards were out in force at Number 9. Workers inside feigned a takeover and gave the UAW the needed time to occupy Number 4. Governor Murphy was furious about the deception, and authorized another 1,200 guardsmen, who briefly cut off power and food supplies. But services were restored when Walter Reuther threatened to light bonfires inside the plant to ward off the winter's chill. Nor did Governor Murphy execute a new court order requiring the UAW to vacate all buildings by February 3.

With its production down to just 1,500 cars per week and dividends slashed by 50 percent, GM relented. On February 11, GM and the UAW struck an agreement, and workers left the plants behind a marching band, singing lusty choruses of "Solidarity Forever," and enjoyed a citywide celebration. The UAW was still in a precarious situation. Its agreement with GM was only for six months, and the union was not recognized as the sole bargaining agent for GM workers. Moreover, the agreement only covered seventeen of GM's sixty-nine plants. The UAW gambled that Flint would be a symbolic victory that would increase its strength, and that proved to be the case. Still, it took several years of hard negotiations and new strikes before all GM workers could opt for the UAW, and the union also had to negotiate with Chrysler and Ford, the latter of which was not organized until 1941.

The immediate aftermath of the Flint strike was electric. Workers across the nation were inspired by the UAW's victory. Between late 1936 and the end of 1937, nearly half a million workers sat down; their occupations ranged from rubber workers to Woolworth's clerks. The Steel Workers Organizing Committee was especially energized by Flint, and union-resistant steel soon found itself organized. The strike also made the CIO into a legitimate alternative to the AFL and catapulted John L. Lewis into the national limelight.

Historians and union activists have debated the long-term significance of the Flint strike, especially since the 1980s, when labor unions began to lose strength. To some, the contemporary labor movement needs to rekindle the militancy of the sit-down strikers, and they call upon today's workers to replicate the latter's willingness to defy court orders, public opinion, and corporate might. Many historians are less sanguine. Courts ruled the sit-down strike illegal in 1939, and success at Flint also took place within a specific political context in which national New Deal leaders and elected Michigan officials refrained from using state power against workers. Such conditions, argue the critics, are unlikely to be duplicated, and labor unions would do well to stop dwelling on the past. Regardless of the conclusions one draws, the General Motors Sit-Down Strike was a key moment in American history and a memorial to the bravery and persistence of the men and women who took part in it.

Suggested Readings: Sidney Lens, *The Labor Wars: From the Molly Maguires to the Sitdowns*, 1974; Nelson Lichtenstein, *Walter Reuther: The Most Dangerous Man in Detroit*, 1995; Victor Reuther, *The Brothers Reuther and the Story of the UAW: A Memoir*, 1976.

Robert E. Weir

General Strike. A general strike is defined as the organized withdrawal of labor by workers in a multitude of industries at the same time. By this definition, numerous nineteenth-century American work stoppages qualify as general strikes. However, the term acquired a more specific meaning with the rise of **anarcho-syndicalism**. Within the United States, general strikes became increasingly associated with larger purposes such as the "abolition of the **wage** system" or the "downfall of **capitalism**." A general strike involves a paralysis of sizable segments of the economy and society, and violence has been a common—but not omnipresent—element of most general strikes. Among revolutionaries, the overall aim of a general strike is nothing less than a mass overthrow of existing social, economic, and political institutions.

Most major general strikes, including the 1886 general strike centered in Chicago that culminated in the tragic **Haymarket** affair, the 1919 Seattle general strike, and the 1934 San Francisco general strike, reflected social and political issues that superseded the workplace and wages. Even when general strikes do not result in revolutionary upheaval, they generally involve such large numbers and diverse alliances that they disrupt society to a much greater degree than conventional actions involving a single union.

The general strike waves extending from the late nineteenth century through the first three decades of the twentieth century did not continue in the post–World War II United States. The meaning of a general strike since then has become less clear, with some observers applying it to industrywide stoppages. General strikes are infrequent in the United States, but those taking place throughout the world attest to the fact that general strikes remain a possibility.

Suggested Readings: Jeremy Brecher, *Strike!* 1997; Georges Sorel, *Reflections on Violence*, 1908; "The General Strike," http://bari.iww.org/culture/official/strike/index.shtml.

Alex Corlu

George, Henry (September 2, 1839–October 29, 1897). Henry George was a journalist, reformer, social philosopher, economist, Irish nationalist, and labor advocate. Among nineteenth-century figures, few had the influence of Henry George. He was born in Philadelphia, the second of ten children to Richard S. H. and Catherine (Vallance) George. He was raised in a fervent Protestant household, left school at age fourteen, and worked as a clerk for two years, before signing on as a cabin boy for an around-the-world voyage on the *Hindoo*. He kept a detailed account of his travels and later won acclaim for his writings. He returned to Philadelphia in 1857, and briefly worked as a typesetter before setting sail again in 1858. Later that year he disembarked in San Francisco, where he worked for several newspapers and the local Democratic Party. An independent publishing venture failed, and George and his wife, the former Annie Fox, whom he married in 1861, were deeply in debt. A political appointment as a gas-meter inspector rescued George.

The job also afforded George the opportunity to complete his seminal book, *Progress and Poverty* (1879). When no publishing house would print the work,

George scraped together resources to self-publish 500 copies. The book suggested the abolition of all taxes except a single-tax on the unearned increments on land. George attacked the rising trend of land speculation, advocated setting aside land for actual settlers, and called for a 100 percent tax on land value increases due to social advances rather than improvements made by its owners. George believed that such a tax would generate sufficient revenues to fund needed social reforms and would obviate the need for any other taxes.

This cartoon comments on Henry George's 1886 third-party campaign for the office of mayor of New York City. George, surrounded by his various writings and proposals, is seated on the left. © George Meany Memorial Archives.

George's attack on landlords and speculation struck a responsive chord on the heels of the economic depression of 1873 through 1878. *Progress and Poverty* went through numerous printings and made George an international celebrity. He moved to New York in 1880, joined the **Knights of Labor**, and immersed himself in politics. His travels to Ireland and England in 1881 and 1882 led to blistering articles attacking English landlords that won him the admiration of the Irish American community. In 1884, George published *Social Problems* and, in 1886, *Free Trade*. Although the latter work cooled the ardor of some **protectionism**-minded labor reformers, the labor community wholeheartedly endorsed his 1886 third-party bid for New York City's mayoralty. He polled more than one-third of the total vote and outdistanced the Republican candidate (Theodore Roosevelt), but fell short to Democrat Abram Hewitt. His United Labor Party briefly challenged two-party hegemony in many communities.

In 1888 and 1889, George again traveled to Great Britain and, in 1890, he visited Australia and New Zealand, where his single-tax proposal spawned numerous social experiments and government policies. He returned home in 1891 and suffered a stroke. He nonetheless continued to write and lecture. He published a synopsis of his theories in *The Science of Political Economy* in 1897. In that year, the ailing George made another quixotic bid to become mayor of New York. He died of a stroke a week before the election and his son, Henry Jr., polled only 22,000 votes, though over 100,000 people were said to have attended his father's funeral. Although George's single-tax plan never came to pass in its entirety, his thoughts and writings inspired countless laborers in the Gilded Age and influenced Progressive Era and New Deal reform movements.

Suggested Readings: Charles Barker, *Henry George*, 1955; Steven Cord, *Henry George: Dreamer or Realist?* 1965; Special Issue Commemorating the 100th Anniversary of the Death of Henry George, *The American Journal of Economics and Sociology* 56:4 (October 1997) pp. 385–683.

Teri Voight

Robert E. Weir

Glass Ceiling. The term glass ceiling refers to barriers that prevent women and minority groups from advancing in their occupations. It is dubbed a "glass" ceiling because those who encounter it are aware of the customs and discriminatory practices that impede their upward mobility. In essence, they can "see" what's above them, but find it difficult to "shatter" the barrier. Many complain that they are better qualified than those above them. In some cases, those below the glass ceiling actually trained their future supervisors. The earliest known coinage of the phrase was by Henry Bradford Smith in 1932, in a review article about geometry and inductive reasoning. It appears to have been given its current meaning by a 1984 *Adweek* magazine article and passed into the common vernacular shortly thereafter.

Skilled positions and management have been dominated by white males since colonial times, but social changes after World War II have challenged that hegemony. Both the civil rights and women's movements stimulated important legal changes that opened society to those once marginalized. The 1963 **Equal Pay Act** stipulated that those who do the same job must receive identical pay. The 1964 Civil Rights Act tore down most of the remaining racist **Jim Crow** barriers that excluded people of color, and Title VII of that bill extended civil-rights protections to women. **Affirmative action** programs forced employers to consider women and minorities when hiring and promoting staff. Other **protective labor legislation** mandated further changes.

By the 1960s, women and minority groups could be found in many occupations historically considered reserved for white males. It soon became apparent, though, that the penetration of said groups into the workplace was shallow, and groups complained that tokenism circumvented substantive social change. This was especially apparent at the upper levels of work. A 1986 survey of Fortune 1000 industrial firms and Fortune 500 service corporations revealed that 95 percent of all senior managers were male and that 97 percent of them were white. Of the remaining 5 percent who were female, 95 percent of them were also white. These percentages have changed only slightly since then, despite the fact that by the mid-1990s, 45 percent of the workforce was female and a mere one-third was male and white.

The 1991 Civil Rights Act established the Federal Glass Ceiling Commission to study ways to redress the imbalances, but has had only modest success. A 1996 report indicated that female managers and chief executives work as many hours as their male counterparts, but receive on average only two-thirds as much compensation. As of 1999, women workers averaged seventy-four cents for every dollar earned by males. Studies further indicate that women and minorities usually only advance in large firms by adopting the management styles of entrenched white males. The record is better with smaller firms where women controlled some 40 percent of small businesses by the year 2000.

In principle, most labor unions oppose the glass ceiling, though they have been selectively active in countering it. Many union hierarchies mirror business in being dominated by white males. Even "progressive" unions like the **United Auto Workers** have been rocked by challenges from **rank-and-file** women and minorities. Groups like the **Coalition of Labor Union Women** have worked hard to increase the number of women in union leadership ranks, while civil rights groups have applied pressure to increase representation for people of color. Unions have fought hard in recent years to eliminate wage discrimination, but do not see it as their issue when it involves decisions on the management level.

Suggested Readings: Nancy Gabin, *Feminism in the Labor Movement: Women and the United Auto Workers, 1935–1975*, 1990; Ann Weiss, *The Glass Ceiling: A Look at Women in the Workforce*, 1999; Glass Ceiling Research Center, http://www.glass-ceiling.com/.

Robert E. Weir

Globalization. Globalization occurs when a business or company begins operating at an international level. In modern **capitalism**, globalization has become the new norm, supplanting older arrangements whereby production of goods and services took place within specific national boundaries. Globalization has posed big problems for American unions, many of which lack the resources to undertake transnational organizing campaigns.

The global economy is dominated by large, elite corporations. These companies are the backbone of the economy, restructuring production and distribution, while moving jobs and money aggressively around the world. Corporations are looking for the cheapest and least-regulated means of labor. From a labor perspective, the fundamental struggle of globalization is securing basic worker rights, environmental and consumer protection, workplace health and safety, and antitrust and financial regulations that restrain corporations. In practice, massive industrialization produces wealth and power for corporations, but displaces farmers and workers.

During World War I and through the 1920s, advances in science and technology changed the world in dramatic ways. The combination of tight labor markets and a rising threat of unionization led many large corporations to establish professional personnel departments under the guise of scientific management **(Taylorism)**. Personnel departments were established to assist management in avoiding union challenges and in reorganizing work by tying a worker's **wage** to output. Management's function was to design and supervise the job, compensate the workforce, and eliminate conflicts between workers and employers. A corporate **open-shop** movement sought to discourage unionization by expanding **pensions**, profit-sharing, and other **fringe benefits**. These "corporate welfare" programs faltered during the Great Depression, and the New Deal and World War II brought about new capital/labor arrangements.

Nonetheless, key components of globalization were already in place. Technology, such as the assembly line, increased efficiency while breaking the production process into simple one-step components that deskilled workers could perform. Industrial unions sought to organize production and maintenance workers in all industries, regardless of their skill level or craft, thereby offering a counter to management initiatives, but corporations continued to seek greater control over the production process to maximize production at the cheapest possible labor cost. Moreover, long-standing international trade networks facilitated the movement of goods around the globe. Prior to the 1970s, the usual practice of American business was to shift jobs domestically, moving operations from unionized high-wage regions to **right-to-work** states. A 1976 change in the tax code encouraged businesses to move operations outside of the United States. Tax credits were given for companies setting up divisions in U.S. possessions like Puerto Rico. Corporations were able to dodge heavy taxes on subsidiaries while writing off losses on aging American operations. Runaway inflation and the stagnating economy of the 1970s flooded the American market with cheaper imports, while loosened tax codes allowed more overseas investment under the guise of making American companies more competitive.

The steady stream of capital flight became a flood in the 1980s, when the Reagan administration revamped the tax code, launched an assault against business regulations, and privatized many state-owned enterprises. Moreover, favorable tax laws even allowed foreign investors to set up American subsidiaries that paid lower taxes than U.S.-based companies. American firms increasingly shifted operations to low-wage nations to compete in the global economy.

Based on the continued imbalance of power between corporations and workers, the **American Federation of Labor–Congress of Industrial Organizations (AFL-CIO)** aggressively seeks to organize on both the national and international level to bring a power balance to the international economy. This has proved a daunting task. New technology, a changing workforce, outsourcing, **subcontracting**, and moving businesses out of the country mean that United States workers no longer have job security. Unions are further challenged by transnational trade agreements like the **North American Free Trade Agreement** among the United States, Canada, and Mexico. Globalization has given rise to an increasing rate of **child labor** worldwide, while eliminating jobs for workers in the United States. This is seen in Northern Mariana Islands, where products are produced outside the continental states but bear the "Made in the USA" label. Workers are paid very little and have poor working conditions. The AFL-CIO seeks to challenge the new internationalism with global solidarity, which would benefit workers around the world and hold corporations accountable for the use of child labor, wages, and working conditions. To date, its campaign has been largely rhetorical, though global campaigns like the one conducted during the 1990–92 **Ravenswood lockout** dispute show promise.

Suggested Readings: Donald Bartlett and James Steele, *America: What Went Wrong?* 1993; Andy Crump and Wayne Ellwood, *The A to Z of World Development*, 1999; Barry Lynn, "Unmade in America: The True Cost of a Global Assembly Line," *Harper's* (June 2002): 33–41; Jo-Ann Mort, *Not Your Father's Union Movement*, 1998.

Danielle McMullen

Goldman, Emma (June 27, 1869–May 14, 1940). Emma Goldman was one of the most feared radicals of the early twentieth century. She was the editor of *Mother Earth*, an anarchist journal she established in 1906. Goldman was a professional agitator and lecturer for the anarchist cause. She worked as a garment worker, a writer, an editor, and a publisher, but was best known for her fiery speeches and powerful lectures on **anarchism**.

She was born in Kovno, Russia (Kaunas in modern Lithuania), the daughter of Abraham and Tuave Goldman. Her family moved their family to St. Petersburg in 1881, and Emma left school to work in a factory. There, she suffered sexual abuse that colored her view of male and female relationships for the rest of her life. She was also introduced to radical politics while in St. Petersburg. When she was fifteen, Goldman joined a sister who had already settled in Rochester, New York. Goldman quickly realized that the life awaiting a poor, Jewish immigrant in the United States was one of toil, **sweatshops**, and slums. She turned to anarchism in the wake of the **Haymarket** Riot of 1886, and later claimed she became an anarchist the day the convicted were hanged.

At twenty, Goldman moved to New York City and became the protégé of Johann Most, editor of a German anarchist newspaper. Through her anarchist education, Goldman decried the workers' fight for an eight-hour workday and instead called for overturning **capitalism**. Unsatisfied with Most's beliefs, Goldman distanced herself and studied the writings of Peter Kropotkin. His writings helped Goldman develop beliefs in the individual and of self-expression. She was an early and strident advocate for free speech, free love, personal freedom, birth control, and women's equality. Goldman took numerous lovers, and her personal life shocked conservatives almost as much as her ideology.

In 1892, she and fellow anarchist Alexander Berkman planned the assassination of Henry Clay Frick, who had suppressed the **Homestead** Steel **lockout**. Goldman and Berkman both believed that violence was necessary in achieving widespread social change, and hoped that Frick's death would raise comrades-in-arms. The assassination attempt failed. Although Goldman escaped detection, she was imprisoned on numerous occasions for causes like distributing illegal birth-control literature, advocating that hungry workers take bread by force, and for establishing "No Conscription" leagues during World War I. Goldman often coordinated her free-speech battles to coincide with campaigns led by the **Industrial Workers of the World** and was briefly a member of that organization. Roger Baldwin, founder of the American Civil Liberties Union, acknowledged Goldman as a civil liberties tutor.

Goldman and Berkman were arrested for obstruction of the draft, stripped of their citizenship, and deported to Russia in 1919. It is reported that J. Edgar Hoover, who directed Goldman's deportation hearing, referred to her as "one of the most dangerous women in America."

In Russia, Goldman quickly grew disenchanted by the Bolshevik Revolution. She considered it a counterrevolution and penned her dismay in *My Disillusionment in Russia*, followed by *My Further Disillusionment in Russia*. She left Russia in 1921, moved briefly to Berlin, lectured in Great Britain, and wrote her autobiography, *Red Emma Speaks*. Goldman married a Welsh miner in 1925 so that she would not be deported. With a British passport in hand, Goldman traveled to Canada and across Europe to agitate on behalf of anarchism. She was allowed only one brief visit to the United States in 1934.

At the age of sixty-seven and in the aftermath of Berkman's suicide, Goldman went to Spain to support the Republican cause during the Spanish Civil War. Attempts to regain permanent entry into the United States failed, and Goldman died in Toronto, where she was aiding Spanish refugees. She is buried in Chicago.

Goldman represents the revolutionary pole of the labor political spectrum. She was convinced that no worker could ever be free under capitalism and devoted her life to denouncing that system and calling for its overthrow. She remains a controversial figure even within the radical movement, and was accused of various deeds and plots in which she probably had no hand.

Suggested Readings: Candace Falk, *Love, Anarchy, and Emma Goldman*, 1990; Emma Goldman, *Living My Life*, 1931; Alice Wexler, *Emma Goldman in America*, 1988.

Cristina Prochilo

Gompers, Samuel (January 27, 1850–December 13, 1924). Samuel Gompers was one of the founders and the first president of the **American Federation of Labor (AFL)**. Gompers was born to a **working-class**, Dutch Jewish immigrant family in London, England. His father, Solomon, was a cigar maker. The family's difficult financial circumstances led them, with financial assistance from Solomon's union, to emigrate to America in 1863. In New York City, Samuel initially worked alongside his father, rolling cigars in their Lower East Side tenement. By 1865, Gompers entered the cigar factory as a skilled worker. It was customary for cigar shops to have a "reader," one worker who read aloud while the others worked. In this atmosphere, Gompers became acquainted with political and social issues, the condition of labor, and the works of labor advocates such as Karl Marx and Ira Steward. Gompers joined with others, "the ten philosophers," who met after work to continue their discussions, particularly those involving trade unionism, **socialism**, and politics.

Gompers witnessed firsthand the influence of technology on work processes. Mechanized equipment was developed to replace the skilled hand cigar makers. Employers were eager to employ the new equipment by which workers were effectively deskilled, and workers were determined to resist. Gompers and his fellow cigar maker and local union leader, Adolph Strasser, saw the inevitability of increasingly mechanized production and sought out ways of maintaining union strength in the face of technological challenge. When Strasser became president of the national union in 1877, he and Gompers sought to strengthen the Cigarmakers International Union (CMIU) by introducing plans to provide for unemployment, sick relief, assistance in traveling in search of work, **strike** funds under the administration of the national, higher **dues** structures, and centralized control of the CMIU. These policies allowed the national union to exert power over the **locals** and dampen the influence of **rank-and-file** workers.

Samuel Gompers in 1905. © George Meany Memorial Archives.

Following the **Tompkins Square Riot**, Gompers grew convinced of the vulnerability of the labor movement. He abandoned his active socialism and embraced the idea that only through strong national unions, and not through autonomous but weak locals, could organized labor survive the onslaught of hostile employers, courts, and politicians. Convinced that workers must achieve class consciousness to bring about political action or social change effectively, Gompers and others founded the Federation of Organized Trades and Labor Unions (FOTLU) in 1881 in Pittsburgh. Gompers, as president, sought to exclude all but skilled workers and to minimize the influence of the dominant national union of the time, the **Knights of Labor**. In 1886, the FOTLU was transformed into the American Federation of Labor with Gompers as president, a position he would hold every year except one until his death. Unlike the Knights, the new organization sought to attract only skilled craft workers, and to distance itself, in the wake of the **Haymarket** incident, from the popular image of labor unions as centers for radicals, **anarchists**, and assassins. The new organization affirmed the principle of **voluntarism**, by which it meant both the autonomy of individual national unions and their right to join (or to leave) the federation, and the need for workers themselves, acting through their unions and employers, to establish specific conditions in the workplace. Gompers rejected the role of government interference in industrial relations.

Workers themselves, he believed, must solve their own problems. In the AFL, the national unions had **jurisdiction** within their own crafts and were regarded as independent of influence from either other national unions or the AFL itself. Thus Gompers's job as president was not to be an authoritarian leader, but to use his powers of speech, persuasion, diplomacy, and organization to achieve a positive public image for labor unions. Gompers did this by tirelessly traveling, writing, and speaking to foster a positive reputation for the labor movement, and to urge workers to organize and join unions. Part of the image of labor unions that Gompers sought to project was one of institutions free of socialist influence. Thus, in the wake of the **Pullman Strike** of 1894, Gompers publicly rebuffed **Eugene V. Debs**, whose affection he had previously cultivated. While this cost Gompers the support of a segment of the labor movement and was, in part, responsible for his one-year loss of the AFL presidency, in the long run, AFL membership grew under Gompers's administration.

By 1904, AFL unions boasted 1.7 million members. Gompers sought acceptance of the labor movement nationally by allying himself with the chiefs of the country's largest corporations who served on the **National Civic Federation (NCF)**, a group that labeled itself as a business reform organization. NCF members pledged themselves to such social welfare plans as employee stock-option plans and company pension plans, while still avowing the principles of management's right to set conditions of employment. Gompers justified his cooperation with the NCF in terms of the advantages it provided by giving labor access to, and influence with, the captains of industry. Gompers saw the NCF as a vehicle for promoting mediation in industrial disputes, but the industrialist members, while tolerant in general toward the principle of mediation, resisted employing this principle in their own establishments.

In addition to seeking influence with industrialists, Gompers gradually abandoned his earlier avoidance of partisan political commitment. Gompers sought support from both Republican and Democratic leaders, but, by 1912, he had allied himself with the Democratic Party under President Woodrow Wilson. The alliance seemed to pay off for labor when a series of issues that had long troubled labor was addressed in the **La Follette Seamen's Act of 1915**, the **Adamson Act** of 1916, and the legislation which Gompers referred to as "Labor's Magna Carta," the **Clayton Anti-Trust Act** of 1914. The Clayton Act provided apparent protection for labor from prosecution under the **Sherman Act of 1890** as a conspiracy in restraint of trade. By 1917, 2.4 million workers were members of AFL unions, and the AFL's support for no-strike pledges during World War I further cemented the alliance between labor and the Wilson administrations. Gompers strongly supported the war effort and refused to tolerate antiwar sentiment within the union movement. He welcomed the **National War Labor Board (NWLB)** as a vehicle for assuring labor peace and uninterrupted wartime production. The board openly acknowledged labor's right to organize, and unions used the wartime détente imposed by the NWLB to increase union membership to four million by war's end. Gompers used the board to increase his own personal influence and the clout of organized labor, both of which reached their high-water mark by the end of the war. Following the war, though, employers were anxious to reassert their prewar autonomy and reverse the gains made by labor during the war. With Woodrow Wilson's death and the election of Republican Warren G. Harding, the favorable climate in Washington evaporated, and Gompers spent the last years of his life fighting to halt a precipitous decline in union membership and increased employer hostility toward unions. Gompers's one success with the Harding administration was the use of what little influence he then had to bring about a pardon for his onetime friend, then nemesis, Eugene V. Debs, who had been imprisoned for his antiwar activities. Samuel Gompers died on December 13, 1924. Except for one year out of office, he had been the only president that the AFL had known since its founding.

Suggested Readings: Philip Taft, *The AFL in the Time of Gompers*, 1957; Gerald Emanuel Stearn, ed., *Gompers*, 1971.

James P. Hanlan

Goon. A stock character in labor history, a goon is a hired thug. A goon works to intimidate, terrorize, and, if necessary, harm or kill his target. He may be working for organized crime, for management, for corrupt unionists to coerce dissidents, or for the government at the behest of big business. Goons are always hired mercenaries beholden only to their employers. They have been a staple of American industrial strife, which has produced the bloodiest conflicts in the history of industrial democracies.

Goons of the Ford Service Division beat a striker during a 1937 strike against the Ford Motor Company. © George Meany Memorial Archives/AP Wide World Photos.

The term has been applied to hired guards like **Pinkerton** detectives, and to squads of strong-armed temporary employees hired by unscrupulous employers to beat up picketing workers and union organizers. It came into wider circulation due to reports issued by the 1937 **La Follette Sub-Committee** on Violation of Civil Liberties. Goons have been visible in such ongoing conflicts as the attempts to organize Ford Motors from 1937 to 1941, but much of their nefarious activity has taken place in remote mining and mill towns further from media attention. Goons continue to harass organizers and strikers, though the term is seldom used in contemporary society, and intimidation methods tend to be more subtle.

Suggested Reading: James David Horan and Howard Swiggett, *The Pinkerton Story*, 1951.

Simon Holzapfel

Granite Workers. Granite workers have fought important, though often underappreciated, battles to improve the lives of stoneworkers in the United States. Although coal mining has received the bulk of attention from labor historians, granite and marble workers have been at the fore of campaigns against silicosis, a deadly lung disease. The struggles of granite workers parallel those of others who have attracted less scholarly attention, including marble workers, glassworkers, construction blast crews, and others who breathe air laden with particulates.

Granite workers have generally been better organized than marble workers, though work was similar within the industries. Granite was a key building material for public structures from the early-nineteenth through the mid-twentieth centuries. Numerous unions emerged within an industry whose constituent parts break down into numerous categories, including quarrying, cutting, carving, and polishing. One of the earliest unions to appear was the Granite Cutters' National Union, which was formed in 1877, and established its headquarters in Quincy, Massachusetts. In 1905, it changed its name to the Granite Cutters' International Association (GCIA). The GCIA represented carvers, cutters, and polishers. It was an early leader in protesting prison labor and took that battle to Texas in 1885, when it learned that the new state capitol was being built in part by prisoners. The GCIA received a charter from the **American Federation of Labor (AFL)** in 1888, but quit the organization two years later when the AFL tried to impose an assessment to support the carpenters' union's battle for an eight-hour day. At the time, the GCIA complained that the carpenters were stealing jobs from GCIA members. The GCIA rejoined the AFL in 1895, and in 1900, the AFL supported the granite cutters in their own battle for an eight-hour day.

The quarry workers who blasted the stone from the pits also formed unions. Many of them joined forces in 1903 to create the Quarry Workers International Union of North America (QW), with headquarters in Barre, Vermont. The QW also joined the AFL. Marble workers were less successful in their efforts, though the **Knights of Labor** briefly organized the sheds and pits around Rutland, Vermont, in the late 1880s.

From the outset, stoneworkers faced daunting obstacles. Quarries were often owned by self-made entrepreneurs who were loath to deal with unions. Many enterprises were small, and competition was fierce. This made owners reluctant to invest in either expensive equipment to improve safety for quarrymen or dust ventilation systems for polishing and carving sheds. The granite cutters was probably the first union in the United States to win sick-leave benefits for its members, but that was cold comfort in an industry where, in the early twentieth century, the average age at death for carvers and cutters in Barre, Vermont, was forty-two.

Both the GCIA and QW organized workers as far away as Indiana, Kansas, Missouri, and Texas, though their strength was usually in the Northeast, especially Vermont, Maine, New Hampshire, and New York. Stoneworkers belied AFL assumptions that immigrant workers were difficult to organize. By 1900, only the textile industry could rival stoneworkers for ethnic diversity. Much of the industry in the Northeast was established by Scots in the 1870s, but within two decades there were also myriad Italians, Spaniards, Germans, Norwegians, Swedes, Finns, French Canadians, Poles, and others. Politics helped establish a cross-ethnic class identity, with many immigrants holding **socialist** or **anarchist** beliefs. By 1900, more than 90 percent of all Barre stoneworkers were unionized. Many stoneworker families in Quincy and Barre took in children from Lawrence, Massachusetts, during the famed 1912 "Bread and Roses" **strike**.

Worker solidarity was tested sorely after World War I when the **open shop** movement spread to the stone industry. Workers who had only gained a forty-four-hour workweek in 1914 found themselves facing longer hours and renewed antiunion sentiment on the part of larger employers within a consolidating industry. Unsuccessful strikes in 1922 and 1933 further curtailed GCIA and QW demands for higher **wages** and improved health standards. Although silicosis was recognized as an occupational disease in 1917, and states passed bills to reduce the amount of dust inhaled by workers, ventilation systems within the stone industry proved inadequate.

Quarry workers expressed their frustration with conservative AFL leaders. Many within the QW felt they received little support in their attempts to organize marble workers. In 1938, the QW left the AFL for the new **Congress of Industrial Organizations**. In 1940, it changed its name to the United Stone and Allied Products Workers of North America (USAPW). The USAPW continued to press for improved safety conditions and engaged in periodic strikes, usually localized and of brief duration. In 1971, the USAPW was absorbed into the **United Steel Workers of America**, and is today an affiliate of the AFL-CIO.

The GCIA continued as an AFL union. Some locals, like those throughout Vermont, unsuccessfully struck for a seven-hour day in 1952. The Northeast granite industry was also struck in 1970 and 1980. Technological changes led to a contraction of employment throughout the stone industry and, in the early 1980s, the GCIA and most of its locals merged with other groups to form the Tile, Marble, Terrazzo, and Granite Cutters Union. It, in turn, was absorbed into Brotherhood of Carpenters and Joiners in the 1990s. Two 1996 Supreme Court decisions *(Acme Tile and Terrazzo Company v. NLRB* and *Roman Tile and Terrazzo Company v. NLRB)* dealt a serious blow to organizing efforts by ruling against closed shop provisions in several **contracts**.

Despite recent challenges in the industry, stone workers achieved great success in calling attention to the dangers of silicosis and played a key role in pressing for national legislation to control dust. Their efforts culminated in important legislation like the 1969 Mine Safety and Health Act, and the 1970 **Occupational Safety and Health Act**.

Today, the bulk of stonework is in memorials, building trim, and curbs. There are fewer workers within the industry now than in the early twentieth century. Some former GCIA locals, including those in Barre, Vermont, resented the high per capita taxes associated with the AFL-CIO and disaffiliated in 1986. There are numerous small unions among granite workers that are independent of the AFL-CIO.

Participants in a farmworkers demonstration against California grape growers. The grape boycotts of the 1960s and 1970s led to the formation and growth of the United Farmworkers of America (UFW). © Ted Streshinsky/Corbis.

Suggested Readings: Public Occurrence, *Vermont's Untold History*, 1976; David Rosner and Gerald Markovitz, *Deadly Dust: Silicosis and the Politics of Occupational Disease in the Twentieth Century*, 1994; Philip Taft, *The A.F. of L. in the Time of Gompers*, 1957.

Robert E. Weir

Grape Boycott. The grape boycott was a series of actions taken by California farmworkers to publicize the plight of workers. The first **boycott** of 1965 to 1970 was the signal event that led to the formation of the **United Farm Workers of America (UFW)** and catapulted UFW leader **Cesar Chavez** to international fame.

The grape boycott began as disputes between California grape growers in the Delano/Bakersfield area and Filipino pickers complaining of low wages, horrendous sanitary conditions, a lack of potable water in the fields, and brutal conditions. Most of the workers were American citizens, but their wages were lower than those of guest *braceros* still working in the fields, despite the official termination of that program a year earlier. On September 8, 1965, Filipino workers organized in the **Agricultural Workers Organizing Committee (AWOC)** struck nine California farms. An attempt to import Chicano **scabs** backfired when Chavez convinced his National Farm Workers Association (NFWA) to support the **strike**. By September 20, pickers on more than thirty farms were out.

The strike was marked by violence on the part of growers, but the AWOC and the NFWA used tactics of passive resistance en vogue in the African American civil rights movement and studiously practiced by the deeply religious Chavez. Chavez was able to convince numerous Roman Catholic clerics and Protestant ministers to join the cause. Violence against strikers and the arrests of peaceful pickets galvanized support for the workers.

Chavez and **Dolores Huerta** convinced the NFWA/AWOC coalition to call for a boycott of California grapes. Chavez proved a skilled grassroots organizer, and soon boycott support chapters crisscrossed the United States. Chavez also held a fast and a 340-mile march from Delano to Sacramento to call attention to the farmworkers' cause. Churches, citizens' groups, student organizations, and social activists pressured local supermarkets to stop carrying grapes until the growers settled. The first to do so were corporate giants Schenley and DiGiorgio, who settled in the spring of 1966. In August, the NFWA and the AWOC officially merged and the United Farm Workers was born. It took nearly five years to bring most growers into compliance, at which time the grape boycott was called off. The UFW then stood at its peak membership of around 80,000 members. The events of 1965 to 1970 stand as one of the most successful uses of the boycott tactic in American labor history.

The UFW called two more grape boycotts whose achievements were more modest. In 1972 and 1973, the UFW renewed its grape boycott to call attention to growers who were still not in compliance with UFW demands, as well as to protest the **raiding** practices of the **International Brotherhood of Teamsters**. Still a third boycott lasted from 1984 to 2000 to call attention to pesticide dangers that cause cancers and miscarriages among farmworkers. The third boycott began with a flourish, but passed from public awareness as it lingered. Chavez's death in 1993 also diverted attention from the boycott. By the time it was called off in 2000, some UFW activists questioned whether the boycott remained an effective tactic. Nonetheless, in 2002, the UFW announced a boycott of Pictsweet mushrooms.

Suggested Readings: Susan Ferriss, Ricardo Sandoval, and Diana Hembree, *The Fight in the Fields: Cesar Chavez and the Farmworkers' Movement*, 1998; Patrick H. Mooney and Theo J. Majka, *Farmers' and Farmworkers' Movements: Social Protest in American Agriculture*, 1995; "The 1965 Grape Boycott: A Case Study in Strategy," http://www.lib.berkeley.edu/~ljones/UFW/.

Robert E. Weir

Great Labor Uprising. The Great Labor Uprising is the name historians and commentators use to refer to a two-week railroad **strike** in numerous American cities in July 1877. The strike progressed quickly into a popular revolt against the growth of railroads, the excesses of corporate power, and the treatment of workers in an industrializing nation. As the first major national strike in the United States, the uprising was a turning point for American labor. The same railroads that carried eastern markets and industry into western states (and connected the Atlantic and Pacific Oceans in 1869) also fostered a sense of national identity for workers who felt mistreated by their employers. Coming just twelve years after the Civil War ended, the violent uprising shocked business and political leaders and confirmed labor leaders' fears about the collaboration of industry and the state. In the span of two weeks, more than 100 people died in clashes with state militias and federal troops called out to reestablish order and get trains moving again.

The seeds of the strikes were sown in the context of a five-year economic depression that followed the panic of 1873. Amid escalating unemployment and railroad companies' hostility toward trade unions, workers' **grievances** and resentment were ignored. Broader concerns also existed, however; merchants in cities such as Pittsburgh and St. Louis criticized discriminatory railroad rates, and city dwellers throughout the country resented the encroachment of dangerous and inconvenient railroad lines into their busy city streets. Building upon these tensions, the direct cause of the uprising was railroad companies' 10 percent **wage** cuts announced in May, June, and July of 1877.

Strikers drag firemen and engineers from trains during the 1877 railroad strike known as the Great Labor Uprising. © George Meany Memorial Archives/Public Affairs Press.

By the time the Baltimore and Ohio Railroad cut its workers' wages on July 16, railroad workers in many parts of the nation had had enough. The most prominent of the established railroad workers' unions, the **Brotherhood of Locomotive Engineers**, counseled its members to show restraint, stressing that employers and employees ultimately shared the same interests. A new association formed in June 1877, the Trainmen's Union, was unable to mount an effective challenge to the announced wage cuts, and railroad companies took swift action to stop its organizing efforts.

Thus, when groups of workers stopped trains in Baltimore, Maryland, and Martinsburg, West Virginia, on July 16 in response to the wage cuts, they did so without the coordination of a central union. Trains in both cities ground to a halt as firemen, brakemen, and engineers acted locally to express their dissatisfaction to their employers. The states' governors ordered troops to restore service, but local militia soldiers sympathized with strikers. Their defection prompted President Rutherford B. Hayes to send federal troops on July 18. The next morning, trainmen in Pittsburgh blocked the railroad lines leading out of the city. Pennsylvania's governor ordered National Guard troops from

Philadelphia to clear the way for rail traffic. The resulting confrontation between strike supporters and Philadelphia troops left scores of dead and wounded Pittsburghers and a city under the control of an outraged crowd. In Pittsburgh alone, protestors destroyed thirty-nine buildings and over 1,000 train cars and engines owned by the Pennsylvania Railroad Company.

From the intense but isolated struggles in Martinsburg, Baltimore, and Pittsburgh, the strike spread quickly westward, creating a variety of popular protests in Chicago, St. Louis, and San Francisco. In Chicago, deadly battles raged on July 26, between workers and an assortment of police officers, militia soldiers, federal troops, and private security forces. In St. Louis, police and federal troops arrested the leaders of a crippling **general strike** coordinated to demand an eight-hour workday. In San Francisco, a gathering of over 8,000 workers that began as a show of solidarity with workers in the East evolved into a protracted assault on the city's Chinese population.

This illustration from the August 11, 1877, issue of *Frank Leslie's Illustrated Newspaper* shows federal cavalry charging railroad strikers in Chicago during the Great Labor Uprising of July 1877. © George Meany Memorial Archives/Chicago Historical Society.

At the height of the uprising, over 100,000 strikers had stopped working nationwide. One contemporary observer noted that the nation's middle class was gripped by a "profound dread of impending ruin" as disturbances jolted city after city. Adding to middle-class fear was the fact that the Workingman's Party of the United States, a loose confederation of Marxist and **Lassallean** socialists, tried to coordinate strike activities in Cincinnati, Chicago, Louisville, New York, and several other cities. Journalists for the nation's major newspapers and magazines treated the waves of strikes as a contagious disease that infected the nation quickly and insidiously.

In each city rocked by protests, security forces managed to regain control of streets and rail yards within several days. By August 1, railroad traffic resumed across the United States under the watchful eyes of state militias and federal soldiers. The uprising left mixed results for American labor. Strikers successfully stopped their employers' practice of wage-cutting, if only temporarily, and many companies attempted to appease their workers with new life insurance and medical relief programs. Other lines, such as the Reading and Pennsylvania Railroads, strengthened their police forces in response to what political and business leaders saw as a threat to state authority and private property. Thomas Scott, the president of the Pennsylvania line, argued that greater federal protection of railroads was necessary if business was to be safeguarded from the masses. For the most part, the mainstream press blamed the strike on communists, **Molly Maguires**, tramps, and immigrant radicals. A spate of National Guard armories rose in American cities, ostensibly to protect the middle class from impending civil insurrection.

For organized labor, July 1877 was a catalyst for decades of heightened political and organizational activity. The strike forced some American workers to see themselves as a class with common interests and needs. More than a fight against a mere cut in wages, the Great Labor Uprising was an acute expression of social and economic defiance that enjoyed broad appeal because its targets—railroads in particular and corporate power in general—transformed life in the United States in often troubling and unbalanced ways.

Suggested Readings: Robert V. Bruce, *1877: Year of Violence*, 1959; Philip S. Foner, *The Great Labor Uprising of 1877*, 1977; David O. Stowell, *Streets, Railroads, and the Great Strike of 1877*, 1999.

Edward Slavishak

Great Upheaval. *Great Upheaval* is a somewhat elusive term used by historians to designate the period between roughly 1885 and 1888 (or 1890) to describe a social climate marked by labor organizing, **strikes**, third-party electoral success, and massive unrest. A few past historians used the term in connection with the 1877 railroad strikes, but most contemporary historians confine its use to the later 1880s. Almost all agree that it was a pivotal period in American history that, in the end, solidified the permanence of industrial **capitalism**.

The signal event of the Great Upheaval occurred in September 1885, when the **Knights of Labor (KOL)** won an unexpected strike victory against Jay Gould and his Southwestern Railway conglomerate. Gould was one of the most-hated robber barons of the Gilded Age, and his capitulation led tens of thousands to join the KOL. KOL membership mushroomed from fewer than 112,000 before the strike to between 729,000 and a million by mid-1886. Although the KOL lost many of its 1885 gains in a new strike during early 1886, the initial victory unleashed pent-up frustrations across the country.

The Great Upheaval reached its zenith in 1886. That year, more than 1,400 strikes took place, idling over 400,000 workers. This posed a dilemma for the KOL, which officially opposed strikes, but its discomfort did little to deter an aroused **working class**. The **eight-hour movement** designated May 1 as a nationwide **general strike** for shorter hours. The world's first **May Day** did not command as much interest as organizers hoped, but it did lead to one of the most traumatic episodes in American history: the **Haymarket** Square bombing in Chicago which resulted in the deaths of eight policemen and an untold number of workers. The wrongful arrests of eight anarchists and the execution of four of them led to massive protests. In the fall, workers cast ballots and working-class candidates running on third-party tickets swept to victory in numerous municipalities. A dozen members of Congress claimed sympathy with the KOL. **Henry George** narrowly lost his bid to become New York City mayor as a United Labor Party (ULP) candidate, but his run inspired a flurry of organizing work on behalf of the ULP. Socialist parties also experienced a surge in membership, while more cautious skilled craftsmen found expression in the newly formed **American Federation of Labor (AFL)**.

Strike pressure mounted in 1887, and some employers granted an eight-hour day rather than face labor's fury. The KOL, however, found itself the victim of a fierce capitalist backlash as it was more concentrated in mass production industries than the AFL. Cash-rich industrialists often precipitated KOL strikes as an excuse to quash the organization. Labor candidates lost ground in the 1887 elections. Industrial capitalists and their political allies succeeded in generating fear among the middle class. In the minds of many, the labor movement was associated with bomb-throwing anarchists, immigrant radicals, violence, and misrule.

By 1888, the tide was turning, though the publication of Edward Bellamy's utopian novel *Looking Backward* inspired myriad **Bellamyite Nationalist** clubs to seek a peaceful means to dismantle capitalism. The Nationalists notwithstanding, the KOL was reeling from strike losses, bitter **jurisdiction** battles with the AFL, internal dissension, a shrinking membership base, financial woes, and negative publicity. Republicans and Democrats frequently cooperated to defeat third-party candidates, while politicians and judges used their powers to stymie workers. By 1890, most third-party officials had lost reelection bids. In that same year, the KOL lost a strike against the New York Central Railroad, eventuating a cascade effect that eviscerated the organization in most Eastern and Midwestern cities.

The Great Upheaval ended in a rout by the forces of organized capital over those of organized labor. Had the tables been turned, subsequent American history would have unfolded quite differently. Despite the collapse of the Great Upheaval, not all was lost. The 1890s was also an unstable decade, with over a thousand strikes per year in the 1890 through 1896 period. Political challenge shifted to rural America where the Populists battled the entrenched two-party system. The decade was also marked by a prolonged financial crisis that lasted from 1893 into 1897. The Great Upheaval, coupled with the crises of the 1890s, did much to convince the urban middle class of the need for social reform. The ensuing Progressive Era was hardly what Great Upheaval activists had in mind, but it did institute needed business regulations, social reforms, and political changes.

Suggested Readings: Leon Fink, *Workingmen's Democracy*, 1983; Bruce Laurie, *Artisans Into Workers*, 1989; Robert E. Weir, *Beyond Labor's Veil*, 1996.

Robert E. Weir

Green, William (May 3, 1870–November 21, 1952). William Green was an important official of the **United Mine Workers of America (UMWA)** and served as the second president of the **American Federation of Labor (AFL)**. Born in Coshocton, Ohio, he was the eldest of the five children of Welsh immigrants Hugh and Jane Oram Green. The son of a miner, Green experienced a poor but secure childhood. Very early in life, Green developed an unshakeable commitment to evangelical Christianity. He most wanted to be a Baptist minister, and religion remained the centerpiece of his union career. He completed eight years of education and was a superior student, but family finances precluded further education or a career in the ministry.

William Green. © George Meany Memorial Archives/Harris & Ewing.

At the age of seventeen, he began a twenty-two-year stint in the mines. In 1892, he married Jenny Mobley, the daughter of a local miner and mother of his six children. Green continued his work in the mines, but gradually became involved in union activities. He joined the Progressive Miners Union in 1886, and remained an active member when it merged with the UMWA in 1891. Green rose rapidly in union leadership, serving as his local's secretary-treasurer, business agent, vice president, and president. This activity enabled him to extol the virtues of Christian idealism and the Social Gospel within union circles.

An unyielding commitment to capital/labor cooperation was the second major principle of Green's union philosophy. Green combined this principle with his dedication to Christian idealism to guide his actions. His rise to higher offices in the Ohio subdistrict of the UMWA led to national stature. In 1909, he was a candidate for the UMWA presidency but lost. In 1910, he was defeated in a bid to become UMWA secretary-treasurer.

Afterward, Green temporarily turned his attention to political office. He was elected to the Ohio State Senate in 1910 and 1912, and served as senate president pro tempore in both terms. An effective legislator, he successfully guided legislation that provided workers' compensation and better safety measures for Ohio miners. He also presented legislation aimed at developing better labor-management relations.

In 1913, Green returned to UMWA activities and was elected national secretary-treasurer. Over the next few years, he combined leadership, ambition, and good fortune to become a major figure in the American labor movement. In 1913, UMWA President John White turned down a position as a vice president on the AFL executive council and offered it to Green. In 1920, **John L. Lewis** became president of the UMWA. Green and Lewis had a problematic working relationship that steadily deteriorated.

Longtime AFL President **Samuel Gompers** died in 1924, touching off a bitter succession battle between Lewis and Matthew Woll of the Photo Engravers' union. Green emerged as a compromise candidate and, in 1925, began a twenty-seven-year stint as AFL president. Green's tenure was as controversial as it was long. He saw himself primarily as a facilitator and servant of the executive committee. Green focused on his lifelong passions of Christian idealism and labor/management cooperation.

As AFL president, Green functioned as a public-relations leader for organized labor, and as a missionary to the nonunion world. Green took his messages to various business groups, churches, and fraternal organizations. He was a dedicated adherent of the free-enterprise system, a rabid anticommunist, and an outspoken patriot. And even though he was personally committed to **industrial unionism** and an active political program, he deferred to the craft union leadership within the AFL.

Green's deference was exacerbated by his general alienation from labor's **rank and file**, especially mass production and unorganized workers. When New Deal legislation provided organized labor with a much-needed catalyst for major organizing drives, Green naively believed that industrial captains would allow unions to organize their workers. Green was strongly opposed to militant organizing campaigns. As a result, the AFL's organizational effort in mass production was uninspired and largely unsuccessful. Militant industrial unionists were expelled from the AFL and formed the separate **Congress of Industrial Organizations (CIO)**. New CIO President John L. Lewis, in turn, expelled Green from the UMWA.

Green had some success in increasing total AFL membership, but as the Great Depression gave way to World War II, he still believed that corporations would cooperate fully with organized labor. He was devastated when conservative business leaders not only refused to work with labor, but also led efforts to pass the Smith-Connally and **Taft-Hartley acts**, that placed greater restrictions on unions. As early as 1939, AFL leaders recognized Green's ineffectiveness and placed increasing responsibility with Secretary-Treasurer **George Meany**, though Green remained president until his death in 1952.

Suggested Readings: Irving Berstein, *The Lean Years: A History of the American Workers, 1920–33*, 1970; Irving Berstein, *The Turbulent Years: A History of the American Worker, 1933–41*, 1969; Craig Phelan, *William Green: Biography of a Labor Leader*, 1989.

R. David Myers

Greenbackism. Greenbackism was a populist movement of various political shades that resulted from the sweeping economic changes, industrialization, and the series of panics and depressions between the 1860s and 1890s. Primary among reformers' concerns was the growing power of monopolies such as railroads and financial institutions. All of these issues were folded into the deceptively simple political goal of financial reform. The term *Greenbackism* denotes the desire to have the nation's money supply be based on paper money (greenbacks). It often fused with the Free Silver Movement, which advocated a silver standard and/or silver combined with greenbacks. Both movements were opposed by the "goldbugs," who desired maintenance of the gold standard and more comprehensive controls on the financial system. The root of the debate lies in differences over how the nation's money supply should be guaranteed. In broad terms, greenbacks and silver systems increase the money supply and favor producers and debtors, while the tighter gold standard reduces the flow of capital, thus favoring lenders and (in theory) consumers. The battle over the nation's money supply spawned numerous third-party movements in the nineteenth century, and was a key idea among **labor parties**.

The roots of the greenback movement lie in the congressional establishment of the national banking system and currency reform during the Civil War to finance the war effort and stimulate commerce and trade. To that end, both Union and Confederate treasuries floated paper money during the war, those in the North being dubbed "greenbacks." After the war, fiscal conservatives wanted to lower the volume of paper money in circulation, reestablish the gold standard, and allow the National Banking System (NBS) to manage currency and credit. (All Confederate debt was repudiated, and its currency declared worthless.) They were opposed by those who felt the NBS established a monopoly over the economy and provided unfair advantages to the financial elite. Greenbackism therefore was about more then just the money system; it was also a movement against financial centralization, big government, monopolies, and chartered corporations. Ideologically, it had its roots in the Jacksonian ideals of small business and free enterprise. Numerous advocates of the **Workingmen's Movement** supported banking and currency reform.

Since it contained many issues, Greenbackism attracted urban labor, small businessmen, farmers, craftsmen, and especially Southerners and Westerners who resented the growing power and influence of the Northeastern establishment. The first Greenback Party was organized by farmers in 1875, but its 1876 presidential candidate was the elderly New York Jacksonian, Peter Cooper. The party also attracted the attention of labor activists like **Ira Steward**, John Siney, George Trevellick, and Uriah Stephens, the founder of the **Knights of Labor (KOL)**. The **National Labor Union** was especially enamored of the greenback cause, with **William Sylvis** openly embracing theories developed by Edward Kellogg in the 1840s to put interest-bearing notes into circulation to break the power of banking monopolies and cause controlled inflation that would benefit farmers.

The post–Civil War Democratic and Republican Parties were in the process of redefining themselves, and both tried to suppress debate on the volatile issue of monetary reform. The Republicans eventually committed to the gold standard, and the Democrats leaned more towards the greenback ideal. However, reformers correctly ascertained that neither party was truly responsive to their concerns. Accordingly, from 1872 through 1896 there were third parties participating in every presidential election and most congressional races. Many of these third parties were local in nature, but several—including the Labor Reform Party, the Antimonopolist Party, the Union Labor Party, and the Greenback Labor Party (GLP)—tried to build national organizations. The GLP was especially successful and, in 1874, elected fourteen members of Congress. In addition, KOL President **Terence Powderly** was elected mayor of Scranton, Pennsylvania, on the GLP ticket. The party's fortunes waned dramatically, however, when the Resumption Act of 1878 recalled Civil War–era paper and returned the United States to the gold standard.

Greenbackism at various times counted everyone from socialists to archconservatives in its ranks. Its popularity fluctuated according to the national economy, with downswings tending to stimulate renewed interest. Greenbackers resurfaced in the mid-1880s under the guise of labor reform, and the KOL endorsed it in principle, though it was fuzzy on specifics. Third parties during the **Great Upheaval** often embraced greenback principles. By the late 1880s, various people's parties formed. Many of them—especially in New York and in the South—attracted a fair amount of support from organized labor as they tended to also endorse the eight-hour day, the establishment of **cooperatives**, mechanics' **lien laws**, and other reforms important to labor unions. Numerous KOL members attended the 1892 convention in Omaha, Nebraska, where a national people's party (Populists) was formed.

By then, the call for greenbacks had been largely subsumed by the Free Silver Movement. At the time, the value of sixteen ounces of silver was equal to one ounce of gold. A move toward silver coinage, advocated especially by farmers and by western states where silver mines proliferated, would essentially cause controlled inflation, thereby driving up the price of commodities. Such a move would have been a boon to farmers seeking to pay off mortgages and bank loans. Some reformers also believed the overall effect would be to break the power of banks and railroads. As logic ran, the economic stranglehold of banks and large corporations allowed them to "buy" political influence; cheapening the value of money would restore some clout to producers and consumers.

The election of 1896, however, exposed a basic contradiction in the farmer/labor alliance, and Republican candidate, William McKinley, parlayed it to victory over William Jennings Bryan, the Democrat who endorsed some aspects of the Populist platform and won their endorsement. The inflationary aspects of both greenbackism and the Free Silver Movement were rooted in passing agrarian ideals. Farmers—whose percentage of the workforce dwindled each year—were producers whose income derived from commodity production. Industrial workers, however, were largely consumers. Higher farm prices translated into lower earning power for consumers. McKinley's victory sent the Populists into steep decline. In 1900, McKinley signed the Gold Standard Act, which required all paper money to be backed by gold.

Both labor and farm groups continued to lobby for monetary reform in the twentieth century. The tight grip of the gold standard was relaxed somewhat by the Federal Reserve Act (FSA) of 1913, which made the money supply more flexible and decentralized banking. (Twelve federal district banks lend money to commercial banks and can raise or lower interest rates to decrease or increase the amount of money in circulation.) The full power of the FSA did not become apparent until 1933, however, when President Franklin Roosevelt took the United States off the gold standard.

Since 1933, labor groups have continued to press for banking reforms, though they now tend to center on investment policies rather than currency issues. In hard economic times, however, labor leaders often call upon the Federal Reserve Board to loosen credit by lowering interest rates.

Suggested Readings: Norman Pollock, *The Populist Response to Industrial America*, 1962; Gretchen Ritter, *Goldbugs and Greenbacks: The Antimonopoly Tradition and the Politics of Finance in America*, 1997; Allen Weinstein, *Prelude to Populism: Origins of the Silver Issue, 1867–78*, 1970.

Jeff McFadden

Grievance. A grievance is a complaint filed by an employee or union against management for inaccurately or unfairly implementing the terms or working conditions of a **contract**. Procedural machinery is usually provided in union contracts to reach a resolution. The grievance procedure provides ways for workers to file a complaint when management is not living up to its end of a contract. Formal grievance procedures can also be used to change management's perception or force compensation for contract violations. In addition, the grievance procedure can be used to resolve issues that are not explicitly outlined in a contract and to warn management about problems that may be overlooked.

Grievance language is now standard in union contracts, though it was not widespread until the twentieth century and did not become ubiquitous until after World War II. By the 1950s, it was instilled in U.S. **collective bargaining** that management's job is to manage and the union's job is to grieve. Management and union leaders jointly sought grievance clauses to resolve disputes formally and avoid spontaneous **wildcat strikes** as well as arbitrary management decisions. Many unions rely on dispute resolution and **arbitration** provisions that outline the steps that an employee or union can take to resolve complaints against management. The final step in most grievance procedures is binding arbitration.

Suggested Readings: Henry Campbell Black, *Black's Law Dictionary*, 1999; Harry C. Katz and Thomas A. Kochan, *An Introduction to Collective Bargaining and Industrial Relations*, 2000.

Danielle McMullen

Guaranteed Annual Wage. A guaranteed annual wage is a plan that provides a minimum sum or minimum number of hours per year to a worker under a **contract**. It has the effect of stabilizing an employer's workforce as well as providing income security for an employee. This type of arrangement is especially desirable in industries, like automotives and household appliances, prone to frequent layoffs during economic downturns. Employees continue to collect **wages**, while the employer retains his trained workforce. Unions frequently seek agreements that include a guaranteed annual wage as a hedge against short-term fluctuations in the demand for work.

As a response to the frequent layoffs in the post–World War II workplace, unions began to seek more security for their members. In 1955, the **United Auto Workers** sought a guaranteed annual wage from the Ford Motor Company. A compromise was struck that produced the world's first Supplemental Unemployment Benefit Plan, a private, employer-financed plan providing payments to laid-off workers in addition to unemployment insurance benefits. This model spread to other companies. By 1995, 16 percent of all union contracts provided work or pay guarantees.

Suggested Readings: Harry Katz and Thomas Kochan, *An Introduction to Industrial Relations*, 2000; R. Emmet Murray, *The Lexicon of Labor*, 1999.

Howard Davis

H

Hard Hat Riot (1970). *See Blue-Collar Workers.*

Haymarket Bombing. The Haymarket Bombing occurred on May 4, 1886, in Chicago's Haymarket Square. A dynamite bomb was thrown at the end of a protest rally. The explosion and subsequent gunfire from police left eight police officers and four workers dead, and scores more wounded. Although the identity of the bomber was never established, eight anarchists were convicted in a trial that most legal scholars agree was a miscarriage of justice. In the short run, Haymarket galvanized workers already caught up in the Great Labor Upheaval and helped **labor parties** at the polls. In the long run, however, Haymarket was a public-relations and political disaster seized upon by opponents of organized labor as pretext for crushing **working-class** movements. The **Knights of Labor (KOL)** was particularly hurt by Haymarket.

Haymarket took place against the backdrop of struggles of the **eight-hour movement**. Although some federal employees and a few workers in the private sector had won the eight-hour day by 1886, most workers toiled ten or more hours. Various groups discussed a nationwide **general strike** to pressure employers to grant shorter workdays, including the KOL; the Federation of Organized Trades and Labor Unions (FOTLU), the forerunner of the **American Federation of Labor**; and the International Working People's Association (IWPA), a radical group that blended **socialism** and **anarcho-syndicalist** precepts. May 1, 1886, was chosen as the date for the strike. (*See* **May Day**.)

The presence of the IWPA led KOL leaders to back away from the protest. By 1886, the KOL was in the midst of a growth spurt that left leaders scrambling to control the increasingly unwieldy organization. The KOL repudiated the use of violence, which many IWPA leaders seemed to embrace. Several key KOL local and district assemblies were influenced by Lassallean socialists, who saw the ballot box as the key to labor's emancipation and were thus distrustful of FOTLU **craft unionism**, as well as the perceived recklessness of the IWPA. This was particularly true in New York, where many local leaders were Lassalleans, and where the organization maintained friendly ties with the Socialist Labor Party, which advocated a peaceful road to social change. Moreover, as the KOL expanded, its national leader, **Terence Powderly**, grew more cautious, hoping to foster a positive public view of the KOL. Powderly openly criticized **anarchism** and maintained that anarchist Knights were unwelcome in the KOL. He even ordered Knights to stay away from the May 1 demonstrations.

This depiction of the Haymarket Bombing appeared in the May 15, 1886 issue of *Harper's Weekly*. © George Meany Memorial Archives.

Lacking the KOL's endorsement, the May 1 general strike was a bust. Organizers had hoped for a million demonstrators, but fewer than one-third of that number participated. The situation in Chicago, however, was quite different. Anarchist ideals were much stronger there, and its advocates less prone to ideological debates that caused schisms elsewhere. Many Chicago Knights defied Powderly and joined the city's eight-hour protest, and at least 80,000 workers turned out, a figure that represented nearly 20 percent of the nationwide total. A key IWPA leader, who also held KOL membership, was Albert Parsons, a Texas-born radical married to Lucy Parsons, an African American woman who was his equal in radical passion. The two were perhaps the nation's most-famous left-wing couple.

Albert Parsons led Chicago's May 1 parade, and the day passed without incident. Two days later, however, flush with feelings of **solidarity**, some veterans of the May 1 demonstration joined protestors on strike against McCormick Harvester Machine Company, a manufacturer of mechanical reapers and one of the city's largest employers. At the behest of police captain John Bonfield, Chicago police beat strikers, fatally shot two (some accounts say six), and wounded several others. In the wake of the unprovoked attack on unarmed workers, the IWPA called for a protest to be held the next day in Haymarket Square. IWPA leaflets were peppered with provocative language like "revenge" and a call "to arms."

Haymarket Square could accommodate up to 20,000 people, but the actual turnout on May 4 was disappointing, with estimates varying from 1,800 to

3,000. Numerous speeches were given, most filled with anger and anguish, but the gathering was peaceful. Chicago's mayor, Carter Harrison, attended and left satisfied that no trouble was brewing. As the last speaker, Samuel Fielden, was finishing his remarks, Captain Bonfield marched 180 policemen into the square. Fielden's remark, "we are peaceful" was interrupted by a bomb blast that killed policeman Mathias Degan. Police opened fire, and several of the seven other officers who subsequently died may have been crossfire victims. At least four protestors were killed, and approximately fifty were wounded.

Four of the men convicted of the Haymarket bombing are executed in the Cook County Jail. © George Meany Memorial Archives.

The mainstream press and political conservatives cried out for a crackdown on anarchism. Within three weeks, thirty-one people were indicted for Degan's murder, his being the only one directly attributable to the bombing. Only eight men actually stood trial in June: August Spies, Adolph Fischer, George Engel, Michael Schwab, Oscar Neebe, Louis Lingg, Fielden, and Parsons. (Parsons had not been apprehended when the trial opened; he dramatically turned himself in as jury selection was taking place.) The presiding judge was Joseph Gary. None of the defendants was charged with actually throwing the bomb, rather they stood accused of conspiracy to commit murder. Judge Gary allowed prosecution such wide latitude that it put anarchism itself on trial. Essentially, the eight men stood accused of creating the very atmosphere of violence that led to the bombing. Despite worldwide protests—only Parsons was native-born—and the general perception that the trial was a farce, on August 19, 1886, all eight men were convicted. All but Neebe—who got a fifteen-year sentence—were sentenced to hang. By November 2, all appeals were exhausted.

The Haymarket trials and the repression of radical groups initially galvanized American workers. Most labor organizations, except the KOL, protested the arrests, trial, and sentence. Powderly tried to distance the KOL from anarchism, but succeeded mainly in angering workers, including many Knights who were angry that he refused to support either Parsons or Spies, who held KOL membership. Powderly's intransigence notwithstanding, Haymarket actually stimulated more strikes for the eight-hour day, and trade unions picked up strength. (In December, the surging FOTLU was reconstituted as the AFL.) In elections held days after the final appeals, **working-class** voters turned out in droves. In New York, **Henry George** was unsuccessful in his bid for the mayoralty, but numerous labor party candidates took office elsewhere. Several locales saw KOL candidates gain control of city government. In most places, a clemency movement arose to spare the lives of the Haymarket men, and many cities saw renewed strikes. Lucy Parsons embarrassed Illinois governor Richard Oglesby by "confessing" her own guilt and demanding that she too be hanged.

Labor flexed its muscles in the short run, but its hopes were soon dashed. Powderly shocked many labor supporters by refusing to endorse clemency and joining the conservative call for the annihilation of anarchism; thousands quit the KOL in disgust, and many KOL elected officials were repudiated in subsequent elections. (KOL strength in Chicago fell from around 400,000 to around 17,000 despite the fact that the city's KOL paper published autobiographies of each Haymarket victim, and local leaders denounced Powderly.) Governor Oglesby commuted the sentences of Fielden and Schwab, but on November 11, 1887, Parsons, Spies, Fischer, and Engel went to the gallows. (Lingg committed suicide in his cell by biting a dynamite cap the day before his scheduled execution.)

Radical groups embraced their departed comrades as martyrs, but the general crackdown of left-wing groups continued unabated. So too did the precipitous decline of the KOL and of once-promising labor parties. In 1893, Illinois Governor John P. Altgeld pardoned Fielden, Schwab, and Neebe and denounced the trial itself, implying that none of the men were guilty. By then, however, the **Great Upheaval** was over, and most of the causes for which the Haymarket Eight stood lay in tatters.

Progressives and radicals alike have subsequently used Haymarket as a symbol of capitalist repression, justice miscarried, and idealism trampled. Historians tend to view it as a key moment in capital/labor struggles in which capital gained the upper hand.

Suggested Readings: Paul Avrich, *The Haymarket Tragedy*, 1984; Philip Foner, ed., *The Autobiographies of the Haymarket Martyrs*, 1969; Bruce Nelson, *Beyond the Martyrs: A Social History of Chicago Anarchism, 1870–1900*, 1988.

Robert E. Weir

Haywood, William Dudley (February 4, 1869–March 18, 1928). William Haywood was an organizer and activist in the Western Federation of Miners (WFM), **Socialist** Party, and **Industrial Workers of the World (IWW)**. Haywood was born in Salt Lake City. His father, a Pony Express rider, died when Haywood was three, and his mother remarried a miner. At the age of nine, Haywood lost his right eye in a farm accident, a misfortune that brought him the nicknames "Squint Eye" and "Dick Dead-Eye." His formal education ended at age fifteen, when he left home and took a series of mining jobs in Nevada and Idaho. Although he was under six feet tall, the burly-framed Haywood was soon known to fellow miners as "Big Bill." In 1889, he married Jane Minor, a rancher's daughter, with whom he fathered two daughters. He was largely an absentee parent due to his activism and a penchant for heavy drinking.

In 1894, Haywood moved his family to Silver City, Idaho, where he joined the Western Federation of Miners (WFM), an early **industrial union**. He rose quickly within the WFM, joining the executive board in 1900, and becoming secretary-treasurer the next year. In 1901, Haywood moved to Denver and was active in several bitter Colorado coalfield strikes. Haywood helped convert the WFM into an organization that espoused revolutionary unionism. Haywood was also present at the 1905 founding of the Industrial Workers of the World. The next year, he, WFM President Charles Moyer, and two others were jailed on a charge murdering ex-Idaho governor Frank Steunenberg.

Haywood and his compatriots were acquitted when defense attorneys demolished the testimony of **Pinkerton** agent James McParland, who had once infiltrated the **Molly Maguires**. The court victory valorized Haywood among labor radicals. He was briefly a victim of internal fighting within the IWW and from 1908 through 1912 was an organizer for the Socialist Party. He rejoined the IWW just in time for its victory in the **Lawrence textile strike** and became general secretary of the IWW, its highest office. He led the IWW to the height of its influence and presided over the IWW's drive to organize agricultural workers. His fiery rhetoric led to his expulsion from the Socialist Party in 1913, when that group renounced violence. It also led to his arrest in 1917. Haywood and other IWW members vehemently opposed militarism and U.S. involvement in World War I. His comments were found in violation of the 1917 Espionage Act and on August 17, 1918, he was sentenced to twenty years in prison.

Haywood appealed his conviction, skipped bail, and fled to the Soviet Union in 1921. He managed a mine there, married a Russian woman who knew little English, set up an international fund for imprisoned radicals, and wrote his autobiography. When he died in 1928, he was buried in the Kremlin wall.

Suggested Readings: Peter Carlson, *Roughneck: The Life and Times of Big Bill Haywood*, 1983; Joseph Conlin, *Big Bill Haywood and the Radical Union Movement*, 1969; William Haywood, *Big Bill's Book*, 1929.

Cheryl Conley
Robert E. Weir

Highlander Folk School. The Highlander Folk School has been an important adult education center for social activists for over seven decades. Now known as the Highlander Research and Education Center, the Folk School was originally located in Monteagle, Tennessee. In 1932, cofounders Myles Horton and

Don West opened "a school in the mountains for mountain people." West soon left to pursue other projects, but the school remained faithful to his and Horton's vision that it would become a center for fomenting social and economic change through the education of activists and leaders, especially within the emerging Southern labor movement. The Folk School was patterned on Danish schools that combined adult education with the power of cultural expression, like traditional music and storytelling. Originally, Highlander was part of a broader workers' education movement that included college-based programs like the Bryn Mawr Summer School for Women Workers and residential centers like **Brookwood Labor College** and Commonwealth College.

In Highlander's educational program, the staff taught skills courses, like organizing and **collective bargaining**, that were of immediate use to union activists, as well as more theoretical courses on economics and social problems. The Highlander staff enforced strong interracial, nonsegregationist rules on those attending classes; Highlander rejected the racism that many workers and unions had practiced in their home communities and workplaces. During the 1930s and 1940s, Highlander also provided the labor movement with direct support of organizing drives and **strikes**, including singing and presenting labor plays on picket lines. These activities laid the basis for decades of cultural work. Many Highlander staff members worked within unions affiliated with the **Congress of Industrial Organizations (CIO)**, and Horton himself worked as an organizer for the Textile Workers Organizing Committee in 1937. For a time, Highlander was the site for the CIO's Southern School.

Highlander's relationship to the CIO fell victim to the schisms in the federation in the late 1940s and early 1950s. Highlander's continuing relationship with affiliate unions expelled from the CIO, the school's interracial philosophy and practice, and the growing rigidity of the federation made the CIO's tie to Highlander problematic. From 1951 to 1953, Horton ran an education program for the **United Packinghouse Workers Union**, a union that Horton respected for its political beliefs and its dedication to interracial unionism. Highlander was finally dropped from the CIO's list of preferred education providers in 1953.

By the early 1950s, Highlander turned its attention to the role the school could play in the struggle for African American civil rights across the South. Throughout the 1950s and 1960s, Highlander trained civil rights movement activists and leaders and launched a very successful effort to eradicate illiteracy in the South, a common barrier to African American voting. Throughout its existence, Highlander's commitment to economic and social justice earned it powerful enemies that harassed the school through legal and extralegal means. In 1962, the state of Tennessee closed Highlander. After a three-year legal battle, Tennessee sold the school's buildings, library, and other physical assets. In the wake of the closure, Highlander reincorporated as Highlander Research and Education Center and began operations in the city of Knoxville.

In 1972, the center moved to its current home outside Knoxville in New Market, Tennessee. Desiring to build on the visibility and success of the civil rights movement, Highlander attempted to create a nationwide poor people's movement across all races and regions. Highlander began the 1970s adrift and rudderless, however, when this coalition failed to materialize. Highlander staff chose to redirect its vision and focus anew on problems confronting Appalachia. This move led to renewed ties with the Southern labor movement, reinvigorated by organizing drives in textiles and fights over occupational safety and health in the coalfields. Throughout the last decades of the twentieth century, the staff of the center used Highlander's worldwide contacts and reputation to connect Appalachian social and labor advocates with a world network of likeminded activists. Today, Highlander seeks to help Appalachians cope with increasing globalism and focus attention on issues like the link between Tennessee plant closures and the rise of low-wage nonunion work in Mexico's ***maquiladora*** factories.

Today, many of Highlander's union-related functions have passed to the National Labor College, which was opened in Silver Spring, Maryland, in 1971.

Suggested Readings: Frank Adams with Myles Horton, *Unearthing Seeds of Fire: The Idea of Highlander*, 1975; John Glen, *Highlander: No Ordinary School, 1932–62*, 1988; Myles Horton, with Judith Kohl and Herbert Kohl, *The Long Haul: An Autobiography*, 1990; Highlander Research and Education Center, http:// www.hrec.org.

John P. Beck

Hill, Joe (October 7, 1879?–November 19, 1915). Joe Hill (aka Joel Haggland, Joseph Hillstrom) was a songwriter for the **Industrial Workers of the World (IWW** or **Wobblies)** and a member of that organization. In the history of **music and labor**, Hill is probably the most famous writer of all time. His compositions include "Union Maid," "The Preacher and the Slave," "There is Power in a Union," "Casey Jones, the Union Scab," "Mr. Block," and "The Rebel Girl," the last composition being Hill's tribute to **Elizabeth Gurley Flynn**.

Details of Hill's personal life are sketchy. He was born Joel Emmanuel Haggland in Gavle, Sweden, one of nine children to Olof and Margaerta Haggland. His father was a railroad worker who died when Joel was eight. Joel's formal education ended early as he was forced to work to help keep his family afloat. He worked in a rope factory, shoveled coal for a construction firm, and was rumored to have been a seaman. Three of his siblings died before he was ten, and he contracted tuberculosis when he was twelve. Joel survived the disease, but several operations left him with distinguishable nose and neck scars. He supposedly learned English at the YMCA in Gavle and perfected it on ships plying the North Sea between Sweden and England. When his mother died in 1901, Joel and his brother Paul decided to emigrate to the United States, landing in New York in October 1902.

Very little is known about Hill until he surfaced at a 1910 IWW-led dock **strike** in San Pedro, California. Fragmentary evidence suggests that he drifted first to Cleveland, then to the West coast, where he worked aboard merchant ships and as a longshoreman. When and why he changed his name to Joseph

Hillstrom—Joe Hill was his pen name—is unknown, though it was common for immigrants to acquire "Americanized" names, either by choice or because they were imposed by others. One unconfirmed story holds that Joel Haggland was a vagrant and thief who changed his name to escape the notoriety of several minor arrests.

Equally speculative is how Hill came to be associated with the Wobblies. At this phase in IWW history, emphasis was placed on recruiting roustabouts, migrant workers, and other semi- and unskilled workers deemed unworthy of notice by the **American Federation of Labor (AFL)**. Hill may have been among that teeming labor underclass targeted by the IWW's Overalls Brigade to lead free-speech fights across the West. Numerous towns fearful of radical groups adopted ordinances designed to limit public speech and the size of gatherings. From 1907 through 1916, the IWW conducted at least thirty separate free-speech campaigns to protect basic constitutional rights. Hill's "The Preacher and the Slave" indirectly and humorously takes up the attempts some towns made to exempt religious groups like the Salvation Army from newly passed ordinances, a bit of hypocrisy the IWW challenged as well as lampooned.

The IWW's revolutionary fervor found a receptive audience in Hill. The few contemporary accounts of Hill describe him as distant and cynical. How many IWW actions Hill actually took part in is as speculative as most of his biography, though it seems he took part in the San Pedro strike in 1910, an ill-fated 1911 attempt to overthrow the Mexican government and make Lower California a workers' commune, and the 1912 San Diego free-speech battle. His first piece for the IWW was a 1910 letter to the *Industrial Worker* in which he claimed to be a member of a Portland, Oregon, local. He was said to have spent thirty days in a San Pedro jail for vagrancy, though the police claimed he was a robbery suspect who they released for lack of evidence. Hill also claimed he was beaten by police during the 1911 Fresno free-speech campaign.

Hill was a self-taught musician who dabbled with violin, piano, and guitar. He claimed that his songs were based on "scribbles," his notes on his travels and of labor struggles. In 1910, Hill's "Workers of the World, Awaken" was published in an IWW newspaper, perhaps his first published song contribution to the Wobblies. Like many labor songwriters, Hill's favorite tactic was to take an existing tune and set new lyrics to it. Since much labor singing was done on **picket** lines, known tunes made it easier for strikers to learn new songs. For example, Hill's "There is Power in a Union" uses the music of the well-known gospel song "There is Power in the Blood," and "The Preacher and the Slave" is a lyrical adaptation of "Sweet Bye and Bye." Labor songwriters frequently used church music, though only a handful did so with the irreverence of Wobbly bards like Hill.

By 1913, Hill enjoyed minor fame for his songs, several of which appeared in print to support ongoing IWW struggles. In that year, Hill went to Utah, perhaps to work in the Park City silver mines. He was living in a Salt Lake City boarding house on January 10, 1914, when two masked men entered a local grocery store. An ensuing gun battle left owner John Morrison and his son, Arling, dead. (Some sources give the son's name as Alving.) A second son, Merlin, saw two men fleeing the store when he rushed to assist his father and brother. Police investigators concluded—though the only material evidence to support the hypothesis were a few bloodspots in an outside alley—that Arling had wounded one of the assailants. They also speculated that a vendetta was involved as John Morrison's wounds were made at close range and no money was taken from the cash register.

Joe Hill was treated for a gunshot wound the very night of the murders. Hill told Dr. Frank McHugh he had been wounded in a jealous fight over a woman. Hill was carrying a gun at the time, though he allegedly tossed it into a field during the carriage ride back to his boarding house. When Dr. McHugh read that police were seeking a wounded suspect in the Morrison murders, he dutifully notified them of treating Hill's wounds. Officers rushed to the boarding house, awoke Hill from his sleep, and shot him in the hand as he reached for his trousers. Rather than treat Hill's wound, police charged him with the Morrison murders and imprisoned him.

Hill remained in jail for five months, awaiting trial. Once Hill's identity and IWW affiliation became known, public sentiment ran high to convict Hill. The Wobblies were especially feared in Utah, a state where antiunion feelings were strong and where the Mormon church controlled much of the state's political, as well as social, life. Hill acted as his own counsel during his arraignment hearing, but was given two court-appointed attorneys for the trial that opened on June 10, 1914. Hill fired both of them midway through the trial, after an outburst in which he claimed they were in cahoots with the prosecutor. Toward the end of the trial, O. N. Hilton, a lawyer with experience defending miners, was appointed, though Hill apparently seldom followed his advice.

Hill sealed his own fate, either by deciding to represent himself or by taking bad advice from Hilton. (The latter seems implausible given Hilton's hitherto stellar record.) The prosecution's case was weak, relying entirely on the timing of Hill's gunshot wounds and two shaky eyewitness accounts claiming that Hill's TB-ravaged face matched that of a man seen fleeing Morrison's store. Missing from the account was the fact that Morrison was involved in a shootout months before and had told police that his attackers were trying to settle an old grudge from Morrison's days on the police force. No murder weapon was produced, nor did Dr. McHugh retrieve a bullet when he treated Hill's wounds.

But Hill did not acquit himself well either. He never took the stand in his own defense, his alibi was shaky, and his refusal to name his assailant or the woman in question made it appear even more so. His gallant claim that he was defending a woman's honor was out of keeping with known aspects of his character, and his steadfast refusal to provide more details of his alleged domestic quarrel as the firing squad loomed leads an objective observer to one of two conclusions: either Hill was guilty as charged or he longed for a martyr's death. After a ten-day trial, a jury convicted Hill of both murders, and he was sentenced to death. Hill was allowed to choose between hanging or the firing squad and chose the latter.

With execution nearing, Hill's case received much more attention than it had previously. The Wobblies defended Hill and accused "copper bosses" and the Mormon church of railroading Hill. The IWW spent so much on Hill's appeals that it had very little money left to assist Wobblies elsewhere with their own legal woes. The case received worldwide attention, with more than 10,000 letters and telegrams flooding state capitol offices when the Utah Supreme Court refused Hill's appeal. Death threats were levied against Utah governor William Spry. But Hill again did nothing to assist his own cause. He refused to give any more details of his shooting to the Board of Pardons when it met on September 18 and sat idly as protests erupted around the country. In his final days, luminaries like the Swedish ambassador to the United States, the AFL's **Samuel Gompers**, and Virginia Snow Stephen, the daughter of the president of the Mormon church, appealed for clemency, but President Woodrow Wilson refused.

Before he faced the firing squad on November 19, 1915, Hill penned a note to the IWW's **William Haywood** urging him, "Don't waste any time mourning. Organize!" That advice quickly became an IWW slogan, and it factored prominently in the song "Joe Hill," penned by poet Alfred Hayes and composer Earl Robinson in 1925. (That song entered the folk-music canon and remains a staple.) At his request, Hill's body was removed from Utah. He was cremated, and small packets of his ashes were distributed to be cast across the world and the United States (except Utah).

In death, Hill became a martyr and a legend. In IWW lore, Hill, Frank Little, and Wesley Everett stand as testaments of organized capital's resolve to smash the IWW. (Little was lynched by vigilantes in Butte, Montana, in 1917, and Everett died in a shootout with American Legion thugs in Centralia, Washington, in 1919.) Given that "reasonable doubt" is the standard of American jurisprudence, Hill's conviction is troubling, though his case is hardly on par with egregious miscarriages of justice like the executions of alleged **Molly Maguires**, **Haymarket** anarchists, or **Sacco and Vanzetti**. The best-available evidence suggests that Hill was a flawed individual, perhaps the petty thief and murderer his prosecutors claimed. But he was also an enormously talented songwriter, whose works and life—mythical or true—have aided organizing efforts. His songs were published in the IWW's *Little Red Songbook*, and many of them found their way into organized labor's permanent canon.

Suggested Readings: Joyce Kornbluh, ed., *Rebel Voices: An I.W.W. Anthology*, 1968; Gibbs Smith, *Joe Hill*, 1984; Ken Verdoia, "Joe Hill: The Man Behind the Martyr," http://www.pbs.org/joehill/story/biography.html.

Robert E. Weir

Hillman, Sidney (March 23, 1887–July 10, 1946). Sidney Hillman was president of the **Amalgamated Clothing Workers of America (ACWA)** and advisor to President Franklin Roosevelt. Hillman was born in Lithuania, the son of Schmuel and Judith (Paikin) Hillman. He studied economics, was involved with trade unions as a young man, and spent eight months in jail for his radical views on labor. He took part in a 1905 Russian revolution, fled to England after his release from prison, and emigrated to the United States in 1907. He settled first in Chicago where he, like many other Jewish immigrants, gravitated towards the garment industry. Hillman, a garment cutter, was a leader in the 1910 **strike** against Hart, Schaffner, and Marx. Another key leader was Bessie Aranowitz (1889–1971) who, in 1916, became Hillman's wife.

In 1914, when Hillman's garment cutters union merged with several others to create the ACWA, Hillman was elected its first president. The ACWA promoted labor/management accords and set up union **cooperatives**, banks, and housing units. In 1920, the ACWA became the first national union to advocate a five-day workweek. Hillman, a **socialist**, also helped establish a short-lived ACWA factory in Russia. His views on **industrial unionism** were increasingly at odds with the **American Federation of Labor (AFL)**, with which the ACWA was affiliated. Hillman was an early ally of **John L. Lewis** and assisted in the creation of the **Congress of Industrial Organizations (CIO)**. In 1937, he became vice president of the CIO. He used ACWA resources to help organize steel-, rubber-, and autoworkers. He chaired the Textile Workers Organizing Committee which, in 1939, became the Textile Workers Union of America (TWUA).

Although Hillman was an early supporter of the **American Labor Party** (founded in 1919), during the Great Depression he was drawn into the Democratic Party. He served on the Labor Advisory Board of the National Recovery Administration in 1933 and the National Industrial Recovery Board in 1935. Hillman was also on the board of the National Youth Administration and the **Fair Labor Standard**'s Textile Committee. He served on three presidential commissions during World War II, and was cochair of the Office of Production Management. In 1943, Hillman founded the CIO's Political Action Committee (PAC) to support President Roosevelt's reelection bid and was a delegate to the World Federation of Trade Unions in 1945. He died suddenly at his home on Long Island in 1946.

Conservatives despised Hillman, and both he the CIO-PAC were thoroughly investigated by the FBI though, ironically, Hillman tempered his radicalism as he aged. The TWUA operated according to conventional trade-union precepts. Since 1950, the Sidney Hillman Foundation has awarded annual prizes to those it recognizes for public service and social justice. In 1992, Hillman was elected to the Labor Hall of Fame.

Suggested Readings: Melech Epstein, *Profiles of Eleven*, 1965; Steve Fraser, *Labor Will Rule*, 1991; Matthew Josephson, *Sidney Hillman: Statesman of American Labor*, 1952.

Don Binkowski

***Hitchman Coal and Coke Company v. Mitchell* (U.S. 1917).** *Hitchman Coal and Coke Company v. Mitchell* was a Supreme Court decision that upheld an injunction that prohibited unions from organizing workers who had signed **yellow-dog contracts**. In 1932, Congress passed the **Norris-LaGuardia Act**, outlawing yellow-dog contracts.

Suggested Readings: William E. Forbath, *Law and the Shaping of the American Labor Movement*, 1991; Benjamin J. Taylor and Fred Witney, *U.S. Labor Relations Law: Historical Development*, 1992.

Bruce Cohen

Hoffa, James Riddle (February 14, 1913–July ?, 1975). James Riddle Hoffa was a controversial president of the **International Brotherhood of Teamsters (IBT)** from 1957 to 1971. He was the son of John C. and Viola (Riddle) Hoffa. His father was a coal driller who died of lung cancer when Hoffa was seven. His family moved to Detroit, and Hoffa left school at age fourteen to help support his mother's meager laundress's income. He worked as a stock boy until 1930, when he became a freight handler. His union activities began that year when he and four coworkers organized warehouse laborers. In 1936, Hoffa married Josephine Poszywak, with whom he had two children, Barbara and James Hoffa, Jr.

Jimmy Hoffa. © George Meany Memorial Archives.

In 1934, Hoffa joined the IBT. The Teamsters were then among the nation's more progressive unions, organizing warehouse workers and chauffeurs as well as truckers. Hoffa rose quickly in the IBT ranks, holding numerous offices within the organization. He was elected president of his local in 1937 and helped organize the Central States Drivers Council to coordinate regional policy and set rates. He also gained a reputation for his fiery temper and his willingness to resort to fisticuffs. In 1942, he became president of the Michigan Conference of Teamsters and in 1952 became IBT vice president.

Hoffa was accused of bribing a U.S. Senate investigator in 1957, was acquitted, and became IBT president that same year, when the IBT's Dave Beck was jailed for corruption. Hoffa's tenure was marked by controversy from the start, with his detractors claiming he freely borrowed from union pension funds, tied the IBT to organized crime, and cooperated with extortion schemes. But Hoffa also streamlined the IBT bureaucracy and skillfully negotiated a 1964 regional

contract for freight haulers that was the IBT's first national agreement. With said contract, Hoffa had the ability to bring the trucking industry to a standstill, power he used to win concessions for the Teamsters' **rank and file**. His activities were relentlessly investigated, especially by Democrats. Hoffa's confrontations with Robert Kennedy did much to establish the latter's reputation. Hoffa, who flirted with **Trotskyism** in his youth, switched allegiance to the Republican Party. The IBT was one of the few unions in the nation to endorse GOP candidates.

In 1964, Hoffa was convicted of jury tampering, fraud, and conspiracy and sentenced to thirteen years in prison. After three years of appeals, Hoffa entered a federal penitentiary, although he refused to give up the presidency of the IBT until 1971. That year, President Richard Nixon pardoned Hoffa under the promise that Hoffa would not seek another IBT office until 1980. Privately, Hoffa felt that his former protégé and acting president, Frank Fitzsimmons, was plotting to rid the IBT of his presence.

Upon release, Hoffa worked to rebuild his power base. On July 30, 1975, he attended a business luncheon in Bloomfield, Michigan, at which several alleged organized-crime figures were in attendance. Hoffa was never seen again. Allegations and rumors abounded, and the FBI investigated leads for seven years, but turned up nothing. Hoffa was declared legally dead in 1982.

Corruption and **racketeering** charges plagued the IBT for decades after Hoffa's disappearance. It was not until the 1990s that the IBT began to rehabilitate its image, though it no longer commands the might it did when Hoffa ran the organization. His children have tried to rehabilitate their father's image. In 1998, James Hoffa, Jr., became IBT president.

Suggested Readings: Joseph Franco and Richard Hammer, *Hoffa's Man*, 1987; Robert Kennedy, et al., *The Enemy Within*, 1994; Walter Sheridan, *The Fall and Rise of Jimmy Hoffa*, 1972.

Pauline Gladstone
Robert E. Weir

Homestead Steel Strike. The Homestead Steel Strike of 1892 was one of the bloodiest and most infamous battles between labor and capital in American history. Andrew Carnegie was reputed to be the richest man in the world, and Homestead was the showcase manufacturing plant of Carnegie Steel. Carnegie stressed controlling costs. The cost of labor was the last to be controlled and thus the last obstacle to Carnegie's industry dominance. Carnegie, known as the most articulate industrialist that America had ever produced, played the role of the workingman's friend and preached of the social obligations of men of wealth. Carnegie arranged to be incommunicado in Scotland during the Homestead crisis, leaving his company in the hands of Henry Clay Frick, who was known for his hostility to labor. As general manager, Frick was determined to deskill steel making and end unionism in the industry. His last offer to the **Amalgamated Association of Iron and Steel Workers**, after five months of negotiation, was for an

18 percent **wage** decrease. Many workers insisted that if only they could contact Carnegie, he would intervene on their behalf with Frick. On June 30, 1892, Frick closed the plant and **locked out** the workers who had announced their intention of **striking**. Frick hired 300 armed **Pinkerton** detectives and on July 6 sailed them on barges up the Monongahela River to Homestead. As the Pinkertons arrived, thousands of armed workers, along with their friends and families, fought a daylong battle with the detectives which resulted in the deaths of nine locals and seven Pinkertons. Six days after the Homestead battle, Pennsylvania governor Robert E. Pattison sent National Guardsmen to dispossess the workers and impose martial law. On July 23, **anarchist** Alexander Berkman, lover of **Emma Goldman**, attempted to assassinate Frick but succeeded only in wounding him three times. In spite of the fact that neither Berkman nor Goldman had any connection with the striking workers, conservative social commentators linked anarchy with labor unions. Union leaders were arrested on a variety of charges, tried, and acquitted, but were blacklisted by the steel industry. By November 17, the strike was broken, and there would be no effective unionism in the steel industry for the next forty years. In 1901, Andrew Carnegie sold his company, which produced one-third of all American steel, to J. P. Morgan for $480 million. Carnegie devoted the rest of his life to giving away his money, offering to build public libraries for the self-improvement of working men and women. In view of his callous insensitivity to his own workers at Homestead in 1892, however, many social critics argued that Carnegie's rhetoric and his generosity rang hollow, for he failed to show the same charity towards his workforce that he now touted to the nation; it was a thin disguise for an underlying, brutal, **Social Darwinism**. Following the strike, Carnegie and Frick fought bitterly with one another over business matters. When, toward the end of his life, Carnegie sought

Attack of the strikers and their sympathizers on the surrendered Pinkerton men in Homestead, Pa. © Library of Congress.

to reconcile with Frick, Frick reportedly sent the message, "Tell Mr. Carnegie I'll meet him in Hell where we are both going."

Suggested Readings: David P. Demarest, ed., *"The River Ran Red": Homestead, 1898*, 1992; David Montgomery, *The Fall of the House of Labor: The Workplace, the State, and American Labor Activism, 1865–1925*, 1987.

James P. Hanlan

Scenes from the 1892 Homestead Steel Strike. © George Meany Memorial Archives.

Homework. Homework is a labor system in which contractors and subcontractors produce goods, usually in a satellite location separate from the employer's factory. Employees are routinely paid on a **piecework** basis, rather than an hourly **wage**. Historically this sort of output-based pay scale often forced entire families, including children, to work long hours for sustenance pay. It was the very foundation of the **sweatshop** system, although the term *sweatshop* usually refers to many workers under one roof, whereas *homework* involves just individual workers or families laboring from their domiciles.

In the nineteenth century, the industrial homework system, fueled by a large influx of newly arrived immigrants, was important in remaking the American **working class**. A diverse and stratified working class emerged in full force with **capitalism**'s post–Civil War expansion. Working people were deeply divided by race, ethnicity, skill level, age, and gender. Immigrant families often found employment opportunities limited. Employers exploited rifts in the working class to build

Homework often engaged the whole family, including children. © George Meany Memorial Archives/Smithsonian Institution.

a pool of low-paid labor. Thousands toiled in sweatshop tenement buildings in large cities. Industrial homework became associated with harsh conditions, **speedups**, long hours, **child labor**, and low wages.

Although unions have long opposed industrial homework and many laws have been passed to regulate the practice, continued waves of new immigrants have perpetuated it. In addition, rural homeworkers—many of whom take in sewing jobs or perform assembly work—have complained that current labor laws overly restrict their freedom of **contract** rights. Recent investigations of Chinese immigrant labor reveal that many continue to toil under nineteenth-century conditions. Industrial homework remains a fixture of North American production despite efforts to eliminate it.

Suggested Readings: Elizabeth Kolbert, "The Unfashionable Mr. Lam," *Mother Jones* (September/October 2001); Alan Kraut, *The Huddled Masses: The Immigrant in American Society, 1880–1921*, 2001; Philip Taft, *Organized Labor in American History*, 1994.

Howard Davis

Hormel Strike and Lockout. The Hormel Strike and Lockout was one of a series of defeats suffered by organized labor in the 1980s, though some observers feel this one was self-induced. It involved a struggle of meatpackers in Austin, Minnesota, that pitted them against the George A. Hormel Company, the state of Minnesota, and their own international union.

Meatpacking, like many industries in the late 1970s and early 1980s, was hit by employer demands for **concessions**. Aging plants closed, and some jobs were lost, but corporate claims that concessions were necessary to maintain competitiveness were specious as corporations faced no threat from imports. Nonetheless, the **United Food and Commercial Workers Union (UFCWU)** cooperated in a wave of **wage** and benefits cutting, in some cases breaking in-place **pattern bargains** to grant them. The **Department of Labor** noted that average wages in the industry fell from $9.19 in 1982 to $7.93 in January 1985. The UFCWU justified this as a job-saving measure.

The wisdom of UFCWU policy was sorely tested in Austin, Minnesota. Unlike aging Chicago and Kansas City facilities, the Hormel plant in Austin was state-of-the-art, having just opened in 1982. Workers there were affiliated with UFCWU Local P-9 and were covered by three separate agreements, one of which included a **no-strike pledge**, though it also included a promise that wages would not be cut prior to the **contract**'s expiration in August 1985. Workers adhered to contract provisions, despite the fact that the Austin plant employed a **speedup** and had a poor safety record. Nonetheless, Hormel began to demand concessions and in October 1984 slashed wages from $10.69 to $8.25 per hour, even though it had just declared a $29 million annual profit.

P-9 President Jim Guyette spoke out against concessions, even as the UFCWU continued to negotiate wage cuts across the industry. A UFCWU-negotiated agreement with Hormel workers in Ottumwa, Iowa, further undercut P-9's efforts to restore cuts. P-9 continued to honor its no-strike pledge, but it also launched an aggressive pressure campaign against Hormel that involved organizing workers' wives, high-school students, and retirees. The cornerstone of P-9's strategy was hiring a firm to engage in a **corporate campaign** against Hormel. Roy Rogers of Corporate Campaign Incorporated (CCI) came to Austin to direct efforts.

The presence of CCI led to conflict with the UFCWU, with both President William Wynn and Packinghouse division chief Lewie Anderson coming to see P-9 as dangerous dissidents prone to **wildcat** actions. In the meantime, however, CCI targeted banks with ties to Hormel and helped P-9 with its public-relations campaign. It also unearthed agreements between Hormel and the apartheid government of South Africa and was able to elicit support from the African National Congress.

On August 17, 1985, P-9 workers walked off after more than 90 percent of its membership approved the **strike**. Since it came at the end of the contract and was thus a legal strike, the UFCWU was constitutionally obligated to provide strike funds, though Anderson and Wynn worked to undermine P-9. In January 1986, the UFCWU openly denounced the strike and P-9 leader Guyette, going so far as to resort to red-baiting. To UFCWU officials, clashes between strikers and National Guardsmen were further indications of a situation spiraling out of control. Anderson even denounced Guyette on network television.

The net effect of the UFCWU's assault on its own local was to tear Austin apart internally. The strike's solidarity was broken, and some workers returned to their jobs. In some cases, families were torn asunder over the question of whether or not to return to work. P-9 offered to return to work if Hormel agreed to rehire workers based on **seniority**, but the company spurned its offer. This is because it began to introduce **scabs** in late January, who it insisted were permanent replacement workers.

The clash between P-9 and the UFCWU came to a head on March 13, 1985, when the parent union withdrew official sanction of the strike as well as strike funds. This meant the strike was now, technically, a **lockout**. P-9 gamely continued, and it garnered tremendous support from other unions and from activists like the Reverend Jesse Jackson. In June, however, the UFCWU seized P-9 offices and records in Austin and placed the union in trusteeship. It even diverted funds raised by P-9 to replenish its own coffers. About 80 percent of the 1,500 strikers lost their jobs.

In September 1986, the UFCWU negotiated a contract with Hormel that raised wages to $10.70 per hour, a mere penny higher than the rate obtained in 1979, that was in place before the 1984 cuts. Even then Austin workers suffered, as Hormel closed part of the plant and rented it to a firm that paid only $6.50 per hour. The UFCWU was able to use procedural moves to turn aside an attempt by former P-9 members to decertify the union.

Since the strike's bleak denouement, scholars and activists have debated its significance. Some argue that the UFCWU's actions were a shameful betrayal of the **rank-and-file** that highlights the bankruptcy of **business unionism**. Several believe that if CCI had not been undermined, its corporate campaign would have been as successful as that used by **Ravenswood** workers. Nearly all scholars interpret the UFCWU's actions as heavy-handed and autocratic.

Defenders of the UFCWU charge that Rogers was self-aggrandizing and the CCI campaign a chimera. They also interpret the actions of Guyette and P-9 as undisciplined, rash, and dangerous. According to this view, the UFCWU was correct to accept short-term losses to bring all packinghouses into a common wage structure. This allowed the negotiation of a 1986 contract that again raised wages. As noted above, relatively few scholars accept this position in total.

Still others feel that it would not have mattered how P-9 or the UFCWU conducted themselves, as Hormel was not going to negotiate. Hormel refused to rehire most of the strikers even though **scabs** never matched the efficiency of the prestrike workforce. The decision to close part of the Austin plant is seen as proof that Hormel's real interests were profit maximization and workplace control. In the negative political and economic climate of the mid-1980s, the unions simply had no chance. The real issue, from this perspective, is that no existing labor law prevents the hiring of permanent strikebreakers.

The events in Austin were made into an award-winning documentary by filmmaker Barbara Kopple titled *American Dream*. It stands as a powerful testament to the pressures felt by organized labor in the 1980s.

Suggested Readings: Hardy Green, *On Strike at Hormel: The Struggle for a Democratic Labor Movement*, 1991; Kim Moody, *An Injury to All*, 1989; Peter Rachleff, *Hard-Pressed in the Heartland: The Hormel Strike and the Future of the Labor Movement*, 1993.

Robert E. Weir

Hotel Employees and Restaurant Employees International Union (HERE). The Hotel Employees and Restaurant Employees International Union (HERE) was chartered by the **American Federation of Labor (AFL)** on April 24, 1891. Organized along craft lines, locals represented bartenders, waiters, cooks, and waitresses. In 1973, the union was reorganized, and locals were merged to represent all hospitality workers in a city or region. HERE today represents a broad variety of approximately 265,000 hospitality-industry workers: room attendants, desk clerks, hospital workers, cafeteria workers, waiters and waitresses, cooks, bartenders, casino workers, airport workers, and stadium concession workers. The union's membership is ethnically diverse but with a high percentage of African American, Latino, and Asian workers. HERE is politically active, cultivating support from political leaders, and emphasizing organizing the unorganized. The union focuses on the usual issues of **wages**, hours, and working conditions, but also has programs intended to improve the self-image of service workers and emphasize worker dignity on the job and in the workplace. When employers, particularly large corporate foodservice and hospitality employers, resist organizing efforts, HERE publicizes employer actions, thus negatively affecting bookings, reservations, and convention business. In an industry sensitive to its public image and dependent upon goodwill, HERE has found this to be an effective tactic.

Suggested Reading: Hotel Employees and Restaurant Employees International Union, http://www.hereunion.org.

James P. Hanlan

Huerta, Dolores (April 10, 1930–). Dolores Huerta, an organizer for the **United Farm Workers of America (UFW)**, was born Dolores Fernandez, the only daughter of Juan and Alicia (Chavez) Fernandez. Her parents divorced when she was three, and she moved with her mother and two brothers from New Mexico to California. Her mother toiled both as a cannery worker and as a waitress to care for her three children. Huerta took piano, dance, and violin lessons, was a Girl Scout, and sang in her church choir. In 1945, her mother remarried James Richards, a Stockton hotel and restaurant owner. Huerta gained a multicultural perspective through the hotel's numerous Chinese, Filipino, Jewish, and Mexican clients. Her labor union awakening came largely though her grandfather, a coal miner who also worked as an itinerant beet harvester.

A series of unsatisfying postgraduation clerical posts led Huerta to enter Stockton College, where she took education courses before marrying. She got divorced after the birth of her second daughter and returned to college for an associate's degree and a teaching certificate. Her concern for impoverished children deepened her social awareness and in 1955 she got involved with the Community Service Organization (CSO), a Mexican American social-service organization for which she taught citizenship classes and registered voters. The CSO sent her to Sacramento to lobby on behalf of Latino economic and social causes.

Huerta also concerned herself with the plight of migrant farmworkers. She joined the Agricultural Workers Association, a community interest group, and met **Cesar Chavez**, then director of the CSO in California and Arizona. In 1962, she and Chavez formed the National Farm Workers Association (NFWA) which launched the 1965 Delano table **grape boycott** that brought the plight of Latino migrant workers to the public spotlight. Huerta helped organize the boycott on the East coast, where most of the distributors were located. In 1970, growers signed a **contract** with the NFWA. In 1968, she helped coordinate the NFWA's entry into the American Federation of Labor–Congress of Industrial Organizations as the United Farm Workers of America (UFW).

Huerta served in numerous roles with the UFW, but she also encountered intense sexism from both union members and allied groups like the Roman Catholic church. While living in New York City, she met Gloria Steinem and began to incorporate feminism into her labor activities. In the early 1970s, Huerta was also instrumental in organizing boycotts against Gallo wines and against lettuce growers. Her work led California to pass the 1975 **Agricultural Labor Relations Act**, which recognized the right of farmworkers to organize. (Most farm labor was excluded from the **National Labor Relations Act**.)

Huerta remains active with the UFW, despite its heavy personal toll. She has given birth to eleven children, but both her marriages failed. In 1988, she suffered a ruptured spleen and several broken bones when she was clubbed by San Francisco police during a peaceful protest against presidential candidate George H. W. Bush.

Suggested Readings: George Horwitz, *La Causa: The California Grape Strike*, 1970; Jennifer Mossman, ed., *Reference Library of American Women*, 1999; Daniel Rothenberg, *With These Hands*, 1998.

Maria Ruotolo
Robert E. Weir

Hutcheson, William Levi (February 7, 1874–October 20, 1953). William Levi Hutcheson was a conservative, business-minded trade unionist who dominated the carpenters' union during his long tenure as president. Hutcheson learned the trade of carpentry in Saginaw, Michigan, from his father. During his youth, Hutcheson witnessed the labor activism of the **Knights of Labor**, miners' strikes in Coeur d'Alene, Idaho, and **Eugene Debs**'s battle in the **Pullman strike**. The main lesson that Hutcheson took from these incidents was a lifelong suspicion of governmental intervention in labor affairs. After traveling around the country, Hutcheson returned to Saginaw in 1906 and became business agent of the carpenters' local. By 1913, Hutcheson was elected second vice president of the **United Brotherhood of Carpenters and Joiners (UBC)**. Two years later, he would succeed the president and remain head of the international union for the next thirty-seven years, to be followed in 1952 by his handpicked successor, Maurice Hutcheson, one of his four children, who in turn would remain head of the union until his retirement in 1972. As union president, Bill Hutcheson brooked no opposition. He moved quickly to squelch the autonomy of union locals and to eliminate the influence of radical or socialist sympathizers within the locals. New York City carpenters, known for their fierce independence, were put down by Hutcheson between 1915 and 1917. Hutcheson broke a strike, ousted independent leadership, and installed his own followers as leaders of the locals. Hutcheson was never again challenged by a local and the international union retained strict control over bargaining and strike matters. Hutcheson was determined to root out left-leaning leadership in the carpenters and spearheaded anticommunist efforts in the labor movement. Hutcheson oversaw significant growth in the brotherhood. Much of the growth, however, resulted not from organizing drives but from **jurisdictional** battles with other unions. Hutcheson was determined to establish control over any aspect of work that could be defined as carpentry. The carpenters became the largest union in the **American Federation of Labor (AFL)**, and Hutcheson used the union's dominance in the building trades, as well as his membership on the AFL executive board, to win jurisdictional battles by threatening to withdraw from the AFL. Hutcheson was an avid opponent of **industrial unionism** and fought against the efforts of the **Congress of**

Industrial Organizations (CIO) to establish industry-wide unions. The issue came to a head at the AFL's 1935 convention, where Hutcheson and **John L. Lewis**, head of the mine workers, came to blows with one another. Two big men, rolling around in physical battle on the floor of the convention, brought pandemonium to labor and instituted the formal split of the CIO and its industrial unionists from the trade unionist approach of the AFL. With the prolabor policies of Franklin D. Roosevelt's New Deal, Hutcheson fell into political eclipse. He had been a lifelong Republican, had enjoyed close relationships with probusiness Republican leaders, and adjusted poorly to the close ties of organized labor with the Roosevelt administration. In protest, he resigned from his vice presidency of the AFL in 1936. Although he stepped down from the presidency in 1952, and died a year later, his son Maurice assured the continued influence of his father's policies until 1972.

Suggested Readings: Robert A. Christie, *Empire in Wood: A History of the Carpenters' Union*, 1956; Maxwell C. Raddock, *Portrait of an American Labor Leader: William L. Hutcheson*, 1955.

James P. Hanlan

I

Incentive Pay. Incentive pay is a **wage** compensation plan that links increased production to higher pay. Incentive systems are grounded in individual performance and involve variable pay rates. Some of the most common means of providing incentive pay are **piecework** systems, sales commissions, and **bonuses**. When an entire workforce is rewarded, the most common type of collective incentive is the gainsharing plan, wherein wage incentives are tied to performance targets and/or organizational goals. Such plans attempt to tie tangible rewards to performance that exceeds normal expectations.

In an earlier iteration, the pay for performance system emerged in the auto industry during the 1940s and thrived during World War II under the War Production Board. Aspects of this system persist to the present day. Although contemporary contracts often contain incentive clauses, most unions oppose incentive pay. Some see it as little more than updated **Taylorism**, wherein workers' additional pay is disproportionate with their increased production, while others interpret it as a **speedup** under a different guise. Moreover, the individual nature of incentive pay is antithetical to the collectivist ethos of the union movement.

Suggested Readings: Robert Mathis and John Jackson, *Human Resource Management*, 2002; R. Emmet Murray, *The Lexicon of Labor*, 1999.

Howard Davis

Indentured Servant. An indentured servant is a person contracted to work for another for a specified period of time in exchange for services like transportation to another country, room and board, land, or training. It was one of the earliest forms of exploited labor in America. The term derives from the French *dent,* meaning teeth. In the Anglo American tradition, identical indenture contracts were written side by side and the agreement was torn in half in a ragged, toothlike pattern. One half was given to the indentured servant and the other to his master. Valid contracts could be authenticated by fitting the two pieces together.

Although most seventeenth-century European nations practiced some form of indentured servitude, the English model had the greatest impact on North American colonies. When attempts to entice or force Native Americans to work failed, English joint-stock companies and landed gentry turned to the English poor. Population pressures, land enclosure, and increased agricultural yields created a large class of so-called sturdy beggars within the British Isles, many of whom were reduced to casual and occasional day labor. A sizable part of the population lived in dire poverty with few prospects. Many were recruited to work in the American colonies and, in many cases, individuals were sold to sea captains who gave money to struggling families, hoping to resell the contract at a higher price. Between 1620 and 1700, more than 100,000 poor English men and women came to the future United States as indentured servants. Half of all white settlers outside of New England were either voluntary or involuntary servants. (A substantial number were forced into servitude to pay off debts that would otherwise have led to imprisonment.)

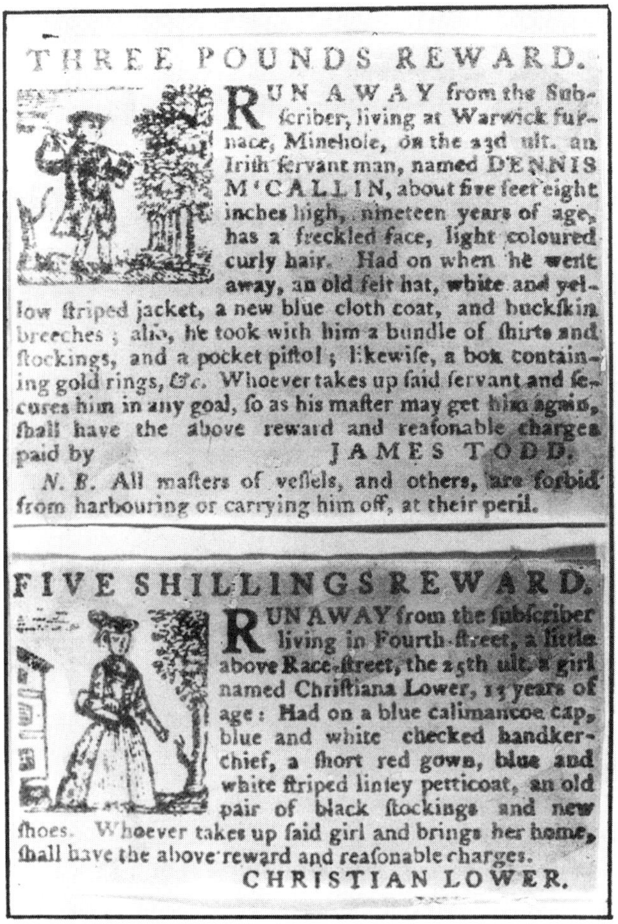

THREE POUNDS REWARD.

RUN AWAY from the Subſcriber, living at Warwick furnace, Minehole, on the 23d ult. an Iriſh ſervant man, named DENNIS M'CALLIN, about five feet eight inches high, nineteen years of age, has a freckled face, light coloured curly hair. Had on when he went away, an old felt hat, white and yellow ſtriped jacket, a new blue cloth coat, and buckſkin breeches; alſo, he took with him a bundle of ſhirts and ſtockings, and a pocket piſtol; likewiſe, a box containing gold rings, &c. Whoever takes up ſaid ſervant and ſecures him in any goal, ſo as his maſter may get him again, ſhall have the above reward and reaſonable charges paid by JAMES TODD.

N. B. All maſters of veſſels, and others, are forbid from harbouring or carrying him off, at their peril.

FIVE SHILLINGS REWARD.

RUN AWAY from the ſubſcriber living in Fourth-ſtreet, a little above Race-ſtreet, the 25th ult. a girl named Chriſtiana Lower, 13 years of age: Had on a blue calimancoe cap, blue and white checked handkerchief, a ſhort red gown, blue and white ſtriped lincey petticoat, an old pair of black ſtockings and new ſhoes. Whoever takes up ſaid girl and brings her home, ſhall have the above reward and reaſonable charges.

CHRISTIAN LOWER.

Colonial newspaper ads offer rewards for the return of runaway indentured servants. © George Meany Memorial Archives.

Many servants faced deplorable conditions in the colonies, and a substantial number starved or died of complications related to poor nutrition and overwork. The situation was particularly dire in Chesapeake Bay colonies where, until the 1640s, many servants died within a year of arrival. The headright system encouraged exploitation. Land was reserved for servants who completed their term—usually four to seven years—but benefits accrued to sponsors if the servant expired before the contract ended. This encouraged some ruthless landowners to work servants to death. Those who survived often ended up working as tenant farmers on plantations as reserved lands were of poor quality, or promised skills necessary for success were never taught.

Indentured servitude began to decline in importance as colonial nutrition and health conditions improved. African slavery largely supplanted the indenture system. Although the first slaves came to Jamestown, Virginia, in 1619, and African slavery was well established in the Caribbean by the 1640s, fragmentary evidence suggests that early North American slaves were few in number and were better treated than white indentures until the 1660s. By 1700, however, fewer indentured servants than slaves arrived in the colonies.

Indentured servitude increased again after 1808, when new slave importation was outlawed. Landowners recruited as far away as India and China for labor, a practice continued by nineteenth-century railroad contractors and manufacturers. Gang labor contracts made with a labor contractor, like the Chinese coolie system or the Italian *padrone* network, could be viewed as forms of indentured servitude even though workers were paid wages. An indentured servitude/slavery amalgam persists in contemporary America. In 2000, *Newsweek* and other news sources revealed that some wealthy Americans employ illegal immigrants as unpaid domestic servants. In addition, successful immigrants often use a form of indentured servitude to bring compatriots to the United States.

Suggested Readings: Gottlieb Mittelberger, *Gottlieb Mittelberger on the Misfortune of Indentured Servants*, 1754; Edmund Morgan, *American Slavery, American Freedom*, 1975; "The New Face of Slavery," *Newsweek* (December 11, 2000).

Lisa Barber
Robert E. Weir

Industrial Unionism. Industrial unionism is a strategy that involves the organization of workers along broad industry lines defined by the production process. Modern industry is complex and includes a wide variety of specialized and nonspecialized labor that contributes to the final product. Often, these processes even take place in different production facilities. For example, automobile assembly line workers produce and handle rubber, plastic, steel, and electrical products to make a single automobile. In addition, the jobs performed in the industry range widely from highly skilled pattern makers and welders to less-skilled line workers. In traditional **craft unionism**, workers would be enrolled in numerous unions instead of a single autoworkers' organization. Industrial unionists argue that organizing workers along craft lines according to skill-based exclusivity reduces the impact and strength of the unions. Instead, unions should follow the lines of production and organize across crafts and industries.

The development of industrial unionism mirrors the spread of mass-production industry. By the 1820s, artisan labor in industries like textiles and shoes faced stiff competition from large-scale factories. After the Civil War, mass production became dominant in most manufacturing firms. Unions like the **Knights of Labor**, the **American Railway Union**, and the **United Mine Workers of America** pioneered in industrial unionism efforts. The **Industrial Workers of the World (IWW)** was the most vocal advocate of industrial unionism in the first two decades of the twentieth century. It criticized the much larger **American Federation of Labor (AFL)** for its restrictive and exclusive organization of skilled craft workers. As mass production industry expanded, craft unionism proved increasingly outmoded. Industrial union advocates rallied to the **Congress of Industrial Organizations (CIO)** after 1935, and the CIO enjoyed success in organizing workers in auto, rubber, textile, glass, electrical, steel, and other heavy industries. The CIO model became the main union organizing strategy in the United States. By the time of the 1955 American Federation of Labor–Congress of Industrial Organizations (AFL-CIO) merger, even the AFL conceded the principle's soundness and sanctioned an Industrial Unionism Department to advance organizing. Industrial unionism remains a key organizational strategy for labor unions in the United States and throughout the world. Its present challenge is adapting to post-industrial economies.

Suggested Readings: Simeon Larson and Bruce Nissen, eds., *Theories of the Labor Movement*, 1987; Ross Martin, *Trade Unionism: Purposes and Forms*, 1989; Michael Poole, *Theories of Trade Unionism: A Sociology of Industrial Relations*, 1981.

Alex Corlu

Industrial Workers of the World (IWW). The Industrial Workers of the World is among the most creative and radical unions to emerge in the United States. It was founded in June 1905 by nearly 200 delegates representing the Western Federation of Miners (WFM) and various smaller unions and **socialist** organizations that were united in their opposition to capitalism and their dislike of the **American Federation of Labor (AFL)**, which they dubbed the "American Separation of Labor." Participating in the Chicago founding convention were many of the American labor movement's most prominent figures, including **Eugene V. Debs**, **Daniel DeLeon**, **William D. Haywood**, **Mary "Mother" Jones**, Lucy Parsons, and **William Trautmann**. While the IWW was never particularly large, it played a leading role in organizing workers previously thought unorganizable, led some of the United States's most dramatic **strikes**, and made remarkable contributions to the culture of the American labor movement. More books and articles have been written about the IWW than about any other union, a testament to the **Wobblies**' (as IWW members are popularly known) pioneering role.

Historians have often described the IWW as an **anarcho-syndicalist** organization, though the union never defined itself that way. Rather, the IWW called for what it alternately called "revolutionary industrial unionism" and "**One Big Union**," concepts that combined commitment to **industrial unionism**, **direct action**, and building a union controlled by its members. IWW organizers believed that such a union would organize workers' power more effectively to battle for better conditions on the job and ultimately bring an end to **capitalism**. The AFL and most unions were organized as **craft unions** that negotiated separately for small groups of workers, which the IWW felt divided workers' collective strength. Moreover, at a time when most unions were reaching an accommodation with capitalism, the IWW preamble reaffirmed that "It is the historic mission of the working class to do away with capitalism." The IWW refused to sign **contracts**, seeing them as dangerous truces in a class war that must be prosecuted to its conclusion.

The New York headquarters of the Industrial Workers of the World (IWW) after a government raid in November 1919. © George Meany Memorial Archives.

The IWW got off to a rocky start, arguing over ideology, organizing strategies, and the wisdom of fighting for higher **wages**. By 1908, the WFM, brewery workers, and followers of Daniel DeLeon had all quit or been expelled, with DeLeon briefly operating an alternative IWW from Detroit. Nonetheless, the small union (fewer than 5,000 members) made impressive gains with silver miners in Goldfield, Nevada (1906), sawmill workers in Portland, Oregon (1907), and smeltermen in Tacoma, Washington (1907). In 1906, Wobblies at a Schenectady, New York, General Electric factory conducted the first-documented **sit-down strike** in American history. The bulk of its strength, however, was in eastern textile mills. By 1911, the IWW had just under 13,000 members. The next year it led massive strikes of textile workers—predominantly unskilled immigrants who had been excluded from the AFL—in Lawrence and Lowell, Massachusetts. The **Lawrence textile strike** became immortalized as the "Bread and Roses" strike. The IWW enjoyed a string of successes in 1912 and 1913, although it lost the 1913 **Paterson silk strike**. That year it formed one of the IWW's longest-lived job branches, an integrated local of longshoremen that controlled the Philadelphia waterfront for a decade. The IWW also organized integrated union locals throughout the South, migratory farm workers on the Great Plains, oil and mine workers in the Southwest, housemaids in Denver, and construction crews across the West. IWW timber workers won clean bedding by burning their infested bedrolls and mattresses and the eight-hour day by stopping work after eight hours.

The IWW showed creative organizational ability, often conducting lightning-quick strikes to win better conditions for workers. It pioneered in reaching workers thought to be unorganizable, like migrant workers and non-English-speaking immigrants. The IWW developed what it called the "thousand mile picket line" to assist Grand Trunk railroad workers in 1912 and harvest workers in 1914 and 1915. It also used multilingual organizers and formed multiethnic locals, thereby belying assumptions that newer immigrants were uninterested in unions.

Few unions have engendered as much opposition as the IWW. Its rhetoric of **sabotage** frightened employers and elites, though most Wobblies defined the word to mean inefficiency rather than destruction. On the West Coast, city councils attempted to curtail IWW activity through ordinances limiting public demonstrations. Between 1909 and 1912, the IWW conducted a series of free speech civil disobedience battles that largely scuttled attempts to erode first amendment rights. Those battles inspired Roger Baldwin, who briefly joined the IWW before founding the American Civil Liberties Union. The IWW also battled the AFL, which often undercut the Wobblies by selling itself to employers as a moderate alternative to the IWW. More damaging, however, were state criminal syndicalism laws that labeled the IWW as a subversive organization and justified official crackdowns of the union, as well as numerous acts of vigilante violence that killed several IWW organizers. The IWW also opposed workers' involvement in World War I, a position that led the federal government to arrest hundreds of union activists for espionage and sedition in 1917 and 1918. One hundred one IWW officials and activists were tried in Chicago. All were convicted and nearly half were given jail sentences ranging from ten to twenty years. State prosecutions for criminal syndicalism continued to hound the organization throughout the 1920s.

Industrial Workers of the World (IWW) demonstration, New York City, April 11, 1914. © Library of Congress.

IWW membership peaked at about 100,000 members in 1917, fell during wartime repression, and rebounded in the early 1920s. However, the IWW never truly recovered from a bitter internal dispute that wracked the union in 1924 and 1925, culminating in the withdrawal of the so-called Emergency Program revitalization faction led by James Rowan and the disruption of promising organizing drives in the construction, maritime, mining, oil, and timber industries. Moreover, a sizable number of one-time members and leaders—including Haywood and **Elizabeth Gurley Flynn**—were inspired by the 1917 Bolshevik revolution in Russia and became communists. Despite the loss of tens of thousands of members, the IWW led two major coal strikes in the Colorado coalfields in 1927, struck the Boulder Dam construction site in 1931, and remained a significant force on the seas and in auto and metalworking into the 1940s. In 1949, the IWW was placed on the U.S. Attorney General's List of Subversive Organizations and it lost National Labor Relations Board representation rights the next year when it voted against signing anti-communist affidavits required by the **Taft-Hartley Act**. Down to a handful of members, the IWW was near extinction when it was revived by an influx of young workers radicalized by the civil rights and antiwar movements during the 1960s. By the 1980s, the IWW had established job control in several small and mid-sized firms primarily in the printing, recycling, retail, and social service sectors. Today the IWW has slightly more than 1,000 dues-paying members, mostly in the United States and Canada.

The IWW is also known for its rich cultural contributions. IWW songwriters—including such notables as Richard Brazier, Ralph Chaplin, and **Joe Hill**—contributed greatly to labor **music**. The IWW's *Little Red Songbook*, now in its thirty-sixth edition, is still used. It has been said that IWW artists invented the labor cartoon, thousands of which illustrated IWW newspapers and appeared as silent agitators—little stickers produced by the thousands to be posted in work sites, bunk houses, and other places workers congregated. The IWW produced scores of labor newspapers, including mimeographed newsletters targeting particular industries; its famous weekly organs, the *Industrial Worker* and *Solidarity*; and dozens of foreign-language titles. Its Finnish-language daily newspaper, *Industrialisti*, appeared for over five decades. While the bulk of the IWW's membership was always in Canada and the United States, the union has also had branches over the years in Australia, the British Isles, Chile, Mexico, New Zealand, and South Africa, while its Marine Transport Workers Industrial Union maintained halls in numerous countries.

Suggested Readings: Stewart Bird, Dan Georgakis, and Deborah Shaffer, *Solidarity Forever: An Oral History of the IWW*, 1985; Melvyn Dubofsky, *We Shall Be All: A History of the IWW*, 1969 (reissued 2000 in abridged edition); Joyce L. Kornbluh, *Rebel Voices: An IWW Anthology*, 1988.

Jon Bekken

International Association of Machinists and Aerospace Workers (IAM). The International Association of Machinists and Aerospace Workers (IAM) represents workers in more than 200 industries, with most of its membership in the United States and Canada. Its forerunner was the Machinists and Blacksmiths' Union founded in 1859, an organization that collapsed shortly after the Panic of 1873. In 1888, Thomas W. Talbott, an Atlanta railroad machinist, revived the union and dubbed it the IAM. The immediate object of the IAM was to raise wages, and membership was restricted to white males.

In 1895, the IAM joined the **American Federation of Labor (AFL)**, two years after AFL President **Samuel Gompers** urged the IAM to drop its whites-only clause. The IAM refused to do so and joined the AFL the one year Gompers was voted out as AFL leader. The IAM maintained racial segregation until 1947, arguing that it was necessary to retain Southern membership. Some critics charged that the IAM had ties with the Ku Klux Klan. The IAM did grow rapidly in the early twentieth century. By 1915, many of its members had won an eight-hour workday, and by 1918, the IAM had more than 331,000 members. In the 1920s, the IAM even experimented with union-owned ship repair yards, print shops, machine shops, and a bank, but few of these thrived. The IAM also lobbied for strong **child labor** laws.

Like many unions, the IAM was weakened during the Great Depression, its membership dropping to 70,000 by 1935. The passage of the **National Labor Relations Act** revitalized the IAM, as did organization efforts in the burgeoning aircraft industry. For much of the 1930s and 1940s, however, the IAM competed for members with **United Auto Workers** in the automotive industry and with the United Aerospace Workers for aircraft workers. In 1949, the IAM signed no-raiding agreements with both unions. These agreements became the model for other unions when the American Federation of Labor and the **Congress of Industrial Organizations** merged in 1955.

The IAM fought to maintain jobs during the reconversion of defense plants to civilian production after World War II. It also took tentative steps to atone for its racist past, and redressing this is a major focus for the IAM today. In 1995, the IAM merged with the United Aerospace Workers. Today the IAM represents more than 730,000 members, making it one of the nation's fastest-growing **industrial unions**. Its 82 percent win rate for certification votes is also one of organized labor's highest. In addition to representing workers in transport, aerospace, railroads, shipbuilding, and woodworking industries, the IAM has been active in the fight to preserve the Social Security system, to reform health care, and to protect worker rights within global trade networks. The current IAM president is Tom Buffenbarger.

Suggested Readings: Derek Bok and John Dunlop, *Labor and the American Community*, 1970; "History of the IAM," http://www.goiam.org/library.asp?N=286.

Maria Ruotolo
Robert E. Weir

International Brotherhood of Papermakers. Although paperworkers have a long tradition of union activity, with their first organizational efforts dating from 1765, modern papermaking unions date from the late nineteenth-century, when a group of paper workers in Holyoke, Massachusetts, organized a local in 1884. From there, union organization spread throughout New England and then throughout the United States and Canada. Initially union membership was restricted to the highly skilled papermakers who passed the "secrets" of their craft from generation to generation, with fathers often introducing sons both to the craft and to the union. The International Brotherhood of Papermakers restricted its membership to the highly skilled craftsmen who mastered the technological complexities of sophisticated paper-making machines and combined that knowledge with closely guarded tricks of the trade. In the early years of the industry, skill and lifelong experience were needed to know when raw materials were properly mixed. It was said that old-time papermakers could tell by tasting the ingredients when the mix of raw materials for the paper machines was correct. A rival organization, the International Brotherhood of Pulp, Sulphite, and Paper Mill Workers evolved to represent skilled, semiskilled, and unskilled workers in the mills. Throughout the late nineteenth and early twentieth-centuries, paperworkers fought to retain the skilled basis of papermaking, while employers attempted to deskill papermaking by employing ever-more sophisticated machinery and technology. The papermakers endured a bitter strike in 1912 in an attempt to secure the eight-hour day and, in an infamous five-year strike in the 1920s, papermakers fought the giant International Paper Company. The battle against International Paper saw strikers and sympathizers evicted from homes in various **company towns**, machine guns erected on company property, and the shooting of strikers by company guards.

During the 1930s, the **Congress of Industrial Organizations (CIO)** established its own organizing committee for paperworkers which resulted in the formation of the United Paperworkers of America. In the 1930s and 1940s, pulp and paper unions enjoyed great success in gaining improvements in wages and benefits. In 1957, following the merger of the **American Federation of Labor** and the CIO, the United Papermakers and Paperworkers (UPP) emerged from combining various **craft** and **industrial unions** in the industry. In 1972, UPP merged with the Pulp and Sulphite Workers to form the United Paperworkers International Union (UPIU), which eventually (1999) merged with the **Oil, Chemical, and Atomic Workers' Union** to form the Paper, Allied-Industrial, Chemical and Energy Workers International Union (PACE).

While paperworkers have made great gains in terms of **wages** and benefits, the industry has largely succeeded in deskilling the trade. Paperworkers now tend sophisticated multi-million-dollar machines, that mixes, measures, calibrates, and manufactures various paper products. Given the ingredients of modern paper, no worker would dare to use the "taste test" employed by the first papermakers. While technology would seem to have given management the upper hand in labor-management relations, the UPIU successfully took on industry giant International Paper in 1983 when, after fifty years of what the union termed "enlightened cooperation," International Paper sought to destroy the union. International Paper brought in new anti-labor executives, hired anti-union consultants, tried to **decertify** existing unions, and sought to discourage unionization at new plants. The paperworkers responded to the challenge by forming **Corporate Campaign, Inc. (CCI)**. CCI used public relations techniques to alert International Paper stockholders, government regulators, institutional investors, and influential business allies to the cost to the company of a potential full-scale disclosure of sensitive labor, environmental, and tax issues. At International Paper's annual stockholder meeting (1983), activists raised questions that proved embarrassing both to the company and to individual executives. Finally, International Paper abandoned its openly anti-union approach. The 1983 battle demonstrated the wisdom of merging the older, smaller unions into an alliance that includes workers from a variety industries, thus giving labor the size and clout to deal effectively with the largest industrial corporations.

Suggested Readings: Harry E. Graham, *The Paper Rebellion: Development and Upheaval in Pulp and Paper Unionism*, 1970; "Paper, Allied-Industrial, Chemical and Energy Workers International Union," http://www.paceunion.org/upiu_history.htm.

James P. Hanlan

International Brotherhood of Teamsters. The International Brotherhood of Teamsters (IBT) was formed in Niagara Falls, New York, in 1903 by the merger of the Midwest-based Team Drivers International Union and the rival Teamsters National Union. **Samuel Gompers**, head of the **American Federation of Labor (AFL)**, was influential in bringing about the merger of the two groups. Two years after its founding, the IBT took on the Chicago-based Montgomery Ward Company. The Ward **strike** lasted 100 days, saw the loss of 21 lives, and cost about one million dollars. Losing the strike, the IBT replaced Cornelius Shea as president with Dan Tobin. Tobin saw that teams of horses, the age-old basis for the teamster's livelihood, were rapidly being replaced by motorized transportation, even as the two modes of transport coexisted and struggled with one another. Tobin stressed organization as the key to the future and won over members by negotiating standardized **contracts**, reduced hours, improved conditions, and overtime pay. During World War I, Tobin made and consolidated union gains. By 1925, the IBT had more than one million dollars in resources, which enabled Tobin to increase strike benefits, seek alliances with the Canadian Trades and Labor Congress, and financially support other struggling unions. The IBT responded to the challenges of the Great Depression by seeking to organize long haul, over-the-road truckers. Key to this effort was gaining control of the truck terminals and using such control to organize the truckers. Tobin welcomed President Roosevelt's New Deal and sought political alliance with the Democratic coalition. During World War II, Tobin led the effort to assure labor peace for the duration of the war, and the IBT stressed war bond sales, scrap metal and rubber drives, and seniority rights for union members returning from the armed services. Under Tobin, the strategy employed by the IBT was to utilize multistate bargaining units, conduct area-wide negotiations, and assure control of trucking terminals. This strategy assured almost certain victory in the event of a strike. In 1952, after 45 years of leadership, Tobin stepped down and was replaced by Dave Beck. In spite of corruption and discord under Beck, the IBT grew stronger, thanks in part of the Federal-Aid Highway Act of 1956, which established the Interstate Highway System and assured the dominance of long-haul trucking in the nation's freight delivery system. In 1957, Dave Beck, tainted by scandal, was replaced by **James Riddle Hoffa** as union president. Under Jimmy Hoffa, IBT's political influence grew, as the union established DRIVE (Democratic, Republican, and Independent Voter Education) as a Political Action Committee (PAC) in 1959. Hoffa, in spite of congressional investigations and notorious clashes with Robert F. Kennedy, was beloved by **rank-and-file** teamsters. In 1964, the Teamsters signed the National Master Freight Agreement (NMFA), a contract for 400,000 members employed by 16,000 trucking companies. The NMFA strengthened benefits, pensions, and working conditions for members and assured that Hoffa would be revered by the rank and file. The NMFA has remained a basic part of IBT's strategy ever since. Following Jimmy Hoffa's imprisonment, Frank Fitzsimmons was named union president. Fitzsimmons never established himself as the beloved leader that Hoffa had been, and the union was troubled with charges of underworld domination. Writer Steven Brill estimated that one-third of IBT locals were squeaky clean, one-third were dominated by organized crime, and one-third were partly tainted. Hoffa's assassination following his release from prison did not help the reputation of the IBT. The IBT, still with truck drivers and warehousemen as its core constituency, is a broad-based union with members in industrial manufacturing, public service, food processing, newspaper, airline, and pipeline industries. Employers fight organizing drives by spreading rumors of IBT corruption, while the IBT emphasizes concrete gains for its members in terms of wages, benefits, and working conditions.

Suggested Readings: Steven Brill, *The Teamsters*, 1978; Walter Sheridan, *The Rise and Fall of Jimmy Hoffa*, 1972.

James P. Hanlan

International Ladies' Garment Workers' Union (ILGWU). The International Ladies' Garment Workers' Union (ILGWU) was one of the twentieth century's most important voices representing needle-trade workers, especially women. The ILGWU sprang to life on June 3, 1900, when eleven delegates from seven local unions representing about 2,000 members met in New York City. It received a charter from the **American Federation of Labor (AFL)** and began fighting for improved working conditions, higher **wages**, and an end to the requirement that workers purchase the equipment they used. The ILGWU was known for the militancy of its early organizational drives, for its work in fighting **sweatshops**, and for initiating both educational and cultural programs for its members. At its onset, the ILGWU was largely comprised of Jewish immigrants who worked in urban sweatshops.

The first great achievement of the ILGWU was an organized walkout of New York City shirtwaist makers in 1909, known as the **Uprising of the 20,000**. That strike was followed by a successful strike of New York City cloak makers in 1910. These back-to-back successes secured the ILGWU's permanency. The cloak-makers' strike, comprised primarily of men as opposed to the shirtwaist makers' strike that was predominantly by women, ended with the first labor-management agreement in the American garment industry. Attributed to John D. Brandeis, the so-called "protocol of peace" created an **arbitration** board for labor disputes, shortened the workweek, created a sanitary commission to eliminate health and safety hazards, and won fixed rates for piecework. The ILGWU was also among the shrillest voices in condemning the 1911 **Triangle Factory fire**, and it increased its membership in the tragedy's aftermath. In 1914, the ILGWU established a union health center to treat tuberculosis among garment workers.

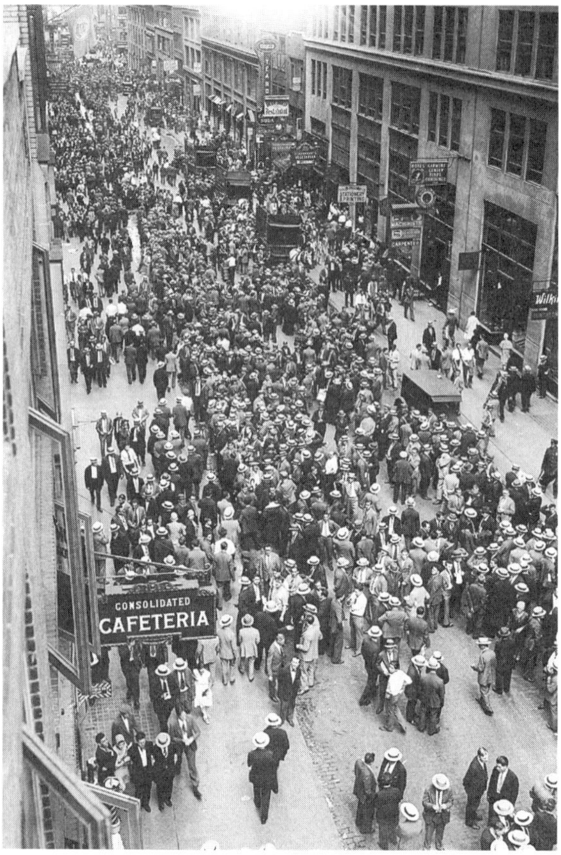

An overhead view of the walkout of 30,000 members of the International Ladies' Garment Workers' Union, the strikers congregating in the garment district in New York, July 3, 1929. © Bettmann/Corbis.

The ILGWU experienced internal upheaval in the 1920s, when communist garment workers attempted to gain control of the union. The upheaval splintered the union until 1932, when **David Dubinsky** was elected president. In 1935, the ILGWU and seven other **industrial unions** formed the Committee for Industrial Organization within the AFL. As a result, the AFL expelled all eight unions in 1937. The following year those unions became the core of the **Congress of Industrial Organizations (CIO)**. The ILGWU, however, withdrew from the CIO in 1940 and resumed its affiliation with the AFL. In the early 1940s, ILGWU contracts included such benefits as paid vacation, health care, and retirement benefits. The ILGWU also commissioned housing developments for workers and opened a summer resort in the Pocono Mountains of Pennsylvania.

The union thrived under Dubinsky's leadership. He is credited with raising membership from approximately 40,000 in 1932 to 450,000 by the 1960s. Dubinsky also helped the ILGWU transform itself from faction-ridden regional organizations into a strong national union with a progressive program focusing on the improvement of pay and working conditions for its members across the country. The ILGWU was involved in the **American Labor Party** in the 1940s and with the Liberal Party in New York state in the 1960s.

The ILGWU's membership began plummeting during the 1970s. By the 1990s, the union had lost approximately 300,000 members due to low-cost imports and the transfer of factories overseas, particularly to Latin America and Asia. In 1995, the ILGWU's remaining 125,000 members merged with the Amalgamated Clothing and Textile Workers' Union to form the 300,000-strong **Union of Needletrades, Industrial, and Textile Employees (UNITE)**.

Suggested Reading: A. H. Raskin, *David Dubinsky: A Life with Labor*, 1977; Gus Tyler, *Look for the Union Label: A History of the International Ladies' Garment Workers' Union*, 1995; "The Triangle Factory Fire," http://www.ilr.cornell.edu/trianglefire/narrative.htm.

Cristina Prochilo

International Union. An international union is a parent union that maintains locals and affiliates outside the United States. Labor unions first applied the term to describe locals established in Canada, but many now seek locals around the globe. The **Knights of Labor** was one of the first unions to have an international presence, with locals as far flung as Australia, Belgium, England, France, New Zealand, and South Africa.

The international is important because it creates a federation that links isolated economic organizations (locals) and enables them to cooperate on issues of mutual importance even while pursuing their own interests. Usually a constitution or sets of bylaws govern the relationship of locals to the international. In most cases, the international also sets the program of locals. An international routinely maintains bureaucratic staffs that administer union affairs. It also hires researchers, organizers, lawyers, and lobbyists that service the locals. That staff assists in recruiting new members, in lobbying politicians and organizations on behalf of workers' issues, and in promoting and supporting broad-based public education. In many cases, locals must also gain the approval of the international before undertaking a work stoppage.

International unions, like the **United Steel Workers of America** or the **United Auto Workers** may be affiliated with a larger labor federation like the American Federation of Labor–Congress of Industrial Organizations, but they are not governed by it and enjoy broad autonomy. In an era of **globalization**, many international unions are looking beyond the United States and Canada and have sought to organize in developing nations as a way to blunt the mobility of **runaway capital**. Locals of American-based unions have formed in Brazil, Japan, Mexico, the Philippines, numerous European nations, and across Latin America and Asia. But, to date, gains have been modest and have not reversed the flight of American corporations abroad.

Suggested Readings: Robert Mathis and John Jackson, *Human Resource Management*, 2002; Kim Moody, *An Injury to All*, 1988; Michael Yates, *Why Unions Matter*, 1998.

Howard Davis

International Union of Electrical, Radio, and Machine Workers of America (IUE). The International Union of Electrical, Radio, and Machine Workers of America (IUE) received a charter from the **Congress of Industrial Organizations (CIO)** in 1949. **James Carey** was installed as the IUE's first international president. The IUE challenged the **United Electrical, Radio, and Machine Workers of America (UE)** for dominance in the electrical manufacturing industry.

Born out of an ideological split within the UE, the IUE allied liberals, Catholics, and Democrats against the UE, whose leadership was accused of coddling communism. The passage of the **Taft-Hartley Act** in 1947 required elected union leaders to sign an affidavit forswearing membership in the Communist Party. The UE was among a small group of unions that refused to sign Taft-Hartley affidavits. Between 1947 and the IUE's birth in 1949, the UE was **raided** by rival unions more than 500 times and lost members and entire locals to unions like the **United Auto Workers (UAW)** and the International Brotherhood of Electrical Workers (IBEW).

After 1949, the IUE began organizing new locals in the electrical manufacturing industry as well as incorporating locals that chose to leave the UE. By 1950, the IUE represented about half of all organized General Electric and Westinghouse workers and the UE a mere 10 percent. This made the IUE the leading union in the electrical manufacturing industry. At its peak in 1955, the IUE claimed about 325,000 members. By the early 1950s, the IUE's leadership core centered around Carey, Secretary-Treasurer Al Hartnett of St. Louis, and Western states' regional director James Click. All three were ardent anticommunists, though Hartnett and Click were later purged by Carey over policy differences. In 1966, Carey was ousted from the presidency by Paul Jennings.

By then, both the IUE and the electrical industry were undergoing a shakeup. In 1960, IUE leaders called an ill-advised industrywide **strike** against General Electric. Despite elaborate preparations, numerous IUE locals refused to honor the strike call, leaving the IUE in total disarray. During this period, union membership in the electrical manufacturing industry fell to 56 percent. Market competition, aggressive corporate antiunion strategies, and fierce interunion fighting led to a overall weakening of the IUE.

By the 1970s, the IUE recovered enough to unite forces with the UE and other unions and to secure a series of contracts with General Electric that delivered high wages and good benefits to members. These proved temporary victories, however. Severe economic downturns in the late 1970s and into the 1980s led to layoffs and plant closings that made it difficult for industrial unions to maintain membership services and benefits. Consolidation of the electrical industry was mirrored by unions. In 2000, the IUE merged with the Communications Workers of America (CWA).

Suggested Readings: Ronald Filippelli and M. D. McColloch, *Cold War in the Working Class: The Rise and Decline of the United Electrical Workers*, 1995; James Green, *The World of the Worker: Labor in Twentieth Century America*, 1998; Ron Schatz, *The Electrical Workers: A History of Labor at General Electric and Westinghouse, 1923–60*, 1983.

Mike Bonislawski

International Union of Mine, Mill, and Smelter Workers. The International Union of Mine, Mill, and Smelter Workers (IUMMSW) was founded on May 15, 1893, as the Western Federation of Miners (WFM), a union of hard-rock miners with a reputation for feisty radicalism in the tough mining communities of the American West. The WFM was active in the founding of the **Industrial Workers of the World (IWW)** in 1905. The union adopted its present name in 1916. In 1936, the union helped to found the **Congress of Industrial Organizations (CIO)** but was expelled thirteen years later in the CIO's purge of radical unions. From 1949 through 1967, the organization maintained an independent identity. In 1967, convention delegates voted to merge with the **United Steel Workers of America (USWA)**. At the time of the merger, the IUMMSW had 37,000 members in 300 locals.

James P. Hanlan

Iron Molders' Union. Since it was formed in 1859 by **William Sylvis** as the National Union of Iron Molders, the Iron Molders' Union has gone through a number of name changes, reflecting changes in membership, for example, the addition of core makers in 1903, brass molders in 1911, and foundry workers in 1943. In 1899, the Iron Molders reached an arbitration agreement with the National Founders' Association (NFA), called the New York Agreement. This agreement was abrogated in 1904 by the NFA and the **open shop** was established, leading to a national **strike** from which the union never recovered.

Suggested Readings: Florence Peterson, *Handbook of Labor Unions*, 1994; Benjamin J. Taylor and Fred Witney, *U.S. Labor Relations Law: Historical Development*, 1992.

Bruce Cohen

J

Jim Crow. Jim Crow is a term that refers to a system of laws and customs that enforced racial discrimination and segregation in the United States from the nineteenth century through the late 1960s. The term derives from popular nineteenth-century minstrel shows in which white actors blackened their faces to lampoon African American song and dance. Jim Crow was a stock figure in such productions. During Reconstruction after the Civil War, Southern states enacted various Black Codes to keep newly freed slaves in a subordinate status. But, it was not until the collapse of Radical Reconstruction after 1877 that Jim Crow systems emerged in full force.

African American carpenters working in a segregated shop. © George Meany Memorial Archives/Library of Congress.

Despite the passage of the Thirteenth, Fourteenth, and Fifteenth Amendments to the Constitution, white supremacy increasingly gained legal as well as cultural and social status. This was cemented by the Supreme Court's 1896 *Plessy v. Ferguson* decision that ruled segregation legal under the rubric of "separate but equal." By the early twentieth century, most public facilities and transportation systems in the South and much of the North were segregated, and many states had laws outlawing racial mixing and miscegenation. Moreover, the black voting franchise was severely curtailed through legal statutes, unfair taxes, and terror.

After the decline of the **Knights of Labor** in the 1890s, most American labor groups rejected its multiracial approach, and practiced discrimination and segregation. Numerous constituent unions within the **American Federation of Labor** forbade black membership, although the **United Mine Workers of America**, dock workers, and the **United Packinghouse Workers of America** made noble efforts to combat racism, as did communists, **socialists**, and members of the **Industrial Workers of the World**. But black workers would not come into the mainstream labor movement in large numbers until the late 1930s, when unions affiliated with the **Congress of Industrial Organizations** challenged Jim Crow assumptions. Even then Jim Crow systems did not lose legal acceptance until the Civil Rights Act of 1964, and racism remains in some areas of the deep South.

Suggested Readings: Philip Foner and Ronald Lewis, eds., *Black Workers*, 1989; William Harris, *The Harder We Run*, 1982; David Roediger, *The Wages of Whiteness*, 1992; C. Vann Woodward, *The Strange Career of Jim Crow*, 1974.

Shalynn Hunt
Robert E. Weir

Joint Agreement. In labor relations, a joint agreement is an accord between a union and a management representative, derived through **collective bargaining** or mutual consensus. Joint agreements usually center on specific issues and involve cooperation rather than adversarial relations. Where unions and businesses form joint agreements, they often take the form of labor-management councils. Both sides become equal partners in creating the joint effort. Labor-management processes are used in dealing with collective bargaining issues during the life of a **contract**. These agreements foster open communication and enable a consensus decision-making pattern. Joint agreements are largely a product of the post–World War II era and reflect a mature relationship between the parties.

Suggested Reading: National Labor Management Association, http://www.nlma.org.

Kenneth Ferus

Jones, Mary Harris "Mother" (May 1, 1830?–November 30, 1930). Mary Harris "Mother" Jones was an important activist for the cause of laborers, especially miners. Her career is among the most colorful in American labor history. She was born in Cork, Ireland, the daughter of Richard and Helen Harris. Her date of birth is in dispute, with dates varying from as early as 1830 to as late as 1837. Her family emigrated to Canada in the 1840s, and Harris received both a public and convent school education. She taught at a convent school in Monroe, Michigan, went to Chicago and worked as a dressmaker, and returned to teaching when she moved to Memphis, Tennessee. In 1861, she married George Jones, an ironworker and a member of the **Iron Molders' Union**, with whom she had four children. Jones introduced her to the labor movement and the social injustices that workers endured.

Mary Jones's life was shattered in 1867 when her husband and children all died of yellow fever. Devastated, she returned to Chicago and resumed making dresses, only to lose everything she had in the Great Chicago Fire of 1871. Destitute, she began attending **Knights of Labor (KOL)** meetings because of her interest in the KOL's campaign for better working conditions. Jones identified with the laborers' plight and found her voice. Inflamed by the **Haymarket** riot of 1886, Jones began a full-fledged career as a labor activist, though she was well into her fifties. Workers dubbed the gray-haired crusader "Mother" Jones.

Mary Harris "Mother" Jones. © George Meany Memorial Archives/Public Affairs Press.

Jones's fiery rhetoric and tenacious advocacy for workers' rights earned her other nicknames—"the grandmother of all agitators," "hell-raiser," and "the miners' angel." She was involved in a number of labor campaigns throughout her career but is best known for her organization of coal miners. She traveled across the country as an official organizer for the **United Mine Workers of America (UMWA)** as well as an independent lecturer. Grandmotherly in demeanor, but a fierce rabble-rouser, Jones referred to the coal miners as her "boys" and thought of them as a surrogate family. Without a house or family of her own, Jones traveled wherever there "was a fight worth fighting" and lodged with working-class families. Her activities included organizing coal miners in West Virginia in 1902 and 1903 and those in Colorado in 1903 and 1904. In 1903, she drew public attention to the plight of textile workers through a dramatic march of their impoverished children to Oyster Bay, New York, where she embarrassed President Theodore Roosevelt at his summer retreat.

Jones grew disgusted with conservative UMWA leadership in the early 1900s and briefly quit the union. Although never an ideologue, Jones's devotion to working people inclined her toward **socialism**, although her conventional views of gender roles meant that she never embraced suffrage or feminist movements. She attended founding conventions for the Social Democratic Party in 1898 and the **Industrial Workers of the World (IWW)** in 1905. In

1910, Jones agitated on behalf of Colorado copper miners and Union Pacific Railroad employees. She rejoined the UMWA in 1911 and returned to the Colorado coalfields in 1913 and 1914, where she witnessed the **Ludlow Massacre**. She reached the height of her fame during the Colorado struggles, when she was deported from the area numerous times and then jailed for defying court orders to stay away from the area.

Jones was imprisoned many times for her unionizing efforts and was even arrested for conspiracy to commit murder during the West Virginia troubles. She exploited her advanced age and diminutive figure—she stood under five feet tall—to avoid prolonged imprisonment, and Jones's willingness to put her body on the line won her the unflagging admiration of workers. Her mere presence at a **strike** or rally bolstered morale and she was much in demand. She was involved in New York City garment worker strikes in 1915 and 1916, and the **Steel Strike of 1919**. In the 1920s, Jones once again quit the UMWA, citing differences with **John L. Lewis**. Despite deteriorating health, Jones continued agitating well into her nineties. She made her last public appearance in Silver Spring, Maryland, in 1930, where she died in November. At her request, she was buried with her "boys" in the Union Miners Cemetery in Mount Olive, Illinois. Jones's aphorism, "Pray for the dead and fight like hell for the living," is still much quoted among labor activists.

Suggested Readings: Dale Fetherling, *Mother Jones: The Miners' Angel*, 1974; Elliot Gorn, *Mother Jones: The Most Dangerous Woman in America*, 2000; Mary Harris Jones, *Autobiography of Mother Jones*, ed. Mary Field Parton, 1925.

Cristina Prochilo

Journeyman. Journeyman is a term used to describe a person who successfully completes an **apprenticeship** and is qualified to work for the top **wages** in a particular trade. Its origins lie in the medieval guild system, and it derives from the French word for day, *journée*. In artisan-based colonial and early republican times, a journeyman worked for a **master craftsman** and was paid a daily wage. In this system, a journeyman expected that after several years of work and saving, he would become a master craftsman, open his own shop, and employ apprentices and journeymen. By the early nineteenth century, however, market pressures and capital concentration eroded journeymen's prospects. Journeymen began to organize to protect their tenuous status as free republican laborers. They were important in the development of trade unions and the **Workingmen's Movement** in the 1830s and 1840s. Industrialization, mass production, and the decline of craft work changed the status of journeymen. By the early twentieth century, the term came to be understood as denoting a person who completed a trade union apprenticeship and was competent to work independently in that trade.

Suggested Readings: Bruce Laurie, *Artisans to Workers*, 1989; Sean Wilentz, *Chants Democratic*, 1984.

Stephen Micelli

Jurisdiction. Jurisdiction refers to the boundaries of a union's representation. This is usually determined by the type of work an employee performs. Jurisdiction confers **collective bargaining** rights on the union that holds it. Contracts often specify who can do certain jobs. In construction organizing, for example, a question may arise as to whether the job being done by an employee belongs to a bricklayer or carpenter.

Many historical disputes between unions took place over the question of jurisdiction. This is particularly the case when two or more federations seek to organize the same employees. In the nineteenth century, for example, the **Knights of Labor** and the **American Federation of Labor (AFL)** sought to organize workers in a host of overlapping fields. Once each organization got a foothold in a particular industry, it sought to lure workers from its rival. Unfortunately, this sort of **raiding** has been commonplace in labor history. The AFL also sought to raid rivals like the **Industrial Workers of the World** and the **Congress of Industrial Organizations (CIO)**. The 1955 American Federation of Labor–Congress of Industrial Organizations merger established procedures to settle jurisdictional disputes, but these still occur. It is an especially hot topic in the contemporary labor movement as shifts in work have rendered older craft and industrial union models problematic. For example, the **United Auto Workers** represents writers, graduate students, teachers, and numerous other professions as well as autoworkers. Disputes arise from these cloudy jurisdictional boundaries.

Suggested Reading: Bernard Ward and Linda Mullenix, *Understanding Federal Courts and Jurisdiction*, 1999.

Kenneth Ferus

K

Knights of Labor (KOL). The Knights of Labor (KOL) was the largest labor federation of the nineteenth century. Its progressive views on gender and race were well ahead of its time, as were its efforts at international organizing, political lobbying, and **industrial unionism**.

The KOL was founded by Uriah Stephens and six other members of a Philadelphia tailors' union in December 1869, a time in which trade unions were in decline due to economic recession and political repression. When Stephens dissolved his tailors' union, he chose to pattern the KOL after a more successful form of voluntary association: fraternal orders. The new organization, officially the Noble and Holy Order of the Knights of Labor, operated in complete secrecy in accordance with a dense code of rituals freely adapted from Freemasonry. Secrecy and the complexity of KOL ritual meant that growth was quite slow, and the KOL did not expand beyond the greater Philadelphia region until 1874. It did not write a constitution or statement of principles until 1878, at which time it contained about 10,000 members.

The KOL gained momentum from railroad **strikes** associated with the **Great Labor Uprising** and steadily grew. In 1879, Stephens resigned as the KOL's grand master workman (president) to run for Congress and was succeeded by **Terence V. Powderly**, who held the post until late 1893. Powderly, a Catholic, lobbied the KOL to change its focus on ritual and secrecy to mollify Vatican bans on secret societies, and to insulate the KOL from hysteria over the **Molly Maguires**. In 1882, the KOL finally abandoned secrecy, although its ritual practices remained a closely guarded mystery.

The KOL embraced a multipronged reform agenda that embraced everything from land reform and the eight-hour day to equal rights for women and the abolition of the **wage** system. It was not a trade union, but rather a federation of constituent unions. Historians often classify the KOL as a social-reform union, though many of its precepts inclined more towards **utopianism**. In theory, the yearly General Assembly and the executive board it elected were the KOL's highest governing bodies. Local assemblies were an eclectic mix, with some being single-trade locals and others mixed assemblies in which various trades sat. In addition, some locals were single gender or race, while others were mixed. Local assemblies combined into district assemblies, and there were also state assemblies and a few national trade districts that represented the interests of specific trades. Since each level of KOL bureaucracy had officers and courts to resolve disputes, exact lines of authority were murky, and most efforts at centralization met with limited success. Ideological lines were also unclear. Anyone, including employers, was eligible for KOL membership as long as they were not lawyers, bankers, land speculators, gamblers, or liquor traders. (The KOL was officially in favor of temperance.) The KOL's history is marked by contentiousness.

An anti–Knights of Labor cartoon. © George Meany Memorial Archives.

In principle, the KOL opposed strikes, believing that more was lost than was ever gained. Instead, it endorsed **boycotts** (both primary and secondary) as a way of bringing recalcitrant employers to their knees. Ultimately, the KOL hoped that a system of mandatory **arbitration** would settle all capital and labor disputes. The KOL insisted that the interests of workers and employers was mutual, though it felt that arbitration and boycotts would lead to the demise of the wage system in favor of a network of productive and distributive **cooperatives**. The KOL engaged in hundreds of cooperative experiments, most of which were short-lived and unsuccessful.

Despite official reluctance, the KOL did engage in strikes; most were unsuccessful. The KOL was one of the first labor groups to organize mass-production industries and was thus the first to deal with the full economic and political clout of organized capital. In 1885, however, the KOL won a strike against the Southwest Railway conglomerate, controlled by Jay Gould, one of the most-hated robber barons of the nineteenth century. Membership soared from 110,000 in 1885 to over 729,000 dues-paying members a year later with hundreds of thousands more claiming affiliation with the organization.

The KOL quickly contracted from this artificial plateau, but it contained over 250,000 members for the rest of the 1880s and around 100,000 for the first part of the 1890s. Powderly was a figure of international fame, and his advice was sought on a variety of matters by politicians, journalists, and clerics. The KOL sent a paid labor lobbyist to Washington, D.C., the first labor federation to do so. By the mid-1890s, it had also organized over 90,000 African Americans and more than 60,000 women. Its success at organizing unskilled workers, women, and African Americans on an equal basis as skilled white males remained unsurpassed until the 1930s. The KOL also pioneered international unionization efforts, forming chapters in Australia, Belgium, Canada, England, France, Ireland, New Zealand, Scotland, and South Africa. It achieved its greatest success in New Zealand, where more than two dozen Knights were elected to Parliament and where it enacted the bulk of its political and social platform.

The promise of the Knights did not materialize in North America. The KOL was hurt by the 1886 **Haymarket** riot and was weakened by a series of disastrous strikes in the late 1880s and early 1890s. It also got embroiled in ill-advised ideological and **jurisdictional** disputes with trade unions and was burdened with internal conflict. By the mid-1890s, the KOL was in severe decline and was eclipsed by the **American Federation of Labor**, though the latter was much more exclusionary than the KOL. The KOL closed its national office in 1917, though there was one operating local assembly as late as 1949. It is estimated that more than 2.5 million men and women passed through the KOL ranks and that more than 10,000 local assemblies were formed. Despite practices that some critics found archaic, much of what the KOL attempted was far in advance of its time and many of its principles are progressive even by modern standards.

Suggested Readings: Leon Fink, *Workingmen's Democracy,* 1983; Robert E. Weir, *Beyond Labor's Veil,* 1996; Robert E. Weir, *Knights Unhorsed,* 2000.

Robert E. Weir

Knights of St. Crispin (KOSC). The Knights of St. Crispin (KOSC) was a trade union of shoemakers founded in 1867 and named for the third-century figure recognized as the patron saint of the craft. By 1870, after a number of successful **arbitration** agreements and strikes, the KOSC achieved a membership of almost 50,000, briefly making it the largest **craft union** in the nation. Most Crispins felt that a larger labor federation was necessary to give discrete labor unions a combined voice. Many Crispins were present at an 1873 industrial conference that created the short-lived Industrial Brotherhood.

Like many nineteenth-century unions, the KOSC opposed **strikes** on principle and called for mandatory arbitration of labor disputes. Alas, the KOSC often encountered employers who were far less amenable to the peaceful settlement of disputes. In an 1870 strike in North Adams, Massachusetts, employers imported seventy-five Chinese **scabs** rather than submit to arbitration. To its credit, the KOSC attempted to organize the Chinese rather than fall prey to the popular anti-Chinese racism of the day. The KOSC was also more open to organizing women than most unions and, in 1868, formed the Daughters of St. Crispin.

Lost strikes in the early 1870s depleted KOSC ranks, but it was one of the very few craft unions to survive the severe economic downturn known as the Panic of 1873. Survival proved ephemeral, however, and the refusal of manufacturers in Lynn, Massachusetts—the nation's largest shoemaking center—to negotiate with the KOSC killed the union. Key KOSC leaders attended the first national conference of the **Knights of Labor (KOL)** held in 1878, and folded remaining KOSC locals into the KOL.

In the early days of the KOL, numerous important leaders—including Charles Litchman, Richard Griffiths, and Harry Skeffington—were former Crispins. Skeffington played a key role in convincing the KOL to initiate women as Knights. By the early 1880s, the KOL contained several district assemblies dominated by shoemakers and, in 1885, a national trade district of shoe and leather workers formed under KOL auspices, though the details of its structure took almost two years to determine and members began to drift from the KOL by the time it was finalized.

KOL shoemakers initially enjoyed good relations with the Lasters' Protective Union (LPU), the only other national shoemaker's union, but the relationship soured after the loss of a traumatic 1887 strike in Massachusetts. By then, the KOL was involved in **jurisdiction** battles with the newly formed **American Federation of Labor (AFL)**, which made overtures to the LPU and disgruntled KOL shoemakers. In 1889, Harry Skeffington led most of the shoemakers out of the KOL and created the **Boot and Shoeworkers' International Union**, which affiliated with the AFL.

Suggested Readings: Mary Blewett, *We Will Rise in Our Might: Workingwomen's Voices from Nineteenth-Century New England*, 1991; Norman Ware, *The Labor Movement in the United States 1860–95*, 1929.

Bruce Cohen
Robert E. Weir

L

Labor Day. Labor Day is a holiday held the first Monday in September to commemorate the achievements of American workers. It is also celebrated in Canada, though workers in many other nations prefer **May Day**. Though it is now an established fixture on the North American calendar, the first workers' holiday was born out of struggle and defiance. Parades and rallies were a staple of nineteenth-century **working-class** protests, and Labor Day emerged from those patterns.

On Tuesday, September 5, 1882, between 30,000 and 40,000 workers marched in New York City rather than report to their jobs, while thousands more watched. This is considered the first Labor Day, though a smaller rally took place several weeks earlier in Providence, Rhode Island. The term "Labor Day" appears to have been coined by Robert Price, a **Knights of Labor (KOL)** member in Maryland. Price suggested an annual holiday in honor of KOL founder Uriah Stephens, whose birthday was on August 3, making the Rhode Island event closer to Price's original vision. **Peter James McGuire**, a carpenter and KOL member, spoke at the Providence event.

McGuire's presence in Rhode Island has led to confusion over the origins of Labor Day, with McGuire often wrongly hailed as the "Father of Labor Day." In fact, the planning of the New York City event lay in the hands of the city's **Central Labor Union (CLU)**, a cooperating consortium of local unions whose officers largely interlocked with those of local Knights of Labor. A KOL machinist named Matthew Maguire was in charge of the Committee of Arrangements, with Peter McGuire simply an active CLU member. The fact that Matthew Maguire was a committed **socialist** may also explain why later labor mythmakers preferred to credit Peter McGuire as he was a leader in the more respectable **American Federation of Labor (AFL)** in 1886.

The size of the New York City event inspired workers elsewhere, and for the next several years, other cities held their own impromptu parades. It was not until 1884 that New York City celebrated on a Monday, and not until 1886 that workers across the country celebrated on that same day. In 1887, Oregon became the first state to recognize Labor Day as a legal holiday. In the same year, Massachusetts, New Jersey, and New York passed similar measures. Workers elsewhere simply took matters into their own hands until, by 1894, twenty-three states officially recognized Labor Day. On June 28, 1894, Congress declared the first Monday in September Labor Day.

A depiction of the first Labor Day parade in New York City in September 1882. © George Meany Memorial Archives.

Labor Day was marked by large parades and speeches, followed by picnics and other forms of recreation. By 1890, the KOL was in decline and the AFL in the ascendancy, though the economic challenges of the 1890s did much to dampen Labor Day enthusiasm. By the 1910s, some labor leaders complained that workers had forgotten about the true intent of the day. Passions were rekindled during the Great Depression, a time in which public protest rose anew, and, after 1947, unions often organized protests against the **Taft-Hartley Act** on Labor Day. Since the mid-1950s, however, the holiday has largely moved from a day of protest to a more commemorative event. Ideologues hold that Labor Day wraps America's bloody labor history in a false cloak of respectability, while its defenders see it as an important affirmation of working-class heritage and culture.

Suggested Readings: Paul Buhle, Scott Molloy, and Gail Sainsbury, *A History of Rhode Island Working People*, 1983; Michael Kazin and Steven Ross, "America's Labor Day: The Dilemma of a Workers' Celebration," *Journal of American History* (March 1992): 1294–1323; Robert E. Weir, *Beyond Labor's Veil: The Culture of the Knights of Labor*, 1996.

Robert E. Weir

Labor Fakir. Labor fakir is an archaic term of derision used to refer to a labor leader who is self-aggrandizing and does not represent the interests of **rank-and-file** workers. It was popular in the late nineteenth and early twentieth century, but has passed out of fashion.

The term *fakir* is Arabic in origin and was originally associated with Hindu and Muslim ascetics whom the general populace regarded as having magical powers. When applied to a labor leader, however, fakir implies the phoniness of a charlatan rather than the activities of a holy man. Labor fakirs were often lumped with vote-seeking politicians who used hollow flattery and vague promises to solicit **working-class** support for personal advancement. Radicals even claimed such labor leaders were a subclass of capitalist exploiters. Critics like **Daniel DeLeon** charged that labor fakirs sought middle-class respectability and that such pursuits imbued working people with false promises and diverted them from the task of overthrowing **capitalism**.

The term was once so widespread that it was applied indiscriminately to express discontent with any leader's policies. It tended, however, to apply mostly against leaders who headed labor bureaucracies. Both **Terence Powderly** of the **Knights of Labor (KOL)**, and **Samuel Gompers** of the **American Federation of Labor (AFL)** faced charges of being labor fakirs. **Socialists** used the term in their 1894 campaign to unseat Gompers as AFL president, while the **Industrial Workers of the World (IWW)** viewed most AFL leaders as fakirs.

Labor fakir was closely aligned to the term "walking delegate," though the latter was used most often to describe deal makers at union conventions. It is important to note that both terms were used by critics, and the terms often expressed more the ideology of the users rather than the values of those to whom they were applied. Today the term "**business unionism**" is used much the same way. Depending on one's point of view, business unionism is either a wise policy or a betrayal of working-class interests.

Suggested Reading: Daniel DeLeon, "Plain Words to Boston Workingmen, Jew and Gentile," 1897, in Daniel DeLeon Internet Archive, http://www.marxistsfr.cjb.net/archives/deleon.pdf.

Robert E. Weir

Labor Journalism. From its beginnings in early nineteenth-century America, labor journalism has provided working men and women with an outlet not often available in the mainstream press. In the decades leading up to the Civil War, the birth of American industrialism fueled class tensions, and early labor groups formed in protest. Feeling that their interests were not accurately or adequately represented by the standard newspapers of the day, these labor groups created their own newspapers. Two of the most prominent labor newspapers in antebellum America started publication in 1828: the *Mechanics Free Press*, founded by Philadelphia-based labor activist William Heighton; and the *Working Man's Advocate*, published by George Henry Evans as the voice of New

York City's Workingmen's Party. These early labor newspapers reflected the growing concerns of skilled male workers, then known as "mechanics" or "**journeymen**" who felt threatened by the growth of industrial capitalism.

As increasing numbers of white women entered industrial labor, they too expressed their displeasure, especially at the **paternalism** of New England mill owners. As a corrective to the corporation-sponsored journal, the *Lowell Offering*, organized mill women purchased the *Voice of Industry*, which was edited for a short time during the mid-1840s by mill worker and leader of the Lowell Female Labor Reform Association, **Sarah Bagley**. The *Voice of Industry*, like the *Mechanics Free Press* and the *Working Man's Advocate*, argued for the right of workers to form "associations" or unions as a way of protecting their interests in the face of nascent industrial capitalism and advocated for the continued need of political redress.

Title page of the *Lowell Offering*. © Library of Congress.

The second half of the nineteenth century saw the rise of a national labor press in the form of newspapers sponsored by both the **Knights of Labor (KOL)** and the **American Federation of Labor (AFL)**. By the 1890s, the *Journal of the Knights of Labor* and the *American Federationist* represented the constituent unions of these respective organizations, reaching thousands of American working men and women. In these newspapers, as well as in scores published by specific craft unions and KOL locals, news articles regularly appeared about particular trades and commentary on national politics and world events as they related to the concerns of American labor. Unconnected to a specific union but still supportive of labor was *John Swinton's Paper*, which began publication in 1883. During its four years of existence, it sought to expose the exploitative and often dangerous working conditions endured by a growing number of American workers, especially women and children. Other important **working-class** newspapers in the late nineteenth century included the *National Labor Tribune* and the *Irish World and American Industrial Liberator*.

The twentieth century brought a further increase in the number of outlets for labor-oriented news. While the AFL continued publishing the *American Federationist*, the more radical **Industrial Workers of the World (IWW)**, founded in 1905, had its own monthly papers, including the Seattle-based publication, the *Industrial Worker*. Foreign-language periodicals, supported by the massive wave of immigration to the United States at the end of the nineteenth and beginning of the twentieth centuries, also provided access to labor-related news, as did those newspapers associated with radical politics, such as the *International Socialist Review*. The *Daily Worker*, the official voice of the American **Communist** Party, published party news as well as labor-related features for more than thirty years (1924–58). At the same time, mainstream journalists sympathetic to the labor cause, such as **Mary Heaton Vorse**, published gripping accounts of **strikes** and of the horrendous working conditions in widely circulated journals such as *Harper's*, the *New Republic*, and the *Nation*. Vorse, a prolific writer, also published several books based on her labor journalism, which remain useful for historians of labor. These include *Men and Steel* (1920), which focuses on the **steel strike of 1919**, and *Strike!* (1930), an examination of the protracted and violent strike of textile mill workers in Gastonia, North Carolina, in 1929.

In addition to writing for mainstream publications, Vorse was one of several journalists who provided copy for the Federated Press, a left-wing news agency founded by Carl Haessler in 1919 as a counterpart to the more conservative news services such as the Associated Press. For almost forty years, the Federated Press supplied its subscribers, primarily newspapers associated with trade unions or radical political movements, with news features that emphasized the concerns of labor. Labor journalism also took to the airwaves with the 1926 founding of WCFL, a radio station sponsored by the Chicago Federation of Labor, and WEVD in New York City, a station associated with the **Socialist** Party whose call letters honored **Eugene V. Debs**.

In the post–World War II era, much of organized labor became more conservative, reflecting the retrenchment of the Cold War. Nonetheless, at the end of the twentieth century, labor journalism remained alive in some portions of the American press. Large international unions, such as the **United Auto Workers (UAW)** and **Union of Needletrades, Industrial, and Textile Employees (UNITE)**, publish monthly journals, and liberal-oriented outlets such as *The Nation* and *Mother Jones* regularly print labor-related articles. Labor journalism, like all forms of communication, has been touched by the revolution in technology. Founded in 1979, *Labor Notes* "has been the voice of union activists who want to 'put the movement back into the labor movement'" in a printed monthly newsletter and on its Web site. So, too, the weekly newsletter of the AFL-CIO, *Work in Progress*, can be received via fax or online. Despite the impact of revolutionary technological change, the intent of labor journalism has remained the same over the last two centuries: To provide a space for the voices of America's working men and women.

Suggested Readings: Nathan Godfried, *WCFL: Chicago's Voice of Labor*, 1997; Nathan Godfried, "Struggling over Politics and Culture: Organized Labor and Radio Station WEVD during the 1930s," *Labor History* 42, no. 4 (November 2001); Sam Pizzigati and Fred J. Solowey, eds.,

The New Labor Press: Journalism for a Changing Labor Movement, 1992; Rodger Streitmatter, "Origins of the American Labor Press," *Journalism History* 25:3 (Autumn 1999).

Kathleen Banks Nutter

Labor-Management Reporting and Disclosure Act of 1959 (Landrum-Griffin Act). This legislation was a direct result of the political climate of the 1950s and the findings of the Senate Select Committee on Improper Activities in the Labor or Management Field, informally known as the McClellan Committee, after its chairman, Senator John L. McClellan (D-Ark.). Initially the committee concentrated its attention on charges of corruption brought against both labor and management, but over time the focus shifted to allegations of corruption and autocratic methods in labor unions. The committee's work was brought to widespread attention by the newly popular medium of television. Opponents of organized labor used the committee to call attention to the wrongdoings of union officers, the use of violence by certain segments of the labor movement, the diversion and misuse of union funds, collusion between corrupt union officials and dishonest employers, the coercion of both employees and small employers by the use of secondary boycotts and organizational picketing, and interference with employee rights.

Labor leaders misread the results of the 1958 congressional elections, which had returned substantial Democratic majorities in both the House and the Senate. The Democratic sweep was facilitated by active campaigning by organized labor against right-to-work statutes and against anti-labor candidates. After the election, however, conservatives raised fears of a Congress dominated by "labor bosses," and called on Congress to act "responsibly" by passing labor reform legislation. Conflict within the American Federation of Labor-Congress of Industrial Organizations (AFL-CIO) led organized labor to assume too much of their Congressional allies and caused labor to fail to form a united front against anti-labor legislation. Although the AFL-CIO expelled from membership three of the unions identified as the most corrupt by the McClellan Committee (the **International Brotherhood of Teamsters**, the Bakery and Confectionery Workers Union, and the Laundry Workers Union), President Dwight Eisenhower and Congressional leaders insisted that reform legislation was necessary. The result was the Landrum-Griffin Act, the second major revision, after the **Taft-Hartley Act**, to the **National Labor Relations Act**.

The Landrum-Griffin Act provided for the regulation of union internal affairs, including regulation and control of union funds. The legislation banned former members of the **Communist** Party (CPUSA) as well as former convicts from holding union office for a period of five years from either their resignation from the CPUSA or their release from prison. Secondary **boycotting** and organizational and recognition picketing (**picketing** a business where a rival union was recognized) were restricted. Union members were guaranteed a "bill of rights" that protected freedom of speech and provided for periodic secret elections. Individual states were allowed greater freedom to regulate labor relations within their borders, especially in cases that fell outside the jurisdiction of the National Labor Relations Board.

The effect of the act was to strengthen the anti-labor provisions of the Taft-Hartley Act and to weaken labor's ability to organize in the South, the least unionized region in the country. It should be noted that almost none of the provisions regulating unions under the Landrum-Griffin bill actually apply to the business community. Critics argue that this act further tilts capital/labor relations in favor of management and that government has abrogated its role as a neutral mediator.

Suggested Readings: R. Emmett Murray, *The Lexicon of Labor*, 1998; Florence Peterson, *American Labor Unions*, 1963.

James P. Hanlan
Bruce Cohen

Labor Parties. Labor parties are attempts by various aspects of the labor movement to create their own political entities to promote a labor-friendly government. These political parties promote an agenda that they claim is ignored or suppressed by the mainstream two-party system, while presenting their program as one that would benefit the general public, regardless of class lines. Although labor parties in the United States have not enjoyed very much success on the national level, such parties continue to form, exist, and challenge the mainstream two-party system.

The earliest labor parties, associated with the **Workingmen's Movement**, formed during the 1820s and 1830s. The first such party was organized in Philadelphia in 1828, with one created the following year in New York City. The parties' agenda included abolition of debt imprisonment, workers' compensation, free public education, universal manhood suffrage, and the "usual" labor concerns such as shorter working hours and higher pay rates. Unfortunately, most of these parties did not live long, and many were eliminated due to the national economic crisis that began in 1837.

The drive toward forming large national parties emerged after the end of the Civil War with the creation of the Labor Reform Party in 1872, a merging of farmers and workers. As the Industrial Revolution spread, with more workers joining the factory system at an accelerated pace, new labor parties formed not just to protect the rights of the **working class**, but to prevent the ever-growing corporate conglomerates from becoming too economically and politically powerful. These parties were created locally in both urban and rural centers, including the Reform Party, the **Greenback** Party, the Union Labor Party, and the United Labor Party. Many of the issues promoted by these parties included public ownership of utilities and railroads, monetization of silver (to increase the money supply), workers' compensation, abolition of prison labor (whose work was considered to be in competition with that of free workers), and, naturally, wage-and-hour issues. Created in 1890, the People's Party, also known as the Populists, took up many of these causes. However, as many historians have argued, when the Populists supported the Democratic presidential candidate, William Jennings Bryan, in 1896, they killed the chances for an effective mainstream third party in the United States.

Many of the reforms supported by these parties, especially public-ownership issues, were considered socialistic in nature, which frightened mainstream society. This was exacerbated by the fact that several Marxist-influenced political parties emerged in their own right. Starting with the Socialist Labor Party, created in 1876, followed by the Social-Democrat Party, and eventually the Socialist Party, both foreign and American-born radicals wanted to create parties imbued with Marxist ideals. But many of the labor upheavals of the nineteenth century, most notably Chicago's **Haymarket** riot in 1886, were blamed on foreign-born radicals who held left-wing doctrines. However, in the presidential election of 1912, Socialist Party candidate and labor leader **Eugene V. Debs** received 6 percent of the popular vote, a strong showing for a third-party candidate.

This 1881 cartoon criticizes the ongoing disputes between different labor parties. © George Meany Memorial Archives.

After World War I, there was a surge of activity in several locations. First, the Socialist Party suspended the left-wing faction, which then formed two separate groups, the **Communist Party** and the Communist Labor Party. Also, during that same year in Chicago, the Chicago Federation of Labor (CFL) created a local and state labor party, leading to a national party known as the Farmer-Labor Party (FLP). Some of the impetus behind these drives was to protect the gains labor made during the war, and, seeing the success of Britain's Labor Party, many felt their own would succeed.

The FLP was a conglomeration of various labor and political groups, including the famed "Committee of 48," of which the liberal leader Robert La Follette was a part. The FLP, while certainly progressive, was not looking to overturn the system, but rather to work within it. The FLP endorsed many of the planks put forth by other such parties, such as public ownership of utilities, workers' compensation, abolition of prison labor, and abolishing the use of the injunction against labor activities. The FLP faced a host of problems; the CFL was created by the **American Federation of Labor (AFL)**, and the latter group opposed any sort of labor party, preferring to be politically active through other means, such as supporting prolabor candidates. The Socialist Party was also opposed, seeing these new labor parties as competition to itself and not class-conscious. While the FLP had some modest success in some locations, as a whole the endeavor was a failure. When the **communists** overran the FLP during 1924–25, groups like the CFL pulled out and returned to AFL's belief in nonpartisanship.

Labor parties did not cease to exist. Labor leader David Dubinsky helped create the **American Labor Party (ALP)** in 1936. When this group was also taken over by communists, Dubinsky withdrew and helped organize the Liberal Party in 1944. Both the Socialist and Communist Parties continued to exist, although their current and former members faced persecution by the U.S. government, particularly during the Cold War. Currently there is a Labor Party in the United States. With a platform that promotes raising the standard of living for workers and the right to unionize, the party also opposes strong corporate control over the economy, government, and environment.

The main problem that faced labor parties throughout U.S. history was promoting their platform as one that would benefit all levels of society. Unfortunately, mainstream society tended to see such parties as divisive, too class-driven, and too radical, even if the party in question disavowed any Marxist beliefs.

Suggested Readings: Nathan Fine, *Labor and Farmer Parties in the United States, 1828–1928*, 1961; Stanley Shapiro, "'Hand and Brain': The Farmer-Labor Party of 1920." *Labor History* 26 (Summer 1985): 405–22; Murray S. Stedman and Susan W. Stedman, *Discontent at the Polls: A Study of Farmer and Labor Parties, 1827–1948*, 1950.

Mitchell Newton-Matza

Labor Theory of Value. The labor theory of value is the idea that labor itself produces all wealth. From this logic, commodities, land, and goods have little or no intrinsic worth of their own; it is the labor that transforms them and imbues them with value.

Despite the surface simplicity of the concept, its implications are complex and its sources varied. It derives in part from John Locke's influential essay "On Property" from *Two Treaties on Government* (1690); it also finds echoes in Adam Smith's *Wealth of Nations* (1776). English writer David Ricardo evoked it when developing his famed Iron Law of Wages theory, in which he argued that the profit motive and rents doomed workers to subsistence **wages**. Many of the underpinnings of the labor theory of value actually defended **capitalism**, so long as one interpreted "labor" broadly to include groups such as bankers, land developers, importers, and retailers.

Working people and their advocates, however, derived a very different message. Thomas Paine drew upon it to champion the cause of the downtrodden, and the **Workingmen's Movement** in post–Revolutionary America made it a central principle in battles against monopoly and class privilege. By the time of Ricardo's death in 1823, radical reinterpretations of his theories were in place, many of which used the labor theory of value as the centerpiece for envisioning noncapitalist economic systems. Both Robert Owen and his son **Robert Dale Owen** used the theory to justify **profit-sharing** schemes. The Quaker visionary Cornelius Blatchly employed the labor theory of value to develop utopian views of a workers' republic. Later writers like Karl Marx and **Henry George** also drew upon it. Its refocused ideals were also important for leaders of the **National Labor Union (NLU)**, the **Knights of Labor (KOL)**, and the **cooperative** movement. From a **working-class** perspective, the labor theory of value divides the world into producers and nonproducers. "Production" was usually defined in a concrete, tangible manner: by the goods one fashioned from toil. The KOL, for example, excluded bankers, lawyers, gamblers, and land speculators from membership, based on the grounds that they did not "produce" anything, therefore, they added no value to society.

The labor theory of value was such a powerful ideal in the nineteenth century that the assumptions of capitalism were frequently called into question. Some workers concluded that deriving profit from the labor of others was inherently wrong. Indeed, the cooperative movement is largely rooted in the labor theory of value. Although many could not have clearly articulated the labor theory of value, nineteenth-century workers can be said to have had a producer ethos.

The labor theory of value was not the only challenge to capitalism that workers considered; they were also attracted to **anarchism**, **socialism**, **Bellamyite Nationalism**, ballot-box politics, the single-tax movement, and other forms of resistance. In all likelihood, the majority of workers freely mixed popularly understood notions of the producer ethos with whatever other ideals they held. It was not until the triumph of **pure and simple unionism** in the early twentieth century that the bulk of union workers can be said to have accepted the permanence of capitalism.

Suggested Readings: Edward Pessen, *Most Uncommon Jacksonians: The Radical Leaders of the Early Labor Movement*, 1967; Sean Wilentz, *Chants Democratic: New York City and the Rise of the American Working Class, 1788–1850*, 1984.

Robert E. Weir

La Follette Committee. The La Follette Committee was the popular name for the Senate Civil Liberties Committee chaired by Wisconsin Senator Robert La Follette, Jr., between 1936 and 1939. The La Follette Committee investigated allegations of violations of free speech and assembly. It unearthed a mountain of **unfair labor practices** that undermined labor's right to **collective bargaining**.

The committee was established in response to concerns raised in the aftermath of the 1935 **National Labor Relations Act (NLRA)**. Several groups, including the American Civil Liberties Union (ACLU), complained that employers were abrogating the newly established rights of workers and that remedial legislation was needed. Investigations centered on four specific abuses:

industrial espionage, strikebreaking, private police systems, and the stockpiling of munitions. Formal hearings began in 1937, but the committee was forced to subpoena reluctant employers aggressively to ensure testimony. When the NLRA's constitutionality was upheld, the committee became even more adamant about employer cooperation. La Follette and his colleagues gathered substantial and shocking evidence of employer disregard for the law. Set against the backdrop of sharecroppers in the South being beaten and killed as they tried to organize, the committee's work called attention to employer abuses and played a role in labor's success in organizing such giants as General Motors and U.S. Steel. Probably the most sensational part of the investigation came when the committee focused on company use of a private army in Harlan County, Kentucky. Attacks and shootings intimidated organizers and local miners; the brutality defied belief.

As the committee prepared to draft legislation, the **United Steel Workers of America (USWA)** union was embroiled in the **"Little Steel" strike**. Republic Steel President Tom Girdler used citizens' committees as vigilante groups to lead a riot against striking workers. Ten workers were killed and dozens more were injured during the Memorial Day Massacre of 1937. As a result, the roles of such industrial organizations as the **National Association of Manufacturers (NAM)** and the International Metal Trades Association were also investigated and condemned for antilabor activity. It was revealed that the Youngstown Sheet and Tube Company alone had stockpiled enough guns and ammunition to outfit a small army, and that numerous firms employed **Pinkerton** detectives and other labor spies to undermine unions. In all, more than 2,500 firms were investigated, and activists such as author John Steinbeck and economist Paul Taylor even convinced the committee to investigate the conditions of agricultural workers in California. The committee found a consistent pattern of poor **wages**, long hours, and deplorable working conditions.

In late 1939, the committee introduced legislation to correct the worst of the abuses. But, by the time the bills began to emerge in May 1940, government officials and the public were more focused on world conflict than labor abuses. Interest dissipated in legislation due to the fear that new labor legislation would cripple defense production, as well as a sense that the NLRA already provided adequate protection.

Nonetheless, the La Follette Committee had three important consequences. First, it called dramatic attention to the abuses of employers in their relations with labor. Second, it redefined the federal government's role in protecting civil rights, with organizations like the ACLU looking to the government for support. Finally, the committee's work provided a foundation upon which African American civil rights activists could draw in the 1950s and 1960s.

Suggested Readings: Jerald Auerbach, *Labor and Liberty: The La Follette Committee and the New Deal*, 1966; Patrick Maney, *"Young Bob" La Follette: A Biography of Robert La Follete, Jr.*, 1978.

R. David Myers

La Follette Seamen's Act. The La Follette Seamen's Act was the culmination of reforms that developed over a century designed to ameliorate labor and living conditions for sailors. When President Woodrow Wilson signed the bill on March 4, 1915, supporters lauded the measure as "the Emancipation Proclamation for seamen of the world." Although the earliest law protecting U.S. seamen dates back to 1798, early twentieth-century sailors often worked in conditions more closely resembling slavery than those appropriate for highly skilled workmen.

Bills like the Maguire Act (1895) and the White Act (1898) protected only certain categories of sailor, and abuses were widespread. Under fugitive sailor laws, for instance, sailors wishing to quit their jobs were subject to arrest and imprisonment, and those who were allowed to quit had to forfeit all **wages** due them. In addition, profit-hungry shipowners often paid advance wages to recruit sailors, who were held in virtual peonage until the advance was repaid.

The final bill was a collaborative effort between Senator Robert M. La Follette, Jr., of Wisconsin and Andrew Furuseth, president of the Sailor's Union of the Pacific. Furuseth had worked for passage of protective legislation since 1894, and he and La Follette presented bills to Congress during every session from 1910 to 1915. A competing but watered-down bill passed Congress in 1912, but was pocket-vetoed by President William Taft. La Follette again took up the fight in 1913, and used canny political strategy to help ensure the bill's passage. In particular, La Follette added amendments for consumer protection to win public opinion for the labor-oriented bill. Transportation safety was of great public concern and the record of large shipping companies protecting their passengers abysmal. La Follette added various safety measures to Furuseth's bill, including requirements that ships carry sufficient lifeboats for all passengers and that two skilled seamen be available for each lifeboat. La Follette dramatized these measures by emphasizing the 13,000 deaths resulting from ocean disasters between 1900 and 1914, the April 1912 *Titanic* catastrophe highlighting the folly of carrying too few lifeboats and skilled seamen. By publicly railing against the greed, avarice, and negligence of shipowners, portions of the bill protecting the seamen received relatively little public attention. Nonetheless, shipowners and business associations so vigorously fought the bill that La Follette had to threaten a filibuster against appropriations bills to coerce passage of the Seamen's Act. It took an additional personal appeal from La Follette and Furuseth to convince President Wilson to sign the measure.

The La Follette Seamen's Act resulted in a number of significant improvements for those who labored at sea. Among the most important changes were an end to imprisonment for seamen who left their ships before the end of a contracted voyage; a prohibition against corporal punishment for offenses aboard ship; proscriptions against receiving or allotting advance pay; and regulations on those who preyed on sailors' wages in exchange for food, lodging, drinks, and clothing. The law also established a nine-hour workday while in port; banned unnecessary Sunday and holiday work; mandated better food quality; prohibited employers from withholding pay for extended periods; instituted the right of a majority of crew members to demand inspections for a vessel's seaworthiness; defined living space requirements for each sailor; required access to washrooms and sickbays; and established the right of seamen to collect damages from officers' negligence.

The shipping companies attempted to scuttle the Seamen's Act, and played on alarmist bankruptcy predictions that convinced the Secretary of Commerce to grant exemptions forestalling enforcement of many of the act's provisions. This had tragic consequences when the underequipped and undermanned Great Lakes sightseeing vessel *Eastland*, capsized on July 24, 1915, killing more than 1,000 passengers. Public outcry forced the federal government to institute much stricter adherence to the Seamen's Act.

Suggested Readings: Jerold Auerbach, "Progressives at Sea: The La Follette Act of 1915," *Labor History* 2 (Fall 1961): 344–60; Walter MacArthur, comp., *The Seaman's Contract, 1790–1918, A Complete Reprint of the Laws Relating to American Seamen*, 1919; Selig Perlman and Philip Taft, *History of Labor in the United States*, vol. 4, 1935.

John Cashman

Lassalleanism. Lassalleanism is a form of **socialism** that proved especially divisive among nineteenth-century workers and theorists. Although numbers are hard to come by, Lassalleanism may have been the dominant expression of American socialism from the time of the **Great Labor Uprising** of 1877 until around 1890. It derives from Ferdinand Lassalle (1825–64), a German thinker who took part in a failed revolutionary upheaval in 1848. Lassalle was an early follower of Karl Marx, but he eventually clashed with Marx over the role of **craft unionism**, political activity, and the proper path to socialism.

Marx saw trade unions as the vanguard of revolution and the foundation upon which a **communist** society would be built. Through his study of David Ricardo, Lassalle grew convinced that the Iron Law of Wages was a defining feature of **capitalism**. The business community maintained a shifting, but permanent surplus labor pool that undermined the wage structure of all workers. As such, all efforts by trade unions to raise wages or reduce hours were doomed and craft unions would remain too impotent to transform society. Moreover, he felt that organizing unions by craft was an exclusionary and counter-revolutionary act that cut adrift the legions of unskilled and semi-skilled laborers. Lassalle thought **cooperatives** a more likely alternative to capitalism than trade union activity, and saw **boycotts** as a more effective tool to battle capitalist employers than **strikes**.

Based on his experiences in 1848, plus his observations of the failure of Giuseppe Garibaldi to export revolutionary socialism beyond Italy's borders, Lassalle concluded that socialism had passed from a revolutionary to an evolutionary phase in which socialists should use the ballot box to attain their goals legally and peacefully. Existing parties were controlled by capitalists, thus necessitating the formation of separate **labor parties**. Many Marxists also engaged in politics, but continued to see the workplace as the focal point of social change; Lassalleans reversed that emphasis.

Lassalle's ideals found expression in the United States in the Socialist Labor Party (SLP), which rose to prominence when Marxist groups languished after the collapse of the 1877 Great Labor Uprising. It gained followers when German immigrants fleeing repression under the government of Kaiser Wilhelm I poured into the United States after 1878. They were particularly strong in New York City, where Lassalleans and SLP stalwarts led by Phillip Van Patten influenced the direction of the city's **Central Labor Union (CLU)**. They played a key role in organizing the 1882 parades that led to the establishment of **Labor Day**.

Lassalleans advocated forming union auxiliaries of the SLP, but many of them joined the **Knights of Labor (KOL)** when it gained in strength after 1878. They dominated KOL leadership ranks in New York City and aggressively spread their ideals to other assemblies and cities. Lassalleans directed a secret faction known as the Home Club, which battled for control of the KOL and greatly disrupted its internal affairs from 1881 to 1889. While under the influence of Lassalleans, the KOL clashed with trade unions. Lassalleans insisted that the craft and trade unions divided the American workforce and touted the KOL as the only universal expression of labor. A New York City dispute between the KOL and the Cigar Makers International Union was a direct inspiration for the 1886 founding of the **American Federation of Labor (AFL)**.

The **Great Upheaval** proved the high-water mark for Lassalleanism. From roughly 1885 through 1888, third-party activity surged and opposition to capitalist domination intensified. Lassalleans often betrayed their own ideals, however. Many became converts to **anarchism** and the lines between the two philosophies blurred, with self-professed Lassalleans often leading strikes that they supposedly abhorred and advocating violence rather than voting. When strikes failed and political gains evaporated, Lassalleanism's appeal declined. Ranks were further decimated by disputes between English- and German-speaking Lassalleans. By 1890, even the SLP was moving toward a more orthodox Marxism, largely due to the efforts of **Daniel DeLeon**. The precipitous decline of the KOL in the 1890s and the subsequent dominance of the AFL and craft unionism relegated Lassalleanism to minority status within American socialism. The SLP retains vestiges of Lassalleanism, but the socialism of **Eugene V. Debs** and his heirs proved more attractive in the twentieth century.

Suggested Readings: Philip S. Foner, *History of the Labor Movement in the United States*, Vol. 2: From the Founding of the American Federation of Labor to the Emergence of American Imperialism, 1955; Bruce Laurie, *Artisans Into Workers*, 1989; Robert E. Weir, *Knights Unhorsed: Internal Conflict in a Gilded Age Social Movement*, 2000.

Robert E. Weir

Latino Labor. *See Minority Labor. See also specific organizations and individuals.*

Lattimer Massacre. The Lattimer Massacre, one of the most serious acts of violence in American labor history, occurred on September 10, 1897, in Lattimer, a small coal patch near Hazleton, Pennsylvania, where nineteen immigrant miners were killed. This bloody event signaled the emergence of Slavic immigrants as a force in the American labor movement and strengthened the solidarity of the **United Mine Workers of America (UMWA)** in the anthracite region of northeastern Pennsylvania.

The Lattimer Massacre is rooted in the UMWA's attempts to organize workers in the hard-coal region, and the determination of coal operators to crush **strike** activity by force. By August 1897, thousands of immigrant miners joined the UMWA in response to cost-cutting measures taken by coal barons. Strike committees were formed and miners marched from colliery to colliery seeking to shut mines that were still shipping coal. By early September, the UMWA sought to close a major Hazelton-area coal producer, A. Pardee and Company. Miners at the company's operation in Harwood, mostly Slavic, Polish, and Lithuanian immigrants, formed a UMWA local and went on strike. At another Pardee operation near Hazleton, Italian immigrant miners at Lattimer joined the strike and requested assistance from Harwood union members in closing the colliery.

In anticipation of problems in the region, county sheriffs, who were politically allied with coal operators, published a proclamation on September 6 prohibiting parades and demonstrations. In Luzerne County, Sheriff James L. Martin swore in about 100 deputies and armed them with Winchester rifles. On September 10, approximately 400 miners began the ten-mile march from Harwood to Lattimer. Strike leaders demanded that marchers dispense with any potential weapons to ensure a peaceful protest. The strikers marched four abreast, led by two with American flags. Deputies first sought to stop the march in West Hazleton. One miner was injured and one American flag was torn to pieces by a deputy, but police allowed the march to continue with the stipulation that protestors bypass Hazleton. Furious at this setback, Sheriff Martin and his deputies took a trolley to Lattimer and prepared to stop the march there. Word spread of an impending confrontation and additional company police and deputies rushed toward Lattimer.

Lattimer's coal operations lay at the end of Main Street, a jumble of company shanties occupied by newly arrived Italian immigrants. Martin positioned his deputies along Main Street. When the marchers approached Lattimer, Martin came forward with his pistol drawn and commanded them to disperse. The first ranks of the strikers heard the sheriff and stopped, however, those out of earshot pressed forward. A command was given to fire—marchers later claimed that it was Martin who gave the order—and a volley rang out. Some men were cut down in their tracks; others were shot in the back as they scattered to find cover behind a thin row of trees. According to some witnesses, at least 150 shots were fired, and some deputies followed the strikers more than thirty yards before gunning them down. When the gunfire ceased, nineteen miners were dead and thirty-eight were wounded.

Tensions rose in immigrant communities throughout the region. Governor Daniel Hastings sent 3,000 soldiers of the Pennsylvania National Guard to the

Hazleton area to patrol coal-company property. Thousands of miners who were working prior to the event joined the UMWA and went on strike. On the national level, immigrant organizations condemned the killings and provided thousands of dollars to support the victims' families.

Sheriff Martin and sixty-seven deputies were put on trial for the murder of only one victim before a nativist jury. The defense placed the blame for the massacre on labor agitators in the region, and the trial included an oration against Slavs. Predictably, the jury returned a verdict of not guilty on March 2, 1898.

Prior to 1950, historians were largely silent about Lattimer and it has been referred to as "labor's forgotten massacre." One reason the historical record unfolded slowly was because many of the survivors of the incident did not speak English. Moreover, the events of 1897 were quickly overshadowed by the **anthracite coal strike of 1902**. Lattimer received much notice in the foreign press, however, with activists in both Australia and New Zealand citing it as justification for passing mandatory **arbitration** laws. Scholars now place Lattimer among those events that best illustrate the bloodiness of American labor history. They also recognize Lattimer's symbolic importance in campaigns to organize Slavic American workers. On the seventy-fifth anniversary of the massacre, the American Federation of Labor–Congress of Industrial Organizations and the UMWA honored the slain and wounded with a memorial, and in 1997, the Pennsylvania Historical and Museum Commission erected a marker at the site.

Suggested Readings: Michael Novak, *The Guns of Lattimer,* 1978; Edward Pinkowski, *Lattimer Massacre,* 1950; George Turner, "The Lattimer Tragedy of 1897." *Pennsylvania Heritage* 3 (1977): 10–13.

Mark Noon

Lawrence Textile Strike. On January 12, 1912, 20,000 woolen textile strikers went on **strike** to protest **wage** cuts and poor working conditions in Lawrence, Massachusetts. The strike was dubbed the "Bread and Roses strike" because of strikers' placards reading "We Want Bread and Roses Too" (wages and respect). It is also known as the "Lawrence Nationalities strike" as more than forty immigrant groups took part, including Abyssinian, Belgian, Bohemian, English, French, German, Irish, Italian, Lithuanian, Portuguese, Spanish, and Turkish workers.

The strike began the previous day when Polish women walked off their jobs to protest a pay cut instituted by the American Woolen Company in response to Massachusetts **protective labor legislation** that reduced the weekly hours women could work. The **American Federation of Labor (AFL)** was weak in Lawrence and it traditionally disregarded unskilled laborers. The outbreak afforded the **Industrial Workers of the World (IWW)** an opportunity to set up organizing committees. The IWW is often credited with demonstrating the possibility of bringing together diverse nationalities, a task it accomplished by sending organizers who were fluent in multiple languages. The IWW also used

anarcho-syndicalist tactics such as **direct action**, the **general strike**, and select acts of sabotage during the strike.

The IWW sent many of its most capable organizers to Lawrence, including **Elizabeth Gurley Flynn**, **William Haywood**, Joseph Ettor, and Arturo Giovannitti, the latter two of whom directed the strike's early days. Striker Anna LoPizzo was killed by city police, but authorities used her death and an alleged dynamite plot (probably planted by **agent provocateurs**) as provocation for calling in the state militia. Incredibly, Ettor and Giovannitti were charged as accessories to LoPizzo's murder, a farce that led to violent street clashes, a public outcry, and a public-relations nightmare for textile firms and the city of Lawrence. The strike's most dramatic moment occurred when the IWW began to send children out of the city to sympathetic **socialist** families in New York and elsewhere. Faced with eroding public support, Lawrence authorities tried to stop the practice. This led to a clash at the city rail station in which police used truncheons to beat women and children. This led people from all over the country to protest the action and to send money in support of the strike. On March 12, 1912, textile firms capitulated and more than 30,000 city workers received wage increases ranging from 5 percent to 20 percent. Employers also agreed to pay more for **overtime** work, reform their **bonus** systems, and refrain from retaliating against known strikers.

During the Lawrence (Massachusetts) Textile Strike of 1912, the IWW sent these children of strikers to live with sympathetic families in New York City. © George Meany Memorial Archives.

The Bread and Roses strike boosted IWW membership dramatically and is often seen as the organization's high-water mark. It was not able to hold onto new members, however, and within eighteen months was nearly an invisible presence in Lawrence.

Suggested Readings: William Cahn, *Lawrence 1912*, 1977; Melvyn Dubofsky, *We Shall Be All*, 1969; Patrick Renshaw, *The Wobblies: The Story of Syndicalism in the United States*, 1967.

Don Binkowski

Lewis, John Llewellyn (February 2, 1880–June 2, 1969). John L. Lewis was the longtime president of the **United Mine Workers of America (UMWA)**, the first president of the **Congress of Industrial Organizations (CIO)**, and one of the most powerful labor leaders in American history. From the 1920s through the 1950s, Lewis challenged corporate leaders, advised presidents, and battled with politicians. He was born in Lucas, Iowa, the son of Welsh immigrants. After three years of high school, the sixteen-year-old Lewis joined other family members in the coal pits. He joined the UMWA when it was led by **John Mitchell**, a man Lewis felt was too cautious and too conciliatory to mine owners. He opposed Mitchell for the UMWA presidency when he was only eighteen, but reconciled with him long enough to be appointed head of the international organizing staff in 1903. He split with Mitchell again in 1906, blaming him for failing to maintain **wage** scales negotiated in 1903. In 1908, Lewis was elected UMWA secretary-treasurer, a position that gave him access to the union's newsletter, which he used as a personal forum. In 1917, he became vice president of the union and three years later he was elected UMWA president. Lewis held that post until his retirement in 1960.

John L. Lewis. © George Meany Memorial Archives.

Lewis took over the miners' union at a time in which overproduction and sinking wages threatened to cancel many of the gains made during World War I. He launched a campaign to streamline UMWA operations, a task that amassed great power in his office. He was not above using strong-armed tactics, and he frequently manipulated the expulsion of leaders who opposed him. The UMWA was in free fall by the time Franklin Roosevelt took the presidency in 1933, having sunk from about half a million members in 1917 to about 75,000. The deepening depression and sinking UMWA fortunes led Lewis, a lifelong Republican, to endorse Roosevelt in 1932.

Lewis advised Roosevelt on parts of the **National Industrial Recovery Act**, including Section 7(a), which recognized labor's right to **collective bargaining** and which was later enshrined in the **National Labor Relations Act**. In 1935, Lewis joined with the heads of seven other unions to form a committee within the **American Federation of Labor (AFL)** to lobby for organizing **industrial unions**. Those unions and several others were expelled from the AFL, but as the Congress of Industrial Organizations (CIO), went on to organize over four million workers by 1936. Lewis served as CIO president from 1935 to 1940. Lewis supported Roosevelt again in 1936, and many considered Lewis the second most powerful leader in the nation. UMWA membership also revived by the mid-1930s, spurred by New Deal legislation, Lewis's hard-nosed bargaining, **rank-and-file** militancy, and the rising political influence of UMWA and CIO leaders. By 1937, over 90 percent of all coal miners belonged to the UMWA.

By 1940, however, Lewis had grown disenchanted with Roosevelt and the New Deal. He campaigned for Republican Wendell Wilkie and told CIO members he would quit the top post if Roosevelt was reelected. When Roosevelt rolled to victory in 1940, Lewis kept his promise, though he retained his presidency of the UMWA. In that same year, he called a series of **strikes** for increased wages for miners, several of which were expressly designed to challenge government wage formulas hammered out in the steel industry, which the government hoped would be the model for other industrial disputes. Lewis despised the so-called **Little Steel Formula**. In 1942, Lewis also led the UMWA out of the CIO. It briefly rejoined the AFL in 1946, but withdrew in 1947.

Under Lewis, the UMWA was one of the few unions to strike while World War II raged, with Lewis demanding (and winning) a **captive mines** policy in which miners automatically became UMWA members. Strikes in 1946 and 1948 gained the UMWA royalties for each ton of coal mined. Lewis used these to fund the union's Welfare and Retirement Fund, seen by some Lewis admirers as his greatest legacy. Several of these strikes violated **contracts** and laws; Lewis persisted in them even when the UMWA faced stiff fines and he was personally cited for contempt of court. UMWA militancy and its perceived lack of patriotism were cited by several supporters of the **Taft-Hartley Act**, which Lewis denounced as "slave labor" legislation, recommending that unions refuse to comply with its provisions, thereby making it a dead article.

By the 1950s, the UMWA had the most extensive welfare and retirement program of any U.S. union, and funds were also used to fund hospitals and address miner health issues. Lewis also led the charge for mine-safety laws and for greater awareness of mining-related diseases. In 1951, he negotiated an agreement with bituminous-mine owners that led to several years of industrial peace, though critics charged it sapped rank-and-file militancy. Lewis retained his own rebel image, though his views moderated in the 1950s, and he supported the same blend of capital/labor cooperation that he once criticized John Mitchell for holding. He retired as UMWA leader in 1960, though he maintained enormous influence over it until his death nine years later.

Lewis was awarded the Presidential Medal of Freedom by President Kennedy in 1960 and was inducted into the Labor Hall of Fame. Lewis married Myrta Edith Bell on June 5, 1907. The couple had three children, including a daughter, Katherine, who later held important UMWA posts. Some Lewis detractors blame nepotism and Lewis's dictatorial policies as a reason for later UMWA corruption.

Suggested Readings: Melvyn Dubofsky, *John L. Lewis: A Biography*, 1977; *John L. Lewis Papers* (State Historical Society of Wisconsin, microfilm, 1970); Robert Zieger, *John L. Lewis: Labor Leader*, 1988.

Don Binkowski

Lien Laws. Lien laws are claims against property for payment of a debt or obligation. In some situations, a lien can arise from the application of unwritten common-law principles whereas in others, a written law is necessary to grant someone a lien.

The lien of greatest relevance to labor is the mechanics' lien. Mechanics' lien laws grant workers and suppliers a claim to the land and buildings in a construction project if payment is not made for the labor performed or materials provided. In effect, construction workers and suppliers "own" part of the construction project until they are paid for their labor or materials.

Mechanics' lien laws are among the earliest pieces of **protective labor legislation** in the United States, dating back to the first statute in Maryland in 1791. These laws seek to provide security and protection to workers who cannot afford court action to collect their **wages** from bankrupt or unscrupulous employers. By making sure that workers and suppliers will be paid, mechanics' lien laws are also intended to encourage construction.

Mechanics' lien laws were unevenly applied, however, and federations like the **Knights of Labor (KOL)** lobbied to make said laws apply universally. The KOL also broadened the principle to demand that wages be paid before employers discharged any other financial commitments. Over time, mechanics' lien laws have been enacted in all fifty states, though the procedural details vary from state to state. Mechanics' liens have generally not been granted for public-sector construction projects, but federal law (the Miller Act) and many state laws require contractors to post a bond to assure payment to workers and suppliers.

Suggested Readings: James Acret, *National Mechanics Liens Handbook: The Mechanics' Lien Laws of the 50 States and the District of Columbia*, 1998; Daniel Roth, *Lien Laws for Design Professionals: A Survey and Analysis*, 1986.

John W. Budd

Little Steel Formula. The Little Steel Formula was an attempt to control **wage** and price increases during World War II. The **National War Labor Board (NWLB)** was created in January 1941 in hopes of fashioning a labor/management/public committee that would peacefully resolve labor disputes and ensure that wartime production would not be interrupted. NWLB decisions were considered binding.

In July 1942, employees at various "little steel" firms—those not working for industry giant U.S. Steel—complained to the NWLB that their wages were inadequate to cope with wartime inflation. They demanded a one-dollar-per-day increase. Upon deliberation, the NLWB granted a forty-four-cent increase (15 percent), based upon the increase in prices from January 1, 1941. A 15 percent increase was the basis of the Little Steel Formula, and the standard applied to subsequent settlements imposed by the NWLB.

This formula proved unworkable, however, as inflation did not ease as NWLB mediators hoped. During 1943, more than two million workers walked off their jobs to protest the inadequacy of their wages. Most of these were **quickies** that were resolved without impeding war production. Several of these disputes were settled by increasing worker **fringe benefits**, an appeasement that technically did not violate the Little Steel Formula.

Not as easily resolved, however, was a dispute involving the **United Mine Workers of America (UMWA)**. In April, UMWA President **John L. Lewis** demanded an increase of two dollars per day and portal-to-portal pay to compensate miners for time spent being transported underground to the head of coal seams (which could be an hour away). Through a six-month campaign, the UMWA strike of 1943 smashed the Little Steel Formula.

The UMWA victory was problematic. At one juncture, President Roosevelt considered seizing the nation's mines. An increasingly conservative Congress was inflamed by the UMWA and enacted the Smith-Connolly bill, which placed limits on labor's ability to strike in industries deemed essential to the national interest. Some historians feel that the UMWA's action also laid the groundwork for the **Taft-Hartley Act**.

Suggested Readings: Foster Dulles and Melvyn Dubofsky, *Labor in America*, 1984; Joseph Rayback, *A History of American Labor*, 1966.

Robert E. Weir

Local 1199. *See National Union of Hospital and Health Care Employees Local 1199.*

Lockout. A lockout is sometimes confused with a **strike**, but they are not the same. A lockout occurs when an employer closes a facility and prevents employees from entering and working. Lockouts are intended to pressure the union to accept management's **contract** terms. Lockouts have also been used to prevent intermittent walkouts, those strikes in which workers work for a short period of time, then strike, then return to work, often in an effort to avoid replacement. Lockouts are considered legal except in some cases where they violate the terms of a joint agreement or **collective bargaining** contract.

Some of the most famous labor disputes in American history technically began as lockouts, although history books routinely call them strikes. This includes events like **Pullman** (1894), **Paterson** (1913), and **Ravenswood** (1991).

Suggested Readings: P. K. Edwards, *Strikes in the United States, 1881–1974*, 1981; P. K. Edwards, *Social Organization of Industrial Conflict*, 1984.

Kenneth Ferus

***Loewe v. Lawlor* (1908).** *Loewe v. Lawlor* is also known as the "Danbury Hatters Case." The Supreme Court dealt a blow to labor unions by ruling that secondary **boycotts** were illegal restraints of trade under the 1890 **Sherman Antitrust Act**. Even more troublesome, the courts agreed that employers could sue individual union members for damages incurred during illegal boycotts. In the case of *Loewe v. Lawlor*, the Supreme Court unanimously upheld triple damages in excess of $250,000.

The *Loewe* case had its genesis in what had been a series of victories for labor unions in the hat industry. By 1902, the United Hatters of North America (UHNA) had used boycotts to organize all but twelve of 190 hat manufacturers, including Roelef's, a Philadelphia-based firm recognized as an industry leader. The UHNA turned its attention to the C. H. Merritt and D. E. Loewe companies of Danbury, Connecticut, which were among the dozen holdouts. Rather than deal with the UHNA, Loewe sought advice from the American Anti-Boycott Association, an alliance of antiunion business officials, and it received a $20,000 pledge to help battle the UHNA. When strikers were replaced, the **American Federation of Labor (AFL)**, with whom the UHNA was affiliated, placed Loewe on its "We Don't Patronize" list. It also launched a secondary boycott and attempted to convince wholesalers and retailers to stop carrying Loewe hats.

Loewe lost about $33,000 during 1902 and 1903, but struck back. The firm argued that the UHNA boycott was an illegal restraint of trade under the Sherman Act. The company also took advantage of a Connecticut law that allowed property attachments for civil damages, and on September 12, 1903, attachments were placed on the assets of 248 UHNA members who held property and bank accounts. Loewe lawyers then pressed the courts to grant triple damages.

The immediate impact of Loewe's actions was to cripple UHNA organizing efforts. Union membership declined, and numerous firms, including Roelef's, reneged on **contract** agreements. The UHNA received a brief respite in December 1907, when a U.S. circuit court dismissed Loewe's claims against the UHNA on the grounds that it was unclear whether or not the Sherman Act applied to labor unions. The Loewe firm appealed the decision, however, and in 1908 the Supreme Court ruled the Sherman Act was applicable. The case was retried, and in early 1910 the UHNA and its members were held liable for losses incurred by the Loewe firm. A technicality voided that verdict, but a third trial in 1912 upheld the 1910 judgment. On January 5, 1915, the Supreme Court ruled that the hatters had to pay costs and triple damages, a toll that amounted to $252,130.

No hatters lost their homes or savings as a result of the *Loewe* decision; the AFL helped defray the costs, and rallies and contributions raised revenue to pay the judgment. Nonetheless, the *Loewe* decision proved disastrous to organized labor in the short run, despite the 1914 Clayton Anti-Trust Act that exempted unions from precisely the liability under which UHNA members were sued. The *Loewe* decision, along with other antilabor decisions like *Buck's Stove and Range Company v. American Federation of Labor*, *Adair v. The United States*, and *Hitchman Coal and Coke Company v. Mitchell* essentially robbed labor unions of most of the weapons at their disposal. Antiunion court cases, the activities of groups like the **National Association of Manufacturers**, and the suppression of radical groups like the **Industrial Workers of the World** calls into question the legitimacy of the term "Progressive" Era.

Suggested Readings: David Bensman, *The Practice of Solidarity: American Hat Finishers in the Nineteenth Century*, 1985; William Forbath, *Law and the Shaping of the American Labor Movement*, 1991; Benjamin Taylor and Fred Witney, *U.S. Labor Relations Law: Historical Development*, 1992.

Bruce Cohen

Robert E. Weir

Longevity Pay. Longevity pay, which is also known as longevity rate or longevity compensation, refers to an additional **bonus** or **salary** boost provided to employees who have rendered continuous and satisfactory service for a certain number of years. Usually the employee has already attained the maximum pay of their salary grade. For each successive year an employee remains with the company, the enterprise may increase the pay amount incrementally. Longevity payments are sometimes offered in a lump sum amount after an employee leaves the firm.

Suggested Reading: George Milkovich, Jerry Newman, and Jerry M. Newman, *Compensation*, 1998.

Kenneth Ferus

Lordstown Strike. The Lordstown strike was a dramatic three-week strike against General Motors (GM) in Lordstown, Ohio, by Local 1112 of the **United Auto Workers (UAW)** union. It took place in February 1972. Many observers see this **strike**, coupled with a less-famous 174-day strike in Norwood, Ohio, also in 1972, as the swan song of **Taylorism**, **Fordism**, and many other dehumanizing aspects of assembly-line production. The Lordstown strike attracted widespread media coverage because much of the workforce was under the age of twenty-five, and was apparently radicalized by the social upheaval that marked American society in the late 1960s and early 1970s. The strike also took place against the backdrop of retooling auto production to adjust for changing tastes and consumer needs. At the time of the strike, the Lordstown Chevrolet Vega assembly facility was considered the most advanced in the auto industry.

By the mid-1960s, Detroit automakers were saddled with oversized, gas-guzzling fleets. With more women entering the job market, many American families began purchasing second cars. Smaller, more fuel-efficient foreign imports began to capture a broader part of the American market. American manufacturers began to restyle their fleets and introduce their own economy cars. By the late 1960s, Ford was enjoying brisk sales of its Pinto line. In response, the Chevrolet division of GM developed the Vega, production of which began in Lordstown in 1968.

Lordstown was a state-of-the-art facility that had opened less than two years earlier. Chevrolet managers hoped to produce sixty Vegas an hour from its assembly line and to sell over 400,000 units annually. The Vega design, however, proved flawed. Chevrolet General Manager John DeLorean warned GM officials that test results were ominous. The car was top-heavy, noisy, and experienced engine problems. DeLorean suspected that the Vega was simply a bad car, but rather than redesign it, GM pressed for its production to compete with Ford and imports from Datsun, Toyota, and Volkswagen.

As DeLorean predicted, Vega proved a troubled product, and sales lagged. In 1971, GM was forced to recall over 132,000 Vegas to correct potential fire hazards. Vega workers complained of crushing boredom on a highly mechanized assembly line that reduced them to automatons. The plant had high levels of absenteeism, discipline was lax, confrontations between line workers and management were frequent, and allegations swirled that workers used alcohol and drugs on the line.

GM's response to the mounting crisis was curious. On October 1, 1971, Chevrolet management was placed under the General Motors Assembly Division (GMAD), essentially ending Chevy's autonomy within GM's corporate structure. Important decisions were now made in the GM boardroom rather than by Chevrolet production officials. GMAD bureaucrats determined that the answer to Vega's woes was greater workplace discipline. Time-motion studies were ordered, with clipboard-carrying supervisors trawling Lordstown in classic Taylorist fashion. Some 700 "unproductive" workers were furloughed, special work arrangements between foremen and workers were eliminated, mandatory **overtime** was instituted, and **grievance** procedures were stonewalled.

GM's heavy-handed response was out of touch with contemporary social reality. The Lordstown workforce was young; even Local 1112 President Gary Bryner was under thirty. Most workers were disinclined to view the assembly line as much more than a paycheck and were unmoved by appeals (or threats) to their careers. Many sported long hair, some were Vietnam veterans, and few were willing to accept arbitrary authority. Rock music, drugs, and alcohol were part of the culture for numerous Vega workers, as was antimaterialist rhetoric. These workers proved as big a challenge to the UAW as to GM. Rather than embrace precepts of **pure and simple unionism**, Vega workers demanded that UAW officials negotiate items like workplace rules, safety issues, and ways to relieve line-worker tedium.

GM's most provocative act came when it set a new production target of 100 Vegas per hour. This meant that the average line worker had about thirty-six seconds to complete a task before another chassis appeared. The workers' response to the **speedup** was a mutually enforced **stint** that included slowdowns and, if deemed necessary, **sabotage**. Workers lampooned GMAD as "Got to Make Another Dollar," and filed more than 1,400 grievances against management in the four months leading to the strike. Predictably, Vega had poor customer-satisfaction ratings, and GM had acres of unmovable, mechanically unsound stock.

Ninety-seven percent of Lordstown's workers voted to strike. They walked out in early February, demanding a return to pre-1971 production standards. At the time, the strike was hailed by the political left as the vanguard of social revolution that would deliver a hammer blow to inhumane **capitalism**. That assessment proved romantic and naïve. After three weeks, an inconclusive settlement was reached that involved vague promises of addressing workplace alienation. The speedup mostly remained in place, though GM also sped the development of robots and computerized machinery that replaced human labor in some of the most tedious unskilled positions.

In the long run, the Lordstown strike was significant less for its revolutionary potential or the **concessions** it wrought than for its sociological and industrial impact. The field of industrial sociology received more attention during and after the strike, with scholars turning their attention to what was variously labeled as the "Lordstown Syndrome" and the "blue-collar blues." Numerous studies appeared that further probed the phenomenon of worker alienation; many concluded that the classic assembly line was a dehumanizing failure and that time-motion studies were more likely to breed resentment and strife than to increase production. The use of Fordist production and Taylorist management methods declined dramatically in the wake of Lordstown.

Automakers began to rethink production methods, particularly after foreign producers captured even larger segments of the U.S. market after the oil embargo of 1973 and reports of poor American car quality in the late 1970s and early 1980s. Although few found it cost effective to set up bumper-to-bumper production teams like those used by Sweden's Volvo, most sought ways to lessen reliability on human assembly-line workers. The UAW actively lobbied for more worker involvement in decision making, and some manufacturers grew enamored of Japanese production and management styles as practiced by corporations like Honda and Toyota. Several have experimented with **quality circles**, with mixed results. American car manufacturers have been loath to abandon the assembly line altogether, however, and it remains a strike-prone industry.

The Chevy Vega ceased production in 1977, unmourned by American consumers. The Lordstown facility most recently has produced Chevrolet Cavaliers and Pontiac Sunfires, though how either will weather GM's most recent centralization and reorganization plan is unclear.

Suggested Readings: James Green, *The World of the Worker*, 1980; Ruth Milkman, *Farewell to the Factory: Autoworkers in the Late Twentieth Century*, 1997; Studs Terkel, *Working*, 1972.

Robert E. Weir

***Los Angeles Times* Bombing.** The *Los Angeles Times* bombing took place on October 1, 1910, and was the climactic event in a struggle between the city's union and business elements which both sides dubbed the "Forty Years War."

During a bitter 1890 dispute with the International Typographical Union (ITU), editor-publisher Harrison Gray Otis **locked out** his printers, hired **scabs** from Kansas City, and instituted a nonunion policy destined to hold until the 1960s. The *Times* became the very symbol of the **open-shop** movement in Los Angeles. Otis used his paper to resist unions in other occupations as well and was influential in the formation of the Merchants and Manufacturers Association (MMA), a citywide open-shop consortium.

By contrast, San Francisco was a stronghold of organized labor, and the Union Labor Party was an important force in local politics. By 1910, however, labor activists realized that San Francisco's continuance as a union city was dependent on organizing Los Angelenos. The San Francisco labor movement made a concerted effort to organize its open-shop rival to the south. Simultaneously, the Indianapolis-based International Association of Bridge and Structural Iron Workers (BSIW), led by Secretary-Treasurer John J. McNamara, was embroiled in open-shop struggles of its own. Only in Chicago and San Francisco was the BSIW successful in fending off the antiunion challenges of the **National Association of Manufacturers** and the Erectors of Structural Steel. As disputes grew more intense, a series of dynamite explosions rocked several facilities connected with contractors with which the BSIW was in dispute. The Burns Detective Agency linked the BSIW to these bombings.

A bomb exploded in an alley behind the offices of the *Los Angeles Times* in the early morning of October 1. It ruptured a gas line, and a catastrophic fire ensued in which twenty men perished. Unexploded bombs were discovered outside the Otis home, as well as that of MMA Secretary Felix Zeehandler. A nationwide investigation led detective William Burns to focus on James McNamara, brother of the BSIW secretary-treasurer; as well as organized crime figures Ortie McManigal and David Kaplan, whose names had been linked to the San Francisco labor movement. On Christmas Day, a bomb exploded at the Llewellyn Iron Works in Los Angeles. By then, McManigal and James McNamara were already suspects in the *Times* bombing, but Burns avoided accusing them, hoping to link them to John McNamara. In April 1911, police and Burns detectives took McManigal and James McNamara into custody for allegedly attempting to blow up a Detroit railroad station. An interrogation of McManigal provided information that led to the arrest of John McNamara as well, and all three were extradited to Los Angeles.

The trial was slated for December 1911, coinciding with a municipal election in which **Socialist** candidate Job Harriman, a labor attorney with a minor connection to the McNamara defense team, was favored to become the new mayor of Los Angeles. Business and political leaders feared a Harriman victory and equated votes for Harriman with support for the McNamaras. Mainstream party leaders and the business community threw support and resources behind incumbent mayor George Alexander. At the same time, they sought a conclusion to the McNamara trial before election day. Clarence Darrow, lead attorney for the brothers, came to realize his clients' guilt and agreed to a plea bargain, brokered in part by muckraker journalist Lincoln Steffens. On December 1, 1911, just four days before the election, John McNamara pleaded guilty to conspiracy to bomb the Llewellyn plant and was sentenced to fifteen years in prison. His brother James admitted guilt in the *Los Angeles Times* dynamiting and received a life sentence.

The McNamara case was a severe blow to organized labor. Los Angeles remained an open-shop city until New Deal labor reforms in the 1930s, and union efforts were weakened in San Francisco. Harriman lost his bid for the mayoralty, and though the Socialist Party elected three assemblymen, it never regained its prebombing strength.

Suggested Readings: William Burns, *Masked War*, 1913; Dennis McDougal, *Privileged Son*, 2001; Grace Stimson, *Rise of the Labor Movement in Los Angeles*, 1955.

Ralph Shaffer

Ludlow Massacre. The Ludlow Massacre, one of the most dramatic confrontations between capital and labor in American history, occurred on Monday, April 20, 1914. Workers at the Colorado Fuel and Iron Company (CF&I), owned by the Rockefeller family, had gone on **strike** in September 1913 in response to the company's **open-shop** drive, which was an effort to stymie the organizing efforts of the **United Mine Workers of America (UMWA)** and to assure that miners would not join unions. Ludlow was a **company town**, where miners were housed in company-owned houses, required to shop at the company store, paid in scrip (a privately printed currency good only at the company store), and policed by a private company police force. Strikers were evicted from their company-owned homes and settled in hastily erected tent colonies on the outskirts of Ludlow. CF&I called in heavily armed private deputies as well as the state militia. Residents of the tent colony faced constant harassment by the militia, including the threat of machine-gun fire into the tent colony. Immediately following Easter, the troops set fire to the occupied tents and fired machine-guns into the camp. Sixteen people, including twelve children, were killed in the resulting massacre. Ten days of open warfare between strikers and the militia followed until President Woodrow Wilson sent federal troops to restore order in the southern Colorado coalfield.

In 1914, the Colorado Fuel and Iron Company evicted strikers from their company-owned homes in Ludlow, Colorado. These two photos show the tent city both before and after it was burned by the state militia in an action that took the lives of sixteen people. © George Meany Memorial Archives/Public Affairs Press.

In congressional hearings, John D. Rockefeller, Jr., appeared unrepentant, arguing that CF&I had been defending the essential rights of the American worker just as surely as the patriots of the American revolutionary era had fought for individual liberty. Rockefeller denied the reality of the massacre and argued that two small squads of militia were merely defending themselves against a hostile tent colony. Any regrettable loss of life, the Rockefellers held, was not the fault of the "defenders of property," but of outside agitators determined to deny workers their individual freedoms by organizing unions. Rockefeller's seeming indifference to the deaths that shocked the nation was exacerbated by newspaper accounts such as that of the *New York Times* that revealed that women and children "died like trapped rats" in pits under the tents that they had dug for protection in the event of bullets fired into the colony by the well-armed and hostile militia. One pit uncovered the bodies of ten children and two women. The photographs of the horrors of Ludlow repulsed the nation. Writer Upton Sinclair publicly announced his intention to see Rockefeller indicted for murder, and protests erupted throughout the nation in cities such as New York, Chicago, and San Francisco, where large immigrant populations sympathized with the largely Italian, Greek, and eastern European mine labor force. The *New York World* revealed the treachery of the militia in the killing of Louis Tikas, a leader of the miners, who attempted to negotiate safety for women and children under the protection of a white flag. Tikas, the would-be peacemaker, was lured to talk with the militia, then beaten and shot in cold blood by the militia. The *World* reporter, aghast, wrote that this "was the first murder I had ever seen." Rockefeller responded to the massive adverse publicity by bringing in publicist Ivy L. Lee and former Canadian Minister of Labour William L. McKenzie-King. Together they rehabilitated the family image and instituted the so-called Colorado Plan of Industrial Representation, a system combining **paternalist** benefits with company-dominated unions that prevailed in the Colorado coalfields for many years following Ludlow.

Suggested Readings: Howard M. Gitelman, *Legacy of the Ludlow Massacre: A Chapter in American Industrial Relations*, 1988; Zeese Papanikolas, *Buried Unsung: Louis Tikas and the Ludlow Massacre*, 1982.

James P. Hanlan

Luther, Seth (1795–1863). Seth Luther was one of the most memorable figures in the pioneering days of the Rhode Island and American labor movement. He was an orator, writer, organizer, and advocate for numerous labor causes. When he died in 1863, a *Providence Journal* obituary said that he "had considerable talent for both writing and speaking; but he was too violent, willful, and headstrong to accomplish any good." Nothing could be further from the truth.

Luther was born in 1795 in Providence, Rhode Island, the son of a Revolutionary War soldier. He received very little formal education before learning a carpenter's trade. He traveled extensively to find work and became involved with the **Workingmen's Movement**. In 1832, he was back in Providence lobbying the state government to enact a ten-hour workday. When assaulted for his activities, he wrote, "I glory in these wounds knowing they would not have been inflicted had I not advocated the cause of the suffering children incarcerated in the cotton mills of our once happy New England." Such dramatic sentiment appeared in several influential pamphlets authored by Luther, some of the nation's earliest union tracts. These works led to a demand for Luther's services as a speaker and agitator. A recurrent theme in his screeds was the inequality of wealth and political power in the new nation.

Luther and Boston labor reformer Dr. Charles Douglas founded the Boston Trades' Union (BTU) in 1832 and led the BTU during an 1835 **strike** for a ten-hour workday. Luther also sold copies of **working-class** newspapers, like the *New England Artisan*, and then turned his attention to winning universal suffrage rights for white males at a time in which many states, including Rhode Island, restricted voting to property holders, a proviso that shut out a majority of working-class citizens. Luther joined in the unsuccessful legislative and military attempt to force the question during the Dorr War of 1842. He was imprisoned and briefly escaped by setting fire to his cell. Charges were eventually dropped, and Luther went on a national tour for the cause of labor and open suffrage. He remained a crusader for the ten-hour workday into the mid-1840s.

Being a social pioneer took its toll on Luther. In 1846, he entered a Boston bank armed with a sword and demanded $1,000, ostensibly to help in the war against Mexico in 1846. He was incarcerated at Butler Hospital in Providence for a decade before being moved to a cheaper facility in Vermont, where he died some time in 1863. He was buried in an unmarked and unknown grave. Luther was inducted into the Rhode Island Hall of Fame in 2001.

Suggested Readings: Seth Luther, *An Address to the Working Men of New England*, 1832; Scott Molloy, Carl Gesuny, and Robert Macieski, eds., *Peaceably if We Can, Forcibly if We Must! Writings by and about Seth Luther*, 1998; Edward Pessen, *Most Uncommon Jacksonians*, 1967.

Scott Molloy

M

Maintenance of Membership. Maintenance of membership is a provision in some union **contracts** that requires unionists to retain their membership through the life of that contract. These clauses date to the 1940s, a time in which union leaders feared that wartime labor relations might weaken the labor movement. During World War II, most unions took a **no-strike pledge**. With the **strike** weapon withdrawn, union leaders faced challenges in compelling employers to improve **wages** and conditions. They also feared that overall solidarity would wane, making it harder to retain members and recruit new ones. Many unions lobbied the Roosevelt administration to set up closed shops that hired only union workers, a plan vehemently opposed by most business owners. Unions, however, remembered the assault on organized labor after World War I and were determined not to be left vulnerable a second time.

In April 1941, the National Defense Mediation Board proposed maintenance of membership clauses as a compromise between unions and employers. In places where closed shops did not already exist, these clauses stabilized union membership during the life of contracts, thereby protecting union treasuries. Many hail this compromise as the tool that freed leaders to concentrate on **collective bargaining**, though critics cite it as another of the factors that hastened the rise of forms of **business unionism** that ignored **rank-and-file** concerns.

Suggested Readings: James Alteson, *Labor and the Wartime State*, 1998; Nelson Lichtenstein, *Labor's War at Home*, 1982; Joel Seidman, *American Labor from Defense to Reconversion*, 1953.

Andrew E. Kersten

Major League Baseball Players Association (MLBPA). The Major League Baseball Players Association (MLBPA) is perhaps the nation's most powerful and successful union. Since 1966, the MLBPA has reversed over a century of management dominance over the economics of Major League Baseball (MLB). In 2000, the average player **salary** reached nearly $1.9 million per year, and the minimum was $200,000; an agreement struck in 2002 raised the minimum to $300,000 per year.

These numbers represent a spectacular reversal of fortunes; as recently as the mid-1960s, the minimum salary was only $6,000, and most players took other jobs in the off-season. Only a handful of superstars commanded salaries in excess of $50,000. Today, players, coaches, managers, and trainers enjoy full **collective bargaining** rights, binding **arbitration** clauses, and the ability to become free agents after six years of service.

The power today enjoyed by the MLBPA is an outgrowth of a century-long struggle against parsimonious and sometimes abusive MLB owners. The first attempt at a players' union came in 1885 when John Montgomery Ward of the New York Giants formed the Brotherhood of Base Ball Players in response to salary caps imposed by owners, the chattel-like manner in which some owners sold players, and the conditions under which players often had to perform. In 1890, numerous players formed a rival league, the Players' Association. It collapsed after a single season and the Brotherhood was crushed.

The Players' Protective Association (PPA) was formed in 1900, but any hope it had of attaining significant power vanished in 1903. Two years earlier, National League (NL) star Napoleon Lajoie tried to invalidate his **contract** to play for the newly formed American League (AL). NL lawyers argued that MLB's "reserve clause" bound Lajoie to his NL club until such time as it chose to release him. In 1903, the NL and AL signed the National Agreement and agreed to uphold the reserve clause. This doomed efforts of the PPA and successors that followed.

In 1922, the newly formed Federal League challenged the reserve clause as a violation of federal antitrust laws, but the Supreme Court upheld it. The case was revisited in 1951, and the court agreed it erred, but left the matter in the hands of Congress to change antitrust laws. In 1966, players hired former **United Steel Workers of America** official Marvin Miller to represent them, and from this, the current MLBPA was formed. In 1968, Miller helped players negotiate the first-ever professional sports union contract.

Miller directed an effort in which in which St. Louis Cardinals' star Curt Flood challenged MLB's exemption to antitrust laws. In 1972, the Supreme Court again passed the matter to Congress. Although Flood lost his bid to become a free agent, three years later a federal arbitrator ruled in favor of two players, thereby opening the door for future free-agency bids. From 1975 on, MLB salaries began to soar as owners were forced to bid for player services in a competitive market. Players frequently changed teams when their contracts expired.

Labor/management relations have been contentious, with player **strikes** occurring in 1972, 1980, 1981, 1985, and 1994–95. Most of these occurred in the off-season, though eighty-six games were cancelled in 1972 and over 700 in 1981. The 1994 strike was particularly acrimonious; 920 games were cancelled, and the World Series was aborted for the first time since it was instituted in 1904. In addition, owners have locked-out players in 1973, 1976, and 1990.

In 1990, MLB owners were forced to pay the MLBPA over $280 million for colluding to hold down salaries by refusing to sign free agents. Owners in small-market cities lacking lucrative media broadcast contracts complain that they can no longer field competitive teams, and many claim they are losing money. At the end of 2001, the Arizona Diamondbacks claimed to have lost in excess of $40 million, though they won the World Series. During the winter of 2002, MLB Commissioner Bud Selig announced plans to eliminate two teams before the start of the season. The MLBPA, plus groups in several cities rumored to be targets of contraction, sued MLB, which was forced to back down. Owners continue to insist that the MLBPA must make **concessions**, or that only a handful of teams can hope to make a profit or be competitive on the field. Foremost among the owner demands is that the MLBPA accept a salary cap, the likes of which are already in place in professional basketball and hockey.

Critics of MLB point to the record sums new owners shell out to buy teams and owners' refusal to consider revenue sharing or luxury taxes as evidence of the game's financial solvency. Owners have been accused of shady accounting practices to exaggerate their plight. The 2002 agreement put off all talks of contracting teams until 2006. It did not include a salary cap, though it did place higher luxury taxes on high-revenue teams that will, in theory, help subsidize teams in smaller markets. Although a 2002 strike was narrowly averted, most analysts foresee future showdowns between the MLBPA and MLB. The current MLBPA president is Donald Fehr.

Suggested Readings: John Feinstein, *Play Ball: The Life and Hard Times of Major League Baseball*, 1993; "Strike Any Thought of Stoppage," *Boston Globe* (July 7, 2002); Andrew Zimbalist, *Baseball and Billions* (1992); Major League Baseball Players Association, http://bigleaguers.yahoo.com/mlbpa/history.

Robert E. Weir

Maquiladora. *Maquiladora* is a Spanish term deriving from the verb *maquilar*, meaning "to do a task for another." It was once used to refer to the in-kind payment made to millers grinding peasants' grain, but it now refers to foreign-owned companies operating in Mexico. The bulk of maquiladoras are owned by U.S. corporations and are located in cities close to the U.S. border like Ciudad Juarez, Mexicali, Nogales, Nuevo Laredo, Rio Bravo, and Tijuana. The products made or assembled in Mexico are then reimported to the country operating the factory, usually the United States.

American firms have long moved parts of their operations to Mexico to take advantage of lower labor costs, lax environmental standards, and favorable tax policies. The 1965 Mexico Border Industrialization Program led to an upsurge of foreign investment in Mexico, and in the 1980s business **deregulation** and tax cuts made it easier for U.S. companies to move across the border. The 1994 **North American Free Trade Agreement (NAFTA)**—passed over the strenuous objection of organized labor in the United States and in Canada—has sped the process even more.

The benefits for U.S. or Canadian firms desiring to relocate to Mexico are enormous. Under NAFTA, a company can set up either a direct subsidiary or a "shelter agreement," in which it supplies raw materials and manufacturing equipment while a Mexican company provides everything else from labor to legal permits. These operate as de facto **subcontracting** arrangements. Under NAFTA, most maquiladora products are taxed only if they are imported outside of North America. Devaluations of the Mexican peso in 1982, and several more times in the 1990s, have made Mexican labor so cheap that even Asian firms have located some production there. By the mid-1990s, Mexican workers averaged the equivalent of about U.S. $19 per week, a figure eclipsed by the hourly rate of many U.S. and Canadian workers. In 2002, it was estimated that the average maquiladora worker in Tijuana had to work for ninety minutes to earn enough to buy a kilogram of rice.

The business community argues that maquiladoras are good for American consumers as they ensure that products can be sold for lower prices. Beyond that, though, it makes little attempt to hide the fact that it is drawn to Mexico's low-wage, nonunion, weak regulatory environment. There are several consulting firms—like North American Production Sharing, Inc.—that specialize in aiding employers in shifting part or all of their production to Mexico.

Labor unions complain that NAFTA and similar programs are little more than taxpayer-subsidized slave-labor bills used by unscrupulous companies to avoid corporate taxes, eliminate jobs, and drive down **wages**. In addition, Mexico's lack of environmental laws allows companies to pollute in ways that jeopardize regional, if not worldwide, ecosystems. Many U.S.-based unions—like the **United Auto Workers**, the **United Electrical Workers**, and the International Longshoremen's and Warehouse Workers—have begun to organize Mexican workers, though Mexico also lacks many of the labor laws that protect workers from retaliation.

There is little doubt that American jobs have been lost to maquiladora production. According to the **National Association of Manufacturers**, over 3,450 foreign firms now operate maquiladoras. Of the 1.2 million jobs involved, the bulk of them have been shifted from the United States; one estimate claims that over 800,000 jobs were lost between 1994 and 2000. Some economists counter that most of these jobs came in assembly-line and labor-intensive industries that were already in severe decline, while others argue that most of the jobs done in maquiladoras are undesirable ones incompatible with American preferences and lifestyles. Although that is true in some cases, it is equally true that some firms have closed profitable plants in the U.S. simply to make higher profits in Mexico.

The fruits of NAFTA and the maquiladora movement will likely remain a point of capital-labor contention. Labor unions are pressing for the repeal or reform of NAFTA. Although that is unlikely in the near term, future downturns in the American economy could spark support for reforms. In the interim, unions will probably increase their presence along the border in the hopes that driving up Mexican wages will make maquiladora production less attractive.

Suggested Readings: Rachael Kamel and Anya Hoffman, eds., *Maquiladora Reader: Cross Border Organizing Since NAFTA*, 1999; Kathryn Kipinak, *Desert Capitalism: Maquiladoras in North America's Western Industrial Corridor*, 1996; David Bacon, "The Fruits of NAFTA," http://www.maquilasolidarity.org/respurces/maquilas/bacon2002.htm.

Robert E. Weir

Master Agreement. A master agreement is a **contract** involving one or more companies and the unions that represent workers in those firms. Unlike most contracts, a master agreement seeks to set **wage** and **fringe benefits** standards in multiple firms rather than with a single company. The key idea is to create a broad agreement that applies irrespective of where a plant is located.

Master agreements are largely a product of **industrial unionism**. Workers in mass-production enterprises like auto manufacturing, meatpacking, and steel found that wage rates varied widely from firm to firm, and that great regional discrepancies existed. A successful master contract normalized wages and benefits across an industry, though most national unions allowed local unions to negotiate conditions peculiar to specific locales. Unions like the **United Auto Workers** were sometimes successful in convincing employers that master contracts were beneficial, so that Ford, for example, was not forced to pay higher wages than competitors like General Motors or Chrysler. The **International Brotherhood of Teamsters** proved very adept at forcing the trucking industry to sign master contracts in the 1950s and into the 1960s.

Master agreements are hard to negotiate as they often involve multiple firms and more than one union. Moreover, existing labor laws restrain efforts, as protections of **rank-and-file** rights are carefully safeguarded against the usurping of too much power by union officials. These agreements are less common in recent years.

Suggested Readings: Henry Campbell Black, *Black's Law Dictionary*, 1999; Stephen Brill, *The Teamsters*, 1978.

Robert E. Weir

Master Craftsman. A master craftsman is an individual who has attained the designation of "master," the highest and most prestigious level of a trade or craft. It is an old designation dating to the medieval guild system. It was transplanted to North America by colonial craft workers and was an important component of the colonial work structure. Only master craftsmen were able to take in **apprentices** and hire **journeymen**. Master status was also a way to limit the number of workers practicing a trade, regulate the quality of goods produced, and enhance **wage** and price bargaining. Today, the title is generally conferred to trades workers who have completed an approved apprenticeship program. Many apprenticeships are regulated by unions.

In the late eighteenth and into the nineteenth century, the distinction between masters and journeymen began to blur, though skill remained primary to both. Skilled workers—also known as artisans—usually commanded the highest wages for their craft. To protect themselves and their families, skilled workers formed unions or alliances. They set their own prices, forcing businesses and consumers to buy their products based on the quality and limited supply. In the early nineteenth century, skilled artisans dominated crafts like furniture making, brewing, baking, plumbing, carpentry, and masonry.

Industrialization and mechanization began to decrease the importance of skilled craftsmen in the 1830s, most notably in industries like shoes and textiles. Artisans remained important throughout the nineteenth century, however, and numerous craft unions formed to protect their rights. Many unions opposed technological changes that replaced master craftsmen with machines and reduced their status to that of unskilled or semiskilled workers. The **American Federation of Labor (AFL)** formed partly to protect craft workers; founder **Samuel Gompers** headed the Cigar Makers International Union, an organization whose craft was particularly threatened by deskilling.

The expansion of industry in the late nineteenth century doomed older craft ideals, however. In 1892 for example, Carnegie Steel company easily replaced skilled steel producers with imported machinery during the **Homestead lockout**. By the twentieth century, many union activists argued that AFL conceptions of craft ideals were outmoded by technological reality. From this, **industrial unionism** gained force. Skilled craftsmen nonetheless continued to dominate in fields like precision machine grinding, carpentry, and tailoring.

In the popular mind, however, craft work began to lose its association with the everyday work world and become identified with niche markets, specialty goods, leisure pursuits, and the fine arts. Society still requires contemporary craftsmen such as plumbers, electricians, carpenters, pipe fitters, and painters. Ironically, though, older craft ideals are most dominant among white-collar professions like doctors and lawyers and in professional unions like the **National Educational Association**. Union apprenticeship programs keep blue-collar ideals of craft alive, as do vocational technical schools, certification requirements, and licensing boards.

Suggested Readings: Alan Dawley, *Class and Community*, 1976; James Green, *The World of the Worker*, 1990; Nelson Lichtenstein et al., *Who Built America? Working People and the Nation's Economy, Politics, Culture, and Society, Vol. 2: Since 1877*, 2000.

Victor Caron

Matewan. Matewan is a small coal-patch town in Mingo County, West Virginia, where striking coal miners were involved in a bloody shootout with the Baldwin-Felts Agency on May 19, 1920. It was part of the larger West Virginia–Kentucky coal **strike** that convulsed the region between 1920 and 1923. The violence in this section of West Virginia was so severe that the region was dubbed "Bloody Mingo County." The events in Matewan later appeared in fictionalized form in a 1987 film by John Sayles.

The events in Matewan occurred in the midst of a **United Mine Workers of America (UMWA)** campaign to organize West Virginia coal miners. New UMWA President **John L. Lewis** made said effort the centerpiece of his plan to revitalize the moribund UMWA. Despite firings and blacklists of UMWA members, the union began to make major inroads in the southern Appalachians. One estimate holds that more than 15,000 miners in the Tug Creek region of West Virginia near Matewan signed with the UMWA.

Regional coal operators and the out-of-state interests that controlled them kept up steady harassment of the UMWA, including the importation of **goons** and gun thugs. Some activists were shot or beaten, and rumors abounded that coal companies were murdering miners. By the spring of 1920, miners were armed for self-protection. Into this tense atmosphere came the Baldwin-Felts Agency. The firm, like the **Pinkerton** Detective Agency and the Burns Agency, specialized in company "security," a term that generally referred to strong-arm union-busting. Residents complained that agents threatened local citizens and harassed women.

Albert and Lee Felts arrived in Matewan on May 15, 1920, with orders from the Red Jacket Coal Company to evict the families of striking miners from company-owned housing. Several UMWA leaders recognized the potential for violence and sought to have the evictions carried out by the Mingo County sheriff instead of Baldwin-Felts agents, but their efforts were rebuffed by U.S. Attorney General A. Mitchell Palmer, a man whose antilabor biases were well-known. The failure to heed UMWA advice led to tragedy.

On May 19, thirteen new Baldwin-Felts agents arrived in Matewan. They carried out several evictions until confronted by Matewan Chief of Police Sid Hatfield, who was also a UMWA member. Hatfield and Matewan Mayor Cabell Testerman charged that the agents lacked the proper paperwork to continue the evictions. A heated discussion ensued, and legend holds that Hatfield attempted to arrest Albert and Lee Felts, brothers of agency president Tom Felts. When the agents attempted to board a train, gunfire broke out. After a brief volley, the Felts brothers, five other detectives, two miners, and Testerman lay dead.

The shootout at Matewan galvanized miners, and they flooded to UMWA ranks. It also turned the mountains into a war zone marked by periodic sniper fire from both sides. Tom Felts vowed revenge on Hatfield, who along with fifteen miners was charged with the murder of Albert Felts. All were acquitted in January 1921. Felts, however, charged that jury members were influenced by **communists** and the UMWA, and convinced the West Virginia legislature to pass the Jury Bill, which allowed judges and juries to be imported from outside the county. In a move of dubious constitutionality, the Matewan defendants were retried, this time for the murders of the six remaining Baldwin-Felts agents. (They could not be charged with the murder of Albert Felts, as that would constitute double jeopardy.)

Hatfield and UMWA member Ed Chambers were assassinated by Baldwin-Felts agents on August 1, 1921, as they were ascending the courthouse steps on the way to their trial. No one was charged with their murders, but the mountains erupted in violence that culminated in the **Battle of Blair Mountain** which cost at least twenty-five miners their lives and led President Warren G. Harding to place the region under martial law. In the end, the UMWA suffered a brutal setback. By the 1930s, however, the UMWA had organized nearly all the region's miners.

Matewan's notoriety faded quickly, and not many Americans knew of it until the appearance of the labor movie *Matewan* in 1987. Independent director John Sayles thoroughly researched the film, but his account is not a documentary. Sayles did not alter the basic historical truth of the Matewan massacre, but he took artistic license in several key areas. For instance, the film's central character, ex–**Industrial Worker of the World (IWW)** activist Joe Kenehan, is, in fact, a composite character based in part on real-life UMWA leaders Frank Keeney and Fred Mooney. Neither man belonged to the IWW, though Keeney once belonged to the Socialist Party, and both men had been involved in the 1912 Paint Creek strike in which the IWW played a minor role. Sayles also plucked protagonist Few Clothes Johnson from a later episode in the strike to give his film a central African American character.

Suggested Readings: David Corbin, *Life, Work, and Rebellion in the Coal Fields: The Southern West Virginia Miners, 1880–1922*, 1981; Lon Savage, *Thunder in the Mountain: The West Virginia Mine War*, 1990; John Sayles, *Thinking in Pictures: The Making of* Matewan, 1987.

Robert E. Weir

May Day. May Day, held on or about May 1, is celebrated in many nations as a day to honor workers. Long associated with the political left, May Day is not celebrated in the United States with the fervor it evokes elsewhere, though, ironically, the holiday originated there.

The first May Day occurred on May 1, 1886, and was part and parcel of a failed **general strike** in support of the **eight-hour movement**. An alliance of trade unionists, radicals, and **Knights of Labor (KOL)** called for a nationwide walkout on May 1 to force recalcitrant employers to grant laborers an eight-hour workday. At the time, most factories routinely defined a workday as between nine and twelve hours. Despite early enthusiasm for the idea, the idea began to fizzle in advance of May 1, in part due to opposition from KOL leaders who felt the actions premature and were troubled by the presence of anarchist organizers in some cities. Although many **rank-and-file** Knights defied their leaders, May Day turnouts were low except in a few cities. Instead of the one million strikers organizers had hoped for, about 300,000 left their jobs.

The biggest crowds were in Chicago, where May Day happened to coincide with a strike against the McCormick-Harvester company. Within the city, some 40,000 workers turned out. The International Working Peoples' Association (IWPA), an anarchist federation, was active in organizing the event and held several massive parades in support of the eight-hour day prior to May 1. On the day itself, clashes in front of the McCormick factory led to clashes in which several strikers were killed. In protest, the IWPA and others called for a massive protest three days later, a fateful call that led to the **Haymarket** tragedy.

In the wake of Haymarket, May Day became associated with **anarchism** and the political left. May Day rallies were held after 1886, and in 1889 the International Socialist Congress, held in Paris, proclaimed May 1 as International Workers' Day. This, however, served only to distance moderate and liberal workers and unions from the event, who preferred to celebrate a separate **Labor Day**. The **American Federation of Labor** did hold some May Day rallies in the 1890s.

May Day Parade, New York, 1910. © Library of Congress.

May Day dropped further from favor after the 1917 Russian Revolution. The new Bolshevik government enthusiastically embraced May Day as a symbol of **working-class** revolutionary fervor and of the military might of the Soviet state. May Day enjoyed a brief resurgence among U.S. radicals in the 1930s, but even then was avoided by most workers in favor of Labor Day. The suppression of radicals following World War II pushed May Day further into the orbit of the radical left. May Day is still commemorated in the United States, but its appeal is limited mostly to ideologues.

Suggested Readings: Paul Avrich, *The Haymarket Tragedy*, 1984; Eric Hobsbawm and Terence Ranger, eds., *The Invention of Tradition*, 1984.

Robert E. Weir

McGuire, Peter James (July 6, 1852–February 18, 1906). Peter James McGuire was one of the founders of the **United Brotherhood of Carpenters and Joiners (UBC)** and the **American Federation of Labor (AFL)**. During the1880s and the 1890s he competed with **Samuel Gompers** and other conservative figures for the ideological leadership of the labor movement in the United States. McGuire was born on July 6, 1852, in New York City, the oldest of five children. His parents, John J. and Catherine Hand (O'Riley) were immigrants from Ireland. His father was a porter in a department store. McGuire attended parochial schools as a boy, but left at the age of eleven to help support his family when John McGuire enlisted in the Union army during the Civil War. Peter held a variety of menial jobs, including bootblack, stable hand, and newsboy. At age seventeen, he became a cabinetmaker at the Haynes Piano Company and joined the Cabinet Makers Union of New York. Also during this period McGuire attended night classes and lectures at Cooper Union, a free institute for the education of young **working-class** men and women. It was here that he was first introduced to, and debated, various strains of socialist thought. He was particularly attracted to the ideas of the German writer and activist Ferdinand Lassalle. **Lassalleans** argued that workers needed to organize political parties as well as trade unions, so that they could use their votes to establish a socialist state. Throughout his career in the labor movement, McGuire was attacked from the right by conservatives who rejected **socialism**, and from the left by more radical socialists who rejected politics and advocated revolution.

McGuire first became prominent in radical circles in New York during the severe depression of 1873. He was a leader of the Committee of Public Safety that demanded relief for the unemployed and threatened a march on city hall to press for their demands. On January 13, 1874, he led a parade that was attacked and dispersed by mounted police. The **Tompkins Square riot** convinced McGuire of the need for political action and the following May he helped found the Socialist Labor Party. For the next several years, he served as one of the party's most successful recruiters and became well known as a tireless organizer and fiery orator. In 1878, he moved to St. Louis and the following year was instrumental in the passage a state law establishing one of the first state **Bureaus of Labor Statistics** in the United States. During this same period, he also joined the St. Louis Carpenters' Union and became increasingly active in the labor movement. This was a time of profound changes in the lives of American workers. Earlier in the century, a young man was educated in the skilled trades by means of a formal **apprenticeship** system, and once he had completed his apprenticeship enjoyed relative independence, a dependable income, and a certain degree of prestige. But by the 1870s, apprenticeships were becoming rare, and even in highly skilled trades such as carpentry, goods once made painstakingly by hand were increasingly mass produced by machines in factories. As a result, workers made less money and had less power.

McGuire and other labor leaders realized that stable, well-financed, nationwide unions were the best way to protect workers from these changes. In April 1881, he served as secretary of a committee of the St. Louis Carpenters' Union that issued a call for a national federation of carpenters' unions, and at the first convention of the UBC in August, was elected national secretary. McGuire held this office for the next twenty years. In the early years, he ran the national union almost single-handedly and developed it into one of the most powerful in the country. At the same time, he edited the union's journal, *The Carpenter*. Also in August 1881, at a special meeting of trade unionists in Terre Haute, Indiana, McGuire wrote the advertisement for a convention to form a federation of all the national trade unions. He was active in the new organization, the Federation of Organized Trades and Labor Unions, and when it was reorganized five years later as the AFL, he became its first secretary. McGuire saw the brotherhood and the federation as serving both immediate and long-range purposes. First, they protected workers' day-to-day interests by fighting for fair **wages**, reasonable hours, and decent working conditions. In McGuire's view, the ultimate purpose of the UBC and the AFL was to prepare the way for a socialist commonwealth. With money from a government controlled by a labor party, workers would essentially buy out the capitalists and form their own large-scale industrial **cooperatives**. During the 1880s and 1890s, both the UBC and the AFL prospered, and McGuire became one of the most influential figures in the national labor movement.

However, as the century came to a close, more conservative leaders, such as AFL President Samuel Gompers, gained control of the movement. These men were interested solely in immediate aims and rejected McGuire's vision of a socialist commonwealth. In 1900, he was forced to resign as vice president of the AFL due to poor health and alcoholism, and two years later was expelled from the UBC in the wake of trumped-up charges of embezzlement. McGuire died in Camden, New Jersey, on February 18, 1906.

Suggested Readings: Robert Christie, *Empire in Wood: A History of the Carpenters Union*, 1953; Mark Ehrlich, "Peter J. McGuire's Trade Unionism: Socialism of a Trades Union Kind," *Labor History* 24:2, 165–97, Spring 1983; David N. Lyon, "The World of P. J. McGuire: A Study of the American Labor Movement, 1870–90" (Ph.D. diss., University of Minnesota, 1972).

Tom Glynn

McKee's Rock. McKee's Rock is a town in western Pennsylvania where the **Industrial Workers of the World (IWW)** led an important **strike** in the steel mills of the Pressed Steel Car Company in the summer of 1909. Though more than a dozen people lost their lives, and several hundred were injured, the strike ended in partial victory for the IWW. For a brief moment, it appeared that **collective bargaining** would emerge in one of the most union-resistant industries in the United States.

McKee's Rock mirrored nearby **Homestead**, where an 1892 strike ended in a rout of labor. Like Homestead, McKee's Rock was largely a **company town** in which workers rented homes and purchased utilities from the corporation. Also like Homestead, the town was dominated by immigrant laborers who lived in crushing poverty. Nations of origin included Russia, Poland, Austria, Germany, France, and Italy. The **American Federation of Labor (AFL)** represented a small number of skilled workers, but deemed most of the workforce as unorganizable.

Difficulties began in McKee's Rock during the economic recession of 1907. During the downturn, **wages** were slashed and new work rules were implemented, the two most troublesome of which were new standards for computing the piece-rate pay under which many workers were compensated and the introduction of a pooling system in which all line workers were penalized if any one of them failed to meet quotas. In addition, workers were docked for **downtime**. By 1909, the recession was over, but wages were still below pre-1907 levels.

On Saturday, July 10, some workers grumbled that their pay was unfairly computed, and on Monday about forty men refused to work; they were promptly fired. The company's refusal to meet with a workers' committee on July 14 led to a spontaneous walkout of about 600 workers; by afternoon, over 5,000 of the plant's employees were out, with only about 500 skilled AFL men staying on the job. The strike officially began on Thursday, July 15, with demands for a wage increase, a formal **grievance** procedure, and an end to the pooling system. The first day of the strike saw a small-scale repeat of Homestead events twenty-one years earlier, when workers fired upon coal and iron police seeking to enter the plant by boat from the Ohio River.

Violence also broke out when the company sought to evict workers from their homes and house **scabs** there. Wives screaming "Kill the Cossacks" greeted the efforts, and more than a hundred individuals on both sides were injured. It is not certain exactly when the IWW entered the fray, but by the end of July, **William Trautmann** was busy organizing immigrant workers. Violence continued to plague the strike, and on August 22 a clash between immigrant workers and the coal and iron police led to at least seven deaths. State troopers subsequently ransacked workers' homes in search of weapons. Trautmann was arrested on minor charges, but the IWW quickly dispatched Joe Ettor to replace him, and the strike continued.

On September 8, 1909, the Pressed Steel Company capitulated to worker demands. Scabs were dismissed, the pooling system was dismantled, and an immediate 5 percent raise was implemented with 10 percent more promised within sixty days. Pressed Steel no doubt decided to end the strike partly in hopes of deterring rising IWW organizing. Most negotiations were held with AFL machinists and electricians, and that American-born group was not sympathetic to foreigners. Ettor led 4,000 immigrant workers out again on September 14, but violent clashes that led to more deaths and AFL opposition collapsed the strike within twenty-four hours.

The IWW briefly threatened to organize steel. Victory at McKee's Rock was followed by successful actions at two plants in East Chicago, Indiana, and another in Hammond, Indiana. In the end, however, Pressed Steel's strategy worked. By dealing with small AFL unions, steel firms avoided **collective bargaining** with the masses and crippled IWW hopes. The IWW's membership at McKee's Rock plummeted from 6,000 in October 1909 to just twenty in August 1912. The bulk of steelworkers remained unorganized until the emergence of the Steel Workers Organizing Committee in the 1930s.

Suggested Readings: Melvyn Dubofsky, *We Shall Be All: A History of the Industrial Workers of the World*, 1969; Ronald Filippelli, *Labor in the USA: A History*, 1984; Sidney Lens, *The Labor Wars: From the Molly Maguires to the Sitdowns*, 1974.

Bruce Cohen

Robert E. Weir

McNeill, George Edwin (August 4, 1837–May 19, 1906). George Edwin McNeill was president of the International Labor Union, a member of the **Knights of Labor (KOL)**, a founding member of the **American Federation of**

Labor (AFL), and such an active member in the Eight-Hour League that he was dubbed by contemporaries as the "Father of the **Eight-Hour Movement**," though that title ought properly to go to **Ira Steward**. Very few nineteenth-century labor leaders enjoyed as much respect across the ideological spectrum as McNeill.

He was born in Amesbury, Massachusetts, the son of John and Abigail (Hickey) McNeill, Scots-Irish immigrants. He attended school until the age of fifteen, when he began work, first in woolen mills, then as a shoemaker. When he was nineteen, he moved to Boston, where he met Steward and came to agree that eight hours ought to constitute a day's work. He held several positions in Boston's Eight-Hour League after 1863, including that of president from 1869 to 1874.

In 1869, McNeill was appointed as deputy state constable of the Massachusetts **Bureau of Labor Statistics (BLS)**, an agency that he had lobbied the Commonwealth of Massachusetts to create. He helped compile the statistical report of trade unions for 1872, and one of his prolabor reports (later published as *Factory Children: A Report upon the Schooling and Hours of Labor of Children Employed in the Manufacturing and Mechanical Establishments of Massachusetts*) resulted in his dismissal from the bureau. Despite his own problems with the BLS, the Massachusetts bureau was widely hailed and became the model from which a national BLS was later fashioned. McNeill championed the creation of such a body when he joined the KOL in 1883. Both McNeill and the KOL believed that BLS statistics would educate the public about the problems facing working people and make that public more receptive to unions.

After his dismissal from the BLS, McNeill reimmersed himself into the Eight-Hour League and studied Steward's economic theories. McNeill came to attribute depressions and economic upheaval to the evils of the **wage** system and to underconsumption. Both Steward and McNeill also supported the Boston Christian Labor Union, McNeill becoming the senior warden of the Boston parish of Reverend W. D. P. Bliss, an Episcopal priest active in the KOL and founder of several Christian socialist organizations. Like many other future AFL activists, McNeill flirted with various forms of **socialism**, and his later adult writings indicate that he remained influenced by Bliss's Christian socialism into his declining years. McNeill was apparently involved with the Socialist Labor Party (SLP) at its inception in 1876. However, he immediately got caught up in internal SLP tactical quarrels over whether the SLP should be primarily a labor organization or a political entity. McNeill was among those union advocates who insisted that the SLP abide by its initial ban on political activity, even though various other local party groups were fielding candidates in local elections in 1876. As a consequence of this discord, Ira Steward and several others in the Eight-Hour League hesitated to join the party.

This dispute ironically awakened McNeill's interest in **labor journalism**. When the financially strapped *Labor Standard*, a Marxist weekly and official SLP organ, was at the point of suspension in May 1877, the paper's editor J. P.

McDonnell and other labor advocates took over the paper and transferred the paper itself to Boston. When the paper moved to Fall River, Massachusetts, McNeill joined the editorial board. In 1877, McNeill began contributing articles and later that year, he and Steward were listed on the paper's masthead as regular contributors. McNeill and his supporters were absent from the December 1877 SLP convention, and telegrams to the paper from the party's executive committee went unanswered. Finally the *Labor Standard* was removed from the list of official SLP organs, and it became the official journal of the short-lived International Labor Union (ILU).

Though the ILU reportedly had around 7,000 members and branches in seventeen states in 1878, its participation in unsuccessful **strikes** caused its fortunes to decline; by 1881 a branch in Newark was the only one left. By then, McNeill had cast his lot with the KOL. He quickly became one of the most popular members in the organization and one of the few figures aside from its national leader, **Terence Powderly**, whose reputation extended beyond his local region. He served in several posts with District Assembly 30, which represented most of Massachusetts. McNeill ultimately clashed with Powderly and others within the KOL who felt that trade unionism should give way to the KOL's more inclusive organizing principles. At the May 25, 1886, Special General Assembly of the Knights in Cleveland, McNeill was a member of a committee that attempted to negotiate peace between the KOL and various trade unions that had lodged complaints against it. McNeill remained a committed trade unionist, and when the proceedings failed, McNeill participated in the December 8, 1886, founding of the AFL. A month earlier, McNeill failed in his bid to be elected mayor of Boston.

McNeill was the editor of the Boston *Labor Leader* until late 1887 and continued to contribute occasional articles thereafter. Like other former socialists who supported the **pure and simple unionism** of the AFL, McNeill was bitterly denounced in the socialist press. While he was editor of the *Labor Leader*, McNeill was occasionally critical of socialism, though he held out an olive branch to the KOL. (His successor, Frank Foster, was far less charitable.) McNeill quit the KOL in 1886, but remained hopeful for the Knights, despite personal animus towards Powderly. Editorial jealousy probably played a role in his dislike of Powderly, as McNeill published a labor-problems text in 1886, *The Labor Movement: The Problem of To-Day*. McNeill advertised that Powderly had endorsed the volume, which he denied, and in 1889 Powderly published his own *Thirty Years of Labor*, which covered many of the same themes. By then, McNeill had also authored *Eight Hour Primer*.

Ironically, the fight with Powderly spilled into the public eye just as McNeill's most active work with organized labor was winding down. Though he published *The Philosophy of the Labor Movement* in 1893 and continued to work in the AFL—he represented it at an 1897 British Trade Union Congress—McNeill lowered his public profile as a labor activist. He was also active in the Anti-Imperialist League from 1898 until his death in 1906. However, the work for which he is best known after 1890 was with the Massachusetts Mutual Accidental Insurance Company, which he founded in 1883. "Mass Mutual" was originally conceived to be an insurance scheme for workers, along the lines of a modernized mutual-benefits society, but it evolved into a modern insurance underwriter and remains one of the biggest firms in Massachusetts. In 1903, McNeill published a volume of poetry, *Unfrequented Paths: Songs of Nature, Love, and Men*. He died in Somerville, Massachusetts.

Suggested Readings: Samuel Bernstein, *The First International in America*, 1962; Herbert Gutman, *Work, Culture, and Society in Industrializing America*, 1976; Robert E. Weir, *Knights Unhorsed: Internal Conflict in a Gilded Age Labor Movement*, 2000.

Jeff McFadden

Meany, George (August 16, 1894–January 10, 1980). George Meany was a gruff, burly, cigar-smoking labor administrator from the Bronx who was the most powerful figure in the American labor movement in the middle years of the twentieth century. He served as president of the **American Federation of Labor (AFL)** from 1952 to 1955, fashioned the AFL's merger with the **Congress of Industrial Organizations (CIO)** in 1955, and thereafter presided over the AFL-CIO until his retirement in 1979.

Meany was born into a **working-class** family in New York City. His father, Michael, was a plumber and local union official; his mother, Anne, worked at home. He attended New York public schools until age fourteen, when he left to begin training in his father's trade. He worked as a plumber from 1916 to 1922, then took a paying position with the local branch of the plumbers' union. From that time until his death fifty-eight years later, Meany worked as a trade-union official. A skilled bureaucrat, effective lobbyist, and ferocious political infighter, he rose steadily through the labor movement's ranks. He directed the AFL's organization in New York State during most of the 1930s. Meany's success in that post brought him to the attention of AFL President **William Green** who, in 1939, named him the AFL's secretary-treasurer, the second-ranking position in the federation. When Green died in 1952, Meany was named his successor.

George Meany. © George Meany Memorial Archives.

Meany immediately put his stamp on the federation. For almost two decades, organized labor had been divided into two competing camps, one dominated by the more traditional **craft unions** of the AFL, the other by the more progressive **industrial unions** of the CIO. Meany set out to heal the rift. After two years of painstaking negotiations, AFL and CIO leaders agreed to merge their organizations in 1955. Because the AFL had almost twice as many members as the CIO, Meany was the obvious choice to head the new federation. He was elected the AFL-CIO's first president in December 1955. Sixty-one years old, thirty years removed from his plumber's job, Meany had become the spokesman for more than fifteen million working people.

He used his position to give the AFL-CIO a powerful voice in national affairs. Meany enjoyed easy access to the White House. Democratic Presidents John Kennedy and Lyndon Johnson, in particular, welcomed his support and advice. He promoted economic policies designed to foster economic growth. He continually prodded Congress to pass social-welfare legislation he believed would benefit union workers. At critical points in the 1960s, he put the AFL-CIO's considerable weight behind civil rights legislation. As much as he promoted progressive causes, however, Meany also kept his distance from many liberal and radical initiatives. He distrusted social movements, like the Southern civil rights movement, that operated outside the rarified halls of Congress and the White House. He also had no time for activists who criticized **capitalism**. A staunch anticommunist, he considered even the mildest critique of the Cold War as bordering on treason. He was appalled when many Americans condemned the Vietnam War, which he considered a noble cause.

Meany's caution also extended to his handling of union affairs. While he worked hard to preserve labor's gains, he had no interest in extending the AFL-CIO's reach by expanding organizing efforts. He swiftly marginalized those union officials who wanted the federation to be more aggressive. In his most dramatic move, Meany essentially forced the **United Auto Workers (UAW)**, one of the AFL-CIO's largest affiliate unions, out of the federation when the UAW's president, **Walter Reuther**, criticized Meany's leadership.

Meany's conservative approach to union affairs left the federation ill prepared for the economic and political changes of the 1970s. In mid-decade, corporations began to slash industrial jobs, the heart of unionization. And the federal government, once a reliable ally, increasingly turned its back on the labor movement. Although Meany was not equipped to respond to these profound challenges, he refused to relinquish his iron grip on the AFL-CIO. Though wracked by ill health, he remained the federation's president until November 1979, when he turned over the reins of power to his handpicked successor, Lane Kirkland. Meany died three months later.

Suggested Readings: Joseph Goulden, *Meany: The Unchallenged Strong Man of American Labor*, 1972; Archie Robinson, *George Meany and His Times: A Biography*, 1981; Robert Zieger, "George Meany: Labor's Organization Man," in *Labor Leaders in America*, eds. Melvyn Dubofsky and Warren Van Tine, 1987.

Kevin Boyle

Mechanics Educational Society of America (MESA). The Mechanics Educational Society of America (MESA) was founded by Detroit automobile tool-and-die makers and was an important forerunner of the **United Auto Workers (UAW)**. Although Henry Ford's introduction of assembly-line production in 1913 had done much to routinize work and deskill laborers, the automobile industry was still dependent on skilled tool-and-die workers for precision metal cutting, patterns, and templates. MESA was formed in February 1933 in the wake of several failed auto **strikes** in the greater Detroit area. Under the dynamic leadership of English-born Matt Smith, MESA spread to Flint and Pontiac, Michigan. In the fall of 1933, MESA conducted a six-week strike that crippled over 100 shops. Its partial victory is considered an important first step in establishing **collective bargaining** rights for autoworkers and is considered by many historians as auto's first industrywide settlement.

By early 1934, MESA claimed over 21,000 members, most of whom were skilled workers. MESA was known for its militancy, and some leaders were also **communists** or **socialists**. It did not shy from confronting the government, and its 1933 strike was in partial response to the failure of the New Deal's National Industrial Recovery Act to apply the same standards to **captive-shop** autoworkers that applied elsewhere. Many MESA members and leaders endorsed shop-floor **direct action** militancy. During World War II, MESA refused to endorse a **no-strike pledge**.

Despite the presence of some production workers in its ranks, MESA was dominated by skilled workers, retained a craft-union focus, and was heavily dominated by workers of English and German heritage. Its industrywide perspective set it apart from the weaker **American Federation of Labor federal unions**, but when the UAW emerged as a full-fledged **industrial union**, more militant MESA workers began gravitating to it. By May 1936, many of MESA's important locals merged with the UAW. By 1937, MESA was a truncated organization confined to tool-and-die makers in just a few shops. One by one its locals joined the UAW until, shortly after World War II, MESA folded.

Former MESA members were instrumental in organizing a 1936 action against Midland Steel which was Detroit's first **sit-down strike** and a precursor of future autoworker job actions. They also supported the decision of the Committee on Industrial Organizations to quit the AFL.

Suggested Reading: Steve Babson, *Building the Union: Skilled Workers and Anglo-Gaelic Immigrants in the Rise of the UAW*, 1991.

Robert E. Weir

Mechanics' Lien Laws. *See Lien Laws.*

Mediation. *See Arbitration/Concession/Mediation.*

Memorial Strike. A memorial strike is a vigilant and peaceful demonstration that commemorates earlier labor disputes. The most notable **strike** of this nature occurred on May 4, 1886, when a group of **socialists**, **anarchists**, **commu-**

nists, **Knights of Labor**, and members of the **American Federation of Labor** rallied to protest the killing of protestors who assembled on May 1 to call for the **eight-hour** day. Unfortunately, the **Haymarket** bombing led to more violence and the condemnation of eight anarchists unjustly accused of precipitating the violence. Many subsequent labor protests, especially those held on **May Day**, led to memorial strikes to honor the Haymarket martyrs. Thousands of workers held memorial strikes and work stoppages shortly after May 1886 to honor their fallen comrades.

Memorial strikes also occasionally proved an effective way to circumvent impediments to conventional strikes, like **contract** provisions or **no-strike pledges**. **John L. Lewis** and the **United Mine Workers of America** employed memorial strikes during World War II to maintain pressure on employers without leaving the union vulnerable to official sanctions. Spontaneous strikes to memorialize workers killed on the job in disaster-prone industries like mining have occurred many times, especially when workers deemed those deaths to have been the result of company negligence. The **United Farm Workers of America** also used memorial strikes to draw attention to pesticide dangers to which agricultural workers are exposed.

Most unions seek to avoid memorial strikes, as most are unsanctioned by the national or **international union**. In many cases, memorial strikes violate signed agreements and thus could be deemed **unfair labor practices**. In practice, though, most have been short in duration and have not led to prolonged battles between workers and management. Today, they are seldom held; **Labor Day** ceremonies often perform many of the honorific duties of memorial strikes.

Suggested Readings: Richard Boyer and Herbert Morais, *Labor's Untold Story*, 1955; Ronald Taylor, *Chavez and the Farm Workers*, 1975.

Victor Caron

Merit Raise. A merit raise is an increase in an individual's **wage**, usually at the discretion of management, to reward what it deems to be outstanding job-related performance. Workers who achieve a satisfactory rating from a supervisor generally earn an annual raise; merit raises are paid in addition to annual raises. Also known as "pay-for-performance," merit pay is based on criteria predetermined by the employer and is a private arrangement between management and the wage earner.

Merit raises are an integral mechanism of **Taylorism**, along with other tools such as **bonus** pay, **piecework**, and **profit sharing**. On the surface, it rewards efficiency, loyalty, and hard work. But it also involves a very subjective interpretation on the part of management, which sometimes discriminates against labor or uses it to discourage **solidarity** and **stints**. Merit raises are rare in union agreements, as opposed to democratic, across-the-board pay raises. Merit raises are more common among white-collar professionals, though their potential to engender resentment and jealousy often leads employers to adopt a polite fiction in which part of a predetermined annual raise is designated as a "merit" increase and is given to all workers within a particular unit.

Occasionally, merit raises have been used as a union-busting tactic by management, whereby selected employees are favored in return for antiunion activism. To date, the **Fair Labor Standards Act** has not addressed this issue.

Suggested Readings: Robert Heneman, *Merit Pay,* 1992; Bill Hopkins and Thomas Mawhinney, eds,. *Pay for Performance*, 1992.

Victor Caron

Minimum Wage. The minimum wage is a threshold set forth by the **Fair Labor Standards Act** to which all covered workers are entitled. It establishes a minimum baseline that individual states must meet or exceed. In 2001, the federal minimum wage was $5.15 per hour. Several states have set minimums that exceed the federal standard, but none may go below it. Certain workers, including bartenders and restaurant workers, are excluded from minimum-wage laws, as it is assumed they earn the bulk of their income from gratuities. Agricultural and farmworkers are also excluded, as are certain other types of work that pay **piecework** rates.

The minimum wage was first established in 1938, through the Fair Labor Standards Act, which was signed into law by President Franklin D. Roosevelt. In the 1950s, when the U.S. economy was strong, the federal minimum wage was raised from $0.75 to $1.00 per hour. Although the 2001 rate of $5.15 was more than five times higher, increases in the minimum wage have not kept pace with inflation. It has only been increased eight times since 1938.

On October 26, 2000, the United States House of Representatives passed legislation to increase the minimum wage immediately from $5.15 to $5.65 per hour, and to $6.15 per hour on January 1, 2002. That date passed, and the United States Senate has yet to approve the House bill thus the rate remained at $5.15. Raising the minimum wage has been a constant rallying cry for unions, though some activists now favor scrapping it in favor of laws guaranteeing a living wage that more realistically reflects how much one needs to support one's self.

Suggested Readings: David Card with Alan Krueger, *Myth and Measurement*, 1997; Barbara Ehrenreich, *Nickel and Dimed*, 2001; Lawrence Glickman, *A Living Wage*, 1999.

Victor Caron

Minority Labor. Minority labor has had an ambiguous and often troubled relationship with organized labor. In many respects, the tensions between unions and minority groups mirror the larger social patterns within American society. Minority-group status is based on power relationships, not raw numbers. A member of a minority suffers some form of discrimination at the hands of the dominant group, whether it is in direct form, or an offshoot of institutionalized power arrangements reinforced by social custom and/or statute. Within U.S. society, white males of western European ancestry have been and remain the defined majority power group, though they have never been numerically so.

Other factors, including religion, education, and family background further constrict entry into the majority. Within the labor movement, skill has also served to stratify workers.

Unfortunately, the record of many labor unions is less than exemplary in combating discrimination. Federations like the **Knights of Labor (KOL)**, the **Industrial Workers of the World (IWW)**, and the **Congress of Industrial Organizations (CIO)** made some attempts to combat racism and sexism, but the record of the **American Federation of Labor (AFL)** is rather grim except in isolated cases. Very few unions can boast a long or distinguished record in advancing minority labor. The KOL, for example, demonstrated vicious anti-Chinese prejudice, the IWW did little for women workers, and some CIO members were involved in anti-Mexican incidents in the 1940s.

African American defense plant workers during World War II. © George Meany Memorial Archives.

Racism is partly responsible for the exploitation of Native Americans by colonial Europeans, and transplanted sexism placed female workers in a subordinate status. The imprecision in defining minorities means that many groups have suffered discrimination. Catholic workers, for example, were barred from many jobs in the nineteenth and early twentieth centuries, and discriminatory patterns against southern and eastern European immigrants during the same period parallels those later borne by Latino and Asian immigrants. Although many have endured unfair treatment, labor scholarship on minorities has centered on African Americans, women, and Latinos.

The most obvious examples of African American discrimination were the brutal system of chattel slavery that prevailed in America from 1619 until 1865, and the dehumanizing **Jim Crow** patterns that ensued and were not legally dismantled in their entirety until 1964. Prior to the Civil War, most Northern workers were profoundly racist, and free black laborers experienced great difficulty in securing decent jobs. In the postwar period, groups like the **National Labor Union (NLU)** and the KOL attempted to organize African Americans, often meeting resistance from their own members. Most AFL unions banned black workers, thus few were organized until CIO efforts in the 1930s. Employers often exploited labor's own racism and employed black **scabs** during strikes. The Colored NLU formed in the 1870s, but the 1925 **Brotherhood of Sleeping Car Porters** was the first independent black union to enjoy more than momentary success. Several unions, including the **United Auto Workers**, the **United Mine Workers of America**, and the **United Packinghouse Workers of America** took tentative steps in combating union racism, and the civil rights movement forced the entire labor movement to reevaluate its position on black workers. The 1950s through the 1970s saw often vitriolic battles to dismantle discriminatory practices within organized labor's ranks. Although the contemporary AFL-CIO is committed to racial equality, there are still clashes with **rank and file** over issues like **seniority** and **affirmative action** hiring.

With thousands of men in the armed forces, the need for workers to produce war material brought many women into industrial plants during World War II. © George Meany Memorial Archives.

Women have also battled for equal recognition in organized labor. Ironically, women were the earliest industrial workers in America and made up the bulk of line workers in antebellum textile manufacturing. Women were also heavily represented in all the needle trades, shoe and cigar making, clerical and sales positions, and in teaching. Most domestic servants were women. The Lowell Female Labor Reform League may have been the first women's labor union. The KOL organized female workers under the leadership of **Leonora Barry**, and women have been proactive in forming their own unions. Strategic leaders often exploited presumptions about domesticity to argue in favor of organizing women. Among the groups in which women played central roles are the **Women's Trade Union League** and the **International Ladies' Garment Workers Union**. The 1930s and 1940s eroded some of the gains made in the early twentieth century, even though women played a militant role in labor struggles during the period. Both the AFL and CIO supported bans on employing married women during the Great Depression, just as both championed replacing women workers with returning male veterans after World War II. By the 1950s, women began to press unions to redress their sexism, a process that accelerated when the women's movement emerged with new vigor in the late 1960s. Several labor union women were involved in the founding of the National Organization for Women in 1966. Soaring numbers of women in low-wage retail and office positions also stimulated militancy and led to the creation of groups like **9 to 5**. Recessions in the 1970s and 1980s also led to increases in women wage earners and laid to rest sexist myths that women only worked to secure discretionary funds. Unions have yet to address fully their unequal treatment of women, a condition that groups like the **Coalition of Labor Union Women** seek to counter. Seniority, affirmative action hiring, comparable worth, child care, women's health, and sexual harassment are among the issues with which women unionists are currently concerned.

Problems facing Latino workers were widely ignored until the 1960s. The Mexican War (1846–48) led to the first large absorption of Latino workers, and the opening of the Great Plains to white ranchers led to another increase. Contrary to American myth, the bulk of cowboys were Mexican *vaqueros* and African American cattle hands. Borders between the United States, Mexico, and the Caribbean have long been porous. By the twentieth century, many Latino workers were located in Florida, the Southwest, New York, and California where they worked in jobs as diverse as cigar making, agricultural labor, the garment trades, railroads, and the canning industry. More than a million Mexicans settled in the Southwest alone between 1900 and 1930. During World War I and again in the 1940s and 1950s, the federal government supported the *braceros* program to recruit contingency agricultural "guest" workers. Since the 1950s, much of the American harvest has been picked by Mexicans, Puerto Ricans, Jamaicans, and other Latinos. (Filipinos have also played a large role, as have other Asians in recent years.) Agrarian laborers have been exploited, a condition that led to the formation of the **United Farm Workers of America**, the best-known Latino union. Today, Latinos work in all sectors of the American economy, though they are disproportionately concentrated in the low-wage service sector. Latinos join blue-collar unions at a higher rate than most Anglo workers and have been at the fore of groups like Justice for Janitors. Latino workers have also been leaders in advancing the concept of international organizing and have been better attuned to the implications of **runaway shops**, movable capital, and economic **globalization** than many Anglos.

Suggested Readings: Stanley Aronowitz, *From the Ashes of the Old*, 1998; Philip Foner and Ronald Lewis, eds., *Black Workers*, 1989; Camille Guerin-Gonzalez, *Mexican Workers and the American Dream*, 1994; Alice Kessler-Harris, *Out to Work*, 1982.

Robert E. Weir

Mitchell, John (February 4, 1870–September 9, 1919). John Mitchell was the president of the **United Mine Workers of America (UMWA)** from 1899 to 1908 and is remembered for his leadership in the **Anthracite Coal Strike of 1902**.

At one time one of the most beloved leaders of the UMWA, Mitchell's popularity was rooted in his familiarity with the hard work and poverty that confronted coal miners. He was born in the tiny coal patch of Braidwood, Illinois, the son of coal miner and farmer, Robert Mitchell, and Martha (Halley) Mitchell. Mitchell was orphaned at age six and was raised by his stepmother. He had to work to support his siblings and stepmother, thus his schooling in

Braidwood public schools was meager. He entered the coal mines when he was twelve, joined the **Knights of Labor** in 1885, and spent time as an itinerant miner in the Southwest and West before drifting back to Illinois.

Mitchell joined the UMWA when the union was founded in 1890. He rose through the ranks quickly, an indication of his organizational skills. He was a prolific reader with a thirst for knowledge and joined numerous debating societies and social organizations to develop his communication skills. In Illinois, Mitchell worked hard as a UMWA organizer, traveling to virtually every coal-mining village in the state. One of Mitchell's great accomplishments was easing the ethnic division between Irish miners and more recent immigrants from Germany and Poland. He was elected secretary-treasurer of the state's UMWA District 12 in 1895. Two years later, he was appointed as an international organizer and worked in southern Illinois and West Virginia with **Mary "Mother" Jones** and John H. Walker. In 1897, he was elected international vice president, and upon the resignation of UMWA President Michael Ratchford, became acting president in September 1898. He was elected international president in 1899, and his leadership of the UMWA led to a substantial growth in membership—from approximately 34,000 to 300,000.

Mitchell's greatest success came in the Anthracite Coal Strike of 1902, which lasted from May 12 until October 23. During his travels through the anthracite region, the thirty-two-year-old Mitchell earned the trust and respect of the miners, who referred to the labor leader as "Johnny d'Mitch." Mining families placed Mitchell's photograph in their homes next to religious icons and prints. The labor dispute was highlighted by the intervention of President Theodore Roosevelt, who was forced to act in response to a developing coal shortage. Mitchell and the leading coal operators were summoned to the White House on October 3 for a negotiating session. Mitchell's courteous conduct during the sessions provided sharp contrast to the arrogance of the operators and disposed Roosevelt to favor the miners. While the miners did not get all that they wished, they achieved substantial gains that included **wage** increases and limited union recognition.

The demands of the **strike** took a toll on Mitchell's health and personal life. He became increasingly mired in the bureaucratic demands of his office and was increasingly distant from the **rank and file**. As a result, he was voted out of the UMWA presidency in 1908, succeeded by Thomas L. Lewis. Afterwards, he increased his involvement in the **National Civic Federation (NCF)**, a conservative organization based on cross-class collaboration that he helped form in 1900. He served as chairman of the Trades Agreement Department of the NCF from 1908 to 1911. He was a member of the New York State Workmen's Compensation Commission from 1914 to 1915 and chairman of the New York State Industrial Commission from 1915 until his death from pneumonia in 1919. He is buried in Scranton, Pennsylvania, where a statue and memorial in his honor can be found at the city's Courthouse Square. Miners still celebrate the second Monday in April as John Mitchell Day.

Suggested Readings: Robert Cornell, *The Anthracite Coal Strike of 1902*, 1957; Elise Glück, *John Mitchell, Miner: Labor's Bargain with the Gilded Age*, 1929; Craig Phelan, *Divided Loyalties: The Public and Private Life of Labor Leader John Mitchell*, 1994.

Mark Noon

Molly Maguires. The Molly Maguires were an alleged Irish and Irish American terrorist organization active in the anthracite coal region of Carbon, Columbia, Luzerne, Northumberland, and Schuylkill Counties of Pennsylvania from 1870 to 1876. Some have argued that the Mollies were a chimera created by coal and railroad companies to justify their crackdown on unionization attempts. It is certain that anti-Irish nativism heightened fears of the Molly Maguires. Between 1846 and 1854, more than 1.2 million Irish emigrated to the United States, where they were subjected to discrimination. Popular anti-Irish, anti–Roman Catholic sentiments were widespread in the mid- and late nineteenth century. Irish immigrants often located in ethnic enclaves where the church, saloons, and fraternal organizations like the Ancient Order of Hibernians (AOH) offered solace.

A scene from the 1969 film *The Molly Maguires*. © George Meany Memorial Archives/Paramount Pictures.

Irish miners faced harsh working conditions, low **wages**, and long hours. Many mine hamlets were **company towns**, controlled through a combination of **paternalism** and authoritarianism. The isolated coal-mining villages of northeastern Pennsylvania also bred ethnic rivalry between largely Irish workers and their Welsh- and English-heritage supervisors. Violence and unsolved murders abounded.

In 1870, John Siney organized the Workingmen's Benevolent Association (WBA), and it struck area mines. By 1873, the region was rife with rumors that Irish miners belonged to the Molly Maguires, a clandestine terrorist group. The origin of the term *Molly Maguire* is obscure. It was alleged that Molly Maguire was an Irish woman who rallied opposition to British landlords in Ireland, but some historians believe the term derives from popular protest traditions in which men disguised themselves as women.

The Philadelphia, Reading, and Lehigh Valley Railroad controlled many of the area's mines. In 1873, corporate president Franklin Gowen hired **Pinkerton** Agency detective James McParland to infiltrate the Mollies. McParland claimed to have unearthed a labyrinthine conspiracy across the region involving the AOH, saloon keepers, and miners. The Mollies supposedly operated independent cells headed by a "bodymaster." The cells coordinated plans via interlocking membership, furtive meetings, and a complex message network through which they threatened and harassed opponents. McParland also asserted that Molly Maguires were responsible for numerous murders of mine superintendents, police officers, and local citizens. The first arrests came in May 1876, and by 1879, nineteen alleged Mollies had been hanged, including Jack Kehoe, who McParland claimed was a major ringleader.

Evidence for the Molly Maguires conspiracy rests solely on rumor and McParland's testimony. Siney and other Irish Americans accused Gowen and McParland of inventing the Molly Maguires to legitimate crushing the WBA, whose five-month "Long Strike" in 1875 vexed Gowen. They also charged anti-Irish xenophobia. All those arrested were Irish; most were miners who had participated in strikes, and several were members of the Irish Land League. The WBA declined after 1876, and recruitment for heavily Irish organizations like the **Knights of Labor** was hampered by Molly Maguire innuendoes. Molly Maguire references fueled anti-Irish discrimination and were used to justify crackdowns against radicals throughout the Gilded Age.

Suggested Readings: Anthony Bimba, *The Molly Maguires*, 1989; Wayne Broehl, *The Molly Maguires*, 1964; Sidney Lens, *The Labor Wars*, 1974.

Robert E. Weir

Mr. Block. Mr. Block was a term used by members of the **Industrial Workers of the World (IWW)** to parody laborers who felt they could benefit from the existing economic and political system. It was a synonym for a naïve worker who uncritically accepted the capitalist system and blindly did as he was told by employers and the government. Unlike a **scissorbill**, Mr. Block was presented as more stupid than malicious. It is related to the term blockhead, a popular slang phrase for a person who is unable to grasp the obvious.

Mr. Block first appeared as cartoon strips drawn by Ernest Riebe in the *Industrial Worker*. It gained wide popularity in the IWW due to a song penned by **Joe Hill**. In it, Hill added the employment sharks and the **American Federation of Labor** to the list of those who victimized the unsuspecting Mr. Block. Like much IWW terminology, the use of Mr. Block faded as the organization declined.

Suggested Readings: Joyce Kornbluh, *Rebel Voices*, 1968; Gibbs Smith, *Joe Hill*, 1984.

Robert E. Weir

Mullaney, Kate (1845?–August 17, 1906). Kate Mullaney was the founder of the Collar Laundry Union (CLU) in 1864, which became a model for subsequent women's labor unions. Mullaney was also the first woman to be appointed to a national union office when, in 1868, she became assistant secretary and women's organizer for the **National Labor Union (NLU)**.

Very little is known about Mullaney's early life or formal education. She was born in Ireland, and her family emigrated when she was a teen. Like many Irish Catholics, the Mullaneys were destined for a **working-class** life. Her family settled in Troy, New York, an industrial city that featured numerous iron foundries as well as commercial laundries that cleaned detachable shirt collars and cuffs. (These items were first developed in Troy in 1827, and the city manufactured about 90 percent of the nation's stock by the 1860s. In the nineteenth century, one usually laundered collars and cuffs far more frequently than entire shirts.) Her father died when Mullaney was nineteen, and her mother's delicate health required that Kate become the family breadwinner. More than 3,000 women toiled in Troy's fourteen commercial laundries, often working up to fourteen hours per day for as little as $3 per week. In addition, caustic chemicals, hot water, bleach, and the rapid pace of work exposed laundry workers to burns and other dangers. Newly developed starch machines were especially infamous for inducing horrifying burns.

Mullaney entered this world to provide for her mother and four siblings. Troy was a strong union town, anchored by the Iron Molders Union (IMU) and its dynamic president and future NLU leader **William Sylvis**. Inspired by the molders and by unions like the Cigar Makers International Union which had begun to accept female members, Mullaney decided to organize Troy's laundresses into the CLU. Some sources credit this as the first women's labor union in the United States, though the Lowell Female Reform Association formed by **Sarah Bagley** in 1845 predates it.

On February 23, 1864, Mullaney, aided by the IMU, led a **strike** of about 300 women. In just a week's time, fourteen Troy laundry establishments granted pay rises of over 20 percent and agreed to address safety concerns. In 1866, Mullaney led another successful strike that raised laundress **wages** to about $14 per week. In that same year, William Sylvis and other labor activists formed the NLU. Sylvis launched a rhetorical call to organize women based on the CLU's success. In 1868, Mullaney attended a New York City labor congress and was elected as second vice president of the NLU. Mullaney declined that honor, but Sylvis appointed her as an NLU assistant secretary and organizer for women's work.

Mullaney showed great acumen in building up the collar union's treasury, whose resources she occasionally used to show **solidarity** with other New York workers. In 1868, for example, the CLU donated $500 to striking New York City bricklayers. In March 1869, Mullaney helped CLU starchers win a strike. The CLU's phenomenal success ended later that year, however. When the CLU struck again in May, laundry owners decided to break the union. Workers received substantial financial assistance from the IMU and moral support from the NLU, but Troy laundry owners offered wage increases only to women who agreed to quit the CLU. Mullaney was briefly the president of the Union Line Collar and Cuff Manufactory, an attempt at a worker-owned **cooperative**. The co-op actually landed a major contract to supply A. T. Stewart, then New York

City's largest department store, only to run afoul of technological change. The development of paper collars altered the equation, and both the CLU and Troy quickly faded as suppliers of collars, cuffs, and shirts.

The CLU was also damaged by the death of William Sylvis in July 1869. Sylvis was a champion of women's rights, and with his death, both financial support from the molders' union and the NLU's rhetorical commitment to working women declined. Both the CLU and the NLU disappeared shortly after Sylvis's death. In February 1870, Mullaney dissolved the CLU, and she and other women returned to work according to pre–May 1869 wage scales.

The CLU was an important forerunner and model for subsequent efforts at organizing women, especially those of the **Knights of Labor**. Not much is known about Mullaney's career after 1870. She eventually married John Fogarty and died in 1906. For many years her body lay in an unmarked grave in Troy. In the 1990s, Mullaney was belatedly recognized for her precocious accomplishments. Her Troy home became a National Historic Landmark in 1998, with Hilary Rodham Clinton adding her voice to those praising Mullaney. In 1999, local labor leaders and Irish cultural organizations adorned Mullaney's grave with a suitable monument.

Suggested Readings: David Montgomery, "William Sylvis and the Search for Working-Class Citizenship," in *Labor Leaders in America*, eds. Melvyn Dubofsky and Warren Van Tine, 1987; Carole Turbin, *Working Women of Collar City*, 1978; "Kate Mullaney: A True Labor Pioneer," www.pef.org/katemullaney.htm.

Robert E. Weir

Muller v. Oregon. *Muller v. Oregon* was a landmark 1908 Supreme Court decision that affirmed the right of states to pass legislation limiting the conditions of women's employment based upon their sex. During the Progressive Era, advocates of protective labor legislation repeatedly sought to address the worst effects of industrial labor through laws designed to ensure safe working conditions, often with both the consumers and producers of goods in mind. In 1905 the U.S. Supreme Court found in *Lochner v. New York* that a recently passed New York state law limiting the workday to ten hours interfered with the right of male bakery workers to their freedom of **contract** and was thus unconstitutional. In its 1905 decision, the court argued that neither the health of the bakers, nor of the consumers of their bread, was at risk if the bakers' workday exceeded ten hours.

Three years later, when Oregon business owners challenged that state's law limiting the hours of women working in laundries and factories, the question of the threat posed to workers' health was once again a major factor. The state of Oregon secured the services of activist attorney Louis Brandeis who, along with his sister-in-law Josephine Goldmark, presented more than 100 pages of evidence. In their brief, Brandeis and Goldmark convincingly argued that women's physical differences from men justified special protection under the law, specifically arguing that long hours of work jeopardized women's abilities to bear and raise children. In *Muller v. Oregon*, the U.S. Supreme Court agreed, claiming that it was in no way reversing its decision in *Lochner*. Justice Brewer, writing for the majority, argued that the physical health of potential mothers was a matter of public interest, and that special protection was needed to "preserve the strength and vigor of the race."

The *Muller* decision cleared the way for a wave of **protective labor legislation** that sought to ensure the health of women workers. By the mid-1920s, all but five states had passed some form of law restricting the hours women could work in industrial settings. (Women in domestic service and agricultural work were exempt.) The 1938 **Fair Labor Standards Act** included a federal, maximum-hour law for both men and women in most categories of employment. Critics of sex-based legislation, including many women workers, pointed out that such laws limited their income potential and assigned them to a status of dependents of the state rather than full citizens under the law. Proponents argued, on the other hand, that women especially needed protective labor laws. Lacking in most cases even minimal union protection, women instead had to turn to the state for recognition of their double burden as workers and mothers.

Suggested Readings: Nancy Erickson, "*Muller v. Oregon* Reconsidered: The Origins of a Sex-Based Doctrine of Liberty of Contract," *Labor History* 30 (1989): 228–50; Julie Novkov, *Constituting Workers, Protecting Women: Gender, Law, and Labor in the Progressive Era and New Deal Years*, 2001.

Kathleen Banks Nutter

Murray Hill Agreement. The Murray Hill Agreement was a national agreement reached in 1900 between the **International Association of Machinists (IAM)** and the National Metal Trades Association (NMTA) that attempted to remedy the labor strife that permeated the Chicago area at this time. Chicago machinists demanded a nine-hour day, a closed shop, **seniority** priority for lay-offs, recognition of shop committees, and a **minimum wage** of 28¢ per hour. Knowing that local employers did not have enough power to win the Chicago **strike**, the NMTA sought to negotiate a national agreement with the IAM. Both sides eventually agreed to reduce the workweek nationally to fifty-seven hours within six months and fifty-four hours within a year. In return, the union agreed to call off current strikes in the Chicago area. The agreement also prohibited discrimination by employers against union members. Machinists were defined according to the union, **wages** were set for each locality through future **arbitration**, and strikes were outlawed during the life of the agreement. The NMTA also enjoyed the IAM's repudiation of the **sympathy strikes** that was a standard feature of late-nineteenth-century battles between management and unions.

The Murray Hill Agreement was forged by the **National Civic Federation**, a capital-labor board that sought to create industrial harmony through mutual cooperation. It stands not only as a testament to the idealism of early-twentieth-century labor and business leaders, but also to their naïveté. It lasted less than a year before both sides resumed adversarial relations.

Suggested Reading: David Montgomery, *The Fall of the House of Labor*, 1989.

Jaime Barnes

Murray, Philip (May 25, 1886–November 9, 1952). Philip Murray was born in Blantyre, Scotland, on May 25, 1886. His father, William Murray, was a coal miner and a local union official in Scotland. The elder Murray taught Philip about important social questions and unions, as well as Catholicism. The eldest of thirteen children, Philip began working in the mines at age ten after a short stint in the public schools. He immigrated to the United States with his father in 1902. The two worked in mines in southwest Pennsylvania, saved money, and brought the rest of the family to the U.S. the following year. Murray had little formal education, but studied math and science through correspondence courses as an adult. In 1910, he married Liz Lavery, a miner's daughter whose father had been killed in a mine accident.

Philip Murray. © George Meany Memorial Archives/ Acme Photo.

Murray's long career as a union official began soon after entering the mines in the United States. In 1905, he was elected president of his **United Mine Workers of America** union (UMWA) local in Horning, Pennsylvania. In 1912, Murray was appointed to fill a vacant seat on the executive board of the UMWA. And, in 1916, he became president of UMWA District Five (western Pennsylvania). Murray's advances in the UMWA and early career as a labor leader were intimately connected with **John L. Lewis**. Murray supported Lewis's rise to union vice president in 1917 and president in 1920. Soon after gaining the presidency, Lewis appointed Murray, still just thirty-three years old, as vice president of the union. Murray would remain Lewis's able lieutenant until the two split in 1940.

Murray was an early supporter of government involvement in labor relations. A lifelong Catholic, Murray supported cooperative industrial-relations plans based on the guild system advanced by Monsignor John A. Ryan. These industrial-union plans were supported by Catholic teachings as advocated by the 1891 papal encyclical ***Rerum Novarum*** (and reaffirmed by the Vatican later in *Quadregisimo Anno* in 1931). During World War I, Murray served on the National Bituminous Coal Production Committee and on the Pennsylvania Regional War Labor Board. Both of these agencies, composed of labor, management, and government representatives, sought to limit labor conflict through cooperation. After World War I, however, Republican administrations and business had little interest in encouraging **collective bargaining** through tripartite organizations. Throughout the 1920s, Murray witnessed the erosion of the UMWA membership as the mining industry became increasingly nonunion.

By the mid-1930s, the fortunes of the UMWA improved. Roosevelt's New Deal passed a number of bills, most importantly the **National Labor Relations Act** (Wagner Act) in 1935, which provided federal government support for collective bargaining. UMWA President John Lewis, with Murray's assistance, formed the Committee later known as the **Congress of Industrial Organizations (CIO)** in 1935. Murray was made a vice president in the CIO. The CIO sought to organize all workers—skilled, semiskilled, and unskilled—by industry in the mass-production facilities like auto, steel, and rubber. Lewis appointed Murray the chairman of the Steelworkers Organizing Committee (SWOC), one of the CIO's most important industrial targets. To the surprise of many, SWOC gained a **contract** with the stridently antiunion and massive U.S. Steel in 1937. But a Murray-led **strike** against most of the remaining steel companies (usually called "**Little Steel**") in the middle of 1937 was violent and unsuccessful. Picket-line violence left more than a dozen strikers dead.

Murray succeeded Lewis as president of the CIO in 1940. The long alliance between Murray and Lewis ended soon after Lewis voluntarily left the CIO presidency in response to his failed support of Wendell Wilkie's presidential campaign in 1940. There were many personal differences between Murray and Lewis, but there were also policy disputes. Lewis distrusted federal-government involvement in labor relations, while Murray continued to vigorously support it. Murray's support of federal-government involvement proved somewhat fruitful during World War II. Through the help of the federal government, the Little Steel companies finally signed contracts, as did important nonunion employers in other CIO organized industries; the Ford Motor Company signed a contract with the **United Auto Workers** union, for example. Murray introduced his own plan for permanent, industrial-union councils that would continue the tripartite organizations established during World War II, like the **National War Labor Board**, after the war ended. But the permanent industrial councils Murray sought never materialized.

After World War II ended, Murray continued as the president of both the CIO and the **United Steelworkers of America (USWA)** union. (SWOC was reorganized as the USWA in 1942.) The years following World War II were difficult for Murray. Employer opposition to the growth of the CIO led Congress to pass, over President Truman's veto, the antiunion **Taft-Hartley Act** in 1947. The increasingly conservative political climate encouraged Murray to support the purging in 1949 and 1950 of eleven unions from the CIO under charges that they were **communist** dominated. Murray had led massive, national USWA strikes in

1946 and 1949, but a 1952 strike tested the aging Murray. Murray enlisted the support of the federal government, through the Wage Stabilization Board, and the personal involvement of Democratic President Harry Truman, during the difficult steel-industry negotiations. Although the USWA gained a satisfactory contract, it came with significant costs. Soon after, Democratic Party candidate Adlai Stevenson lost to Dwight D. Eisenhower. More than any other national CIO labor leader, Murray had encouraged and relied on government involvement in labor relations. But when the Republicans gained control of the White House for the first time in twenty years, Murray must have wondered what this meant for federal government support of collective bargaining. But Murray did not live to see the Eisenhower presidency. On November 9, 1952, within a week of the presidential election, Philip Murray died. He was sixty-six.

Suggested Readings: Paul F. Clark, Peter Gottlieb, and Donald Kennedy, eds., *Forging a Union of Steel: Philip Murray, SWOC, and the United Steelworkers*, 1987; Ronald Schatz, "Philip Murray and the Subordination of the Industrial Unions to the United States Government," in *Labor Leaders in America*, eds. Melvyn Dubofsky and Warren Van Tine, 234–57, 1987.

Joseph Turrini

Music and Labor. Working people have long used music as a weapon in their fight for justice. Most labor songs were written as spontaneous responses to immediate conditions, not with an eye toward posterity. They were created in the hope that mutual singing would build **solidarity** among workers and strengthen them in their struggles. Only a select few have endured. Many labor songs put new words to well-known tunes to facilitate their use in a **strike**, **boycott**, or protest. A prime example is "Solidarity Forever," the song now considered the anthem of American workers. The words were written in 1915 by **Industrial Workers of the World (IWW)** songwriter Ralph Chaplin, who set the lyrics to the well-known tune "John Brown's Body."

"The Marseillaise" and "The International" are popular worldwide, though less so in the United States. This is because most American labor songs are part of an indigenous protest tradition. Common themes include lampoons of privilege, exposés of harsh conditions, pleas for social justice and civil rights, political commentary, and parodies of labor's enemies. Many professions also created music designed to keep cadence with work patterns or to wile away long hours. Miners, sailors, cattle drovers, and textile workers are among those with strong work-song traditions. North American slaves created extraordinarily rich songs to ameliorate their harsh conditions, encode protest messages, set the pace of work, and build community.

In Colonial times, workers parodied both the British and their bosses. **Journeymen** used music to protest against **master craftsmen** before and after the American Revolution, and organized labor's song tradition developed in earnest when journeymen's organizations became full-fledged trade unions in the 1820s. **Labor journalism** helped popularize protest songs, with papers associated with the **Workingmen's Movement** publishing songs in the 1830s.

Factory conditions led to labor protest songs. Lowell women sang "I Will Not Be a Slave" during an 1836 strike, and other songs appeared in the pages of the *Lowell Offering* and *The Voice of Industry*. Both the ten- and **eight-hour movements** produced songs to rally supporters, as did reactionary nativist and antiabolitionist groups with large **working-class** followings. Irish and German immigrants brought musical traditions that they adapted to American conditions. German *turnverein* groups often functioned as a combination gymnastics club, singing society, and impromptu labor organization.

Nineteenth-century trade unions created more songs than labor federations, with the exception of the **Knights of Labor (KOL)**, which produced hundreds of songs. One KOL song, "Storm the Fort Ye Knights of Labor" was reworked as "Hold the Fort" and is still sung. The KOL also popularized I. G. Blanchard's "Eight Hours," the rallying song of the eight-hour movement. Followers of both **Henry George** and various socialist groups produced numerous songs, as did the Populist and **Bellamyite Nationalist** groups. By the 1880s, it was a rare picnic, parade, strike, or protest at which workers did not sing.

Music was always an important tool of American labor organizers. © George Meany Memorial Archives.

Singing declined somewhat in the late 1890s, as the **American Federation of Labor (AFL)** lacked the musical vibrancy of preceding labor groups. But music was revived spectacularly by the IWW, which nurtured skilled songwriters like Ralph Chaplin, Harry McClintock, T-Bone Slim, and **Joe Hill**. The last contributed songs like "The Preacher and the Slave," "Mr. Block," "The Rebel Girl," and "There Is Power in a Union." The IWW continues to publish its *Little Red Songbook*, and it has helped perpetuate songs like "The Popular **Wobbly**," "Hallelujah, I'm a Bum," and "Solidarity Forever." Also popular is "Bread and Roses," a James Oppenheim song-poem that honors women's participation in the 1912 **Lawrence textile strike**.

Repression of labor marked the 1920s and early 1930s. The violent Gastonia-Loray textile strike of 1929 claimed the life of North Carolina songwriter Ella May Wiggins, and Appalachian balladeer Aunt Molly Jackson was forced to flee Kentucky for New York, where she sang of the miners' plight and influenced Woody Guthrie. The bloody Harlan County (Kentucky) coal strike of 1932 influenced **Florence Reece**, whose "Which Side Are You On?" is now a labor standard. Socialist and communist groups introduced songs like "We Shall Not Be Moved," whose theme of class struggle found receptive audiences among the victims of 1920s repression and 1930s depression. Many left-wing organizers were found in the **Congress of Industrial Organizations (CIO)**, especially after 1935, when the **Popular Front** emerged.

Because union singing generally peaks during crisis periods or when a movement struggles to gain recognition, the 1930s was a fruitful period for music. Labor-themed radio stations like WCFL in Chicago and WEVD in New York spread labor songs, as did the labor and left-wing press. Both the CIO and the Communist Party sponsored folk-music concerts at which labor songs were sung. Old and new songs like "Step by Step" and "Sit Down" found their way into labor's repertoire.

More significantly, the flurry of left-wing and labor activity in the 1930s attracted professional musicians who brought labor songs into the musical mainstream. This group included Woody Guthrie, Lee Hays, Millard Lampell, Huddie Ledbetter (Leadbelly), Earl Robinson, and Pete Seeger. Guthrie's "Dust Bowl ballads" have been hailed as a musical snapshot of rural America during the Great Depression. He also penned famed offerings like "Union Maid," "Pastures of Plenty," "You Gotta Go Down," and "This Land Is Your Land," the last written to protest the discrepancies between rich and poor during the Great Depression. Robinson cowrote "Joe Hill," which became a classic, while Leadbelly, Josh White, Bill Broonzy, and Paul Robeson added powerful black voices to working-class struggle.

In 1940, Guthrie, Hays, Lampell, and Seeger formed the Almanac Singers. The Almanacs became a changing musical lineup that brought labor songs to the masses. This included their 1941 composition "Talking Union," written to assist the CIO. In 1945, Seeger formed People's Songs, Inc., whose *People's Songs Bulletin* and *People's Songsters* publicized labor music. In 1950, The People's Songs gave way to *SingOut!* magazine, which continues to publish labor-themed songs, though it is now a general folk-music publication. Among the important labor songs distributed by these sources are "Banks of Marble," "Roll the Union On," and "The Hammer Song."

"The Hammer Song" and left-wing politics brought problems for Hays and Seeger during the post–World War II crackdown on the political left. Right-wing thugs broke up labor rallies featuring leftist performers, most infamously at a 1949 Peekskill, New York, concert in which Paul Robeson narrowly escaped lynching. By the 1950s, many performers were blacklisted, radio was reluctant to play controversial songs, and organized labor actively purged its left wing. Labor music suffered during the decade, though a few noteworthy performers came into their own right, including the AFL's Joe Glazer.

The folk-music revival of the 1960s pumped new life into labor songs, with artists like Seeger, Bob Dylan, Joan Baez, and Phil Ochs performing old and new tunes. By the 1970s, however, music's importance as an organizing tool was in deep decline, a victim of changing popular culture tastes shaped by television and Top 40 radio, as well as competing social concerns like civil rights and the Vietnam War. Moreover, **deindustrialization** and declining union membership dramatically reduced the blue-collar workforce that nurtured much of labor's singing tradition. Music was most vital in newer movements and played an important role during **United Farm Workers** campaigns of the 1970s. Women used music to call attention to inequity in the workplace; Dolly Parton's 1980 hit "**9 to 5**" inspired a movement, and Fred Small's "Fifty-Nine Cents" addressed gendered wage differentials. For the most part, however, labor songs addressed the disappearance of work. Songs like "Aragon Mill," "The L & N Don't Stop Here Anymore," and "The Run Away Shop Song" express that theme.

Currently, labor songwriting is moribund. Occasionally, recording stars like Bruce Springsteen, Billy Joel, and Willie Nelson address working-class concerns, but only as a small part of their total repertoire. (Also, pop music is usually too ephemeral to produce long-term interest.) Very few current performers write or perform labor songs. Among those who do are Pete Seeger, Joe Glazer, Tom Juravich, Si Kahn, Larry Long, John McCutcheon, and Peggy Seeger. By far the most prolific living artist is Bruce "U. Utah" Phillips.

Suggested Readings: R. Serge Denisoff, *Great Day Coming: Folk Music and the American Left*, 1971; John Greenway, *American Folksongs of Protest*, 1953; Pete Seeger and Bob Reiser, *Carry It On! A History in Song and Picture of America's Working Men and Women*, 1985.

Robert E. Weir

Muste, Abraham Johannes (January 8, 1885–February 11, 1967). Abraham Johannes Muste was a pillar of progressive labor, pacifism, and social activism. He was born in Zeeland, The Netherlands, the son of Martin and Adriana (Jinker) Muste. His family emigrated to the United States when he was six and settled in Grand Rapids, Michigan. Muste grew up in a conservative Dutch Reformed family, and his deep religious commitment stayed with him throughout his life, and that faith led him to engage the principal material and intellectual issues of the day. He got a bachelor of arts degree from Hope College in 1905, graduated magna cum laude from Union Theological Seminary in 1909, and received ordination in the Dutch Reformed church. That same year, he married Anna Huizenga. Later, his pacifist tendencies sharpened by World War II, Muste became attracted to the personalized spirituality exemplified by the Society of Friends (Quakers).

Muste could not countenance a life strictly dedicated to the soul, but also sought to aid the oppressed, exploited, and powerless. Textile **strikes** following World War I initiated the young minister into labor issues, as strikers actively sought support from the religious community. He was a leader during the Lawrence strike of 1919 and served as secretary of the strike committee. He also served as secretary of the Amalgamated Textile Workers union from 1919 into 1921, when he resigned to assume the directorship of the **Brookwood Labor College** in New York, where the curriculum emphasized both theory and praxis in labor organization. By then, Muste was a committed pacifist, having joined the Fellowship of Reconciliation (FOR) in 1916. He served as FOR chair from 1926 through 1929. Muste also left the Dutch Reformed church and became a Congregationalist. In 1923, Muste joined the **American Federation of Teachers (AFT)**. He later became an AFT vice president and served on worker-education committees for the **American Federation of Labor (AFL)**.

By 1929, Muste, increasingly attracted to the left, joined efforts by the Conference for Progressive Labor Action (CPLA) to transform from within the staid AFL. He was an early convert to the cause of **industrial unionism** and pushed the AFL to embrace the idea. He was not successful in that pursuit, but the CPLA served as the springboard for creating the American Workers Party in 1933, the year he resigned from Brookwood. Increasingly influenced by Marxism—especially as refocused by Soviet-style Leninism—he played key roles in the **sit-down strike** movement of the Great Depression years and cooperated with James Cannon in forming the **Trotskyite** Workers Party of America. Throughout the 1930s and 1940s, the peripatetic labor activist continued to pursue industrial democracy at the same time he moved further leftward.

A. J. Muste's significance in the labor movement, however, cannot be isolated from his spiritual and political crusades, for each facet of his persona represented the totality of his commitment to social justice and human dignity. Even before working for the rights of labor, Muste felt the tug of social conscience in relation to politics and voted for the Socialist Party's **Eugene V. Debs** in the 1912 presidential election. For the next quarter of a century, Muste sought a democratically oriented movement to fight for **working-class** interests. After a trip to Norway, where he spoke with Leon Trotsky, Muste recommitted himself to spiritual mysticism and embraced a radical pacifism. In 1936, Muste became the industrial secretary for the FOR and the director of New York City's Presbyterian Labor Temple. From 1940 through 1953, he was the executive secretary of the FOR.

Muste's embrace of pacifism and social-justice issues lessened his active involvement with the labor movement. His pacifism was unpopular during World War II, but it was rekindled by the Vietnam War in the 1960s. FOR involvement also led Muste to embrace the civil-rights movement. During the 1960s, Muste was active in the Committee for Nonviolent Action and the broader antiwar movement. His unique blend of labor activism, religious faith, and progressive political vision represented the core of his personality and life's work. When he died in New York City in 1967, his passing brought notes of condolence from figures as diverse as liberal Democratic Senator Robert F. Kennedy and the Communist leader of North Vietnam Ho Chi Minh.

Suggested Readings: Nat Hentoff, *Peace Agitator: The Story of A. J. Muste*, 1963; A. J. Muste, *Non-Violence in an Aggressive World*, 1940; Jo Ann Robinson, *Abraham Went Out: A Biography of A. J. Muste*, 1981.

Timothy Draper

N

National Agreement. National agreement refers to a multi-employer agreement that extends across an industry regardless of where individual employers are located geographically. The term also refers to an agreement that sets a national pattern, even though it may not cover all plants in an industry. Unions seek national agreements to reduce the risk of employers moving their operations to low-wage regions. National agreements help to set a standard wage so workers are not forced to undercut each other and drive **wages** down. They are also beneficial to unions because they create greater cohesion and unity. In recent years, **deindustrialization** and **concessionary** bargaining have greatly weakened labor's ability to structure such contracts.

Suggested Reading: Brian Moskal, "Supplier Bonanza?" *Industry Week* (April 7, 1997).

Jaime Barnes

National Association of Manufacturers (NAM). The National Association of Manufacturers (NAM) is one of the most influential business organizations in American history. For over a century, the NAM has promoted the values of free-market **capitalism** by lobbying politicians for probusiness legislation and by conducting public-relations campaigns. Furthermore, the NAM has been active in fighting the political influence of labor unions, believing that organized labor prevents economic growth by impeding the authority of employers.

The NAM was formed in 1895, when more than 500 manufacturers gathered in Cincinnati, Ohio, to discuss ways of responding to the period's financial crisis. The founders of the NAM discussed ways of establishing new markets for their goods. Throughout the Progressive Era (1901–17), the NAM lobbied the government for probusiness policies, including higher tariffs. The NAM also helped establish a number of business-friendly political organizations, including the National Industrial Council, as well as the National Council of Commerce, the predecessor of the U.S. Chamber of Commerce.

While the NAM was started primarily to promote the expansion of trade, it soon focused on ways of curtailing the numerical strength and political influence of trade unions, believing that trade unions posed a significant challenge to the free-market system. In the face of union activism, NAM leaders promoted the idea of the **open shop**, which would allow employers to decide the terms of workplace relations without organized labor's influence. NAM strategies ran counter to the **welfare capitalism** policies advocated by social reformers, benevolent capitalists, and some union leaders. The NAM also opposed programs established during World War I that encouraged union growth, set price controls, and stipulated production goals. After the war, NAM ideals prevailed and the organization helped contain the power of organized labor throughout the 1920s.

To the NAM, the 1930s was a decade of setbacks. Responding to the emergence of the **Congress of Industrial Organizations (CIO)** and the prolabor New Deal, the NAM launched a far-reaching campaign to educate workers on the virtues of free-market capitalism over state control. The NAM produced corporate-friendly radio shows, newspaper columns, and movie shorts. Its efforts were largely unsuccessful in changing popular opinion; large numbers of Americans greeted the growth of organized labor and political liberalism with enthusiasm.

The NAM succeeded in rehabilitating its pre-New Deal influence during World War II and the postwar period. Troubled by numerous workplace **strikes** and the New Deal, particularly the 1935 prolabor **National Labor Relations Act**, the NAM lobbied Congress for probusiness legislation and engaged in more public-relations campaigns. In both its political lobbying and public-relations campaigns, the NAM presented itself as a responsible organization fighting the excessive power of organized labor. Politically, the NAM scored a major victory when Congress passed the **Taft-Hartley Act** in 1947, an act designed to limit the power of organized labor by barring certain types of strikes. The Taft-Hartley Act also prevented foremen from joining trade unions and forced trade unionists to sign anticommunist affidavits. Most importantly, the Taft-Hartley Act gave workers the right *not* to join labor unions.

In the postwar era, the NAM continued to highlight the marvels of capitalism to the general public and lobby politicians for the expansion of trade. In the 1950s, the NAM launched short television programs on the triumphs of industry. Throughout the century's last decades, the NAM has sought tax breaks for business. Representing more than 14,000 members, the NAM remains a powerful probusiness organization that retains its antilabor union bias.

Suggested Readings: Robert Collins, *The Business Response to Keynes, 1929–64*, 1981; Elizabeth Fones-Wolf, *Selling Free Enterprise: The Business Assault on Labor and Liberalism*, 1994; Howell Harris, *The Right to Manage: Industrial Relations Policies of American Business in the 1940s*, 1982.

Chad Pearson

National Civic Federation. The National Civic Federation (NCF) was founded in an era of industrial conflict at the turn of the twentieth century. Intended to provide a place for business and labor to resolve their problems through discussion and **conciliation**, the NCF was founded in 1900 by reformist newspaper editor Ralph Montgomery Easley. Early NCF members included industrialist and political powerhouse Mark Hanna, **American Federation of Labor** President **Samuel Gompers**, and **United Mine Workers of America** President **John Mitchell**. Easley and other members—representatives of business, labor, and the public—signed on with the idea that extremes on either the business or the labor side were undesirable. Reform and discussion, not **strikes** or political radicalism, could resolve the important issues between them. Antitrust measures and other government regulations could be one way of reforming the system. Furthermore, various departments within the NCF promoted such measures as **workman's compensation** laws and **welfare capitalism** programs. All these were ways to moderate the excesses of the modern industrial world.

During World War I, the NCF's antiradicalism manifested itself as patriotism. Fully behind America's war effort, it saw **socialists**, pacifists, and other critics of the war as disloyal. It vigorously denounced such forces in society and promoted the war effort.

By the 1930s, the NCF had largely lost its reason for being, as New Deal labor legislation helped unions gain rights for **collective bargaining**. The National Labor Relations Board provided a formal government mechanism for handling labor-management strife, thus obviating the NCF's role.

Suggested Readings: Marguerite Green, *The National Civic Federation and the American Labor Movement, 1900–1925*, 1956; John Zerzan, "Understanding the Anti-Radicalism of the National Civic Federation," *International Review of Social History* 19, no. 2, 1974.

Elizabeth Jozwiak

National Education Association (NEA). The National Education Association (NEA) is the nation's largest union representing teachers and other academic professionals. Its 2.5 million members are drawn from all levels of public and private education. It was founded in Philadelphia, Pennsylvania, in 1857, but did not engage in **collective bargaining** until after 1962.

For much of its history, the NEA functioned more as a teachers' guild than a trade union. It often drew leaders from among university presidents concerned with issues such as teacher preparation, curriculum development, college-entrance standards, and technical education. The NEA also operated as an effective lobbying organization for educational reform, supporting such important bills as the Morrill Act (1862) and state legislation that protected teacher tenure. The NEA's relationship to classroom teachers proved more amorphous than its commitment to principles, however, and by 1920, it was losing members to other organizations.

The NEA began to revive when it adopted a more aggressive stance over issues affecting individual teachers. Its 1928 resolution Freedom of the Teacher marked its entrance into the issue of academic freedom. In 1934, the NEA moved its offices to Washington, D.C., from whence it tackled emergent issues such as teacher loyalty oaths and ideological biases in the awarding of teacher contracts. In 1941, the NEA Defense Commission (later the DuShane Defense Fund) was set up to assist legal battles over academic freedom. In the 1950s, the NEA was among the few labor organizations to oppose censorship and red-baiting aggressively and openly.

Nonetheless, it was the **American Federation of Teachers (AFT)** that took the lead in collective-bargaining rights for teachers. The NEA did not even study the issue until 1962, and it was in 1966 when an NEA junior-college affiliate won a contract, and not until 1969 that a university did so. Even then, growth came slowly, with several organizations set up to organize colleges and universities declaring independence from the NEA. In 1974, the NEA restructured its efforts under the National Council for Higher Education.

Success proved far greater among elementary and secondary teachers, who spurred much of the NEA's dramatic growth from the 1970s on. The NEA was outspoken in defending public school teachers against attacks on education during the 1980s, and it offered tactical and logistical support to numerous locals engaging in tough bargaining situations and job actions. The NEA's various state affiliates were given wide latitude to bargain and set policy, a structural arrangement that encouraged growth on the local level, while freeing the parent organization to lobby for teacher rights and teacher-friendly educational reforms. It also allowed the healing of rifts and jurisdictional battles between the NEA and AFT. In recent years, the NEA has fought against mandatory testing of veteran teachers and other imposed standards that it feels should be bargained collectively. It also set up task forces to study the impact of the electronic revolution on teaching and has voiced suspicion over the proper place of distance learning in the curriculum. It also takes a strong stand on matters of racial and gender equity.

Suggested Readings: Marjorie Murphy, *Blackboard Unions*, 1990; Bob Peterson and Michael Charney, eds., *Transforming Teacher Unions: Fighting for Better Schools and Social Justice*, 1999; Joel Spring, *Conflict of Interests: The Politics of American Education*, 2001.

Robert E. Weir

National Industrial Recovery Act (NIRA). The National Industrial Recovery Act (NIRA) was one of the most important components of what is now referred to as the First New Deal. It was also the most controversial of the New Deal agencies and sowed the seeds of its own undoing. The purpose of the NIRA was to stabilize American industry during the early years of the Great Depression by reducing destructive competition within industries through cartels, which could cooperate in setting prices and other industry standards. The NIRA, which also created the National Recovery Administration (NRA) to administer the act, was to be in effect for two years, and it granted significant authority to the U.S. president to develop industrial codes.

The NIRA came into being, in part, in response to the demands of industrialists who, since the nineteenth century, had tried various ways of combining to achieve stability in the frequently volatile American economy characterized by recurring boom-and-bust cycles. The late-nineteenth century efforts to combine as trusts were outlawed by the **Sherman Antitrust Act**, and later efforts at looser confederation in the form of trade associations were entirely voluntary in character, which limited their effectiveness. By the onset of the Great Depression, business and labor leaders from major industries were turning to the federal government to help achieve business stability through national planning that would involve industrial self-regulation, with relaxation of the antitrust laws. The **National War Labor Board** from World War I provided the closest model for the kind of industrial cooperation and self-regulation that the NIRA prescribed.

After leaving the Dust Bowl states for California, many people were temporarily housed in National Resettlement Administration camps. The camps were part of a New Deal effort to meet the needs of such displaced families as the one pictured here. © George Meany Memorial Archives.

However, the resulting legislation was not merely a result of industry's lobbying efforts. Early into the Roosevelt administration, Alabama Senator Hugo L. Black proposed a bill that would reduce the workweek to thirty hours to help relieve unemployment by spreading work. The Black Bill would have also imposed trade sanctions on companies that violated the proposed thirty-hour workweek. When the Black Bill was passed by the Senate, on April 6, 1933, President Franklin Delano Roosevelt, alarmed by its rigidity, immediately set about drafting an alternative, with the assistance of his Brain Trust, both to the Black Bill and to the efforts of the business community to promote simple revision of the antitrust laws. Secretary of Labor **Frances Perkins**, U.S. Senator Robert Wagner, and Roosevelt's adviser Hugh Johnson proposed alternative measures to stabilize industry, regulate wages and hours, and introduce public-works projects to provide immediate employment. The resulting bill, created by a committee that included Wagner and Johnson, among others, passed through Congress and was signed into law on June 16, 1933.

The NIRA included a variety of provisions for stabilizing American industry, but the most significant measure for working Americans was the extensive set of labor regulations in Section 7(a) of Title I. The most important components of Section 7(a) included the right of employees "to bargain collectively through representatives of their own choosing . . . free from the interference, restraint, and coercion of employers" and the right to choose their bargaining agent, which included the *de facto* outlawing of company unions and **yellow-dog contracts**. Section 7 also legislated **minimum wages** and maximum hours among other labor standards.

Another part of the NIRA especially significant for working Americans was Title II, which established the Public Works Administration (PWA). It included a budget of $3.3 billion to provide people with work on public-works projects, such as highways and federal buildings. The NIRA was crafted not to conflict with the Agricultural Adjustment Act (AAA), and, while particular codes for each industry were being established, the NRA provided a very general basic code or blanket code—the President's Reemployment Agreement (which included a thirty-five hour workweek and a forty forty-cent minimum wage). While compliance with the code was voluntary, it was strongly encouraged, along with the display of the Blue Eagle, the official symbol of the NRA.

The industrial harmony that the NIRA was designed to achieve, however, was achieved with difficulty at best, and sometimes not at all. The active participation of industries in drawing up the codes made them responsible for self-policing, and many industrialists found ways to duck the codes, sometimes by "changing" industries. Owners of small businesses argued that the NIRA favored the interests of big business at their expense. At the same time, labor maintained a healthy skepticism and wariness toward government intervention in labor relations, even while unions took full advantage of Section 7 to rebuild from the serious decline of organized labor in the 1920s. Disputes over the interpretation of the law, especially regarding the closed shop, resulted in **strikes**, sometimes as a way of enforcing employer compliance. Additionally, organized labor had little, if any, say in the development of the codes.

The end of the NIRA and the NRA came in May 1935, in the Supreme Court decision in *Schecter Poultry Co. v. U.S.*, which declared that the NIRA vested too much legislative authority in the executive branch. Nonetheless, the federal effort to regulate industry, and, with it, labor conditions, continued in other forms, having by that time become somewhat more acceptable. Successor legislation to the NIRA included the **National Labor Relations Act** (or Wagner Act) and the **Fair Labor Standards Act (FLSA)**, as well as other regulatory efforts in what became known as the Second New Deal. Despite its limitations, the NIRA proved to be of lasting benefit to organized labor. It spurred an unprecedented level of organization that broadened beyond the traditional craft unionism to include an unprecedented variety of workers, which resulted in the formation of the **Congress of Industrial Organizations (CIO)**. The legislation that followed (and was ultimately modeled on) the NIRA also brought marked and lasting improvements in working conditions, including minimum wages, maximum hours, and curtailment of **child labor**.

Suggested Readings: Colin Gordon, *New Deals: Business, Labor, and Politics in America, 1920–1935*, 1994; Emmanuel Stein, Carl Raushenbush, and Lois MacDonald, *Labor and the New Deal*, 1934; Fiona Venn, *The New Deal*, 1998.

Susan Roth Breitzer

National Labor Relations Act (NLRA). The National Labor Relations Act (NLRA), also known as the Wagner Act after its sponsor, New York Senator Robert Wagner, is a 1935 law hailed by many as the single most important piece of prolabor legislation in U.S. history. Its provisos continue to shape basic labor laws. The NLRA was first introduced in 1933, and languished until President Franklin D. Roosevelt concluded that corporate interests were hostile to most New Deal programs and turned to the resurgent labor movement for support. The NLRA passed Congress in 1935, but remained ineffective until 1937, when the Supreme Court declared it constitutional. Most historians believe the court was influenced by labor militancy and successful organizing drives led by the **Congress of Industrial Organizations (CIO)**. The NLRA in essence legitimized what workers had already won at the point of production.

Under the NLRA, unions gained legitimacy from the state. The very principle of **collective bargaining** is enshrined in the NLRA, which established the National Labor Relations Board (NLRB) to oversee labor-management relations. The NLRA establishes procedures under which workers can petition the NLRB for a secret-ballot union representation election. Employers are forbidden to interfere by using threats, spies, bribes, or intimidation. In addition, other management union-smashing tactics were abolished, including **company unions** and **yellow-dog contracts**. The NLRA requires both sides to bargain in good faith, defined as reaching an agreement that can be reduced to writing and signed. It preserves the right of workers to **strike** and unions gained the right to file an **unfair labor practice** claim and ask the NLRB to investigate. In theory, the NLRB is an impartial board and its decisions have the weight of law.

The NLRA has been weakened and management rights expanded by legislation such as the 1947 **Taft-Hartley Act** and the 1959 **Landrum-Griffin Act**. Employers are now allowed to file unfair labor practice charges against unions. In the 1980s, President Ronald Reagan was accused of staffing the NLRB with members hostile to organized labor. Some observers believe that the NLRA is no longer impartial or effective, and some unions have sought to circumvent it in organizing campaigns that put direct economic and community pressure on employers.

Suggested Readings: Stanley Aronowitz, *From the Ashes of the Old*, 1998; Foster R. Dulles and Melvyn Dubofsky, *Labor in America*, 1993; United States Government Printing Office, ed., *A Guide to Basic Law and Procedures Under the National Labor Relations Act*, 1990.

Albert V. Lannon

National Labor Relations Board. *See National Labor Relations Act.*

National Labor Relations Board v. Jones and Laughlin Steel Corporation. *National Labor Relations Board v. Jones and Laughlin Steel Corporation*, 301 U.S. 1 (1937), is a landmark U.S. Supreme Court decision that ruled that the **National Labor Relations Act** (**NLRA**, also known as the Wagner Act) was constitutional. The NLRA was passed by Congress in 1935 and protected employees' rights to form labor unions and made some employer actions illegal. Opponents of organized labor and New Deal policies succeeded in challenging the **1933 National Industrial Recovery Act (NIRA)**, whose famed Section 7(a) guaranteed **collective-bargaining** rights. The Supreme Court struck down the NIRA in 1935, the same year the Wagner Act became law. At the time of its passage, many believed Congress exceeded powers granted by the U.S. Constitution, and that the NLRA would also be deemed unconstitutional.

Congressional supporters justified its ability to govern labor unions and collective bargaining through its constitutional authority to regulate interstate commerce, but this justification was not widely accepted in 1935. Many argued that a **strike** at a single manufacturing facility disrupted production, but not interstate commerce. Earlier Supreme Court decisions did not find a connection between collective-bargaining issues and interstate commerce. Others argued that legislative restrictions on employment matters violated the rights of employers and individuals to enter into contracts and deprived them of property and liberty without due process of law.

Shortly after the NLRA was passed, the newly formed National Labor Relations Board (NLRB) found steel manufacturer Jones and Laughlin guilty of violating the NLRA when they fired the employees who were trying to form a union. After a federal appeals court denied enforcement of the NLRB's order, the Supreme Court heard the case. By a five-to-two vote, the Supreme Court upheld the NLRA in the 1937 Jones and Laughlin decision by ruling that strikes in manufacturing affected interstate commerce and that employers were not denied due process of law.

The Jones and Laughlin decision came on the heels of President Franklin D. Roosevelt's controversial plan to pack the Supreme Court by adding one new justice for each one over the age of seventy. The Jones decision, coupled with intense opposition to Roosevelt's proposal, led the president to abandon his court-packing scheme. For labor, this landmark decision not only upheld the constitutionality of the NLRA, thus giving legitimacy to the U.S. system of collective bargaining, but also provided the legal foundation for additional government laws pertaining to employment such as **minimum wage** and civil rights legislation.

Suggested Readings: Richard Cortner, *The Jones & Laughlin Case*, 1970; James Gross, *The Making of the National Labor Relations Board: A Study in Economics, Politics, and Law*, 1974; Jethro Lieberman, *The Enduring Constitution: An Exploration of the First 200 Years*, 1987.

John W. Budd

National Labor Relations Board v. Yeshiva University. *National Labor Relations Board v. Yeshiva University*, 444 U.S. 672 (1980), was a Supreme Court decision that makes it exceedingly difficult for faculty at private colleges and universities to unionize. By a five-to-four decision, the court ruled that faculty members in private schools are managers, not employees. The decision was hailed by trustees of private and religious colleges, but has been assailed by labor unions and professors.

The original case involved full-time faculty members at Yeshiva University, a private, Jewish university in New York City. In 1974, faculty in ten of Yeshiva's thirteen undergraduate and graduate schools sought representation for the Yeshiva University Faculty Association (YUFA) and petitioned the National Labor Relations Board (NLRB) for certification as a **bargaining unit**. The NLRB granted that petition, and in 1975, the faculty voted to unionize. Yeshiva University refused to recognize the election and it ignored a NLRB order to open negotiations with the union, choosing instead to file a lawsuit challenging the legitimacy of the YUFA. In 1978, the Court of Appeals for the Second Circuit denied the NLRB's petition to force Yeshiva to bargain with the YUFA. In 1980, the Supreme Court upheld the university's position.

Writing for the five-to-four majority, Justice Lewis Powell asserted that no evidence was given to prove that Congress ever intended faculty to be covered by the **National Labor Relations Act** or the **Taft-Hartley Act**. Moreover, the court ruled that faculty were substantially independent decision-makers who determined matters related to curriculum, admission policies, grading standards, graduation requirements, the academic calendar, and numerous other matters. It also advised university administration on such things as hiring, promotion, tenure, and sabbaticals. By Powell's reckoning, this meant they were essentially management rather than employees, as few of the latter have such broad autonomy.

Justice William Brennan wrote a blistering dissenting opinion endorsed by three fellow justices, the essence of which was a rebuttal of the idea that faculty members could be considered part of the very group charged with their supervision. Both sides agreed that current statutes are unclear in the matter of university faculty.

Since the 1980 decision, groups such as the **American Federation of Teachers (AFT)**, the **National Educational Association (NEA)**, and the American Association of University Professors (AAUP) have called upon Congress to amend labor laws to include faculty members at private colleges and universities. To date, Congress has failed to act on this proposal, other than in a vague component of the unsuccessful 1994 Teamwork for Employees and Managers Act, which organized labor opposed as a backdoor attempt to reintroduce **company unions**. President William Clinton vetoed the so-called TEAM Act.

The Yeshiva decision has been consistently upheld in private religious colleges. In 1995, faculty at the University of Great Falls (in Montana), a Roman

Catholic school, was denied the right to organize, even after several previous decisions found its mission to be primarily secular. Efforts at the University of St. Francis in Chicago were similarly frustrated.

The Yeshiva decision has not been a universal precedent, however. Faculty at state colleges and universities—many of whom are unionized—have not been deemed management, raising the question of how their duties differ in substantive ways. Further muddying the waters is the fact that some private colleges are organized, their administrations having chosen not to challenge the legitimacy of faculty to unionize. It is also unclear as to what degree the Yeshiva decision applies to nonreligious private schools. In recent years, potent challenges have arisen to the Yeshiva ruling. In 2001, part-time and adjunct faculty at Emerson College in Boston were organized by the AAUP, their part-time status insulating them from being considered management. Other questions have arisen as to whether faculty at institutions without tenure who are classified as employees at will can reasonably be considered as management. Currently, most teachers' unions seek changes to labor laws and steer clear of attempting to organize faculty at private schools.

Suggested Readings: "Labor Law Reform: To Do or Not to Do?," http://www.aaup.org/publications/Academe/98nd/WW_ND98.htm; "NLRB v. Yeshiva University, 444 U.S. 672," http://www.faculty.senate.villanova.edu/yeshiva.htm.

Robert E. Weir

National Labor Union (NLU). The National Labor Union (NLU, 1866–73) is considered by many to be the first national federation of trade unions, though others believe that honor belongs to the **National Trades' Union** (1834–37). Most historians credit the NLU over the latter organization as the former was largely a pressure group formed by shipyard workers to lobby for a ten-hour workday and made little effort to evolve a permanent bureaucratic structure.

The NLU was the brainchild of Baltimore iron molder **William H. Sylvis**, an activist in the **eight-hour movement**. In 1866, seventy union activists and seven leaders from Eight-Hour Leagues announced the formation of the NLU, whose vague goal was to supplant **capitalism** with **cooperative** ventures. A loose federation was set up in which yearly labor congresses planned an agenda relevant to all constituent unions and eight-hour leagues. In 1867, farmer organizations were added to the eligibility list. Affiliates received one delegate per 500 members.

In addition to a call for an eight-hour workday and **cooperatives**, NLU congresses fashioned a general reform platform that embraced land and currency reform, a ban on the sale of prison-made goods, mandatory **arbitration** laws, women's suffrage, and an end to **child labor**. There were also rhetorical calls for gender and racial equality (except for the Chinese). **Kate Mullaney**, a Troy, New York, laundress, was an NLU vice president, and the organization also had loose links with the **Colored National Labor Union (CNLU)** led by Issac Myers.

In many respects, the NLU was more impressive in theory than in reality. The yearly congress format was more meaningful to union leaders and reformers than to the **rank and file**. Estimates run from as few as 60,000 to as many as 800,000 members of the NLU, but many had little grasp of the organization and were members only by virtue of belonging to an affiliated group. Moreover, members were deeply divided ideologically. Divisions deepened upon Sylvis's premature death in 1869. Rural members were devoted to the **greenback** cause, but less interested in unionization, the opposite of how many urban workers felt. Relations with the CNLU cooled when that group remained devoted to the Republican Party, while the NLU gravitated toward third-party politics. The NLU was dominated by trade unionists, but it also contained many **Lassallean** socialists who favored political agitation.

This illustration graphically depicts the ideology of the National Labor Union (NLU), with its emphasis on the value of hard work. © George Meany Memorial Archives/Library of Congress.

In 1872, the NLU transformed itself into the National Labor Reform Party (NLRP) and nominated Illinois judge David Davis as its presidential candidate. His campaign and the NLRP were equally disastrous. The NLU held its final congress in September 1872, with only seven delegates showing up. Ironically, the NLU collapsed on the eve of its greatest success. In 1872, President Ulysses Grant granted most federal workers an eight-hour day, but the NLU failed to survive the Panic of 1873.

Suggested Readings: Foster Dulles and Melvyn Dubofsky, *Labor in America*, 1993; Gerald Grob, *Workers and Utopia: A Study of Ideological Conflict in the American Labor Movement 1865–1900*, 1961; George McNeill, *The Labor Movement: The Problem of To-Day*, 1887.

Robert E. Weir

National Trades' Union (NTU). The National Trades' Union (NTU) was formed in New York City in 1834 and is often cited as the first attempt at forming a nationwide labor federation, although its loose structure and focus on general reform render such a claim problematic. The NTU drew upon a variety of Jacksonian-era reformers, including those associated with ten-hour societies, the **Workingmen's Movement**, land reform, and trade unions. Key leaders included John Ferral, a Philadelphia weaver; William English, a radical Philadelphia shoemaker; **Seth Luther**, a well-known New England labor activist; and Charles Douglas, a labor editor and Workingmen's advocate. Its first president was Ely Moore, a **journeyman** printer.

The NTU grew out of the desire for a federation that could amass a strike fund from national contributions that could assist walkouts of constituent unions. What it might have become was demonstrated in 1836, when striking Philadelphia bookbinders received financial aid from New York City's General Trades' Union, a body that resembled a prototype **central labor union**. The NTU, however, never forged strong ties with trade unions and was never much more than an annual labor congress, where delegates debated the pressing issues of the day and issued various resolutions. It also sought to exert political influence, though it was officially nonpartisan. In the sense that its rhetorical force exceeded its concrete actions, the NTU presaged the **National Labor Union (NLU)**, though the latter had much better relations with trade unions.

The NTU—like the Workingmen and numerous trade unions—failed to survive the economic downturn known as the Panic of 1837. Although it accomplished little in its own right, it deserves credit for bringing labor reformers together from various parts of the country. Periodic labor conferences kept alive NTU ideals, which coalesced with the founding of the NLU in 1866 that, in turn, gave way to more powerful federations like the **Knights of Labor** and the **American Federation of Labor**.

Suggested Readings: Paul R. Taylor, *The ABC-CLIO Companion to the American Labor Movement*, 1993; Foster R. Dulles and Melvyn Dubofsky, *Labor in America: A History*, 1984; Bruce Laurie, *Artisans into Workers: Labor in Nineteenth-Century America*, 1989.

Bruce Cohen
Robert E. Weir

National Union of Hospital and Health Care Employees Local 1199. From its humble beginnings in New York City during the Great Depression, the National Union of Hospital and Health Care Employees Local 1199 has become America's largest organization of health-care workers. The union is noted for its connections to the civil rights movement and efforts at bringing women and minority workers into the labor movement.

The dramatic growth of Local 1199 owes much to Leon Julius Davis, the organization's vibrant founder and leader for nearly fifty years. In 1932, Davis, who attended Columbia University's School of Pharmacy, was among a small group of mostly Jewish pharmacists and clerks who, with the help of the **Communist** Party's Trade Union League, formed the Pharmacists Union of Greater New York. An **industrial union**, the organization represented not only pharmacists but also clerks, porters, "soda jerks," and cosmeticians. Davis assumed the presidency of the organization in 1934 and brought his tireless energy to the picket line and negotiating table. In 1936, the union joined the **American Federation**

of Labor (AFL) and was named Local 1199. In that same year, Davis became the union's first full-time organizer. His determination was clearly demonstrated in 1962, when he spent thirty days in jail for refusing to call off a **strike**.

In the decades following its inception, Local 1199 won gains for its membership and experienced substantial growth. It faced its first strike—involving just one worker—in 1933; however, it faced a larger struggle in 1936, helping African Americans to win the right to work in Harlem drugstores. By 1959, Local 1199 had organized approximately 90 percent of pharmacy workers in New York City. About this time, the ties of its leadership to the Communist Party were severed, and 1199 turned its attention to organizing workers in the city's voluntary, nonprofit hospitals. The **wages** for hospital workers in the city—mostly African Americans and Latinos—were at the poverty level and benefits were nonexistent. A major organizing victory was scored in 1958 at Montefiore Hospital in the Bronx, spurring a successful effort to unionize minority and women hospital service workers at other facilities. By 1963, Local 1199 had secured legal rights to **collective bargaining** for its **rank and file**.

In the 1960s, the union extended its organizing call to hospitals, nursing homes, and mental health clinics in other sections of the country. For example, when nurses' aides in Charleston, South Carolina, sought to address their **grievances** in 1969, they turned to Local 1199 for help. The organizing drive stimulated by events in Charleston would lead to the creation of the National Union of Hospital and Health Care Employees in 1973.

The union advocated social and economic justice for all workers and closely allied itself with the civil-rights movement. Davis and 1199 formed a coalition with civil-rights groups and leaders such as Bayard Rustin, **A. Philip Randolph**, and Martin Luther King, Jr. In 1988, Local 1199 endorsed Reverend Jesse Jackson for president. The union took the lead in protesting the involvement of the United States in Vietnam and also voiced opposition to South African apartheid and U.S. activities in Central America.

Local 1199 intensified its efforts to grow and enhance its political strength by devoting more funds to organizing unorganized workers and through affiliation with other unions. In 1984, Local 1199 received a direct charter from the American Federation of Labor-Congress of Industrial Organizations (AFL-CIO). In separate 1989 moves aimed at increasing its political strength, the union affiliated with both of the **American Federation of State, County, and Municipal Employees (AFSCME)** and the Service Employees International Union (SEIU). SEIU affiliation strengthened Local 1199's efforts to bring Head Start workers as well as library and higher-education workers into the union. Another indication of the union's efforts to include new industries and workers also occurred in 2001, when members of the Social Agencies Employees Union (SAEU) voted to merge with Local 1199. Local 1199 is often cited as a model of militancy, flexibility, and adaptation to the changing workplace of postindustrial America.

Suggested Readings: Leon Greenburg and Brian Greenburg. *Upheaval in the Quiet Zone: A History of Hospital Workers' Union, Local 1199*, 1989; Peter Levy, *The New Left and Labor in the 1960s*, 1994.

Mark Noon

National War Labor Boards: World War I and World War II. When the United States joined World War I in 1917, industries had to increase production drastically if they were to contribute to the war effort. This was difficult, as many Americans had gone to fight in the war. The people left behind to work in these industries had to work under difficult conditions, working harder and much longer than ever. Their difficult working conditions, the quickened pace of production, and an increase in the cost of living upset many people and resulted in an atmosphere of work stoppages and **strikes**. This situation had to be solved since it was essential to produce the items that contributed to the economy and the war effort. To solve this problem, the government felt that a permanent agency was needed to improve the labor situation and resolve disputes between workers and employers. The result was President Woodrow Wilson's crea-tion of the National War Labor Board, in April 1918. The board consisted of twelve members: five labor representatives (workers), five employer representatives (business), and two co-chairs (one from each group). The goal of the National War Labor Board was to disallow strikes and **lockouts** and to keep the economy moving for the duration of the war. To do so, they listened to complaints, considered approximately 1,250 cases, and made decisions in almost 500 of them. World War I ended on November 11, 1918, and the National War Labor Board was discontinued in March 1919.

To resolve labor disputes that arose during wartime, especially in defense industries such as this airplane plant, the government established national war labor boards during both World War I and World War II. © George Meany Memorial Archives/Official U.S. Navy Photograph.

The attack on Pearl Harbor, on December 7, 1941, drew the United States into World War II. Like World War I, the situation created many social and economic problems for Americans. President Franklin D. Roosevelt immediately asked representatives of labor and business to agree that all wartime disputes would be settled peacefully and there would be no strikes. On January 12, 1942, President Roosevelt created the National War Labor Board of World

War II. Although this board also consisted of twelve members, members of the public were included as well. Instead of five labor and five employer representatives, there were now four labor representatives, four employer representatives, and four public representatives. Once again, unions signed **no-strike pledges** and employer **lockouts** were outlawed. In addition, the board was given permission to settle any dispute and force a settlement on those involved if their dispute might interrupt the work contributing to the "effective prosecution of the war." World War II officially ended in August 1945, and the National War Labor Board was discontinued on December 31, 1945.

The war labor boards, for the first time, enabled workers to determine federal policy alongside employers. They kept workers on the job and effectively balanced the demands of both workers and employers. In addition, the boards established many policies that provided great advantages to labor and were subsequently continued after both wars ended. The National War Labor Board of World War I confirmed the rights of workers to join trade unions and bargain collectively with their employers. They also acknowledged a worker's right to a living wage, supported the concept of working an eight-hour day, and supported women in their fight for equal pay for equal work. Unfortunately, after the end of the war in 1918, many of the problems that had existed before the war simply returned.

There were numerous strikes in 1919 as workers tried to improve upon the gains they had made during World War I. More improvements were made after the end of World War II, as its National War Labor Board left a legacy of positive changes to the labor situation as well. Many of its policies, such as providing workers with sick leave and paid holidays, helped unions and became a part of postwar bargaining. The board also encouraged workers and employers to bargain and negotiate instead of striking. Finally, some of the board's members became skilled in mediation and **arbitration** and offered these skills to help both workers and employers.

Suggested Readings: James B. Atleson, *Labor and the Wartime State: Labor Relations and Law During World War II*, 1998; Valerie Jean Conner, *The National War Labor Board: Stability, Social Justice, and the Voluntary State in World War I*, 1983; Marc Allen Eisner, *From Warfare State to Welfare State: World War I, Compensatory State Building, and the Limits of the Modern Order*, 2000.

Lisa J. Wells

Newspaper Guild. The Newspaper Guild was founded in 1933 (as the American Newspaper Guild) by newspaper editorial workers who were dissatisfied with their salaries. Led by well-known columnist Heywood Broun, the union's first president, the Guild had to overcome a long tradition of fierce independence and individualism that permeated its members as well as overcome the intense hostility from newspaper owners who attempted to argue that the very existence of the union was a threat to freedom of the press. Broun argued relentlessly for opening the Guild to other newspaper employees. By 1936, the Guild had affiliated with the **American Federation of Labor (AFL)** and, in 1937, with the **Congress of Industrial Organizations (CIO)**. As the Guild grew, it expanded its areas of concern from **salary** issues to issues of newspaper hiring and promotion practices, including concerns over racial and gender discrimination. In recent years, the Guild has been a leader in matters of workplace safety, including the hazards posed by repetitive motion tasks and cathode-ray tube display radiation. In 1995, in response to changes and consolidation in the newspaper, publishing, and media industries, the Guild merged with the Communication Workers of America (CWA) to become a union with over 700,000 members, encompassing workers in the broader communication media industry, including broadcast news, magazines, and electronic media. The CWA absorbed the membership of the older International Typographical Union (ITU) in 1987, when that union's craft was rendered obsolete by changing technology. The typographers had formed a union before George Washington was elected president, but computer technology and the rise of desktop publishing made both hot and cold typesetting obsolete, and the remaining ITU locals were folded into the CWA. Cooperation between the ITU and the Guild had often been tenuous, with the highly skilled ITU often holding a stronger bargaining position with employers. Technology completely undercut the printers, though, and ultimately it was the newspaper workers who had the stronger organization.

Suggested Reading: John Howells and Marion Dearman, *Tramp Printers*, 1996.

James P. Hanlan

Newspapers. *See Labor Journalism.*

New York City Teachers Strike. The New York City Teachers Strike of 1960 was the job stoppage that led to the first **collective-bargaining** agreement for public schoolteachers in a major U.S. city, and it ushered in two decades of unrest and union organizing among teachers nationwide. Previously teachers and other public-sector employees were excluded from the provisions of the **National Labor Relations Act** of 1935. By the late 1950s, the **American Federation of Teachers (AFT)** had failed to obtain collective-bargaining rights, and was unable to organize the vast majority of public schoolteachers.

Under the leadership of former teachers David Selden, from Michigan, and **Albert Shanker**, from New York City, New York teachers in an AFT-affiliated local called the United Federation of Teachers (UFT) started a campaign to attain collective bargaining for New York City's 50,000 public-school teachers. Complaining of low **wages**, few fringe benefits, large classes, and student unrest in the classroom, and inspired by the gains of organized workers in the private sector, in March 1960 Charles Cogen, president of the UFT, threatened a teachers' strike in the country's largest school district. In response, the New York Board of Education announced that if 30 percent of New York's teaching staff requested a bargaining election, they would allow one to take place. They also offered higher **salary** scale and sick leave. With no sign of the agreement, the UFT voted to strike in the fall of 1960.

Although the Condon-Wadlin Act passed in 1947 prohibited public-sector strikes in New York State, more than 5,000 teachers participated in a one-day strike on November 7, 1960, to demand a collective-bargaining election. In response, Democratic Mayor Robert F. Wagner, Jr., and the New York Board of Education authorized a union-recognition election and, in June 1961, New York's teachers overwhelmingly voted for collective-bargaining rights. In another ballot in December of the same year, New York teachers voted to have the UFT as their sole bargaining agent. When the first contract talks between the UFT and the Board of Education broke down over a salary issue in April 1962, the union called another strike, and more than 20,000 teachers responded to the strike call. The strike was abandoned after a day when the state Supreme Court ruled the strike illegal. Once it was over, however, New York Governor Nelson Rockefeller agreed to increase aid to the city to meet the UFT's demands, and the UFT successfully negotiated the first comprehensive collective-bargaining agreement in a major U.S. city. The teachers received a substantial raise in salary, improvements in working conditions, and the establishment of a **grievance** procedure.

In the following years, teachers all across the country, encouraged by the success of the New York teachers, went out on strike to force boards of education to conduct bargaining elections. In 1963, the AFT repealed its no-strike pledge, and numerous U.S. cities experienced strikes by public schoolteachers. Between 1960 and 1974, there were more than 1,000 teacher strikes involving over 800,000 teachers. The frequent strikes for the purpose of obtaining bargaining rights led states to adopt legislation allowing or mandating public-sector collective-bargaining agreements. By the end of the 1970s, more than 70 percent of public schoolteachers were covered by collective-bargaining agreements. Membership of the AFT grew from 59,000 in 1960 to over 200,000 in 1970, and to over 900,000 by the end of the century. The AFT was now one of the biggest affiliates of the American Federation of Labor-Congress of Industrial Organizations and a major influence in national politics. The two leaders of the New York strike, David Selden and Albert Shanker, became AFT presidents. From 1974, when Shanker became AFT president until his death in 1997, Shanker became one of the most recognizable union leaders and educational experts in the country.

Suggested Readings: Marjorie Murphy, *Blackboard Unions: The AFT and the NEA, 1900–1980*, 1990; Philip Taft, *United They Teach: The Story of the United Federation of Teachers*, 1974; United Federation of Teachers, http://www.uft.org.

John F. Lyons

New York City Textile Strikes, 1909–10. The garment industry was expanding rapidly in the early twentieth century. Mechanization, mass immigration, and the emergence of a ready-to-wear clothing market contributed to its spread. Operatives had long complained about working conditions in the textile shops. Competition was intense, and employers regularly lowered workers' **wages** to cushion their own losses. Inner-city textile shops suffered from overcrowding, bad ventilation, insufficient lighting, and sanitation. Work hours often exceeded ten hours per day. An arbitrary fine system further angered textile workers and the common practice of inside **subcontracting** was a constant source of complaint. Here, a skilled worker distributed work to a number of unskilled helpers who were not paid directly by the employer but by the subcontractor. This practice led to huge inequalities in the pay scales of textile shops. Despite these shortcomings, few workers in the garment trades were unionized. Employers reacted with open hostility to employees who were union members and frequently tried to get rid of them. In general, they refused to recognize unions as representatives of their workforce. In the summer of 1909, workers from three Manhattan shirtwaist factories walked out of their shops. The strikers, primarily Jewish and Italian immigrant teenage girls, met rough treatment on the **picket** lines. Shop owners hired thugs to harass striking workers, and the police, in open collaboration with employers, arbitrarily arrested pickets and protected **scabs**. The abuse incensed textile operatives all over the city. When, on November 22, 1909, workers met with prominent union officials such as the **American Federation of Labor (AFL)** President **Samuel Gompers** and Mary Dreier from the **Women's Trade Union League (WTUL)**, the garment workers voted enthusiastically in support of a **general strike**. Over the next couple of days, about 20,000 shirtwaist workers, mostly women, walked out of their shops. They demanded a 10 percent wage increase, paid **overtime**, an end to strikers' harassment, the abolition of the subcontracting system, and, most fundamentally, union recognition.

Union leaders soon realized the publicity value of a large female presence on the picket lines. The strikers gained the support of middle-class ladies active in the WTUL. These women, often stemming from very prominent New York families, organized regular picket watches to prevent beatings and arrests of strikers. Gradually, public opinion began to shift. By January 1910, most employers were willing to grant wage increases and reduce working hours, but stalled when it came to the issue of union recognition. Determined not to settle for compromises, the strikers continued their pickets through the hard winter months of January and February. Their insistence on union recognition, however, cost them the support of some of their more conservative supporters from WTUL and AFL. When in mid-February the strike was officially declared over, operatives from 150 shops still had not gained a contract, and even those who did often had to sacrifice their goal of union recognition.

But conflicts in the textile trades were not over yet. Only five months after the shirtwaist makers' strike had been settled, an estimated 60,000 of New York's cloak makers went on strike. The cloak makers profited from public outrage over the mistreatment of pickets to a far lesser extent than the female shirtwaist workers. Nonetheless, their bargaining position was a more powerful one. New York's cloak manufacturers were divided in their interests; bigger factories feared the growing competition of smaller shops. The former hoped that the latter would not be able to keep up with the rising standards and higher wages upon which the unions insisted. Small shops, on the other hand, hoped that a long strike would weaken their large competitors. The strikers profited from this division. Prominent progressives and social-welfare advocates such as the lawyer, and later Supreme Court judge, Louis D. Brandeis, served as mediators between strikers and the manufacturers' association. The September 1910 agreement between unions, strikers, and employers became a remarkable union success. In addition to higher wages, shorter hours, better sanitary conditions, and the abolition of inside subcontracting, the agreement guaranteed a **preferential shop**. This meant that employers would select new workers only from a pool of union members. The recognition of unions as representatives of their workforce made possible the establishment of permanent bodies of negotiation. In future conflicts, the parties would resort to a tripartite board consisting of a representative of the union, the manufacturers' association, and a member of the public. The establishment of such a mediating instance constituted an important change in the way labor conflicts were conducted.

The impact of the New York textile strikes was not limited to the city alone. Textile workers in Chicago, Cleveland, and Philadelphia followed the New York example and took to the streets. Although the outcome was not always as favorable for the strikers as in the case of the cloak makers, the walkouts in the garment industry had long-lasting effects. Formerly an industry in which the majority of the workforce was unorganized, the textile trades became a union stronghold. Four weeks before the shirtwaist makers walked out, New York's radical Local 25 of the **International Ladies' Garment Workers' Union (ILGWU)** had a membership of only 800 persons. At the end of the strike, it boasted 13,000 members. Successes such as this made the socialist-dominated ILGWU the third-largest union inside the AFL. Other organizations profited as well. The United Garment Workers received an initial boost in membership but, because of the union's reluctance to endorse the strikes, a radical segment of workers split off. Jewish American garment workers, such as **Sidney Hillman**, became founding members of a new industrial textile union born out of the conflicts of 1910, the **Amalgamated Clothing Workers of America (ACWA)**. Further, the WTUL established itself as an important force in the organization of female workers and an ally in the labor struggle.

Suggested Readings: Joan M. Jensen and Sue Davidson, *A Needle, A Bobbin, A Strike: Women Needleworkers in America*, 1984; Carolyn D. McCreesh, *Women in the Campaign to Organize Garment Workers, 1880–1917*, 1985; Gus Tyler, *Look for the Union Label: A History of the International Ladies' Garment Workers' Union*, 1995.

Babette Faehmel

9 to 5: National Association of Working Women. 9 to 5: National Association of Working Women (9 to 5) is a lobby and pressure group with organizations in more than 200 cities and in all fifty states. It focuses on issues of concern to working women, including sexual harassment, employment discrimination against women, pay inequity, **glass ceiling** impediments to women's advancement in their jobs, and perceived antifamily business practices. Since its birth in 1973, it has been a major force in helping **minority labor** groups assert their rights.

9 to 5 began life in 1972 as the newsletter *9 to 5 News*, published by disaffected Boston office workers. The organization's founder was Harvard University clerical worker **Karen Nussbaum**. Local efforts in Boston resonated with women's experiences elsewhere and a national organization soon evolved. 9 to 5 emerged in part because of both change and lag in the American workforce. Women's participation in the workforce has increased dramatically since World War II, but progress in combating gender discrimination has not proceeded apace. By 1996, women made up more than 46 percent of the labor force, and more than 62 percent of all women are now employed. Yet women's wages are, on average, only about 70 percent of those of men. By 9 to 5's reckoning, despite the 1963 Pay Equity Act, the gap between male and female wages has closed by less than a penny per year. 9 to 5 has been very active in trying to get more women into labor unions as the union **wage differential** between men and women is far better than in nonunion workplaces.

9 to 5 has been at the fore of many social justice issues. It has been a champion of **affirmative action** policies, has fought for better conditions and pay for **contingency labor**, supports nonpunitive welfare reform, and has been a leader in a broad-based civil rights agenda. It was a major supporter of the **Family and Medical Leave Act**, though it maintains that the program's limited scope needs to be expanded. It is currently embroiled in efforts to assist low-wage workers. Of particular interest is a desire to make family leave and sick leave available to low-wage workers, as well as to address serious inequities in Social Security benefits for workers who were trapped in low-paying jobs for most of their careers. It maintains the Job Problem Hotline, through which women can request assistance in dealing with workplace discrimination.

The organization's high public profile spawned a fanciful namesake Hollywood film in 1980 and a song from country/pop artist Dolly Parton. Neither was directly about 9 to 5, and some critics complained that these popular culture expressions trivialized women's work issues, but they engendered publicity that aided the organization. It operates a national office out of Milwaukee and has cordial links with the American Federation of Labor-Congress of Industrial Organizations and other workplace reform groups.

Suggested Readings: Ellen Bravo, *The Job/Family Challenge, A 9 to 5 Guide—Not for Women Only*, 1995; "9 to 5: National Association of Working Women," www.9to5.org/.

James P. Hanlan
Robert E. Weir

Non-Wage Labor. Non-wage labor is a growing concern in American society. There are large numbers of people whose work is important to society, but who receive little or no compensation for their efforts. These workers are not covered by labor laws and few of them are organized. For the most part, unions have ignored or made half-hearted attempts to represent non-wage workers. In some cases—like prison labor and volunteer work—unions have interpreted non-wage labor as a threat to worker wage security.

Historically, the largest group of non-wage laborers are domestic homemakers, a trade customarily dominated by women. From Colonial times on, the agrarian-based American economy relegated wage-earners to minority status. This began to change with the advent of industrialization in the early nineteenth century. The yeoman ideal held that agrarian workers were independent and self-employed. In such an economy, each family member was both a producer and a consumer, and the work of each was integral to financial security, even if all jobs were not valued equally. (So-called women's work associated with child-rearing and food production was often viewed as less prestigious.) Workers who did not own farms might receive a wage, but this condition was viewed as temporary; even artisans were presumed to be working toward a goal of land ownership.

The advent of industrialization altered these assumptions. As more workers became lifelong wage-earners, the family economy gave way to ideals of a **family wage** in which a single wage-earner would be able to support an entire family. This mixed with prevailing gender notions and usually meant that men were supposed to be the breadwinners, while women would continue customary domestic duties. This had a profound impact on women. By the mid-nineteenth century, dominant social ideals held that men should have public roles, while women ought to assume only private ones associated with the household. Since men received payment for their work, it was viewed as more important. In effect, this made males producers and relegated the rest of the family to the consumer role. Even when women worked—a necessity for most nineteenth-century working-class families—their work was denigrated. Women usually received lower wages in the belief that they were not as capable as men, and that they would soon return to their homes to take up their "natural" roles. During economic downturns, laws sometimes forbade married women from wage work on the assumption that jobs should be reserved for male breadwinners.

Propaganda supplemented social custom in reinforcing the idea that women belonged in the home. Occasionally—as in both World War I and World War II—equally powerful propaganda was used to convince women they could temporarily assume public roles, but mostly women were told that they *should* be performing domestic duties and that these tasks were not as valuable as wage work. Women nonetheless entered the workforce in increasing numbers, especially in the latter half of the twentieth century. Even as women worked and the family-wage ideal eroded, women were still expected to perform the bulk of domestic chores.

The rebirth of the feminist movement in the 1960s challenged the way in which non-wage work for women was valued. Women complained of the double shift, as studies revealed that after-hours domestic chores meant that many working women held the equivalent of two full-time jobs. There were even proposals to pay women for housework, an idea that was much ridiculed in popular culture but that was based on sound economic calculations of the true value of women's unpaid labor and the potential cost to society if it were to be withdrawn. Advocates also pointed out that non-wage laborers have no health-care benefits, **workman's compensation**, sick leave, or **pensions**; they do not even accrue Social Security benefits unless they take paid positions. The rising divorce rate—which stood at 50 percent by the 1990s—made homemakers especially vulnerable. Feminists pointed out that many American women were but one death or divorce away from poverty.

To date, not much progress has been made on compensating homemakers for their labor and not much is anticipated, as the full-time homemaker is an ever-diminishing group. In recent years, concern over non-wage labor has shifted to other fronts. Many artists, writers, musicians, and performing artists often donate work and services. When they do not get paid for their work, they fall prey to many of the same issues as the full-time homemaker. For example, newspapers and on-line publications often pay nothing to publish the work of nonestablished writers. These writers are pressured to donate their work in exchange for an in-print credit they hope will give them credibility. Unions like the National Writers Union have pushed for standards that would require payment for published work. Similar campaigns have been launched in other professions.

Even more troublesome is labor that some unions dub coerced volunteering. The push to move welfare to workfare has, in some cases, forced individuals into job training or educational programs for which they might not be compensated; some programs require volunteer work in exchange for benefits. In some cases, welfare recipients even work **apprenticeships** in which they produce goods and services, but receive no pay. Unions like the **American Federation of State, County, and Municipal Employees** have complained that some workfare programs are abused by cost-cutting towns and cities seeking to trim budgets by replacing paid workers with coerced volunteers. In addition, some states—like Maine and Georgia—sell a wide range of prison-made goods to the general public, thereby reopening battles with unions and consumer groups that date back to the nineteenth century.

Volunteerism in the larger sense will likely become a contentious issue in the future. Teachers, nurses, social workers, and others complain that an influx of well-meaning individuals into nonpaid positions has led schools, hospitals, and agencies to rely upon volunteers while laying off paid aides and counselors. Ironically, though, the rise of non-wage labor has fueled the campaign for a living wage, which would link wages to local indices of what it actually costs to survive in a particular locale.

Suggested Readings: Jane Collins and Martha Gimenez, eds., *Work Without Wages: Comparative Studies of Domestic Labor and Self-Employment*, 1990; Jean Hinton, *What is a Wife Worth*, 1989; Susan Straser, *Never Done: A History of American Housework*, 1982.

Robert E. Weir

Norris-LaGuardia Act. The Anti-Injunction Act of 1932 is popularly known as the Norris-LaGuardia Act. Often thought of as the first of President Franklin Roosevelt's New Deal labor laws, this legislation was actually introduced into law during the last year of the presidency of Herbert Hoover, who signed the bill on his last day in office. The bill's sponsors were Senator George Norris, a Nebraska Republican, and Representaive Fiorello LaGuardia, a New York Republican. The legislation did not create any specific new rights for workers or unions, but it helped workers by forbidding judicial enforcement of **yellow-dog contracts** and by severely restricting the use of judicial injunctions or restraining orders, temporary or permanent, during labor disputes. Freedom from fear of adverse judicial intervention made it easier for labor unions to organize, **strike**, **picket**, and use other forms of leverage against management.

Prior to Norris-LaGuardia, federal courts had often viewed strikers or union members as engaged in unlawful combination or conspiracy in restraint of trade. The courts utilized injunctions and restraining orders to limit the activities of unions, union members, and their supporters. Thus the federal courts effectively became an ally of employers in their resistance to unionization. After Norris-LaGuardia, federal courts were allowed to use injunctive relief only if strikers threatened to break the law or were doing irreparable property damage. Even in these cases, a five-day waiting period and public hearings were required before an injunction could take effect. The legislation specifically assured the peaceful right to join a union, strike, pay or receive strike benefits, publicize a labor dispute, and, without fraud or violence, induce others to engage in such actions as were protected under the law. The **American Federation of Labor (AFL)** lobbied energetically for the passage of this legislation and viewed the law as one of its greatest accomplishments. Antilabor members of Congress described the law as "a long march in the direction of Moscow." While federal courts could still issue injunctions, their power to do so was limited by requiring detailed findings of facts. Additionally, the courts would no longer be the first resort of employers, for injunctions were allowed only after attempts at negotiation and mediation had failed. For a court to find fact sufficient cause to issue an injunction, they had to establish that illegal acts had been committed or threatened, that irreparable harm would occur, that law enforcement officials were unable or unwilling to provide adequate protection, and that there were no remedies at law for threatened illegal actions.

Norris-LaGuardia's great contribution was that unions and employers were put on a more equitable basis of negotiation than in the past, when power clearly rested with the employer and the federal courts were the employers' willing allies.

Suggested Readings: Richard Lowitt, *George W. Norris: The Persistence of a Progressive, 1913-1933*, 1971; "Labor Education Program," University of Missouri, http://www.missouri.edu/~labored/1997-32.html.

James P. Hanlan

North American Free Trade Agreement (NAFTA). The North American Free Trade Agreement (NAFTA) went into effect in January 1994, after a bitter political battle. The goal of NAFTA was to foster economic growth in Canada, the United States, and Mexico by eliminating barriers to trade and investment among the three nations. Labor unions oppose the agreement and assert that its effect has been to enrich international corporations while leaving both workers and the environment by the wayside. Labor maintains that one million U.S. and Canadian jobs have been lost to the agreement. While Mexican wages were supposed to increase, American unions charge that Mexican manufacturing wages have dropped by 21 percent, while environmental and public-health regulations have been ineffective in all three countries. Mexican workers lack union protections and toxic waste is spewed into the environment. The American Federation of Labor-Congress of Industrial Organizations (AFL-CIO) further charges that displaced manufacturing workers in the United States have been forced into the service sector, where wages are 23 percent lower than in manufacturing, and employers are using their flexibility to move across borders as a ruse to avoid **collective bargaining** through threats of **runaway shops**. The Free Trade Area of the Americas (FTAA) proposal would extend NAFTA to an additional thirty-one countries and 400 million people and, the AFL-CIO maintains, exacerbate the problems created by NAFTA.

Suggested Readings: *NAFTA at Seven*, Economic Policy Institute; *Trading Away Rights: The Unfulfilled Promise of NAFTA's Labor Side Agreement*, Human Rights Watch.

James P. Hanlan

No-Strike Pledge. A no-strike pledge is a contractual provision that states that a union will not issue a work stoppage during the life of the contract. Under this type of agreement, all strikes are deemed illegal. There is also a more limited type of no-strike pledge in which a list of conditions must be met before an industrial action can be deemed permissible. With the latter, there is usually the condition that employee **grievances** and disputes over the interpretation of contractual provisions be submitted to a mediation procedure, with resolution, if necessary, in final and binding **arbitration**.

No-strike pledges provide a peaceful work environment without interruption and provide a way for workers to resolve conflict through grievance procedures. This explains why **strikes** normally occur after a contract has expired. Unions have historically signed such pledges when the United States was at war to ensure the production of military goods and to demonstrate the patriotism of union members. During World War II, however, some unions—including the **United Mine Workers of America (UMWA)**—withdrew adherence to the pledge when they deemed that employers violated their part of the bargain.

No-strike pledges are also sometimes used on an entire project with the stipulation that only union workers will be employed on the job. Unions are currently embracing project-labor agreements on large job sites in just such a manner. This strategy greatly contributes to a union's likelihood of winning a contract because it dampens employer fear of organized work stoppages.

Suggested Readings: Nelson Lichtenstein, *Labor's War at Home*, 1987; "Padres Ballpark Work to Proceed Uninterrupted; No-Strike Clause Part of 'Historic Agreement,'" *San Diego Union-Tribune* (January 15, 2000); Robert Zieger, *John L. Lewis*, 1988.

Jaime Barnes

Nussbaum, Karen. Karen Nussbaum is the founder of **9 to 5: National Association of Working Women** (9 to 5), has served as an officer in the **Service Employees International Union (SEIU)**, headed the Women's Bureau at the **Department of Labor**, and currently leads the Working Women's Department of the American Federation of Labor-Congress of Industrial Organizations (AFL-CIO).

Nussbaum was born in Chicago, Illinois, on April 25, 1950. She attended the University of Chicago, dropped out, and finished her bachelor's degree at Goddard College in 1975. After leaving the University of Chicago, Nussbaum moved to Boston and took a clerical job at Harvard University. Even by the standards of the early 1970s, her $2 per hour pay was too low to allow a decent standard of living. She began to meet with other female Harvard workers and, in 1972, began publishing a newsletter to draw attention to their situation. In 1973, she formed 9 to 5 and expanded its reach throughout the greater Boston area. Its campaign against Harvard greatly embarrassed the university but also improved **salaries** and conditions for working women. Nussbaum was aided by SEIU, which chartered office workers as a **local**, which, in 1981, became the national District 925 of the SEIU. Nussbaum served as executive director of 9 to 5 from 1977 to 1993 and was president of SEIU District 925 from 1981 to 1993. (The two are allied, but are distinct.) Nussbaum also served on SEIU's executive board and headed its Office Workers Division, which served more than 170,000 members.

Nussbaum left both 9 to 5 and SEIU District 925 in 1993, when President William Clinton appointed her to head the Women's Bureau at the **Department of Labor**, a post she held through 1996. Nussbaum helped rebuild the Women's Bureau, which had been downsized by President George H. Bush, of whom Nussbaum was a harsh critic. She was especially scornful of his decision to close numerous Women's Bureau regional offices. Nussbaum is also credited with the survey "Working Women Count!," a comprehensive look at working women in the 1990s. She supported President Clinton's initiative that led to the **Family and Medical Leave Act**. In 1995, SEIU national president **John Sweeney** became the president of the AFL-CIO. He eventually convinced Nussbaum to become director of the AFL-CIO's Working Women's Department (WWD), a Sweeney initiative that began in 1997. Nussbaum was placed in charge of overseeing policy, outreach, political activity, and organizing efforts for the WWD.

Suggested Readings: Ellen Cassedy and Karen Nussbaum, *Nine to Five: The Working Woman's Guide to Office Survival*, 1983; Karen Nussbaum and John Sweeney, *Solutions for the New Workforce*, 1989; Mary Hartman, ed., *Talking Leadership: Conversations With Powerful Women*, 1999.

James P. Hanlan
Robert E. Weir

O

Occupational Safety and Health Act (1970). At the end of the nineteenth century, an increase in industrial activity, as well as population growth, led to the subsequent development of a **working class**. This increase in industrial activity meant an increase in poor, unhealthy, and unsafe working environments. During the 1920s, for example, almost 20,000 workers were killed and 2.6 million were injured every year. In 1945, 16,500 workers were killed and 2.6 million were injured. Although the poor working conditions of many Americans were a social problem in existence for many decades, it was not until the 1960s that a movement began promoting the need for government intervention.

During the 1960s, the number of workers injured or killed remained high. Injuries increased by approximately 20 percent and there were still approximately 14,000 workers killed each year. It was also at this time that the public became more aware of the high numbers of workplace accidents and deaths, many of which were caused by negligence on the part of employers who consistently forced people to work in dangerous environments. Some speculate that the increasing concern about the environment might have played a role as well. However, the greatest voice for change was heard from the workers themselves. They began to voice their concerns to their unions and their representatives about unsafe working conditions, as well as occupational diseases, which were not well known at the time. As many workers felt that union officials were not properly handling their concerns, they organized **wildcat strikes**, filed **grievances**, and used any other tactic that would help them publicize their concerns.

Increased public awareness and pressure from workers led to the introduction of health and safety legislation in 1968. The **Occupational Safety and Health Act** became law on December 29, 1970, and the Occupational Safety and Health Administration came into being on April 28, 1971. Known initially as the safety bill of rights, its purpose is to "assure safety and healthful working conditions for working men and women." The act established three permanent agencies: (1) the Occupational Safety and Health Administration, to administer the act and set and enforce workplace health and safety standards, (2) the National Institute for Occupational Safety and Health, to conduct research, and (3) the Occupational Safety and Health Review Commission, to hear cases where employers are charged with not obeying the standards of the act.

Employers in the United States must obey the Occupational Safety and Health Act and its standards. To do so, they must keep records of injuries and illnesses, as well as employee exposure to toxic materials. It is through inspections, either in response to employee complaints or as part of a regular inspection program, that the government makes sure all businesses are following the act. In addition to this act, states can also use their own standards as long as they meet certain criteria and establish an agency to enforce the standards.

The Occupational Safety and Health Act was the first federal legislation in the United States that granted the government the right to inspect and punish those employers who made people work in unsafe and unhealthy environments. When it was enacted, it covered 56 million workers at 3.5 million workplaces. Today, the act covers 105 million workers at 6.9 million workplaces. The U.S. occupational injury rate is now 40 percent lower than when OSHA first enacted regulations in 1971, and deaths from occupational injuries are 60 percent lower. Since its beginnings, administration of the act has led to the establishment of training programs, the formation of partnerships with companies that wanted to improve their records, and continuous studies on new hazards and chemicals in the workplace. Its administration even offers loans to small businesses that want to improve the workplace for their employees and meet the act's requirements, but find it financially difficult to do so. The Occupational Safety and Health Act, from its beginnings, was considered to be a compromise as no one interest group got everything it wanted. Labor organizations often feel the act is not effective enough, while employers feel it is often overly concerned with trivial standards. Regardless, the enactment of the Occupational Safety and Health Act was an important piece of legislation for all workers in the United States.

Suggested Readings: Patrick G. Donnelly, "The Origins of the Occupational Safety and Health Act of 1970," *Social Problems* 30, no.1 (October 1982); Susan Hall Fleming, "OSHA at Thirty: Three Decades of Progress in Occupational Safety and Health," *Job Safety and Health Quarterly* 12, no. 3 (Spring 2001), also available, "OSHA's 30th Anniversary," http://www.osha.gov/as/opa/osha-at-30.html; Robert Stewart Smith, *The Occupational Safety and Health Act: Its Goals and Its Achievements*, 1976.

Lisa J. Wells

Oil, Chemical, and Atomic Workers Union (OCAW). The Oil, Chemical, and Atomic Workers Union (OCAW) grew from a **strike** by oil rig workers demanding an eight-hour day in California's San Joaquin Valley in 1917. In 1918, the **American Federation of Labor (AFL)** granted a rare **industrial-union** charter to the Association of Oil Field, Gas Well, and Refinery Workers. In the 1930s, the union, with its membership based largely in small towns and rural areas, joined the **Congress of Industrial Organizations (CIO)** and, in 1955, united with other gas and oil workers' unions to form OCAW. Among the union's successes was the establishment of nationwide bargaining as the norm for oil industry workers. Due to the nature of the industry, OCAW focused on both safety and occupational health issues, taking on the federal government in legal challenges, as employer in addition to employers in private industry. The Department of Energy, as regulator or operator of nuclear facilities, is the focus of OCAW legal challenges. OCAW was among the leaders in lobbying for the passage of the **Occupational Safety and Health Act** in the late 1960s. By 1973, OCAW's **collective-bargaining** agreements included specific health and safety clauses. The last holdout against such clauses was the Shell Oil Company, and a four-month strike in 1973 drew support from unions around the world and from a wide coalition of environmental activists. Among OCAW's other prominent fights was the case of Karen Silkwood, a worker for the Kerr-McGee Nuclear Corporation in Oklahoma who was exposed to massive plutonium radiation in 1974.

Longtime OCAW official Tony Mazzocchi (1926–2003), who had been active in the campaign to create OSHA, was a personal friend of Silkwood's, and he pressured the OCAW to lobby even harder for improved workplace safety standards. Silkwood's death galvanized many OCAW members and some of its **rank-and-file** moved sharply to the left politically. The BASF **lockout** of the 1980s further angered OCAW members. The lockout of OCAW workers at the Geismar, Louisiana, facility began in 1984, spawned an international **corporate campaign**, and lasted until 1989, when a settlement was finally reached. It was perhaps the longest lockout in American labor history.

The antilabor climate of the 1980s led Mazzocchi and other OCAW activists to contemplate the need for a **labor party**. In 1990, Mazzocchi announced the formation of Labor Party Advocates (LPA) to explore that possibility. In 1991, Mazzocchi left his post as secretary-treasurer of the OCAW to devote more energy to the LPA. Despite Mazzocchi's departure, the OCAW remained the driving force behind the LPA, which in 1996 reformed as the Labor Party. The party, unlike its LPA predecessor, does not endorse candidates from other parties. As of 2003, the Labor Party has been mostly a moral voice and has not enjoyed electoral success.

The OCAW has found itself at the fore of battles to stop **runaway shops**. In 1992, it won a $24 million settlement against American Home Products, which abused the tax code to relocate profitable plants to tax havens in Puerto Rico and other Caribbean islands. It also lobbied for tightening tax loopholes, though most of the production jobs were lost. In 1999, the OCAW merged with the **United Paperworkers** to form PACE, the Paper Allied-Industrial, Chemical, and Energy Workers International Union. PACE represents more than

300,000 workers in pulp, paper, chemical, petroleum, nuclear, and pharmaceutical industries. PACE continues to place emphasis on independent political action, environmental action, workplace safety, and employee health issues.

Suggested Readings: "OCAW," http://www.webshells.com/ocaw/; Timothy Minchin, *Forging a Common Bond: Labor and Environmental Activism during the BASF Lockout*, 2002.

James P. Hanlan

One Big Union (OBU). The One Big Union (OBU) was one of the central elements in the vision of society advocated by the **Industrial Workers of the World (IWW)**. Founded in 1905, the IWW's **anarcho-syndicalist** worldview produced what became an alternative vision of social and economic organization.

At its core, the OBU model is a union of unions, formed by the gathering of all industrially organized labor unions into one organization. In a sense, the OBU replaces the state, the government, the capitalist class, and everything else that has a role in organizing or shaping production in modern society. The OBU was not envisioned as a centralized governing body, rather it was an amalgam of loosely organized collectives and federations in which social-class differences would dissolve when citizens were integrated by a common state and a common purpose. The IWW never clearly articulated what the OBU would look like, but it became an effective rallying cry and expression of displeasure with existing power structures.

What made the OBU model more than simply a large union organization was the IWW's revolutionary intent. As workers assumed control of industries through their unions, the capitalist class would disappear, as would allied appendages like the central government. In theory, the OBU would fill the vacated void.

The concept of the OBU did not become a dominant influence in the labor movement, and its decline in popularity largely mirrored that of the IWW. It remained a vital organizing principle for militant unionists, and an IWW offshoot in Canada adopted the term as its official name. Conceptually, the term mutated after World War I to refer to a generalized **solidarity** among workers and coordinated activity among unions. However, large federations of unions should not be considered as continuations of the OBU model, as they are not rooted in the revolutionary ideals that underpin it. With some exceptions, the OBU model is not common in the contemporary labor movement.

Suggested Readings: Paul Brissenden, *The I.W.W.: The Study of American Syndicalism*, 1919; Melvyn Dubofsky, *We Shall Be All: A History of the Industrial Workers of the World*, 1969; "One Big Union," http://bari.iww.org/culture/official/obu/.

Alex Corlu

Open Shop. An open shop is a workplace that hires employees regardless of their union status. Individual employees may be union members and are legally free to join them, but the employer treats them as individuals and not members of a labor organization. The open shop is thus unorganized and nonunion. Recently, nonunion employers in the construction industry have used the term merit shops to stress the fact that employees are dealt with individually based on their productivity, rather than the traditional union style of **seniority**. In open shops, even if some employees organize and certify a union, nonunion employees enjoy the benefits of their union counterparts, but they are not required to pay **dues**. Some contracts do impose an **agency fee** on nonunion employees to reimburse the union a percentage of the cost of negotiating contracts. Unions generally oppose both open shops and agency fees and complain that the latter creates "free riders," who receive union benefits at cut-rate costs.

The open-shop movement emerged in the early twentieth century as an antilabor ploy to discourage union membership. In 1903, the **National Association of Manufacturers (NAM)** unveiled its first open-shop drive. The NAM enjoyed its greatest success in the 1920s when the so-called **American Plan** lent an air of patriotism and moral superiority to the **union shop** system. Supporters exploited American individualism and accused unions of coercing membership. Closed shops reemerged in a new guise after the form of **right-to-work** laws after the passage of the **Taft-Hartley Act** in 1947. Many observers cite open shops and right-to-work laws as two of the biggest obstacles to organization for the contemporary labor movement.

A cartoon of the 1920s depicting the hidden dangers of the open shop. © George Meany Memorial Archives.

Suggested Readings: Irving Bernstein, *The Lean Years*, 1960; Mike Davis, *Prisoners of the American Dream*, 1988; Foster Dulles and Melvyn Dubofsky, *Labor in America*, 1984.

Jaime Barnes

Operation Dixie. Operation Dixie was a largely unsuccessful attempt by the **Congress of Industrial Organizations (CIO)** to unionize southern states during the years 1946 through 1953. By the end of World War II, the CIO had more than a quarter-million southern members, largely in textiles, mining, and the steel industry. Nonetheless, CIO leaders worried that the spread of **right-**

to-work laws in the South would cause cost-conscious northern capitalists to relocate operations in the region unless it was more thoroughly unionized. Affiliated unions donated more than a million dollars to support the efforts of over 400 organizers.

Operation Dixie began to unravel quickly. The CIO's commitment to racial equality faced stiff opposition from southern segregationists, and its organizers were often the targets of threats and violence. Many employers, newspapers, law-enforcement officials, white-supremacy groups, and churches launched vicious propaganda campaigns to discredit the CIO. Accusations that CIO leaders were **communists** proved especially damaging. Against all odds, organizers managed to organize over 300 new unions and enjoyed modest success among timber workers, especially African Americans.

In the end, however, opposition proved too powerful and the passage of the 1947 **Taft-Hartley Act** signaled political hostility toward organized labor. Most regional offices closed before the end of 1949, a time in which there were only about 400,000 CIO members in the South. Remaining campaigns ceased in 1953, the union admitting that its efforts were a failure. By the mid-1950s, most southern states had right-to-work laws and union membership declined below pre-1946 levels. The South remains a sparsely organized region.

Suggested Readings: Barbara Griffith, *The Crisis of American Labor: Operation Dixie and the Defeat of the CIO*, 1988; William Jones, "Black Workers and the CIO's Turn Toward Black Liberalism: Operation Dixie and the North Carolina Lumber Industry, 1946–1953," *Labor History* 41, no. 3 (August 2000): 279–306; Robert Zieger, *The CIO, 1935–1955*, 1995.

Robert E. Weir

O'Reilly, Leonora (February 16, 1870–April 3, 1927). Leonora O'Reilly, a labor organizer, reformer, and feminist, was born in New York City, the daughter of Irish immigrants John and Winnifred (Rooney) O'Reilly. Her father, a printer, died when Leonora was only a year old, forcing her garment-worker mother to work even longer hours to support Leonora and her brother. O'Reilly was forced to leave school at age eleven to work in a collar factory. She joined the **Knights of Labor (KOL)** when she was sixteen and joined the Comte Synthetic Circle, a Lower East Side self-education group. There she met Victor Drury, a French-born intellectual, anarchist, and KOL activist, who became her mentor. Drury exposed her to books and ideas that more than compensated for her interrupted formal education.

The KOL organized women, a cause that became O'Reilly's lifelong endeavor. In 1886, she cofounded the Working Women's Society and caught the attention of philanthropist and activist Louise Perkins, who introduced her to the Social Reform Club, a New York gathering devoted to discussions of the political economy. O'Reilly supported herself in the garment industry. In 1897, she set up a **cooperative** shirtwaist shop at the Henry Street Settlement House, but the project faltered. With Perkins's help, she began taking art courses at Brooklyn's Pratt Institute in 1898 and obtained a degree from there in 1900.

She simultaneously served as head resident at the Asacoq House settlement. From 1902 through 1909, she taught sewing at the Manhattan Trades School for Girls.

O'Reilly's greatest fame came after 1903, when she cofounded the national **Women's Trade Union League (WTUL)**, a coalition of middle- and working-class women devoted to bringing women into the fold of organized labor. In 1909, O'Reilly became a full-time WTUL organizer. She served as vice president of New York City's WTUL. As a WTUL activist, O'Reilly helped organize the 1910 New York City shirtwaist **strike** and she galvanized protest following the **Triangle Factory Fire of 1911**. O'Reilly also became involved in the fights for women's suffrage and civil rights; she joined the National Association for the Advancement of Colored People (NAACP) in 1909. She was a peace activist before and after World War I.

In 1915, O'Reilly attended the International Congress of Women at The Hague. Upon returning home, she resigned from the WTUL because of policy differences and failing health. A weak heart curtailed her efforts at the 1919 International Congress of Working Women. She was able to teach labor-history courses for the New School for Social Research in 1925 and 1926 before dying of heart disease in 1927.

Suggested Readings: Domenica Barbuto, *American Settlement Houses and Progressive Social Reform: An Encyclopedia*, 1999; Edward James, ed, *Notable American Women 1607–1950*, 1971; *Women's Trade Union League Papers: Leonora O'Reilly file*, Radcliffe University.

Robert E. Weir

O'Sullivan, Mary Kenney (January 8, 1864–January 18, 1943). Mary Kenney O'Sullivan was a labor organizer and social reformer. She was born in Hannibal, Missouri, the daughter of Irish immigrants, Mary Kelley and Michael Kenney. Her father was a railroad machinist who participated in the **Great Labor Uprising** of 1877 and the young Mary Kenney's labor consciousness was formed then. A year later, at the age of fourteen, she was **apprenticed** in a bookbindery and was the main support for her now-widowed mother.

Over the next decade, Mary Kenney worked in bookbinderies in Hannibal and Keokuk, Iowa, before moving to Chicago in the late 1880s. Despite her status as a skilled bookbinder, she was limited by her gender, as men routinely held the high-paying jobs within binderies. In her frustration, she turned to the labor movement, hoping that through organization, wage-earning women such as she could improve their working conditions. In Chicago, Kenney organized Women's Bindery No. 1 and accepted the invitation of Jane Addams to use the recently opened settlement, Hull House, as a meeting place. There she founded the Jane Club, a cooperative living space in an adjacent apartment building. In 1892, **American Federation of Labor (AFL)** President **Samuel Gompers** appointed Kenney as the AFL's first woman organizer. She spent several months organizing women workers in and around Boston, but she was soon frustrated by the notion that working-class women only worked for "pin money" before marriage and the reality that most were confined to unskilled jobs usually not represented by **craft unions**. The AFL shared these prejudices and let Kenney go after only six months in the field.

Kenney returned to Chicago but moved back to Boston in 1894 when she married local labor leader John F. O'Sullivan. In the next eight years she gave birth to four children, one of whom died in infancy, while continuing to organize women workers. As in Chicago, Kenney O'Sullivan relied on the support of both the local labor movement and the settlement houses. She was also involved in Denison House, a settlement in Boston's South End. In 1903, she was a cofounder of the **Women's Trade Union League (WTUL)**, a cross-class alliance of women wage-earners and their middle- and upper-class allies, that sought to agitate for **protective labor legislation** and organize women workers into AFL-affiliated unions. During the next decade, Kenney O'Sullivan was a leader in the WTUL, on both the national level and in Boston, but she withdrew in protest during the **Lawrence textile strike of 1912**, when both the AFL and the WTUL refused to support the strike of more than 15,000 workers, many of whom were immigrant women. In 1914, she was appointed a factory inspector for the Massachusetts Board of Labor and Industries, retiring in 1934. She died at her West Medford home in 1943. A committed pacifist as well as an ardent supporter of women's suffrage, Mary Kenney O'Sullivan was first and foremost an advocate of the rights of wage-earning women, especially their right to organize.

Suggested Readings: Robin Miller Jacoby, *The British and American Women's Trade Union Leagues, 1890–1925*, 1994; Kathleen Banks Nutter, *The Necessity of Organization: Mary Kenney O'Sullivan and Trade Unionism for Women, 1892–1912*, 2000; Meredith Tax, *The Rising of the Women: Feminist Solidarity and Class Conflict, 1880–1917*, 1980.

Kathleen Banks Nutter

Overtime. Overtime refers to hours of work beyond the normal workday and/or workweek for which higher rates must be paid either by contract or pertinent state law. Hours in excess of the standard are paid at usually one and one-half times the normal rate. The **Fair Labor Standards Act (FLSA)** of 1938 established minimum wages and maximum hours beyond which overtime pay is mandatory, setting a weekly threshold of forty hours before overtime premiums must be paid. Employers are required to pay workers for all time worked, whether the employer requested the work or not. Management bears the burden of preventing unwanted work.

Overtime pay emerged from organized labor's long battle to establish the **eight-hour** workday. It discourages employers from forcing workers to toil long hours as it costs them more to do so. Overtime pay usually applies only to those who work for **wages** as opposed to **salary**, however, and the long hours of salaried employees constitute a current issue of concern. In addition, some unscrupulous employers seek to circumvent the law.

Suggested Readings: "Defining 'Hours Worked' Under the Fair Labor Standards Act," *The CPA Journal*, (June 2001); "Workers' Winning Claims for Back Overtime Shake Employers," *Restaurant News* (September 24, 2001).

Jaime Barnes

Owen, Robert Dale (November 9, 1801–June 24, 1877). Robert Dale Owen spent a brief portion of his long reform career aligned with New York's **Workingmen's Movement** in 1829–30, primarily using it as a vehicle to advance a state education plan he developed with Frances Wright. His broad reform agenda tinged with **utopianism** was typical of many early-nineteenth-century labor activists.

The son of Scottish reformer Robert Owen and Ann Caroline Owen, Robert Dale Owen lived and worked at his father's industrial reform community, New Lanarck, Scotland, before emigrating to the United States in 1825 to join the elder Owen's utopian community at New Harmony, Indiana. There, he participated in the attempt to build a **cooperative**, rationalist, community akin to New Lanarck on American soil. He met Fanny Wright—another Scots reformer—at New Harmony and traveled with her to her experimental community in Nashoba, Tennessee, that sought to prepare slaves for freedom. After coediting newspapers with Wright at both New Harmony and Nashoba, Owen followed her to New York City in the spring of 1829. Through a new journal, the *Free Enquirer*, and public lectures at a converted church renamed the Hall of Science, the pair advocated an education plan that included state guardianship of all children as a cure for social and economic inequalities.

Numerous labor reformers embraced free public education as central in helping **working-class** families escape a life of permanent wage-earning. Moreover, Owen's editorials supported the fight of a New York City Workingmen's Party for a ten-hour day, and by the fall of 1829, he was included in the group's leadership. Owen also edited the *Daily Sentinel*, a workers' newspaper, and was associated with George Henry Evans's *Working Man's Advocate*. In December 1829, Owen participated in a coup that ousted the radical agrarian **Thomas Skidmore** and his backers from the Workingmen, only to be expelled himself in the spring of 1830, when political opportunists gained party control.

Owen later served three terms in the Indiana legislature and two terms in the U.S. House of Representatives. In each position, he advocated free public education. An outspoken abolitionist, Owen also championed women's rights. Although he was never again directly associated with labor organizations, his plans for public education continued to capture working-class imaginations and many subsequent organizations embraced his plan.

Suggested Readings: Richard Leopold, *Robert Dale Owen: A Biography*, 1940; Celia Morris, *Fanny Wright: Rebel in America*, 1984; Sean Wilentz, *Chants Democratic: New York City and the Rise of the American Working Class, 1788–1850*, 1984.

Robert D. Sampson

HISTORICAL ENCYCLOPEDIA OF

AMERICAN LABOR

HISTORICAL ENCYCLOPEDIA OF AMERICAN LABOR

VOLUME 2
P–Z

Edited by
Robert E. Weir and James P. Hanlan

GREENWOOD PRESS
Westport, Connecticut • London

Library of Congress Cataloging-in-Publication Data

Historical encyclopedia of American labor / edited by Robert Weir and James P. Hanlan.
p. cm.
Includes bibliographical references and index.
ISBN 0–313–31840–9 (set : alk. paper)—ISBN 0–313–32863–3 (vol. 1 : alk. paper)—ISBN 0–313–32864–1 (vol. 2 : alk. paper)
1. Labor—United States—History—Encyclopedias. 2. Labor movement—United States—History—Encyclopedias. 3. Industrial relations—United States—History—Encyclopedias. 4. Labor laws and legislation—United States—History—Encyclopedias. I. Title: Encyclopedia of American labor. II. Weir, Robert, E. 1952– III. Hanlan, James P.
HD8066.H57 2004
331.88'0973'03—dc21 2003052847

British Library Cataloguing in Publication Data is available.

Library of Congress Catalog Card Number: 2003052847

ISBN: 0–313–31840–9 (set)
0–313–32863–3 (vol. 1)
0–313–32864–1 (vol. 2)

First published in 2004

Greenwood Press, 88 Post Road West, Westport, CT 06881
An imprint of Greenwood Publishing Group, Inc.
www.greenwood.com

Printed in the United States of America

The paper used in this book complies with the Permanent Paper Standard issued by the National Information Standards Organization (Z39.48–1984).

10 9 8 7 6 5 4 3 2 1

Every reasonable effort has been made to track down the owners of copyright materials in this book, but in some instances this has proven impossible. The editors and publisher will be glad to receive information leading to more complete acknowledgments in subsequent printings of the book and in the meantime extend their apologies for any omissions.

Contents

Acknowledgments

The magnitude of this project makes it inevitable that small errors will occur. We take full responsibility for such slip-ups, although we have taken pains to ensure that the overall integrity of the historical record has not been compromised.

Our codicils aside, we are very proud of this work. That is in no small part due to the outstanding support we got from the labor history community and from Greenwood Press. When we put out a call for contributors to the H-Labor LISTSERV discussion group, we were overwhelmed by the number of those who responded, as well as by their generosity, knowledge, and desire to help. There are too many to list individually, but their names are listed with their entries and in the front matter, and we encourage readers to seek out their work. We thank each and every contributor.

Several individuals went above and beyond the call of duty in helping bring this project to fruition. Professor Weir's undergraduate labor history class at Bay Path College helped with some of the initial research in the fall of 2000. He wishes to thank Lisa Barber, Michele Bernier, Cheryl Conley, Yasmin Correa, Pauline Gladstone, Heather Hite, Shalynn Hunt, Leslie Juntunen, Maria Medina, Sara Pleva, Carina Reid, Maria Ruotolo, Aryu Sunyoto, and Teri Voight for their invaluable assistance. Professor Hanlan also drew upon the hard work of the students at Worcester Polytechnic Institute enrolled in his labor history seminar. They served as a sounding board and an inspiration. His colleagues Kent Ljungquist, Robert W. Thompson, Edmund Hayes, and Penny Rock provided companionship, counsel, and the best of friendship that any college faculty member could hope for. They showed me the joys of interdisciplinary and interdepartmental collegiality. I owe them much. Likewise I thank Provost John F. Carney for providing release time.

Our friend Scott Molloy, who directs the labor center at the University of Rhode Island, toiled long and hard on behalf of the project. Scott not only served on the advisory board, but he also enlisted his graduate students in the project and wrote numerous entries. A special thanks goes to another good friend and colleague, Bruce Cohen of Worcester State College. Other than our own names, Bruce's name appears more than any other in these volumes. Whenever we were stuck for coverage, we contacted Bruce and he took over our troublesome topics, to say nothing of the dozens of entries for which he actually volunteered. Bruce inspired both of us through his dedication to teaching and scholarship and especially through his genuine and heartfelt commitment to the well-being of the men and women who work and struggle to earn their livings.

The staff at the George Meany Memorial Archives at the National Labor College in Silver Spring, Maryland, were extremely generous in helping track down images and in providing support materials for the project. A special thank you goes to Lynda DeLoach at the archives and to Bob Reynolds, who edits the wonderful *Labor's Heritage* from the same location. They helped make Professor Weir's research and visit to the archives an absolute delight.

Greenwood Press could not have been more accommodating. Barbara Rader, the executive editor of the School and Public Library Reference division, got the ball rolling and showed great confidence in the editors' ability to get the job done. She then turned the editors over to the capable hands of Kevin Ohe and John Wagner, who shepherded the project to completion. Elizabeth Kincaid did a fine job of tracking down photos. The editors are indebted to Greenwood for their faith in them and for making this a quality work.

* * *

I would like to thank my wife, Emily, for her ongoing love and support. She is also the most affable research partner that one could hope to have. I am truly blessed to be able to share life's road with her.

In the middle of this project, I was fortunate enough to be a Fulbright scholar in New Zealand. I want to thank Jim Hanlan for taking up the slack while I was on the adventure of a lifetime. I had endless hours of fascinating discussions with Kiwi colleagues like Melanie Nolan and Pat Moloney at Victoria University, Jim McAloon at Lincoln University, Kerry Taylor at Massey University, Miles Fairburn and Graeme Dunstan at the University of Canterbury, and Tom Brooking and Erik Olssen at the University of Otago. My conversations with these individuals helped shape my words and thoughts in more ways than I can count. So too did my time at the Alexander Turnbull Library in Wellington, where I learned so much more not only about New Zealand labor history but also about American history. Many thanks to Frank Rogers, who came to one of my Turnbull talks and proceeded to share his wisdom with me, and to John Martin, the senior historian with the historical branch of the Department of the Interior and one of the most careful researchers I've ever met. A special thank you to Janet Horncy and Margaret Calder at the Turnbull Library, who gave me the freedom to pursue various research interests, but also made me feel like part of their extended families. And finally, a thank you to Jenny Gill and her staff at Fulbright New Zealand. You folks are simply the best!

I would like to dedicate my part of this work to my father, Archie Weir, a longtime union member, who died on April 11, 2002. His loss is deeply felt, but his fighting spirit lives on.

Robert E. Weir

I am indebted more than I can express to my wife, Gaye D. (Francis) Hanlan. She tolerated my distractions and absences and eased my burdens through this long project. Likewise, my children, George, Janet, and Jamo, served as promise for what the future can hold. I would like to express my thanks to the Lowell Central Labor Council, which, many years ago, provided a scholarship for my undergraduate education.

I dedicate my part of this work to the memory of my father and mother, George J. and Cecilia G. (Tynan) Hanlan. They knew what it was to endure a long and painful strike and to persevere. My father's pride in craftsmanship was exemplary. Together my parents inspired my life.

James P. Hanlan

Preface

Compiling the *Historical Encyclopedia of American Labor* has been a daunting task, to say the least. Like most historians, each of us is trained in a narrow specialty. Our long years of teaching experience have broadened us, but there were, invariably, gaps in our knowledge. Luckily, the labor history community is stocked with numerous bright and affable individuals who were ready to lend their expertise to the project. We thank them profusely and without them could not have finished these volumes.

The project was imposing because we knew from the outset that some professional labor educators were going to take umbrage with how we covered certain topics, what we covered, and what we left out. Our only defense is to say that this is *not* a collection for experts in the field. Ours is a guide for those starting research projects, writing school reports, or familiarizing themselves with hitherto unknown people, ideas, events, and organizations. It is designed primarily for public libraries, college and university library reference sections, high school libraries, and general repositories. Although we certainly hope that labor research centers, unions, and graduate schools find our efforts useful, we would be the last to say that the *Historical Encyclopedia* is the final word on *any* of the subjects it contains.

The *Historical Encyclopedia* offers almost 400 entries covering unions, union leaders, labor-related events, important statutes and court cases, and labor terminology. The entries are thoroughly cross-referenced, with mentions of other related entries highlighted upon their first appearance in the text of any particular entry. Entries conclude with a listing of suggested readings for those wishing to read in more detail on a particular subject. The *Historical Encyclopedia* is also illustrated with numerous photographs and includes an appendix containing excerpts from fifty-eight labor-related primary documents, including items such as statutes, interviews with workers, passages from the autobiographies of labor leaders, union documents, congressional testimony, and newspaper and magazine articles on labor topics and events. Finally, as a quick reference supplement to the entry readings, the *Historical Encyclopedia* offers a bibliography of important books and Web sites on labor-related topics and also includes a detailed subject index to provide quick, in-depth access to the information in the entries.

It is easy for experts immersed in the intricacies of research to forget that the general public knows little or nothing about American labor history. Most high school textbooks give scant attention to labor history, and our recent perusal of a half dozen popular college U.S. history survey texts reveals that among labor leaders only Terence Powderly, Samuel Gompers, A. Philip Randolph, Mary Jones, John L. Lewis, and Cesar Chavez are mentioned with any degree of regularity. Likewise, the only labor actions to warrant much coverage are the eight-hour-movement, the railroad strikes of 1877, the Pullman and Homestead strikes in the 1890s, the sit-down strikes of the 1930s, and the Professional Air Traffic Controllers Organization (PATCO) walkout of 1981. And even then, the operative word is "mentioned." Thorough discussions of the arc of labor history are noticeably absent. It has been more than four decades since the new social history admonished historians to consider race, class, and gender when writing history. Our observations reveal that class largely remains a junior partner within the troika.

When we began this project, we met with many people, scoured the indexes of numerous labor history textbooks, put out calls on the World Wide Web, and endlessly brainstormed. Our question was a basic one: *What would individuals with little or no background in labor history need to learn if they wished to begin studying the subject?* We tried to remember our own initial forays into the subject and Professor Weir recalled his high school teaching days. Experts may be dismayed to discover that cherished topics they've been researching for years are absent from this work. Our exclusion of topics is in no way a value judgment of their relative importance. Neither of us holds to elitist views of history that privilege some topics and individuals as more important than others. Our main criterion for choosing topics was simply the likelihood of a researcher to encounter it in the initial stages of a bigger project. We also endeavored to be as inclusive as possible on matters pertaining to race, gender, and ethnicity, but the fact is—and we decry it in numerous entries—the organized labor movement in the United States has been distressingly dominated by white males. Numerous entries on nonorganized labor made their way into the work as a way of partially addressing this imbalance.

Throughout the project, we remained cognizant that we were writing an encyclopedia. In that spirit, we opted to present general knowledge rather than specialized research, though we apologize in advance for what will seem to experts gross simplifications. We also opted, whenever possible, to avoid technical language, jargon, and arcane terminology. The staff at Greenwood continually reminded us that our target audience is a general one, and we tried our best to serve that readership. Those seeking to expand their understanding of American labor leaders not covered in these volumes are directed to another Greenwood publication, Gary Fink's superb *Biographical Dictionary of American*

Labor Leaders. We had to be very selective in choosing specific unions to include, but most labor unions past and present can be researched further on the World Wide Web, and several have outstanding Web sites that surpass any efforts on our part. The same is true for most of the events and terms we present. Good public, college, and university libraries are also filled with fine works from professional historians—many of whom we are proud to name as friends and colleagues—and we hope readers will consult them. Like all encyclopedias, this one is designed to make readers want to learn more. If it inspires novices to plumb depths we could not, our job will have been well done.

Robert E. Weir
Florence, Massachusetts

James P. Hanlan
Worcester, Massachusetts

Entry List

Film and Labor
Flynn, Elizabeth Gurley
Foran Act
Fordism
Foster, Frank Keyes
Foster, William Zebulon
Fraser, Douglas Andrew
Free Labor
Frey, John Phillip
Fringe Benefits

Gastonia Strike
General Agreement on Tariffs and Trade (GATT)
General Motors Sit-Down Strike
General Strike
George, Henry
Glass Ceiling
Globalization
Goldman, Emma
Gompers, Samuel
Goon
Granite Workers
Grape Boycott
Great Labor Uprising
Great Upheaval
Green, William
Greenbackism
Grievance
Guaranteed Annual Wage

Haymarket Bombing
Haywood, William Dudley
Highlander Folk School
Hill, Joe
Hillman, Sidney
Hitchman Coal and Coke Company v. Mitchell
Hoffa, James Riddle
Homestead Steel Strike
Homework
Hormel Strike and Lockout
Hotel Employees and Restaurant Employees International Union (HERE)
Huerta, Delores
Hutcheson, William Levi

Incentive Pay
Indentured Servant
Industrial Unionism
Industrial Workers of the World (IWW)
International Association of Machinists and Aerospace Workers (IAM)
International Brotherhood of Papermakers
International Brotherhood of Teamsters
International Ladies' Garment Workers' Union (ILGWU)
International Union
International Union of Electrical, Radio, and Machine Workers of America (IUE)
International Union of Mine, Mill, and Smelter Workers
Iron Molders' Union

Jim Crow
Joint Agreement
Jones, Mary Harris "Mother"
Journeyman
Jurisdiction

Knights of Labor (KOL)
Knights of St. Crispin (KOSC)

Labor Day
Labor Fakir
Labor Journalism
Labor-Management Reporting and Disclosure Act (Landrum-Griffin Act)
Labor Parties
Labor Theory of Value
La Follette Committee
La Follette Seamen's Act
Lassalleanism
Lattimer Massacre
Lawrence Textile Strike

Lewis, John Llewellyn

Lien Laws

Little Steel Formula

Lockout

Loewe v. Lawlor

Longevity Pay

Lordstown Strike

Los Angeles Times Bombing

Ludlow Massacre

Luther, Seth

Maintenance of Membership

Major League Baseball Players Association (MLBPA)

Maquiladora

Master Agreement

Master Craftsman

Matewan

May Day

McGuire, Peter James

McKee's Rock

McNeill, George Edwin

Meany, George

Mechanics Educational Society of America (MESA)

Memorial Strike

Merit Raise

Minimum Wage

Minority Labor

Mitchell, John

Molly Maguires

Mr. Block

Mullaney, Kate

Muller v. Oregon

Murray Hill Agreement

Murray, Philip

Music and Labor

Muste, Abraham Lincoln

National Agreement

National Association of Manufacturers (NAM)

National Civic Federation

National Educational Association (NEA)

National Industrial Recovery Act (NIRA)

National Labor Relations Act (NLRA)

National Labor Relations Board v. Jones and Laughlin Steel Corporation

National Labor Relations Board v. Yeshiva University

National Labor Union (NLU)

National Trades' Union (NTU)

National Union of Hospital and Health Care Employees Local 1199

National War Labor Boards: World War I and World War II

Newspaper Guild

New York City Teachers Strike

New York City Textile Strikes, 1909–10

9 to 5: National Association of Working Women

Non-Wage Labor

Norris-LaGuardia Act

North American Free Trade Agreement (NAFTA)

No-Strike Pledge

Nussbaum, Karen

Occupational Safety and Health Act (1970)

Oil, Chemical, and Atomic Workers Union (OCAW)

One Big Union (OBU)

Open Shop

Operation Dixie

O'Reilly, Leonora

O'Sullivan, Mary Kenney

Overtime

Owen, Robert Dale

Part-Time Labor

Paternalism

Paterson Silk Strike

Pattern Bargaining

Pensions

Perkins, Frances Corlie

P

Part-Time Labor. Part-time labor is, according to the **Bureau of Labor Statistics**, any job in which an employee works fewer than thirty-five hours per week. Part-time work has been a feature of American labor from Colonial times, but it has taken on new urgency in recent years. As many as 25 percent of all jobs are now part-time, with critics charging that this trend impoverishes workers while enriching companies that could afford to hire workers on a full-time basis. Part-time jobs usually pay less than full-time jobs; benefits are often prorated or nonexistent.

Critics and defenders of contemporary hiring practices agree that as many as 80 percent of all part-time workers choose their status. Students, retirees, parents seeking flexible hours, and those making lifestyle choices make up the bulk of part-time workers. Their numbers are highest in the retail, food, and service industries, where over 30 percent of the workforce is part-time. They are also found in large numbers in manufacturing (18.7 percent) and farming (19 percent). Increasing numbers are also found in higher education; at some colleges and universities, more than half of all courses are taught by graduate students or adjunct faculty. Most part-time workers are younger than twenty-four or older than fifty-five. In 1998, 36.5 percent of women worked part-time, as did 21.2 percent of men.

Disagreements rage as to whether involuntary part-timers constitute a social problem. The Employment Policy Foundation claims that the percentage of involuntary part-time workers has remained around 18 percent of the total workforce since the 1970s, and that only one-fifth of these workers remain unwilling part-timers for more than a year. Feminists point to the gender discrepancies of part-time work and note that women are more likely to head single-parent households. Their critique has gained potency due to recent welfare reforms that require part-time "workfare" as a precondition for drawing benefits. Social reformers point to educational inequities; the less education a worker has, the more likely he or she is to be an involuntary part-time worker.

Unions note that full-time workers averaged $15.77 per hour in 1997, while part-timers earned only $8.89. In addition, many employers use part-time work as a way to avoid paying health care and other benefits. Unions also charge that part-time work is often used to discourage unionization; about 6.8 percent of part-time workers belong to unions, as opposed to nearly 15 percent of full-time employees.

Suggested Readings: Kathleen Barker and Kathleen Christensen, eds., *Contingent Work: American Employment Relations in Transition*, 1998; Employment Policy Foundation, "Part-Time Work: Not a Problem Requiring a Solution," http://www.epf.org/polpartwork.htm; "Share of Part-Time Workers by Industry."

Robert E. Weir

Paternalism. Paternalism is the principle or practice of administration in a fatherly manner. It can refer to the claim or attempt to provide, protect, and control a community as a father would his children. The *Chicago Times* coined the term in 1881 from the root *paternal* and applied it to industrial enterprises. Historians have applied the term to industries during the antebellum period as one dimension of the social relations of production, as well as to later businesses. The New England textile mill communities of Samuel Slater and the Lowell model provide two distinct examples. Slater built entire communities that included churches, shops, schools, and all other necessities for families in an attempt to obtain, retain, and control his workforce. The owners of the Lowell mills provided supervised dormitory accommodation for their largely female workforce, maintained strict moral codes of behavior, and provided what the mill owners deemed to be suitable recreational activities. Other forms of paternalism are found in industrial communities, but all retain the basic principles of provision and control.

One aspect of the paternalistic practices of some nineteenth-century industries was the issuing of scrip, a privately printed form of "currency" that was redeemable only at the company store. Workers paid in scrip had no alternative but to purchase their necessities at company prices. © Bettmann/Corbis.

Theoretically, paternalism has also been applied to the southern slave communities, whereby a master provided all the physical needs for his slaves and regulated their behavior, as a father might his children. In the late nineteenth and into the early twentieth century, paternalism became less formal and took the form of a master-worker relationship. Employers might provide steady work, education for workers' children, and deflect immoral influences such as alcohol in exchange for workers' loyalty, certain levels of conduct on the shop floor, and employees' surrender to factory routines. During the first half of the twentieth century, paternalism evolved into corporate welfare schemes that were created to address labor-relations problems and that were characterized by new technology and routines within a more humane workplace. Thus, paternalism provided a distinct alternative to individualistic factory **capitalism**, despite the many forms it adopted over time in the various regions of America.

Suggested Readings: L. J. Alston and J. P. Ferrie, *Southern Paternalism and the American Welfare State: Economics, Politics, and Institutions in the South, 1865–1965*, 1998; Eugene Genovese, *Roll Jordan Roll: The World the Slaves Made*, 1972; Phillip Scranton, "Varieties of Paternalism: Industrial Structures and the Social Relations of Production in American Textiles," in *American Quarterly* 36, no. 2 (1984): 235–57.

Janet Greenlees

Paterson Silk Strike. The Paterson, New Jersey, silk mill strike began in January 1913, when the city's largest company, Doherty and Company, increased employee workloads by demanding each laborer tend four looms instead of two. This **stretch-out** meant faster, harder work. When Doherty fired members of a **grievance** committee seeking redress, 800 silk workers walked out. Strikers appealed to the **Industrial Workers of the World (IWW)** for help, and, flush with success from the **Lawrence textile strike**, the IWW sent organizers to Paterson. The IWW extended the **strike** to all of the city's 300 silk mills and virtually its entire workforce of 25,000 laborers, nearly a third of whom were Polish Jews.

Standing between two large American flags, Ann Burlak, secretary of the Textile Workers' Union, is shown addressing the large crowd of Silk Mill strikers, October 21st. © Bettmann/Corbis.

Using tactics honed in Lawrence, Massachusetts, the IWW set up soup kitchens and nationality committees, and organized mass rallies. Leaders like **William Haywood**, Patrick Quinlan, and **Carlo Tresca** took part in the strike, and **Elizabeth Gurley Flynn** organized women workers. Unlike Lawrence, however, Paterson officials avoided public-relations debacles whilst engaging in a brutal crackdown against strikers. Several strikers died, over 4,800 workers were arrested, and some 1,300 were jailed, including Flynn, Haywood, Quinlan, and Tresca. The opposition of the **American Federation of Labor**'s United Textile Workers union, which tried to **raid** IWW members and undermined its efforts, aided company efforts. In attempt to rally flagging support, journalist John Reed organized a strike pageant of over a thousand workers. The pageant was an artistic triumph but an economic boondoggle, despite selling out Madison Square Garden and attracting financial support from bohemian Greenwich Village socialites.

After a bitter twenty-two-week battle, oppression, hunger, and deprivation forced strikers to surrender and accept prestrike conditions. Paterson was the first of a series of post-Lawrence IWW setbacks in eastern industrial cities. Some of the events of Paterson in 1913 were dramatized in the 1981 film *Reds*, directed by and starring Warren Beatty.

Suggested Readings: Melvyn Dubofsky, *We Shall Be All*, 1969; David Goldberg, *A Tale of Three Cities*, 1989); Anne Trip, *The IWW and the Paterson Silk Strike of 1913*, 1987.

Don Binkowski

Pattern Bargaining. Pattern bargaining is the negotiation of a **contract** based on what has already happened to similarly situated firms in an industry and/or region. It is most often associated with the attempt to take **wages** out of competition in a particular field by examining other comparable contracts. The settlement of the first contract in the industry sets the terms for others to follow. Although the relationship between the companies is not formal, a trend becomes established due to the previous conduct of the parties. While pattern bargaining may eliminate some individual choice for businesses and unions, it does offer some advantages. Companies in highly regulated or monopolistic industries tend to like pattern bargaining because it stabilizes their workforce. If everyone is paying the same wage, they will be better able to retain their workforce, since the market has been set for workers' wages and they cannot go somewhere else for better remuneration. If all companies are paying the same compensation, then the firm with the best management or product will be the strongest.

Unions also favor pattern bargaining as it dissuades management from using regional wage differentials to undercut what all workers get paid. In addition, it mediates against rogue employers who pay substandard wages and thus unfairly compete against firms that employ union workers. The problem with this from a membership standpoint is that a local union may be unwilling to negotiate a better contract than the other locals for fear that it will cause disruption in the **international union**. An example occurred when the Canadian branch of the **United Auto Workers (UAW)** disaffiliated from the parent group in 1984 and created the Canadian Auto Workers when the UAW accepted a **profit sharing** plan that was not acceptable to the Canadian workers.

While pattern bargaining can work from the viewpoint of either side, it is most commonly sought by unions. The **International Brotherhood of Team-**

sters was quite successful in establishing pattern bargaining in the 1950s and 1960s. **Deregulation** of the trucking industry dealt a blow to Teamster pattern bargaining. In like fashion, many other unions lost pattern bargaining leverage with the onset of **globalization** in the 1970s. Wages in most industries have been put back into competition, making pattern bargaining difficult to achieve.

Suggested Readings: John W. Budd, "The Internal Union Political Imperative for UAW Pattern Bargaining," in *Journal of Labor Research,* Vol. 16: 1 (Winter 1995); Gary Samuels, "Bargaining in Detroit: One Size No Longer Fits All," in *Business Week* 30 (September 1996).

Joseph F. Rodgers

Pensions. Pensions are private plans, primarily employer-sponsored, intended to supplement the Social Security benefits a person receives upon retiring. They have come to be an extension of the government's minimalist approach in Social Security legislation. An employer makes the payments, usually a fixed amount, to retirees or their beneficiaries in consideration for the worker's years of service to the company. Normally the employee is entitled to collect these payments upon reaching a certain age, after working a number of years for the same employer, or a combination of both. The formula used to derive the compensation generally takes into consideration the years of service and the employee's previous compensation. There are several types of qualified pension plans that are allowed under the law, with a general restriction that the formulas cannot discriminate in favor of management.

The American Express Company established the first private pension plan in 1875. Five years later, the Baltimore and Ohio Railroad set up a plan; by 1930, some 400 pension plans were in place. Unions were often ambivalent about employer-managed pensions, with many voicing concern that they were little more than forms of **paternalism**. Labor organizations often offered their own pension plans; several railroad brotherhoods had modest plans in effect by the early twentieth century. Most unions embraced the 1935 Social Security Act, but soon realized that Social Security provided inadequate retirement benefits. In 1946, the **United Mine Workers of America (UMWA)** succeeded in negotiating the first employer-financed pension program that was jointly administered by employers and the UMWA. In 1948, the National Labor Relations Board ruled that unions could negotiate pensions in the **collective bargaining** process. That right was confirmed by the Supreme Court in the 1949 decision *Inland Steel v. the National Labor Relations Board.* Since then, pensions have become a standard negotiating item. Recent controversy centers on the rights of employers to move pension funds into other accounts, shifts that employees claim threaten the solvency of pension systems.

Suggested Readings: Everett Allen, *Pension Planning: Pensions, Profit Sharing, and Other Defined Compensation Plans,* 7th ed., 1992; Jay Conison, *Employment Benefit Plans in a Nutshell,* 1998.

Joseph F. Rodgers

Perkins, Frances Corlie (April 10, 1880–May 14, 1965). Frances Perkins was a reformer and the first female cabinet officer. Perkins was born in Boston, the only daughter of Frederick W. and Susan (Bean) Perkins. The family moved to Worcester, where Perkins attended Worcester Classical High before going on to Mount Holyoke College, where in 1902 she received a bachelor of arts in chemistry and physics.

A speech by Florence Kelly of the National Consumer's League (NCL) inspired Perkins toward social service. She taught at several New England girls' schools from 1902 through 1904, and then at Ferry Hall in Chicago from 1904 through 1907. While in Chicago, Perkins also worked for both Hull House and Chicago Commons, which were settlement houses. She then moved to Philadelphia, where she became the executive secretary of the city's Research and Protective Association, a social agency aimed at protecting immigrant women and recent African American arrivals from the South. She also studied economics and sociology at the Wharton School of Finance and won a Russell Sage Foundation fellowship that took her to the New York School of Philanthropy in 1909. She obtained her master of arts from Columbia, her thesis dealing with malnutrition among slum children.

In 1910, Perkins became NCL executive secretary and was mentored by Kelly. Perkins investigated safety and health conditions in **sweatshops** and bakeries and was profoundly affected by the **Triangle Factory Fire of 1911**. The tragedy led to the creation of the New York State Investigating Commission, for which Perkins served as executive secretary from 1912 through 1917. On September 26, 1913, Perkins married economist Paul C. Wilson; in 1916, the couple had a daughter, Suzanne.

Perkins's activities drew the attention of New York Governor Al Smith, whom Perkins advised on progressive factory legislation. Smith's successor, Franklin Delano Roosevelt, appointed her state industrial commissioner in 1929. When Roosevelt was elected president in 1932, he asked Perkins to serve as his secretary of labor, the first woman to hold a cabinet post. She advised the president during a chaotic period for organized labor that saw such events as the **sit-down strikes**, the birth of the **Congress of Industrial Organizations**, and the passage of the **National Labor Relations Act**. She was also instrumental in incorporating into the **Department of Labor** key New Deal programs like the Civilian Conservation Corps, the Civil Works Administration, **the Federal Emergency Relief Administration**, and the Public Works Administration. Perkins was at the forefront of advising Roosevelt on issues like the **minimum wage**, **child labor**, and public-works projects. She also reorganized both the Bureau of Immigration and the **Bureau of Labor Statistics**. Perkins pushed Roosevelt to sign both the Social Security Act of 1935 and the **Fair Labor Standards Act** of 1938.

During World War II, Perkins oversaw the Department of Labor's efforts to shift the economy from domestic to military production. She also thwarted FBI director J. Edgar Hoover's plan to keep dossiers on all American citizens.

Perkins resigned her post when Roosevelt died in 1945, but President Truman appointed her to the Social Security Commission in 1946, and asked her to attend the International Labor Organization's founding meeting in Paris. She also found time to pen *The Roosevelt I Knew*, a memoir of her service with the deceased president.

Perkins retired from government service in 1952, the same year her husband died. She taught at the University of Illinois until 1954, when she joined the industrial and labor relations faculty at Cornell. At the time of her death, she was working on a biography of Al Smith, which became the basis for a book by historians Hannah and Matthew Josephson.

Suggested Readings: George Martin, *Madame Secretary*, 1976; Lillian H. Mohr, *Frances Perkins*, 1979; Frances Perkins, *The Roosevelt I Knew*, 1946.

Robert E. Weir

Permit Cards. Permit cards establish a procedure whereby a union member can pre-pay **dues** and travel to a new area where another branch or local of their **international union** has **jurisdiction**. Presentation of one's card gains access to union hiring halls. The practice began in the late 1800s when union activists and strikers often found themselves on a blacklist that prevented them from obtaining local employment. Permit cards allowed blacklisted workers to relocate. Some unions, notably the **International Association of Machinists**, even gave card carriers shelter and meal money. Workers were expected to reimburse the union, and the names of deadbeats were published in union journals.

Albert V. Lannon

Pesotta, Rose (November 20, 1896–December 7, 1965). Rose Pesotta was an important activist in the **International Ladies' Garment Workers' Union (ILGWU)**. Her career illustrates both the militancy of Jewish women in organized labor and the problems encountered by **minority labor** within unions. Pesotta was born in Derazhyna, Ukraine (Russia), the daughter of grain dealers. She became an anarchist in her teens, and she fled Russia when she was sixteen to avoid an arranged marriage. She emigrated to New York City in 1913 and moved in with her older sister, Esther. Like many Jewish women, she found employment in the city's clothing industry and took a job sewing in a shirtwaist factory.

Despite a so-called protocol of peace negotiated between major employers and the ILGWU in 1911, industrial relations remained tense, with many employees remembering the **Uprising of the 20,000 (1909)**, smaller strikes in 1910, and the tragic **Triangle Factory Fire of 1911**. Pesotta joined a heavily Yiddish ILGWU local and quickly rose through the ranks, despite her involvement with the **anarchist** and free-love movements and her outspoken opposition to World War I. In 1920, she was elected to the ILGWU's executive board and also served as a national organizer. She was also active in the unsuccessful clemency campaign for **Sacco and Vanzetti**. The ILGWU sent Pesotta to Los

Angeles in the late 1920s, where she enjoyed success in bringing Latina members into the union. In 1933, new ILGWU president David Dubinsky promoted Pesotta to one of the union's vice presidencies, and he encouraged her work in Los Angeles.

Pesotta helped some 7,500 women spread among more than 200 **sweatshops** develop a Spanish/English bilingual newspaper and assisted them in a 1933 cloakmakers' strike that saw men break ranks and return to work. The fiery Pesotta used creative tactics to maintain **solidarity** among the women, including broadcasting strike messages from Mexico when a local station refused to air updates and holding a mock fashion show on a **picket** line outside a Los Angeles hotel where new spring fashions were being unveiled. Her tactics helped the women win a **contract** despite a lack of support from male cloakmakers.

From 1934 through 1942, Pesotta traveled across the continental United States, Puerto Rico, and Canada organizing women garment workers. Despite her successes, she was not comfortable inside the ILGWU, largely because of her political and personal views. She complained of sexism within the union, a charge made manifest by the fact that she was the sole woman officer for an organization whose membership was 85 percent female. Moreover, her advocacy of anarchism and free love made Dubinsky nervous, especially given his desire to purge the union of **communists** and other radicals.

In 1942, Pesotta helped Los Angeles workers win a contract against several important dress retailers, but her tactics and abrasive personality led to clashes with the ILGWU's male West Coast director, Louis Levy. When Dubinsky sided with Levy and removed Pesotta from the very local she founded, she abruptly resigned her ILGWU vice presidency and returned to work as a sewing-machine operator. In 1944, she also resigned from the ILGWU executive board. Although she continued to take part in some local activities, Pesotta's career within the ILGWU was over. After World War II, Pesotta toured Europe and took up the cause of refugees. The experience also enhanced Pesotta's Jewish identity. She won some acclaim for two autobiographical books, *Bread Upon the Waters* (1944), which recounted her union organizing efforts, and *Days of Our Lives* (1958), the story of her Ukranian childhood.

Pesotta's difficulties within the ILGWU underscored the sexism of much of the organized labor movement, an issue not fully addressed until feminists challenged unions in the 1960s and 1970s. Pesotta died in Miami in 1965, having retired from the dressmaker profession several years earlier.

Suggested Readings: Naomi Shepherd, *A Price Below Rubies: Jewish Women as Rebels and Radicals*, 1993; Ann Schofield, *"To Do & Be": Portraits of Four Women Activists, 1893-1986*, 1997; Elaine Leeder, *Gentle General: Rose Pesotta, Anarchist and Labor Leader*, 1993.

Bruce Cohen
James P. Hanlan

Phelps Dodge Strike. The Phelps Dodge strike was a brutal struggle against copper interests in Arizona during 1983 and 1984 that ended in a complete rout of over 2,000 strikers and the thirty local unions that represented them. The Phelps Dodge **strike** is viewed by many as one of the worst **downsizing**, **decertification**, and **concessions** strikes of the 1980s. Evidence suggests that the Phelps Dodge Corporation's intent from the start was to break its unions. The strike had a devastating effect on heavily Hispanic communities like Ajo, Clifton, and Morenci, Arizona.

Long before the 1983 strike, the Phelps Dodge Corporation was infamous for poor labor relations. In 1903, the company rounded up and deported Mexican activists attempting to unionize, and in 1917 a company-sponsored vigilante committee in Bisbee, Arizona, herded members of the **Industrial Workers of the World** into unventilated railroad boxcars and transported them to the desert. In 1941, the company was forced to rehire thirty-five members of the **International Union of Mine, Mill, and Smelter Workers (IUMMSW)** after Justice Felix Frankfurter blasted Phelps Dodge's union-busting record in his Supreme Court brief of *Phelps Dodge v. National Labor Relations Board*. Conditions remained tense, and in 1953 a strike broke out among largely Hispanic miners. It was immortalized in the documentary *Salt of the Earth*, a classic labor movie. The IUMMSW also had to endure red-baiting, as it contained communist members objectionable to both the company and the **Congress of Industrial Organizations**.

The IUMMSW was eventually forced to purge extreme left influences. In 1967, its remnants merged with the **United Steel Workers of America** (USWA), which became the dominant union in the copper fields. Copper production was booming by 1970, and the USWA negotiated **pattern bargaining** agreements with most producers in the Southwest. Phelps Dodge was forced into pattern bargaining by a USWA-led strike in 1967. The next year, the company began relations with the University of Pennsylvania's Wharton School of Business, which was in the process of developing strategies for businesses wishing to break unions. (Today, the Wharton School's methods are considered the definitive way to defeat unions.)

Pattern bargaining held at Phelps Dodge into 1983, and the USWA and other unions had raised **wages** to an average of $12 per hour. Although copper-field wages were slightly below that of many other miners, a key element was the existence of provisions that granted periodic **cost-of-living adjustments (COLA)**. Company officials complained that high wages and COLAs made the firm uncompetitive against imported copper. It demanded concessions from various unions, including the right to pay new hires lower starting wages. When the **contract** with Phelps Dodge expired on June 30, 1983, and no progress emerged in negotiations, Phelps Dodge workers authorized a strike. The two locales most affected were the adjacent towns of Morenci and Clifton, the former a virtual **company town**, and the latter a union stronghold with a heavily Hispanic population.

It soon became apparent that Phelps Dodge intended to break the unions. It pulled out of pattern bargaining agreements with other producers, won injunctions to limit the number of **pickets**, threatened union workers, and began to recruit **scabs**. The company even tried to get courts to ban the word scab, though they were rebuffed in that effort. It did, however, take full advantage of the current political climate. In the wake of the Reagan administration's firing of **Professional Air Traffic Controllers Organization (PATCO)** workers, unions found themselves on the defensive. Court rulings that allowed firms to hire **replacement workers** during economic strikes gave Phelps Dodge the opening it wanted. Arizona's **right-to-work** laws allowed the firm to replenish its workforce quickly.

During the months that ensued, Phelps Dodge resorted to brutality seldom seen since the 1930s. Labor spies infiltrated union locals, and company **goons** precipitated violent clashes with strikers. That violence, in turn, was used to convince Arizona's Democratic Governor Bruce Babbitt to call in the National Guard on August 19, 1983. The Guard was also involved in violence, and several communities were transformed into armed camps, with tanks, helicopters, and camouflaged troops patrolling company property and town streets. Phelps Dodge also exerted influence on the media's reportage of the strike. All attempts at mediation were dismissed by company officials. It also played off ethnic and religious tensions by hiring mostly Protestant Anglos to take the places of Catholic Hispanics.

The affected towns suffered tremendously. Some strikers broke ranks and returned to work, raising tensions considerably. The Morenci Miners Women's Auxiliary set up food banks, day-care centers, clinics, and other community services, but faced inadequate capital and supplies. The women did, however, demonstrate more militancy than many of the men. They constantly harassed scabs, confronted police and guardsmen, and pressured local merchants and doctors to aid strikers. The unions seemed powerless to offer much more, however, and some strikers complained that leadership was out of touch. The USWA did bring in consultant Ray Rogers to launch a **corporate campaign** against Phelps Dodge. An attempt to pressure Manufacturers Hanover Investment Company—which dealt with Phelps Dodge and held union **pension** funds—yielded only minor results. Singer Bruce Springsteen donated $10,000 to strikers, but deprivation raged.

In the end, Babbitt's decision to use the National Guard doomed the strike. With strikers unable to disrupt production, there was little incentive for Phelps Dodge to negotiate. Unions filed several **unfair labor practices**, but given that the regional director of the National Labor Relations Board (NLRB), Milo Price, had once clashed with unions, they stood little chance of succeeding. For all intents and purposes, the strike was broken by September 1983. Production continued despite ongoing protests, and Phelps Dodge put into place all of its demands, including a two-tier wage system and an end to COLAs. Price called an October 9, 1984, union **decertification** vote. Strikers could not cast ballots, and the replacement workers voted out all thirty unions. Price announced the official results on January 24, 1985, and appeals lingered until February 19,

1986. As expected, the NLRB ruled against the unions, officially ending the strike.

One study calculated that Phelps Dodge invested about $92,000 per replacement worker rather than negotiate with union workers earning roughly $26,000 annually. The firm lost money during 1983, but copper prices quickly rebounded, and it began to post large profits. In 1988, it paid workers an $8,000 **bonus**, after posting a profit of over $420 million. The company could not buy goodwill, however, and it did not remain union-free. The USWA rebuilt some of its base, as did the International Brotherhood of Electrical Workers and the Office and Professional Employees International Union. In 1996, unionized workers in Chico, New Mexico, found themselves without a contract. Having learned a lesson in 1983, workers stayed on the job while their unions applied pressure through community groups, filed NLRB complaints, and exposed company environmental violations that stood to cost it tens of millions in fines. Phelps Dodge again tried to play hardball, threatening to lay off over 300 workers, but in the end was forced to capitulate. On November 19, 1998, the company signed a four-year contract with several unions.

The Phelps Dodge strike stands as a testament to corporate arrogance and to the unequal power relationship between capital and labor in the 1980s and beyond. Some observers draw more conclusions. The actions of Governor Babbitt led some to argue that labor's historic alliance with the Democratic Party is unwise. (President Clinton appointed Babbitt secretary of interior in 1993, further angering activists.) Moreover, NLRB actions suggest that the board has become a tool of partisan politics rather than industrial peace. Critics of **deregulation** see the Phelps Dodge struggle as emblematic of the abuse potential of laissez-faire economic policies. Still others argue that labor laws are tilted too far in favor of the business community. Optimists view strikes in the 1980s as a wake-up call for organized labor that showed a new generation needs to evolve new tactics. However one wishes to interpret it, the 1983–84 events devastated several small Arizona communities in ways that will take several more decades to repair.

Suggested Readings: Barbara Kingsolver, *Holding the Line: Women in the Great Arizona Mine Strike of 1983*, 1989; Jonathan Rosenblum, *Copper Crucible: How the Arizona Miners' Strike of 1983 Recast Labor-Management Relations in America*, 1996.

Robert E. Weir

Philadelphia Carpenters' Strike (1791). In one of the earliest **strikes** in the building industry, **journeymen** carpenters organized the first strike for a ten-hour workday in 1791. Following the American Revolution, wageworkers began to exercise independence in employment decisions. They became mobile and, in some instances, opened their own businesses in new locations. The pressures to earn a suitable living and find skilled and able laborers had already compelled masters to consolidate their efforts to control their trade. Philadelphia's master carpenters formed the Carpenters' Company in 1724 and created a book of prices to regulate their income and journeymen's **wages**. In 1786, masters drafted a new rule book, changing the measuring system that determined a journeyman's wage. It became practice to pay journeymen by the day instead of by the piece.

By the 1790s, journeymen carpenters who were concerned about meeting the cost and improving the quality of living formed a temporary union to confront what they perceived to be exploitation. Though they were disgruntled over their wages, the major issue of the strike was the length of the workday. Their chief complaint was that they were made to "toil through the whole course of the longest summer's day" without having their "labour sweetened by the reviving hope of an immediate reward." The journeymen resolved that a day's work should "commence at six o'clock in the morning, and terminate, at six in the evening of each day." This included two hours for meals and compensation for **overtime**. Master carpenters argued that the strikers' complaints were unfounded, when in fact they shrewdly paid journeymen carpenters by piece wage during the shorter days of the winter months, and a flat wage during the longer summer days. Furthermore, since journeymen were denied access to their employers' rulebook, they could not estimate the value of their work. Recognizing the inequities of this arrangement, they demanded a standard workday regardless of the season. By specifying the hours they would spend at their occupation, workers were defining the limits an employer could place on their time. Unlike slaves or indentured servants, who were coerced into working whatever hours a master determined, wageworkers sequestered time for personal pursuits. In this way, they were asserting personal liberties and establishing a basis for the equality of all free citizens. Nevertheless, master carpenters did not acquiesce to the strikers' demands and depicted journeymen as lazy agitators and themselves as victims of an insecure trade. The journeymen lost the strike, but did not abandon the issue. From this point forward, the carpenters saw the expediency of establishing permanent labor organizations to address their needs. In 1827, Philadelphia's journeymen carpenters joined with other trade unions to form the Mechanics' Union of

A membership certificate of the New York Mechanick Society dated 1791, the same year as the Philadelphia Carpenter's Strike. © George Meany Memorial Archives.

Trade Associations. This citywide coalition of workers raised the ten-hour issue again in the 1820s and 1830s, and in 1835 they won the ten-hour strike plus increased wages for **piecework**. Thus, while the journeymen carpenters lost the 10-hour strike of 1791, they set in motion a chain of events that forever altered the relationship between laborers and employers. American workers began to distance themselves from a **paternalistic** system in which an employer controlled almost every aspect of a worker's life. Although the needs of a worker and his family were cared for, the system sustained a social hierarchy that prohibited upward mobility and stifled political equality. Because of the democratizing philosophies of the Revolution, workers no longer accepted the idea that employers were their natural superiors. Workers began to confront exploitation in the workplace and diligently press issues that would secure political equality and personal autonomy. In just a few years, Philadelphia's carpenters and other workers would establish a centralized, politically vital labor organization that ushered in the era of the modern labor movement.

Suggested Readings: David Brody, *In Labor's Cause: Main Themes on the History of the American Worker*, 1993; Philip S. Foner, *History of the Labor Movement in The United States, vol. 1: From Colonial Times to the Founding of the American Federation of Labor*, 1962; Sharon V. Salinger, "Artisans, Journeymen, and the Transformation of Labor in Late Eighteenth-Century Philadelphia," in *William and Mary Quarterly*, vol. 3 (January 1983): 62–84.

Dinah Mayo

Philadelphia Shoemakers' Strike (1805). The first case of an organized labor **strike** in the United States involved the **Federal Society of Journeymen Cordwainers** (shoemakers) of Philadelphia. Philadelphia's journeyman shoemakers began to organize as early as 1792 and formed the Federal Society of Journeymen Cordwainers (FSJC) in 1794. In 1805, the society organized a strike to protest low **wages**. Consequently, in 1806, George Pullis, head of the journeymen's society, along with seven others, was charged with conspiracy (*Commonwealth v. Pullis*). The cordwainers' trial was one of the first labor conspiracy trials in the United States. The strike and conspiracy trial revealed Americans' emerging notions of equality and independence, which encompassed both personal and political freedom as well as the right to govern the conditions of their labor. It also addressed the political contention over the place of British common law in the United States.

Before the eighteenth century, wages and prices were established through the English government by statute or ordinance. Often, workers' wages were decided by justices of the peace or local magistrates who consulted with prominent members of a craft. By the 1760s, revolutionary rhetoric encouraged master cordwainers to form an organization to control the trade. They established prices for their products, payment for themselves, and the wages of **journeymen**. Soon, the same notions of independence that motivated master cordwainers to organize also compelled journeymen to take control of their labor. By attempting to establish the value of their labor, the strikers were rejecting a social hierarchy that had dominated every phase of their lives. After the Revolution, the United States became a major exporter of shoes, exporting close to 50,000 pairs in the late 1790s. The earnings of master cordwainers rose and remained high throughout the decade, but the wages of journeyman cordwainers did not. Journeymen earned approximately £117 annually, while the yearly cost of living was £120. Thus, their income did not meet the cost of living. When master cordwainers attempted to reduce journeymen's wages during the slow winter months of 1805, the journeymen's frustrations led to a strike. In return, master artisans brought charges of conspiracy against the journeymen.

The conspiracy trial raised questions concerning the new nation's recognition of, and adherence to, English common law. In the eighteenth century, conspiracy, as defined in English law, prohibited workers from acting collectively, and although the range of offenses was not restricted to labor, it was interpreted to include restraint of trade. Thus, the FSJC itself was in defiance of common law, and their strike strengthened the claims against the union. The court found the journeymen cordwainers guilty of "a combination to raise their wages." Although none of the strikers was sentenced to jail, the fines imposed, which were between $1 and $10, equaled as much as seven-days' wages. The FSJC did not survive the strike, but workers continued to form labor organizations to address their concerns, monitor employer-employee relations, and stage strikes against unfair labor practices. The Philadelphia cordwainers' strike is significant for many reasons. The resulting trial tested the limits of individual freedom, the right of workers to organize, the role of the judicial system in labor disputes, and the contours of economic growth in the United States. While the conspiracy trial of 1806 was one of several involving American cordwainers, only in the Philadelphia trial would the court declare it illegal for workers to organize. Thus, issues raised over the rights of American workers probed the nation's commitment to equality and, by making demands of their employers, the cordwainers expanded the precincts of democracy into the workplace. Finally, although employers continued to charge striking workers with conspiracy as late as the twentieth century, the Philadelphia cordwainers' strike signaled the beginning of laborers' willingness to flout tradition, challenge social hierarchies, and exercise the prerogative to organize and strike for fair wages and acceptable working conditions.

Suggested Readings: John R. Commons, et al. *History of Labour in The United States*, 1961; E.E. Cummins, *The Labor Problem in The United States*, 1932; Billy G. Smith, *The Lower Sort: Philadelphia's Laboring People, 1750–1801*, 1990; Christopher L. Tomlins and Andrew J. King, eds. *Labor Law in America: Historical and Critical Essays*, 1992.

Dinah Mayo

Picketing. Picketing is a form of "speech" used by an individual or a group to publicize concerns by marching or protesting at a location where a perceived offense is being committed. Although characterized mostly by **strikes**, picketing can achieve social goals as well. Labor has long used picketing as a tool to publicize **grievances**, **contract** stalemates, or other issues affecting employer-employee relations. In these situations, workers try to exert pressure through peaceful means by informing the public about the controversies that exist in the workplace. The goal is to bring public pressure to bear and force employers to improve working conditions.

Section 7 of the **National Labor Relations Act** (NLRA) specifically protects the rights of striking workers to picket to gain public support, but this right does not extend to intimidating others, deliberately misinforming the public, or inflicting more economic harm on an employer than is necessary to achieve their goals. Although considered a form of free speech, a worker's right to picket is limited by the harm it may cause the public.

Chicago picketers in 1910. © George Meany Memorial Archives.

There are other forms of labor picketing that are not part of strikes or **lockouts**. Workers use informational picketing to educate the public about mutual concerns and place external pressure on employers. A union that attempts to get a company to recognize it as the representative of the workers is participating in organizational or recognition picketing. Prior to the enactment of the NLRA, this type of picketing was the only way most unions could achieve negotiations. It is illegal for a union to picket for recognition if there is already a certified union in place. Unions may also apply "force" to the struck employer by picketing businesses that have no direct dispute with the union, but whose relationship is important enough that the protest might encourage a third party to intercede. So-called secondary picketing was common in the nineteenth century, but is now legal only in a limited number of situations. Picketers may not enjoy job protection for such an activity, and thus unions tread very carefully in this contested legal terrain. It has proved useful in recent **corporate campaigns**.

Suggested Readings: Kenneth Jenero and Mark Spognardi, "Defending Against the Corporate Campaign; Selected Legal Responses to Common Union Tactics," in *Employee Relations Law Journal* 22 (Autumn 1996); Douglas Leslie, *Labor Law in a Nutshell*, 4th ed., 2000.

Joseph F. Rodgers

Piecework. Piecework—the practice of paying workers by the item produced, rather than by the hour or week—has been a familiar practice in many sectors of American manufacturing, although it is most commonly associated with the clothing industry. Other, more euphemistic terms for it include "working on commission" and "payment by results." Piecework has been favored by employers—and some employees—as a way of rewarding faster, more diligent workers, and has been allowed into some labor agreements. Over the course of the twentieth century, however, it has fallen out of favor among labor organizations on the basis that it leads to general **speedups** of work and decrease in pay. Piecework has been the subject of many significant labor disputes, especially in the garment trades from the 1890s through the 1930s. Even when this form of payment was generally accepted, the question of which side (or both) had the power to set piece rates was an ongoing struggle. In the clothing industry, piecework and piece rates were an especially lively issue, in part because changing fashions necessitated near-continuous renegotiations of piece rates. Efforts to make piecework less exploitative, and hence more acceptable, including the introduction of a base pay rate, were attempted during the early twentieth century with varying degrees of success. Piecework remained, and even increased in frequency, as a form of payment through the 1940s, and then went into decline in the 1950s.

Suggested Readings: International Labour Office. *Payment by Results*, 1984; Louis Levine, *The Women's Garment Workers: A History of the International Ladies' Garment Workers' Union*, 1924; Gus Tyler, *Look for the Union Label: A History of the International Ladies' Garment Workers' Union*, 1995.

Susan Roth Breitzer

Pink-Collar Workers. *See Blue-Collar Workers. See also Minority and Labor.*

Pinkertons. Pinkertons were agents employed by the Pinkerton Detective Agency, the most notorious of numerous private companies contracted by capital to sabotage the efforts of labor unions. The agency was founded by Scottish immigrant Allan Pinkerton in 1850 and is often considered the first modern American detective agency. Its earliest days were devoted to investigating counterfeit rings, train robberies, and outlaw gangs. Pinkerton detectives also proved effective spies for the Union cause during the American Civil War.

After railroad **strikes** associated with the **Great Labor Uprising** of 1877, and the passage of state laws giving corporations the power to hire private militias, the Pinkerton agency expanded its activities to include union-breaking. Between 1875 and 1877, Pinkerton spy James McParlan gave testimony at a series of trials that sent ten men to the gallows for allegedly belonging to the **Molly Maguires**. McParlan's exposure of this supposed Irish American terrorist group in Pennsylvania's anthracite coal region led to an increase in demand for Pinkerton services. Its industrial policies took two main forms: planting labor spies within unions to identify activists or expose their tactics, and providing private armies for employers engaging **scabs** or **locking-out** their employees.

Although other firms, including the Burns Detective Agency, also provided these services, the Pinkertons became synonymous with repression and corporate brutality in the minds of many workers. Groups like the **Knights of Labor** lobbied for the passage of laws to curtail the hiring of private industrial armies. The Pinkertons gained especial notoriety when they precipitated violence during the 1890 New York Central strike and when they engaged in shootouts with workers during the 1892 **Homestead Steel strike**, which left over a dozen people dead. It did not help the company's reputation that many of those it hired during labor disputes were little more than thugs. The firm's reputation was further tarnished when **William Haywood** and several associates were acquitted of murder charges stemming from the 1903–04 Colorado coal strikes when it was revealed that James McParlan blatantly lied and falsified evidence. (McParlan was so discredited that some historians have come to doubt his Molly Maguire revelations.)

The Pinkerton agency's role in industrial disputes began to diminish as a result of poor public relations, an outcry against private industrial armies, and the formation of federal agencies like the Federal Bureau of Investigation. The agency did provide information used to repress the **Industrial Workers of the World**, a campaign that employed future author Dashiell Hammett, but public outrage from the 1914 **Ludlow Massacre** eventually led to the passage of laws curtailing private armies, as did revelations from the 1937 La Follette Civil Liberties Committee. Many of the worst practices were expressly forbidden by the **National Labor Relations Act**.

The Pinkerton Detective Agency logo. © Library of Congress.

Although the Pinkertons and similar agencies engaged in many worthy law-enforcement activities, they stand for many as veritable symbols of the oppression of working people, and Pinkerton was a term that aroused hatred and fear among workers from roughly 1875 to 1940. The Pinkerton agency still exists, though its 47,000 employees are mainly engaged in building security, conducting employee background checks, providing personal-protection services, and investigating fraud. Both it and the Burns agency—once its chief rival—are wholly owned subsidiaries of the Swedish firm Securitas.

Suggested Readings: Alan Axelrod and Charles Phillip, *Cops and Crooks and Criminologists*, 2000; Wayne Broehl, *The Molly Maguires*, 1964; Leon Wolff, *Lockout: The Story of the Homestead Steel Strike of 1892*, 1965.

Robert E. Weir

Pittston Coal Strike. The Pittston Coal strike was a successful 10-month **strike** during 1989–90 led by the **United Mine Workers of America (UMWA)** against the nation's second-largest coal exporter. It was an important victory for organized labor, coming after nearly a decade of lost **downsizing**, **decertification**, and **concessions** strikes. To many analysts, it also suggested that labor unions should engage in militant actions and ignore labor laws tilted in favor of employers.

The strike began on April 5, 1989, and involved miners employed by the Pittston Coal Group in Virginia, West Virginia, and Kentucky. Workers had already labored without a **contract** for fourteen months. At the heart of the dispute were working conditions and benefits. Pittston sought to operate its mines around-the-clock, abolish the eight-hour day, and require Sunday work. One company official even claimed that workers feigned interest in church to avoid work. Matters came to a head when the company announced plans to eliminate medical benefits for more than 1,800 individuals, including widows, disabled miners, and those on **pensions**. Company arrogance led 1,700 miners to walk out on April 5. Eventually nearly 9,000 miners took part in the strike. Because the National Labor Relations Board (NLRB) ruled Pittston guilty of **unfair labor practices**, the company could not hire permanent **replacement workers**, though it did import more than a thousand **scabs**.

Aside from the initial NLRB ruling, most other official actions went in favor of the company. Virginia state police were used to escort scabs, and company property was patrolled by Vance Security, a firm specializing in antiunion activity. Numerous court rulings went against the UMWA, including injunctions limiting **picketing**. At one point, strikers attempted to bottleneck roads in and out of Pittston mines by driving slowly. Slow driving was ruled a violation of federal injunctions, and drivers were arrested; several spent up to ninety days in jail, and the UMWA was slapped with fines.

Strikers and the UMWA responded with a variety of tactics. Some militants tossed jackrocks (a welded assemblage of spikes designed to flatten tires) on the roads, while others pelted scabs with rocks. The UMWA did not sanction acts of violence, but was nonetheless fined. (A decision was made early in the strike to engage in acts of nonviolent civil disobedience.) When UMWA officials told a Virginia judge, Don McGlothin, Jr., that the strike was a "class war," he slapped more than $30 million in fines on the union. The UMWA responded with roving pickets and public demonstrations. It also briefly sanctioned **wildcat** and **sympathy strikes**, which broke out in eleven states and idled 46,000 miners, calling them **memorial strikes**. The UMWA quickly retreated from this and withdrew its official sanction, though it did little to discourage acts of **solidarity**. It did, however, authorize a **corporate campaign** against Pittston that picketed Shawmut Bank in Boston and led the Boston City Council to remove funds from the bank. (Shawmut later went out of business.)

Key to winning the strike was the remarkable level of unity sustained. A sympathetic council in New Jersey petitioned the **American Federation of Labor-Congress of Industrial Organizations (AFL-CIO)** to call a one-day sympathy strike by all AFL-CIO members. That request was turned down, but more than 30,000 supporters went to the UMWA's Camp Solidarity in Virginia between June and September 1989, including the Reverend Jesse Jackson. Jackson's presence symbolized the unity of black and white miners during the strike. Strikers also received assistance from the International Confederation of Free Trade Unions, which convinced Secretary of Labor Elizabeth Dole to visit Camp Solidarity. In an evocation of the 1937 **General Motors sit-down strike**, ninety-nine individuals illegally occupied Pittston's Moss Number 3 mill between September 17 and September 20. Miners and the UMWA ignored an NLRB order to vacate Moss and the $13.5 million fine it levied; occupiers left after seventy-seven hours on their own accord, defiantly waiting until an NLRB-imposed deadline had passed.

Also key to the strike was the role of women. Wives, daughters, and sympathizers of the mostly male strikers formed the Daughters of **Mother Jones** (DMJ) to offer support. Unlike women's auxiliaries in previous eras, the DMJ went well beyond support that extended traditional domestic roles to strikers. In addition to supplying food and child care, women also helped plan and participate in militant tactics. Many of them were among the more than 4,000 individuals arrested for acts of civil disobedience, and they played the central role in planning public demonstrations and taking charge of public relations. Several newspapers and television stations gave positive coverage of the strike, a rarity in the 1980s. Women also helped get out the vote. The UMWA rejoiced when one of its members upset twenty-two-year incumbent Don McGlothin, Sr.—father of the judge who fined the union—for a seat in the Virginia state legislature after only a three-week write-in campaign.

Pittston lost over $25 million in the last quarter of 1989, and it was clear the company was losing the strike as well. Secretary Dole appointed a federal mediator, and West Virginia Senator Jay Rockefeller introduced successful legislation to protect miner pensions. An agreement was hammered out on December 31, 1989, that gave Pittston the right to operate its mines twenty-four hours per day, but which did not allow the company to make miners work during daylight hours on Sundays. The UMWA also won preservation of health and pension benefits, and a guarantee that laid-off miners would be offered jobs when openings occurred in Pittston's nonunion mines. Most of the fines levied against the UMWA were lifted. UMWA officials like **Richard Trumka** received praise from many **rank-and-file** members for their willingness to use militant tactics. The rank and file insisted on several minor changes in the December settlement before ratifying a new contract on February 19, 1990. Three days later, miners returned to work.

The Pittston strike was an important symbolic, as well as actual, victory for organized labor. After years of antiunion activity sanctioned by the Reagan administration, victory during successor George H. W. Bush's tenure signaled the possibility of reversing the downward trend. Many came away from Pittston convinced that militancy led to success. Some activists openly advocated ignoring U.S. labor laws in favor of **direct action** at the point of production. Few AFL-CIO officials shared such sympathies, but **John Sweeney** did make renewed militancy a component of his successful bid for the AFL-CIO presidency. In 1995, documentary filmmaker Anne Lewis recounted the strike in *Justice in the Coalfields*. It has proved a popular film among union advocates.

The strike contained notes of irony. By 1995, only about one-third of the strikers still had union jobs. Technological change and a declining demand for coal led to layoffs in the Pittston Group. In December 1997, the UMWA reopened a contract with the Bituminous Coal Operators Association nine months early and signed a new five-year agreement with operators, which included Pittston. Militants protested the UMWA's agreement to work rules that allow workers to be scheduled two Saturdays out of every three, as well as a requirement that they must continue operating equipment until relieved by the incoming shift. Some complained that Trumka had become a **business unionist** and had quashed rank-and-file militancy. Overall, UMWA strength declined from around 120,000 in 1982 to about 40,000 in 1998.

Suggested Readings: Adrienne Birecree, "The Importance of Women's Participation in the 1989–90 Pittston Coal Strike," in *Journal of Economic Issues* 30:1 (March 1996): 187–211; Jeremy Brecher, "Resisting Concessions," http://www.zmag.org/ZMag/brechermay98.htm; James Green, *Taking History to Heart: The Power of Building Social Movements*, 2000.

Robert E. Weir

Popular Front. The Popular Front was a loose alliance of politically and socially minded activists, which was active between 1935 and 1949 and dedicated to aggressive organizing and the establishment of a social democratic America. Its support from organized labor was almost entirely restricted to unions associated with the **Congress of Industrial Organizations (CIO)**. The Popular Front included relatively moderate voices, like CIO President **Philip Murray** and CIO Secretary-Treasurer **James B. Carey**, as well as **communists**, **socialists**, Trotskyites, and **anarchists**. Popular Front radicalism led enemies of labor to assert communist domination of individual unions and the CIO itself. Conservative backlash ultimately led to the demise of the Popular Front.

Before the 1930s, communists had some successes, but mostly endured a troubled relationship with American labor unions. Shifting tactics sometimes led communists to forge alliances with other groups, at others to denounce former friends. Abroad, hostility between the powerful socialist and communist parties in Germany contributed to the triumph of Nazism in 1933. In France in 1934, socialist and communist workers cooperated in physically battling and defeating an attempted fascist coup. During 1935 at the World Congress of Communist Parties in Moscow, Georgi Dmitrov proclaimed the new policy of the Popular Front as a bulwark to defeat fascism. In the United States, such a policy of left-wing cooperation was already operating informally in many locations as a means to combat the Great Depression and organize desperate, increasingly radicalized American workers.

The biggest boost to the Popular Front in the United States came with the surge of **industrial unionism**. **John L. Lewis** had actually banned communists from membership in the **United Mine Workers of America** in 1927. **Sidney Hillman** of the **Amalgamated Clothing Workers of America** fought his own battles with the communists during the 1920s. Yet both men embraced former opponents in their aggressive drive to organize America's production workers. Communists provided organizational expertise and dedication needed to galvanize industrial workers.

Though prominent, communists were hardly alone in labor's Popular Front. In addition to members of other organized political groups, individuals called "fellow travelers" were an important part of the CIO's success. At the national level, Lee Pressman, CIO general counsel, not only negotiated and drew up **contracts** with employers, but also brokered affairs between the differing factions. **Leonard De Caux**, editor of the *CIO News*, was also influential. Among national unions, Mike Quill of the Transport Workers Union and Joseph Curran of the National Maritime Union maintained alliances with the Popular Front that enabled their unions to make major gains.

At its most influential, American labor's Popular Front alliance provided a united, powerful, and more radical counterpart to the New Deal. During World War II, it supported the establishment of the new United Nations and brought American labor into the new, inclusive World Federation of Trade Unions (WFTU). However, pressures generated by the deepening Cold War and conservative backlash at home shattered the Popular Front. Beginning in the **United Auto Workers (UAW)** with the election of **Walter Reuther** as president, the balance of forces within the CIO decisively shifted.

Many union leaders, such as Mike Quill, president of the Transport Workers Union, maintained a close association between their organization and the Popular Front. © George Meany Memorial Archives.

As the external environment for labor grew more hostile, CIO leaders felt the need to become even more dependent on government largesse. The price was the exclusion of communists. The antiunion **Taft-Hartley Act** in 1947, congressional committees like the House Committee on Un-American Activities, and state investigating boards like California's Tunney Committee were intent on rolling back labor gains, which forced the CIO to retrench. By February 1948, markers of CIO loyalty included demands that unions support the Marshall Plan and renounce the presidential campaign of progressive candidate Henry Wallace. The following year, the CIO withdrew from the WFTU and began expelling unions it deemed unduly influenced by communists. Nearly one-third of the CIO's total membership was purged. The Popular Front among American labor was finished, and communist influence was eventually eradicated. But along with it, the progressive nature of American unions suffered, and militancy declined.

Suggested Readings: Michael Denning, *The Cultural Front: The Laboring of American Culture in the Twentieth Century*, 1996; Robert H. Zieger, *The CIO, 1935–1955*, 1995.

Stephen Burwood

Postal Strike of 1970. The Postal Strike of 1970 was the first nationwide strike of federal employees. It began in New York City on March 18, 1970, and quickly spread to over 200,000 letter carriers, clerks, and mail handlers nationwide. The **walkout** was prompted by the poor pay earned by urban postal workers and the difference in pay rates between the government and private sectors. Although the **strike** ended within one week, it was responsible for a dramatic overhaul of the relationship between the federal government and organized labor.

The strike had a long gestation period. As inflation and the cost of living rose throughout the 1960s, in part because of the war in Vietnam, post office employees' real **wages** fell drastically. Full-time postal employees earning the top pay rate after twenty-one years' service in New York City received only $8,400 per annum. Many full-time employees qualified for welfare benefits. The United Federation of Postal Clerks and the National Association of Letter Carriers (NALC), the two largest of seven national unions representing post office workers, deleted no-strike clauses from their constitutions in 1968. Both unions repeatedly warned of worker discontent and the impossibility of keeping their members on the job without significant improvements. Under prevailing federal law, however, strikes were illegal, unions could not bargain directly with post-office management, and they had to lobby Congress for pay increases. On March 12, 1970, the House of Representatives' Post Office and Civil Service Committee offered a pay raise that was rejected by the **rank and file**. New York City Letter Carriers Local 36 was especially angry over the congressional inactivity and timid union leadership. When President Richard Nixon announced that the next scheduled wage increase would be postponed for six months, workers responded. Rejecting pleas by their representatives—at one point they hanged NALC President James Rademacher in effigy—Local 36 voted to strike. They were joined by the Postal Clerks Union as well as other New York locals, and within two days postal workers in Buffalo, Boston, Pittsburgh, Detroit, and other locales walked off in **solidarity** with the New Yorkers.

At its peak, approximately 25 percent of the nation's postal employees were on strike, shutting down New York–based financial and business centers and halting national mail delivery. Rademacher claimed that radical students affiliated with Students for a Democratic Society had infiltrated the NALC and precipitated the strike. Although some younger workers were influenced by 1960s social movements, the strike was the product of the workers' desperation and government inaction, not outside agitators. The *New York Times* blamed Congress and the White House, and public sentiment was generally favorable toward the strikers. Nevertheless, the federal government obtained a court injunction requiring postal unions to compel their members to return to work. When the unions found Postmaster General Winton Blount unwilling to concede any issue that would encourage workers to abandon the strike, representatives from all seven postal unions asked Secretary of Labor George Shultz to intervene. Shultz pressured Blount into a secret meeting with union officials on March 20, the day the NALC met to decide whether to make the strike official. When union members rejected the secret meeting's modest compromise, President Nixon announced that if the strike did not end by March 23, he would move to ensure mail delivery. Ignored by the workers, Nixon declared a state of national emergency and ordered 25,000 soldiers and National Guardsmen to New York City to sort and move mail. Nixon did stipulate that troops be unarmed, dress in uniforms without battle gear, and that they avoid confrontations with strikers. There was no way that federal troops could hope to replace the 57,000 striking New Yorkers, thus they concentrated on moving mail vital to business interests and did not make home deliveries. The administration won additional injunctions that would have levied crushing fines on locals remaining on strike after March 25, and these forced most strikers back to work.

With the workers once again delivering the mail, public and political pressure shifted to post-office management. Both sides quickly reached agreement on a new contract that included an immediate 6 percent wage increase, with a slightly larger increase coming after congressional approval; reduction of length-of-service for top pay from twenty-one years to eight; withholding disciplinary action against individual strikers; and future **collective bargaining** with binding **arbitration**, which relieved Congress of the responsibility for post-office wage negotiations. Strikes remained illegal. Congress quickly approved the agreement, and President Nixon signed the bill into law on April 15, less than one month after the strike began. The strikers' gains reverberated among other federal workers, including truckers, who engaged in a **wildcat strike**, and air traffic controllers, who held a **sick-out** in the wake of the postal-workers strike. (The latter was successful, but during the **Professional Air Traffic Controllers Organization (PATCO) strike** of 1981, President Ronald Reagan fired striking air traffic controllers.)

On August 12, Nixon signed into law the Postal Reorganization Act, which changed the relationship between the post office and the federal government. For unions to bargain collectively, the post office was transformed into an autonomous and self-supporting government corporation. In exchange, postal employees gave up the right to strike and agreed to binding arbitration. The strike marked the beginning of a long process that brought a living wage to postal workers. Workplace issues related to work conditions and work-related chronic medical ailments are still unresolved.

Suggested Readings: Joseph Lowenberg and Michael Moskow, eds., *Collective Bargaining in Government: Readings and Cases*, 1972; Stephen Shannon, "Work Stoppage in Government: The Postal Strike of 1970," in *Monthly Labor Review* 101 (July 1978): 14–22; John Walsh and Garth Mangum, *Labor Struggle in the Post Office: From Selective Lobbying to Collective Bargaining*, 1992.

John Cashman
Robert Shaffer

Post–World War I Strikes. After the November 1918 armistice ending World War I, working people worldwide declared their own war against employers by

striking in record numbers. In the United States, the 1919 postwar strike wave included an unprecedented four million workers, who staged more than 3,500 strikes. These included national strikes of coal miners and steelworkers, a regional New England telephone operators' strike, the Seattle general strike, and the famed **Boston police strike**. Clothing workers in New York, textile workers in the East, copper miners in Montana, and streetcar workers in the Midwest also staged **walkouts**. In all cases, strikers faced intense opposition from employers, who used local police, state militia, and, in some cases, federal troops to force workers back on the job. Though the **steel strike of 1919** did not result in union recognition, others strikers succeeded. Clothing workers won shorter hours, coal miners won a **wage** increase, and telephone operators won a better **contract**.

The explosion of postwar strike activity had several causes. Most strikers responded to massive wartime inflation. Between 1914 and 1918, the cost of living rose an average of 17 percent a year. Even **working-class** families who managed to keep pace with inflation during the war through **overtime** and war **bonuses** could not make ends meet once war-production lapsed. Not only did workers face common hardships, but their wartime experience raised expectations of change. President Woodrow Wilson had pledged that the United States was fighting a "war to make the world safe for democracy," leading many workers to expect a measure of "industrial democracy" after the war. But when employers instead sought to lower wage rates, campaign for the antiunion **open shop**, and dismantle federal agencies such as the National War Labor Board, many working people felt betrayed. The strikes also took place in the shadow of the 1917 Bolshevik Revolution in Russia, which some early observers proclaimed the first workers' republic. This event was reflected in the radical demands of some strikers. A group of Illinois coal miners called for "mines to the miners," while workers in Seattle refused to load a shipment of arms destined for the anti-Bolshevik white armies in Russia. The event was reflected as well in the accusation by business and political leaders that the communists lurked behind every American striker. Though untrue, this charge paved the way for the red scare and Palmer Raids of 1920.

Suggested Readings: Jeremy Brecher, *Strike!*, 1997; Philip Foner, *History of the Labor Movement in the United States, Volume 8: Postwar Struggles, 1918–1920*, 1988; David Montgomery, *The Fall of the House of Labor: The Workplace, the State, and American Labor Activism, 1865–1925*, 1987.

Carl Weinberg

Powderly, Terence Vincent (January 22, 1849–June 24, 1924). Terence V. Powderly, the national leader of the **Knights of Labor (KOL)** from 1878 through 1893, later served as commissioner general of immigration and in the **Department of Labor**. Powderly was born in Carbondale, Pennsylvania, the son of Terence and Margery (Walsh) Powderly. He attended Carbondale schools until age thirteen, at which time he became a railroad worker. In 1866, he **apprenticed** as a machinist and worked at various shops in the greater

Scranton area until 1877. He married Hannah Dyer on September 19, 1872. The couple had a child that died in infancy.

In the early 1870s, Powderly got caught up in the various causes that defined his life: Irish nationalism, temperance, politics, and labor. As the son of an Irish immigrant father, Powderly was deeply interested in Irish politics. He was an active member of the Irish Land League, supported Irish independence, and was an outspoken critic of British policy towards the Irish. Powderly was also a teetotaler and an ardent supporter of temperance causes. During his tenure as leader of the KOL, the organization established a working relationship with the Women's Christian Temperance Union.

Terence Powderly. © George Meany Memorial Archives.

The exploitation of labor after the Civil War had a profound effect on young Powderly. Though he later denounced radicalism and supported the Republican Party, for a brief period he paid **dues** to the Socialist Labor Party. He was also caught up in the **Greenback** Labor Movement and in 1878 rode that ticket to victory as mayor of Scranton. He served three, two-year terms.

Powderly came to fame as a labor leader. He joined the Machinists and Blacksmiths Union in 1871. Like many unions, the machinists were badly hurt by the panic of 1873. He gravitated towards the ultrasecret Noble and Holy Order of the KOL and probably joined it in 1874. Appointed an organizer in 1876, he helped expand the KOL westward from its Philadelphia base. In that same year, he became president (master workman) of his local, then corresponding secretary for his district assembly.

In 1879, Powderly became the general master workman of the entire KOL when founder Uriah Stephens resigned. Powderly led the Knights from secrecy and obscurity to national prominence as an open organization. There were fewer than 10,000 members in 1878; by mid-1886, there were perhaps a million. Powderly lectured and organized tirelessly on behalf of the Knights and managed administrative affairs admirably given the KOL's inadequate bureaucratic development. He supported the organization of both women and African Americans into the KOL and oversaw the KOL's greatest triumph: its 1885 strike victory over Jay Gould's Southwest railway conglomerate. Powderly also called for an end to the **wage** system and its replacement by producer and distributor **cooperatives**. By the mid-1880s, Powderly was the nation's most famous labor leader. Politicians and reformers sought his advice, and local assemblies, retail products, and children were named for him.

Powderly's KOL tenure was controversial, however. Despite the victory over Gould, Powderly was bitterly opposed to **strikes** and called for mandatory **arbitration**, a position that angered many trade unionists and radicals. He was also lukewarm to the idea of independent labor parties and, after the **Haymarket bombing** of May 4, 1886, an outspoken critic of **anarchism**, **socialism**, and radicalism. Critics claimed he was vain, argumentative, petty, and self-serving. Some accused him of trying to make the KOL into a personal power machine, while others said he was part of an internal conspiracy that was opposed to trade unions. When the KOL began to decline in the wake of the **Great Upheaval**, Powderly often bore the brunt of criticism. A coalition of urban socialists and agrarian radicals removed Powderly from office in late 1893. He battled the KOL over **back pay** and other matters and was briefly expelled from the Knights.

Tenth annual convention of the Knights of Labor, at Richmond. Frank J. Farrell, African American delegate, introducing General Master Workman Powderly to the convention. © Library of Congress.

He worked as a lawyer for several years until 1897, when President William McKinley appointed him U.S. commissioner general of immigration. But his xenophobic, anti-immigrant diatribes did little to distinguish him. He left his post in 1902 and served in several positions with the Department of Labor. His wife, Hannah, died in 1901, and on March 31, 1919, he married Emma Fickenscher, his former secretary. He died in Washington, D.C., on June 24, 1924. At the time, he was nearly forgotten, but in many respects, Terence Powderly was the first prominent leader of an American labor federation. In January 2000, Powderly was inducted into the Labor Hall of Fame.

Suggested Readings: Harry Carman, Henry David, and Paul Guthrie, *The Path I Trod: The Autobiography of Terence V. Powderly*, 1960; Craig Phelan, *Grand Master Workman: Terence Powderly and the Knights of Labor*, 2000; Robert E. Weir, *Knights Unhorsed: Internal Conflict in a Gilded Age Labor Movement*, 2000.

Robert E. Weir

Preferential Shop. The preferential shop, also known as the preferential union shop, was one of the cornerstones of the Protocols of Peace, one of the earliest successful efforts to harmonize labor-management relations in New York's garment industry in the 1910s. The term, first coined by Louis Brandeis, was an attempt to compromise between the irreconcilable demands of management for an open shop, in which union membership was not required, and labor's demand for the **closed shop**, or union shop, in which employees must belong to the union, either upon hiring, or within a limited time thereafter. In the preferential shop, the employer was required to give preference to union over nonunion workers, provided that they were of equal competence. The preferential shop quickly became a compromise that pleased neither side, with the **International Ladies' Garment Workers' Union** initially rejecting the offer, and the **National Association of Manufacturers** later arguing that the preferential shop was little different from the union shop. Even when the protocols were accepted as a matter of industrial law, labor and management alike attempted to manipulate the preferential union shop to their own advantage. By the 1920s, with the effective demise of the protocol, the preferential union shop also declined in practice as shops became either open or closed, depending on union strength or weakness.

Suggested Readings: Louis Levine, *The Women Garment Workers: A History of the International Ladies' Garment Workers' Union*, 1925; National Association of Manufacturers, *Open Shop Encyclopedia for Debaters: A Reference Book for Use of Teachers, Students, and Public Speakers*, 1921; Gus Tyler, *A History of the International Ladies' Garment Workers' Union*, 1995.

Susan Roth Breitzer

Premium Pay. Premium pay is an adjustment made to the hourly **wage** in consideration for working outside of normal hours or job classification. Often, companies use premiums as an incentive to entice workers to accept undesirable conditions or schedules. Employees may earn extra compensation for night, weekend, or holiday work, or for working in uncommon situations with greater risk.

The most common form of premium is **overtime** pay, which is mandated by the **Fair Labor Standards Act**, which requires that nonsalaried, nonmanagerial employees receive one-and-a-half times their regular hourly wage for time worked in excess of forty hours per week, or past their normally scheduled day. (Unions may negotiate a higher premium in the **collective bargaining** process.)

Suggested Reading: Robert Covington and Kurt Decker, *Individual Employee Rights in a Nutshell*, 1995.

Joseph F. Rodgers

Prevailing Wage. Prevailing wage refers to the pay standards for construction workers within a given geographical territory. The thirty-one states that have prevailing-wage laws stipulate that an employer must pay **wages** in line with local custom on any job open to public bid or involving state or federal **contracts**. Employers must meet that minimum standard whether or not the workforce is unionized, though they may pay more. The prevailing wage is an outgrowth of the 1931 **Davis-Bacon Act**.

Prevailing-wage laws are designed to protect local wage structures. They apply mainly in the building industry where large public projects are usually put out for competitive bids. Prevailing-wage laws emerged to prevent nonlocal firms from gaining contracts funded by local taxpayers, then importing low-wage workers who would undercut local wage rates. Employers must pay prevailing wages if they accept a contract, even if their workers customarily work for lower rates. States publish the prevailing wage for various regions, and that information is available to contractors before they put in bids. The **Department of Labor** also maintains current data on prevailing wages. There are also nonprofit agencies, like the Prevailing Wage Contractors Association, that assist firms in complying with existing laws.

Some states establish thresholds that stipulate the total value of a contract before prevailing wages must be paid, though eight states have no minimum threshold whatsoever. This figure is usually low, though it is $400,000 for new construction in Connecticut and $500,000 in Maryland. With the exceptions of New Hampshire and Vermont, all of the states without prevailing wage laws are located in the South or west of the Mississippi River.

The construction and business communities are generally opposed to prevailing-wage laws and have funded expensive campaigns to overturn them. Since 1979, Colorado, Florida, Idaho, Louisiana, New Hampshire, and Utah have repealed prevailing-wage legislation. Studies reveal that those states experienced an immediate 2 to 4 percent decline in construction industry wages and about a 10 percent decline for unionized workers. In recent years, unions have done a better job of fending off attacks. No state has repealed a law since 1988, despite well-financed efforts to do so.

Suggested Readings: David Francis, "The Effect of Repealing Prevailing Wage Laws," National Bureau of Economic Research, http://www.nber.org/digest/amy00/w7454.html; Prevailing Wage Contractors Association Web site, http://www.pwca.net/; U.S. Department of Labor Web site, http://www.dol.gov/esa/programs.

Robert E. Weir

Professional Air Traffic Controllers Organization (PATCO) Strike. The Professional Air Traffic Controllers Organization (PATCO) strike was a pivotal 1981 battle between PATCO and the administration of President Ronald Reagan that ended in the complete rout of the union. Many observers see the crushing of PATCO as the event that legitimized organized capital's ongoing program to break the power of labor unions.

On August 3, 1981, roughly 13,000 air traffic controllers employed by the Federal Aviation Administration (FAA) refused to report for duty in airport control towers and in control centers which managed traffic between air hubs. This **walkout** of nearly 80 percent of the FAA's air traffic control personnel was organized by their union, PATCO. Staged in defiance of federal law, which forbids **strikes** by U.S. government employees, the job action crippled the flow of air traffic, prompting a showdown between PATCO and President Reagan. PATCO demanded a thirty-two-hour workweek, improved retirement benefits, and an immediate $10,000 per year raise. The media seized upon the seemingly exorbitant **salary** demands, though it was largely a bargaining chip to address what many workers felt was the central issue: reducing the stress of air traffic controllers who worked long hours with few breaks staring at radar screens. Lost in the drama of the strike was PATCO's appeal to public safety. The union claimed that the flying public was at risk due to conditions guaranteed to impair controllers' judgment. Also lost in subsequent events is the fact that PATCO had been negotiating with the FAA for months preceding the strike.

Striking air traffic controllers walk the picket line at the New York air route traffic control center in Ronkonkoma, N.Y., on August 5, 1981. With an 11:00 A.M. deadline passed, the traffic controllers continue their court-prohibited strike. © AP/Wide World Photos

Hours after the strike began, President Reagan issued an ultimatum, warning strikers that if they did not resume work within forty-eight hours, they would be terminated. The 11,350 controllers who ignored the president's ultimatum were fired on August 5. With a sweep of the pen, President Reagan replaced 70 percent of the nation's air traffic controllers. This action made him enormously popular with the business community and political conservatives, and it also played well with the public at large. Years of declining membership reduced organized labor's clout among the public and made it more receptive to corporate antiunion messages. Unions were blamed for a host of ills, including the stagnating economy. Reagan's actions also appeared decisive and bold, a welcome change to the political malaise of the 1970s.

The breaking of PATCO was one of the most dramatic labor events of the post–World War II era, and it had lasting negative consequences for organized labor in general. PATCO was formed in 1968 by air traffic controllers who expressed dissatisfaction with the long hours, low pay, and high stress that then characterized their jobs. After two stormy years, which saw PATCO stage a slowdown and two major **sick-outs**, PATCO finally established a stable organization and affiliated with the Maritime Employees Benevolent Association,

American Federation of Labor-Congress of Industrial Organizations (AFL-CIO), in 1970. It won its first **contract** with the FAA in 1973. Relations between PATCO and the FAA were generally troubled, with the union organizing sick-outs and slowdowns in 1974, 1975, and 1978. Relations deteriorated further after 1978, due to federal budget constraints, **pension** disputes, transfer policies, and several quality-of-work issues. Two separate studies indicated that morale among air traffic controllers was dangerously low, though the FAA ignored said findings. The FAA even ignored reports showing that controllers handled duties in excess of the FAA's own standards.

In response to this unrest, PATCO leaders initiated a strike plan for the expiration of the union's contract in 1981. The implementation of that plan accelerated when Robert Poli replaced longtime PATCO President John Leyden in 1980. The union's hopes that a strike could be averted rose briefly when Poli extracted vague promises to improve conditions from candidate Ronald Reagan. PATCO subsequently endorsed Reagan's 1980 presidential candidacy, only to become bitterly disappointed by the Reagan-staffed FAA during the contract negotiations of 1981. In July 1981, an angry union **rank and file** rejected an FAA offer that would have paved the way for significant wage increases, even though that offer broke new ground by including wage considerations in a federal contract. (Federal wage increases normally require congressional approval.) Insisting that the FAA's final offer did little to address most of their **grievances**, controllers staged the most significant strike of white-collar technical workers in U.S. history.

The Reagan administration was well prepared for the strike, using every legal means at hand to break it. Federal judges issued costly injunctions that assessed PATCO for damages resulting from the strike, quickly bankrupting the organization. Several strike leaders were arrested and jailed for defying the injunction, and a swift **decertification** vote among **scab** controllers removed PATCO as a bargaining unit. Meanwhile, military controllers, FAA supervisors, and hastily trained replacements were marshaled to break the strike. The AFL-CIO publicly supported PATCO and nationwide grassroots **solidarity** efforts sprang up as workers expressed their collective outrage at Reagan's antiunion tactics. International support for the strike came from several quarters as well, including the Canadian Air Traffic Controllers Association, which staged limited actions in support of PATCO. But unions in the U.S. airline industry did not honor PATCO picket lines, and the volume of air traffic steadily rose in the months following the walkout. As previously noted, PATCO also lost the battle for public opinion. About 90 percent of PATCO members were white males, who were perceived to be well-paid and privileged. PATCO credibility suffered further when long-delayed technological changes automated many of the more tedious air-traffic-controller tasks, thereby eliminating many of the quality-of-work issues that partly prompted the strike.

By the end of 1981, PATCO had been broken. This realization sent ripples throughout the United States, as Reagan's action was widely seen as encouraging private-sector companies to break unions as well. The PATCO strike touched off a new wave of **downsizing**, **decertification**, and **concessions** strikes. Within a few years, private employers had opted to replace permanently strikers at **Phelps Dodge**, International Paper, **Hormel**, and other major companies, contributing to a dramatic drop in strike rates in the United States that was not reversed by the end of the twentieth century.

Suggested Readings: Willis Nordlund, *Silent Skies: The Air Traffic Controllers' Strike*, 1998; Rebecca Pels, "The Pressures of PATCO: Strikes and Stress in the 1980s," in *Essays in History*, 1995; Michael Round, *Grounded: Reagan and the PATCO Crash*, 1999.

Joseph A. McCartin

Profit Sharing. Profit sharing is a plan that links a portion of a worker's yearly income to the company's profitability. Instead of an annual percent increase, the employee receives an added **bonus** when the company meets its expectations, but receives only his or her normal **salary** if the company fails to achieve expected goals. Profit sharing is designed to make workers feel that they have a stake in the continued success of the business. This has been a standard feature in American corporations since the Progressive Era and was a key component of **welfare capitalism**. By the late 1920s, over a million workers were enrolled in profit-sharing plans, though many of those systems collapsed during the Great Depression (1929–41).

Since employees are usually not given access to employer accounts, critics complain that profit-sharing plans are subject to abuse and can be dodges designed to avoid giving raises. Making pay raises contingent can also harm employees' long-term buying power. Deferred compensation can cause **wages** to lag behind the inflation rate. Because most profit-sharing plans pay their bonuses as a lump sum, it does not have the same cumulative effect as an annual raise, since the base wage remains stagnant. Moreover, these payments cannot be relied on for long-term financial planning.

Unions have long claimed that profit-sharing plans are also designed to deter unionization by creating the false impression that management will take care of workers without being pressured to do so. Despite problems associated with profit sharing, such plans began to reemerge in the 1970s as employers enlisted them as a way of being more competitive in an era of **globalization**. In theory, motivated employees with a vested interest are more productive. Many **contracts** contain profit-sharing language, despite union skepticism of its merits.

Suggested Readings: Everett Allen, *Pension Planning: Pensions, Profit Sharing, and other Defined Compensation Plans*, 7th Ed., 1992; Jay Conison, *Employment Benefit Plans in a Nutshell*, 1998; Douglas Krause, *Profit Sharing: Does it Make a Difference? The Productivity and Stability Effects of Employee Profit Sharing Plans*, 1993.

Joseph F. Rodgers

Protectionism. Protectionism is a term most commonly used in economics to describe regulations preventing free trade between countries. Although some economists do not believe that protectionist policies benefit a country's ability to distribute goods and services effectively, most find that these plans help developing "infant industries" that are new to the market of trade and exchange. Protectionism is usually created in the form of tariffs, import quotas, and trade regulations. Trade regulations are sometimes used when there is a concern regarding the quality of imports, such as automobiles.

Working people and their unions often favor some form of protectionism and argue that cheap imports endanger American jobs. Occasionally they find allies among manufacturers seeking alleviation from foreign competition to their products. Americans have hotly debated tariff issues related to protectionism since Colonial times. Past and present advocates of free trade argue that it benefits workers as both consumers and producers by providing low-cost goods for purchase while providing open markets for the goods and services workers create. A handful of labor activists, most notably **Henry George**, was dedicated to free trade, but most nineteenth-century workers favored protectionism; groups like the **Knights of Labor** employed paid lobbyists to pressure Congress to support protectionist legislation. In the twentieth century, protectionism's grip on workers relaxed somewhat, especially among urban consumers seeking cheaper products, but free trade remains a minority viewpoint. Farmers are split on the issue as they simultaneously fear competition from imported foodstuffs, yet want easy access to potential foreign markets. Most labor groups have been adamantly opposed to recent free-trade measures like the **North American Free Trade Agreement**, as well as the attempts of groups like the World Trade Organization to knock down international trade barriers.

The term protectionism is also used regarding **child-labor** issues. Used within this context, it refers to agencies, organizations, and institutions that advocate child-labor legislation to prevent children from being exploited in the workplace. Many contemporary critics of globalism cite child-labor abuses as another reason to oppose free-trade agreements.

In terms of labor law, protectionism refers to any legislation on the federal, state, or local level to increase the safety of employees at a workplace. These laws are also developed to promote the general welfare and interests of employees. This type of law is often called **protective labor legislation**.

Suggested Readings: Anne Krueger, ed., *The Political Economy of Trade Protection*, 1996; Charles Rowley, Willem Thorbecke, and Richard Wagner, eds., *Trade Protection in the United States*, 1995; Bureau of Labor Statistics Web site, http://www.bls.gov.export-import.

Amanda Busjit

Protective Labor Legislation. In its broadest terms, protective labor legislation refers simply to laws designed to protect human beings from the potentially damaging effects of work demands by their employers or inherent within work itself. It has proved problematic when designating special categories of workers as more deserving or needy of protection than others. It has been most often applied to children and women.

Protective labor legislation evolved out of Colonial debates between free labor and the reality of the changing nature of work. In theory, each Colonial worker was free to negotiate **wages**, hours, and working conditions according to the best bargain he or she could fashion. Custom generally dictated said terms, and a relatively closed economic system reinforced them. In an increasingly **capitalist** economy, however, competition rendered customary practices less viable. One of the first groups to push for work regulations was **journeymen**. After the American Revolution, journeymen carpenters led the move to regulate the number of hours that constituted a legal day's work. Despite the fact that courts often declared journeymen associations illegal, the associations' efforts led to, first, the ten-hour movement and, later, the **eight-hour movement**. Female textile workers also played an important role in both movements. One of the earliest versions of protective labor legislation was an 1840 ten-hour bill for federal employees.

Child labor laws, one important type of protective labor legislation, sought to protect the rights and health of child workers, such as these coal mine breaker boys, who sorted the slag from the coal. © George Meany Memorial Archives/Library of Congress.

After the Civil War, however, protective labor legislation often broke down along gender lines, with state and federal courts playing a pivotal role. Courts routinely struck down laws regulating hours and conditions for male workers, but left them intact for women. Court decisions dovetailed with Victorian social and cultural systems that assumed women to be inferior in physical strength and intelligence. Victorians advocated separate spheres for men and women, with males suited for the public world of business, commerce, and work, while women's "natural" roles were those of homemaker and mother. Ideally, a male worker would earn a **family wage** sufficient to support his spouse and children. Few **working-class** males actually earned that amount, and women usually did not have the luxury of confining themselves to the private realm. However, Victorian customs excluded women from many jobs, especially those involving heavy toil or those that exposed women to moral dangers, like bartending or night work. Courts often opined that special protections for women were necessary to protect their presumably fragile reproductive systems and their delicate psychological health.

Ironically, nineteenth-century women were often protected better than children, as **child-labor** laws were notoriously lax throughout the century. This changed dramatically during the Progressive Era; by 1912, thirty-eight states adopted at least rudimentary child-labor laws. Progressive Era legislation and court decisions had far different implications for women, however. By 1900, many states regulated the number of hours women could work, and many male workers had won reduced hours. In 1905, the Supreme Court ruling in *Lochner v. New York* declared unconstitutional a New York state law regulating bakers' hours. Subsequent rulings stripped male workers of hard-fought reduced hours, but left shorter hours in place for women. Practice was cloaked in law in 1908 when the Supreme Court's ***Muller v. Oregon*** upheld shorter hours for women. Justice Louis Brandeis's majority opinion relied heavily on Victorian assumptions about women's health. By 1917, nineteen states fashioned laws based on the *Muller* decision.

Women's-rights activists faced a dilemma. On one hand, women were granted reduced hours, weightlifting restrictions, hazardous-waste-handling safeguards, and other protections that male workers still struggled to obtain through **collective bargaining**. To accept them without challenge, however, meant to accept an inferior status that many feminists found unacceptable. Groups like the **Women's Trade Union League** and the **International Ladies' Garment Workers' Union** were embroiled in hot debates over whether or not to acquiesce to gender-based protective legislation. Feminists correctly asserted that in lieu of an Equal Rights Amendment, women workers were vulnerable to unfavorable protective labor legislation.

New Deal legislation in the 1930s resolved some protective labor issues and engendered new ones. Job shortages during the Great Depression led numerous states to enact laws forbidding married women from holding most wage-earning jobs. New Deal job programs largely left said custom in place and excluded married women. However, programs like the **National Industrial Recovery Act** and the **Fair Labor Standards Act** instituted the eight-hour day, **minimum-wage** laws, **overtime** rules, and child-labor laws without regard to gender. Labor shortages during World War II negated bans on married-women's work. (World War II workplaces nonetheless continued to mandate rest periods for women, pay them lower wages, and restrict women from certain jobs.)

In the post–World War II period, protective labor legislation expanded. Greater awareness of workplace safety issues culminated in the 1970 **Occupational Safety and Health Act**, child-labor laws were tightened, and **workman's compensation**, minimum wage, and overtime laws were periodically updated. Customary gender biases remained, however, with entire categories of work being considered as gender-specific. Secretarial work, for example, was so heavily female (and so poorly compensated) that commentators spoke of it as a "pink-collar ghetto." Feminists in the 1960s began to challenge social customs, especially as they extended to the workplace. The 1963 **Equal Pay Act** outlawed differing wage scales for the same work, and Title VII of the 1964 Civil Rights Act referred sexual discrimination allegations to the Equal Employment

Opportunities Commission (EEOC). Other bills and executive orders took down more discriminatory barriers.

By the 1970s, women were found in numerous occupations once thought to be the preserve of men. Full equality was dealt a blow in 1982, however, when a proposed Equal Rights Amendment to the United States Constitution was not ratified. Many women complain that de facto protective legislation continues. Some jobs, most notably in the construction and parcel-post industries, continue to limit the amount of weight women can lift, and custom continues to dictate that certain jobs are inappropriate for women. Some critics also note that EEOC equal-pay provisions are circumvented by manipulating job titles instead of actual duties, a complaint that has spurred discussions of comparable worth. Women in many workplaces complain that their representation is more token than real, and that a **glass ceiling** prevents them from advancing.

Gender and race have also proved sticking points in protective labor legislation. **Affirmative Action** programs have led to complaints that women and people of color have been given unfair preference in hiring and promotion. Hiring quotas have been especially controversial, though rigid quotas were struck down by the Supreme Court's 1978 decision in *University of California Board of Regents v. Bakke*. Unions have steadfastly opposed any affirmative action interpretations of long-held **seniority** systems.

In recent years, workplace sexual-harassment complaints have skyrocketed. Ironically, the call for special rules to reduce sexual harassment have rekindled Progressive-Era dilemmas. The vast majority of complaints have been lodged by women, causing some males to raise questions of women's ability to cope in competitive and pressure-packed work environments. The same charges are leveled when women lobby for family leave, flexible hours, job sharing, or increased medical coverage for women's health issues. Once again the challenge is to adopt rules that protect workers in gender-neutral ways.

Overall, the track record of protective labor legislation is mixed. Obtaining it in some form or another is central to the mission of organized labor. Few would argue the wisdom of implementing child-labor laws, minimum-wage protection, and workplace-safety provisions, but laws that have applied only to certain categories of workers have proved controversial.

Suggested Readings: Rosalyn Baxandall and Linda Gordon, *America's Working Women: A Documentary History*, 1995; Alice Kessler-Harris, *Out to Work: A History of Wage-Earning Women in the United States*, 1982; Susan Lehrer, *Origins of Protective Labor Legislation for Women, 1905–1925*, 1987.

Robert E. Weir

Pullman Strike/Lockout. The Pullman Strike/Lockout of 1894 embodied many of the social ills and injustices of the late Gilded Age. Despite the crushing defeat dealt to the **American Railway Union (ARU)**, the strike catapulted **Eugene Debs** to national prominence, focused attention on the woes of the laboring classes, contributed to political realignment, and paved the way for needed reforms.

The events of 1894 took place against a backdrop of deep conflict and economic depression. The crushing of a nationwide railroad **strike** during the **Great Labor Uprising** of 1877 did little to bring quiescence to an industry that was marked by numerous subsequent strikes, especially during the **Great Upheaval** of the mid-1880s. Because rail workers were split into six brotherhoods, and the **Brotherhood of Locomotive Engineers (BLE)** was particularly loath to cooperate with other groups, rail workers' gains were modest during the 1880s. The **Knights of Labor (KOL)** proved more successful than any of the brotherhoods, but its decline after 1888 again left rail workers in a weak position. In 1893, Debs formed the ARU, an attempt at **industrial unionism** among railroad workers. His fledgling union won a victory against the Great Northern Railroad in 1893, but was ill-prepared to tackle the Pullman Palace Car Company in 1894. Debs, in fact, cautioned against the strike.

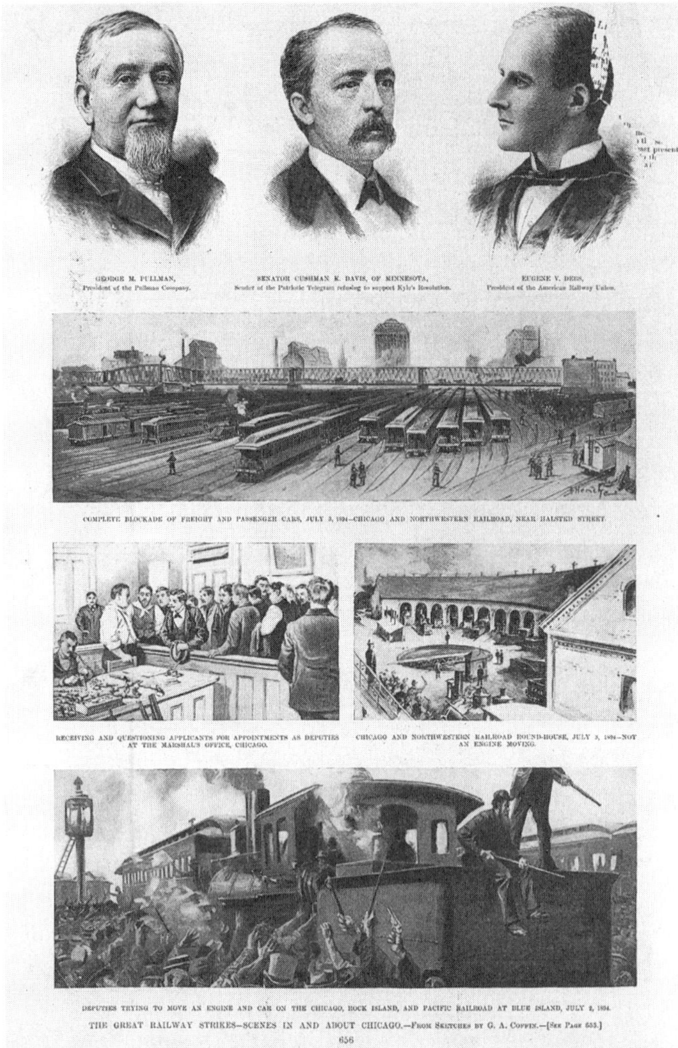

Three bust portraits showing George Pullman, Cushman K. Davis, and Eugene V. Debs; and four illustrations showing "blockade of railroad cars, applicants for appointments as deputies at the marshal's office, roundhouse, and deputies trying to move an engine and car at Blue Island." © Library of Congress.

Industrialist George Pullman held a monopoly share of the lucrative sleeping-car industry. In 1880, Pullman purchased land twelve miles south of Chicago's central business district and constructed a new manufacturing facility. Pullman also responded to the growing urban social problems of the day and constructed what he hoped would be a model industrial town around his factory: Pullman, Illinois. The wide streets, sturdy homes, manicured lawns, and city services of

Pullman stood in marked contrast to Chicago's slums, but Pullman was also a **company town** and workers' lives were much more controlled. Saloons and labor unions were banned from Pullman, and the town library did not even carry information on the latter. In addition, rents and utilities cost more in Pullman, and the company actually turned a profit on rent and services.

George Pullman's **utopian** vision was challenged by the collapse of financial markets in 1893. Tension between workers and employers was already high, and memories of the **Haymarket bombing** of 1886 remained vivid. The Panic of 1893 led to wide-scale business failures, bank closings, and massive layoffs. The Chicago area was hit even harder as the area had attracted numerous temporary laborers lured to construction jobs in preparation for the World Columbian Exposition that opened in 1893. Pullman exacerbated the region's unemployment by laying off nearly half of his 5,500 workers in 1893. His workforce rose to over 3,300 by April 1894, but Pullman slashed the **wages** between 25 and 40 percent. He did not, however, lower rents, utilities, or prices at company stores.

The immediate catalyst for the strike came in May, when Pullman rejected the pleas of a **grievance** committee that approached him for relief on rents. Despite his promise not to seek reprisals against the committee, he fired three members of it, possibly with the knowledge that all three belonged to the ARU. The ARU had a small presence at Pullman. Ironically, Pullman himself violated the no-union proviso by allowing a small **company union** to form; some of its members also joined the ARU. Pullman refused to submit the firings to **arbitration**, and on June 21, ARU locals in Pullman voted to issue a **boycott** of Pullman Palace cars unless he reconsidered. Rather than wait, Pullman preemptively closed his factory, thus officially making the events of 1894 a **lockout**. His actions were backed by a consortium of railroad executives, known as the General Managers Association (GMA), which was anxious to cripple the ARU.

The ARU officially issued its boycott on June 26, with union members staying on their jobs but refusing to handle Pullman cars. When companies attempted to fire those who refused to work with Pullman cars, entire crews walked off. Within days, the ARU tied up much of the freight traffic from Chicago to the West Coast, and the boycott threatened to expand to East Coast lines. At the height of the strike at the end of June, more than 25,000 workers were out. Public opinion was initially on the side of the workers, and Republican leaders like Mark Hanna called upon Pullman to arbitrate the dispute. The GMA, however, secretly schemed to create legal conflicts and incite violence to justify crushing the strikers and boycotters. This was accomplished largely through the importation of **scabs** from Canada and by attaching mail cars to Pullmans. The GMA also convinced Attorney General Richard Olney—a board member and stockholder in several railroads—to deputize more than 3,400 agents to make sure trains ran. Mainstream newspapers also fed the public a steady diet of antistrike propaganda.

Predictably, strikers clashed with scabs and deputies, and railroad property was destroyed. This prompted Olney to request that President Grover Cleveland send federal troops to protect the mails. Four divisions were dispatched over the protests of Illinois Governor John P. Altgeld. These actions initially energized strikers, but on July 2, Olney used several obscure Civil War–era laws and the recently passed **Sherman Antitrust Act** to obtain a court injunction from Judge Peter Grosscup expressly forbidding interference with mail delivery and interstate commerce. By early July, strikers faced more than 6,000 federal and state militia troops, in excess of 5,000 marshals, and some 3,100 police officers. Debs and the ARU contemplated a **general strike**, but those hopes were dashed when the **American Federation of Labor (AFL)** refused to sanction **sympathy strikes**. Despite support from the KOL and several unions that defied AFL leadership, the Pullman strike was doomed.

Several strike leaders, including Debs, were arrested for conspiracy to obstruct the mails, made bail, then were rearrested for contempt of court. The strike was officially raised on August 2, though troops were withdrawn several weeks earlier. Judge Grosscup sentenced Debs to six months imprisonment, an experience that Debs later claimed converted him to **socialism**.

Twenty-five workers died during the Pullman conflict, and 406 were seriously injured. Railroad losses totaled more than $5.3 million, and workers lost more than $1.7 million in wages. Many workers were blacklisted, and those who got their jobs back were forced to accept employers' terms as the ARU quickly collapsed. More damaging was the widespread use of injunctions during future strikes, Pullman supplying the model for their issuance.

Despite the rout, not all was lost. The Pullman strike, plus other traumatic events like the **Homestead Steel strike** and the march of **Coxey's Army**, convinced many Americans that reform was needed. The Panic of 1893 lasted until 1898, another indicator that industrial **capitalism** needed to be reined in, and even Olney was a reluctant convert to that conclusion. In 1898, some railway abuses were corrected by the **Erdman Act**. The Democratic Party was thoroughly repudiated by **working-class** voters and did not hold the White House again until 1912, after party officials reevaluated the party's overt probusiness biases. This paved the way for the election of a series of prolabor Democratic governors and legislators. Eugene Debs emerged from prison as a heroic figure and rallied tens of thousands to the socialist cause before his death in 1926.

Suggested Readings: Almont Linsey, *The Pullman Strike*, 1964; Richard Schneirov, Shelton Stromquist, and Nick Salvatore, eds., *The Pullman Strike and the Crisis of the 1890s*, 1999; Stanley Buder, *Pullman*, 1967.

Robert E. Weir

Pure and Simple Unionism. The term pure and simple unionism refers to the idea that a labor union's primary task is the pursuit of higher **wages**, shorter hours, and better conditions for its members. The concept derives from **Adolph**

Strasser and **Samuel Gompers**, officials in the Cigar Makers International Union (CMIU). Gompers made it a centerpiece of the ideology underpinning the **American Federation of Labor (AFL)**. The AFL was the first important labor federation to embrace pure and simple unionism.

Capitalism was still a contested concept in the nineteenth century, and most labor federations spoke of supplanting it with a more just economic system. By the 1880s, the nation's largest labor federation was the **Knights of Labor (KOL)**, and the CMIU was affiliated with it. Like most groups, the KOL embraced a broad reform agenda whose ultimate goal was nothing less than remaking the nation's cultural, economic, political, and social systems. Instead of capitalism, the KOL called for **cooperation**. **Socialist** and **anarchist** groups also called for the dismantling of capitalism and had equally broad reform agendas.

Socialist cigar makers in New York City quarreled with the CMIU in the early 1880s and eventually founded a rival organization. When the KOL backed the challengers, Strasser and Gompers led the CMIU out of the organization. Gompers, who claimed to have been a socialist in his youth, grew to have great disillusionment over what he thought their naïve and utopian views. He reached similar conclusions about the KOL and most other versions of reform unionism. To him and Strasser, too much energy was siphoned in pursuit of unobtainable goals, and both men felt the KOL's opposition to **strikes** was wrongheaded. They saw the strike as labor's weapon to force employers to grant what they did not wish to give. They further concluded that only individuals within the same trade unions would be able to maintain sufficient levels of **solidarity** to sustain strikes. Moreover, Gompers rejected popular sentiments to form a labor party, as he felt the two-party system was too entrenched and that politics only diverted energy from the workplace.

When the AFL was founded in 1886, Gompers and Strasser had effectively pared labor's agenda to that of wages, hours, and conditions. Many workers, reformers, and labor advocates of the time found the AFL's more modest goals too narrow, though its view ultimately prevailed. By stripping the AFL of partisan politics and social agitation, the organization gave implicit acceptance to the legitimacy of capitalism. That, plus its exclusionary membership policies, earned it the opprobrium of the **Industrial Workers of the World (IWW)**, which called the AFL the "American Separation of Labor." Ironically though, the IWW was the last important labor federation to call for the dismantling of capitalism.

Since the early twentieth century, most labor unions have accepted the permanence of the capitalist system. This has made the pure and simple approach the everyday operating philosophy of most unions, even if they adhere rhetorically to loftier future visions.

Suggested Readings: Bruce Laurie, *Artisans Into Workers*, 1989; Nick Salvatore, ed., *Seventy Years of Life and Labor: An Autobiography of Samuel Gompers*, 1984.

Robert E. Weir

Q

Quality Circles. Quality circles, in which small groups of managers and laborers work in tandem to plan and accomplish tasks, are an alternative to assembly-line production. Unlike the specialization of the assembly line (**Fordism**) or the relentless efficiency of scientific management (**Taylorism**), quality circles stress task diversity and cooperation between management and labor. Instead of individual workers performing a single task, each member of a quality-circle team performs multiple, changing tasks and sees the product through from planning to completion. The goal is to make workers feel less alienated toward the products they create, thereby ensuring high quality and a happier workforce.

Quality circles originated in Japan, though in many ways its central tenets hark back to 1930s human-relations theories developed by people like Elton Mayo. They began to catch on in the United States in the 1980s, especially in the auto industry, which had been hard hit in the 1970s by foreign imports and declining consumer confidence in domestic auto quality. Honda Motors was the world leader in using quality circles, with General Motors the first domestic auto manufacturer to adopt the method. By the 1990s, over 90 percent of all Fortune 500 corporations used quality circles to some degree. Some unions remain suspicious of quality circles, seeing them as a way for management to change work rules without negotiating such changes, though two National Labor Relations Board decisions in the early 1990s ruled that quality circles were subject to the **National Labor Relations Act**. An attempt by conservative Republicans to circumvent those decisions (the "TEAM Act") was vetoed by President Clinton in 1996.

Suggested Readings: Steve Babson, *The Unfinished Struggle: Turning Points in American Labor, 1877-Present,* 1999; Richard Florida and Martin Kennedy, "Transplanted Organizations: The Transfer of Japanese Industrial Organization to the US," in *American Sociological Review* 56 (1991): 381–98.

Robert E. Weir

Quickie. Quickie is another term for an unauthorized **wildcat strike**, a work stoppage that occurs without notice or approval by union officials or the national union. Such action usually violates **collective-bargaining** agreements and may, in some cases, be illegal. It can also refer to an authorized action of limited duration whose purpose is to demonstrate worker strength and serve warning to employers.

Quickies peaked during specific periods of labor history. During the 1930s and 1940s, quickies were frequent, despite management opposition. By the 1950s, one-third of all **strikes** were of this type, and **rank-and-file** members used them to force companies to renegotiate workplace-rights provisions. Even though these strikes seemed successful initially, they proved unsuccessful in the long run. The reason for the long-term failure is that companies agreed to increase **wage-** and benefit-packages demanded by workers but never shifted the balance of power of production and workplace issues to the employees. Such a loss of power forced employees to strike repeatedly over work conditions. Over time, wages and benefits weakened the impetus for such action.

Suggested Readings: Eugene C. Friedman, "Illegal and Unauthorized Strikes in Violation of Collective Bargaining Agreements: A Union View," in *NYU 36th Annual National Conference on Labor,* 1983; Martin Glaberman, *Wartime Strikes,* 1980; Florence Peterson, *American Labor Unions,* 1963.

Amanda Busjit

R

Racketeer Influenced and Corrupt Organizations Act (RICO). Passed by Congress in 1970, the Racketeer Influenced and Corrupt Organizations Act is designed to help the federal government prosecute organized crime. Although it does not pertain to labor as such, some unions have been involved in **racketeering** and other forms of union corruption. In fact, unions have been pursued as aggressively under RICO as groups like the Mafia and drug dealers. This has prompted some critics to charge that RICO has been applied against organized labor as much for political and ideological reasons as for actual corrupt practices.

The federal government has long found it difficult to break crime syndicates. Merely arresting corrupt individuals often does little to lessen crime; intact organizations simply replace them. The Federal Bureau of Investigation (FBI) was created in 1924 to replace a less-effective federal anticrime unit, and turned its attention to organized crime activities like bootlegging, gambling, extortion, and prostitution. Labor unions have also been investigated by the FBI and other federal agencies. A variety of pre-RICO federal legislation deals with possible union corruption. The 1935 **National Labor Relations Act** contains language to protect union members and employers from potential abuse by union officials. The rights of each were greatly enhanced by the 1946 **Taft-Hartley Act**. The Hobbs Act was also passed in 1946 to curtail union racketeering and protect employers during negotiations. Under the Hobbs Act, it became a federal crime to even attempt robbery or extortion in activities that involve interstate or foreign commerce. The latter provisions were directly incorporated into RICO. The 1959 **Labor-Management Reporting and Disclosure Act (Landrum-Griffin Act)** contained a union members' "bill of rights," as well as numerous provisions requiring union disclosure of internal procedures, use of union funds, and limits on an **international union's** rights to place locals in trusteeship.

Unfortunately, some unions have been guilty of racketeering. The **International Brotherhood of Teamsters** forged an alliance with organized crime that dates to the early 1950s, if not before. Some officials of the International Longshoremen's union were so infamous for their connections to the criminal underworld that their practices gave rise to the 1954 Hollywood film *On the Waterfront*. Smaller unions—like the bakers, laundry workers, and hotel and restaurant employees—have come under scrutiny. Beginning in 1957, the Senate Select Committee on Improper Activities in the Labor Management Field—better known as the McClellan Committee—investigated the Teamsters and others. Eventually, Teamster boss **James Hoffa** went to prison.

RICO was fashioned to aid the government's efforts to break crime syndicates. It makes it a federal crime punishable by up to twenty years in prison—or life, if the crime is one for which a life sentence can be imposed—to "conduct or conspire to conduct an enterprise whose activities affect interstate commerce by committing or agreeing to commit a pattern of racketeering activity." To be convicted under RICO, an individual must be proven to be a part of an organization whose history contains two or more racketeering episodes. RICO prosecutions take place for murder, extortion, jury tampering, gambling, mail fraud, counterfeiting, pornography distribution, drug trafficking, and a host of other activities. Usually, government agents are given wide leeway in investigating potential RICO violators.

One problem with RICO has been its ambiguity. Terms like "enterprise," "conspiracy," "pattern," and "racketeering" are subject to overly broad interpretation. Almost immediately, some employers saw RICO as a potential weapon to counter unions. A **strike**, for example, could be interpreted as affecting interstate commerce, and holding several could be seen as a pattern. A 1973 Supreme Court decision clarified this by exempting unions from prosecution if their activities were related to legitimate union objectives. One controversial section of that ruling also extended protection to illegal acts committed by members when the union itself was pursuing legitimate goals. RICO could not, for example, be used against an international union merely because some members of a local conspired to commit acts of vandalism.

RICO has been applied against unions on numerous occasions. The two best-publicized cases involved the Teamsters in 1988, and the Longshoremen two years later. Both were placed under federal trusteeship until **rank-and-file** reform groups could reorganize the unions along democratic lines. But there have also been many misapplications of RICO. In the late 1990s, for example, California building trades unions began setting up protect-labor agreements (PLAs) that required contractors to sign union contracts with at least one union on public-works projects. Contractor groups tried to sabotage PLAs by bringing RICO suits against the unions. (None was successful.) In 2000, AK

Steel brought suit against the **United Steelworkers of America (USWA)** and numerous officials, including USWA President **Richard Trumka**, charging them with RICO violations ranging from extortion and threats to attempted murder of AK Steel families. In 2002, those suits were dismissed as having no merit.

RICO remains a prosecutorial weapon with the potential to rid unions of corrupt practices, but also one that can be used unscrupulously.

Suggested Readings: Foster Dulles and Melvyn Dubofsky, *Labor in America*, 1984; U.S. Department of Labor, "Employment Law Guide," http://www.dol.gov/asp/programs/handbook/unions.htm.

Robert E. Weir

Raiding. Raiding is an inter-union squabble in which one union tries to represent organized employees already under another union's **jurisdiction**. Raiding does not exist when employees work within another union's jurisdiction but are not organized. A common motive for raiding occurs when a union seeks to increase its membership for purposes of bargaining power. Another reason a union may raid another union's membership is to retaliate against another for not cooperating on particular issues or with other organizations.

The American Federation of Labor-Congress of Industrial Organizations (AFL-CIO) created a no-raiding agreement as a precondition for merger in 1954. Affiliates pledged not to organize or represent employees where "an established bargaining relationship" already existed between the employer and another union. The agreement was effective for four years and, in 1958, its principles were incorporated in Article II, Section 8 and Article III, Section 4 of the AFL-CIO constitution, making the agreement mandatory for all affiliates. Raiding usually results in bitterness and it weakens the labor movement. In 1967, the **International Brotherhood of Teamsters** sought to raid Chicano workers allied with **Cesar Chavez** and the **United Farm Workers of America**. It took many years before the two unions cooperated with trust in one another. Raiding and jurisdictional issues have surfaced again recently in the wake of union mergers and the expansion of older industrial unions into workplaces outside their traditional constituencies.

Suggested Readings: Susan Ferriss, Ricardo Sandoval, and Diana Hembree, eds., *Fight in the Fields: Cesar Chavez and the Farmworkers Movement*, 1998; David Prosten, ed., *The Union Steward's Complete Guide*, 1998.

Amanda Busjit

Railroad Strikes of 1877. *See Great Labor Uprising.*

Railroad Strike of 1922. The Railroad Strike of 1922, also known as the Big Strike or the Great Railroad Strike of 1922, is often considered the largest strike in U.S. history. Between July and September 1922, some 400,000 skilled craft workers, known as shopmen, walked off their jobs to protest wage cuts and work-rule changes. It saw the most widespread use of injunctions in American labor history and resulted in a loss for the six unions involved.

The strike was a direct result of the breakdown of the **National Agreement**, a measure set up during World War I. The National Agreement created the Railroad Labor Board (RLB) to mediate wage and work disputes that might otherwise lead to stoppages that would jeopardize the movement of troops and war materiel. The RLB included representatives from the government as well as those from railroad carriers and unions. Vague promises of future cost-of-living increases were made, and the tripartite RLB resolved most wartime disputes peacefully. In 1920, however, the government's direct role in the RLB ended and power shifted to private carriers.

A postwar economic slump and a desire to break the power of **craft unions** led carriers to slash wages on July 1, 1921. Several lines, led by the Pennsylvania Railroad, also announced intentions to cease paying **overtime** rates for work on Sundays and holidays, and to change how **seniority** was calculated. The Pennsylvania Railroad added insult to injury by cutting more than 8,000 jobs during the winter of 1922, largely by **subcontracting** work once done by shopmen. Many of the Pennsylvania's actions were inspired by the **National Association of Manufacturers**, which had launched an **open-shop** drive to break the power of unions. In all, companies foisted about $60 million in wage cuts upon their employees, and most of their actions were in violation of the National Agreement. Craft unionists protested to the RLB, but the RLB acquiesced to carrier demands.

THE PERFECT ANTIDOTE FOR ANTI-LABOR PROPAGANDA IS 'LABOR' IN REGULAR DOSES

Keep it Moving

LABOR

Must Be Done NOW

WASHINGTON, D. C., SATURDAY JULY 15, 1922.

Price, Five Cents

Strikers' Ranks Grow; Train Service Is Breaking Down

LABOR BOARD COMES TO INEVITABLE END, DECLARES B. OF L. E.

"THE VOICE IS JACOB'S VOICE, BUT THE HANDS ARE THE HANDS OF ESAU"
Genesis 27:22

600,000 IN WALKOUT; 100,000 VOLUNTEERS HELP SHOP CRAFTS

"Company Union" Pronouncement of Chairman Hooper Touch Needed to Solidify Rail Workers—Paralysis Creeps Over Transportation Lines

HIGH SPOTS OF SHOPMEN'S STRIKE

ROADS BREAKDOWN; MANAGERS APPEAL FOR FEDERAL HELP

NORTHWEST FACING WINTER AND EMPTY BINS, AVERS PREUS

Help Wanted Ads Belie Hooper Claim Show Inadequacy of Rail Board Rates

OLD GUARD ATTACKS RALLY ITS FRIENDS TO SIDE OF PRIMARY

Newspaper coverage of the 1922 Railroad Strike. © George Meany Memorial Archives.

As conditions deteriorated in 1922, unions and carriers alike readied themselves for confrontation. Skilled shopmen had the potential to inflict severe economic damage to both railroads and the nation at large. Automobiles were not yet a fixture of American society, thus a sizable percentage of the nation's mail, commerce, and passengers was transported by rail. The carriers were dependent upon skilled carpenters, machinists, welders, repairmen, and others to keep the railroads running smoothly.

The first workers to leave their jobs were those employed in Pennsylvania Railroad shops, but it soon spread to other lines. A July 1 strike vote received the approval of 97 percent of the **rank and file** of the affected labor organizations, despite the fact that the RLB declared their strike illegal. Within days as many as 400,000 workers walked out. The strike was confined to skilled shopmen in six unions, including the **International Association of Machinists**, which negotiated through a joint Railway Employees' Department. Railroad brotherhoods like the carmen, firemen, and the **Brotherhood of Locomotive Engineers** were covered by separate agreements and continued to work after shopmen laid down their tools. This meant the railroads could continue to operate, and carriers recruited **scabs** from among management, the unemployed, college students, clerks, and those ideologically opposed to labor unions. The RLB authorized the hiring of scabs, and it turned a blind eye as machine guns and hired guards appeared in railyards across the East and Midwest.

The scabs were ill-prepared to take on such highly skilled work, leading railroad officials across the United States to seek injunctions to force workers back on the job; thousands faced arrest rather than yield. On July 28, President Warren G. Harding tried to broker an agreement that would have done little except protect seniority rights. The Railroad Employees' Department expressed reluctant acceptance, but railroad executives refused to discuss even Harding's modest proposal. Both the unions and President Harding were undermined by Harding's own attorney general, Harry Daugherty.

Daugherty played much the same role during the 1922 strike as Attorney General Richard Olney assumed during the **Pullman** boycott thirty years earlier. He sought broad injunctions against strikers, partly to protect his own investments, and partly because he had a pathological fear of communism. The Bolshevik Revolution took place in Russia five years earlier, and Daugherty claimed that railroad workers sought to emulate it. His interpretation was ludicrous, but red-baiting proved a successful strategy. Daugherty convinced Federal District Judge James Wilkerson to issue restraining orders on September 1, based on rather convoluted interpretations of the **Sherman Antitrust Act**. Again, like Pullman, alleged interference with the U.S. mail was used as one justification for injunctions.

Wilkerson's restraining order involved the widest use of injunction powers in U.S. labor history. He placed a total gag order on the unions, officials, and rank and file. Strikers were forbidden to **picket**, call strike meetings, issue press releases, or in any manner encourage the strike. His orders even forbade use of the mail or telegrams; in essence, Wilkerson outlawed free speech. Wilkerson's temporary restraining order also contained his defiant intent to defend **open shops**.

Hundreds of union members were jailed as a result of the injunction. In San Francisco, a $9 million judgment was ordered against striking unions; elsewhere even individuals filed lawsuits against the strikers. There was little unions could do in the face of such opposition except surrender. On August 25, 1922, less intransigent employers of the New York Central and Baltimore and Ohio Railroads settled with their workers. The so-called "B & O Plan" retained seniority systems and rehired most of the strikers at existing wage rates. This became the blueprint by which disputes on other lines were settled. Most strikes were over by mid-September, though some Pennsylvania Railroad workers remained on strike for more than two years.

In the short-term, the strike was a disaster for unions. Unions were weakened to the point where they couldn't muster opposition even when promises on seniority were broken. Tens of thousands of railroad workers were forced to quit their organizations and join **company unions**. It stands as the most dramatic example of the fate that befell most strikers in the 1920s. Union membership across the nation plummeted in the wake of a full-scale assault on the part of aggressive anti-union employers.

But rail carriers also paid the price. The Daugherty/Wilkerson injunctions were so outrageous than even some conservatives saw them as unreasonable. Daugherty's subsequent role in the Teapot Dome scandal crippled his credibility, and some awards against unions were either overturned or drastically reduced. Many workers responded to the political heavy-handedness of the strike by supporting the 1924 Progressive Party campaign of Robert La Follette, who garnered more than 4.8 million votes, more than half as many as Democratic challenger John Davis. In 1926, Congress passed the **Railway Labor Act of 1926 (RLA)** to correct some of the problems within the industry. In 1935, the **National Labor Relations Act** outlawed many of the abusive injunction methods used in 1922.

Suggested Readings: Irving Bernstein, *The Lean Years*, 1960; Foster Rhea Dulles and Melvyn Dubofsky, *Labor in America: A History*, 1984; Leonard Painter, *Through Fifty Years with the Brotherhood of Railway Carmen of America*, 1944.

Robert E. Weir

Railway Labor Act of 1926 (RLA). The Railway Labor Act of 1926 is the federal law that governs labor relations and **collective bargaining** in the U.S. railroad and airline industries. The act's objective is to avoid strikes and other forms of conflict which interrupt interstate commerce and weaken the economy. To do this, the act protects employee rights to form labor unions and mandates mediation of disputes by a federal agency.

The railroad industry receives special attention from lawmakers because of its critical importance in commerce and transportation. Stemming from disruptive and violent strikes during the **Great Labor Uprising** and the **Great Upheaval** from 1877 through 1888, a series of laws tried to achieve industrial peace in the railroad industry. The first of these laws was passed in 1888, and the 1926 Railway Labor Act was enacted to address the shortcomings of previous laws. It was a direct outgrowth of the **railroad strike of 1922**, which saw abusive use of injunction power against workers. Initially the RLA applied only to the railroad industry; airlines were added in 1934.

The act promotes collective bargaining and is administered by the National Mediation Board (NMB). When bargaining over pay and working conditions, strikes can only occur after the NMB releases the parties from mediation. The president of the United States can further delay a strike by creating a Presidential Emergency Board to investigate the dispute. Over 230 Presidential Emergency Boards have been formed since 1934. There are also provisions to prevent work stoppages over grievances.

To prevent strikes caused by employees trying to force an employer to recognize a union, the RLA authorizes secret-ballot elections conducted by the NMB. If a majority of workers vote for union representation, the union is certified and the employer must bargain with it. In addition to regulating railroad and airline labor relations, the RLA is significant because of its legal and operational influence on the drafting of the **National Labor Relations Act** of 1935, which governs labor relations in the rest of the private sector.

Suggested Readings: Douglas Leslie, ed., *The Railway Labor Act*, 1995; Charles Rehmus, ed., *The Railway Labor Act at Fifty: Collective Bargaining in the Railroad and Airline Industries*, 1977.

John W. Budd

A. Philip Randolph in about 1930. © Bettmann/Corbis.

Randolph, Asa Philip (April 14, 1889–May 16, 1979). Asa Philip Randolph was a trade unionist and civil-rights leader. He was the son of the Rev. James William and Elizabeth (Robinson) Randolph and completed high school in Jacksonville, Florida. In 1914, he married Lucille Greene. Shortly thereafter he moved to the Harlem section of New York City, and worked as an elevator operator while taking classes at City College of New York. Randolph's arrival in New York coincided with a flowering of political and cultural activity within the black community known as the Harlem Renaissance. He became a **socialist** and, in 1917, set up the United Brotherhood of Elevator and Switchboard Operators union. That same year, he and Chandler Owen began publication of *The Messenger*, an independent socialist journal. That paper was sympathetic to the **Industrial Workers of the World** and critical of African American involvement in World War I. Randolph was arrested as a suspected **communist** in 1918, was briefly jailed, then drafted into military service, but the war ended and charges against him were dropped.

The Messenger advocated that African Americans join labor unions and was highly critical of both capitalism and the National Association for the Advancement of Colored People (NAACP), which Randolph felt was too conservative. In 1919, Randolph served on the executive board of the National Brotherhood Workers of America and, in 1920, he set up Friends of Negro Freedom, an organization to protect migrant and tenant rights. Randolph quit the Socialist Party when it moved too slowly on black issues. In 1925, he founded the **Brotherhood of Sleeping Car Porters (BSCP)** and commanded its twelve-year struggle to obtain a contract with the Pullman Corporation. In 1936, the BSCP affiliated with the **American Federation of Labor (AFL)**. He continued as president of the BSCP until his retirement in 1968.

Randolph was one of the most important civil-rights advocates of his era. He served on numerous commissions on race and, in 1936, co-founded the National Negro Congress to promote black job opportunities under the New Deal and protect black workers. His threat to organize a march of black workers on Washington, D.C. prompted President Franklin Roosevelt to establish the **Fair Employment Practices Committee** in 1941. During and after World War II, Randolph was an outspoken critic of military segregation. He was equally outspoken within the labor movement. As a delegate to the International Confederation of Free Trade Unions in 1951 and a member of the executive council of the American Federation of Labor-Congress of Industrial Organizations (AFL-CIO) after its 1955 merger, Randolph forcefully argued for full inclusion for people of color. In 1960 he founded the Negro American Labor Council to advance black union members. His militancy led to numerous clashes with cautious AFL-CIO leaders and, in 1961, the executive council censured Randolph. He was the national director of the 1963 March on Washington for Jobs and Freedom and addressed the rally just before the Rev. Martin Luther King, Jr. By the time of his death in 1979, the AFL-CIO had adopted many of the protections for black workers that Randolph advocated.

Suggested Readings: Jervis Anderson, *A. Philip Randolph: A Biographical Portrait*, 1972; Mari Jo Buhle, et al., *Encyclopedia of the American Left*, 1992; William Harris, A. Philip Randolph, "Black Workers, and the Labor Movement," in Dubofsky and Van Tine, *Labor Leaders in America*, 1987.

Robert E. Weir

Rank and File. Rank and file describes ordinary union members who do not hold office in the local union. Often, these workers are referred to as the union's grass roots. These are the participants whose interests the officers and other union officials represent during collective bargaining negotiations. In theory, these individuals belong to a democratic union whose procedures were formally stated in the **Labor-Management Reporting and Disclosure Act** of 1959. A union's bargaining power is established by the rank and file since, without the majority vote of workers, officers cannot be elected or undertake negotiations with an employer. Currently, there is insufficient worker-rights legislation to protect democracy within some unions. Unions like the **International Brotherhood of Teamsters** and the **United Mine Workers of America**

have witnessed rank-and-file insurgency movements to restore democratic union principles, but many unions continue to concentrate power in the upper echelons of their bureaucracies and employ complex rules and procedures that isolate officials from the rank and file.

Suggested Reading: Harry Kelber, "Why Drop Workers' Rights?" in *Weekly Labor Talk*, April 10, 1999.

Amanda Busjit

Rate Cutting. Rate cutting is a general term that applies to an employer's attempt to motivate workers to perform their jobs faster and more efficiently by reducing their pay or **piecework** rate. This type of reduction usually occurs in enterprises like textiles or the garment trade where the quantity of goods produced is essential to the firm's overall profit margin. Trade unionists usually oppose this type of system for two reasons. First, it is a de facto **speedup** in which increased efficiency and production far outstrip worker remuneration. Second, employers often abuse employees who have already mastered their skill and usually don't reward them financially for increased productivity. Sometimes, this term may refer to work situations where the pay rate to motivate employees has been higher than the salary of workers within the industry or in similar operations.

Rate cutting is primarily associated with jobs that pay either piece rates or a fixed sum for each article produced. It was also more common in the years before World War II than it is today. It was a key component in scientific management principles associated with **Taylorism** and often engendered fierce opposition from workers. For example, demand for production of wartime supplies in the early 1940s generated conflict and safety concerns at automotive plants such as Chrysler and Packard Motors. Workers challenged management consistently during this time over the right to maintain production standards and **incentive pay** rates. However, rate cutting still occurs wherever incentive pay is based on output, and in businesses intent on reducing costs and maximizing human resources.

Suggested Readings: Joyce Bagot, ed., *Source Book on Collective Bargaining*, 1998; Frederick Winslow Taylor, *The Principles of Scientific Management*, 1998.

Amanda Busjit

Ravenswood Lockout. The Ravenswood Lockout was a protracted struggle between the **United Steelworkers of America (USWA)** and the Ravenswood Aluminum Company (RAC). To some observers, the USWA's partial victory in 1992 signaled an important reversal of union fortunes in the 1980s and is a portent for organized labor's potential for renewal.

Problems at Ravenswood were part and parcel of the merger mania that marked American corporate culture in the 1980s. The aluminum reduction and fabrication plant in this small West Virginia Ohio River town opened in

1954, as part of the Kaiser Aluminum Company (later known as ALCOA). In 1958, the USWA organized plant workers in local 5668. For many years, capital/labor relations were marked by **paternalism**, union/management cooperation, and civic benevolence on the part of the corporation. By the 1970s, however, ALCOA's market share declined in the face of competition from imports and its own outmoded manufacturing processes. Jobs were eliminated in Ravenswood and other facilities. ALCOA management forced local 5668 to accept deep **concessions** in 1984. By 1986, however, ALCOA was still deeply in debt. Two years later, Ravenswood was part of an ALCOA sell-off that placed the RAC under the control of an international holding company clandestinely financed by corporate raider and tax-evader Marc Rich.

Safety conditions and morale were already in decline at the RAC and the plant's new management was openly hostile to the USWA. The deaths of several Ravenswood workers brought matters to a head in 1990. On November 1, RAC management issued a **lockout** of the plant's 1,700 workers, declared it a non-union facility, and began hiring **scabs** to replace USWA members. For the next eighteen months the USWA battled the company on the picket line, in domestic and international courts, before the National Labor Relations Board, in the political arena, and on the public-relations front. The USWA launched an especially effective **corporate campaign** that exposed Ravenswood's ties to Marc Rich, by then an international fugitive from justice living in Switzerland. It also showed how cost-cutting measures took place in violation of the **Occupational Safety and Health Act (1970)**, and how the firm routinely violated provisions of the Clean Air and Clean Water Acts.

RAC workers also maintained inspiring levels of solidarity throughout the struggle. Even more impressively, local 5668 was able to build bridges with overseas union movements that collectively placed pressure on Rich, banks doing business with Ravenswood, and politicians who coddled questionable corporate practices. The union also convinced important RAC clients—like Coca Cola and Anheuser-Busch—to stop purchasing scab-made cans. The union's anti-Rich campaign took them to Australia, England, Finland, France, The Netherlands, Romania, Russia, Spain, Switzerland, and five other nations. It successfully linked Rich's consortium to labor struggles around the globe and pressured Rich holdings worldwide. Faced with international pressure, mounting legal bills, and overwhelmingly negative public opinion, the RAC settled its dispute with USWA local 5668. On June 12, 1992, members ratified a new contract and, on June 29, jubilant workers marched into the plant singing "Solidarity Forever."

For many observers, Ravenswood—like 1990s victories by United Parcel Service workers, NYNEX workers, Fieldcrest employees, and others—shows that organized labor is on the cusp of a renewal. Ravenswood workers received high praise for their creativity, their international organizing efforts, and their steadfast refusal to cave in. Some observers see the Ravenswood lockout as proof that modern labor conflicts must go beyond traditional trade union reliance on strikes. The final settlement was not a complete victory for the USWA. Ravenswood nearly went bankrupt during the lockout and its uncertain financial future threatens to delay promised safety improvements, job guarantees, and pension schemes. The $2,000 in back pay given to each worker hardly compensated their loss, and several hundred workers did not get their jobs back. Moreover, the USWA had to welcome into the union over 300 scabs who took vacant positions. In 2001, President William Clinton pardoned Marc Rich, an act seen by many USWA members as an insult. It remains to be seen if Ravenswood truly was a turning point for labor.

Suggested Readings: Tom Juravich and Kate Bronfenbrenner, *Ravenswood,* 1999; Joshua Green, "Union Square Off," www.thenewrepublic.com/express/green.020801.html; Russell Mokhibu and Robert Weissman, "A Rich Pardon," www.sfbg.com/focus/120.html.

Robert E. Weir

Reece, Florence (April 12, 1900–August 3, 1986). Florence Reece was a social activist, poet, and songwriter. Born in Sharps Chapel, Tennessee, she grew up in a coal camp at Fort Ridge, Tennessee. Florence Reece was the daughter of a coal miner who loaded a ton and a half of coal for thirty cents. At age of fifteen, the year after her father was killed in a slate fall, she married Sam Reece. Reece was also a coal miner, who had gone to work in the mines at the age of eleven to earn sixty cents a day. Her mother opposed the marriage and the two crossed the state line to Kentucky where her mother's permission was not needed. Reece had ten children, some of whom went into the mines as boys to help support the family.

Florence Reece lived in Harlan County, Kentucky in the 1930s when the **United Mine Workers of America** attempted to unionize coal miners. She saw miners and their families—hard-working people—going hungry. She saw thugs prowling her county to keep coal miners from affiliating with the union. Her husband Sam would come home wearing frozen clothes after lying in water all day to mine coal. Sam Reece was one of the labor organizers for the United Mine Workers of America in "bloody" Harlan County. During the Harlan County strike, which is called the Battle of Evarts, Sheriff J. H. Blair led his deputies on a violent rampage of beating and murdering union leaders. One night in May 1931, while Reece was alone with her children, Sheriff Blair and a band of deputies broke into her home. She demanded of the sheriff, "What are you here for? You know there's nothing but a lot of little hungry children here." The men ransacked the house in search of Sam, but could not find him. While the sheriff and his thugs waited for Sam, she managed to get word to her husband not to come home. Days later, while waiting for her husband to return, she wrote "Which Side Are You On?" on an old wall calendar, written to the tune of an old Baptist hymn called "Lay the Lily Low." The Battle of Evarts, immortalized in this Appalachian woman's coal-miner protest song, is one of the most famous labor songs in history and communicates hope and inspiration.

Come all you poor workers,
Good news to you I'll tell,
How the good old union
Has come here to dwell.
Which side are you on?
Which side are you on?
We're starting our good battle,
We know we're sure to win,
Because we've got the gun thugs
A lookin' very thin.
Which side are you on?
Which side are you on?
If you go to Harlan County,
There is no neutral there,
You'll either be a union man
Or a thug for J. H. Blair.
Which side are you on?
Which side are you on?

In 1941, a version recorded by the Almanac Singers—comprised of Woody Guthrie, Lee Hays, Millard Lapell, and Pete Seeger—made the song famous. The song is still sung at labor worker gatherings and other social causes, worldwide. (See **Music and Labor**.)

A lifelong activist, Reece wrote *Against the Current*, a collection of short stories and poems. Reece also criticized President Reagan for his cuts in programs for the poor and needy in her song "You Can't Live On Jellybeans," which is a reference to one of the president's favorite foods.

Florence and Sam lived happily together for sixty-four years, until he died in 1978 of pneumoconiosis, or Black Lung Disease. Florence died from a heart attack in Knoxville, Tennessee.

Suggested Readings: William Serrin, "Labor Song's Writer, Frail at 83, Shows She Is Still a Fighter," in *The New York Times* no. 160 Late City Final Edition (March 18, 1984, Sunday); Hilda Wenner, *Here's to Women*, 1987; Deana Martin, "Appalachian Protest Songwriters," http://athena.English.vt.edu/~appalach/writersM/protestsongs.htm.

Patricia Shackleton

Reeves v. Sanderson Plumbing Products, Inc. *Reeves v. Sanderson Plumbing Products, Inc.* is a Supreme Court decision rendered in June 2000 that makes it easier for employees to file bias lawsuits against their employers. The plaintiff, Roger Reeves, was a supervisor in the Sanderson Plumbing Products firm of Columbia, Mississippi. In 1995, he was fired after working for the firm for forty years. The company alleged that Reeves was dismissed for poor record keeping and lax supervisory skills, but Reeves maintained that he was fired because of his age. A company manager told the fifty-seven-year-old Reeves that he was "too damn old," several months before his dismissal. This followed a similar slight several months before.

Reeves's job reviews were exemplary and he thus filed suit alleging that he was a victim of age discrimination. Reeves won, but the original verdict was overturned by a federal appeals judge who ruled that Reeves failed to demonstrate discrimination, even though the company's stated reasons for firing him were untrue. In June 2000 the Supreme Court unanimously sided with Reeves and reinstated the original verdict. The court also ruled that employees need only demonstrate that an employer's explanation for a hiring or promotion decision was false, and that it was the task of juries to determine whether or not discrimination occurred. Unions and worker advocates hailed the decision, which no longer requires employees to provide concrete evidence of discrimination. Legal scholars predict it will dramatically increase discrimination suits against employers.

Suggested Readings: Marcia McCormick, "Reeves v. Sanderson Plumbing: Turning Back the Tide on Summary Judgment in Federal Employment," in *Washington Post,* June 13, 2000. "DCBA Brief Online," http://www.dcba.org/brief/octissue/2001/art31001.htm; *Reeves v. Sanderson,* http://supct.law.cornell.edu/supct/html/99–536.ZS.html.

Robert E. Weir

Replacement Worker. Replacement worker is the term used to describe a person who takes the place of another during a **strike** or **lockout**. It has only gained currency since the late 1970s and has been part of concerted, professional attempts to defeat and discredit unions. The term has been actively promoted in an attempt to escape the opprobrium associated with the older term "**scab**."

Although businesses have long attempted to operate as non-union concerns and many have succeeded in routing organized labor from their businesses, the usual practice was to rehire most strikers once a union was broken. In strikes like the **Professional Air Traffic Controllers Organization (PATCO) strike** in 1981, the **Phelps-Dodge strike** in 1983 (miners), and the **Hormel strike** in 1985 (meatpackers), however, management replaced their entire workforce. A 1993 attempt by the 103rd Congress to amend the **National Labor Relations Act** and prohibit the hiring of permanent replacement workers was killed by Republican filibuster. Under current law, permanent replacement workers remain legal hires if the strike is deemed purely an economic action on the part of the union. Unions have countered by filing **unfair labor practices** in order to refute the right to hire replacement workers. (An unfair labor practice would mean the strike was not entirely economic.)

Suggested Readings: Stanley Aronowitz, *From the Ashes of the Old,* 1998; Charles Baird, "Strikers and Scabs," http://www.libertyhaven.com/theoreticorphilosophicalissues/economics/employmentandunemployment/strikersandscabs.html; Thomas Geoghean, *Which Side Are You On?,* 1991.

Robert E. Weir

Republicanism. Republicanism was the political ideology that formed Americans' core political beliefs and institutions. In the antebellum years, republicanism helped shape the views of workers and their unions as well. Throughout the eighteenth and nineteenth centuries, many denounced the inequalities of colonialism, slavery, and industrialization by employing the tenets of republicanism: virtue, citizenship, community, liberty, and equality. British labor agitator Thomas Paine, for example, emigrated to America, where he wrote *Common Sense* (1776). Seeking farmers' and artisans' participation in the American Revolution, Paine proclaimed "the floor of Freedom is as level as water." Many workers were attracted to Paine's challenges to constituted authority and his insistence that true liberty was radically democratic. Among artisans, Thomas Paine's birthday was a de facto workers' holiday. Thomas Jefferson was also much honored for his perceived radicalism and support for farmers and other commoners.

Vague republican precepts also resonated among slaves. In 1800, Gabriel Prosser rallied more than 1,000 slaves under the slogan "Death or Liberty." Prosser invoked the same principles as Patrick Henry's famous revolutionary proclamation, thereby demonstrating that the promises of republicanism were being denied to slaves.

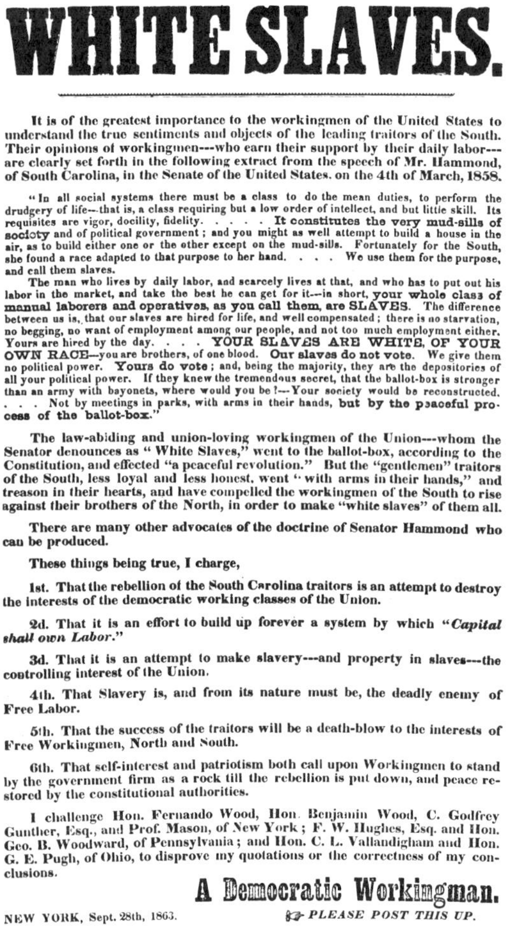

WHITE SLAVES.

It is of the greatest importance to the workingmen of the United States to understand the true sentiments and objects of the leading traitors of the South. Their opinions of workingmen---who earn their support by their daily labor---are clearly set forth in the following extract from the speech of Mr. Hammond, of South Carolina, in the Senate of the United States. on the 4th of March, 1858.

"In all social systems there must be a class to do the mean duties, to perform the drudgery of life---that is, a class requiring but a low order of intellect, and but little skill. Its requisites are vigor, docility, fidelity. . . . . It constitutes the very mud-sills of society and of political government; and you might as well attempt to build a house in the air, as to build either one or the other except on the mud-sills. Fortunately for the South, she found a race adapted to that purpose to her hand. . . . We use them for the purpose, and call them slaves.

The man who lives by daily labor, and scarcely lives at that, and who has to put out his labor in the market, and take the best he can get for it---in short, your whole class of manual laborers and operatives, as you call them, are SLAVES. The difference between us is, that our slaves are hired for life, and well compensated; there is no starvation, no begging, no want of employment among our people, and not too much employment either. Yours are hired by the day. . . . YOUR SLAVES ARE WHITE, OF YOUR OWN RACE---you are brothers, of one blood. Our slaves do not vote. We give them no political power. Yours do vote; and, being the majority, they are the depositories of all your political power. If they knew the tremendous secret, that the ballot-box is stronger than an army with bayonets, where would you be?---Your society would be reconstructed. . . . Not by meetings in parks, with arms in their hands, but by the peaceful process of the ballot-box."

The law-abiding and union-loving workingmen of the Union---whom the Senator denounces as "White Slaves," went to the ballot-box, according to the Constitution, and effected "a peaceful revolution." But the "gentlemen" traitors of the South, less loyal and less honest, went "with arms in their hands," and treason in their hearts, and have compelled the workingmen of the South to rise against their brothers of the North, in order to make "white slaves" of them all.

There are many other advocates of the doctrine of Senator Hammond who can be produced.

These things being true, I charge,

1st. That the rebellion of the South Carolina traitors is an attempt to destroy the interests of the democratic working classes of the Union.

2d. That it is an effort to build up forever a system by which "*Capital shall own Labor*."

3d. That it is an attempt to make slavery---and property in slaves---the controlling interest of the Union.

4th. That Slavery is, and from its nature must be, the deadly enemy of Free Labor.

5th. That the success of the traitors will be a death-blow to the interests of Free Workingmen, North and South.

6th. That self-interest and patriotism both call upon Workingmen to stand by the government firm as a rock till the rebellion is put down, and peace restored by the constitutional authorities.

I challenge Hon. Fernando Wood, Hon. Benjamin Wood, C. Godfrey Gunther, Esq., and Prof. Mason, of New York; F. W. Hughes, Esq. and Hon. Geo. B. Woodward, of Pennsylvania; and Hon. C. L. Vallandigham and Hon. G. E. Pugh, of Ohio, to disprove my quotations or the correctness of my conclusions.

A Democratic Workingman.

NEW YORK, Sept. 28th, 1863.

☞ *PLEASE POST THIS UP.*

This Civil War declaration of a workingman contains a description of the concept of "wage slavery," which many southerners, and some northerners, viewed as the North's version of slavery. © George Meany Memorial Archives.

Despite most Americans' use of republicanism to stress economic individualism, workers employed republicanism to critique industrialization and commercialization that they believed amassed wealth and power and threatened their independence. The **Workingmen's Movement** of the 1820s and 1830s helped shape labor republicanism. An Albany paper proclaimed that "the farmers, mechanics, and workingmen are assembling [with] those principles of liberty and equality unfolded in the Declaration of Independence." By the 1830s, labor republicanism was a loose nexus of ideas that critiqued existing social and economic elites and called for equal rights, essentially demanding American society honor the democratic ideals embedded within the Declaration of Independence and the Bill of Rights. To that end, advocates called for banking regulations, land reform, mechanics' **lien laws**, shorter work hours, reform of inheritance-tax laws, and universal public education. They also called for the abolition of debtor prisons, laws requiring males to drill in local militias, and the formation of monopolies. A key idea was expansion of suffrage; some even supported women's right to vote.

Women working in New England textile mills employed the term "wage slavery" to denounce class structures and workplace injustices. Over time, this became a key link for those who associated labor's cause with abolition. After the Civil War, workers joined the **eight-hour movement** to bring about the "republicanization of labor, as well as a republicanization of government." In the 1880s, the **Knights of Labor**'s motto, "an injury to one is the concern of all," tapped workers' republican idealism. From Virginia to California, Knights participated in labor parties and took control of local politics, causing a San Francisco newspaper to proclaim that the Knights were "regenerators of the Republic."

The post–Civil War period also saw the penetration of imported ideologies, like **anarchism**, **Lassalleanism**, Marxism, and other varieties of **socialism**. In addition, American-style liberalism began to cast off its associations with laissez-faire **capitalism** and merge with republican precepts. By the 1890s, the term republicanism began to fall out of favor, though its ideals continue to resonate in working-class movements. In recent years, labor historians have found republicanism a useful idea in helping explain why socialist movements in the United States have been weaker than those in other western industrialized nations. According to this line of reasoning, American workers were less susceptible to imported socialism because they were grounded in an older and better-entrenched radical tradition that drew on Paine's democratic idealism and Jefferson's rural (and rhetorical) radicalism.

Suggested Readings: Leon Fink, *Workingmen's Democracy: The Knights of Labor and American Politics*, 1983; Eric Foner, *Tom Paine and Revolutionary America*, 1976; Sean Wilentz, *Chants Democratic: New York City and the Rise of the American Working Class, 1788–1850*, 1984.

John Whitmer

Rerum Novarum. *Rerum Novarum* was an encyclical issued by Pope Leo XIII in 1891 that, among other things, removed the Roman Catholic Church's blanket condemnation of secret societies and recognized the legitimacy of labor unions. It offered critiques of both **socialism** and **capitalism**, arguing that capital and labor must recognize that their interests are inextricably linked.

Prior to *Rerum Novarum*, Catholic workers faced a dilemma. In the wake of the anti-Masonic agitations in the early nineteenth century and violence associated with the clandestine **Molly Maguires** in the 1870s, the Catholic Church reaffirmed views against secret societies that dated to medieval times. The Church similarly took a dim view of burgeoning socialist movements, both in Europe and in the United States. Catholics joining any sort of secret order faced the threat of excommunication.

In the United States, however, the church's position ran afoul of other social trends. First, the post–Civil War period saw a proliferation of fraternal orders, most of which practiced some degree of ritual secrecy. Second, many labor unions also maintained levels of secrecy. In the absence of labor laws protecting **collective-bargaining** rights, workers faced severe sanctions merely for associating with a labor union. To protect membership, many chose to operate clandestinely. For Irish, German, and French-Canadian Catholic immigrants the church's condemnation imposed a special burden: obeying the church's prohibition meant avoiding fraternal groups and labor unions important to helping immigrants assimilate into American society. It also fueled already deep nativist suspicions of foreign-born workers. Moreover, many workers were attracted to socialism, and many immigrants had been involved in movements prior to arriving in America.

The Catholic Church's position became untenable with the growth of the **Knights of Labor (KOL)** in 1880s. Because the KOL practiced a concealed ritual and operated in complete secrecy until 1882, it was roundly condemned by Catholic clerics. In Canada, Catholic workers were forbidden to join the KOL, and those in America faced church discipline. The KOL's leadership, however, was heavily Roman Catholic and, at least until 1886, so too was the bulk of its membership. Forced to choose between their church or their union, many choose the latter.

The KOL took the lead in attempting to ameliorate disputes with Rome. In 1879, Knights changed wording in their ritual to allow communicants to reveal parts of it to their priests, and KOL head **Terence Powderly**, a practicing Catholic, led the move to make the KOL a public organization in all but its ritual. He also cultivated an alliance with the powerful James Cardinal Gibbons of Baltimore, who admired the KOL and saw no threat to the faith in its precepts. Gibbons lobbied Rome to make policy changes. At first he was rebuffed, but after 1885, so many workers were joining the KOL that Gibbons argued that the Church would be irreparably harmed by continuing a blanket ban against secret orders and labor unions.

The Catholic Church was still officially a mission church in the United States for much of the nineteenth century. Catholics were suspect, and outbreaks of anti-Catholic discrimination were common, especially against Irish and Irish-Americans. Powderly himself came in for intense criticism for attempting to placate the Church. Gibbons parlayed all of this into a successful plea in Rome. Canadian parishes were ordered to cease excommunicating Knights and, in 1891, Pope Leo XIII issued *Rerum Novarum*.

Rerum Novarum pales when compared with the pronouncements of Protestants involved in the Social Gospel movement. The document offers only tepid acceptance of labor organizations, though it did recognize their struggle for social justice. It did, however, place the blame for industrial strife upon the shoulders of capital rather than labor. It also valorized manual labor, echoing views of the dignity of toil found in popular labor manifestos. Officially, it endorsed neither capitalism nor socialism. Instead, the encyclical upheld a vague mutualism rooted in principles of Christian fraternity and charity.

Nonetheless, it had a profound impact on the American labor movement. Ironically, the KOL was in deep decline by 1891 and *Rerum Novarum* did little to revive its sagging fortunes. But many future labor leaders were Roman Catholic, and the encyclical allowed Catholic workers to join unions with a clear conscience. Rome's periodic reaffirmations of *Rerum Novarum* also insulated it somewhat from charges of complicity with oppression. The most significant of these was *Quadragesimo Anno* issued by Pope Pius XI in 1931, which contained blistering condemnations of unemployment. As an ironic footnote, *Rerum Novarum* also led to the founding of a large Catholic fraternal order that uses secret rituals: the Knights of Columbus.

Suggested Readings: Sidney Ahlstrom, *A Religious History of the American People*, 1975; Henry Browne, *The Catholic Church and the Knights of Labor*, 1949; Ken Fones-Wolf, *Trade Union Gospel: Christianity and Labor in Industrial Philadelphia 1865–1915*, 1989.

Robert E. Weir

Reuther, Walter (September 1, 1907–May 9, 1970). Walter Reuther was born in Wheeling, West Virginia, the son of German immigrant parents. Reuther's father, Valentine, worked as a brewery-wagon driver and insurance agent and was active in the trade union and **socialist** movements. Walter Reuther and his two younger brothers, Roy (1909–1968) and Victor (1912–), were inculcated with their father's working-class idealism and commitment to social justice. In 1923, Walter dropped out of high school to become an apprentice die maker and, in 1927, moved to Detroit where he worked as a die maker for Ford Motor Company. While working full-time at Ford, Reuther finished high school and enrolled at Detroit City College (later Wayne State University). Reuther was involved in campus politics and worked actively for the election of Norman Thomas, socialist candidate for the presidency in 1932. Reuther joined the Auto Workers Union, affiliated with the communist Trade Union Unity League, but found himself laid off, a victim of the Great Depression. In 1933, Walter and his brother Victor traveled abroad where they witnessed the Nazi seizure of power

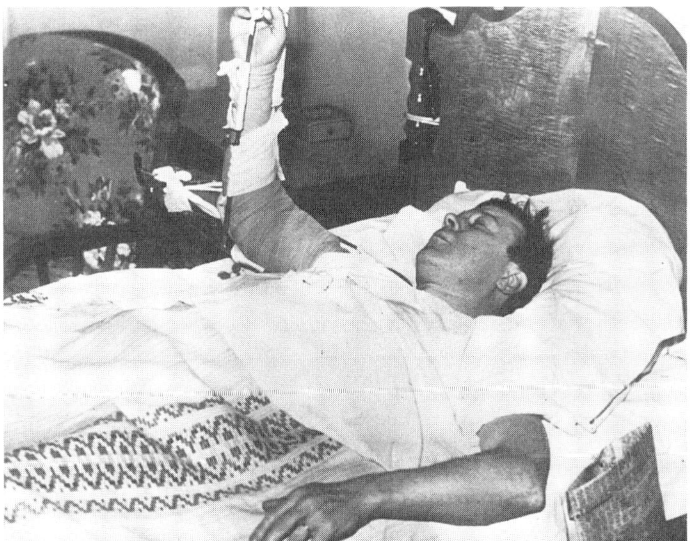

Walter Reuther recovering after an assassination attempt. © George Meany Memorial Archives.

and briefly worked with the underground resistance. Traveling to the Soviet Union, the Reuther brothers were employed at the Gorki automotive factory where their experience at Ford proved valuable. The Stalinist regime proved too oppressive for the Reuthers and they remained in the Soviet Union for only two years. Upon return to the United States, Walter Reuther became involved in the labor movement. He attended the 1935 **American Federation of Labor (AFL)** convention, where **John L. Lewis** led the movement for industrial unionism, arguing that mass organization on an industry-wide basis rather than organization by skilled craft was the future of organized labor. Reuther, without a job, obtained a union card in a small **United Auto Workers (UAW)** local of GM workers. Reuther was a delegate at the UAW's South Bend, Indiana, convention in 1936, where his ambition, self-confidence, ability, left-leaning reputation, and oratorical skills propelled him to a position of leadership. Reuther became president of the tiny Local 174. Reuther and his brothers led a **strike**, in December 1936, against Kelsey-Hayes Corporation, a brake and wheel supplier for Ford. This strike spurred tremendous growth for Local 174. Immediately following the Kelsey-Hayes settlement, the Flint, Michigan, General Motors (GM) **sit-down strike** began. Walter's brothers Victor and Roy were deeply involved in the Flint strike. On May 26, 1937, Reuther and other UAW organizers were viciously attacked by Ford Service Division goons at the Battle of the Overpass, outside the River Rouge plant. Newspapers throughout the nation published vivid photographs of Reuther, Richard Frankensteen, and other bloodied UAW organizers, thus establishing Reuther as one of labor's heroes.

Walter Reuther (speaking) and his younger brother Victor Reuther (seated). © George Meany Memorial Archives/Nate Fine Photo.

Between 1936 and 1939, the UAW was fraught with internecine warfare between numerous factions, not only communists and conservatives, but also those who feuded with the leadership over tactics, strategy, and organization. By 1939, Reuther had emerged as head of the potentially important GM Department, which Reuther transformed from a paper organization into a critical part of the UAW by organizing the tool and die makers. Reuther saw that, without the labor of the tool and die makers, GM would be unprepared to roll out its 1940 models, thus the company was compelled to recognize and bargain with the UAW.

As the United States entered World War II, Reuther proposed the conversion of auto plants to military production, with the goal of 500 aircraft per day. Reuther saw the war as an opportunity for labor to achieve a more nearly equal voice with the companies in workplace management. Reuther proposed a series of new ideas that gained him national attention. Once reconversion to peacetime production began, Reuther challenged GM's argument that it could not afford wage increases without increases in the cost of automobiles. Reuther challenged GM to "open the books" to prove the company's contention. No other labor group joined Reuther in his challenge, though, and labor obtained wage increases while companies passed along significant price increases to consumers.

In 1946, Walter Reuther defeated the ineffective R. J. Thomas for UAW president. Thomas and George Addes, UAW secretary-treasurer, had been among Reuther's staunchest opponents. Reuther purged the UAW leadership of all remnants of the Thomas-Addes caucus and, in 1948, was the subject of a shotgun assassination attempt. In 1949, his brother Victor was the subject of a similar attempt; Walter suffered a paralyzed arm, Victor lost an eye. Neither crime ever resulted in an arrest, but Reuther beefed up personal security for the remainder of his life. Following 1948, Reuther led the purge of communists from the **Congress of Industrial Organizations (CIO)**. In 1949, eleven communist-dominated unions were expelled and Reuther, once seen as a leftist himself, was the most prominent leader in the movement to purge the left-wing unions. Politically, Reuther had slowly become more centrist. He abandoned the Socialist Party and became a stolid supporter of Franklin D. Roosevelt's New Deal, coming to believe that the Democratic Party was the only practical way for labor to achieve national political influence. He dreamed of a realignment of American politics whereby the Democrats would take on the role of Europe's labor and social democrats. He became a force within the Democratic Party, solidly backing John F. Kennedy and Lyndon B. Johnson and enthusiastically supporting Johnsons's civil rights and Great Society programs.

Reuther's labor strategy evolved to the identification of one target firm among auto's big three. That firm would bear the brunt of strike actions. Then, once a settlement was reached with the target firm, the gains made there would be used as a model for settlement with the other two giant auto firms. Under Reuther's bargaining strategy, tremendous gains were made for auto workers in the postwar era. Productivity increases were linked to **cost-of-living** increases at GM in 1948; employer-funded pensions were introduced at Chrysler in 1950; medical insurance for workers began at GM in 1950; unemployment benefits that supplemented those available through the government were introduced by Ford in 1955. Reuther's strategy in a prosperous postwar world was to offer shop-floor stability and discipline in exchange for gains in wages, benefits, and job security. Reuther's critics charged that this transformed the union from a vital, radical force for social change into a disciplinary arm of the auto companies' personnel departments.

Reuther's practical successes made the UAW the largest union in the CIO, however, when President Philip Murray died in 1952, Reuther succeeded him. As CIO president, Reuther started the negotiations that would lead to the merger of the AFL and CIO in 1955 under the presidency of **George Meany**. Reuther eventually clashed with Meaney, largely over Meaney's support of the Vietnam War, but also over issues such as minority rights and environmental abuses. By 1968, the UAW left the AFL-CIO. Following this, Reuther devoted his efforts to the UAW's Black Lake Recreation and Education Center. He and his wife were killed in an airplane crash in Pellston, Michigan, on May 9, 1970, while traveling to inspect the construction of the center. Roy Reuther worked as an organizer for voter-registration drives as well as for progressive political causes, continuing his formal association with the UAW until his death in 1968. Victor Reuther remained active with the UAW until 1971, but grew disaffected with the union's leadership and direction and became a harsh critic of UAW leaders and policies.

Suggested Readings: John Barnard, *Walter Reuther and the Rise of the Auto Workers*, 1983; Nelson Lichtenstein, *The Most Dangerous Man in Detroit: Walter Reuther and the Fate of American Labor*, 1995; William Serrin, *The Company and the Union: The "Civilized Relationship" of the General Motors Corporation and the United Automobile Workers Union*, 1973.

James P. Hanlan

Rice, Monsignor Charles Owen (November 12, 1908–). Charles Owen Rice was born in New York City on November 12, 1908. After his mother (Anna O'Donnell) died in 1912 while giving birth to her third child (Ellen), Charles and his older brother Patrick were sent to Ireland to live with his father's family. (The sister, Ellen, died a month after birth.) The two brothers moved from Ireland to Pittsburgh in 1920 and lived with their Uncle Joe and their father, Michael, who was an A & P food store warehouse foreman. Michael Rice had remarried his dead wife's eldest sister, Jennie. Charles's Uncle Joe eventually became an organizer in the **Congress of Industrial Organizations (CIO)** and had a significant influence on the political development of his nephews.

The family was strongly Irish Catholic. Charles and his brother both attended parochial schools in Pittsburgh. Charles graduated from St. Mary's Elementary School (1922) and St. Mary of the Mount High School (1926). Charles followed his older brother when he entered Duquesne University in 1926, Patrick's senior year at the college. After graduating from Duquesne in 1930, Charles entered St. Vincent's Seminary and was ordained as a priest in 1934.

Coming of age as a priest during the Depression impacted Rice. He became socially active soon after being assigned assistant pastor of St. Agnes Parish in Pittsburgh in 1935. Between 25 percent and 50 percent of his parishioners were on public assistance. Rice's own father lost his job at the market in the 1930s and had great difficulty finding work. In 1931, while Rice was a student in the seminary, Pope Pious XI issued *Quadregisimo Anno*, a papal decree that reaffirmed Pope Leo XIII's ***Rerum Novarum*** (1891). These papal pronouncements encouraged Catholic social activism in organized labor and guided a generation of socially active priests who supported trade unions and a more organized form of capitalism.

Rice and two other Pittsburgh priests, Father Carl Hensler and Monsignor George Barry O'Toole, formed the Catholic Radical Alliance (CRA) in 1937. The CRA initially followed the philosophy of, and was allied with, Dorothy Day's Catholic Worker (CW) Movement. The CRA established a CW-type hospitality house to help clothe, shelter, feed, and comfort Pittsburgh's poor. But the CRA also focused on supporting organized labor causes in Pittsburgh. Rice and the others formed a Pittsburgh chapter of the **Association of Catholic Trade Unionists (ACTU)** in 1938. A number of fissures developed between the CW movement and Pittsburgh's CRA. Rice did not agree with the CW movement's uncompromising pacifism and opposition to U.S. entrance into WWII. The CW movement was also less critical of individual Communist Party members' activities in reform and labor organizations than Rice and the Pittsburgh ACTU.

Monsignor Charles Rice. © George Meany Memorial Archives.

Rice and many of the other Pittsburgh ACTU activists (often called actists) were vigorous anticommunists who redbaited their foes in the labor movement. Indeed, a strong strain of the motivation for ACTU was for Catholics to counter Communist Party influence in the working class, as well as a sincere support of unionism. By the time that Rice and the Pittsburgh ACTU hosted the first national ACTU convention in 1940, the connections with the CW movement had been severed, and Rice was well on his way to becoming one of the best-known and most influential labor priests in the country.

Through the Pittsburgh ACTU, Rice became increasingly enmeshed in the political battles in the labor movement throughout the 1940s. He was very close to important Catholic national labor leaders, like CIO President **Philip Murray**. Rice sought to rid the CIO unions of communist influence. He was perhaps the most visible, forceful, and active anticommunist cleric involved in the labor movement. He wrote, spoke, and actively red-baited the left in the CIO, particularly in the years immediately following World War II. He was especially active, for example, in the bitter internal battle for control in the **United Electrical Workers (UE)** union. ACTU, Rice, and the other anticommunists supported the CIO's purge of eleven CIO international unions, including the UE, for being communist dominated in 1949 and 1950. They supported the CIO's creation of the **International Union of Electrical Workers (IUE)**, which was formed to replace the UE in the CIO. Rice also provided information to the FBI and collaborated with the House Un-American Activities Committee (HUAC) when it held hearings in Pittsburgh in August 1949. After the death of Rice's friend, Philip Murray, in 1952, he receded from the limelight and, in 1958, he was made pastor of a large parish in Washington, Pennsylvania.

Although he was never again as active or nationally important as in the 1940s, Rice continued to champion social causes. In the 1960s he opposed the U.S. military role in Vietnam. Rice also became critical of the complacency and inactivity of the labor movement in the 1960s. He supported progressive **rank-and-file** reform movements in a number of national unions, including the **United Steel Workers** and the **United Mine Workers** in the 1960s and 1970s. In the 1980s, he also supported activists and steelworkers who attempted to keep their plants from closing in the Monongahela Valley, Pennsylvania.

Rice has openly questioned the stridency of his anticommunism of the 1940s. He regrets some of the red-baiting tactics he used in the internecine labor battles then and how they may have contributed to the general conservatism of organized labor.

Suggested Readings: Neil Betten, "Charles Owen Rice: Pittsburgh Labor Priest, 1936–1940." *The Pennsylvania Magazine of History and Biography* XCIV no. 4 (1970): 518–32; Charles J. McCollester, ed., *Fighter With a Heart: Writings of Charles Owen Rice, Pittsburgh Labor Priest*, 1996; Patrick McGeever, *Reverend Charles Owen Rice: Apostle of Contradiction*, 1989.

Joseph Turrini

Right-to-Work. Right-to-work is the belief that workers should not be forced to join a labor union or pay union **dues** to work. If a union contract contains a **union shop** or agency shop clause, all employees must pay union dues to continue their employment. Opponents argue that this is compulsory unionism which violates individual freedoms: individuals have a right-to-work, that is, the right to choose whether or not to join a union and/or pay union dues.

Since unions must represent all employees, members and nonmembers, unions argue everyone should have to join or pay dues because it is unfair to allow free riders to benefit from union representation without sharing the costs. Also, in democratic institutions, everyone is bound by what the majority decides and a union or agency shop clause is only present when a majority approves it. Many unions also charge that right-to-work campaigns are little more than thinly disguised attacks on **collective bargaining** rights and are part and parcel of an overall campaign of union-busting on the part of unscrupulous employers and ideological conservatives.

U.S. labor law does not prohibit union and agency shop clauses, but Section 14 (b) of the 1947 **Taft-Hartley Act** allows states to pass right-to-work laws, thus making agency and union shops illegal. States with these laws are called right-to-work states. As of 2001, there were twenty-two right-to-work states, primarily in the South and Midwest. The National Right to Work Committee lobbies for right-to-work legislation and the National Right to Work Legal Defense Foundation provides legal representation for workers trying to challenge union membership requirements. Right-to-work laws have made union organizing drives quite difficult in some areas, especially in the South and Southwest. Most unions call for the overturn of right-to-work laws, but have made little headway in accomplishing said goal.

Suggested Readings: Thomas Haggard, *Compulsory Unionism, the NLRB, and the Courts: A Legal Analysis of Union Security Agreements*, 1977; Fred Witney, Fred Taylor, and Benjamin J. Taylor, *Labor Relations Law*, 1995; "National Right-to-Work Committee," http://www.right-to-work.org.

John W. Budd

Robinson, Cleveland Lowellyn (1915–August 23, 1995). Cleveland Robinson was the authoritative voice of the Coalition of Black Trade Unionists (CBTU), a civil rights advocate, and labor official. He and his long-time associate, **A. Philip Randolph**, were considered the leading voices for greater participation by African Americans inside the American Federation of Labor-Congress of Industrial Organizations (AFL-CIO). The two frequently clashed with AFL-CIO President **George Meany** in efforts to get the organization to take a stronger stance on **minority labor**.

Robinson was born in Swabys Hope, Jamaica, in 1915 and emigrated to the United States in 1944, settling in New York City. He took employment with a Manhattan dry goods store and quickly took up the task of unionizing workers. In 1947, Robinson became an organizer for District 65 of the Distributive Workers of America, a union of about 30,000 retail and wholesale employees affiliated with the Retail, Wholesale, and Department Stores Employees Union. Both were absorbed by the **United Auto Workers (UAW)** in 1969. District 65 was one of the nation's more liberal labor organizations in matters of civil rights, and Robinson became one of its vice presidents in 1950. He held that post only two years and, in 1952, became the secretary-treasurer for District 65, a post he held until his retirement in 1992.

Robinson himself was active in the civil-rights movement. He served as a labor advisor to the Reverend Martin Luther King, Jr. and was the administrative chair of the 1963 march on Washington. He was also served mayors Robert Wagner and John Lindsay on New York City's Human Rights Commission. Robinson felt that the causes of labor and civil rights were inextricably linked and challenged the AFL-CIO to make said connection. He served as vice president, then president of the Negro American Labor Council, the forerunner of the CBTU. By the late 1960s, black workers inside the AFL-CIO were restive, and militant **rank-and-file** groups like the **Dodge Revolutionary Union Movement** were on the rise. Robinson grew convinced that the AFL-CIO's **voluntarism** was untenable. When Meany pledged the federation to neutrality in the 1972 presidential election, Robinson admonished that the re-election of Richard Nixon would result in "four more years of favored treatment for the rich and powerful . . . and [insensitivity] to the rights of workers, minorities, and the poor." He and four other black leaders announced the formation of the CBTU to pressure the AFL-CIO to pay more attention to the concerns of African American trade unionists. The CBTU greatly increased the number of African Americans in union leadership positions. He played an active role in the CBTU even when his personal life was marked by tragedy. In 1976, his wife, Susan Jenkins Robinson, passed away. In 1977, he married the former Doreen McPherson.

Robinson continued to merge interests in labor and civil rights. In 1985, he became the vice chairman of New York state's Martin Luther King, Jr. Commission, a group lobbying to make the Reverend King's birthday an official holiday and, later, in charge of commemorative events, educational programs, and social justice programs to honor King. Robinson became chair when Harry Belafonte stepped down in 1987, and he continued to serve on the commission until his death. He was also an outspoken opponent of the apartheid system in South Africa and pressured the AFL-CIO to call for boycotts of the nation and its products. In 1990, he co-chaired the committee that sponsored Nelson Mandela's visit to New York City.

Robinson retired from District 65 and the labor movement in 1992. When he died in 1995, the mourners and speakers at his funeral included such political and civil-rights luminaries as Mayor David Dinkins of New York, former United Nations ambassador Andrew Young, singer Harry Belafonte, the Reverend Jesse Jackson, and Coretta Scott King, the widow of Martin Luther King, Jr. Both President Mandela of South Africa and President William Clinton also sent condolences. The CBTU remains an active force in advancing the cause of African American union members.

Suggested Readings: "Coalition of Black Trade Unionists," http://www.cbtu.org/2003website/aboutcbtu/robinson.html; Wolfgang Saxon, "Cleveland Robinson, 80, Civil-Rights Advocate," obituary in *New York Times*, August 26, 1995; Philip Foner, *Organized Labor and the Black Worker, 1619–1981*, 1982.

James P. Hanlan
Robert E. Weir

Runaway Capital/Shops. The term runaway capital/shops refers to the business practice of moving operations in whole or in part to another state, area, or country to escape the effects of a unionized workforce or government regulations. Historically the Northeast and northern Midwest regions of the United States contained the greatest density of industrialization. For this reason, unions and protective labor laws were more prominent. Beginning in the early nineteenth century, some employers sought to circumvent the countervailing power of strong employee representation. Early captains of industry like Samuel Slater did not hesitate to close textile mills and build entirely new **company towns** to avoid challenges to his authority. After the Civil War, however, the customary practice was to move (or threaten to move) operations to regions—often the South—where unions were weak and wages were lower.

Ironically, the 1935 **National Labor Relations Act** exacerbated this trend by further encouraging union membership in those areas where it was already strongest. The 1947 **Taft-Hartley Act** allowed state legislatures to pass **right-to-work** laws that prohibited compulsory union membership. Since 1947, twenty-two states in the South and the Midwest have passed right-to-work laws, the most recent of which was Oklahoma in 2001. These states have been favored by labor-intensive industries as a way to lower production costs through reduced wages. The Northeast, for example, saw most of its textile, shoes, and machine-tool industries leave the region and relocate in the South.

The debate over runaway shops has become ideological and is seen by opponents of unions as a way to curb their political influence and power. It has taken on new urgency now that the practice of runaway industries has become global. By the 1970s, even right-to-work states began to experience job losses as businesses left to secure even cheaper labor outside the United States' border. Moreover, new investments frequently take place in low-wage nations. The controversial **North American Free Trade Agreement (NAFTA)** removed many tariff barriers between the United States, Canada, and Mexico. Many free-trade advocates wish to extend NAFTA throughout Central and South America. To opponents, this move toward **globalization** threatens the very future of American jobs and wages.

Suggested Readings: Thomas A. Kochan, Harry C. Katz, and Robert B. McKersie, *The Transformation of American Industrial Relations*, 1994; John Mehring, "Labor Loses 'Right-to-Work' Fight in Oklahoma," *Labor Notes*, vol. 272, (November 2001); Robert B. Reich, *The Work of Nations: Preparing Ourselves for 21st Century Capitalism*, 1992.

Pete Gingras

S

Sabotage. Sabotage is a commonly (or deliberately) misunderstood word when applied to labor relations. In common parlance it refers to wanton destruction of property resulting from a dispute between two parties. It is often used to refer to damages inflicted by workers on the property of recalcitrant employers, especially during a **strike** or **boycott**. Most labor unions, however, adhere to a definition developed by the **Industrial Workers of the World (IWW)**, in which sabotage meant a systematic withdrawal of worker efficiency. For example, assembly line workers might deliberately slow the pace of their work so they meet only exact production quotas, or fail to meet them altogether. Many labor supporters advocate sabotage as a form of what the IWW called "striking on the job." Workers can disrupt work processed by withholding specialized knowledge they possess that management does not. A group of workers might, for instance, feign ignorance of how to repair a broken machine, thereby slowing production.

Unions have, however, engaged in direct destruction of property. Destructive sabotage was quite common during the **Great Labor Uprising** of 1877, and some IWW members used it as part of a larger program of **direct action** aimed at disrupting **capitalism**. Many observers claim the term comes from the French word *sabot*, or wooden shoe. One school of thought credits the term to a 1910 French rail strike in which workers damaged the shoes (*sabots*) holding rails together. Still others claim it comes from the practice of disgruntled machine tenders hurling their *sabots* into machines in the early days of the French industrial revolution. The latter claim seems more probable, as the practice of both wanton and passive forms of sabotage assuredly predates 1910. As numerous IWW supporters were fond of pointing out, the act of ancient Hebrew slaves spoiling Egyptian bricks was a form of sabotage, as were acts of antebellum slaves filling the bottoms of cotton bags with stones.

Destructive sabotage has often provided the pretext for employers to request government assistance in defeating strikes. When several hotheaded strikers derailed a train during an 1890 strike against the New York Central Railroad, for example, the railroad used the incident to justify the hiring of **Pinkerton** detectives (which was actually done before the incident) and to convince reluctant state governments to send National Guard troops into numerous locales. Likewise, striking miners who dynamite pits or commit other acts of destructive sabotage have often found themselves subject to state repression in the wake of their violence.

For the most part, however, destructive sabotage has been less common than striking on the job. Management often exaggerates or invents sabotage threats to justify heavy-handed crackdowns. In some cases, management employs **agent provocateurs** to either incite strikers to commit property damage or make it appear that unions did damage that was done by company thugs. The 1936 **La Follette Committee** revealed that this was a widespread tactic. The use of agent provocateurs, like destructive sabotage itself, is illegal, but both continue to occur occasionally. For the most part, however, destructive worker sabotage has been an act of frustration, not a tactic authorized, endorsed, or condoned by their unions.

The modern form of sabotage as a way of withdrawing efficiency is the **work-to-rule** tactic. In such a case, workers follow the letter of the law in their contracts and refuse to take on any task not specifically enumerated in the contract. Truckers in the **International Brotherhood of Teamsters** have several times won employer concessions simply by driving the speed limit at all times, taking breaks exactly as mandated in the contract, and by refusing to do any loading or unloading of cargo not specifically mandated. Teachers have found work-to-rule an especially effective tool when contract talks stall. Since most teachers perform myriad tasks not required under their contracts—like staying after hours to work with students, supervising bus loadings, advising clubs, meeting with parents, making photocopies, correcting homework at night, informally handling discipline problems, and taking on extra duties during unexpected emergencies—a well-run work-to-rule campaign can severely disrupt how schools operate. Work-to-rule and striking on the job campaigns of all sorts have gotten more attention in recent years as strikes have become harder to win and **replacement workers** easier to obtain.

Suggested Readings: Frank Bohn, "Some Definitions: Direct Action—Sabotage," and Ben William, "Sabotage," in Joyce Kornbluh, ed., *Rebel Voices: An I.W.W. Anthology*, 1968; Martin Sprouse, ed., *Sabotage in the American WorkPlace: Anecdotes of Dissatisfaction, Mischief and Revenge*, 1992.

Robert E. Weir

Sacco and Vanzetti. Nicola Sacco and Bartolomeo Vanzetti were Italian immigrants convicted of murdering two people during a 1920 payroll robbery in suburban Boston. They were executed in 1927, despite the lack of credible evidence against them. In the annals of American jurisprudence, their executions rank among the **Molly Maguire** executions, the convictions following the **Haymarket bombing**, and later cases like the Scottsboro Boys and the Rosenberg electrocutions as severe miscarriages of justice that violate the rules of evidence.

Both Nicola Sacco, a shoemaker, and Bartolomeo Vanzetti, a fish peddler, were anarchists attracted to the views of Italian theorist and revolutionary Luigi Galleani, and members of the East Boston anarchist debate society Gruppo Autonomo. This combination proved fatal in the aftermath of World War I when a red scare broke out. Attorney General A. Mitchell Palmer's near pathological fear of radicalism led to authorized crackdowns against **anarchists**, **communists**, members of the **Industrial Workers of the World**, and even moderate **socialists** who advocated ballot-box politics. Such famed radicals as **Eugene Debs**, **Bill Haywood**, and **Emma Goldman** were arrested; Goldman and various other resident aliens were deported. A bad situation was exacerbated when some anarchist groups responded with the very violence the public feared. In June 1919, anarchist bombs rocked seven U.S. cities.

On April 15, 1920, a payroll heist occurred outside a shoe factory in East Braintree, Massachusetts, a Boston suburb. Robbers made off with $16,000 and killed two guards in the process. Sacco and Vanzetti were arrested on May 4, when they went to pick up a car police had connected with the robbery. The trial that ensued was marked by many unethical procedures, including the prosecution's coaching of witnesses and Judge Webster Thayer's overt prejudice against the defendants. More seriously, the prosecution quashed evidence that exonerated Sacco and Vanzetti. Both were convicted in a case that, in essence, put their anarchism on trial. Shortly after both were indicted in September 1920, an anarchist bomb planted on Wall Street in New York City killed forty people. In such a tense atmosphere, neither defendant stood much of a chance. Both were convicted on July 14, 1921 and sentenced to death. Lengthy appeals and worldwide protests served only to delay their electrocution until August 23, 1927. Their deaths took place even though another man confessed to the crime in 1925.

Organized labor had little connection to Sacco and Vanzetti; their anarchist beliefs made them unwelcome in most unions. Although several unions held strikes to protest their impending execution and many union workers endorsed clemency, organized labor was largely silent on the matter. Only unionists associated with the political left dared to speak vociferously in defense of Sacco and Vanzetti. This was partly because all unions were under attack in the 1920s. Post–World War I red-baiting proved a disaster for labor unions, irrespective of their ideological leanings. The **open-shop** movement was in full swing, and workers across the country found themselves subject to indignities like **company unions** and **yellow-dog contracts**. The dramatic Sacco and Vanzetti case was another tool used by employers to tar labor unions and other progressives with murderous intent and to justify crackdowns.

Neither man was the martyred saint that romantics made them out to be. It is possible, even probable, that both were involved in some aspect of the June 1919 bombings. That said, however, few legal scholars believe either should have been convicted for the East Braintree murders. In the end, theirs appears to be a state-sanctioned murder. Sacco and Vanzetti have never been exonerated, though in 1977, Massachusetts Governor Michael Dukakis declared that they had not received a fair trial and proclaimed Sacco and Vanzetti Day on the fiftieth anniversary of their execution.

Suggested Readings: Paul Avrich, *Sacco and Vanzetti: The Anarchist Background*, 1991; Irving Bernstein, *The Lean Years*, 1960; Katharine Porter, *The Never-Ending Wrong*, 1977.

Robert E. Weir

Salary. Salary is the compensation for the time during which an employee is required to be on the employer's premises or on duty at a prescribed work place. Salary is the total remuneration paid by an employer to an employee for labor or services in accordance to a previously agreed upon rate, secured either via collective bargaining or individually. Unlike **wages**, salaries are usually not pegged to an hourly rate.

The 1938 **Fair Labor Standards Act (FLSA)** governs most employment relationships, though six major categories of employees are exempted: executive, administrative, professional, elected officials, recreational (i.e. entertainers), and agricultural employees. Under the exemptions these employees are to be considered salary-based and thus receive a fixed payment for any pay period without regard to the number of days or hours worked. Unless contracts specifically stipulate otherwise, salary deductions can be made for all such work absences as personal reasons, illness, or disability. The FSLA forbids deductions for jury duty, court service, or temporary military leave. Many salaried employees complain of long work hours, burdensome job duties, and abusive supervisors. Some labor observers believe that professional and white-collar workers are ripe for union-organizing drives. Many professions, including teachers, nurses, and journalists, have already organized in some areas.

Suggested Readings: Maurice B. Better, *Contract Bargaining Handbook for Local Leaders*, 1993; David B. Lipsky and Clifford B. Donn, *Collective Bargaining in American Industry*, 1987; Juliet B. Schor, *The Overworked American: The Unexpected Decline of Leisure*, 1991.

Pete Gingras

San Francisco General Strike (1934). *See Depression-Era Strikes.*

Scab. Scab is the term used to refer to workers who refuse to participate when their colleagues strike, or to workers who are hired by management to replace strikers. To loyal union supporters, there is no greater insult than to be dubbed a scab.

The exact origin of the term is disputed. Its first known use in English occurred in 1529 as a synonym for moral decay. By 1590 it was used generally to refer to persons of low character. Its first recorded use to refer to strike breakers occurred during a 1777 cordwainers' strike in Bristol, England, though it's likely the term was in currency long before then. The term appeared in the United States as early as 1806 during a boot and shoemakers' strike. For much of the nineteenth century it vied with blackleg as the favored term of abuse, though the latter has fallen from popular use. Printers also commonly used the terms fink, rat, and/or ratfink.

During the 1877 railroad strike, strikers in Chicago attack scab switchmen and brakemen. © George Meany Memorial Archives/Public Affairs Press.

Imported scabs have long been a staple of capital/labor disputes, with management attempting to maintain production and thus break strikes. Until recently, most scabs have been recruited from among the ranks of immigrants, itinerant laborers, and the unemployed. In some cases, workers were unaware that they were strike breakers until they arrived at their jobs. Some of the tension between African American and Caucasian labor can be traced to the deliberate importation of blacks into strike-torn situations. Since the late 1970s, employers have turned increasingly to professional strike-breaking firms and the hiring of permanent **replacement workers**. This supplants an older practice in which scabs were terminated once a dispute was settled and all or most strikers were rehired. Labor advocates have taken some solace in the fact that the term scab has withstood several legal challenges from those claiming they were libeled or injured by its use. Most recently, a 1999 11th Circuit ruling in *Dunn v. ALPA* stated that the use of scab to describe pilots who crossed picket lines was accurate and non-libelous.

Suggested Readings: Stanley Aronowitz, *From the Ashes of the Old*, 1998; Archie Green, *Wobblies, Pile Butts, and Other Heroes*, 1993.

Robert E. Weir

Schneiderman, Rose (April 6, 1884?–August 11, 1972) Rose Schneiderman was an important leader of the **Women's Trade Union League (WTUL)**, the **International Ladies' Garment Workers' Union (ILGWU)**, and numerous other organizations. She was born in either 1882 or 1884 in Saven, a Polish town then controlled by Russia, the daughter of Samuel and Deborah (Rothman) Schneiderman. Her Jewish parents emigrated to the United States in 1890, and settled in New York City's Lower East Side. Soon after their arrival, Schneiderman's father, a tailor, died of influenza. Economic pressure dispersed the Schneiderman children to orphanages and the homes of relatives. Rose's public-school education ended when she was thirteen, and she went to work in a department store. She left for a factory job stitching cap linings.

The brutal conditions of factory work led Schneiderman to **socialism** and trade unionism. She was instrumental in the formation of New York Local 23 of the United Cloth Hat and Cap Makers of North America (UCHCM), and was elected its secretary. At the time, the UCHCM did not even officially admit women, a policy Schneiderman helped reverse. She also helped direct a successful 1905 strike that increased wages for city hat makers. Schneiderman's efforts attracted notice and, in 1907, she was elected as vice president of the New York Branch of the WTUL. She also received a scholarship to attend classes at a preparatory school while working as an East Side organizer. She and Leonora O'Reilly were key figures in organizing a 1908 strike against the Cohen Company for better wages and an end to the **piecework** system. The strike was successful and the dressmakers' union affiliated itself with the ILGWU.

Schneiderman came to national attention following a rousing speech she gave after the **Triangle Factory Fire of 1911**. Schneiderman spoke at a funeral held by the city for the unclaimed dead and marched in the procession to represent the WTUL. After the fire, Schneiderman organized workers with increased vigor. She was an ILGWU organizer from 1914 to 1916. Her ILGWU duties took Schneiderman across the country to unionize workers in Boston, Philadelphia, Cleveland, and Chicago. In Chicago, Schneiderman was a valuable contributor in the successful Herzog glovemaker strike of 1915. She also served as WTUL vice president from 1919 to 1926, and as its president in 1918 and from 1926 to 1947. She spent much of her career organizing Jewish and Italian working women in the garment industry of the Lower East Side. Schneiderman claimed that Eastern European Jewish women were the most loyal unionists. In addition, she was an ardent believer in women's suffrage and campaigned heavily for the right to vote.

Schneiderman attended the 1920 International Congress of Working Women, and served as a trustee of **Brookwood Labor College** from 1924 to 1929. She was an early supporter of Franklin Roosevelt and, in 1933, became the sole female labor unionist on the board of the National Industrial Recovery Administration. She also served as secretary to the New York Department of Labor from 1937 to 1944. Her friendship with Eleanor Roosevelt provided White House access and some consider Schneiderman to have been among the brain trust that helped Roosevelt formulate New Deal policy. By the 1940s, however, the WTUL was in severe decline, and some critics fault Schneiderman for distancing the WTUL from the **Congress of Industrial Organizations**. Others blamed her for holding onto the WTUL reins for too long. She finally dismantled the national WTUL in 1949 and retired. Schneiderman died in 1972.

Suggested Readings: Alice Kessler-Harris, "Rose Schneiderman and the Limits of Women's Trade Unionism," in Melvyn Dubofsky and Warren Van Tine, *Labor Leaders in America*, 1967; Rose Schneiderman and Lucy Goldthwaite, *All for One*, 1967; Leon Stein, *Out of the Sweatshop: The Struggle for Industrial Democracy*, 1977.

Cristina Prochilo

Scientific Management. *See Taylorism.*

Scissorbill. Scissorbill is an out-of-fashion term for a worker who lacks class consciousness, has bourgeois pretensions, and refuses to join a union. The term was sometimes spelled scissorsbill. It was a favored slang insult among members of the **Industrial Workers of the World (IWW)**. Scissorbill was first applied to refer to late-nineteenth-century law-and-order vigilantes in Western states and probably came to the IWW through Western miners who changed its meaning. IWW members were especially scornful of scissorbills and songwriter **Joe Hill** parodied them in verses set to the popular "Steamboat Bill." In the song, Hill called them "the missing link Darwin tried to trace." The term faded from use when the IWW declined.

Suggested Reading: Joyce Kornbluh, *Rebel Voices*, 1968.

Robert E. Weir

Secondary Labor Force. Secondary labor force is a pool of reserve and/or less skilled laborers whose labor is deemed less valuable than that of workers in the top echelon of a particular job or trade. Historically, **child labor** and **minority labor** (including women) made up the bulk of the secondary labor force. Workers in smaller firms in industries dominated by large-scale, high-wage companies were also included in the secondary labor market. Craft workers and labor unions argued that these workers were used by unscrupulous employers to depress across-the-board wages within an industry. Employers frequently drew upon secondary labor during labor disputes when seeking replacement workers.

In more recent times, unions and some economists maintain that the American capitalist system continues to exploit the secondary labor market through two-tier wage systems, the use of temporary workers, the recruitment of foreign and immigrant labor, and the maintenance of a vast low-wage underclass. As these critics view it, workers find it difficult to press for better wages and benefits when management can draw upon large labor reserves that will work more cheaply. Debate rages as to whether such conditions are natural within **capitalism** or if they are part of a deliberate management strategy to hold down costs, increase stockholder profits, and discipline the work force.

Suggested Reading: David Gordon, Richard Edwards, and Michael Reich, *Segmented Work, Divided Workers*, 1985.

Robert E. Weir

Senate Civil Liberties Committee. *See La Follette Committee.*

Seniority. Seniority is customarily defined as the length of full-time service or work by an employee without a break in service. Less than full-time employment can be credited on a prorated basis. Seniority determines a worker's standing relative to fellow employees. Those with greater service or work time usually receive more privileges with regard to appointments, promotions, consideration for vacant positions, work-location preferences, scheduling of vacations, and overtime opportunities. Seniority also frequently determines who gets laid off during economic downturns, with employees lacking seniority being the first to lose their jobs and the last to be recalled when conditions improve.

Seniority has concerned the labor movement since the nineteenth century. Many unions sought seniority considerations to curb the practice of dismissing older workers in favor of younger ones who employers felt would be more productive. Many craft unions struck bargains that recognized seniority, though not always for the protection of all workers. While the length of service rewarded employees for service time, some unions barred African Americans from bargaining units. Other programs made it impossible for black workers to move out of unskilled job classifications. As women entered the labor market in greater numbers during World Wars I and II, they experienced unequal treatment due to a union's rigid seniority provisions. Even the **United Auto Workers**, prior to World War II, maintained a privileged seniority list for the all-white skilled and semi-skilled job categories, and separate lists for women, and yet another for all-black unskilled classifications.

During World War II, the War Labor Board established principles of nondiscriminatory seniority known as industrial jurisprudence. In 1961, President Kennedy created the President's Committee on Equal Employment Opportunity (PCEEO), to administer a fair seniority system for federal employment. Such legislation helped ease past discrimination, but problems remain in some industries and unions where the seniority principle of last hired, first fired prevails.

Suggested Readings: Richard Freeman and James Medoff, *What Do Unions Do?*, 1984; Clark Kerr and Paul Staudohar, *Labor Economics and Industrial Relations: Markets and Institutions*, 1994.

Pete Gingras

Service Employees International Union (SEIU). The Service Employees Internation Union (SEIU) represents more than 1.6 million workers, most of whom are employed in the service sector of the economy. Its members range in occupation from custodians and nurses to taxi drivers and window washers. At a time in which many unions have struggled to maintain their strength, SEIU has more than doubled its ranks since 1980. It is also one of the most diverse unions in the United States. More than thirty percent of its **rank-and-file** are racial minorities, and fifty-three percent is female.

SEIU was founded by a group of Chicago janitors in 1921 and was chartered by the **American Federation of Labor (AFL)**. It was known as the Building Service Employees International Union (BSEIU) until 1968, when it changed its name to SEIU. Although the BSEIU has not received the attention from scholars that the **industrial unions** of the 1930s have, it organized hospital workers and public employees during the 1930s at a time in which no other major union was attempting to do so. It was most active in large cities, including New York, where local 32B won several strikes that resulted in wage increases for members.

The BSEIU began to grow in the 1960s, due in no small part to shifts in the American economy that led to an expanding service sector. Its growth coincided with the resurgence of feminism and the union found itself inexorably drawn into the organization of women, especially in the health care industry. In 1974, the newly renamed SEIU was one of the major supporters of the **Coalition of Labor Union Women (CLUW)**, a group that seeks to address women's issues and place more women in union leadership roles. In 1975, the SEIU chartered **9 to 5**, a union of women clerical workers. Although 9 to 5 has since spun off into a separate organization, the SEIU maintains a powerful clerical **district** number 925. The SEIU was also deeply affected by the civil rights movement, as many custodians and office support staff have been (and are) African American and Latino. In 1985, SEIU members in Denver created Justice for Janitors, a campaign to organize office cleaners and custodians. Since its inception, it has spread to other cities, including Los Angeles and Boston, where heavily non-English-speaking immigrant workforces won wage and benefit concessions in the 1990s.

The SEIU has also enjoyed a reputation for being among the more democratic unions in the modern American Federation of Labor-Congress of Industrial Organizations (AFL-CIO). Its individual locals maintain a high level of autonomy within the **international union**. The SEIU suffered a minor setback in 2000, when its Canadian affiliates representing 30,000 workers disaffiliated. Publicly, Canadian leaders claimed a desire for a more uniquely Canadian perspective, but most observers cite dissatisfaction with lower wage rates in negotiated settlements in the United States. Nonetheless, the SEIU's aggressive organizing successes coupled with its reputation for diversity sensitivity have led many observers to see it as a model for future union organizing. The AFL-CIO itself recognized this when, in 1995, it tapped SEIU President **John Sweeney** to head the AFL-CIO. The current president of the SEIU is Andrew Stern.

Suggested Readings: Thomas Beadling et. al., *A Need for Valor: The Roots of Service Employees International Union, 1902–1992*, 1992; John Jentz, "Citizenship, Self-Respect, and Political Power: Chicago's Flat Janitors Trailblaze the Service Employees International Union," *Labor's*

Heritage 9, no. 1 (Summer, 1997), pp. 4–23; Anne Kornhauser, "Reader's Companion to U.S. Women's History—Service Employees International Union," http://college.hmco.com/history/readerscomp/women/html/wm_019611_serviceemplo.htm.

Robert E. Weir

Shanker, Albert (September 14, 1928–February 22, 1997). Albert Shanker was an advocate for teacher unions and president of the **American Federation of Teachers (AFT)** from 1974 until his death in 1997. He was born in New York City to Jewish immigrant parents. His father, Morris, delivered newspapers and his mother, Mamie, was a garment worker. After he graduated from high school in 1946, Shanker attended the University of Illinois and earned a B.A. in philosophy. He earned an M.A. in mathematics and philosophy from Columbia, but never finished the Ph.D. program in which he enrolled. In the early 1950s he became a mathematics teacher in the New York City public schools.

Shanker soon became active in the local teachers' union, the Teachers' Guild. He helped to organize the school in which he taught and, in 1959, became a full-time organizer for the union. In 1960, the guild merged with the High School Teachers' Association to form the United Federation of Teachers (UFT). Even though New York state laws prohibited teachers' **strikes**, on November 7, 1960, over 5,000 UFT members struck to demand **collective bargaining** rights. In 1961 New York teachers chose the UFT as their sole bargaining agent, and it negotiated the first comprehensive collective bargaining agreement in a major city. The 1960 **New York City Teachers' Strike** inspired public schoolteachers across the country to demand collective bargaining rights.

Shanker's New York activities thrust him into the national limelight. In 1962, Shanker was elected UFT secretary and in 1964, he succeeded Charles Cogen as the second UFT president, a position he held until 1986. In the 1960s he was twice jailed for breaking the state law that barred public-employee strikes. The first time was in 1967 during a strike over smaller classes and more funding for public education, and the second came after the 1968 Ocean Hill-Brownsville strike, which centered on an African American community's attempt to replace white schoolteachers.

During the 1970s, Shanker was one of the most widely known labor leaders in the United States. In 1972, he helped to bring about the merger between the New York State AFT affiliate and the state chapter of the rival **National Education Association (NEA)** to form the New York State United Teachers (NYSUT). NYSUT became the largest and most influential statewide union in the country, and Shanker served as its executive vice president from 1973 to 1978. He wrote a regular "Where We Stand" column in *The New York Times*, and made such regular appearances on radio and television that comedian Woody Allen satirized him in the 1973 futuristic film, *Sleeper*. In 1974, Shanker was elected AFT president and became a member of **American Federation of Labor-Congress of Industrial Organization (AFL-CIO)** executive council. During New York City's fiscal crisis in 1975, he was widely credited with helping save New York from bankruptcy by using the UFT's pension money to buy the city's financial bonds.

Shanker used his position with the AFL-CIO executive council as a platform for supporting government Cold War policies. As head of the AFL-CIO's International Affairs Committee, he financially backed pro-American labor unions around the world. In 1993, Shanker became the founding president of Education International, the pro-Western worldwide teacher-union federation. Education International had been formed by the merger of the International Federation of Free Teachers' Unions (IFFTU), to which the AFT belonged, and the World Confederation of Organizations of the Teaching Profession, with which the NEA affiliated.

Shanker also increasingly supported the call of conservative commentators for national educational standards. He espoused greater classroom discipline and teacher testing and blamed parents for student failure. From 1976 to 1996, he was a regular delegate to the Democratic National Convention, and was an education advisor to U.S. presidents from Jimmy Carter through Bill Clinton. Shanker died of cancer in 1997 at the age of 68, leaving behind four children from two marriages.

Suggested Readings: Dickson A. Mungazi, *Where He Stands, Albert Shanker of the American Federation of Teachers*, 1995; Philip Taft, *United They Teach: The Story of the UFT*, 1974; United Federation of Teachers web site: http://www.uft.org.

John F. Lyons

Shape-Up. The term shape-up refers to a method of hiring for short-term work. Usually this system applies to unskilled day laborers. A shape-up occurs at a gathering spot for unskilled workers looking for short-term job assignments. The gathering could take place at a work site—such as on the docks—in a union hall, or a streetscape known by both workers and employers as a place where men and women in search of work tend to gather. Economists refer to this as the "casual labor market."

Workers were typically selected by hiring foremen from a milling crowd seeking jobs at the morning shape-up, or call. This system was particularly infamous on the docks well into the 1950s. The decasualization of longshore labor was a struggle that took decades. Under the shape-up system, the hiring foreman controlled access to work. The system encouraged kickbacks to the foreman, favoritism, and an arbitrary method of selecting workers in which a wide variety of discrimination was possible. The inequities of the shape-up system gave rise to repeated **strikes**, job actions, and corruption. Union officials, employers, and politicians attempted to work within the shape-up system. Union officials tried to use the shape-up to favor the selection of union members. Politicians often sought preferential hiring for particular ethnic groups. Employers saw the system as a way to prevent casual workers from gaining strength in the workplace. The shape-up allowed union officials, employers, and politicians alike to exploit workers and keep them in line. One of the more famous films about labor, *On the Waterfront*, is based on shape-up abuses among dock workers. (See **Films and Labor**.)

While the evils of the system were widely recognized, the solution to the arbitrariness of the shape-up was different in various labor markets. San Francisco and New York, for example, found different solutions to the problem of longshore workers. On the West coast, a 1939 arbitrator's decision, written by Wayne Morse, opened the door for a new era of industrial relations when it replaced the shape-up system with the union hiring hall. Under the hiring hall system, workers still shaped-up, but work opportunities were assigned on a fair rotational basis among all union members who sought work. The **rank-and-file** elected dispatchers who assigned work, via a set of posted rules, and employers were forbidden from bypassing the hiring hall. The International Longshore and Warehouse Union (ILWU) used union hiring halls on the West coast docks, while in New York, arbitrary work assignments on the docks persisted into the 1950s.

The shape-up continues to be practiced in agricultural labor and in day labor, where labor contractors use the system as a means to avoid regulations governing workplace health and safety. It also thrives among immigrant laborers, illegal aliens, and homeless individuals anxious to secure employment under any condition. In 2003, the General Accounting Office estimated the **contingent workers** comprised thirty percent of the workforce. On July 24, 2003, Rep. Luis Gutierrez (D-IL) introduced legislation (H.R. 2870) aimed at protecting day laborers from the abuses of the contemporary shape-up system.

Suggested Readings: Charles P. Larrowe, *Shape-up and Hiring Hall: a Comparison of Hiring Methods and Labor Relations on the New York and Seattle Waterfronts*, 1955; Wayne Morse Center for Law and Politics, University of Oregon, http://libweb.uoregon.edu/speccoll/exhibits/morse/; Howard Kimledorf, *Reds or Rackets?*, 1988.

James P. Hanlan
Albert V. Lannon

Sherman Antitrust Act. The Sherman Antitrust Act was passed by Congress in 1890, ostensibly to curtail monopolistic business methods. In practice, the Sherman Act was applied more vigorously against labor unions than monopolists. The bill was drafted by Senator John Sherman of Ohio in response to the rise of trusts and monopolies in the two and one-half decades after the Civil War. The Sherman Act outlawed combinations deemed a restraint of trade or commerce, including cartels, price-fixing schemes, and other impediments to competition. Moreover, the act allowed the federal government, as well as private parties, to initiate restraint-of-trade lawsuits. The act was enforced by the Department of Justice, and violators could be fined and/or imprisoned. If the courts so desired, triple damages could be levied against violators.

From its inception, organizations like the **National Association of Manufacturers** opposed applying the Sherman Act to regulate business practices, but sought to use it against labor unions. The Sherman Act was invoked during the 1894 **Pullman lockout** and the courts obliged by issuing injunctions against the **American Railway Union (ARU)**. ARU President **Eugene Debs** spent six months in prison for violating court injunctions. In 1895, the Supreme Court ruled in *United States v. E. C. Knight* that manufacturing was not covered by the commerce clause of the Constitution. This effectively eviscerated much of the act's original intent and opened the door for broader use of the act against labor. President Theodore Roosevelt used the Sherman Act against the Standard Oil Corporation and several other trusts, but government pursuit of business monopolies remained rare.

The **American Federation of Labor (AFL)** made reform of the Sherman Act a high priority for its legislative lobbyists. This stand later caused tension within the **National Civic Federation**, a labor/management board upon which AFL President **Samuel Gompers** sat, but the importance of reform was obvious to most working people. By 1901, eighteen suits had been brought, but half of them were against labor. The following year saw the D. E. Loewe Company of Danbury, Connecticut, bring suit against the striking **United Hatters, Cap, and Millinery Workers International Union**. The courts awarded Loewe $240,000 in damages and declared most secondary **boycotts** illegal. Liens were placed on both union bank accounts and the homes of individual hatters. The AFL was stunned when the Supreme Court upheld the awards. In 1903, the Kellog Switchboard and Supply Company and the American Anti-Boycott Association brought a successful suit against the **International Brotherhood of Teamsters**, who urged a boycott to support Kellog strikers.

The AFL included the use of the Sherman Antitrust Act against labor among the list of wrongs it presented to Congress in its 1906 Bill of Grievances. In that same year, however, an AFL boycott of the **Buck's Stove and Range Company** of St. Louis led to injunctions against the AFL. Gompers was sentenced to a year in jail for contempt, though the conviction was later overturned and Gompers never served the sentence. The Sherman Act remained a thorn in labor's side until most labor activity was placed beyond "restraint of trade" interpretations by the 1914 **Clayton Antitrust Act**.

Suggested Readings: Ronald Filippelli, *Labor in the USA: A History*, 1984; Philip Foner, *History of the Labor Movement in the United States*, Vol. 3, 1964; Walter Licht, *Industrializing America: The Nineteenth Century*, 1995.

Robert E. Weir

Shoemakers Strike of 1860. The Shoemakers Strike of 1860 took place in New England and was the largest strike to take place before the Civil War. As many as 20,000 workers left their jobs in Massachusetts, New Hampshire, and Maine. The strike is notable also for the role women played and for the manner in which sexism undercut the strike's potential.

Although shoemaking was a highly skilled craft during the Colonial era, it was not a lucrative one and even **master craftsmen** were often quite poor. It remained a poorly paid profession into the nineteenth century, even as it was transformed by centralization and mechanization. The introduction of machines, especially sewing machines, deskilled shoemaking. Paralleling changes in textile production, by the 1830s, shoes were being produced in urban centers like Lynn, Massachusetts. Like textile workers, increasing numbers of shoemakers were women, especially those involved in pattern-making, stitching, and binding. Although firms centralized, a substantial amount of shoemaking still took place in private homes. As in cigar making and the needle trades, married women took on a lot of shoemaking **homework**. Technological advances gradually reduced the number of homeworkers and, by extension, the number of women working in the shoe trade; but by 1860, women still made up about 40 percent of Lynn's shoeworkers.

Union organization was weak in the shoe industry. In 1831, Lynn women formed the short-lived Society of Shoebinders, which demanded that women be treated as equals as well as receive higher wages. Two years later they created the Female Society of Lynn and Vicinity for the Promotion of Industry. Men formed the Society of Cordwainers, best known for its labor paper, the *Awl*. The Society also admitted women in a special auxiliary. However, neither men nor women had an organization strong enough to challenge manufacturers.

Industry downturns led to discontent in the 1850s. The roots of the 1860 strike lay in a **journeymen**'s dispute in 1859 related to wage cuts the previous year. What came to be called the Great Strike began on February 22, 1860, Washington's Birthday. It began in Lynn and quickly spread to other shoe towns like Danvers, Haverhill, Natick, Newburyport, and Marblehead in Massachusetts; and Dover, Farmington, and Rochester in New Hampshire. The early morning of February 23 saw the strike's only violence, when some Lynn strikers attempted to prevent a shipment of bottoms and uppers from leaving town. Boston police and militia were called in and strike leaders denounced both their presence and all acts of violence. Initially, women were called upon to support the strike in the hope that their involvement would lend moral force to the strikers' demands.

The role of women proved more complicated than mere appeals to morality, however. Male workers touted the ideal of a **family wage** to demand higher compensation. Basic to the family wage is the principle that a man's wage ought to be sufficient to support his dependents. The concept of the family wage resonated with married female homeworkers, but Lynn also contained hundreds of young, single women employed as factory stitchers who had their own issues. Led by Clara Brown, more than 300 Lynn factory women voted their own strike and issued separate wage demands. Several meetings were held that affirmed Brown's actions and, by the end of February, as many as 2,000 women supported the strike. Ruptures soon occurred in their ranks, however.

The men's efforts were being coordinated by Willard Oliver and Alonzo Draper, head of the Lynn Mechanics' Association and editor of the *New England Mechanic*. They planned a massive parade for March 7. On March 2, Clara Brown learned that the demands of women strikers had been softened without her knowledge. She protested this action and was told by Oliver and Mary Damon that existing demands were unreasonable. Damon represented female homemakers who supported a family wage; both she and Oliver argued that high wages on the part of women factory workers threatened to destroy homework jobs and undermine the male-wage structure.

Heated meetings and discussions took place, bifurcating women's ranks. In the end, about 800 women joined the March 7 protest parade in Lynn. Many carried banners bearing defiant slogans like "American Ladies Will Not Be Slaves." Some estimates put the total number of marchers at around 4,000, making it one of the largest antebellum protests in American history. The march marked the highwater mark of the strike, and solidarity and resolve weakened in the ensuing weeks. Brown's refusal to endorse the actions of Draper, Oliver, and Damon isolated her and her followers, as did Brown's outspoken remarks about the folly of the others' decision. Manufacturers also sought to undermine unity by offering wage increases that affected only homeworkers. Those offers bred resentment, but the strike began to fizzle after most male workers obtained wage increases. On March 31, Oliver advised all women remaining on strike to return to work under existing low-wage scales and without signed agreements.

Some have interpreted the shoemakers strike of 1860 as a partial victory, though the historical record suggests that is an overly optimistic reading of the events. The strike was dramatic because of its size but strikers accomplished very few of their goals and manufacturers refused to recognize any unions. One could easily conclude that male strikers undermined chances for success by remaining committed to the concept of the family wage and by refusing to meet Brown and her charges as equals.

Suggested Readings: Mary Blewett, *Men, Women, and Work: Class, Gender, and Protest in the New England Shoe Industry, 1780–1910*, 1988; Alan Dawley, *Class and Community: The Industrial Revolution in Lynn*, 1976; Walter Licht, *Industrializing America: The Nineteenth Century*, 1995.

Robert E. Weir

Shop Steward. The shop steward is the frontline union representative who carries out the business of the union in the workplace. Shop stewards handle grievances, collect dues, and recruit new members. Generally the shop steward is elected by union members in the workplace or appointed by higher elected union officials. Most shop stewards continue to work a regular job and handle union duties on a part-time or release-time basis. Often the term is now interchangeable with union steward.

The evolution of the shop steward over the history of the labor movement symbolizes the dynamic nature of employee representation. Initially, the position of steward embodied strength; typically it was a male able to intimidate employer and co-worker alike. Before labor laws assured unions a legal right to exist, the steward had to fight the employer as well as wrangle dues from colleagues. Now that laws like the **National Labor Relations Act** legitimate the existence of unions, agents are able to enforce mutually-agreed-to work policies. This has transformed the shop steward from a physical enforcer to a legal enforcer, as well as a generalist who combines many roles in servicing the representational needs of fellow workers. The major obligations of this duty are to serve the interests of all union members without discrimination, and to exercise discretion with good faith and honesty.

Suggested Readings: Bruce S. Feldacker, *Labor Guide to Labor Law*, 2000; Terry L. Leap, *Collective Bargaining and Labor Relations*, 1991.

Pete Gingras

Sick-Out. A sick-out is a concerted job action, sometimes sanctioned, in which a large number of workers do not report to work on a predetermined day. Uniformed workers like police and fire fighters sometimes refer to this as the blue-flu. The purpose of this type of job action is to force concessions from an employer without resorting to a formal strike or other job action that would negatively impact workers' wages or threaten their jobs.

Sick-outs have been a form of labor protest since Colonial times and have been an occasionally effective tactic since. Unions like the **United Mine Workers** have used it to demonstrate workers' collective might and hasten stalled contract negotiations. Sick-outs have also been used as a form of protest when a **no-strike pledge** or **contract** language precludes the possibility of a formal work stoppage. Diverging from strikes has taken on renewed urgency since the 1980s, given the relative ease with which employers now utilize temporary and **replacement workers** to replace strikers. Although some sick-outs violate existing labor laws, they often prove safer than formal actions, and they frequently generate publicity for worker grievances.

Suggested Readings: Bruce S. Feldacker, *Labor Guide to Labor Law*, 2000; William Gould, *Agenda for Reform: The Future of Employment Relationships and the Law*, 1993; David B. Lipsky and Clifford B. Donn, *Collective Bargaining in American Industry*, 1987.

Pete Gingras

Sit-Down Strikes. Sit-down strikes occur when workers refuse to leave their place of employment or continue production until a grievance or contract is settled. This form of job action has its roots within the **Industrial Workers of the World (IWW)** at the beginning of the twentieth century, although IWW tactics did not catch on until a generation later during the Great Depression of the 1930s. The **Congress of Industrial Organization (CIO)** split from the **American Federation of Labor** in this period to organize mass production workers. The CIO employed a number of IWW methods, especially the sit-down strike. While the **General Motors Sit-Down Strike** in Flint, Michigan in 1936–37 was not the initial use of a sit-down strike by the CIO, it garnered national publicity for the fledgling organization as it took on the world's largest corporation. The sit-down in Flint featured a disciplined group of auto workers who stayed warm and dry in the confines of their factory, while supporters surrounded the perimeters. Because of insurance regulations, General Motors was unwilling to shut off utilities and was unable to introduce **scabs**. Instead the National Guard was mobilized. However, public and political support for the strikers eventually carried the day and General Motors finally agreed to recognize the union in February 1937.

Subsequently, workers around the globe engaged in a series of sit-down strikes that brought the labor movement great success and influence. Culturally, the seizing of private property by a group of workers claiming "sweat equity" in a facility clashed head-on with an endearing tenet of free enterprise mentality. Although the United States Supreme Court outlawed the practice in 1939, the use of the tactic continues sporadically.

A striking autoworker reclines on an automobile bench-seat during the 1930s sit-down strikes against General Motors. © George Meany Memorial Archives/Library of Congress.

Suggested Readings: Richard O. Boyer and Herbert M. Morais, *Labor's Untold Story*, 1955; Jeremy Brecher, *Strike!*, 1972; Sidney Lens, *The Labor Wars*, 1973.

Scott Molloy

Skidmore, Thomas (August 13, 1790–August 7, 1832). Thomas Skidmore was an important early labor radical and a member of New York's Workingmen's party. He was born in Newton, Connecticut, the eldest of ten children, to John and Mary Skidmore. He was a precocious and brilliant child who, at the age of thirteen, became a teacher in the Newton school district. He taught there for five years before moving on to teach in Connecticut, New Jersey, Virginia, and North Carolina. He left teaching in 1815 to pursue an interest in the chemical properties of gun powder. He moved to New York in 1819 and married Abigail Ball two years later.

Skidmore held exceedingly progressive views for his day. He advocated free, universal education; the ten-hour workday; racial equality; property redistribution; and equal rights for women. He worked for the presidential campaign of John Quincy Adams in 1828, and was a cofounder of the New York Workingmen's party in 1829. He was largely responsible for writing the party platform. His 1829 book, *The Rights of Man to Property*, stands as a radical testament to his views on land reform. In it, Skidmore advocated the abolition of inheritance rights, a nationalization of property, and land redistribution by lottery. Skidmore's views gained immediate currency and he narrowly lost an 1829 bid for the New York legislature. He published a short-lived labor paper, *The Friend of Equal Rights*.

Skidmore was a temperamental man who quarreled with other leaders. As the Workingmen began to splinter and falter, he tried to salvage a radical wing that he called the Original Workingmen, or the Poor Men's Party. In 1832, he was ousted from the very party he founded, and he died that summer of cholera. His work stands as a radical example of the emphasis that nineteenth-century labor activists placed on land reform.

Suggested Readings: Edward Pessen, *Uncommon Jacksonians*, 1967; Ronald Walters, *American Reformers 1815–1860*, 1978; Alden Whitman, ed., *American Reformers*, 1985.

Michele Bernier
Robert E. Weir

Smith-Connally Act. *See War Labor Disputes Act.*

Social Darwinism. Social Darwinism was a philosophy embraced by the business community and many members of the middle and upper class in the middle- and late-nineteenth century. It sought to apply Charles Darwin's evolutionary models to society, particularly his assertion that within nature a struggle for existence rages, and that survival of the fittest dictates which species gets access to limited resources. Proponents of Social Darwinism perverted Darwin's biological findings to argue that wealth and poverty were natural products of social struggle, therefore, those who made great fortunes were more "fit" than those who lived in poverty. Quite conveniently, Social Darwinists ignored factors like inherited wealth, corrupt financial and political practices, and exploitation. In their eyes, entrepreneurs of the emerging business class, investors, and the rich were a more completely evolved species than the toiling masses. Eugenicists, nativists, and racists also cast these principles in ethnic and racial terms.

Social Darwinism was, in some respects, a logical outgrowth of the underlying principles of **capitalism**. In Adam Smith's classic treatise, *The Wealth of Nations*, he argued that economic activity ought to be free of external regulations and controls and subject only to the natural laws of supply and demand. Those views found few adherents among Colonial-American artisans, and were roundly challenged by workers after the American Revolution. Many advocates of the **Workingmen's Movement** in the 1830s offered devastating critiques of an unregulated economy and lambasted any attempts to institute special privileges or class legislation.

Capitalism expanded during the antebellum period, but did not reach its take-off phase until after the Civil War. The rise of mass industry, the birth of modern corporate structures, and the advent of new managerial techniques gave rise to manufacturers, investors, and business owners who had fewer ties to local communities and/or the customary social arrangements of the past. With sheer profit as the driving motive for many such individuals—who were dubbed "robber barons" by their critics—business competition was often cutthroat and the exploitation of workers brutal. Yet these same ruthless forces helped the national economy expand exponentially, pushing the United States to first-tier status among the world's economic and military powers. Enormous fortunes were made in the last third of the nineteenth century, and they were used to buy political influence. Economic expansion also led to more complete articulation of the middle class, which was small by contemporary standards, but more stratified. Its upper echelon consisted largely of the nouveau riche who were wealthy, but who lacked the social pedigrees of long-standing elites. New industrialists, managers, and professionals tended to identify with the social and cultural practices of the elites but, like the working classes, had to work for their compensation. Social Darwinism thus served to both justify amoral business practices and confer social status on the upwardly mobile.

The primary theorists of Social Darwinism were English philosophers Herbert Spencer and Walter Bagehot, and American sociologist/economist William Graham Sumner. Industrialists like John Rockefeller and Andrew Carnegie also added to Social Darwinian thought through their many speeches and essays. By the 1870s, Social Darwinism was the hegemonic social philosophy within the United States. Ministers, mainstream newspapers, orators, and writers praised its virtues and lampooned its critics. In practice, Social Darwinism was a marriage between laissez-faire economics and conservative politics, and the courts routinely turned aside legal challenges. Social Darwinists justified their great wealth and power by arguing that their alleged virtues—like sobriety, thrift, investment acumen, and hard work—were hallmarks of being more highly evolved than those who failed to attain their levels of success. Such thinking was in accord with late-Victorian beliefs. The concept of social problems had not yet been articulated; rather, misfortune was associated with sin and personal moral failings.

Not surprisingly, the American working class begged to differ. Trade unions and the **Knights of Labor** mounted powerful rhetorical challenges, with the labor press churning out stories of exploitation, graft, and illegalities on the part of allegedly moral and upright Social Darwinists. Among workers, the writings of **Henry George**, Victor Drury, David Ricardo, Karl Marx, and other social critics were widely discussed, as were various forms of **anarchism**, **communism**, **socialism**, **Bellamyite nationalism**, cooperation, and other ideas that challenged capitalism and Social Darwinism.

More than rhetoric, however, it was workers' direct challenges to Social Darwinism that loosened its grip. So many workers boycotted Social Darwinian churches that conferences were held to discuss ways to win them back to the pews. The Vatican summoned American cardinals and priests to Rome because many Catholics were giving up the church for their unions. In 1891, Pope Leo XIII issued the encyclical ***Rerum Novarum***, which removed the Vatican's objections to organized labor and contained strong condemnations of unbridled capitalism (as well as most forms of socialism). By the 1890s, many Protestant churches were abandoning Social Darwinism in favor of the Social Gospel movement, with its messages of alleviating poverty and its warnings against materialism.

Even more powerful were the challenges offered at the workplace and the voting booths. **Strikes** were frequent and violent after the Civil War, including the 1877 railroad strikes of the **Great Labor Uprising** and the voluminous work stoppages during the **Great Upheaval** of 1885 through 1890. Labor- and agrarian-based third parties dislodged numerous Republicans and Democrats on the local and state level, and threatened to do so nationally. The social Darwinian cause was hurt further by the numerous panics and recessions that threw the nation into economic turmoil. In all, the late-nineteenth century was so chaotic that even members of the middle class—especially those of moderate wealth or less—concluded that reform was necessary. The Gilded Age gave way after 1901 to the Progressive Era, the first significant reform movement that also involved local, state, and federal governments. Many of that period's leading reformers were members of the middle class, while unions and labor advocates continued to press for economic and social changes.

The American labor movement deserves credit for exposing the inequities, fallacies, and ruthlessness of Social Darwinism. The development of modern sociology also helped reveal the naiveté of attributing social problems to individual weakness. By the early-twentieth century, Social Darwinism had lost its moral force and was widely viewed as indefensible. The business community contained numerous individuals who were as heartless as their Gilded Age predecessors, but Social Darwinism was no longer the dominant social or cultural philosophy within the United States. Those who openly practiced its precepts were roundly criticized by many of the same forces that once defended its practices: the church, the media, and liberal politicians. Most people in the business community gave at least rhetorical support to philanthropy and moderate reform; some even experimented with **welfare capitalism**. It would be a mistake, however, to assume that Social Darwinism passed from the American scene. Its major assumptions continue to be held by many conservatives and some modern business practices are as cruel as those of an earlier age. Though social Darwinism is no longer the prevailing philosophy, it retains vigor.

Suggested Readings: Richard Hofstadter, *Social Darwinism in American Thought*, 1955; Robert McCloskey, *American Conservatism in the Age of Enterprise 1865–1910*, 1951; Norman Pollack, *The Populist Response to Industrial America*, 1962.

Robert E. Weir

Socialism. Socialism refers to an ideology whereby the means of production are in collective hands and are used for the benefit of the larger society rather than for a restricted group of individuals. For the most part, socialists envision a greater role for the state than communists or anarchists support. Socialists distrust many forms of private property and seek to make all wealth serve the broader community rather than single individuals. It rejects capitalist logic that links wages, prices, and the supply of goods and services to market forces.

It is a broad term encompassing many forms of collectivism, ranging from faith-based idealism to state-planned economies.

Socialist groups have suffered repression, though usually not as much as companion leftist ideologies. Because its ideals run counter to the logic of American **capitalism**, its overall impact on U.S. society has been less than that of most other industrial societies. At various moments, however, socialism has resonated with sizable segments of the population. Numerous religious groups, like the Shakers and various German Pietist groups, practiced rudimentary forms of socialist collectivism. Many labor activists and organizations have supported at least limited forms of socialism.

Like Marxism and **anarchism**, to which many forms of socialism are related, socialism was largely conceived in Europe and imported to the United States through literature and the influx of class-conscious immigrant laborers and social activists. The wide popularity of the *Manifesto of the Communist Party* (1848) by Karl Marx and Frederic Engels stimulated discussions about socialism in the United States. Many nineteenth-century European immigrants contributed to the discourse. In the antebellum period, German immigrants like laborer Herman Kriege and political activist Wilhelm Weitling sought to organize their comrades under socialist ideas. In New York City, Joseph Wedemeyer organized the Proletarian League that lasted until 1854. After the Civil War, doctrinal reinvigoration brought by Karl Marx and Ferdinand Lasalle inspired American socialists to organize socialist associations. The 1876 Union Congress tried to unite the disparate groups. That attempt largely failed; diversity is a hallmark of American socialism. The Socialist Labor Party, founded in 1877, and the Socialist Party (SP)—formed in 1901 when the Social Democratic Party absorbed several smaller groups—have been the foremost organized political expressions of American socialism.

Throughout the late-nineteenth and early-twentieth centuries, socialists wrestled with internal and external challenges. Internally, the socialist movement was both invigorated by the participation of new immigrants and hampered by the cultural contradictions brought by ethnic diversity. American-born socialists like **Eugene V. Debs** did not always agree with immigrant radicals like **Daniel DeLeon**. In addition, ideological disputes arose. **Lassallean** socialists placed more hope in the ballot box than did many Marxists, but socialists frequently clashed over whether or not socialism could be achieved peacefully. Despite disagreements, ongoing economic decline in the 1890s and the repression of labor activism helped socialism gain supporters. Debs became the leading SP politician of the day. In 1912, he gathered nearly a million votes for president, and there were over 300 socialist newspapers in circulation. The 1917 Russian Revolution also reinvigorated socialism, as well as the debate over how to achieve it. Socialists won a variety of state and local offices between 1910 and 1918, and the independent socialist Victor Berger was elected to Congress in 1910. The SP reached its highwater mark in 1918, when it had over 100,000 dues-paying members and many more supporters.

Externally, socialism faced three challenges: electoral politics, bourgeois reformers, and political repression. Groups that embraced electoral politics saw Republicans and Democrats co-opt many of their more moderate ideas. Moreover, ballot-box politics did not appeal to potential allies like the **Industrial Workers of the World**, which advocated anarcho-socialism. Reformers outside the major parties also borrowed from socialism: **Henry George**, Edward Bellamy, Jacob **Coxey**, and others borrowed socialist language and concepts, though their exact ideology was more hazy. Periodic repression has been an even bigger obstacle. Federal, state, and local governments frequently used repressive devices to muzzle socialist leaders. Many, like Debs, were persecuted for opposition to World War I. Postwar repression of better-established socialist groups and disappointment over Robert La Follette's failed 1924 presidential bid partly explain why communists held a higher profile during the Great Depression than did the SP. The SP did revive under the leadership of Norman Thomas, who garnered 800,000 votes for president in 1932. Upton Sinclair polled well in his bid to become governor of California in 1934, but the SP proved unable to avoid renewed doctrinal debates or compete with Franklin Roosevelt's popularity among working-class voters. Roosevelt's New Deal incorporated moderate socialist ideals in programs like Social Security and unemployment compensation.

Few radical groups weathered post-World War II political repression well, and most socialist groups declined precipitously even though most socialists became ardent anticommunists during the Cold War. In the 1950s, labor unions increasingly embraced **business unionism** and distanced themselves from leftist ideology of all sorts. A few advocates like Michael Harrington and the League for Industrial Democracy served left-labor interests well into the 1960s, and socialism as a whole enjoyed a brief revival during the 1960s. Nonetheless, socialism as a movement is small and its impact on American society remains marginal. A few unions continue to espouse socialist collectivist principles, but their current profile is low.

Nonetheless, socialism continues to provide an ideological critique of capitalism, potential connections to the international workers' movement, and language for conceptualizing leftist political activism in the United States. It also provides intellectual critiquing tools popular in American universities. Most recently, socialist criticism of **deregulation** and **globalization** has energized protest groups. Ideals of personal politics, open processes, democratic participation, social capital, community enterprise, human rights, and other progressive sentiments spring from age-old socialist doctrines.

Suggested Readings: Paul Buhle, *The Immigrant Left in the United States*, 1996; John Diggins, *The American Left in the Twentieth Century*, 1973; James Weinstein, *Ambiguous Legacy: The Left in American Politics*, 1975.

Timothy Draper

Social Reform Unionism. Social reform unionism refers to an activist philosophy that sees the labor movement as a force for larger change in society. Social unionism runs the gamut from socially sanctioned reform efforts to revolutionary ideology. Government authorities and business leaders have historically viewed organized workers with suspicion and treated them with antagonism—except during wartime when labor peace is deemed necessary to maintain uninterrupted production. Labor's programs over the decades thus reflected not only the **pure and simple unionism** principles of wages, hours, and working conditions, but also a need to tackle larger social problems to ensure the acceptance of unions. The liberal and, at times, radical outlook on society required a freer social structure and involved working-class movements in broad-based reform efforts. This often made labor a target for corporate and political opponents whose wealth and influence gave them greater access to those channels influencing public opinion.

The first real flowering of unions in the 1830s combined demands for shorter hours and higher wages with a political program that attacked child labor, municipal corruption, and property requirements for voting that disqualified working men in some states. Child labor usually went hand in hand with illiteracy, thereby subjugating factory hands to a de facto manufacturing caste system, and the ineligibility to vote often translated into a prohibition against workers serving on juries. These shackles severely undermined unions' ability to fight for smaller pure-and-simple objectives. This led early worker movements like the **Workingmen's Movement** and the **National Labor Union** to call for wholesale revamping of political and economic conditions.

During the Gilded Age, the **Knights of Labor (KOL)**, with its broad constituency, advocated changes as sweeping as mandatory **arbitration** of strikes, the abolition of the wage system, racial and gender equality, temperance, and land reform. A determined employer counteroffensive eliminated the Knights, but paved the way for the more exclusive **American Federation of Labor (AFL)** and its conservative craft mentality, which tried to match a skilled worker monopoly against corporate trusts. The AFL largely rejected the KOL's social unionism in favor of a pure-and-simple agenda. In the early 1900s, however, an insurrectionary version of social unionism found expression in the **Industrial Workers of the World**, which called for the overthrow of the free-enterprise system.

The AFL outlasted its union and corporate foes by maintaining a hard-nosed fixation on everyday working conditions and by using tactics that did not threaten the larger political framework. This evolutionary approach brought the AFL through the depression of 1893 and helped it gain acceptance as an alternative to the IWW during World War I. Even the AFL declined in the 1920s when businesses returned to prewar hostility and eviscerated all of organized labor by the time of the stock market crash and the onset of the Great Depression.

Ironically, the economic disaster of the 1930s rekindled social reform unionism, especially in the unskilled and semi-skilled ranks of the new **Congress of Industrial Organizations (CIO)**. The upsurge in labor militancy dovetailed with the radical policies of President Franklin Roosevelt's New Deal. The CIO embraced Roosevelt programs that liberalized the nation's archaic and restrictive labor laws, precipitating a large scale organizing drive, especially in mass-production industries. Labor's new **rank and file**—swelled by previously ignored immigrants, women, and people of color—became an army for social change. Leftists were instrumental in fashioning this alliance, though their socialist and communist ties later haunted the labor movement.

After World War II, the United States abandoned its alliance with the Soviet Union and the Cold War ensued. Opponents of the labor movement, as well as conservative forces within the AFL, found it easy to discredit progressive labor forces through red-baiting. By extension, other forms of social activism—like African American civil rights—were deemed suspicious, if not disloyal. The red scare in the 1950s provided the rationale to expel radicals from the labor movement. By the time the AFL and CIO merged in 1955, most unions had banned radicals from membership. The purge included small numbers of actual communists, but the climate of fear also sacrificed larger numbers of progressives espousing less extreme versions of social reform unionism. This sanitized version of the labor movement temporarily enjoyed the fruits of economic expansion and the emergence of a consumer society.

By the 1970s, however, the energy crisis, **runaway shops**, and the pressures of **globalism** caught the AFL-CIO unprepared for the new world order. Labor's first line of defense, its left-wing militants had been muzzled or expelled. The conservative forces of **business unionism**, confronted by economic change and a hostile political environment, discovered that their roles as junior partners in a corporate-dominated society served only to make them an easy target for those managers seeking to discredit the labor movement. This downward spiral for the labor movement also included massive job losses in former union strongholds like steel making, automobile production, and machine shops. Sophisticated personnel relations also undercut the union appeal, as management practiced enlightened workplace policies during flush economic times. Many unions began to lament lost militancy and question their blithe acceptance of prevailing economic and political arrangements. In 1995, **John Sweeney** was elected president of the AFL-CIO, largely on the strength of promises to reinvigorate the federation with social reform unionism principles. To date, the AFL-CIO's versions of social unionism and activism seem tepid when compared with that of the KOL, IWW, or early CIO, but they mark a promising revision of business unionism. How well it will play out in the new global economy remains to be seen.

Suggested Readings: Simeon Larson and Bruce Nissen, eds., *Theories of the Labor Movement*, 1987; Kim Moody, *An Injury to All*, 1989; Philip Taft, *The Structure and Government of Labor Unions*, 1962.

Scott Molloy

Solidarity. Solidarity is a term that encapsulates the central organizing principle of most labor unions. It denotes the collective ideal that only in unity can working people attain their objectives and goals. It implies mutualism and community and entails both rights and responsibilities for individuals. Solidarity unionism, ideally practiced, educates and supports individuals and their families, but individuals are expected to forgo private goals if doing so would better serve the union. Solidarity can express itself in classic Marxist perspectives on social class, or in less precise notions of interdependence, fellowship, or comradeship. The goal of most unions is to foster solidarity among the **rank and file** though, in practice, solidarity is usually strongest in moments of struggle and challenge, like **strikes, contract** negotiations, or external oppression.

The term derives from the French *solidarité* and was used by those intellectuals and workers who formed the short-lived Paris Commune in 1871. It probably came to the United States via immigrant anarchists and communists shortly after 1871. The term was used in the late-nineteenth century, but greater popularity came after 1915, when **Industrial Workers of the World** songwriter Ralph Chaplin penned "Solidarity Forever." That song became the unofficial anthem of the American labor movement for workers of all ideological dispositions. (See **Music and Labor**.)

Since 1915, solidarity has passed into general usage and has become a shorthand phrase for organizers and unionists expressing the need for unity. Appeals to solidarity are used to mute internal union bickering, justify coalitions with other groups, and substantiate calls for greater rank-and-file involvement in their unions. It has also come to imply a near-mythic ideal of unity, harmony, and strength. In 1980, unionized Polish workers opposed to the ruling Soviet-style government dubbed themselves *Solidarność*. Their struggles revitalized use of the term solidarity within the United States. In 1981, the American Federation of Labor-Congress of Industrial Organizations called a Solidarity Day to oppose the economic policies of President Ronald Reagan. An estimated half million people rallied in Washington, D.C., perhaps the largest labor protest in American history. That same year, Pope John Paul II defended the concept of solidarity in the papal encyclical *Laborem Exercens*.

Despite the imprecision of the term and the abstractions for which it sometimes stands, solidarity remains the highest ideal of the labor union movement.

Suggested Readings: Jeremy Brecher, *Strike!*, 1972; Bang Jee Chun, *The Impact of Solidarity or Conflict on Participation in a Labor Union*, 1997; Simeon Larson and Bruce Nissen, eds., *Theories of the Labor Movement*, 1987.

Robert E. Weir

Speedups. Speedups are any form of increased work and productivity requirement without a parallel increase in pay or benefits. In a manufacturing facility, a company might accelerate the movement of the assembly line or require workers to produce a greater number of goods. In a service-sector scenario, delivery routes might be increased or office personnel assigned a larger number of tasks. The speedup was once a standard feature in industries like textiles and automobiles, with companies often employing it to build up excess inventory prior to contract negotiations as a hedge against possible **strikes**. Such unilateral work changes occur most frequently in non-union settings, however, because many **collective bargaining** agreements have provisions blocking such management practices without prior negotiations.

Today, many multinational corporations with labor-intensive operations avoid speedup prohibitions by relocating North-American and European production plants to developing nations where unions are weak. The new era of labor-management relations, beginning with the energy crisis and the dawn of **globalism** in the 1970s, introduced a host of new work practices which circumvented earlier restraints against speedups. For example, computers measuring in nanoseconds can also be used to monitor and time employee tasks. Although such acceleration predominates in union-free environments, the competitive pace has affected labor contracts as well. Telephone operators, postal workers, and keypunch operators are among those groups of workers who have complained of modern-day speedups.

Suggested Readings: Carroll R. Daugherty and John B. Parrish, *The Labor Problems of American Society*, 1952; Mike Parker and Jane Slaughter, *Working Smart: A Union Guide to Participation Programs and Reengineering*, 1994.

Scott Molloy

Staley Lockout. The Staley Lockout took place between June 1993 and November 1995. It was one of three labor disturbances in Decatur, Illinois during the early- to mid-1990s, making the city of about 85,000, in the words of workers, a "war zone." In addition to the A.E. Staley Manufacturing Company, a corn processor, local facilities of **Caterpillar** Tractor and **Bridgestone-Firestone** were involved in clashes that pitted multinational corporations against workers' rights. The fundamental importance of the lockout to U.S. workers and unions was captured in occasional references to Decatur as the **Homestead** of the 1990s, a comparison to the infamous 1892 labor-management confrontation in Homestead, Pennsylvania. Like Homestead, the Decatur actions ended badly for affected workers and their unions. Some pessimists cite these three incidents as proof of organized labor's inexorable decline toward irrelevance.

The battle began in the fall of 1991, when members of the **United Auto Workers** (UAW) struck two Caterpillar factories in Decatur and Peoria, and the company responded by locking out union workers at two other Illinois plants. Caterpillar management sought a six-year **contract** that would break UAW **pattern bargaining** in the tractor industry and create a two-tier wage system that would establish a lower wage scale for new hires. The issues remained unresolved when, in the spring of 1992, Caterpillar threatened to hire **replacement workers**. In response, the UAW ended the **strike**, but without a new contract. Nearly two years of tense relations on the shop floor followed, marked by frequent disputes between union members and managers, and firings of union activists.

Also in 1992, officials of Tate & Lyle, PLC, a London-based multinational corporation that purchased the nearly century-old Staley company in 1988, sought to lower labor costs and increase management flexibility by insisting on a new contract featuring twelve-hour, rotating shifts. Workers affiliated with the Allied Industrial Workers Union (AIW) refused to discuss the contract proposal. Although the plant employed as many as 2,300 workers in the late 1960s, the 1992 workforce was about 740 and the company indicated its intent to make further reductions. A brief walkout by AIW workers in early June 1993 was followed a few weeks later by the company's **lockout**. Staley workers retained labor consultant Ray Rogers and launched a **corporate campaign** against Tate & Lyle, hoping to marshal public and financial pressure to end the lockout and soften the company's contract demands.

Confrontation also brewed at the Bridgestone/Firestone plant, located midway between Staley and Caterpillar on Decatur's east side. Bridgestone, a Japanese firm, purchased Firestone in 1988. Six years later, claiming it was responding to increasing competition in the industry, Bridgestone/Firestone sought a new contract with the **United Rubber Workers (URW)** that also included twelve-hour, rotating shifts; productivity-linked wage hikes; cuts in vacation time, and a two-tiered wage system. In July 1994, the URW struck and the company responded by hiring **scabs** at 30 percent lower wages. Efforts by the Clinton administration to withdraw government contracts from the tire maker in response to its hiring of replacement workers failed. Massive demonstrations, civil disobedience—including the arrest in June 1994 of a priest and several nuns and police use of pepper gas against peaceful demonstrators at Staley—Rogers's corporate campaign, and the efforts of Staley "road warriors," who traveled about the United States rallying support from other unions, focused national attention on Decatur. It did little, however, to cushion the crippling losses that ensued.

Following a late 1995 change in the local's leadership, Staley workers—reorganized as members of the **United Paperworkers International Union**—accepted the company's contract. Of the 740 workers employed at the time of the lockout, just 146 returned to work. As the decade ended, the plant employed only 270 laborers with that figure projected to drop to 200. In June 1994, UAW leadership called a new strike against Caterpillar that continued until December 1995 when, despite rejection of a contract offer by the membership, workers were ordered by the union to return to their jobs. Within three years, UAW members ratified a new contract similar to Caterpillar's original offer. Firestone workers, now affiliated with the **United Steel Workers of America**, ratified a new contract in late 1996, an agreement that included twelve-hour, rotating shifts.

To workers and students of labor history, the Decatur disputes placed in doubt the future of working-class gains in hours, wages, and conditions won over the previous sixty years. Organized labor has not yet fashioned an adequate response to the aggressive demands of multinational corporations in labor relations. Two of the unions involved—the AIW and the URW—disappeared into mergers that were, in part, brought on by the disputes. Relations between unionized Firestone union workers, picket-line crossers, and replacements were improving when, in December 2001, the plant closed following negative publicity involving tire problems in certain Ford vehicles that used their tires. About 1,500 men and women were left unemployed.

Suggested Readings: Stephen Franklin, *Three Strikes: Labor's Heartland Losses and What They Mean for Working Americans*, 2001; Tom Juravich and Kate Bronfenbrenner, *Ravenswood*, 1999.

Robert D. Sampson

Standard Time. Standard time was a creation of **Taylorism**. Scientific management experts calculated the exact time necessary for a worker to complete a particular task. Frederick Winslow Taylor, who founded this school of thought, employed stopwatches to standardize every movement that went into assembling a product. In a quest for total efficiency, management dissected jobs into steps and taught employees how to repeat processes in a more time-efficient way. The savings in time, multiplied by each worker over the course of the year, created a gargantuan leap in productivity, at least on paper. The robotic nature of the system was not lost on workers, who faced deskilling of their jobs and dehumanizing conditions. Taylor and his followers tried to entice factory hands by offering **incentive pay** to those who could beat the clock. Time, rather than the making of so many items, became the benchmark of this accelerated work life.

Labor unions bitterly contested this **speedup** and many workers imposed an informal **stint** that applied pressure to workers who bought into standard time. Assembly-line workers sometimes even resorted to sabotage to resist the dehumanizing effects of standard time. Ultimately, most firms determined that strict adherence to standard time was impractical. Despite eventual widespread societal disillusionment with the system, however, it lingers into the present and permeates the up-tempo life of contemporary America. Computerization modernized the old concepts of time-and-motion studies by fracturing time into humanly unfathomable bits, such as nanoseconds. Some vestiges of the old assembly line speedup can still be witnessed in fast food restaurants, where even the shaking of salt on french fries is carefully timed. For the most part, high-end production facilities have abandoned standard time in favor of team management.

Suggested Readings: American Social History Project, *Who Built America?*, Vol. 2, 2000; Eric Schlosser, *Fast Food Nation*, 2001.

Scott Molloy

Steel Strike of 1919. Like other strikes that occurred this same year, the Steel Strike of 1919 had its origins in World War I. The National Committee for Organizing Iron and Steel Workers, led by John Fitzpatrick of the Chicago Federation of Labor and former **Industrial Workers of the World (IWW)** organizer

William Z. Foster, began a campaign to unionize steelworkers nationwide in 1918. At first, steel producers were reluctant to fight organization because the administration of President Woodrow Wilson would not have tolerated labor disruptions that put government war contracts at risk. For this reason, the committee signed up thousands in the waning days of the war. This was the first sustained effort to organize steelworkers since the **Homestead lockout** of 1892 had largely driven unions from the industry.

When the war ended, union leaders requested negotiations with industry executives in the hope of receiving a contract. Steel producers refused to recognize or even meet with them. Even though the National Committee wanted more time to organize before striking, **rank-and-file** pressure forced it to call a nationwide steel strike on September 22. The two main issues were union recognition and a reduction in working hours from the ten- to twelve-hour days that remained a steel-industry standard.

Strike leader at Gary, Ind., advising steel strikers, 1919. © Library of Congress.

The strike affected firms differently. On the first day of the strike the majority of workers did not show up at most of the facilities owned by industry-giant U.S. Steel. By contrast, Bethlehem Steel, U.S. Steel's largest competitor, experienced only scattered disruptions. Best estimates put the total number of strikers at 250,000 nationwide, approximately half the workers in the industry.

Steel producers fought the strike by using three successful strategies. First, they immediately hired **scabs** to replace as many strikers as possible. Since the committee tended to attract unskilled workers, it proved relatively easy to replace them. Second, steel producers deliberately inflamed racial and ethnic tensions in the workforce. For example, U.S. Steel paid African Americans in Gary, Indiana, to march through the streets rather than to make steel, anticipating that this would engender fear among white strikers that blacks would take their jobs. Finally, the industry encouraged the media to attack the politics of the strike and its organizers. Most of these attacks centered on Foster, whose previous career with the IWW gave the committee's enemies an easy way to make the campaign seem dangerously radical.

The committee's best hope for winning concessions of any sort came during an industrial conference called by President Wilson in October. But when U.S.

Steel Chairman Elbert Gary refused to accept voluntary government **arbitration**, all hopes for compromise disappeared. Striking workers gradually returned to their jobs—without union contracts—all across the country. The committee formally ended the strike on January 8, 1920, although production had returned to normal levels weeks before. Steel remained largely nonunion until the Steel Workers Organizing Committee won major victories in the late-1930s.

Suggested Readings: David Brody, *Labor in Crisis: The Steel Strike of 1919*, 1987; Interchurch World Movement, *Public Opinion and the Steel Strike*, 1921; Interchurch World Movement, *Report on the Steel Strike of 1919*, 1920.

Jonathan Rees

Steel Strike of 1959–60. The Steel Strike of 1959–60 was the last nationwide and industry-wide strike of steelworkers. One of the largest and most successful strikes in United States' history, it was the culmination of many decades of labor's efforts to establish and consolidate its power in basic industries. For steelworkers, it evoked memories of historical struggles like the **Homestead steel strike**, the **steel strike of 1919**, and the **Depression-era strikes**. On July 15, 1959, more than 500,000 steelworkers, all members of the **United Steel Workers of America (USWA)**, struck the twelve major steel companies, including U.S. Steel. The strike closed over 90 percent of the American steel industry and idled close to one percent of the United States' entire labor force. In terms of idled hours, the strike was the largest in U.S. history. The workers were out for 116 days, returning to the mills November 7 by mandate of the **Taft-Hartley Act**. In early January 1960, the steel companies gave up. The settlement was a sweeping victory for the steelworkers and a humiliating defeat for management.

The steel companies sought a strike to roll back much of what the steelworkers had gained in previous contracts. Management precipitated the walkout in hope that a long strike would cause the **rank-and-file** to abandon USWA leaders. Ultimately, the companies wanted to severely reduce the union's and workers' power on the shop floor. Section 2-F of the steelworkers' contract forced company management to negotiate with the union over work processes. The companies' goal was to force the union to abandon section 2-F, thus returning all shop-floor power to management. The USWA saw section 2-F as vital to protecting jobs and workers and refused to negotiate changes to it.

The strike became a battle of attrition, and a settlement was reached only due to the intervention of the federal government. In October, the strike began to affect the national economy and President Dwight Eisenhower declared it a threat to national security. On October 9, Eisenhower invoked the eighty-day cooling-off provision of the Taft-Hartley Act to force the steelworkers back into the mills. USWA President David McDonald accused Eisenhower of strike-breaking, but once Taft-Hartley was in effect, negotiations began in earnest for the first time. In mid-October, Kaiser Steel agreed to the USWA's terms. Under order by the U.S. Supreme Court, the workers returned to work on November 7. The cooling-off period expired in January 1960. Recognizing the rank-and-file's willingness to renew their strike, the Eisenhower administration convinced the companies to settle on the USWA's terms. A settlement was announced on January 5. The steelworkers earned a wage increase and no reduction in their various benefits. Section 2-F remained intact.

The USWA maintained **solidarity** among steelworkers. Despite a four-month strike and two more months of intense management lobbying to convince workers to drop their support of the union, the rank-and-file remained committed to their union. This was all the more remarkable given that few younger steelworkers favored the original strike. Veterans of previous strikes argued that a show of force was necessary to defend the union and preserve wages, various benefits, and shop-floor power. Management intransigence served only to focus rank-and-file anger, determination, and solidarity. Left with little choice, the federal government allied with the workers and convinced the steel companies to capitulate. The USWA hailed the contract as its best ever. Ironically, it may remain so. By the 1970s, the steel industry was in deep decline, with foreign imports undercutting domestic prices, hastening the closing of aging plants, and leading to overall retrenchment. Giants like U.S. Steel began to shift assets out of production and diversify their investments. USWA membership declined among a shrinking steelworker pool until it expanded organizing efforts to workers in other fields.

Suggested Readings: Anthony F. Libertella, "The Steel Strike of 1959: Labor, Management, and Government Relations," Ph.D. dissertation, Ohio State University, 1972; Jack Metzgar, *Striking Steel: Solidarity Remembered*, 2000.

Mark Marianek

Steel Workers Organizing Committee. *See United Steel Workers of America.*

Steward, Ira (March 10, 1831–March 13, 1883). Ira Steward was a machinist who was one of the influential early advocates for the **eight-hour movement**. He was born in New London, Connecticut. His father was a laborer, and Steward was largely self-educated. By 1850, Steward was an apprentice machinist whose grueling twelve-hour workdays kindled his interest in reducing the strain of long hours on workers. He joined the International Machinists' and Blacksmiths' Union (IMBU)—a forerunner of the International Association of Machinists—which, in 1863, passed resolutions demanding an eight-hour workday. Steward quickly became a leader, and the IMBU provided him with seed money to build a workers' movement in support of the eight-hour goal.

Steward set up several organizations in the greater Boston area, including the Labor Reform Association and the Grand Eight-Hour League (which later was known as the Boston Eight-Hour League). In 1868, federal employees won an eight-hour day. He ran afoul of progressive Massachusetts labor advocates like Wendell Phillips for his anti-Chinese views, but Steward did help pressure the Massachusetts legislature to grant a ten-hour day for women and children in 1874. In 1878, he and J. P. McDonnell founded the International Labor Union (ILU). Although the ILU was short-lived, many of its views on **cooperation**, shorter workdays, and redistributing wealth inspired future labor leaders, especially **George McNeill**, who idolized Steward.

Steward is credited with being among the first to make cogent arguments about how shorter hours would improve workers' lives and society. His numerous articles and pamphlets were often mined by others seeking to defend shorter hours. Among Steward's claims was the argument that shorter hours would lead workers to improve themselves morally. He even argued that the overall economy would benefit because reduced hours would give workers more time to become consumers. That said, there can be no doubt that Steward saw the eight-hour day as part of a larger program to undermine capitalism through redistributing wealth.

Steward married twice. His first wife, Mary, died in 1878, and, in 1880, he married Jane Henning. He died in Plano, Illinois, in 1883. Steward remained an important symbol for the eight-hour movement for most of the nineteenth century, but he was largely forgotten by the time the 1938 **Fair Labor Standards Act** put the force of federal law behind the eight-hour day.

Suggested Readings: David Montgomery, *Beyond Equality: Labor and the Radical Republicans, 1962–1872*, 1967; Timothy Messer-Kruse, "Eight Hours, Greenbacks, and Chinamen: Wendell Phillips, Ira Steward, and the Fate of Labor Reform in Massachusetts," *Labor History* 42, no. 2 (2001); Paul R. Taylor, *The ABC-CLIO Companion to the American Labor Movement*, 1993.

Bruce Cohen

Stint. Stint refers to an informal agreement among workers as to what constitutes a reasonable pace and amount of work. Often expressed under the rubric a fair day's work for a fair day's pay, the stint was an important part of the nineteenth-century work mentality that persists to the present. Employers routinely attempt to break worker stints through methods ranging from **piecework** rates to **speedups**, but frequently encounter resistance when they do so. Unlike organized protests, the stint requires little more to maintain than tacit agreement among workers. It is considered an important aspect of shop-floor culture that illustrates how laborers exert some degree of control over production, even in nonunionized companies. Overly zealous workers who do not respect the stint are usually ostracized by others. Employers face resistance ranging from deliberate slowdowns and **grievance** filings to sabotage.

Suggested Reading: David Montgomery, *Workers' Control in America*, 1984.

Robert E. Weir

Stool Pigeon. A stool pigeon is an informer used as a decoy to entice individuals into a trap. In the workplace the term stool pigeon is used to describe a company or government spy in the ranks of workers. A stool pigeon is comparable to an **agent provocateur**, though the latter also incites illegal actions as well as spying. Other terms with similar connotations include: company spy, company spotter, fin, rat, and labor spy. Stool pigeon derives from a fowling practice in which a pigeon was tied to a stool to attract birds of prey. Stool is a variant of the archaic stale, meaning decoy or, more specifically, of the French *estale*, a pigeon that entices hawks or other pigeons into a net. The modern sense of the term dates from the fifteenth-century alternative spelling *stall*, which was jargon for a pickpocket's accomplice who distracted a victim while the co-conspirator fleeced a victim. By the end of the sixteenth century, a person who worked to entrap another was generally referred to as a stool pigeon.

In the United States, one of the earliest known uses of the phrase was in an 1830 *Workingman's Gazette*, which used it to illustrate how political parties used human decoys to attract voters, much as a huckster might use a fake testimonial to peddle his goods. Its first use in the context of industrial espionage is difficult to pinpoint. The rise of factory spies and the use of **Pinkerton** detectives in the labor struggles of the Gilded Age certainly provided the opportunity for the use of the term. In one famed incident, Pinkerton detective James McParlan allegedly infiltrated the **Molly Maguires**. His evidence sent ten Pennsylvania miners to the gallows in 1875, and fourteen more to jail. During the West Virginia-Kentucky bituminous coal strikes of the 1920s, stool pigeons acted as agent provocateurs and committed illegal acts that justified harsh crackdowns. The use of police informants to break organized crime rings during the Prohibition era brought the term to greater prominence, but stool pigeons continued to be used against labor unions as well. The practice was condemned by the 1937 **La Follette Committee**, but the report did little to stop the practice. Many 1960s social reform movements, including unions, were troubled by internal spies. Stool pigeons also kept management apprised of union activities during the 1997 Detroit newspaper strike.

Suggested Readings: Edward Levinson, *I Break Strikes!*, 1969; Jean Spielman, *The Stool Pigeon and the Open Shop Movement*, 1923.

Mark Noon

Strasser, Adolph (1844–January 1, 1939). Adolph Strasser was a major figure in the early Socialist Labor Party, Cigar-Maker's International Union (CMIU), the **Knights of Labor (KOL)**, and was a cofounder of the **American Federation of Labor (AFL)**. Strasser is credited with being the ideological father of **pure and simple unionism**.

Strasser was a German-speaking Hungarian who emigrated to America around 1872. Not much is known of his early life. His knowledge of British trade unionism indicated that he probably spent some time in England, and some people—including AFL leader **Samuel Gompers**—surmised that Strasser had upper-class origins. Upon his arrival New York City, the twenty-eight-year-old Strasser became an active participant in the socialist movement, joining the American Section of the International Workingmen's Association of the Marxist First International. He also took an active role in the CMIU, where he worked with Samuel Gompers.

Strasser was disappointed in the faction-ridden, German immigrant character of the International, and joined a group of American-born activists in organizing the **Tompkins Square** unemployment demonstration on January 13, 1874, which ended in violence. His participation violated the rules of the American Section, and Strasser, **Peter J. McGuire**, and several others were expelled. Strasser and McGuire then organized the Social Democratic Workingmen's Party (SDWP), Strasser becoming its executive secretary. He contributed extensively to its paper, *The Socialist*, which was later renamed *The Labor Standard*.

Though Strasser was an active, visionary force in the SDWP, he was never able to stem the arguments raging in the German-American community on the tactical merits of trade union organization versus political action. This issue was hotly debated in the pages of the SDWP's journal, and it caused serious disruption at an April 1876 Unity Convention in Philadelphia of various socialist groups. Strasser's statements on the need to focus on immediate achievements—provision of jobs, high wages, short working hours, unemployment insurance, and sick benefits—as opposed to participation in political campaigns, was the major point of contention in the meetings. After much debate, the Workingmen's Party of the United States—soon to be re-christened the Socialist Labor Party (SLP)—was formed. Most of the other participants insisted upon the primacy of political campaigning, and Strasser was removed from his leadership position.

In 1877, Strasser was promoted from organizer to president of the CMIU, a position he occupied for the next fifteen years. When he took over the CMIU, membership had sunk to just over 1,000 members. Within three years, the CMIU membership climbed to over 4,000. Both Strasser and Gompers soon shed their socialism and developed pure and simple unionism. Strasser insisted unions should focus on **collective bargaining** and short-range political action. Although this strategy was the antithesis of the utopianism of the Socialist Labor Party, pure and simple unionism became the bedrock model for American trade unionism by about 1890.

The first major action of the Strasser/Gompers-led CMIU was the campaign against tenement cigarmaking. The CMIU organized a campaign that emphasized the unsanitary conditions of tenement labor, and introduced a **union label** on cigars to distinguish them from the tenement-made brands. In 1878, the union appealed to the federal and state legislatures to ban commercial production in residential dwellings. The several bills introduced all failed, and further alienated socialists within and without the CMIU. In consequence, CMIU members of the SLP bolted from the union to form the SLP-affiliated Progressive Cigar-Maker's Union (PCMU). In New York City, the PCMU was chartered as a Knights of Labor local assembly, a move that angered Strasser and Gompers, who were nominal members of the KOL. The fight between the

CMIU and the PCMU weaned Strasser from any remaining vestiges of socialism and touched off bitter jurisdiction battles between the CMIU and the KOL. Strasser actively worked to subvert the PCMU. He also became a harsh critic of the KOL and, in 1886, demanded that the Knights stop organizing workers in skilled trades.

Though Strasser was a central figure in the formation of the AFL in 1886, he preferred thereafter to focus his energies on the CMIU. He did serve the AFL's legislative committee and on its executive council. In the latter position Strasser is credited with pushing through the expulsion of the **Brewery Workers** Union in 1907, when it embraced an **industrial unionism** philosophy. Strasser vacated the CMIU presidency in 1892, but continued to serve the cigar makers in a variety of lower-level capacities. Later in life he moved a great deal, first from New York City to Buffalo, then to Chicago from 1905 to 1911, and then back to Buffalo in 1914 when he retired from the labor movement and spent four years as a real-estate agent.

Little is known of Strasser's personal life. A CMIU newspaper article published at the end of his presidency said "personally, or rather socially, he makes few friends. . . . " In 1930, Strasser moved to Florida, and his apparently deliberate low profile left him an almost-forgotten figure in the AFL. He had no further contact with the CMIU, and spent his last years living in the home of a dressmaker, dying there on January 1, 1939. Strasser's considerable stock portfolio and savings were depleted during the Depression. He died nearly penniless, his burial expenses being paid by the state of Florida. Several years later the CMIU paid to have his remains exhumed and shipped to Chicago for reburial. Only three people attended Strasser's interment in the Forest Home Cemetery.

Suggested Readings: Patricia Cooper, *Once a Cigarmaker: Men, Women, and Work Culture in American Cigar Factories, 1900–1919*, 1987; H. M. Gitelman, "Adolph Strasser and the Origins of Pure and Simple Unionism," *Labor History* 6, no. 1 (Winter 1965): 71–83; Julie Greene, *Pure and Simple Politics: The American Federation of Labor and Political Activism, 1881–1917*, 1988.

Jeff McFadden

Strike. A strike is the cessation of work initiated by employees in protest against perceived injustices on the part of an employer. It is also commonly referred to as a work stoppage, suspension, or walkout. Issues like low pay, poor working conditions, long hours, or fringe benefits are among those that precipitate strikes. The strike is the primary weapon of organized labor and is one of the most significant forms of social protest in the United States. Strikes can take a variety of forms including the **sit-down strike**, the **sympathy strike**, or the **wildcat strike**. However, the most common form involves a decision among workers to withhold their labor by walking off their jobs and staying away until their demands are negotiated. A dominant feature of the strike is the use of a **picket** line in which workers voice their demands, alert the public of their plight, and attempt to prevent strikebreakers from entering the business or factory.

The first recorded use of the term in the context of a concerted refusal to work dates from 1768, and likely originated in the sailors' practice of striking, or lowering, a ship's sails to symbolize their refusal to go to sea. The first documented strike in the United States occurred in Philadelphia in 1786, when printers sought a minimum wage of $6 per week. With the development of labor organizations in the late-nineteenth century, strikes became more frequent, with the first nationwide strike occurring in 1877, when railroad workers protested a series of wage cuts. The opening decades of the twentieth century witnessed several important industry-wide strikes by miners, steelworkers, and autoworkers. Significantly, until New Deal legislation in the 1930s gave unions the right to organize, courts routinely ruled that strikes were illegal and forced employees back to work. Since World War II, the number of strikes has been on the decline with some of the most significant strikes occurring among public employees such as teachers and municipal workers.

In 1948, during a strike at the Univis Lens Company in Dayton, Ohio, replacement workers enter the plant under the protection of Ohio National Guardsmen. © George Meany Memorial Archives.

Suggested Readings: Jeremy Brecher, *Strike!*, 1997; E. T. Hiller, *The Strike: A Study in Collective Action*, 1969.

Mark Noon

Subcontracting. Subcontracting is the practice whereby production and/or services purchased from one firm are assigned to another by the firm under contract. It is especially commonplace in the building trades. A consumer—which could be an individual, a municipality, or even the federal government—signs an agreement with a contractor. The contract usually specifies the amount the consumer will pay for the project and the time in which the contractor will complete it, or reasonable estimates in the case of larger undertakings. Contracts are often quite detailed regarding the nature and quality of the work to be completed. In addition, building codes and consumer laws may apply.

It is the contractor's responsibility to complete the project, but that individual or firm may have great flexibility in how to do so. Few general contractors complete all the work themselves. They may choose, for example, to subcontract the plumbing to one firm, landscaping to another, and electrical work to still a different company. It is usually the original contractor's responsibility to make certain all work is completed properly.

Subcontracting has long been a feature of American industry, and not just in the building trades. Auto manufacturers, for example, often subcontract parts fashioned in one place, but assembled at another. The same is true in the apparel industry, where cloth or even basic garments might be woven or cut in one location and tailored somewhere else.

Organized labor concerns itself with subcontracting when it undermines the jobs and wages of union workers. In recent years, subcontracting has emerged as another way for less scrupulous firms to subvert wages under the guise of frugality. Hospitals, for example, have replaced staff nurses with subcontracted care from firms that generally pay lower wages. Many airlines now subcontract plane maintenance, a practice that has cost jobs among union workers in the **International Association of Machinists and Aerospace Workers**. Abuses are widespread in the building trades, where large construction firms may actually set up nonunion subsidiaries toward which they channel projects. Apparel-industry workers complain that subcontracted **homework** is little more than **sweatshop** production in a new guise. Malls and office complexes routinely subcontract services like security, maintenance, rubbish removal, and cleaning to outside firms. In larger cities, badly paid subcontracted work often goes to immigrants and the poor, though campaigns by groups like Jobs with Justice and Justice for Janitors have helped in some cities. For the foreseeable future, subcontracting is likely to remain a point of contention between unions and management.

Suggested Reading: Barbara Ehrenreich, *Nickel and Dimed*, 2001.

Robert E. Weir

Sugar, Maurice (August 12, 1891–February 15, 1974). Maurice Sugar was born on August 12, 1891, in Northern Michigan. His parents were Lithuanian Jews who immigrated to the United States in the early 1880s. His father was a salesman who eventually opened his own small shop in the lumber boom town of Brimley, Michigan. The family moved to Detroit in 1900, but returned to live in Brimley in 1906. When Maurice entered University of Michigan law school, there was no indication of the radicalism that would motivate much of his legal career. At University of Michigan, Maurice met and fell in love with Jane Meyer, a committed **socialist**. By the time Sugar graduated in 1913, he firmly embraced the Socialist Party of **Eugene Debs**. Meyer and Sugar eloped in 1914 and moved to Detroit.

The politically active and motivated Sugar quickly gained the trust of the local labor movement and the Socialist Party of America (SP) in Detroit. In the few years after he moved to Detroit, and prior to World War I, Sugar worked for the International Typographical Union Local #18 (Detroit) during a strike, and assisted the Detroit Federation of Labor in its attempts to stop the use of injunctions in labor disputes in Michigan. Sugar and his wife also became leaders in the Detroit and Michigan chapters of the SP. Sugar supported the SP's antiwar and anticonscription positions as the United States entered World War I.

Like other SP members, Sugar was convicted and jailed for his opposition to United States entrance into World War I and for failing to register for conscription. On November 25, 1918, two weeks after WW I ended, the Supreme Court refused to hear his appeal and Sugar entered the Detroit House of Corrections. He spent the next ten months in jail. Perhaps more alarming to the young attorney, the Detroit Bar Association argued successfully for Sugar's disbarment soon after he was sentenced in early 1918.

Frank Murphy, in 1923 a young, ambitious Detroit judge, thought Sugar's disbarment unjust. Murphy had been an opposing attorney at some of Sugar's earlier labor cases and respected Sugar as an attorney and as a person. Murphy, who later became mayor of Detroit (1930–33), governor of Michigan (1937–38), and then a Supreme Court justice (1940–49), prepared and argued successfully Sugar's case for reinstatement to the Michigan Bar. The paths of Murphy and Sugar continued to intersect, sometimes as allies and sometimes as adversaries, throughout their careers.

Now able to practice law again, Sugar returned to the labor movement and worked on civil-liberties cases as well. He was a local advisor to Clarence Darrow in the Ossian Sweet defense case, a landmark Detroit civil-rights trial. Although he did not return to membership in the SP in the 1920s, he remained close to the left in Detroit and provided legal assistance to both the International Labor Defense (ILD) and the Unemployed Councils (UC). Both the UC and the ILD were close to the Communist Party (CP). Although he does not appear to have been a member of the CP, he was also active in other CP-allied organizations like the John Reed Club. He and his wife visited the Soviet Union in 1932.

By the mid-1930s Sugar became more formally connected with the local labor movement. In 1933 he was hired as the legal counsel for the **Mechanics Educational Society of America** (MESA), an independent union of skilled craftsmen located primarily in the Detroit area. While working for MESA he became an expert on the legal workings of the New Deal agencies that had increased the federal government's involvement in labor relations. He represented MESA, for example, at the Automobile Labor Board hearings of the National Recovery Administration (NRA). Perhaps more important, he was called upon as an advisor for the fledging **United Auto Workers** union (UAW) at the historic Flint **sit-down strike**. Sugar penned "Sit-Down," one of the better known labor songs of the twentieth-century in 1938, as Detroit exploded in sit-down strikes in the wake of the Flint workers' success. More than a few of Detroit's sit-down strikers called Sugar for advice and legal representation.

His association with the UAW grew quickly and, in 1939, he was hired as the UAW general counsel. Sugar established a modern and quite skilled legal department in the UAW. Although Sugar became increasingly skeptical of the labor movement's reliance on the federal government, he and his UAW staff utilized federal-government-established labor relations machinery, like the National Labor Relations Board and the **National War Labor Board**, as successfully as any other union in the country. But Sugar was much more than the UAW's general counsel. From the beginning he was deeply involved in the overall functioning, decision-making, and politics of the union. He helped develop strategies in the drive to organize the Ford Motor Company, particularly between 1939 and 1941, for example. Although not an elected official, he regularly attended executive board meetings. Sugar also participated in the factional political struggles that wracked the union after World War II. He opposed the rise of **Walter Reuther** to the presidency in 1946 and Reuther's successful campaign to gain control of the executive board eighteen months later in 1947. Soon after gaining control of the UAW, Reuther moved to fire many of his factional enemies' supporters, including Sugar. Many unsubstantiated charges were filed against Sugar as the executive board debated his disposition for eight hours before deciding to terminate his relationship with the union. Sugar was clearly a casualty of the left-wing faction's loss to Reuther.

Sugar was politically and personally committed to the UAW and his ouster was unpleasant. Especially difficult for Sugar was that the UAW did not allow him to respond to unfair accusations made by his political opponents. After being released from the UAW, Sugar receded from politics and moved north to Black Lake. His private practice was the first integrated law firm in Detroit. It included African American George Crocket, who was also fired by Reuther from a UAW post in the late 1940s, and Ernest Goodman. Sugar died on February 15, 1974.

Suggested Reading: Christopher Johnson, *Maurice Sugar: Law, Labor, and the Left in Detroit, 1912–1950*, 1988.

Joseph Turrini

Supplemental Unemployment Benefits. *See Guaranteed Annual Wage.*

Sweatshop. Sweatshops are generally defined as small manufacturing concerns, often within a residential setting, in which men and especially women and children labor under substandard conditions, for long hours and low pay. Beginning in the nineteenth century, American workers, many of them recent immigrants, toiled in urban tenements making clothes, shoes, and cigars, paid by the piece. During the 1880s, the Cigarmakers International Union was among the first trade unions to demand regulation of sweatshops. Progressive Era social reformers also expressed concern for sweatshop workers, as well as the possibility that disease could be spread to unwary consumers through goods produced in unhealthy settings. The garment industry was especially dependent on "sweated" labor, which trade unionists argued kept all garment makers' wages low. The **International Ladies' Garment Workers' Union** in particular lobbied against the proliferation of sweatshops. The horrible **Triangle Factory Fire of 1911** focused public attention on sweatshop and factory conditions and stimulated ordinances to control them. Federal laws, passed during the New Deal in the 1930s, further restricted the use of sweatshop labor. Nonetheless, inhuman labor conditions, especially in the production of clothing, continue in the twenty-first century. In addition, many unions charge that **subcontracted homework** replicates sweatshop conditions in private homes. Moreover, many American-based firms have moved their manufacturing operations to low-wage nations where sweatshop conditions are the norm. In response, activist groups like Sweatshop Watch and labor organizations like UNITE seek to publicize both American and global sweatshop labor by mounting **boycotts** and sponsoring organizing campaigns.

An 1888 illustration depicting the evils of New York sweatshops. © George Meany Memorial Archives/Library of Congress.

Suggested Readings: Eileen Boris, *Home to Work: Motherhood and the Politics of Industrial Homework in the United States*, 1994; Miriam Ching Yoon Louie, *Sweatshop Warriors: Immigrant Women Workers Take on the Global Factory*, 2001.

Kathleen Banks Nutter

Sweeney, John Joseph (May 5, 1934–). John J. Sweeney is the current president of the American Federation of Labor-Congress of Industrial Organizations (AFL-CIO). He was elected in 1995, and has pledged to reverse decades of declining union membership in the United States. He is the son of working-class Irish immigrants and was raised in the Bronx borough of New York City. His father, a bus driver, was an active member in the Transport Workers Union and his mother was a domestic worker. Sweeney attended Roman Catholic schools and obtained a B.A. in economics from Iona College in 1956. He is married and has two children.

He worked briefly for IBM, before leaving to earn substantially lower pay as a researcher for the **International Ladies' Garment Workers' Union**. By 1960, he was working for the Building Service Employees International Union (BSEIU) as a contract director. His affiliation with the BSEIU grew as he steadily took on tasks more central to the union's operations. Four years after the BSEIU changed its name to the **Service Employees International Union (SIEU)** in 1968, Sweeney became a part of the union's executive board. Soon after, he became a vice president. In 1976, Sweeney assumed the presidency of SEIU Local 32B in New York City and confronted two problems hampering union efforts: corporate disregard of workers and union passivity. In the first four years of his presidency of Local 32B he addressed both concerns. Two fierce and swift **strikes** won important wage and job security **concessions** for 70,000 workers.

Sweeney was elected SEIU international president in 1980 and was also elected as a vice president of the AFL-CIO. During the 1980s, Sweeney led a number of successful campaigns including Justice for Janitors in 1985, and the Work and Family Campaign begun in 1986. Sweeney also agitated for legislative changes, including the federal Family and Medical Leave Act. Under his watch SEIU also made a concerted effort to bring gender and racial diversity to the union. In addition, gays and lesbians found expression in the union's Lavender Caucus.

In response to what Sweeney saw as AFL-CIO apathy and its inability to confront conservative politicians and deteriorating working conditions, he challenged Lane Kirkland's hand-picked candidate for the presidency of the AFL-CIO in 1995. Sweeney won the election and vowed to expand SEIU policies and militancy throughout the federation. He also announced intentions to concentrate on recruitment drives. As SEIU president, Sweeney spent one-third of its budget on organizing campaigns, and SEIU was one of the few AFL-CIO unions to experience growth during the antiunion administrations of Presidents Ronald Reagan and George H. Bush. Similarly, when Sweeney assumed the presidency of the AFL-CIO, he immediately launched an aggressive organizing drive backed by $20 million of newly allocated funds. This campaign also sought to diversify AFL-CIO membership and leadership through active recruitment of women and minorities. Sweeney also vowed to promote union democracy, a call that ruffled several notoriously autocratic affiliate heads.

Another constant in Sweeney's leadership has been his dedication to consider the plight of all working Americans, not just union members. He is an outspoken critic of modern corporate management strategies used to maximize profit: **deregulation**, **downsizing**, capital flight, reducing employee benefits and **pensions**, and ignoring worker security. He also maintains that corporate managers have persuaded the government to enact laws that protect property but not people. Current and recent AFL-CIO campaigns include making workplaces conform to principles of ergonomics, enforcing workplace safety laws, safeguarding the right of workers to organize, recognizing new categories of occupational injury, preserving the current Social Security program, and equalizing incomes as a means to achieve greater social stability worldwide.

The **Teamsters**' 1997 victory in the **United Parcel Service strike** heartened many union supporters, and AFL-CIO unions reversed a 1980s trend by winning more strikes than they lost. Sweeney, however, has not been successful in stopping the AFL-CIO's membership slide; in fact, it has decreased at a faster rate than it did under Kirkland. Very few unions have honored Sweeney's call to devote 30 percent of their budgets to organizing. Attempts to assist the **United Farm Workers** in organizing strawberry pickers flopped, as did an expensive campaign to unionize Las Vegas construction workers. The federation has also been plagued by defections, most notably the United Transportation Union, which quit over conflicts with the **Brotherhood of Locomotive Engineers**, and the 500,000-strong **United Brotherhood of Carpenters and Joiners**. Some critics charge that methods used by SEIU will not work in businesses subject to movable capital, though most analysts feel it is too early to evaluate Sweeney's effectiveness.

Suggested Readings: *Current Bibliography Yearbook*, 1996; Jo-Ann Mort, *Not Your Father's Union Movement: Inside the AFL-CIO*, 1998; "Leadership: AFL-CIO Top National Officers," www.aflcio.org/aboutaflcio/leaders/.

Simon Holzapfel

Sweetheart Contract. Sweetheart contract is a sarcastic term for bargaining agreements worked out secretly between a few union officers and management without the input or even knowledge of **rank-and-file** unionists. Historically such arrangements have been associated with corrupt practices by either party and usually involve a kickback to a labor official. The **American Federation of Labor-Congress of Industrial Organizations** condemned this method as a violation of trade union ethics. Although the practice was never widespread, except in a handful of local and national unions with ties to organized crime, most corrupt vestiges had been eliminated by the start of the twenty-first century. The term itself, however, lingers on in the lexicon of the rank and file as a simile for an unpopular **contract**, even if it was negotiated legally. Some union leaders simply find it easier to work out an agreement in private and then sell the contract to a skeptical membership, or purposefully avoid grassroots involvement fearing that the rank and file will not understand the larger issues and problems facing the industry. The negotiator tries to address these concerns privately in good faith to avoid temporarily the wrath of the union constituents. Such procedures invariably lead to cynicism among union members' ranks and are now a hallmark of **business unionism** rather than criminal intent.

Suggested Reading: Florence Peterson, *American Labor Unions: What They Are and How They Work*, 1963.

Scott Molloy

Swinton, John (December 12, 1829–December 15, 1901). John Swinton was one of the leading **labor journalists** and reform activists of the late-nineteenth century. He was born in Salton, Scotland, the son of William and Jane Swinton. He received little formal education before emigrating to Montreal, Canada, with his parents at the age of fourteen. He worked briefly as a **journeyman** printer at the Montreal *Witness*, before his family moved to New York City, and then to Illinois, where Swinton worked on small-town newspapers. Swinton studied theology for a short time at the Williston Seminary in Massachusetts, however, his interests in writing and social reform led him toward a career in labor journalism.

John Swinton. © George Meany Memorial Archives.

As a journeyman printer, Swinton traveled extensively through the South and the West, trips that sharpened his sympathies for the oppressed. In South Carolina, he confronted the horrors of chattel slavery, an experience that converted him to abolitionism. As a compositor in the state printing office, he taught African Americans to read and write at considerable personal risk. His antislavery sentiments drew him to Kansas in 1856, where he edited the *Lawrence Republican*, aided Kansas free-soil forces, and took part in a raid led by John Brown. In 1857, he briefly studied medicine at the New York Medical College, but did not complete his courses.

On the strength of some articles on medicine, he joined the staff of the *New York Times*. By 1860, he was its chief editorial writer. He left the *Times* in 1870 and worked at the rival *New York Sun* until 1883. Swinton's special interest was union news, and he gained a reputation as an inspirational speaker on behalf of labor groups. On January 13, 1874, he was the principal speaker at a demonstration at **Tompkins Square** to protest injustices to workers. Swinton's speech was interrupted when police and militia moved in to disperse the crowd, resulting in a riot. His popularity inside the labor movement prompted the Industrial Political Party, an affiliate of the Socialist Labor Party, to nominate him for mayor of New York City in 1874. Although he did not win, Swinton worked to abolish tenement house cigar making—a notoriously exploitative practice—and helped lead an 1875 mill **strike**. Swinton also spoke out against **child labor** and deplorable conditions in the **sweatshops**. In 1886, he provided testimony at a U.S. Senate Committee on Labor and Education hearing and offered ideas on legislation to benefit working people.

Swinton is best remembered for his effort to create a newspaper whose content was free from the influence of big business. The first issue of *John Swinton's Paper* debuted on October 14, 1883. The six-column, four-page weekly sought to improve the economic welfare of the laboring classes by organizing protests, promoting reform legislation, and encouraging organized labor. Many readers relied on Swinton for news of the **Knights of Labor** and the **American Federation of Labor**. *John Swinton's Paper* also reported on living and factory conditions, strikes, wage-and-hour statistics in individual trades, and the abuse of power by Gilded Age robber barons like Jay Gould and William H. Vanderbilt. The paper's 1885 exposés on contract immigration labor led to legislation prohibiting the practice.

Swinton's insistence on the paper's independence eventually brought about its downfall, as he refused to accept financial backers or gifts. In addition, Swinton turned down opportunities to affiliate the paper with specific unions. Subscriptions and advertising were not enough to keep up with expenses, and the paper was forced to fold in August 1887. Swinton lost his life savings—approximately $40,000—on the venture.

After the collapse of the paper, Swinton made an unsuccessful bid for the New York State Senate on the Progressive Labor Party ticket. He then continued his campaign for social justice as a freelance writer and a public speaker. Swinton eventually returned to the New York *Sun*, and he wrote for European journals. Failing eyesight plagued Swinton and he depended on his wife to assist him. Despite being totally blind by 1889, he continued his crusade for social reform by completing two books, *Striking for Life: Labor's Side of the Labor Question* (1894) and *A Momentous Question: The Respective Attitudes of Labor and Capital* (1895). He died in Brooklyn Heights in 1901. Swinton's career embodied many of the virtues and frustrations of the independent labor crusader. Autonomy and outspokenness won Swinton scores of admirers and provided labor with a truly independent advocacy voice. In the end, however, Swinton's lack of affiliation and firm alliances provided little cushion against insolvency, nor did he possess the means to widen his audience beyond its small devoted core.

Suggested Readings: Sender Garlin, *John Swinton, American Radical, 1829–1901*, 1976; Frank Reuter, "John Swinton's Paper." *Labor History* 1, no. 3 (Fall 1960): 298–307.

Mark Noon

Sylvis, William H. (November 26, 1828–July 27, 1869). William H. Sylvis was a Philadelphia iron molder and the founder of the **National Labor Union (NLU)**. He was born in Armagh, Pennsylvania, the son of Nicholas and Maria (Mott) Sylvis. His father was a failed wagon maker who moved his family frequently as he searched for work. When he was eleven, William boarded with a Whig politician, and his several years there provided his only formal education. At eighteen, Sylvis was apprenticed as an iron molder. He married fifteen-year-old Amelia Thomas in 1852, and moved to Philadelphia two years later.

Molders, who made stoves and other iron products, were highly skilled craftsmen whose wages exceeded that of most other trades. Until the 1850s, they retained great control over their craft and often operated their own foundries. Sylvis himself was briefly part owner of a foundry, though he usually worked as a **journeyman** molder. By the mid-1850s, however, a separate proprietary class was emerging in the molding trade, with owners seeking to wrest workplace control from mechanics. Sylvis participated in a **strike** in 1857, and was soon chosen as secretary for his local union. In 1859, he organized a Philadelphia convention to explore forming a national molders union. In 1860, the National Union of Iron Molders came into being, with Sylvis serving as treasurer. He also authored a fiery constitution that accused organized wealth of degrading common labor.

William H. Sylvis. © George Meany Memorial Archives.

The Civil War threw the union into disarray. Sylvis, a Democrat, was an ardent supporter of the Union cause and served in a workers' militia during the war. He left active duty in 1863, returned to union activism, reorganized his trade as the Iron Moulders' International Union (IMIU), and served as its president. Sylvis was a tireless organizer and by 1865, two-thirds of all molders belonged to the IMIU. Employers responded by increasing the number of unskilled hands in the foundries, thereby driving down journeymen's wages. Several also banded together to combat the IMIU, hoping to rid the trade of union activity. Sylvis, however, built a strong strike fund and brought union locals under the control of the parent organization. A 1866 strike forced owners to capitulate.

Despite success, Sylvis recognized that the coming struggle between capital and labor required greater coordination between unions. Like many others of his time, he was also a booster of worker-controlled **cooperatives**. Although several appeared in the iron molding trade, they did not supplant **capitalism** as Sylvis and other advocates hoped. Sylvis felt that labor needed a national umbrella organization that would represent all trades in order to press for legislation beneficial to workers. He was the moving force behind the 1866 Baltimore labor congress that created the NLU, though he did not attend. Sylvis became the co-editor of the NLU's journal, the *Working Man's Advocate*. At an 1868 convention, Sylvis was elected NLU president.

The NLU proved to have more rhetorical than political clout, but Sylvis did what he could to put teeth into the organization's demands. He was among the many voices that urged President Ulysses S. Grant to enforce a recently enacted eight-hour-day law for federal employees. He was also an ardent supporter of the **greenback** movement seeking to reform the nation's monetary policy. Sylvis grew convinced that a working-class/middle-class alliance was necessary to advance favorable labor legislation and thus urged the seating of non-workers as NLU convention delegates. Already an advocate of limited suffrage for women, he also welcomed Susan B. Anthony, **Kate Mullaney**, and two other women to the 1868 convention, despite some organization resistance. When Sylvis ascended to the NLU presidency, he promptly appointed Mullaney as an assistant secretary in charge of organizing female workers.

Sylvis also pressed the NLU to work closely with the International Workingmen's Association (IWA), a European socialist organization, and he attended an 1869 IWA congress in Switzerland. He also urged African Americans to join the NLU, and several attended its 1870 congress, a mere two years after the NLU had rejected a proposal to admit black members. For a time, the NLU worked closely with the **Colored National Labor Union**.

Alas, much of the NLU's promise evaporated after Sylvis's death. Never a robust man, Sylvis died in July 1869, shortly after returning to his Philadelphia home from an organizing tour of the South. Without his guidance, NLU ties to women, African Americans, and the IWA weakened and the organization disappeared shortly after the 1872 election. Sylvis is considered by many scholars to have been the prototype of a more modern labor leader. Many of his ideas and tactics were well in advance of the times.

Suggested Readings: John R. Commons, *History of Labour in the United States*, Vol. 2, 1946; Jonathan Grossman, *William Sylvis: Pioneer of Labor*, 1945; David Montgomery, "William Sylvis and the Search for Working-Class Citizenship," in Melvin Dubofsky and Warren Van Tine, eds., *Labor Leaders in America*, 1987.

Ralph Shaffer

Sympathy Strike. A sympathy strike is a work stoppage in support of another group of workers who have walked out or been locked out, rather than a grievance against one's own employer. It is rooted in ideals of class **solidarity** and in the hope that capitalists will exert pressure on each other to resolve labor disputes. For example, during the 1934 San Francisco dock **strike**, Atlantic dock workers considered using the tactic to express their solidarity with the struggle of their west coast comrades. The 1947 **Taft-Hartley Act** outlawed use of sympathy strikes, though many workers ignore the law. Between 1980 and 2000, a variety of workers have engaged in sympathy strikes. In 1996, members of the **United Auto Workers** walked off jobs in Michigan in support of striking Dayton, Ohio, brake workers. Pilots and flight attendants have ignored the ban, as have teachers striking in support of support workers. The sympathy strike remains a potent, if risky, tactic.

Suggested Readings: Helen Marot, *American Labor Unions*, 2001; United Transportation Union, http://www.utu.org/worksite/history/LaborHistory.htm.

Evan Daniel

T

Taft-Hartley Act. Taft-Hartley Act is the popular name for the Labor-Management Relations Act, a bill sponsored by Senator Robert Taft (Ohio) and Representative Fred Hartley (New Jersey). It became law in June 1947, when the Republican-dominated Congress overrode President Harry Truman's veto, and is regarded by unions as one of the worst pieces of antilabor legislation in U.S. history. It was consciously designed to weaken the **National Labor Relations Act (NLRA)**, which the business community and its Republican allies felt gave unions too much power.

By the end of World War II, nearly 25 percent of the workforce was unionized, and half of the existing union **contracts** contained closed-shop, or **preferential-shop**, hiring provisions. Conservative attempts to scuttle the NLRA faltered in 1937, when the Supreme Court affirmed its constitutionality. Tactics then switched to securing legislative remedy. The Taft-Hartley Act represents the culmination of over a decade of opposition to the NLRA, although it was often touted as merely correctives and amendments to the NLRA.

The law has nine major clauses. Among its most important provisions, it outlaws closed shops, allowing a union-controlled shop to exist only if a union represents the majority of eligible voters and accords new members equal rights with existing members. The act mandated a sixty-day cooling-off period before a union could resort to a **strike**, and another provision gave the federal government the authority to seek injunctions for an eighty-day cooling-off period in essential industries. Both employers and unions were empowered to sue each other for breach of contract. Republicans also exploited the emerging red scare to secure a clause that required union officers to file affidavits stating that they were not members of the Communist Party, a proviso that had the effect of silencing some of labor's more radical voices. Moreover, unions were required to file their constitutions and yearly financial statements with the **Department of Labor (DOL)**. This section rankled many union leaders, as private corporations were not required to make their finances public. Reacting to the union-Democratic Party alliance forged by the New Deal, another clause forbids unions from making direct or indirect campaign contributions, a proviso largely sidestepped when unions set up political action committees. The act also allowed employers to discontinue the **dues checkoff** system, if they so choose.

A labor rally against the Taft-Hartley bill. © George Meany Memorial Archives.

Congressman Hartley hated unions and hoped his bill would destroy them. That did not happen, but Taft-Hartley's impact has been devastating. The right to strike was severely curtailed and the wave of postwar militancy that emerged in 1945 quickly petered out. Anticommunist provisos and the need for leaders to quash **wildcat strikes** further depleted militant ranks. Under the Taft-Hartley Act, employers gained the right to initiate **decertification** hearings, a power that unions charge has led to intimidation and unfair labor practices. There is no question that labor-management relations grew more litigious after the passage of Taft-Hartley, with disputes often moving from the shop floor to the courtroom.

In the late 1940s and early 1950s labor lost a golden moment to overturn Taft-Hartley, which did not enjoy popular support initially. Unions, however, failed to mobilize uniform working-class opposition. Some unions, like the **United Mine Workers of America (UMWA)**, openly defied the law. The **Congress of Industrial Organizations (CIO)** threatened to conduct **general strikes** until the bill was repealed, but it failed to follow through on its bluster. Most unions placed their hopes in a political solution, backing liberal politicians and lobbying for prolabor appointments to the National Labor Relations Board. The Taft-Hartley Act moved unions even more solidly into alliance with the Democratic Party, which has consistently supported—though never implemented—changes to the law. Nearly every union in the nation has called for repeal of the Taft-Hartley, but it remains law. It is not solely responsible for the demise of organized labor in recent decades, but it has hurt labor's ability to defend itself, and current labor law remains tilted in favor of employers.

Suggested Readings: James Alteson, *Values and Assumptions in American Labor Law*, 1983; Melvin Dubofsky, *The State and Labor in Modern America*, 1994; Christopher Tomlins, *The State and the Unions*, 1986.

Andrew E. Kersten

Taylorism. Taylorism is a production system based on principles outlined by Frederick Winslow Taylor in 1911 and somtimes known as scientific management. Efficiency, defined as maximizing worker output, is the key to Taylorism. Taylor sought to break down all labor into a series of easy-to-learn tasks. He then used time-and-motion studies pioneered by Frank and Lillian Gilbreth to reorganize work tasks efficiently by eliminating needless motion. All work was designed by a planning department, which delegated the overseeing of worker efficiency to line supervisors. Taylor recommended separate supervisors for setup, line speed, quality, and repairs. Taylor recommended using motivational tools such as **incentive pay** and **piecework** to get workers to increase their output, but a major component of the system was the constant surveillance of the workforce.

Taylor's methods were so harsh and dehumanizing that most business leaders adopted modified versions. In 1933, sociologist Elton Mayo challenged Taylor's assumptions and redefined efficiency as a worker's social capacity. He developed methods today known as human relations, which focuses on benefit packages, group work, respect, and workplace culture. In some form or other, though, Taylorist central planning, time-and-motion studies, incentive pay, piecework, and worker surveillance became common features in American business firms. Most workers deeply resented Taylorism, especially when combined with assembly-line production **(Fordism)**. As Mayo predicted, workers found informal and formal ways to resist Taylorism, ranging from **stint** or **sabotage** to union organizing and **strikes**.

Suggested Readings: Frank Gilbreth and Lillian Gilbreth, *Cheaper by the Dozen*, 1949; Frank Gilbreth and Lillian Gilbreth, *Motion Study*, 1911; Elton Mayo, *The Human Problems of Industrial Civilization*, 1933; Frederick Winslow Taylor, *Scientific Management*, 1911.

Robert E. Weir

Team Act. *See Company Union.*

Textile Strikes (1934). *See Depression-Era Strikes.*

Textile Workers Union of America. *See Amalgamated Clothing Workers of America.*

Time and Motion. *See Taylorism.*

Tompkins Square Riot. The Tompkins Square Riot was an 1874 clash in New York City that signaled worsening relations between capital and labor. Some see it as a harbinger of the **Haymarket** Square riot that convulsed Chicago in 1886.

General insecurity and unemployment resulting from the depression of 1873 led to calls for direct governmental intervention and public-works programs to assist unemployed workers. Though this movement was widespread, efforts were largely uncoordinated. By late 1873, only New York City workers had managed to unite many of their various factions. On January 1, 1874, several thousand workers, including **socialists**, trade unionists, and antimonopolists, founded the Committee of Safety to pressure the city government to provide unemployment relief. All efforts to meet with authorities were rebuffed, and the city press furiously denounced the committee.

After the failure to schedule a meeting with officials, the Committee of Safety distributed a circular demanding that $100,000 be allotted to a Labor Relief Bureau comprised of committee members and city aldermen, and announced a January 13 meeting in Tompkins Square to show the strength of the movement. Meanwhile, a rival organization headed by bricklayer Patrick Dunn denounced the committee and its leaders as **communists** and tried to organize a march to City Hall on January 5. Dunn was almost universally discredited, but some workers did turn up on January 5. They were greeted by two committee leaders, **Peter James McGuire** and Theodore Banks, who led the march to City Hall. Mayor William Havemeyer was absent, and the committee had an unfruitful meeting with the Board of Aldermen.

Meanwhile, impatience on the part of the workers for action caused Banks to reschedule the next meeting for January 8. On that date, approximately 1,000 workers met in Union Square, but another proposed march to City Hall was cancelled, and participants marched instead to Tompkins Square, where McGuire and about 200 others were waiting. McGuire asked the assembled to join together in ward organizations set up by the committee and to meet again on January 13. McGuire also called upon the city government to halt the evictions of unemployed tenants and to deliver public aid to them. He also affirmed the willingness of the ward organizations to distribute food to the needy.

But while the participants were satisfied, the city government was alarmed. At the January 5 meeting, more than 150 police officers stood outside City Hall, and several hundred others entered Union Square after the crowd's departure for Tompkins Square. On January 8, the press reported that several thousand cases of ammunition had arrived at the armory on 35th Street, and the mayor and police commissioner held a meeting to decide on tactics for the upcoming demonstration. The committee was granted a permit to meet in Tompkins Square, but the police refused its request to march to City Hall. Police officers were instructed to arrest anyone who encouraged workers to leave their posts to take part in the demonstration. McGuire protested these restrictions and pled the case of suffering immigrant workers, only to be chided by Police Commissioner Oliver Gardner that he should confine his concerns to American citizens. When told that the police would arrest anyone nearing

City Hall, McGuire pointed out that no city statute gave the police such power. Gardner told him pointedly that it didn't matter; protestors would be arrested anyway. Appeals to Mayor Havemeyer were ignored.

While having difficulties with city officials, the committee's tenuous hold over its factions began to unravel. The committee president George Blair resigned; the New York City local of the Iron Molder's International Union denounced the committee as communists, internationalists, and **anarchists**; and Patrick Dunn and a group of his supporters appeared before the police board and warned of the committee's communistic character. The latter charge was based on the involvement of the American Section of the International Workingmen's Association (IWA).

On the morning of January 13, plans for the demonstration were unclear. At first, the mayor was scheduled to speak, then rumors circulated that the parade permit had been revoked. The permit had, in fact, been revoked, but word did not reach most of those who turned out. Though the temperature was well below freezing, between four and six thousand people gathered in Tompkins Square that morning; most were immigrants, and many were women and children. Among the crowd were about 1,200 members of the German Tenth Ward Workingmen's Association, and among the participants were future **American Federation of Labor (AFL)** dignitaries **Samuel Gompers** and **Adolph Strasser**, as well as Lucian Sanial, later prominent in the Socialist Labor Party.

At the office of the police board, meanwhile, the First Mounted Squad of the city police department awaited instructions, along with the rest of the 1,600 members of the police force who had been mobilized en masse that morning. Because of IWA's involvement and the intent of radicals to speak, superiors were given orders to suppress all meetings held during the day. Several dozen officers were stationed at public buildings throughout the city; others were posted outside of Tompkins Square, prepared to arrest anyone who showed seditious intent. Later that morning the *New York Graphic* published its daily issue with the headline "A Riot Is Now in Progress in Tompkins Square."

Around 11 A.M., the First Mounted Squad was ordered to fall in behind a group of the committee members who were marching toward Tompkins Square. By then, about 7,000 people were crowded into the square. Police Commissioner Abram Duryee and several policemen with nightsticks walked into the center of the crowd and ordered them to go home. The police officers immediately began clubbing bystanders, and the crowd began to scatter. In the corner of the square, however, the German Tenth Ward Workingmen's Organization refused to move. One German, Joseph Hoefflicher, hit an officer with a cane. An officer who then attacked Hoefflicher was hit with a hammer by another German, Christian Mayer. Just then, a group of mounted police entered the square and chased away the remaining protesters.

After Tompkins Square was sealed, more mounted policemen chased the fleeing crowds down the city streets, clubbing and beating them in what Samuel Gompers later called "an orgy of brutality." According to Gompers, for the next several hours squads of policemen attacked any group of poorly dressed persons standing or moving together. Those who gathered outside of the Fifth Street Police Station and protested the forty-six arrests made that day were also beaten. In other parts of the city, wild rumors circulated about immigrant plots to steal diamonds to trade for weapons, or of Hungarian workers planning to burn a schoolhouse. Most of the protesters arrested that day were foreign-born; most were charged with disorderly conduct, and a young German socialist named Justus Schwab was charged with inciting a riot and waving a red flag. None of those arrested could afford bail, and all remained in jail pending their arraignments.

City officials and most local newspapers defended the actions of the police, as did Mayor Havemeyer and Police Commissioner Duryea. *Harper's Weekly* evoked the specter of the Paris Commune and reminded its readers that such ways were "alien to American thought and methods." *The Philadelphia Inquirer* advised police to deal similarly with future demonstrations, even advocating lethal force to suppress such activities. Only a handful of newspapers were even mildly critical of the police; they included the *New York Sun*, the *New York Graphic*, and the *Cincinnati Enquirer*.

The protest coalition fell apart after the riot. The Committee of Public Safety reorganized as the Industrial Political Party, and several other parties were formed, but all were short-lived. Some in the labor movement saw Tompkins Square as an indication that democratic political institutions could no longer contain their demands. Many were radicalized by the experience, among them *New York Sun* editor **John Swinton**, who ran for public office on a labor ticket in 1874, and later started his own labor newspaper; and P. J. McGuire, who with Adolph Strasser, organized the Social Democratic Workingmen's Party later in 1874. Samuel Gompers, however, came to the conclusion that organized labor's association with radicalism was injurious to the movement and began to repudiate the socialism of his youth. Eventually, Strasser also adopted that position.

The police board created a special detective bureau to spy on socialist and trade-union meetings. The two German workers charged with assault on police, Joseph Hoefflicher and Christian Mayer, were both sentenced to several months in prison. On January 30, 1874, a large meeting in support of free speech and against police brutality was held at the Cooper Institute. A large and diverse coalition of groups and individuals, especially Germans, supported the right of workers to petition for public aid. Their call came to naught, as did efforts to punish or dismiss the police board. Another meeting was held in Tompkins Square on August 31: it secured the pardon of Christian Mayer. The meeting was peaceful, though it attracted little attention. One exception was in Chicago, where newspapers began warning authorities of the possibility of similar incidents in their city. The *Chicago Tribune* encouraged the wealthy in the city to fund and support a local militia to deal with agitators. In October, Cyrus McCormick became an honorary member of the First Regiment of the

Illinois National Guard. Chicago was therefore on its way toward mobilizing its police forces well before the 1886 **Haymarket** incident.

Tompkins Square heralded a more confrontational phase in capital/labor relations. Violence erupted in the coalfields of northeast Pennsylvania, where the **Molly Maguires** were rumored to be responsible and, in 1877, the traumatic railroad strikes associated with the **Great Labor Uprising** led to the loss of many lives and millions of dollars in property damage. An unfortunate legacy of Tompkins Square and ensuing clashes is that U.S. labor history has been stained by violence.

Suggested Readings: Iver Bernstein, *The New York City Draft Riots: Their Significance for American Society and Politics in the Age of the Civil War*, 1990; Samuel Gompers, *Seventy Years of Life and Labor: An Autobiography*, 1925; Herbert Gutman, "The Tompkins Square Riot in New York City on January 13, 1874: A Re-examination of Its Causes and Its Aftermath," *Labor History* 6, no. 1 (Winter 1965): 44–70.

Jeff McFadden

Trade Union Unity League. The Trade Union Unity League (TUUL) was the labor federation of the **Communist** Party-USA (CP); it was initiated in 1929 and officially dissolved in 1935. The Trade Union Unity League was an outgrowth of the Trade Union Educational League (TUEL), which had been started by **William Zebulon Foster** in 1920 and supported by the CP since 1922.

The TUEL's objectives were to work within the existing **American Federation of Labor (AFL) craft unions**, advocating for **industrial unionism** and organizing the most militant workers into the TUEL. However, the TUEL was largely unsuccessful. By 1928 a campaign to expel communists from the AFL and a string of TUEL failures coincided with a change in the perspective of the Communist International (Comintern): the capitalist economies were held to be entering a third period in which stability was threatened and revolution was on the agenda. CP-affiliated labor groups such as the TUEL were instructed to organize workers into revolutionary unions. This policy of **dual unionism**—setting up organizations in competition with existing unions—directly contradicted the official TUEL strategy of "boring from within," but actually reflected its more recent practice. (For example, the TUEL set up the National Miners Union [NMU] and the National Textile Workers Union [NTWU] in 1928 after being expelled from AFL unions.)

After its formal creation in 1929, the TUUL organized dozens of dual unions along with new unions in industries untouched by the AFL. Together, these industries included mining, textiles, steel and metal, auto, the needle trades, shoe and leather, tobacco, lumber, cannery and agricultural, packinghouse, machine tool and foundry, food, marine transport, furniture, and lumber. In addition, the TUUL organized in specific locales, such as pharmacies and dried goods in New York City.

Industrial unionism, **direct action**, **rank-and-file** independence, and the centrality of interracial solidarity characterized the TUUL unions. The slogan of the organization was "Class against Class," and it was overtly and unapologetically a part of the Communist Party. However, class-war rhetoric and pro-Soviet propaganda for the most part took a back seat to the demands for union recognition, better wages, and better conditions, which dominated most TUUL organizing work. The organizers were admirably audacious or disastrously foolhardy, depending on whom you ask; hardworking or fanatical, their ideological commitment certainly helped to provide the courage and perseverance necessary for organizing when and where they did. Sometimes, TUUL unions would plan **strikes**, but more often, the TUUL provided leadership during spontaneous workplace actions.

Nearly all of the TUUL battles followed identical trajectories: committed political and organizational work, direct action, violence from various authorities, and defeat. The first TUUL union to gain substantial recognition was the NTWU, in a tragic and bloody battle at the Loray Mill in **Gastonia**, North Carolina, in 1929. The NMU led a series of similarly failed strikes in Pennsylvania, Ohio, West Virginia, and, most famously, in Harlan County, Kentucky, where the struggles were immortalized in the **Florence Reece** song "Which Side are You On?" From 1930 through 1934, TUUL activities in the south and west among farmworkers resulted in multiracial unions like the Share Croppers Union and the Cannery and Agricultural Workers Industrial Union. They fought against evictions and for government relief. TUUL also led strikes, some of which eventually met with some success. The Marine Workers Industrial Union was one of the strongest in the TUUL, and its waterfront actions helped transform hiring practices in the industry on the East Coast.

Alongside trade-union work, the TUUL participated in much of the CP organizing among the unemployed. By early 1930, under TUUL auspices, the Communist Party began to create a network of unemployed councils, which fought for public work, government relief, unemployment insurance, and mortgage moratoriums, and against evictions in communities around the country. In 1930, the TUUL helped mobilize the March 6 Hunger March, simultaneous nationwide demonstrations that brought out close to one million jobless into the streets of most major cities. In 1932, the local TUUL led the Ford Hunger March from Detroit to the Ford River Rouge plant in Dearborn, Michigan. Autoworkers and their families presented Ford with a series of demands at the gate and, as fights with security and local police broke out, police began to fire into the crowd. The march became known as the Ford Massacre after four marchers were killed and twenty-three others shot.

By 1933, in spite of extraordinary levels of activity, the TUUL had little concrete to show for its efforts, and its membership consisted, in the main, of unemployed and blacklisted workers. The staggering number of unemployed, the despair and fear felt by many, and the extreme reaction against unions by employers accounted for most of this failure. The propagandizing of the red unionists during the third period surely contributed as well: Their revolutionary ideology isolated them from many workers, and gave employers and local authorities greater impetus and leverage for retaliation. Additionally, the TUUL's principled insistence on racial equality in its campaigns and organizations generated intense hostility in the South in particular, and was used as a divisive tactic by employers to break **solidarity**. However, the radicalism of the TUUL also stood it in good stead with those workers who were drawing radical conclusions in light of the country's depression, while, for many others, the TUUL's willingness to fight overrode political questions they might have about the organization. In the end, accurately assessing the extent to which the TUUL's politics stood in its way is difficult: Organizing attempts by the AFL in textiles, mining, and other industries proved just as unsuccessful during the early depression era.

The events of 1933–34 tested the TUUL's dual unionism even further. With a partial economic recovery and the passage of the National Recovery Act, thousands of workers were now streaming into unions, and the AFL and other traditional unions gained the vast number of new recruits. Although its membership stood at an impressive 100,000, the traditional unions dwarfed the TUUL; in response, it began disbanding its unions to join with AFL or other independents in their industries. The end of the TUUL corresponded with another change in the CP line toward a united, or Popular Front, with reformists against fascism. In this sense, the TUUL could be interpreted as a mistaken revolutionary experiment that was ultimately rejected by its own initiators.

Viewed in another light, however, the TUUL's legacy of militant, industrial, antiracist organizing laid important groundwork for the industrial unionism of the mid-1930s. Thousands of organizers and workers who cut their teeth in the TUUL played crucial roles in building the **Congress of Industrial Organizations (CIO)** and its member unions. Beyond the skills of its organizers, much of the organizing in the mid-1930s owed a great deal, tactically and at times politically, to the TUUL. Finally, unions from the TUUL were themselves, alone or in combination with others, the nuclei of later CIO affiliates: The **United Auto Workers (UAW)**, New York City's Transport Workers Union, the **United Electrical, Radio, and Machine Workers of America (UE)**, and the International Longshoremen's and Warehousemen's Union were among the more important unions formed with TUUL influence. Finally, the influx of communists and communist supporters from the TUUL into the traditional unions set the stage for the reaction to their presence, which itself had profound effects on the overall shape of the U.S. labor movement.

Suggested Readings: Michael E. Brown, et al., eds., *New Studies in the Politics and Culture of U.S. Communism*, 1993 (cf., Roger Keeran, "The Communist Influence on American Labor"); Irving Howe and Lewis Coser, *The American Communist Party, a Critical History*, 1957; Fraser M. Ottanelli, *The Communist Party of the United States: From the Depression to World War II*, 1991.

Penny Lewis

Trautmann, William Ernest (1869–?). William Ernest Trautmann was a radical unionist and cofounder of the **Industrial Workers of the World (IWW)**. He was born in New Zealand to German American parents and was raised in Germany and Poland, where he served an **apprenticeship** in the brewing industry. Trautmann moved to Germany after he became a master brewer, but was eventually expelled for agitation on behalf of child bottling-shop workers and exploited brewery workers. He immigrated to the United States in the 1890s, settled in Ohio, and became an organizer for the United **Brewery Workers** Union (UBW), an early **industrial union**. In 1900, he became editor of the UBW newspaper, *Brauer-Zeitung,* and used its pages to criticize the exclusionary policies of the **American Federation of Labor (AFL)**, whose **craft union** perspective sacrificed the welfare of workers who were female, African American, and unskilled.

When the UBW moved closer to the AFL, Trautmann gravitated toward the militant Western Federation of Miners (WFM). In 1905, Trautmann quit the UBW and joined forces with WFM and Socialist Labor Party leader **Daniel DeLeon** to form the Industrial Workers of the World (IWW). At a 1908 convention, IWW members were split over their tactics. Trautmann supported the **direct action** tactics espoused by former WFM colleague Vincent St. John over the electoral strategy advanced by DeLeon. DeLeon's faction quit the organization and formed a rival IWW based in Detroit.

Between 1909 and 1912, Trautmann was an IWW organizer, and he participated in several **strikes**. The 1909 Pressed Steel Car strike at **McKee's Rock**, Pennsylvania, led to a gun battle in which a dozen workers died, but it resulted in a partial victory for workers, one of the few in the steel industry until the 1930s. Trautmann was also an organizer and bookkeeper in the famed 1912 Bread and Roses strike in **Lawrence**, Massachusetts. When $20,000 turned up missing, Trautmann blamed St. John and other IWW leaders for misusing funds.

Trautmann resigned because of the fund debacle and, in 1913, joined DeLeon's Detroit IWW. He was an outspoken critic of U.S. involvement in World War I and penned the pamphlet *War Against War.* In 1915 and 1916, he worked as a carpenter in Universal City, California, where he constructed sets. He also appeared as an American Indian extra in a film, and he claimed to have written several scripts that were used by studio executives. He also worked on the Los Angeles-Owens Valley aqueduct, but was fired for trying to unionize workers.

In 1919, Trautmann moved to Chicago and became a factory worker. He became disillusioned with unions, but helped workers organize informal workshop councils. In the 1920s, he participated in a strike by sugar-beet workers in Colorado. He wrote two books, *Riot,* a novel based on the Pressed Steel Car strike, and *America's Dilemma,* a book critical of labor unions. In the 1930s he moved back to California where he worked on a New Deal highway project and finished his autobiography, *Fifty Years: The Rise and Fall of the Industrial Workers of the World.* He was known to have lived until 1939, but the date and place of his death are unknown.

Suggested Readings: Melyvn Dubofsky, *We Shall Be All,* 1969; Patrick Renshaw, *The Wobblies,* 1968.

Jay Miller

Travel Card. *See Permit Cards*.

Tresca, Carlo (March 9, 1879–January 11, 1943). Carlo Tresca was a radical, an organizer for the **Industrial Workers of the World (IWW)**, and a crusader against fascism. He was born in Sulmona, Italy, the sixth child of Filippo and Filomena Tresca. He finished secondary school and harbored ambitions of becoming a lawyer, though his mother wanted him to become a priest. His family fell into debt in the 1890s, lost their land, and Tresca embraced free thought and **socialism**. He joined the Italian Railroad Workers Federation, and in 1900, he became a branch secretary and editor of their newspaper. Tresca organized peasant workers, was arrested several times, and faced a libel charge that spurred him to immigrate to the United States in 1904 where he settled in Philadelphia. He married Helga Guerra shortly before fleeing Italy. She joined Tresca in 1905 and the couple had a daughter, but their marriage quickly failed. In 1908, Carlo was indicted for assault, rape, and adultery for a liaison with a fifteen-year-old girl; he served nine months in jail for adultery.

From 1904 to 1906, Tresca edited *Il Proletario*, the official journal of the Italian Socialist Federation of North America, then began his own paper. He edited three short-lived Italian-language radical papers between 1906 and 1917. Tresca immersed himself in the struggles of Italian immigrant workers, especially miners and mill workers in Pennsylvania. His editorials in *La Plebe* engendered opposition from the Catholic Church, as well as capitalists, government officials, and the Italian consulate. His exposés of the "Black Hand" Mafiosi figures he alleged had ties to the church and right-wing political movements also gained him enemies.

Nonetheless, Tresca embodied a strong radical tradition among Italian immigrant workers, many of whom joined socialist and anarchist movements. Over time, Tresca converted to **anarchism**, though socialism was so strong among Italian workers that Tresca easily deflected charges of anarchism by claiming to be a socialist. Tresca was not an ideologue, though opposition to **capitalism** and authoritarianism of any sort remained constants in his speeches and writing. His popularity was such that the IWW invited him to speak during the 1912 **Lawrence textile strike**, and his powerful oratory helped maintain solidarity among Italian workers that was threatened when officials arrested Joseph Ettor and Arturo Giovanniti. He met **Elizabeth Gurley Flynn** at Lawrence, and the two became lovers shortly thereafter.

Tresca took part in several IWW job actions, including the **Paterson silk strike** in 1913, and a miners' strike in the Mesabi Range in Minnesota in 1916. During the latter strike, Tresca was charged with murder and was almost lynched. Tresca was freed from the trumped-up charge in a complicated plea bargain in which some IWW members agreed to plead guilty to other charges. IWW secretary **William Dudley Haywood** lashed out against the agreement, and Tresca soon quit the IWW. He, like many IWW members, was arrested in 1917, but he moved to have his case tried separately and charges were dropped, although he was under surveillance for much of the rest of his life.

For most of the 1920s and 1930s, Tresca was an independent voice in defense of freedom and worker rights. He raised money and public support on behalf of **Nicola Sacco and Bartolomeo Vanzetti**, two Italian anarchists accused of bank robbery and murder in 1920. He also worked hard on their appeal efforts, although the two were executed in 1927. Tresca was embroiled in numerous free-speech fights, several of which elicited support from the American Civil Liberties Union. In 1922, fascists under Benito Mussolini took control in Italy. Mussolini's government pressured the United States to silence Tresca and his latest publishing venture, *Il Martello*. In 1925, Tresca was arrested and jailed for obscenity, because *Il Martello* ran an advertisement for birth control. He was sentenced to a year in jail, but served only four months before President Calvin Coolidge yielded to public outrage and commuted his sentence. Tresca redoubled his editorial attacks on fascism and many observers claim his efforts did much to sour Italian Americans on Mussolini. He was active in the antifascist Mazzini Society. Tresca originally supported the Bolshevik Revolution in Russia, but he reluctantly attacked Josef Stalin when he concluded that Stalin was as authoritarian as Mussolini. The expulsion of Leon Trotsky from the Communist Party in 1927 and the Spanish Civil War in the 1930s deepened Tresca's anarchism and his hatred for all forms of fascism. Tresca took part in the Italian American Victory Council in the early 1940s and zealously weeded out those he felt were fascists, mafiosi, or communists.

Tresca was gunned down in New York City on January 11, 1943, and his murder has never been solved. Assassination theories range from the possible to the fanciful, with the motives of everyone from communists to the Catholic Church being suspect. Most historians point the finger at future Mafia boss Vito Genovese who, in 1943, was a lieutenant in the Luciano crime syndicate and was perhaps acting on behalf of pro-Mussoloni forces. Recent evidence bolsters this theory, but the controversial Tresca never lacked enemies.

Tresca holds significance for the labor movement on several levels. He was an important radical voice in the immigrant community, a group often spurned by more conservative union leaders as unorganizable. Tresca's efforts at Lawrence and elsewhere proved the unsoundness of that assertion. He is also an important example of an independent drive for workers' rights that takes place outside the formal structure of unions. Finally, he illustrates the way in which labor rights are linked to broader questions of freedom and social justice.

Suggested Readings: Dorothy Gallagher, *All the Right Enemies*, 1988; Nunzio Pernicone, "Tresca, Carlo," in *Encyclopedia of the American Left*, eds., Paul Buhle, et al., 1992.

Robert E. Weir

Triangle Factory Fire of 1911. The Triangle Factory Fire of 1911 was one of America's most infamous industrial accidents. For many, it symbolized rapacious unbridled **capitalism** at its worst, and the tragedy became a rallying cry for reformers and labor activists. The official cause of the fire remains unknown. It began on the eighth floor of New York City's Asch Building near the close of business on Saturday, March 25, 1911. (The exact time of the fire is in dispute as factory owners commonly set back the clocks to extract a longer workday from employees.) The fire started as workers collected their paychecks and belongings to go home for the weekend.

Initially, the fire was small but it quickly raged out of control as flames engulfed the shirtwaist fabric. As the workers, largely young women, fled the fire, panic ensued when they found doors locked, an elevator out of order, and the windows blocked. When the fire department arrived, its ladders only reached to the seventh floor. By then, floors eight through ten were engulfed in flame. As the fire spread and the workers grew increasingly desperate, some chose to jump from the windows. Firefighters tried to save the workers by holding nets to brace their falls, but the plummeting bodies tore through their nets. The result was macabre, with corpses piling as women jumped to imminent death. At the end, 146 workers had died in the blaze. Many of those who remained inside were burned beyond recognition and remained in the city morgue for days before family members could retrieve their loved ones.

The New York Times reported that the Asch Building was fireproof, but the building did not meet safety codes. Doors opened inward instead of outward, and the doors were bolted during working hours to ensure workers would be unable to take breaks. Additionally, there were only two narrow staircases in the building. Manslaughter charges were brought against Triangle Factory owners Max Blanck and Issac Harris, both of whom escaped the building unharmed. They were acquitted on December 27, 1911. On March 11, 1913, Harris and Blanck settled, agreeing to pay seventy-five dollars for each life lost.

Firefighters try to put out the catastrophic 1911 fire at the Triangle Shirtwaist Factory Building which killed 146 workers as a result of locked doors and missing fire escapes. © Underwood & Underwood/Corbis.

The 1911 fire culminated a series of labor disasters associated with the Triangle Factory. A spontaneous walkout in 1909 failed to address worker concerns and both the **Women's Trade Union League (WTUL)** and the **International Ladies' Garment Workers' Union (ILGWU)** failed in their numerous attempts to organize Triangle Factory workers. The company also remained relatively unaffected by the 1910

Uprising of the 20,000 (1909) in which New York City's immigrant female shirtwaist workers successfully struck for better working conditions, shorter hours, and wage increases.

After the blaze, ILGWU Local 25 organized relief services and proposed a day of mourning. Thousands of people poured into the streets for the memorial and public funerals. The ILGWU also organized a rally against unsafe working conditions at which **Rose Schneiderman** made a scathing speech about the inequities of working conditions.

The fire's graphic horror and senseless deaths attracted nationwide attention and outrage. Unions and reformers used the tragedy to advance their causes, and the fire became a symbol of the horrendous working conditions under which factory workers toiled. The WTUL fought for sweeping code regulations and building inspections. Although reforms were not as sweeping as advocates desired, the fire did lead to a spate of state and local factory safety laws.

Suggested Readings: *New York Times*, (March 26, 1911); Leon Stein, *The Triangle Fire*, 1962; "The Triangle Five" http://ilr.cornell.edu/trianglefire/.

Cristina Prochilo

Trolley Wars. The Trolley Wars were a series of understudied **strikes** that bridged the Gilded Age and the Progressive Era and that illuminate late-nineteenth- and early-twentieth-century labor-management relations. Conflicts regularly erupted between horsecar and trolley companies and the drivers, motormen, and conductors who operated their vehicles in small cities and urban metropolises in this period. For almost forty years, streetcar workers and legions of their riders waged a relentless war to reform and politically control traction companies.

The earliest battles involved horsecar employees who, spontaneously or under the leadership of the **Knights of Labor (KOL)**, rocked the urban landscape beginning in the 1880s. Drivers and conductors usually triggered walkouts with demands for shorter workdays, higher **wages**, and union recognition. Surprisingly, the public joined in street demonstrations that often ended in mayhem, transportation paralysis, and mobilization of the local militia. Citizen hostility targeted the corporate influence of transit companies who did everything in their considerable power to obtain inexpensive, long-term charters to monopolize the streets of any given city. Owners resisted lower fares, refused to implement transfer tickets, and packed their vehicles like freight cars. Although the concerns of the public, especially the emerging middle class, differed from the demands of the car men, they made common cause to curtail the power of urban transportation firms whose machinations undermined the democratic process, especially in city councils and state legislatures.

As the urban, mass-transit industry switched from horsepower to electricity during the 1890s, the changeover to an accelerated system only aggravated earlier worker and patron complaints. Streetcars the size of steam locomotives could reach blistering speeds on suburban, private rights of way, which led to accidents and carnage rivaling that of the railroad system. Gone, too, were the amenities that a slower-paced world provided through horsepower and accommodating drivers and conductors. Employees chafed under the ruthless dictates of systemized routes, which eliminated time for layovers or passenger courtesy. The protests packaged together a host of these complaints, sometimes spawning clean-government campaigns in their wake. Several hundred strikes punctuated the quarter century before World War I.

In 1892, a new militant national union, the Amalgamated Association of Street Railway Employees, organized the industry's discontented workers. Combining the ugly threat of class warfare on the streets with a civilized offer to arbitrate any differences with hostile companies, the Amalgamated provided the organizational muscle to bring parity and progress to the workforce. The union displayed tremendous resiliency despite many dramatic losses. In some cities, the **strikes**—like those in St. Louis in 1900 and Philadelphia in 1909—resembled insurrections rather than industrial conflict. Eventually, efforts during the Progressive Era ushered in a system of nationally standardized wages and conditions. One of the nation's most unusual alliances between service workers and passengers held firm, especially when traction companies turned to **scabs** to replace admired motormen and conductors. The establishment of a **National War Labor Board** during World War I mediated disputes and solidified the union, which is now over a century old.

Suggested Reading: Scott Molloy, *Trolley Wars: Streetcar Workers on the Line*, 1996.

Scott Molloy

Trumka, Richard Louis (July 24, 1949–). Richard Louis Trumka is a union organizer and secretary-treasurer of the American Federation of Labor-Congress of Industrial Organizations (AFL-CIO). Trumka was born to Italian- and Polish-American parents in the coal-mining town of Nemacolin, Pennsylvania. He received an excellent education and obtained several degrees from Pennsylvania State University and Villanova University Law School. Upon graduation from Villanova, Trumka joined the legal staff of the **United Mine Workers of America (UMWA)**.

At the time, the UMWA was moribund, and Trumka quit his post and worked as a miner for five years. In 1981, he was elected as the southwest Pennsylvania representative on the international executive board of the UMWA. A year later, Trumka rode a tide of **rank-and-file** insurgency to the presidency of the UMWA. At age thirty-two, he became the youngest-ever president of a major union. Trumka set out to reestablish militant unionism at a time in which many other labor organizations were moving sharply rightward. He helped reverse a downward spiral in UMWA membership. By 1998, the union's 240,000 members represented about 42 percent of the nation's miners.

Trumka left the presidency of the UMWA when he became the youngest secretary-treasurer in the history of the AFL-CIO in 1995. He, along with president **John Joseph Sweeney** and Linda Chavez-Thompson, promised to reinvigorate the labor movement by focusing on organizing, independent politics, and coalition-building. Trumka is an unabashed liberal who rejects the **business unionism** of the post–World War II labor movement and calls upon labor to commit acts of civil disobedience when necessary. He served on President Clinton's Bipartisan Commission on the Deficit, where he argued vociferously against changes in the Social Security system. Trumka is also an outspoken opponent of the **North American Free Trade Agreement (NAFTA)** and of the World Trade Organization.

Suggested Readings: *The Columbia Encyclopedia*, 2000, s.v. "Trumka, Richard"; *Current Biography*, 1986 s.v. "Trumka, Richard."

Don Binkowski

Two-Tier Wage Structure. *See Concessions*.

U

Unfair Labor Practices. The term unfair labor practice stems from Section 8 of the **National Labor Relations Act (NLRA)**. The NLRA creates rights and obligations for unions, management, and employees in a workplace represented by a labor union. If either labor or management fails to perform its obligations, an unfair labor practice charge may be filed with the National Labor Relations Board. Such a charge may also be filed if either side interferes with the rights of the other party. Employees are empowered to file charges against either employers or representative unions.

The NLRA makes it illegal for management to threaten or retaliate against employees for seeking union representation or refuse to provide information necessary for the union to fulfill its representational responsibilities. At the same time, unions are not allowed to intimidate management, retaliate against other employees who do not join the union, or refuse to represent nonunion workers during contract talks. Each group is required to bargain with the other in good faith. If any party fails to do so, the NLRA is empowered to compel good-faith bargaining.

Historically, unions have filed the most unfair labor practice suits, often during organizing drives during which management oversteps its legal authority in seeking to dissuade workers from joining a union. Suits are also common during **contract** talks in which negotiations stall. More recently, some employers have used unfair labor practice charges as a prelude to **decertification** votes, or to sap union strength by bottlenecking them in the cumbersome and slow bureaucracies associated with legal challenges.

Suggested Readings: American Bar Association, *The Developing Labor Law*, 2001; Frank and Edna Elkouri, *How Arbitration Works*, 1997.

Cornelia McAndrew

Union Label. The union label, or *bug* as it is known in printing trades, is a tag, imprint, or design attached to an article as evidence that it was produced by union labor. The invention of the union label is credited to the Carpenters' Eight-Hour League in San Francisco, which adopted a stamp in 1869 for labeling products produced by mills employing men working an eight-hour day (as opposed to ten). Six years later, in 1874, the cigar makers of San Francisco created a white labor label as part of an ongoing campaign against a cheaper (and greatly exploited) nonunionized Chinese labor force, which had come to dominate that industry in California. The Cigar Makers International Union quickly recognized the potential support that working-class consumers could provide in encouraging the production and sale of union products, especially as new technologies in cigar manufacturing began pushing out skilled (unionized) labor. The union adopted the first national union label in 1880. Other unions quickly followed suit in the next decade, including those representing typographers, garment workers, coopers, bakers, and iron molders.

Labels of unions affiliated with the American Federation in 1903.

The labels of unions affiliated with the American Federation of Labor in 1903. © George Meany Memorial Archives.

A Union Label Department, created by the **American Federation of Labor (AFL)** in 1909, worked vigorously to spread the label's use. **William Green**, president of the AFL in 1939, noted that the label's appearance on a product was "emblematic of a high standard of living, of tolerable conditions of employment, of those conditions surrounding working men and women, which makes for a higher and better standard of living." A modern "look for the union label" campaign was launched by the **International Ladies' Garment Workers' Union (ILGWU)** in 1975 to build consumer awareness about the products that Americans buy. The campaign is an effort that the Union Label and Services Department of the American Federation of Labor-Congress of Industrial Organizations (AFL-CIO) carries on today.

Suggested Readings: Ira B. Cross, *A History of the Labor Movement in California*, 1935; Tony Hyman, "'Look for the Union Label': A Guide to Union Labels for Collectors," *The Antique Trader Weekly* (11 March 1987): 68–72; Union Label Section of San Francisco, *1939 Union Label Catalogue-Directory*, 1939; Union Label and Service Trades Department, AFL-CIO.

Susan Sherwood

Union Local. In simplest terms, a union local is the smallest **bargaining unit** in the union process. It refers to those members of a particular union who are defined as a bargaining unit. The union local takes care of the day-to-day operations that concern workers the most. It negotiates **contracts**, oversees the **grievance** procedure, galvanizes members for political activity, collects and distributes **dues**, supervises **business agents**, and leads **strikes** and **boycotts**, should they become necessary.

A union's locals usually comprise workers within a single locale, although that's not always the case. Often, not even all members of a certain profession working in a single place belong to the same local. Procedures for defining a local are determined by each parent union. Union locals usually have their own bylaws, officers, and procedures. Locals then cooperate with one another in larger alliances, like district councils and national (or international) unions. Many of the latter send representatives to larger federations with which they are affiliated.

The **United Auto Workers (UAW)** typifies the above structure. Its 750,000 members are spread across more than a 1,000 union locals. Each elects a nine-member executive board to coordinate important member services. For example, Local 160 represents 1,600 General Motors (GM) employees in Warren, Michigan. The same city also sports Local 909, which represents GM workers at its Powertrain facility. Local 400 is an example of a union local that spans several locations, as it represents 5,500 Visteon and Ford workers in Chesterfield, Highland Park, and Utica, Michigan. All three locals belong to UAW District 1, which has its own executive board and officers; altogether, there are twelve UAW regions and subregions. These regions report to the international UAW, which is affiliated with the American Federation of Labor-Congress of Industrial Organizations (AFL-CIO).

Depending on the union, locals often operate with great autonomy. The term union local came into widespread use only after the founding of the AFL in 1886. Since earlier organizations such as the **Knights of Labor (KOL)** and the **Brotherhood of Locomotive Engineers (BLE)** were modeled, in part, on fraternal orders, the terms lodge and assembly were often preferred.

Suggested Reading: "Welcome to the UAW," http://www.uaw.org.

Robert E. Weir

Union of Needletrades, Industrial, and Textile Employees (UNITE). The Union of Needletrades, Industrial, and Textile Employees was founded in 1995, when the **International Ladies' Garment Workers' Union (ILGWU)** and the **Amalgamated Clothing and Textile Workers Union** voted to join forces as one union. It is the latest attempt to organize workers in the historically union-resistant textile and garment industries, though UNITE's reach extends beyond such firms. At its formation, UNITE represented more than 250,000 workers in the United States, Puerto Rico, and Canada. Since then, UNITE has led drives against **sweatshop** labor, expanded its representation to thousands of other workers, and has been a part of the growing student protest movement against exploitative labor conditions around the globe.

In 1996, in response to news reports of widespread sweatshop labor in the United States, Central America, and Asia, UNITE began a Stop Sweatshops campaign that seeks to bring together trade unions, students, consumers, civil-rights activists, and women's groups to publicly ban sweatshop labor within the United States and abroad. Innovative summer internships with UNITE increased student activism on campuses across the United States and led to the formation of a nationwide organization, the United Students Against Sweatshops, in 1998. A year later, in 1999, UNITE took part in the demonstrations against the World Trade Organization in Seattle and in several other U.S. cities. At the same time, UNITE has continued to organize workers, including 5,000 workers at the **Fieldcrest** Cannon textile mills in North Carolina who, in 2000, ratified a contract that included precedent-setting guarantees such as paid sick days, improved working conditions, and expanded retirement benefits. UNITE has also sought to expand its membership to industries other than the needle trades. Beginning in 1998, UNITE increased its representation among industrial laundry workers when it organized almost 3,000 National Linen workers in twenty-nine plants in southern United States. In 2001, the Laundry and Dry Cleaning International Union joined UNITE, bringing with it almost 40,000 union laundry workers, totaling 90 percent of all union laundry workers in the United States.

UNITE lobbied for a 2001 effort that saw passage of an antisweatshop law in New York City that makes illegal the use of tax dollars to purchase city employee uniforms made under sweatshop conditions. Additionally, UNITE continues its commitment to improved labor conditions around the world with its most recent campaign, Global Justice for Garment Workers. By 2001, UNITE claimed 300,000 active members from a variety of industries including textiles, laundries, auto parts, and in Xerox manufacturing plants across the United States, Canada, and Puerto Rico.

Suggested Reading: "UNITE," http://www.uniteunion.org.

Kathleen Banks Nutter

Union Shop. A union shop, also called a closed shop, is a situation in which a worker is required to join a union as a condition of employment. Unions involved in successful organizing drives have sought such provisions since the nineteenth century, and they proved especially attractive in extractive industries such as mining and timber. Under current law, several sections of the **National Labor Relations Act** allow such arrangements, though the act sets limits. Employees subject to union-shop clauses have at least thirty days to join the union. Furthermore, the union-shop clause can be invoked to secure a discharge only if the employee refuses to pay **dues**, or initiation fees, and only if the requirement is enforced on a uniform, nondiscriminatory basis. Finally, the union's authority to enter into a union-shop agreement can be discontinued by majority vote of employees in an election held pursuant to section 9(e) of the act.

Many critics see union-shop agreements as a violation of an individual's right to free association. Unions often counter that it is unfair to allow single individuals to reap the same benefits as dues-paying members in a union **collective bargaining** unit. Some union advocates also oppose closed shops on the grounds that they breed resentment and that coerced membership is counterproductive. In recent times, union shops are less popular than so-called agency shops in which those employees who opt not to join a union are compelled to pay a fee to the union that negotiates their **contract**.

Suggested Reading: American Bar Association, *The Developing Labor Law*, 2001.

Cornelia McAndrew

Union Steward. *See Shop Steward.*

United Auto Workers (UAW) Strike of 1945–46 (General Motors). After Victory in Japan Day (V-J Day), conversion from wartime to peacetime production went slowly, and more than 300,000 Michigan workers were unemployed. Within the UAW, there was a struggle for the future direction of the union and who would lead it. The most likely leader was **Walter Reuther**, but prominent UAW figures George Addes, R.J. Thomas, Richard Frankensteen, and Richard Leonard allied against Reuther, who warned against a reenactment of the post–World War I **open-shop** drive. *The New York Times* columnist James Reston observed that both labor and management seemed eager for a fight. From the summer of 1945 through the end of 1946, **strikes** were rife in the auto, steel, electrical equipment, meat-packing, longshore, and trucking industries. The most bitterly contested of the battles was the General Motors strike, which began in November 1945, and lasted for 113 days. Walter Reuther's controversial strategy was to demand both a 30 percent **wage** increase and a stipulation that GM hold the line on car price increases. Reuther argued that, in the past, carmakers had simultaneously conducted two sets of negotiations: one with workers for wages and working conditions, and the other in the marketplace with consumers who were seeking price increases to cover more than whatever **concessions** had been made to workers. Reuther argued that labor unions should use their clout to prevent manufacturers' price increases from paying their workers' wage increases with "the wooden nickels of inflation." To the complaint of GM that the UAW demands would prevent the corporation from making a fair profit, Reuther offered to accept less than 30 percent if GM would open its books to the union and show their entire cost and earnings record. GM charged that Reuther's demands would lead to a **socialistic** nation. A fact-finding board appointed by President Harry Truman recommended a 17.5 percent increase, which the board believed the company could easily afford. GM ignored the recommendations, and Truman declined to pursue the matter further. As it turned out, Reuther badly miscalculated the willingness and ability of GM to take a long strike. Under the wartime excess-profits tax, GM had earned what it was allowed for the year. In effect, the federal government would be making strike payments to the corporation. Industry settlements were reached with Ford and Chrysler, which offered approximately eighteen cents per hour. By the end of January, a single cent separated GM and the UAW, and workers' savings were exhausted. On March 13, 1946, GM agreed to eighteen and one-half cents, with additional provisions for plant-pay differentials, vacations, and **overtime**. Although Reuther failed to get the auto companies to open their books, the strike propelled Reuther to national attention with the assurance that he would be elected union president. Later critics viewed Reuther's settlement with GM as a missed opportunity for labor to co-manage the economy.

Suggested Readings: John Barnard, *Walter Reuther and the Rise of the Auto Workers*, 1983; Nelson Lichtenstein, *The Most Dangerous Man in Detroit: Walter Reuther and the Fate of American Labor*, 1995.

James P. Hanlan

United Brotherhood of Carpenters and Joiners (UBC). The United Brotherhood of Carpenters and Joiners (UBC) represents about 520,000 carpenters, millwrights, cabinetmakers, and assorted woodworkers in the United States and Canada. Like many modern unions, the UBC has also absorbed other groups not involved in woodcrafts, including the former **granite cutters** union.

The UBC was founded in 1881 in response to changes in the post–Civil War building trades industry. In Colonial and antebellum America, skilled carpenters and joiners enjoyed tremendous bargaining power. Woodworking trades replicated the medieval guild system with its hierarchy of **apprentice**, **journeymen**, and **master**. They established a book of prices that regulated the trade across North America. Most projects were small and the functions of contractor, master, and capitalist were often identical. Face-to-face negotiations made it easier for skilled artisans to resolve disputes. After the Civil War, however, technological changes, changes in building techniques, and the expansion of the American economy unraveled the already frayed customary arrangements between contractors and carpenters. Masters reappeared as independent contractors, whose incentive was to hold down labor costs, which was also the goal of the venture capitalists, stockholders, developers, and government officials that authorized and funded large-scale projects.

The UBC was largely the brainchild of **Peter J. McGuire**, a New York City carpenter who had witnessed such Gilded Age capital/labor clashes as the 1874 **Tomkins Square riot**, and railroad strikes associated with the **Great Labor Up-**

rising of 1877. McGuire was also a member of the **Knights of Labor (KOL)**. The UBC was founded in August 1881, with just over 2,000 members; McGuire served as union secretary, and Gabriel Edmonston was its first president. McGuire, though a **socialist**, became increasingly committed to **pure and simple unionism**. He and the UBC were instrumental in creating the **American Federation of Labor (AFL)** in 1886.

The UBC supported the **eight-hour movement**, and it took a key part in planning a **general strike** in support of eight hours on May 1, 1886. Although some UBC members won reduced hours, the 1886 strike was not a success, and it culminated in the **Haymarket bombing** in Chicago. In 1890, the UBC led another AFL-sanctioned general strike for the eight-hour day, and it bore better fruit; more than 23,000 carpenters won an eight-hour workday and another 32,000 were reduced to nine. By the early twentieth century, the eight-hour day was the norm for most carpenters.

UBC-AFL **craft unionism** conflicted with the principles of many within the KOL, and the UBC often found itself in **jurisdiction** disputes with the KOL. Relations between the two groups were tense after 1886, but many UBC members held dual membership in the KOL and AFL until the early 1890s. By 1903, the UBC contained 167,200 members, far more than the moribund KOL.

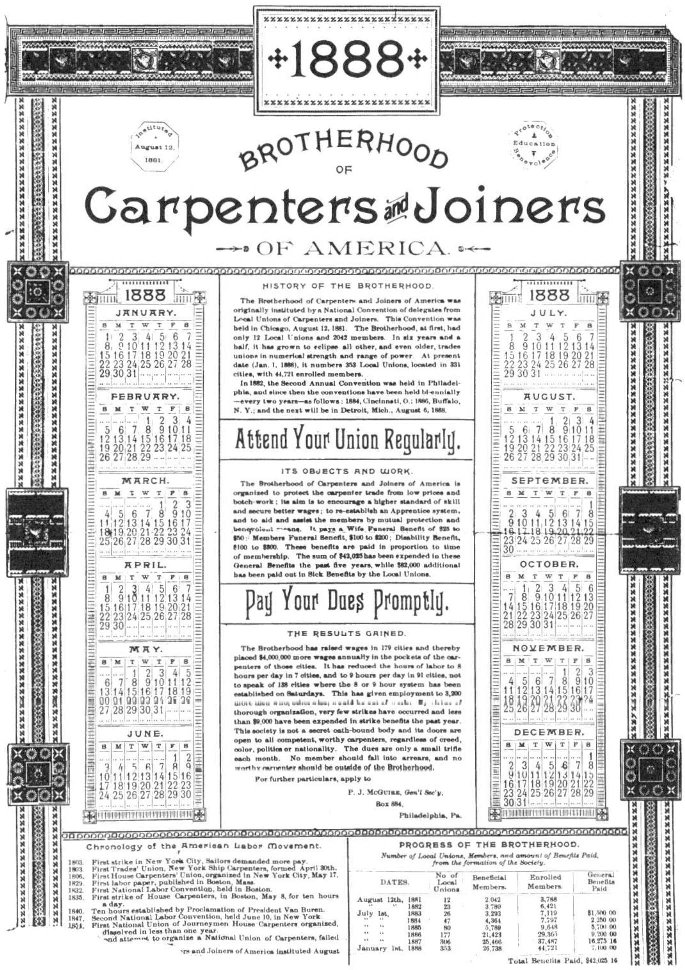

Union literature published by the United Brotherhood of Carpenters and Joiners (UBC) in 1888. © George Meany Memorial Archives.

The first two decades of the twentieth century saw the UBC battle against the **open shop movement**. Employers in numerous major cities engaged in **lockouts** against the UBC in attempts to reduce wages and hire non-union carpenters. For the most part, such efforts served only to increase UBC strength; in 1910, the union contained more than 200,000 members. In 1915, **William Hutcheson** took over as UBC president, and was successful in thwarting the Wilson administration's back-door attempts at open shops during World War I. The 1920s were more difficult, however. Employers advocating the open shop, now under the guise of the **American Plan**, **locked out** UBC members in many cities. The UBC defeated open-shop plans in Chicago and San Francisco, which crippled the American Plan, but UBC membership fell in the 1920s. The union also faced internal challenges from **communists** attempting to assert control over UBC locals.

The Great Depression also proved difficult, with only about 30 percent of UBC members gainfully employed at any moment. Hutcheson grew increasingly conservative and launched bitter attacks against radicals and advocates of **industrial unionism**. At the 1935 AFL convention, Hutcheson called **John L. Lewis** a "bastard" for supporting industrial unionism, and Lewis bloodied him with a haymaker. Many historians credit the intransigence of conservative craft unionists like Hutcheson as hastening the formation of the **Congress of Industrial Organizations**. Even some UBC members complained that leaders were out of touch with **rank-and-file** concerns. UBC leaders historically embraced the AFL **voluntarism** principle with its built-in distrust of government intervention in capital/labor relations, but they reluctantly supported key New Deal programs and lobbied for unemployment compensation and **minimum-wage** programs.

The UBC enjoyed a resurgence during World War II, and Hutcheson's son, Maurice, served on the Wage Stabilization Board. Membership surged from 320,000 in 1940 to over 700,000 by 1945. The UBC lost a key battle in 1946, however, when the **Taft-Hartley Act** was passed over President Truman's veto. Section 14 (b) of that bill gave legal status to hated **right-to-work** provisos against which the UBC had long battled. Nonetheless, the UBC benefited from the building boom of the 1950s, and grew to 850,000 members by 1958. Critics continued to complain that the UBC was a **business union**, and cited its purchase of properties in New Jersey and Florida and its new Washington headquarters (opened in 1961) as examples of its inattention to the rank-and-file. In 1952, Maurice Hutcheson succeeded his father as UBC president, and some complained his style was autocratic.

Whether or not the critics were correct, the UBC took a big hit in the 1970s. Although the UBC was over 800,000 strong in 1973, the end of the construction boom during the recession that began in 1973 and lingered for a decade greatly reduced its ranks. Developers—spearheaded by groups like the Chamber of Commerce and the Business Roundtable—renewed efforts to hire nonunion carpenters. Business efforts were buoyed by conservative politicians, especially the antiunion administrations of Ronald Reagan (1981–89) and George H. Bush (1989–93). In 1969, approximately 80 percent of all carpenters were unionized; by 2000, the figured slipped to about 30 percent.

In the 1990s, the UBC renewed efforts to organize workers, and UBC President Doug McCarron (elected in 1995) reversed some of the policies the rank and file found distasteful. Recently, the UBC has fought campaigns to preserve

prevailing wage structures as established by the 1931 **Davis-Bacon Act**, a law conservatives seek to repeal.

Suggested Readings: Walter Galenson, *The United Brotherhood of Carpenters*, 1983; Richard Schneirov and Thomas Suhrbur, *United Brotherhood, Union Town: The History of the Carpenters' Union of Chicago, 1863–1987*, 1988; "UBC Union History," http://www.carpenters.org/history.

Robert E. Weir

United Electrical, Radio, and Machine Workers of America (UE). The United Electrical, Radio, and Machine Workers of America was founded in 1936 during the wave of **depression-era strikes**. It was once the third largest affiliate of the **Congress of Industrial Organizations (CIO)**, but was badly hurt by the anticommunist red scare that emerged after World War II. In a much reduced state, the UE still exists and is headquartered in Pittsburgh, Pennsylvania.

After a successful strike in 1933, Philadelphia Radio (Philco) locals were recognized by the **American Federation of Labor (AFL)** and granted a union charter. Jurisdictional disputes arose between established **craft unions** within the AFL and the newly federated **industrial unions** like that at Philco. When AFL leadership assigned Philco locals to the International Brotherhood of Electrical Workers (IBEW), they quit the AFL and joined forces with the newly formed electrical manufacturing locals from Lynn, Massachusetts, and Schenectady, New York, and created the United Electrical and Radio Workers of America (UERW). These unions affiliated with the CIO. In 1937, James Matles led the 15,000-member **International Association of Machinists** out of the AFL and into the UERW, with a resultant name change.

As early as 1933, union activists saw New Deal labor legislation as a golden opportunity to build industrial unions. Originating from individual local unions in Westinghouse, General Electric, Philco Radio, and other locations, union activists like **James Barron Carey**, Julius Emspak, Al Coulthard, and William Turnbull joined forces to fight union-recognition battles within the electrical and radio industries. The UE became known for its militant and democratic unionism. It began with about 30,000 members and ballooned to 720,000 by 1944.

The UE did not shy from using talented left-wing organizers, and from its inception, the UE battled charges that it was dominated by **communists**. It faced a constant barrage of attacks from anticommunist crusaders in federal and state government, business, and other labor unions. UE leadership split over the issue of communist influence. At the 1941 UE convention, Carey proposed banning fascists and communists from holding union office. Matles, Emspak, and Albert Fitzgerald, a popular member from Lynn, Massachusetts, united to defeat Carey's motion. The same coalition ousted Carey and installed Fitzgerald as the new UE president.

World War II (1941–45) brought boom years, and the UE's largest membership gains took place during the war. Challenges emerged after the war when the 1947 **Taft-Hartley Act** focused renewed attention on communist influences in organized labor and required leaders to sign anticommunist affidavits. When the UE refused to do so, it became vulnerable to raids from other unions. At the 1949 CIO convention, the UE pressed for a resolution forbidding further union **raiding** of the UE. When the convention refused the UE's request, it stopped paying CIO **dues** and was expelled. The 1949 convention also chartered a rival union, the **International Union of Electrical, Radio, and Machine Workers of America (IUE)**.

Raiding of UE locals continued through the 1950s and into the 1960s. In addition, the IUE operated in the same shops and factories as the UE, thus forcing repeated run-off elections. By the mid-1960s, the once dominant UE was reduced to a shadow of its former self. This proved disastrous for electrical workers. Where the UE had been the main institution representing electrical manufacturing workers, operatives were now represented by sixteen different unions. This made unified **collective bargaining** with conglomerates like General Electric and Westinghouse nearly impossible.

Battered and wounded by the internecine union battles, the UE began to rebuild in the late 1960s, only to suffer greater losses during the 1970s and 1980s due to **downsizing** and plant closings. The UE remains proud and defiant, however, and boasts a core of loyal members that has allowed it to survive into the twenty-first century. It touts its independence from the AFL-CIO and is viewed by some as a model of independent **rank-and-file** democratic unionism. The UE publishes its own monthly newspaper, maintains a vibrant Web site, and represents about 35,000 members. It has expanded its organizing focus to embrace workers as diverse as plastic injection molders, warehouse workers, custodians, and graduate teaching assistants.

Suggested Readings: Ronald Filippelli and M. D. McColloch, *Cold War in the Working Class: The Rise and Decline of the United Electrical Workers*, 1995; James Matles and J. Higgins, *Them and Us: Struggles of a Rank-and-File Union*, 1974; Ed Rosswurm, ed., *The CIO's Left-Led Unions*, 1992.

Mike Bonislawski

United Farm Workers of America (UFW). The United Farm Workers of America is the union that represents about 27,000 agricultural workers in the United States. It has locals across the United States and Canada, though the bulk of its membership is located in California and the Southwest. Members come from many ethnic backgrounds, but historically the UFW has been an important voice for Chicano workers. The UFW is affiliated with the American Federation of Labor-Congress of Industrial Organizations (AFL-CIO).

Despite the political rhetoric of modern-day xenophobes, the border between the United States and Mexico has long been a fluid boundary, and Chicanos a fixture of American society. In the 1820s, Americans moved into what was then Mexican territory in search of new farmlands to replace those worn out by cotton cultivation. Many settlers came despite prohibitions by the newly independent nation of Mexico. The desire of southern agriculturalists to bring slaves into sections of Mexico was among the issues that led to the Texan war for independence in 1836. The United States annexed Mexico in 1845, and border disputes precipitated the Mexican War in 1848. Under terms of the Treaty of Guadalupe Hidalgo, the United States seized about one-third of Mexico, including parts of the present-day states of Arizona, California, Colorado, Nevada, New Mexico, and Utah. Thousands of Mexicans found themselves American citizens overnight. The border proved equally porous during the 1870s and 1880s, with Mexican *vaqueros* providing much of the manpower for cattle drives.

United Farm Workers President Cesar Chavez talks to striking Salinas Valley farm workers during a large rally in Salinas, Calif., on March 7, 1979. © AP/Wide World Photos.

Chicanos, Central Americans, Caribs, and South Americans often sought employment opportunities in the United States. Cubans, for example, played an important role in the south Florida cigar trade by the early twentieth century, Filipino farm laborers entered after the 1898 Spanish-American War, Puerto Ricans began coming to the mainland in the 1920s, and large numbers of Mexicans sought employment in mining, railroading, and the auto industry between 1910 and 1930. The **Industrial Workers of the World (IWW)** had some success in organizing agricultural workers of various ethnic backgrounds in the 1910s.

Fewer Latinos came to the United States during the Great Depression (1929–41) and, in some cases, those who were not U.S. citizens were forcibly repatriated. The U.S. government encouraged new waves of Latino immigration during World War II. Growers complained of manpower shortages, and the government set up the *bracero* program to recruit Mexican agricultural workers, many of whom stayed in the United States irrespective of their temporary guest-worker status. In 1951, the tacit agreement between the United States and Mexico was formalized as Public Law 78, with a stipulation that guest workers could not replace domestic workers, a proviso seldom enforced. Contrary to popular belief, however, the majority of Latino farmworkers are American citizens, with many UFW members having deeper American roots than nativist critics.

Both *braceros* workers and American farmworkers faced appalling conditions. Agricultural labor was exempt from the 1935 **National Labor Relations Act (NLRA)**, leaving farmworkers to negotiate whatever deals they could. Only those in the *braceros* program were regulated to any degree, and even their wages hovered around $1.40 per hour in 1964, the year the program ended; others averaged about $.90 per hour. Moreover, sanitary conditions, health standards, educational opportunities, and housing were inferior to those of America's worst ghettos. Life expectancy for farmworkers was only forty-nine years.

The UFW came about after a series of small steps taken by other organizations. In 1958, **Dolores Huerta** sought AFL-CIO support for a group called the Agricultural Workers Association (AWA); one year later the AFL-CIO absorbed the AWA as part of the **Agricultural Workers Organizing Committee** (AWOC). AWOC contained some Anglo and African American workers, but the bulk of its membership was Filipino and Chicano, with Huerta and Larry Itliong, a Filipino, providing much of AWOC's leadership. In 1962, **Cesar Chavez** and Huerta created the National Farm Workers Association (NFWA) to organize Chicano farm laborers in and around Delano, California. In 1965, the NWFA struck a California rose farm at the same time the AWOC struck California grape growers who were not complying with the end of the *braceros* program. Both **strikes** enjoyed some success, but neither resulted in a union **contract**.

The UFW was born out of a joint NWFA/AWOC strike against grape growers in the Delano/Bakersfield area of California's southern San Joaquin Valley. AWOC called the strike on September 8, 1965, and growers began to import Chicano **scabs**. On September 16, Chavez convinced the NWFA to join the largely Filipino strike. Within weeks, more than thirty farms found themselves unable to field a workforce. By most accounts, the event that made the strike and led to the founding of the UFW was Chavez's decision to launch a nationwide **grape boycott** of California table grapes. Inspired by the nonviolent tactics of Gandhi in India and civil rights leaders like Martin Luther King, Jr., in the United States, Chavez proved a capable and charismatic organizer. Grassroots mobilization spread awareness of the **boycott** across the nation, roving **pickets** tied up a 400-square-mile region, and organizers convinced numerous scabs to leave the fields. Chavez also led a 340-mile protest march from Delano to Sacramento in March, 1966, that gathered intense media attention for the farmworkers' cause.

The giant Schenley conglomerate buckled under the pressure and signed an agreement with the NFWA, the nation's first **collective bargaining** agreement between farmworkers and growers. Several weeks later, the DiGrigorio corporation agreed to hold union elections. That move, however, temporarily hurt the farmworkers' cause when the **International Brotherhood of Teamsters (IBT)** tried to organize farmworkers, touching off bouts of **raiding** and wholesale boycotting of the first election by NWFA members. A second election ordered by California governor Pat Brown resulted in NWFA victory.

Despite victory over Schenley and DiGrigorio, however, other growers remained intransigent. On August 22, 1966, the NWFA and the AWOC merged to form the Farm Workers Organizing Committee (FWOC), under the aegis and with the support of the AFL-CIO. The name was subsequently changed to the United Farm Workers of America (UFW); by 1970, most growers had settled with the UFW. Public opinion largely pressured the settlements, shaped in no small measure by Chavez's twenty-five-day water-only fast to publicize the cause. Contracts covered issues ranging from housing and access to clean drinking water to the handling of pesticides. The UFW also set up a credit union, a health clinic, Radio Campesina, and a union hiring hall. The UFW's stylized eagle became an instantly recognizable icon, and posters emblazoned with *Huelga! (Strike!)* and *Viva La Causa (Long Live Our Cause)* proved so popular that they became UFW slogans.

The UFW grew rapidly in the late 1960s, peaking at about 80,000 by 1970. Each campaign it undertook proved a bruising battle, however. Three picketers were killed in 1972; the UFW renewed its grape boycott; Chavez underwent a second fast; and the Teamsters continued to sign side agreements with growers that undermined UFW efforts. Particularly nasty was the fight to eliminate the short hoe, which took its toll on the backs and posture of workers; growers insisted long hoes damaged plant roots. One of the UFW's biggest victories came in 1975, when California passed the **Agricultural Labor Relations Act (ALRA)**, which extended legal collective bargaining rights to farmworkers and set up structures that parallel those under the NLRA.

UFW fortunes waned in the latter half of the 1970s and into the 1980s. The UFW called a lettuce boycott in 1979, but it failed to capture the same support as had the grape boycott, and many California growers simply refused to comply with the ALRA. Several more farmworkers died during strikes between 1979 and 1983. Studies revealed that farmworkers suffered higher cancer rates and miscarriages than the general public, problems linked to the handling of and exposure to toxic pesticides. The UFW achieved very little in negotiations with growers over pesticide use. In 1984, Chavez and the UFW called for a third worldwide boycott of all sprayed grapes. The boycott lingered until 2001, when the UFW called it off.

By the late-1980s, the UFW was in serious trouble. It lost more union elections than it won, and its official membership plunged to around 10,000; in truth, it was probably about half that. Chavez underwent a thirty-six-day "Wrath of Grapes" fast in 1988 to call attention to pesticide poisoning and the renewed grape boycott. Publicity, however, was perhaps as much due to the support of celebrities like Whoopi Goldberg, Martin Sheen, and Emilio Estevez as to the public's sympathy for the UFW. Some UFW supporters complained that Chavez was autocratic and that too many of the union's strategies revolved around appeals to charisma and public opinion.

But even critics were stunned by Chavez's premature death on April 23, 1993. He was succeeded by Arturo Rodriquez, his son-in-law through marriage to Linda Chavez. Rodriquez has, thus far, attempted to balance dramatic public actions with grassroots organizing. To mark the one-year anniversary of Chavez's death, Rodriquez and the UFW recreated the 1965 Delano to Sacramento march, an event in which 20,000 participated. The UFW has slowly rebuilt its membership base and, since 1994, has won nearly all representation elections. Contracts with Gallo Vineyards, strawberry workers at Coastal Berry, and several mushroom growers represent significant strides forward.

The UFW's future contains numerous challenges. Ending the grape boycott was due as much to public indifference as to tangible gains. To date, two of the five pesticides that sparked the 1984 grape boycott remain in use, and overall pesticide use is up. In 2002, the UFW launched a boycott against Pictsweet mushrooms and encouraged the public to pressure Pizza Hut, a major buyer, to cease its use of Pictsweet products. Taking on United Foods, which owns Pictsweet, has not been an easy struggle. Moreover, studies reveal that nearly half of all growers still flunk field sanitation standards.

Despite its waxing and waning fortunes, UFW achievements for an organization built on large numbers of **part-time** and **contingency** workers is impressive. In addition to winning union contracts, UFW farmworkers have a union pension plan, health benefits, **profit sharing**, and parental leave policies. Its biggest challenge will be to raise wages; in 1999, farmworkers still averaged less than $7,500 per year.

Suggested Readings: Susan Ferriss, Ricardo Sandoval, and Diana Hembree, *The Fight in the Fields: Cesar Chavez and the Farmworkers Movement*, 1998; Patrick Moore and Theo Majka, *Farmers' and Farm Worker Movements: Social Protest in American Agriculture*, 1994; "UFW History," http://www.ufw.org/ufw.htm.

Robert E. Weir

United Food and Commercial Workers Union (UFCW). The United Food and Commercial Workers Union is an international union that represents about 1.4 million workers, mostly in the United States and Canada. Its members are currently concentrated mostly in food retail, food processing, and meatpacking industries, though it also represents workers in a variety of professions including distillery and wine workers, health care workers, garment workers, and those employed in chemical and fertilizer processing plants. The UFCW bears watching, as it hopes to be a major force in organizing the fast food and retail industries, two varieties of service industry work that have grown rapidly since the 1960s, but which are largely nonunion. The UFCW was formed in 1979, when the Retail Clerks International Association and the **Amalgamated Meat Cutters and Butcher Workmen of North America (AMCBW)** merged.

The struggles of butchers and meatpackers are among the most dramatic and difficult ones in American labor history. The invention of refrigerated railcars led to a national meat industry that was dominated by corporate giants like Armour, Cudahy, Morrell, Swift, and Wilson. Both stockyards and meatpacking plants proved hard to organize. A traumatic strike loss in 1886 led by the **Knights of Labor (KOL)** in the Chicago stockyards retarded union efforts for a time, but the AMCBW formed in 1897 and obtained a charter from the

American Federation of Labor (AFL). It made modest gains, but more significant progress was made in the 1930s by the **United Packinghouse Workers of America (UPWA)**, which was affiliated with the **Congress of Industrial Organizations (CIO)**. The two unions ceased **raiding** each other's membership prior to the AFL-CIO merger in 1955, but maintained separate identities until 1968, when the UPWA joined the AMCBW. Many supermarket meat cutters and butchers are union members, though the packinghouses remain a challenge for unions, and membership has declined in recent years.

Retail clerks have been affiliated with the AFL since 1890. Retail has proved a union-resistant industry due to its historically high employee turnover rate, intransigent employers, seasonal employment cycles, and sexism. (Women often dominate the ranks of retail clerks and many unions have, in the past, not given their concerns attention equal to the concerns of male industrial workers.) From the outset, however, the UFCW has had a good record in matters of gender equality. More than half of its members are women, and many hold positions of authority within the UFCW. In 1987, UFCW President Lenore Miller became the first female union president to be elected to the AFL-CIO's executive council.

Much of the UFCW's success has been in organizing grocery and supermarket employees. In 1998, Wal-Mart—the world's largest corporation—entered the supermarket business. Its entry hastened a merger process already underway and placed cost pressures on Wal-Mart competitors. The UFCW has faced pressure to grant **concessions** to unionized supermarket chains. In 1999, it began a campaign to organize Wal-Mart, a virulently antiunion corporation. It has also launched campaigns against so-called big box stores like Home Depot, as well as McDonald's and other fast-food chains.

If the UFCW is successful in its efforts, it could emerge as one of the most important labor unions of the twenty-first century. Its opposition is formidable and commands enormous financial resources, but most UFCW targets are not likely to become **runaway shops**, a factor in its favor.

Suggested Readings: Barbara Ehrenreich, *Nickel and Dimed*, 2001; Eric Sclosser, *Fast Food Nation*, 2001; "UFCW: A Voice for Working America," http://www.ufcw.org.

Robert E. Weir

United Hatters, Cap, and Millinery Workers International Union. In 1934, the United Hatters of North America merged with the Cloth Hat, Cap, and Millinery Workers Union to form the United Hatters, Cap, and Millinery Workers International Union (UHCMWIU). From earliest times, men and women wore functional head coverings to protect themselves from sun, rain, cold, and the hazards of the environment. Early nomadic Asian tribes are believed to have discovered the use of felted sheep's wool for making tents and clothing. By the late fourteenth century, the hat began to be important as a source of fashion as well as practicality, and fancy materials such as silk, velvet, taffeta, leather, and felted beaver were used by hat makers, whose trade would always be subject to the notoriously fickle whims of fashion.

The hat-making trade was long known as a sick trade, largely due to the illnesses to which hatters were prone and the environmental hazards to which they were subjected. Mercury nitrate salt was used to prepare and soften fur and wool fibers in the felt-making process. This was regarded as a trade secret by the hat makers, who would inevitably suffer the effects of mercury poisoning, hence the phrase, mad as a hatter. For hundreds of years, hatters suffered from hatters' shakes, uncontrollable shaking of the hands of hat-industry workers. Hatters struggled to conceal the shakes from employers since the first sign of the shakes endangered continued employment in the trade. It was not until December 1, 1941, that the United States Public Health Service brought an end to the use of mercury by hat manufacturers as a result of individual negotiations with manufacturers in twenty-six states. Union president Max Zaritsky had convinced Surgeon General Thomas Parran to investigate mercury poisoning. The Health Service found that one in five workers in the hat industry suffered from the shakes. The Public Health Service, as well as the union, claimed credit for the elimination of the use of mercury. The efforts on both sides were doubtless boosted by the war-time shortage of mercury.

In addition to the battle to eliminate the workplace environmental health hazards of mercury, the UHCMWIU and its predecessors fought to eliminate prison labor, **sweatshops**, and crippling **jurisdictional** battles. Similarly, the hatters struggled to drive **racketeers** out of the industry and to fight charges of **communist** domination during years of red-baiting following both world wars. Among the most famous of the hat industry struggles was the fight over the use of the secondary boycott during the so-called Danbury Hatters Case (***Loewe v. Lawler***, 1908). The decision in that case was a major setback for all of organized labor but was particularly devastating for the hatters.

In the period immediately after World War II, the hatters were led by Zaritsky, who had been involved in hat unions since 1907. The UHCMWIU advocated labor-management cooperation to promote the hat, cap, and millinery industry in the face of a decline in the fashion of wearing hats by both men and women. In an effort to seek greater strength and form alliances with other unions in the garment and needletrades, UHCMWIU became part of the Amalgamated Clothing and Textile Workers Union (ACTWU) in 1983. In 1995, ACTWU merged with the **International Ladies' Garment Workers' Union (ILGWU)** to form **Union of Needletrades, Industrial and Textile Employees (UNITE)**.

Suggested Readings: Donald B. Robinson, *Spotlight on a Union: the Story of the United Hatters, Cap, and Millinery Workers International*, 1948; David Bensman, *The Practice of Solidarity: American Hat Finishers in the Nineteenth Century*, 1985.

Patricia Shackleton
James P. Hanlan

United Mine Workers of America (UMWA). The United Mine Workers of America has engaged in numerous bitter disputes with coal mine operators over wages, working conditions, and benefits for miners. It represents miners of various kinds, though its historic strength has been in anthracite and bituminous coal fields.

The miners' struggle is among the bloodiest and most bitter in American labor history. Mines were often located in remote areas and mine owners ran their operations as if they were personal fiefdoms. Workers often toiled in **company towns** and were subject to rigid rules that regulated both work and life off the job. Some workers were paid in scrip, and many mining camps were marked by squalor, backbreaking labor, and crushing poverty. The first effort to organize coal miners came in 1860. It and other efforts yielded only modest success. The first miner unions to have more than a regional presence were those affiliated with **Knights of Labor (KOL)** National Trade District 135 and the 1885 National Federation of Miners and Mine Workers, which affiliated with the newly formed **American Federation of Labor (AFL)** in 1886.

A 1902 certificate of membership in the United Mine Workers of America (UMWA). © George Meany Memorial Archives.

The UMWA was formed when the National Progressive Union of Miners and Mine Laborers merged with KOL District 135 in 1890. It affiliated with the AFL. The UMWA constitution forbade discrimination based on race, religion, or ethnicity. In 1898, the UMWA won an **eight-hour** day for most of its members. Dynamic leadership aided UMWA growth. **John Mitchell** was the UMWA president from 1898 to 1908. Although he was a conservative man, Mitchell was a good tactician. He was a member of the **National Civic Federation** and parlayed his contacts into bargaining advantage. In 1902, more than 150,000 miners struck in protest of low pay and appalling safety records in the mines. Mitchell offered to submit **grievances** to binding **arbitration**, and when operators refused, President Theodore Roosevelt intervened on behalf of the miners. This event is widely heralded as the beginning of a change in government attitudes toward organized labor.

Many UMWA campaigns were contentious. Hard-rock miners in the west faced especially difficult conditions, with nearly constant **strikes** involving the UMWA and the Western Federation of Miners from the 1890s through 1914. Many lives were lost in pitched battles that led to such notorious episodes as the 1897 **Lattimer massacre** and the **Ludlow massacre** of 1914. The UMWA agreed to a **no-strike pledge** during World War I and grew to over 500,000 members during this period of industrial peace. Strikes broke out anew after the war, spurring the government to create the Bituminous Coal Commission in 1920 that gave miners large raises and recognized the UMWA as the miners' **bargaining unit**. This did little to prevent horrendous violence in Kentucky and West Virginia, including the infamous 1920 shootout between miners and Baldwin-Felts agents in **Matewan**, West Virginia. Its aftermath led to the **Battle of Blair Mountain** in which more than two dozen lives were lost. In all, some 10,000 miners battled police, company forces, and the government for over a year, until miners were forced to capitulate. The same sort of conflict lived on in Kentucky, where violence was so pronounced that one county was dubbed "bloody Harlan" in 1932.

In 1920, **John Llewellyn Lewis** became UMWA president. Under his tutelage, UMWA members secured retirement **pensions** and higher pay. Lewis grew increasingly restless with the AFL's slowness to recognize the need for **industrial unions** and its parsimony in funding organizing efforts. He was the leading spirit behind the establishment of the Committee for Industrial Organization, that later became the **Congress of Industrial Organizations (CIO)**. Although a formal break did not come until 1937, the UMWA was effectively out of the AFL in 1935. Lewis rose in national prominence becoming the first CIO president and riding a tide of worker militancy to win wage and benefit **concessions** for UMWA members. Lewis supported Franklin Roosevelt in 1932 and 1936, but opposed him in 1940 and resigned as CIO president when Roosevelt was reelected. In 1941, Lewis demanded and won a closed-shop agreement in captive mines owned by steel firms. In 1942, Lewis abruptly pulled the UMWA out of the CIO and, unlike most other unions, the UMWA refused to take a no-strike pledge during World War II. Lewis was twice cited for contempt of court during the **coal miners' strike of 1943**. Some historians believe that UMWA actions during the war fueled postwar antilabor legislation.

The UMWA rejoined the AFL in 1946, then quit in 1947 when Lewis refused to commit the UMWA to noncommunist affidavits required under the **Taft-Hartley Act**. The UMWA also defied the act through a series of short strikes, **memorial strikes**, and other tactics designed to test its limitations. From 1947 through 1950, the UMWA interrupted national coal supplies on numerous occasions, with President Harry Truman issuing an injunction against new strikes in 1950, whilst Congress debated seizing coal mines.

Lewis resigned as UMWA president in 1959. Although his leadership had been dynamic, it was also autocratic. **Automation** began to displace workers by the 1960s, and the UMWA progress stalled on key campaigns like worker safety and occupational diseases like **black lung**. In 1963, William Boyle succeeded to UMWA presidency and almost immediately charges of corruption swirled. A miners-for-democracy movement grew within the UMWA, and it supported **Joseph A. Yablonski**'s bid to unseat Boyle in 1969. Boyle was reelected and Yablonski was murdered several weeks later. A federal judge invalidated Boyle's reelection as fraudulent, and Boyle was later convicted of Yablonski's murder. Reformer Arnold Miller became UMWA president and was in charge during a brutal 1973–74 battle against Duke Power Company in Brookside, Kentucky. In 1982, **Richard Trumka** became UMWA president, and he is credited with completing the restoration of **rank-and-file** democracy. Under Trumka, the UMWA also made headway on black lung disease, though it remains a touchstone issue for the union. Trumka led the UMWA back into the AFL-CIO and became secretary-treasurer of the latter organization in 1995. In that year, Cecil Roberts, Jr., became UMWA president. The UMWA currently has about 240,000 members and represents over 40 percent of all American coal miners.

Suggested Readings: Melvyn Dubofsky, *John L. Lewis*, 1986; J. M. H. Lasslett, *The United Mine Workers of America*, 1996; Paul Taylor, *Bloody Harlan*, 1990.

Shalynn Hunt
Robert E. Weir

United Mine Workers Strike of 1943. *See Coal Miners Strike of 1943.*

United Packinghouse Workers of America (UPWA). The United Packinghouse Workers of America was created in 1943 as the **industrial union** that succeeded the Packinghouse Workers' Organizing Committee (PWOC, 1937–43). Both the PWOC and the UPWA were affiliated with the **Congress of Industrial Organizations (CIO)**, and were the culmination of many decades of struggle to secure **collective-bargaining** rights for workers in the meat industry. In the 1880s, the **Knights of Labor (KOL)** organized packinghouse workers in small firms, but industry giants like Swift and Armour proved intransigent, and the KOL's efforts faltered during a disastrous 1887 strike in Chicago.

The **American Federation of Labor's (AFL) Amalgamated Meat Cutters and Butcher Workmen of North America** formed in 1897 and enjoyed its greatest success during World War I. After the war, however, most firms broke agreements with the Amalgamated Meat Cutters and Butcher Workmen of North America, and other AFL workers **scabbed** on it during struggles against Armour. Moreover, the AFL largely ignored the immigrant workforce that made up the bulk of slaughterhouse workers. The harsh conditions and long hours under which they toiled was the subject of Upton Sinclair's famed novel, *The Jungle*, the title derived from a term used to describe work in the stockyards. If anything, those conditions worsened once the Great Depression began.

Many PWOC leaders were left-wing radicals, and some held associations with the Communist Party. The Autoworkers Organizing Committee also supplied logistical support for the PWOC. Ideology was put into practice, with the PWOC maintaining strict codes of racial and gender solidarity. It also broke down barriers that separated pork butchers from those working in beef, who viewed themselves as more skilled. Although the UPWA probably never contained more than 125,000 members, its activist traditions allowed it to succeed where prior efforts had faltered. Its "night riders" tactic transported workers and leaders from one packing town to another to facilitate quick organizing drives and maintain **solidarity** between cities, thereby lessening the likelihood of scabbing during labor disputes. Kansas City workers defeated Armour in 1937, and the firm soon settled in other cities. Two years later, the PWOC forced firms to pay men and women equal wages for equal work.

The progressive PWOC swamped the Amalgamated Meat Cutters and Butcher Workmen of North America in most elections held under the **National Labor Relations Act** and, by 1943, was the largest union in the stockyards. In 1946, the UPWA elected Ralph Helstein as its president. He was dedicated to maintaining the union's activism. Helstein and the union attacked the segregation policies of southern plants and the glaring **wage differentials** vis-a-vis northern workers. Although the UPWA managed to raise wage rates in the South, it was less successful dealing with Jim Crow policies that relegated African American workers to the worst jobs available.

The UPWA maintained its commitment to racial equality even when it cost them white members. In the 1950s, the union moved its headquarters to the heavily African American "Black Belt" in Chicago's South Side, and when whites dropped out, promoted African Americans to positions of leadership. The UPWA also conducted a militant fourteen-month strike and boycott against Boston's Colonial Provision Company between 1954 and 1956, which saw remarkable levels of racial cooperation despite red-baiting and other brutal company tactics.

The UPWA declined in the 1960s, as mechanization replaced line workers and firms relocated to nonunion areas. In addition, industry consolidation eliminated jobs and new corporate ownership groups instituted antiunion policies. In 1968, the UPWA merged with the Amalgamated Meat Cutters and Butcher Workmen of North America. Further union streamlining resulted in the creation of the **United Food and Commercial Workers Union (UFCW)** in 1979. Its 1.4 million members represent stockyard workers, butchers, grocery workers, and other food-industry employees.

Suggested Readings: Rick Halpern, *Down on the Killing Floor*, 1997; Roger Horowitz, *Negro and White, Unite and Fight*, 1997; Shelton Stromquist and Marvin Bergman, eds., *Unionizing the Jungle*, 1997.

Sara Pleva

Robert E. Weir

United Paperworkers International Union (UPIU). The United Paperworkers International Union (UPIU) was one of two large unions attempting to organize paper industry workers in the twentieth century, the other being the International Brotherhood of Pulp, Sulphite, and Paper Mill Workers (IBPSPW). The UPIU tended to represent skilled workers, whereas the IBPSPW was more of an **industrial union**. The UPIU—under the name of the International Brotherhood of Paperworkers (IBP)—was formed by Holyoke, Massachusetts, paperworkers in 1884 and ceased as an independent entity on January 4, 1999, when it merged with three other **international unions** to form PACE, the Paper, Allied-Industrial, Chemical, and Energy Workers International Union, an organization that represents about 320,000 workers in the United States and Canada.

During its 155-year history, the UPIU changed its name numerous times. The IBP, a forerunner of the UPIU, was chartered by the **American Federation of Labor (AFL)**. Through time, AFL **craft unionism** made increasingly less sense as the paper industry underwent mechanization changes that eroded the centrality of skilled craft workers. Many locals of both the IBP and the IBPSPW cast their lot with the **Congress of Industrial Organizations (CIO)** in the late 1930s, while others remained inside the AFL. CIO locals were reorganized under the banner of the United Papermakers and Papermakers (UPP). In 1957, two years after the AFL and CIO merged, the UPP and remaining AFL locals merged to form the UPIU.

Skilled and semiskilled paperworkers in both the AFL and CIO often battled a common enemy: the International Paper Company, a company that formed in 1898, when it consolidated more than 1.7 million acres of forests in eastern Canada with milling operations in New England and New York. International soon became the world's largest paper, pulp, and forest products industry in the world, a status it retains to the present. The UPIU began its struggle for an **eight-hour** day beginning in 1912, one of many contentious issues that led to a five-year-long strike against International Paper in the 1920s. After that, strikes against International Paper become a relatively constant part of the UPIU's history, although relations took a turn for the better in the 1970s. In 1985, however, a new company management team headed by John Georges demanded wage cuts from employees and announced plans to close several operations. The UPIU found itself embroiled in a well-publicized sixteen-month **downsizing, decertification and concessions strike** against International Paper during 1987 and 1988. At the center of the controversy was **local union** number 14, which represented about 900 workers in the Androscoggin Mill in Jay, Maine. Local 14 attracted world attention and brought luminaries like the Reverend Jesse Jackson, consumer advocate Ralph Nader, and Amy Carter, daughter of the former president, to this remote part of Maine. It also waged a **corporate campaign** against International Paper that exposed the company's deplorable environmental record. The strike was lost when the UPIU struck a deal with International Paper that was unfavorable to Maine workers, many of whom lost their jobs to **replacement workers**. Many union advocates expressed anger against the UPIU and accused it of **business unionism** strategies not in keeping with **rank-and-file** interests.

The UPIU has also struggled to become more racially diverse. From 1975 to 1981, African American workers brought a series of lawsuits against Gilman Paper Company operations in Georgia, charging that it, often in collusion with the union, confined black workers to bottom-rung positions in the company. The UPIU was a codefendant in many of these suits, most of which were won by plaintiffs. The UPIU did improve its civil rights record but negative publicity coupled with losses in the 1980s served to sap its strength.

The UPIU was not alone in its plight. During the late 1980s and into the 1990s, many weakened unions merged to create larger and presumably more powerful entities. PACE was born from this impulse. It brought together the UPIU, the **Oil, Chemical, and Atomic Workers Union (OCAW)**, cement workers in the former Allied Industrial Workers of America, and the Allied Industrial Workers of America, the remnant of autoworkers who did not bolt the AFL for the **United Auto Workers** in 1937.

Suggested Readings: Peter Kellman, *Divided We Fall: The Story of the Paperworkers' Union and the Future of Labor*, 2003; Julus Getman, *The Betrayal of Local 14: Paperworkers, Politics, and Permanent Replacements*, 1998; "One Great Union PACE History," http://paceunion.org/one_great_union.htm.

Robert E. Weir

United Parcel Service (UPS) Strike. The United Parcel Service Strike occurred in 1997 when 185,000 workers walked out on the United Parcel Service. It resulted in a thorough victory for the **International Brotherhood of Teamsters** (IBT). Some analysts hailed the union's victory as a sign that organized labor was poised to reverse its two-decade decline. The **strike** also focused attention on the plight of **part-time** and **contingency labor**.

At the time of the strike, UPS was the nation's largest private handler of packages. Like many companies, it used the rubric of competitiveness to increase its use of part-time and contingency workers. UPS had added 46,300 new jobs in the four years preceding the strike, but 38,500 of them were part-time. In all, nearly 60 percent of the UPS workforce consisted of part-time workers. Also akin to other companies, UPS maintained a two-tier **wage** structure under which new hires and part-timers were paid a lower rate than full-time workers; most part-timers made about $11 per hour, whereas full-time workers averaged more than $23.

The IBT wisely chose to make the plight of part-time workers the centerpiece of its fight against UPS, and it called upon the company to create more full-time positions. This struck a responsive chord as millions of Americans were working part-time, often not by choice. This was certainly the case at UPS, where three-quarters of those leaving the company claimed to have done so because they could not secure full-time work with the firm. In 1996, UPS trained more than 182,000 part-time workers, of whom just over 40,000 remained after a year. (The IBT strategically ignored the fact that a sizable number of these were seasonal employees working on a predetermined limited term.) The issue of part-time work resonated in urban areas—where many UPS terminals were located—because higher costs of living made it more difficult to make ends meet without full-time work. UPS offered to promote 10,000 part-timers, but only to fund 1,000 new full-time jobs; others would have to wait for openings created by retirements, resignations, and firings.

The IBT also opposed UPS's plan to administer the employee **pension** plan. The IBT managed UPS pensions as part of a multiemployer group. Under the UPS proposal, the company would have removed funds from the IBT-managed group and established its own fund. Although it promised higher rates of return than the IBT currently offered, the union feared that future contributions would not exceed the tax breaks UPS received, a level that might not keep pace with rising prices. More importantly, the IBT feared the risks involved in a corporate-run fund in which management would be free to shift money from the pension fund to other accounts.

The IBT and UPS also quarreled over safety issues, weight limits, and **subcontracting**. The company's safety record—though not bad overall—was marred by its seeming indifference to accidents. To many, the company's requirement that line workers be able to lift 150 pounds also appeared excessive. For the IBT, however, a more substantive issue was the company's plan to subcontract feeder driver jobs. Feeder drivers transport parcels between UPS terminals; if subcontracted, such a plan would reduce the number of drivers.

The strike began on August 4, 1997, and ended fifteen days later. From the outset, the IBT won the public-relations battle. IBT president Ron Carey was articulate throughout the strike and came across as more reasonable than UPS officials. It was also apparent that the union was far more prepared for the strike than UPS. UPS tried to move managers onto the line, but it did not have an in-place reserve of **scabs** to make good its threat to layoff or fire strikers. As a result, the IBT was able to reduce the volume of packages from twelve million per day to under one million through a combination of manpower shortages, **picketing**, and encouraging the public to use other shippers.

The IBT maintained remarkable solidarity throughout the fight, even though the union strike fund was low. It received solid support from the American Federation of Labor-Congress of Industrial Organizations (AFL-CIO), whose financial assistance helped strikers draw $55 per week strike pay. AFL-CIO President **John Sweeney** was also instrumental in helping the IBT on the political front, where the IBT's biggest danger lay. Under the **Taft-Hartley Act**, the president of the United States has the authority to order an eighty-day cooling off period if a strike creates a national emergency. President William Clinton had used that power earlier in 1997 to avert a pilots' strike at American Airlines. UPS officials argued that the strike threatened five to seven percent of the national output, as firms were dependent on UPS to deliver parts, contracts, and goods. President Clinton chose not to evoke Taft-Hartley, a decision that conservatives claimed was driven by AFL-CIO and IBT contributions to his reelection campaign. (Politics may have been involved, but the presence of numerous parcel post carriers—the United States Postal Service, Federal Express, Guaranteed Overnight Delivery, Emery, and others—tends to vindicate Clinton's decision that no national emergency existed.)

On August 19, 1997, UPS capitulated. Under the terms of a five-year contract, UPS agreed to create 10,000 new full-time jobs, and that five of every six new full-time openings would be filled by promoted part-time workers. Part-timers also won annual increases of 7 percent, while full-timers won 3 percent raises. The IBT also maintained control over pension funds and got UPS to agree to discuss weight and safety issues. UPS also agreed to abandon plans to subcontract feeder routes.

The IBT victory was marred by one sour note. IBT President Ron Carey was forced to resign when a federal mediator ruled that his 1996 election over James Hoffa, Jr., was tainted by fraud and misappropriation of union funds. New elections were ordered, and Carey was barred from seeking reelection. (Hoffa was elected IBT president in April 1998.) Carey, the IBT, and the AFL-CIO were also alleged to have made illegal contributions to the Democratic National Committee, but investigations did not sustain those charges.

The significance of the UPS strike divides along ideological grounds. Conservatives chastised the ineffectiveness of the Clinton administration and argued that UPS was permanently damaged by a capricious strike. They further claimed that members lost wages that would take years to recover, that UPS lost so much business that it would not be able to create new jobs, that the company pension plan was superior, and that the strike did not change the ratio of full- to part-time workers. As of 2002, only the last charge appears to have merit. The strike's short duration and generous wage increases quickly led to recouped wages, and Wall Street scandals have called into question the long-term viability of employer-administered pension plans.

Liberals hailed the UPS victory as the harbinger of a new labor movement that would reverse losses suffered from the 1970s on. The AFL-CIO drew upon the UPS victory in its campaign to organize new workers and hailed it as an example of workers' hunger to join unions. More than five years after the strike, the liberals' hopes appeared no more prescient than the conservative critique. Organizing gains have barely offset losses, and organized labor struggles to maintain its rate of representing about 14 percent of the American workforce.

There are, nonetheless, concrete lessons to be drawn from the UPS strike. First, the IBT was very well prepared for its action, indicating that offensive strikes are more likely to succeed than defensive ones. Second—as the contingency issue indicated—favorable public opinion is an important issue in helping win strikes. In that regard, actions like the UPS strike and the **Ravenswood lockout** of 1990–92 stand in marked contrast to public relations nightmares like the 1981 **PATCO strike**. Third, organized labor's remarkable **solidarity** during the UPS action was vital in helping achieve victory.

The UPS strike probably also validates those who claim that short, decisive actions have more chance of success than drawn-out clashes. It also shows that politics plays an important role. The neutrality of the Clinton administration contrasts sharply with the antiunion stance of presidents Reagan and Bush in the 1980s. Finally, the strike highlights the problems of contingency workers. This is likely to form the basis of future clashes between capital and labor.

Suggested Readings: Kathleen Barker and Kathleen Christensen, *Contingent Work: American Employment Relations in Transition*, 1998; David Bacon, "The UPS Strike—Unions Win When They Take the Offensive," http://www.igc.org/dbacon/Strikes/07ups.htm; Leo Troy, "The UPS Strike: Labor Tilts at Windmills," http://www.heritage.org/library/backgrounder/bg1165.html.

Robert E. Weir

United Rubber Workers of America (URWA). The United Rubber Workers of America had its roots in the late-nineteenth-century Eastern boot and shoe business, especially in New England. Operatives in the field first organized under the banner of the **Knights of Labor (KOL)** and tried to unite the industry on a national basis before the companies formed a trust in 1892. Internal strife within the KOL and the eventual demise of the organization allowed the cartel—the United States Rubber Company—to dictate labor-management relations without the intervention of labor unions during the 1890s. Production soon outgrew the narrow confines of rubber footwear and expanded into the manufacture of tires for bicycles, then automobiles. Innovations in the creation of rubber, the industry's continual search for **automation**, and periodic **speedups** transformed the workforce from **artisan** bootmakers to semi-skilled and unskilled tire makers.

In the 1890s, the **American Federation of Labor (AFL)**, under **Samuel Gompers**, tried to pick up the organizational pieces left by the KOL by chartering **federal labor unions**. Numerous federal locals banded together to create the short-lived Amalgamated Rubber Workers Union. Both the **Industrial Workers of the World (IWW)** and the machinists' union attempted to organize the field workers at the rubber tire citadel of Akron, Ohio, but were not successful. With the stimulus of New Deal labor legislation in the 1930s, the AFL once again led the field with the establishment of a Rubber Workers Council in 1934. However, the AFL's penchant for splitting mass-production workers into **craft union** affiliates weakened its appeal, but the AFL formed the United Rubber Workers of America in 1935. Almost immediately, URWA leaders rebelled against the AFL's skill mentality and pushed for **industrial unionism**.

The infant union shocked the labor world with a massive **sit-down strike** at the Goodyear Rubber Company in Akron in 1936, as well as subsequent **wildcat strikes**. Such actions moved the rubber workers into the more hospitable orbit of the **Congress of Industrial Organizations (CIO)** that same year and led to a signal triumph against the Firestone Rubber Company. Under government supervision, the URWA won victories over other major tire enterprises, including the United States Rubber Company, the industry pacesetter. The URWA continued its momentum during World War II and expanded its jurisdiction and title to the United Rubber, Cork, Linoleum and Plastic Workers of America (URCLPWA) at the end of the conflict to reflect new categories of workers under the union's jurisdiction.

Like other CIO unions in the postwar era, the rubber workers union split into left-wing and conservative factions that destabilized the organization for several years. As in similarly divided unions, the postwar red scare encouraged the URCLPWA to adopt a middle-of-the-road stance. With a politically acceptable ideology, the union achieved an organizational durability that gained master contracts in the field of rubber and increased membership, especially in the burgeoning field of plastics. By the 1970s, the union had almost a quarter of a million members.

Globalism and **concessionary** bargaining emerged at about the same time the union reached its organizing zenith. Rubber companies continually sought synthetic rubber, instituted automation, and eventually moved many jobs to underdeveloped countries with lower labor costs. As **runaway** plants eroded union membership rolls, the rubber workers merged with the **United Steel Workers of America (USWA)** in 1995.

Suggested Readings: Daniel Nelson, *American Rubber Workers and Organized Labor*, 1988; Bryan D. Palmer, *Goodyear Invades the Backcountry: The Corporate Takeover of a Rural Town*, 1994.

Scott Molloy

United Steel Workers of America (USWA). The United Steel Workers of America grew out of the Steel Workers Organizing Committee (SWOC). The **Congress of Industrial Organizations (CIO)** created SWOC and similar organizing bodies in 1936 to organize nonunion industries that the **American Federation of Labor (AFL)** had previously ignored. The CIO paid particular importance to steel because many steel companies controlled coal mines that the **United Mine Workers of America (UMWA)**, the CIO's largest **industrial union**, wished to organize fully. The UMWA lent the SWOC experienced organizers, including union executive **Philip Murray**, who served as SWOC's chairman. The USWA ultimately organized the notoriously antiunion steel industry, the culmination of decades of struggle that produced upheavals like the 1892 Homestead lockout and the **steel strike of 1919**.

SWOC focused its organization efforts on **company unions** at U.S. Steel, the industry's largest firm. By convincing independent employees that an outside union could offer them more than a company-dominated organization, the SWOC managed to rally workers to their cause. In March 1937, secret negotiations between CIO President **John L. Lewis** and U.S. Steel Chairman Myron Taylor resulted in a SWOC contract. For the first time since the **Homestead** lockout of 1892, an independent trade union represented a significant portion of America's steelworkers. The SWOC hoped that the $5 per day, forty-hour workweek **contract** with U.S. Steel would become an industry standard.

Other large firms, dubbed "Little Steel" simply because they were smaller than U.S. Steel, did not succumb to union pressure until after World War II began.

The SWOC began the Little Steel Strike in mid-1937, but its efforts stalled because the leaders of these firms had a near pathological hatred for organized labor. The Memorial Day Massacre of 1937, during which police killed ten defenseless strikers outside a steel plant in Chicago, demonstrated the resolve of Little Steel to resist unionization. However, once the war began, the administration of Franklin Roosevelt forced most of the industry to recognize unions to ensure uninterrupted war mobilization efforts. The SWOC's June 1942 decision to change its name to the United Steelworkers of America signified its newly acquired permanence.

Steel workers constructing the Chase Manhattan Bank building in New York in the late 1950s. The steel industry was an important sector of industrial employment and industrial unionism. © George Meany Memorial Archives.

With more than 700,000 steelworkers enrolled, the USWA called a nationwide strike in January 1946 in an effort to make its recent contract gains permanent. The **walkout** lasted less than a month. President Harry Truman partially lifted wartime price controls, and steel producers gave workers an eighteen-and-a-half-cent hourly wage increase. Four other industry-wide strikes between 1945 and 1959 resulted in new wage increases for USWA members. It also obtained important **concessions** on job classification and supplemental unemployment benefits during this period. David McDonald became USWA president upon Murray's death in 1952 and served until 1963. He helped ease the USWA into the newly merged American Federation of Labor-Congress of Industrial Organizations (AFL-CIO) in 1955.

In retrospect, the USWA's highwater mark came during the **steel strike of 1959–60**, which lasted 116 days and idled 519,000 steelworkers in addition to 250,000 workers in related industries. Its ripple effect on the national economy was practically unparalleled.

Saddled with aging equipment, high labor costs, and a flood of cheaper steel imports, the American steel industry waned in the mid-1960s. The USWA did what it could to help employers cope, effectively abandoning strikes as a weapon from 1960 through 1983. From 1973 through 1983, the USWA and the steel industry formally agreed to submit their differences to **arbitration** under an arrangement known as the Experimental Negotiating Agreement (ENA). **Wages** continued to increase under the ENA, even as the industry contracted. In the 1980s, though, remaining steel firms demanded concessions and give-backs from the USWA.

Layoffs accompanying the steel industry's decline profoundly influenced the direction of the USWA. Plant closings and production cutbacks created massive unemployment in the union's ranks during the 1980s and 1990s. To compensate for these losses, the USWA began organizing workers in other industries. The merger of the USWA and the United Rubber, Cork, Linoleum, and Plastic Workers union in 1995 is the clearest symbol of this effort.

Hardship also radicalized many of the union's members. Once an organization consisting mostly of conservative, highly-paid white males, the USWA led some of the longest, bitterest strikes of the 1990s, including campaigns like the **Ravenswood lockout** of 1990 to 1992, and the **Bridgestone-Firestone strike** of 1994 to 1996. The USWA has also become more ethnically and racially diverse. Today, it represents about 675,000 members. USWA membership fluctuates monthly, as under its rules members only pay **dues** when they're employed. It also represents about 600,000 retired workers in the United States and Canada. Its broad-based membership includes steel, aluminum, copper, container, brick, glass, and technical workers.

Suggested Readings: Paul Clark, Petter Gottleib, and Donald Kennedy, eds., *Forging A Union of Steel: Philip Murray, SWOC, and the United Steelworkers*, 1987; John Hoerr, *And the Wolf Finally Came*, 1988; "United Steelworkers of America," http://www.uswa.org/uswa/program/content/index.php.

Jonathan Rees

Uprising of the 20,000 (1909). Approximately 20,000 workers, 80 percent of them women, mostly between the ages of sixteen and twenty-four, and almost entirely Jewish, were involved in the manufacture of ladies' garments in New York City in 1909. The strikers were mostly women but the leadership of the **International Ladies' Garment Workers' Union (ILGWU)** was mostly male. The **strike** was called in reaction to the brutality of the police against **picketers** at the Triangle Shirtwaist Factory, where workers were on strike. Employers retaliated by hiring thugs to beat workers and by hiring prostitutes to harass the young women on the picket lines and suggest, lasciviously, that the young women turn to prostitution if they were dissatisfied with garment-industry **wages**. The strike called attention to the ease with which employers could fire troublesome employees, the sixteen-hour workdays during the garment season, and the periods of compulsory unemployment in the off-season. High-paying jobs, such as tailoring and cutting, were reserved for men, while women were confined to labor-intensive sewing, basting, and finishing. Prior to the uprising of the 20,000, women in New York City's garment trade were widely regarded as unorganizable. Although the strike was not a success, it caused the **American Federation of Labor (AFL)** to reconsider its stance on organizing women, and it strengthened the ILGWU.

Suggested Readings: Charlotte Baum, Paula Hyman, and Sonya Michel, *The Jewish Woman in America*, 1976; Elizabeth Ewan, *Immigrant Women in the Land of Dollars*, 1985.

James P. Hanlan

Utopianism. Utopianism is a belief in an ideal society free from social and economic imperfections. The term dates to the early-sixteenth-century writing of Sir Thomas More, though ideological uses of the term utopian are of more recent vintage. During the nineteenth century, numerous workers, thinkers, and social activists sought to reorganize society and ameliorate the ills brought by inequality and industrialization. American labor and social activists imported much of their utopian bent from Europe. During the French Revolution, François-Noël Babeuf led a secret movement that laid the groundwork for early-nineteenth-century schemes in European utopianism. Others followed. Charles Fourier, in his 1820 *Theory of Social Organization*, called for a new social order featuring the phalanx, which would organize labor on a more rational basis and allow greater flexibility in a worker's life. Numerous short-lived Fourier-inspired phalanxes appeared in the antebellum United States.

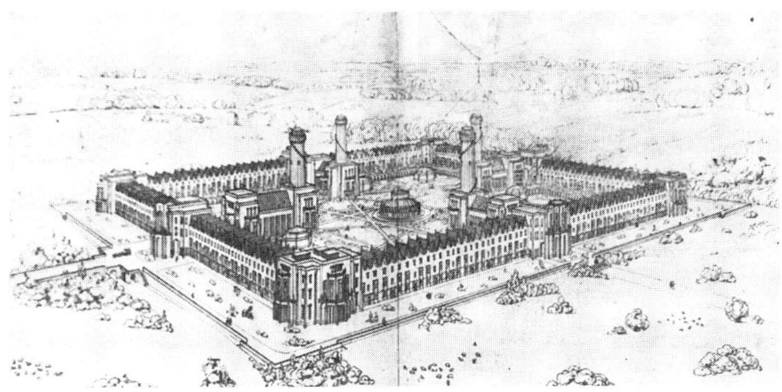

A depiction of Robert Owen's utopian community at Harmony, Indiana. © George Meany Memorial Archives/Library of Congress.

The **Workingmen's Movement** of the 1830s drew inspiration from Robert Owen's experiments in New Lanarck, Scotland. Both Owen and his son, **Robert Dale Owen**, immigrated to the United States in 1824 to establish a New Lanarck spin-off at New Harmony, Indiana, one of the best-known models of American utopianism. While promoting a **cooperative** ethos, New Harmony could not sustain its viability as an independent, cohesive community and soon folded.

In antebellum New York, the Oneida community offered a particularly American version of utopianism by combining radical versions of economic, religious, and sexual life. Under the leadership of John Humphrey Noyes, Oneida lasted for several decades, emphasizing the notions of Biblical communism, Christian perfectionism, and gender equality. Like New Harmony, ideological and cultural differences surfaced and doomed the community. The very nature of these experiments, however, suggested that the revolutionary nature of industrializing **capitalism** forced many Americans to reappraise their relation to the evolving social order and seek new alternative lifestyles.

Radicals often admired utopian experiments, even while criticizing them. In the *Communist Manifesto*, Karl Marx and Frederick Engels viewed the utopian impulse as a significant working-class movement, though one that failed because its adherents lacked an understanding of class struggle. As they saw it, inattention to class dynamics caused utopians to rely on bourgeois interests and place too much hope in nonrevolutionary palliatives. For most of the nineteenth century, however, belief in human perfection remained a powerful ideal. After the Civil War, the Grange, Farmers' Alliances, and the **Knights of Labor (KOL)** engaged in numerous **cooperative** experiments. Utopian novels enjoyed wide popularity, especially Edward Bellamy's *Looking Backward*. That book inspired a movement known as **Bellamyite Nationalism** that involved thousands of Americans in the effort to make the writer's fictive utopia a social reality.

Utopian movements weakened in the twentieth century, though New York City's Greenwich Village fostered a communal movement prior to World War I, and counterculture activists revived those ideals in the 1960s and 1970s. During the 1930s, New Deal programs experimented with collective farms and village settlements. Within the labor movement, however, the utopian impulse largely gave way to concentrating more intently on issues of **wages**, hours, and working conditions.

Suggested Readings: Spencer Klaw, *Without Sin: The Life and Death of the Oneida Community*, 1994; "The Robert Owen Museum," http://robert-owen.midwales.com/index.html.

Timothy Draper

V

Voluntarism. Voluntarism is the reliance on uncoerced action to maintain an institution, carry out a policy, or achieve an end. It is used particularly in reference to joining a union and was one of the foundational principles of the early **American Federation of Labor (AFL)** under **Samuel Gompers**. Voluntarism also involves distrust of governmental authority. It values the liberty of workers to determine their own forms of union organization and methods without outside interference.

According to Gompers, voluntarism advances labor unionism in a number of ways. First, it binds workers to a union that delivers health, unemployment, and retirement benefits. Second, voluntarism isolates workers from hostile state power by limiting government interference in the labor movement and making workers immune from antilabor courts. Finally, voluntarism's values of individual ingenuity and initiative allegedly give workers more power to put pressure on employers to recognize the right of self-organization.

Voluntarism is a vague self-help construct that was more likely clear to Gompers than to most **rank and file** AFL members. In practice, its political nonpartisanship and suspicion of all governmental action often led to decisions that members questioned. The AFL's refusal to endorse political candidates or embrace popular third-party movements engendered tension. Likewise, many AFL members questioned Gompers's logic in 1919, when he opposed unemployment compensation on the grounds that workers and their unions, not the state, needed to solve the problem of joblessness. Although never officially repudiated, the concept of voluntarism was dealt a mortal blow in the 1930s, when New Deal policies altered the relationship of workers to the state.

Suggested Readings: Ronald Filippelli, *Labor in the USA: A History*, 1984; Bruce Laurie, *Artisans Into Workers*, 1989.

Cornelia McAndrew

Vorse, Mary Heaton (October 9, 1874–June 14, 1966). Mary Heaton Vorse was a **labor journalist**, reformer, and feminist. Born in New York City, Vorse was the only child of Hiram and Ellen (Blackman) Heaton. She was raised in Amherst, Massachusetts, in a well-to-do home. Her father owned a prosperous inn in the Berkshires, and Mary regularly traveled to Europe, where she received much of her education. In 1898, she married writer Albert Vorse, and the couple maintained homes in New York and Provincetown, Massachusetts, where she organized a Montessori school and was involved with the Provincetown Players, an experimental theater group. Vorse also began her career as a writer, submitting articles on Italian education to the *Woman's Home Companion*.

In 1910, her husband died, and Vorse turned to her writing for financial and emotional support. Much of Vorse's early writing included sketches and short stories that appeared in various periodicals. Her labor activism dates from the 1912 **Lawrence textile strike**, which she covered for *Harper's Weekly*. Some credit her colorful dispatches as a reason why the **Industrial Workers of the World (IWW)** were able to win said strike. The Lawrence strike led her to befriend IWW leader **Elizabeth Gurley Flynn** and radical journalist Joseph O'Brien. She married O'Brien in 1912, and their son was born two years later.

The Lawrence strike radicalized Vorse, and she began devoting her life and writing to progressive and labor causes. Among the **strikes** Vorse covered were those involving Minnesota iron-ore miners in 1916, the national **steel strike of 1919**, and the 1920 **Amalgamated Clothing Workers of America** strike. Vorse also attended the Women's International Peace Conference at The Hague in 1915, and she covered several international conferences devoted to women's suffrage. During World War I, Vorse worked as a war correspondent for the Hearst newspaper chain, and she reported on the famine gripping the Soviet Union in 1921–22. She also covered the **Sacco and Vanzetti** case and was convinced of their innocence.

Joseph O'Brien died of cancer in 1915; to ease her grief, she was prescribed morphine, to which she became addicted. In 1920, she cohabited with Robert Minor, a cartoonist for *The Masses* and later the secretary of the Communist Party USA. After a miscarriage and separation from Minor, Vorse's morphine addiction worsened, and she did not free herself of its grip until late 1925. Vorse then resumed her career as a labor journalist and reported on numerous upheavals, including textile strikes in Passaic, New Jersey, in 1926, and in Gastonia, North Carolina, in 1929. From those experiences came two novels.

During the 1930s, Vorse chronicled the rise of fascism in Europe, events inside the Soviet Union, and the emergence of the **Congress of Industrial Organizations (CIO)** at home. The latter inspired her 1938 book *Labor's New*

Millions, her best-known book. She also served briefly with the Bureau of Indian Affairs. Vorse was a target of post–World War II red-baiting. Her last major work of investigative journalism was a 1952 analysis of internal corruption in waterfront unions controlled by organized crime. She remained an unrepentant radical throughout the 1950s, a situation that led to de facto retirement. Vorse's commitment to labor, feminism, global peace, and democratic **socialism** helped rehabilitate her image in the 1960s. The **United Auto Workers** awarded her its Social Justice Award in 1962. She died at her Provincetown home on June 14, 1966.

Suggested Readings: *AFL-CIO News* June 25, 1966; Dee Garrison, *Mary Heaton Vorse*, 1989; Barbara Sicherman, *Notable American Women: The Modern Period*, 1980.

Leslie Juntunen
Robert E. Weir

W

Wage Differential. The term wage differential refers to the difference in **wages** earned by workers in the same job. It occurs most often on shift-work jobs, wherein a worker on a late-night shift might get a higher wage than someone on the more desirable day shift. Wage differentials also occur on jobs that require more skill. For example, a worker with knowledge of maintaining a machine might get a higher wage than a line worker. Wage differentials are usually negotiated between unions and management through **collective bargaining**.

Wage differentials also exist regionally, and these regional differentials are of more concern to unions. For many decades, textile workers in the South received lower pay than those in the North. This had the effect of deflating wages across the industry, and made constant the threat to close factories in the North and relocate them in South. In recent years, the same threat looms from low-wage developing nations.

Suggested Reading: American Bar Association, *The Developing Labor Law,* 2001.

Cornelia McAndrew

Wages. Wages are the set amount of monies paid to workers. The term wage does not apply to all remuneration for labor, but more specifically to that paid to the hourly employee. The wage is payment for labor hired on a short-term basis or workers employed in actual production, as distinct from the payment made to hired professional and white-collar employees, which is called **salary**.

Unions generally see wage negotiation as one of their primary tasks during **contract** bargaining, although this has not historically been the case. In the nineteenth and early twentieth centuries, unions like the **Knights of Labor** and the **Industrial Workers of the World** called for an end to the wage system. **Capitalism** was still contested, with many workers seeing wages as a form of social and economic dependency. They were also troubled by the fact that under the wage system, investors, speculators, and management generally made more money than ordinary workers yet did no productive labor. Those opposed to the wage system advocated replacing it with economic arrangements that linked productive labor to remuneration. Those included **cooperatives**, communal labor, and syndicalism.

The **American Federation of Labor** was the first important labor organization to endorse the wage system unequivocally, and today, wage labor is considered the norm. In unionized environments, unions usually negotiate hourly wages. In nonunion businesses, employers unilaterally set monetary scales, but must often take into account the compensation in the industry or a local region. Some businesses will pay a union scale to dampen labor organizing.

Suggested Readings: American Bar Association, *The Developing Labor Law*, 2001; Frank Elkouri and Edna Elkouri, *How Arbitration Works*, 1997.

Cornelia McAndrew

Wage Stabilization. Wage stabilization is a government policy usually instituted during wartime or under extreme economic conditions to control **wages** and prices through legislative action. Beginning in World War I, federal agencies intervened in industrial conflicts as mediators to try to strike a balance between the demands of labor and management to maintain peace in the workplace and ensure uninterrupted production of war material. During the Great Depression, President Franklin Roosevelt's New Deal programs promoted wage increases, but only as a way of taming political and economic unrest until the economy improved. World War II took the economy out of the depression, but that same conflict also ushered in a whole new series of government initiatives like the **National War Labor Board**, which, for the most part, froze wages. However, organized labor managed to gain **concessions** in other areas making it easier to recruit new members on jobs with federal **contracts**. Similar, but less draconian, stabilization efforts reappeared during the Korean and Vietnam Wars. Although labor unions usually chafed under such policies, they routinely bargained for legislative tradeoffs that bore future dividends.

Suggested Readings: Jack Barbash, *The Practice of Unionism*, 1956; Melvyn Dubofsky, *The State and Labor in Modern America*, 1994.

Scott Molloy

Walsh-Healey Public Contracts Act (1936). The Walsh-Healey Public Contracts Act of 1936 provided general employment regulations for employers who received contracts from any department, agency, or instrumentality of the federal government in any amount exceeding $10,000. Federal contractors were required to pay the federal **minimum wage** plus an established **overtime** rate (time and a half) for hours in excess of eight hours per day, or forty hours per week. Males under sixteen years of age and females under eighteen years of age were barred from employment by contractors as was convict labor (except under carefully defined circumstances). Contractors were required to maintain safe and sanitary working conditions. Enforcement of the act was the responsibility of the secretary of labor. Contractors accused of violating the law's provisions were entitled to a hearing, but failure to comply could result in fines, penalties for actual and liquidated damages, and the cost of recontracting the work. Equally as important, violators could be placed on a list of debarred bidders, effectively eliminating a company's ability to obtain work under any federal contract. Contractors were required to keep certain information about their employees, including logs of hours worked, wages paid, and dates of birth for a period of three years and to make a public posting of the law's requirements at the place of employment.

The Walsh-Healey Act has been amended since its enactment but remains in effect to the present time. Its provisions remain a staple of human resouces departments throughout the country.

Suggested Readings: U.S. Department of Labor, http://library.dol.gov/oasam/regs/statutes/41-35.htm; Arnold Thieblot. Jr., *Prevailing Wage Legislation: The Davis-Bacon Act, State "Little Davis-Bacon" Acts, the Walsh-Healey Act, and the Service Contract Act, 1986.*

James P. Hanlan

War Labor Disputes Act (Smith-Connally Act). The War Labor Disputes Act was an attempt by conservative Democrats and Republicans to curtail strikes and rising union might during World War II. It passed in June 1943 and is also known as the Smith-Connally Act for its congressional sponsors, Virginia Democrat Howard Smith and Texas Democrat John Connally. It was precipitated by a series of labor shortages, predominately in the coal industry, that idled some 1.3 million workers in the first half of 1943. Public-opinion polls revealed widespread support for shackling the **United Mine Workers of America (UMWA)** and its president, **John L. Lewis**.

The bill gave the government the right to take over any production facility involved in the war effort if the workforce went on **strike**, and it allowed for the prosecution of those who instigated strikes. The bill further required union leaders to notify management of its intention to walk out, mandated a thirty-day cooling-off period before a strike could proceed, and required the National Labor Relations Board (NLRB) to hold a strike vote after thirty days to determine if workers still wished to strike. The bill also prohibited union contributions to political campaigns.

Both the **American Federation of Labor (AFL)** and the **Congress of Industrial Organizations (CIO)** opposed the bill, while Lewis denounced it as a "slave act." President Roosevelt vetoed the bill, arguing that government-imposed cooling-off periods and strike votes would only encourage **walkouts**. Congress overrode Roosevelt's veto, but his reservations proved prophetic. In the first three months the bill was in effect, the NLRB held fifty-three strike votes resulting in forty-seven work stoppages. Moreover, workers engaged in over 1,900 walkouts in the last half of 1943 without paying any attention to the act.

Ironically, the bill also increased labor's participation in politics. In July 1943, the CIO established its Political Action Committee (PAC) to funnel money to prounion candidates. Following the advice of Lee Pressman, the CIO's general counsel, the CIO advised its affiliates that the Smith-Connally Act did not prohibit contributions for primary candidates, nor did it prevent unions from spending money on candidates through intermediary groups. The PAC ultimately increased interest in politics and led the CIO to push voter education and registration. The act's many loopholes rendered it ineffective, but it nonetheless signaled congressional intent to limit union power. Key parts of the bill resurfaced in antiunion bills like the **Taft-Hartley Act** and the Labor Management Reporting and Disclosure Act.

Suggested Readings: James Foster, *The Union Politic*, 1975; Joel Siedman, *American Labor from Defense to Reconversion*, 1953; Robert Zieger, *The CIO, 1935–1955*, 1995.

James Wolfinger

Watsonville Strike. The Watsonville strike was a **strike** from 1985 to 1987 of some 1,000 women against the Watsonville Canning Company. The strike ultimately pitted the mostly Latina, Mexicana, and Chicana workforce against their own **International Brotherhood of Teamsters (IBT)** union. Although it ended in wage **concessions**, the strike inspired the labor movement because of its **solidarity**, as well as its role in helping reform the Teamsters. It also demonstrated that a supposedly hard-to-galvanize group, Spanish-speaking women, were in fact capable labor unionists.

The Watsonville Canning Company in California's Salinas Valley was among the many firms that demanded concessions during the 1980s. Although its largely female workforce made only $6.66 per hour, Watsonville demanded cuts to $4.25 and an end to health-care benefits. Watsonville officials were also intent on breaking IBT **pattern bargaining** in the region. They were joined by Richard Shaw, Inc., which also demanded wage concessions.

The workers faced seemingly insurmountable odds. First, the strike came during the antilabor administration of President Ronald Reagan, which saw numerous **downsizing, decertification, and concessions strikes** end in routs of the affected unions. Second, the strikers were largely Latina, whereas the local town council and agribusiness management were Anglo. Third, the IBT was a troubled union around which swirled charges of union corruption that were soon verified. By most accounts, Teamster officials were ready to grant concessions to both Watsonville and Shaw.

Teamsters Local 912 managed to unify workers at both plants, and on September 9, 1985, more than a thousand women walked out. Local 912 received logistical support from Teamsters for a Democratic Union (TDU), a reform movement of dissident IBT members. Although TDU could not offer much, it did help strikers organize their own strike committee and set up needed support systems. The women of Watsonville maintained unparalleled levels of solidarity; not a single member crossed **picket** lines. They also proved adroit at soliciting support from other sources, especially Spanish-speaking members of the **Hotel Employees and Restaurant Employees International Union** and the **United Farm Workers of America (UFW)**. UFW President **Cesar Chavez** attended a Watsonville rally, as did the Reverend Jesse Jackson. San Francisco–area women also raised money for the strikers during a 1985 International Women's Day rally.

The most remarkable achievement of the strikers was their ability to cultivate family and transnational networks. Watsonville attempted the popular tactic of importing **scabs**, declaring them **replacement workers**, and encouraging them to **decertify** the union. Since most of the scabs were also Latina, strikers called upon a vast kinship network that applied pressure to families of replacement workers as distant as Mexico and Texas. Watsonville officials were stunned when in August 1986, replacement workers voted to retain Local 912 as its **bargaining unit**.

That action did not bring the strike to a close, however. Wells Fargo Bank loaned Watsonville $23 million in 1985. At the suggestion of Cesar Chavez, a modified **corporate campaign** targeted the bank. In May 1986, Local 912 began encouraging local unions to withdraw funds from Wells Fargo. Within weeks, Wells Fargo drove Watsonville into bankruptcy. It was purchased by Gill Davis, a grower owed millions by Watsonville. The Teamsters immediately accepted his offer to end the strike.

By then, however, the IBT no longer had the respect of the Local 912 **rank and file**. Membership rejected the new **contract**, as some workers lost medical benefits under it. The IBT cut off strike funds to Local 912 and tried to place it under trusteeship. Instead, Local 912 ousted its president, Richard King, and replaced him with Sergio Lopez, who was sympathetic to the strike's continuation. Finally, on March 11, 1987, Davis offered a contract that extended health care to all workers.

The Watsonville strike was not a complete success. In the end, workers saw their **wages** cut to $5.85 an hour, the amount Shaw workers accepted in early 1986. Given their already-low wages, it took years to recoup lost wages. Nonetheless, the willingness of Latina women to hold out for eighteen months inspired union workers across the country. The strikers also brought more light to the internal corruption of the Teamsters, paving the way for long-needed reforms.

Suggested Readings: Jeremy Brecher, "Resisting Concessions," http://www.zmag.org/ZMag/articles/brechermay98.htm; James Green, *Taking History to Heart: The Power of Building Social Movements*, 2000; Kim Moody, *An Injury to All: The Decline of American Unionism*, 1989.

Robert E. Weir

Welfare Capitalism. Welfare capitalism is a practice whereby employers provide a variety of benefits for their workers in the hope or expectation of ensuring a loyal workforce. It has been a popular business practice, especially in good economic times, since the nineteenth century. In the nineteenth century, factory owners sometimes saw themselves in a **paternal** role, taking care of the workers in exchange for their loyalty and hard work. Such employers tended to see worker unions and **collective bargaining** as betrayals of this reciprocal relationship. In the twentieth century, employers utilized welfare capitalist measures often specifically to counteract the appeal of union membership by providing services and benefits as good as, if not better than, those the union could provide. Typical welfare capitalist benefits of the twentieth century included **pensions**, paid vacation, sick leave, and **profit sharing**. Services at the workplace might be provided, such as cafeterias, well-appointed restrooms, libraries, and lounges. Loyalty and a feeling of stake holding might also be obtained through worker-advisory councils and recreational activities such as company picnics or athletic contests. Large companies used welfare capitalism extensively in the prosperous 1920s, but the practice declined quickly during the Great Depression of the 1930s as companies cut costs. As laws became friendly to organized labor in the 1930s, and collective bargaining became the norm in labor management relations, companies increasingly negotiated with unions over providing benefits as part of their labor **contracts**. No longer were pensions and vacations due to the "benevolence" of the company, they were demands to be fought for. By the 1950s and 1960s, they had become expectations.

In the last decades of the twentieth century, many nonunion firms, especially those in technological industries, looked again to welfare capitalism to attract and retain quality workers. Some employers revived earlier practices such as athletic teams and company picnics. Others took into account the modern realities of two-income families or single parenthood by allowing for flexible start times or providing on-site child-care centers. Employee concerns with physical fitness were sometimes met with company-provided exercise facilities, keeping the workers physically and psychologically connected to the workplace. Welfare capitalism has the potential for virtually infinite variations and has been a highly adaptable practice.

Suggested Readings: Stuart D. Brandes, *American Welfare Capitalism, 1880–1940*, 1970; Sanford M. Jacoby, *Modern Manors: Welfare Capitalism Since the New Deal*, 1997.

Elizabeth Jozwiak

West Virginia Mine War, 1919–22. The series of violent confrontations collectively known as the West Virginia Mine War began in late 1919 with the start of the **United Mine Workers of America (UMWA)** organizing campaign in the largely nonunion southern West Virginia coalfields. Mine operators had kept the region nonunion through a combination of **contracts** that prohibited miners from joining unions (commonly called **yellow-dog contracts**) and operatives of the Baldwin-Felts Detective Agency, who enforced the contracts. When the UMWA's organizing campaign began, those miners who joined the union or supported it were fired and evicted from their company homes. As the conflict dragged on into the spring, tent colonies of striking miners and their families began to appear throughout southern West Virginia. The first major confrontation between miners and operators came in May 1920 at the village of **Matewan** in Mingo County. Eleven Baldwin-Felts detectives, including Albert and Lee Felts, brothers of one of the agency's partners, arrived at Matewan by train to evict striking miners in the area. The evictions themselves were carried out without difficulty. However, when the detectives returned to the train station at Matewan, they were confronted by the town sheriff Sid Hatfield, the town's mayor, and a large group of angry miners. Hatfield apparently ordered the detectives to surrender their weapons. When the detectives refused, an argument ensued. At some point, a shot was fired, and the street in front of the station erupted in a gun battle that left seven detectives, including Albert and Lee Felts, dead. The Matewan mayor and two miners were also killed.

The battle at Matewan made headlines all over the nation and inaugurated months of violent conflict. Armed miners throughout the region began closing down the mines. Operators responded by importing strikebreakers and more detectives. Shootouts between prounion miners and mine guards and **scabs** became commonplace. Company property, including shaft houses and coal cars, was also destroyed. Finally, the governor declared a state of martial law and brought in federal troops to maintain order. With the introduction of troops, the fighting stopped. However, when the troops were withdrawn in September 1920, the violence began again. In May 1921, a three-day battle erupted around the town Merrimac on the Tug River between striking miners and a combination of mine guards, state police, and deputy sheriffs. The battle spread up the river and across into Kentucky. When it was finally over, nearly twenty people had been killed.

Tension levels remained high, and President Warren Harding was hesitant to send federal troops into the area again, possibly out of fear that the West Virginia governor saw federal troops as his private police force. Instead, the governor of West Virginia took matters into his own hands. The state police force was enlarged, and the National Guard was reconstituted. Both of these institutions began enlisting and training anyone who would join. Local communities also began deputizing local businessmen for service in the conflict. These new forces quickly moved to suppress the miners. Under martial law, all meetings were prohibited, and any conversation between two or more miners was forbidden. Union miners were also arrested for carrying any prounion literature and were not released until they promised to leave the state. National Guard troops, state police, and local sheriffs invaded and destroyed the tent colonies where the evicted miners lived.

In January 1921, Sid Hatfield and several others who had taken part in the shootout at Matewan were tried for the murder of the seven detectives at Matewan. All the defendants were acquitted. However, Hatfield and his friend, Ed Chambers, were called before a grand jury in McDowell County for questioning in another shooting. When Hatfield and Chambers arrived at Walsh, the county seat, in August, they were gunned down in front of their wives on the courthouse steps by Baldwin-Felts detectives. The murder of Sid Hatfield, who had become a local hero after Matewan, enraged the miners. Throughout the region, miners began to assemble at Lens Creek, south of Charleston, with the intention of marching through Logan and Mingo Counties, breaking martial law and liberating union miners from jail. As the small army of miners began to move toward Logan County, their organization became apparent. Although there was no "general" leading the army, it had its own medical and commissary facilities as well as passwords and patrols. As they marched, they confiscated whatever supplies they needed from local communities, or brought them from Charleston. They also hijacked trains and cars to increase their progress.

In response to the miners army, the sheriff of Logan County, Don Chafin, began to assemble his own army. A combination of National Guard, state police, deputized businessmen, and conscripted strikebreakers, armed with rifles, machine guns, and even a few airplanes, Chafin's army met the miners at **Blair Mountain**. The fighting at Blair Mountain lasted for over a week, but in spite of fierce fighting on both sides, little was accomplished, and neither side could dislodge the other. With the reports of fighting in Logan County, the federal government acted by declaring southern West Virginia in a state of insurrection. Federal troops under the command of General Henry Bandholtz descended on the region from several directions. The presence of federal troops effectively ended the fighting. Although the miners bitterly hated the mine operators and their supporters, they were unwilling to confront the federal government. Miners began turning over their weapons to federal troops, or simply hid them, and returned to their homes. Don Chafin's army returned to a hero's welcome.

In the aftermath of the West Virginia Mine War, some 550 individuals were brought up on charges ranging from treason to murder. However, as the miners' army had no significant leader to blame, it proved very hard to establish treason. Also, the heavy involvement of the mine operators in support of the prosecution cast doubt on the purpose of the trials. As a result, most of the miners were acquitted.

Suggested Readings: David Alan Corbin, *Life, Work, and Rebellion in the Coal Fields: The Southern West Virginia Miners 1880–1922*, 1981; *Matewan* [video] Los Angeles: Evergreen Entertainment, 1996; Lon Savage, *Thunder in the Mountains: The West Virginia Mine War, 1920–21*, 1990.

Jim Riordan

White-Collar Workers. *See Blue-Collar Workers.*

Wildcat Strike. A wildcat **strike** is an unplanned, spontaneous, and short-lived work stoppage. Most occur in response to local conditions and are not authorized by the union. Relatively few of them involve **wages**. Instead they often involve issues to which labor leadership does not attribute much importance or feels lie outside its purview. While radical unions such as the **Industrial Workers of the World** advocate the tactic, most contemporary unions view wildcat strikes as anathema. The 1947 **Taft-Hartley Act** prohibited the use of wildcat strikes, and unions are subject to heavy fines if members engage in them and the union does not do its utmost to end them. Safety issues often trigger wildcats, especially in mining where local stoppages often occur after a worker is injured. During the 1960s and 1970s, some **rank-and-file** workers engaged in wildcat strikes to express their displeasure with union leadership. Wildcat strikes are rare, however, as workers engaging in them abrogate most legal protection. A 1970 Supreme Court decision, *Boys Market Inc. v. Retail Clerks Union Local 770*, dealt a further blow to wildcat strikes when the court ruled that no-strike clauses were implied in union **contracts**, even if they were not specifically stated.

Suggested Readings: Leigh Benin, *The New Labor Radicalism and New York City's Garment Industry: Progressive Labor During the 1960s*, 1999; Jeremy Brecher, *Strike!*, 1997; Martin Glaberman, "Wildcat Strikes" in Mari Jo Buhle, Paul Buhle, and Dan Georgakas, *Encyclopedia of the American Left*, 1992.

Evan Daniel

Winpisinger, William W(ayne) (December 10, 1924–December 11, 1997). William Winpisinger served as president of the **International Association of Machinists and Aerospace Workers (IAM)** from 1977 through 1989 and as a vice president of the American Federation of Labor-Congress of Industrial Organizations (AFL-CIO). Known to his friends as "Wimp" or "Wimpy," he was once described by A. H. Raskin as "the Stanley Kowalski of American Labor," due to his gruff manner and beefy appearance. Winpisinger described himself as a self-conscious seat-of-the-pants **socialist**. He was born in Cleveland, Ohio, the son of a **journeyman** printer at the Cleveland *Plain Dealer*. Winpisinger dropped out of high school to join the navy during World War II, serving in the Mediterranean and the English Channel, where he learned and practiced the trade of a diesel mechanic from 1942 to 1945. Upon discharge, Winpisinger returned to Cleveland and, opposing his father's wishes that he become a newspaper stereotyper, worked as a mechanic. An active member of Lodge 1363 of the IAM, by 1949 Winpisinger was elected president of the 1,300-member local. Winpisinger's skills at **contract** negotiation, **grievance,** and **arbitration** cases, and organizing led to his appointment with the IAM's Midwestern field staff and by 1958 his transfer to IAM headquarters in Washington, D.C. At headquarters, Winpisinger organized truck and auto mechanics, served in the aerospace unit, and performed masterfully as a special troubleshooter for the union's president. He became national automobile coordinator with responsibility for 120,000 members. Eventually his responsibilities included railroad and airline workers as well. By 1977, Winpisinger was administrative chief of staff for the IAM.

The IAM was chiefly for skilled workers, and its members and leaders alike took an elitist viewpoint of restricting membership to the skilled. Winpisinger was an advocate for **industrial unionism** within the IAM and favored mass organizing based on the model of his heroes **John L. Lewis** and **Walter Reuther**. Realizing that his views were in the minority, Winpisinger did not raise the hackles of his fellow union leaders, who tolerated his views because of his superb skills at **collective bargaining** and his tendency to get the best possible deal for his members. When president Floyd E. (Red) Smith retired in 1977, Winpisinger was the natural choice to succeed him.

The union that Winpisinger took over had grown from its 1888 roots as a union of railroad mechanics to encompass the transportation, electronics, and aerospace industries. It was the third largest affiliate of the AFL-CIO and the fifth largest union in North America. Only the **International Brotherhood of Teamsters** had a more diverse industrial base. Nevertheless, membership had dropped from a high of 1 million to about 750,000. Winpisinger insisted that both the IAM and the AFL-CIO needed a dose of old-fashioned activism to restore membership. Within two years, Winpisinger had the membership rolls back to about 900,000. He began quietly by forming alliances with other AFL-CIO leaders known as the "progressive bloc," a group critical of the lethargic and conservative leadership provided by **George Meany**. Winpisinger took to the road to present the case both for the IAM and for unionism in general. His goal was to restore the tarnished image of unions and make a case for stabilizing and improving the economic position of America's union workers. His task, he argued, was formidable, for the reputation of labor unions was "just ahead of Richard Nixon and just behind the used car dealers." Winpisinger began youth programs, sponsored prizes for auto-race mechanics, and insisted that broadcasters present an unbiased view of labor unions or face opposition to license renewal in front of the Federal Communications Commission. Winpisinger did not shrink from political activism and insisted on backing only those politicians whose labor records were solid. In this context, he once referred to President Jimmy Carter as "the best Republican president since Herbert Hoover." Similarly, he referred to Energy Secretary James R. Schlesinger as "a nazi." Winpisinger took public stances on energy policy and limiting defense spending (in spite of his union's large presence in the defense industry). The IAM's Machinists Non-Partisan Political League became the nation's eighth largest nonpartisan political donor and was fifth largest among union political contributors. Winpisinger served as a vice president of the Americans for Democratic Action and was a prominent member of Michael Harrington's Democratic Socialist Organizing Committee.

In spite of his radical views, Winpisinger remained enormously popular within the IAM. He was seen as a man who rose through the ranks, who fought for, and advanced, the interests of his members, who never lost touch with his **working-class** roots, and who bargained pragmatically and creatively with employers. He was even admired by Eastern Airlines President Frank Borman for his willingness to consider innovative **salary** agreements. Thus members of a conservative union could embrace Winpisinger in spite of what Sidney Lens called "the sharpest [recent] indictment of American **capitalism** uttered by a prominent union official." Winpisinger viewed the American worker and the government alike as potential victims of the corporate state, where the rhetoric of a free-market economy and free-enterprise propaganda endangered both economic and political freedoms. His down-to-earth manner, devotion to working for progressive and pragmatic change, as well as the power of his intellect, endeared him to his union. William Winpisinger and his wife, Pearl, had five children, two of whom followed their father into the mechanic's trade. William Winpisinger died in Howard County, Maryland, on December 11, 1997.

Suggested Reading: William Winpisinger, *Reclaiming Our Future: An Agenda for American Labor*, 1989.

James P. Hanlan

Wobbly. Wobbly is a term used to refer to members of the **Industrial Workers of the World (IWW)** and sometimes shortened to "Wob." The exact origins of the term are unknown, and it does not appear in usage until 1913. The term may be related to the verb wobble. Many members of the IWW toiled in unskilled positions on docks and railroads. One theory holds that the term may have originated from either longshoremen wobbling under their loads or from railroad men prying long tamping irons under rails and lifting themselves into the air to gain leverage. The latter created a midair wobble. Still another theory links the term to Chinese members' attempts to pronounce the difficult *w* consonant. Those with little English proficiency might pronounce IWW as "eye-wobble-u-wobble-u." Still others postulate Australian or exotic-dance connections. There is no conclusive proof for any theory. After 1913, however, union members freely and proudly appropriated the term.

Suggested Reading: Archie Green, *Wobblies, Pile Butts, and Other Heroes: Laborlore Explorations*, 1993.

Robert E. Weir

Women and Labor. *See Minority Labor. See also Protective Labor Legislation, as well as specific organizations and individuals.*

Women's Trade Union League (WTUL). The Women's Trade Union League (WTUL) was founded in Boston in 1903 to campaign for shorter hours, higher **wages**, and better working conditions for working women. The WTUL partially filled the void in women's trade unionism left by the decline of the **Knights of Labor**, as most unions affiliated with the **American Federation of Labor (AFL)** either excluded women or showed little interest in organizing them. The American WTUL was patterned after an eponymous group founded in England in 1874. A 1902 **boycott** by housewives of kosher butchers inspired William English Walling, a New York City settlement-house worker, to go to England and learn how the WTUL operated there. Walling and **Mary Kenney**

O'Sullivan drew up plans for an American WTUL with the aid of **Samuel Gompers**, though future AFL support for the WTUL was minimal.

Many of the early WTUL leaders were drawn from the settlement-house movement and included figures like Lillian Wald, Agnes Nestor, Vida Scudder, **Leonora O'Reilly**, and Jane Addams. The WTUL hoped to promote the cause of women trade unionists and convince women workers to join unions, but its membership also included sympathetic middle-class women who were not wage-earners, a structural arrangement for which some criticized it. The WTUL grew under the dynamic leadership of Margaret Dreier Robins, who served as president from 1906 until 1922. The organization played an important role in the 1909 **Uprising of the 20,000**, raising money to support strikers, urging **boycotts** of firms being struck, and organizing mass protests. The strike was said to be the largest strike of women in labor history to that point. The WTUL also investigated the **Triangle Factory Fire of 1911** and used the tragedy to promote its causes. It also supported the **Industrial Workers of the World** during the 1912 Bread and Roses strike in **Lawrence**, Massachusetts.

The all-female staff working in the headquarters of the Women's Trade Union League of New York during the Shirtwaist Strike, January 1910. © Hulton/Archive.

Robins's leadership was marked by controversy. The WTUL supported **protective labor legislation** for women on the grounds that a **minimum wage** and **eight-hour day** were true labor reforms. As these applied only to women, however, feminists decried the essentialist implications of such legislation, and the AFL felt that the WTUL undermined its own **collective bargaining** efforts. Moreover, the WTUL's willingness to work with both the middle class and radicals led some in both camps to distrust it. Thus the WTUL had good relations with some unions—notably the **Amalgamated Clothing Workers of America**—but strained contacts with most AFL trades.

The WTUL also immersed itself in the suffrage movement and provided important **working-class** support for the National American Woman Suffrage Association. By the 1920s, much of its work was more political in nature, with the WTUL continuing to lobby for protective labor legislation for women. The election of Franklin Roosevelt in 1932 gave the WTUL a boost, as First Lady Eleanor Roosevelt was a long-time WTUL member. The WTUL's **Rose**

Schneiderman gained access to the White House and was said to have influenced several pieces of New Deal legislation, including the Social Security Act. The WTUL was less successful in its campaign to remove laws and customs barring married women from working during the Great Depression.

The WTUL's influence waned on the eve of World War II, though it continued to offer classes for working women in everything from history to vocational training. It officially dissolved in 1950, but should be considered the forerunner of such groups as the **Coalition of Labor Union Women** and various women's caucuses within the organized labor movement.

Suggested Readings: Philip Foner, *Women and the American Labor Movement*, 2 vols., 1980; Alice Kessler-Harris, *Out to Work: A History of Wage-Earning Women in the United States*, 1982; Jone [*sic*] Johnson Lewis, "Women's History," http://womenshistory.about.com/.

Robert E. Weir

Working Class. Historian E. P. Thompson argues that the only way to understand class is to see it as a "social and cultural formation" that develops over a long period of time. Any study of class must take place within this context and must consider not only the people, but also their relationships and their environment. Thompson's comments concerned the English working class, but can be applied to the American working class as well.

Classes are groups of people connected to one another, and made different from one another, by the ways they interact when producing goods and services. The working class is an economic and social class, involving both men and women, with a particular income, status, and lifestyle. The people who make up this class do not own their own businesses, but rather are hired, paid labor. It is with the help of these people that businesses, and those who own them, are able to accomplish their work and make money.

The working class only started to appear in the United States in the early nineteenth century. Before that, the majority of the population in the United States was either self-employed or slave labor. An increase in industrial activity, as well as population growth, led to hired labor becoming the majority of the population and the subsequent development of a working class. In the beginning of its development, the United States had an active working-class culture that included theater, magazines, books, newspapers, social clubs, and political parties dedicated to working-class life. However, over the years, this culture has weakened as the working class has become more involved with American culture in general.

There are several reasons why the working class is important to American labor history. First, the majority of Americans are working-class people, myths of a middle-class society notwithstanding. Although these people belong to the same class, it does not mean they always think and act the same way. They work in different industries and occupations, and they have different opinions, attitudes, and feelings. A second reason why the working class is important is that working-class life is imperiled in today's changing economic climate.

Many members of the working class fought for legislation that encouraged the establishment of Social Security, **minimum wages**, and occupational health and safety regulations, legislation from which all Americans benefit. As economic change continues, some analysts predict that **blue-collar** work in high-wage industrial jobs will become largely obsolete. Thus far, service-sector employment offers few of the **wage** and **benefit** comforts that labor unions struggled to attain. The transformation from a production to a service economy is unlikely to occur without social disruption, and it is possible that the future will involve disputes, even conflict, between the working class and those above them on the socioeconomic scale.

A final reason to understand the working class is that it has been and remains an important category of analysis for both scholars and activists. Most labor history is written from the assumption that the interests of the working class have been (and are) in opposition to those of the middle and upper classes. In sociological terms, most labor historians are conflict theorists, who see social change emerging from the clash between competing interests. The working class is the primary analytical tool for **socialist**, **communist**, and left-wing political theorists past and present. Karl Marx saw the working class—which he referred to as the "proletarians"—and their unions as a revolutionary force that would overthrow **capitalism** and construct a producer-based **utopia**. Marx did not anticipate advanced nonindustrial economies, thus neo-Marxists have expanded his original conception of the working class to encompass most wage-earners.

At its base, working class refers to power relationships. As long as the U.S. economy remains one in which profound gaps occur in wages, wealth, status, and decision-making authority, the working class will exist both in reality and as an analytical category.

Suggested Readings: Harry Braverman, "The Making of the U.S. Working Class," *Monthly Review*, vol. 46, no. 6 (November 1994); E. P. Thompson, *The Making of the English Working Class*, rev. ed., 1968; Michael Zweig, *The Working Class Majority: America's Best Kept Secret*, 2000.

Lisa J. Wells

Workingmen's Movement. Workingmen's Movement is the term used to identify unionization and third-party political agitation from 1828 through the Panic of 1837. It was not a unified movement, rather a catchall category to describe **working-class** political agitation that was strongest in eastern seaboard cities in the North.

In the 1820s, many **journeymen** began to transform traditional associations into trade unions. In 1827, Philadelphia carpenters struck for a ten-hour workday. That action failed, but the next year they and several other unions formed the Mechanics' Union of Trade Associations, considered by some historians as the first American labor federation. From it came the Workingmen's Party of Philadelphia, a model for other cities. Between 1828 and 1834, hundreds of **strikes** took place in eastern cities, scores of independent political parties formed, and at least sixty-eight **labor journals** were published, the most famous of which was New York City's *Working Man's Advocate*.

Many of the new parties were critical of both the Whigs and the Democrats, though in some places they allied with the latter. They operated under various names including the Workingmen's Party, the Farmer and Mechanics Society, and the Workingmen's Republican Association. Their platforms also varied, but most workingmen's parties called for land and tax reform, the passage of **lien laws**, free public education, the abolition of debtor prisons, shorter work hours, and strict regulations for banks, limited-liability corporations, and the use of labor-saving machinery. Many also adhered to the **labor theory of value**, the belief that the worth of any good or service is determined by the amount of labor put into it. All Workingmen, nicknamed "Workies," rejected Malthusian explanations for poverty and insisted that class privilege and unfair business practices caused privation. The "Workies" put forth a mixed bag of progressive, preindustrial, and agrarian values that was sometimes called **republicanism**.

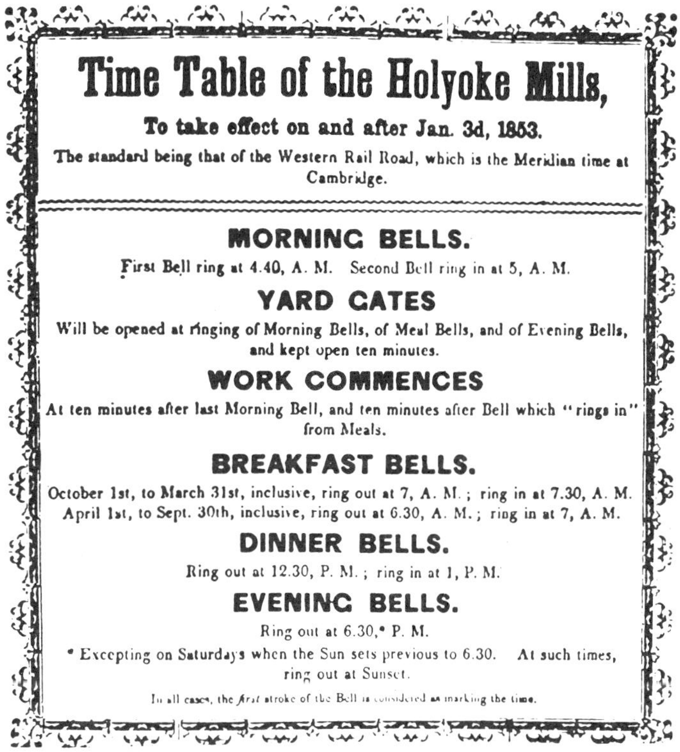

Time Table of the Holyoke Mills,

To take effect on and after Jan. 3d, 1853.

The standard being that of the Western Rail Road, which is the Meridian time at Cambridge.

MORNING BELLS.

First Bell ring at 4.40, A. M. Second Bell ring in at 5, A. M.

YARD GATES

Will be opened at ringing of Morning Bells, of Meal Bells, and of Evening Bells, and kept open ten minutes.

WORK COMMENCES

At ten minutes after last Morning Bell, and ten minutes after Bell which "rings in" from Meals.

BREAKFAST BELLS.

October 1st, to March 31st, inclusive, ring out at 7, A. M.; ring in at 7.30, A. M.
April 1st, to Sept. 30th, inclusive, ring out at 6.30, A. M.; ring in at 7, A. M.

DINNER BELLS.

Ring out at 12.30, P. M.; ring in at 1, P. M.

EVENING BELLS.

Ring out at 6.30,* P. M.

* Excepting on Saturdays when the Sun sets previous to 6.30. At such times, ring out at Sunset.

In all cases, the first stroke of the Bell is considered as marking the time.

Spurred by long workdays imposed by management, such as outlined in this schedule of hours from the textile mills of the Boston Associates, the Workingmen's Movement of the 1830s included a ten-hour workday among its demands. © George Meany Memorial Archives/Public Affairs Press.

Workingmen's parties competed for power throughout the Northeast and initially did very well. New York City sent a carpenter to the state legislature, Philadelphia elected twenty of its fifty-four Workingmen's candidates, and other cities elected Workies to a variety of municipal and state posts. Success proved fleeting, however, and by 1834 the movement was dead in most places. Decline came for many reasons. Coordinated efforts proved difficult because Workingmen leadership varied so greatly. In New York City, for example, **Thomas Skidmore**'s call for the state to seize and redistribute land struck George Henry Evans as so radical that he conspired with others to kick Skidmore out of the party. Another Workingmen's leader, Frances "Fanny" Wright, shocked Southerners and bigoted Northern workers with her attempts at forming a biracial community. Her views on sexual liberation were also widely parodied. Still other leaders, like **Robert Dale Owen**, were **utopian** thinkers whose plans proved unworkable. The Workies also generated religious controversy. Many of its leaders were freethinkers, and few shared the middle class's enthusiasm for the religious revivals of the Second Great Awakening. Critics often accused Workies of being anti-Christian, and this hurt their efforts to recruit workers for whom religion was important.

Mostly, though, the Workingmen were undone by employer opposition and weakening economic conditions. The parties drew much of their strength from nascent trade unions whose membership rolls were unstable due to high turnover. The movement was moribund by 1835, and the Panic of 1837 finished it. Many trade unions collapsed during the depression and would not revive until after the Civil War.

Suggested Readings: Philip Foner, *History of the American Labor Movement, Vol. I*, 1982; Edward Pessen, *Most Uncommon Jacksonians: Radical Leaders of the Early Labor Movement*, 1967; Sean Wilentz, *Chants Democratic: New York City and the Rise of the American Working Class, 1788–1850*, 1984.

Robert E. Weir

Workman's Compensation. Regulation of industrial safety began over 100 years ago in the late nineteenth century. At that time, the amount of money awarded after industrial accidents was based on who was at fault. However, even if the employer was at fault, the employer was often able to avoid payment and thereby leave the injured worker with nothing. It was clear that this system did not work and, as a result, a system of workman's compensation, also known as workers' compensation, was developed that eliminated fault as an issue. It was one of the first social-insurance programs in the United States, beginning in 1908 as part of the Federal Employees Compensation Act. In 1911, various states began to enact their own workman's compensation laws.

Every year, one out of ten workers in private industry is injured while working. The goal of workman's compensation is to alleviate the financial hardship of workers after an injury prevents them from working, as well as to make them more aware of injury and prevention costs. The system protects both the employer and the employee. Under workman's compensation, employers are obligated to pay their employees, or their families, benefits, as determined by the government, regardless of the cause of the injury. In turn, the employer is protected from being sued by the employee. The initial decision about whether to compensate workers is made by employers or insurance companies rather than the state workman's-compensation agencies. The state agencies will only intervene to resolve disputes.

Nearly 90 percent of all workers are covered by workman's compensation, which provides them with cash benefits, health care, and rehabilitation services in response to work-related injury and disease. Payments are provided in five benefits categories: (1) payment of medical expenses for injured workers;

(2) payment of temporary total disability to injured workers who temporarily cannot work, but are expected to fully recover; (3) payment of permanent partial disability to workers suffering from injuries that might affect their ability to work and support their families in the future; (4) payment of permanent total disability to workers permanently prevented from working; and (5) payment of burial and survival benefits to the families of workers killed in work-related accidents. Workman's compensation is important as it ensures that those injured on the job, or the families of those killed, receive adequate support.

Suggested Readings: John F. Burton, ed., *New Perspectives in Workers' Compensation*, 1988; James Robert Chelius, *Workplace Safety and Health: The Role of Workers' Compensation*, 1977; Price V. Fishback and Shawn Everett Kantor, *A Prelude to the Welfare State: The Origins of Workers' Compensation*, 2000.

Lisa J. Wells

Worksharing. Worksharing is a reduction in individual working hours so that more people can be employed. Worksharing was advocated in the United States during the Great Depression in the 1930s and over the last two decades in Europe as a method for reducing unemployment. It has also gained currency among women's organizations seeking greater flexibility for working mothers and among advocates for the elderly, who see worksharing as a way in which senior citizens can secure part-time employment. Government laws often encourage worksharing by requiring employers to pay an **overtime** premium for hours worked in excess of some standard.

The effectiveness of worksharing is controversial. If hourly **wage** rates are not increased when worksharing is implemented, weekly take-home pay will be reduced. If take-home pay levels are maintained, hourly labor costs will increase. This increase, along with the fixed per employee cost of **fringe benefits**, can reduce the number of new jobs created by a worksharing initiative. However, productivity increases accompanying a reduction in work hours can potentially offset these negative factors.

While worksharing is primarily advocated to reduce unemployment, a form of worksharing, job sharing, is offered by some organizations as a family-friendly benefit. Job sharing is an explicit division of one full-time job into two part-time jobs to allow workers to balance work and family responsibilities. Worksharing programs can also be part of a broader push for reduced working hours to improve workers' quality of life.

Suggested Readings: Anders Hayden, *Sharing the Work, Sparing the Planet: Work Time, Consumption, and Ecology*, 1999; Benjamin Hunnicutt, *Kellogg's Six-Hour Day*, 1996; Jennifer Hunt, "Has Work-Sharing Worked in Germany?" *Quarterly Journal of Economics* 114, no.1 (1999): 117–48.

John W. Budd

Work-to-Rule. The work-to-rule is a union pressure tactic employed in **contract** negotiations or a conflict about working conditions. It involves workers following company regulations exactly. In most workplaces, there are many rules that are outdated or ignored by both sides. A union may encourage members to follow archaic practices to slow production and service without violating the **collective bargaining** agreement. There are also many tasks that are routinely undertaken by employees, even though they are not specifically written into job descriptions or contracts. Employees refuse to undertake such tasks during a work-to-rule action. Such concerted actions can severely interrupt output and in some cases involve the public and politicians. For example, police officers might stop all vehicles going above a usually unenforceable minimum speed limit of twenty-five miles per hour, thus bringing an incensed citizenry into the negotiations. Bus drivers in Providence, Rhode Island, once used a regulation to inspect buses thoroughly to have off-duty union mechanics examine vehicles. This pulled several dozen buses off the road for various safety problems during the morning rush hour. In manufacturing facilities, work-to-rule can disrupt assembly by adhering to safety practices or interfering with delivery of parts. Teachers have effectively employed work-to-rule to jump-start stalled contract negotiations. By refusing to undertake tasks not covered by the contract—like coaching duties, helping students after hours, proctoring study halls, and so on—teachers stretch administrative personnel beyond their ability to cope effectively. Some experts in the field of labor-management relations charge that work-to-rule is a type of **strike** or **sabotage**, but is not legally defined as such as long as workers perform all assigned duties. The tactic continues to appear in different guises as the nature of work evolves.

Suggested Reading: Dan La Botz, *A Troublemaker's Handbook*, 1991.

Scott Molloy

World Trade Organization. *See General Agreement on Tariffs and Trade (GATT).*

Wurf, Jerome (Jerry) (May 18, 1919–December 10, 1981). Jerome Wurf, as head of the **American Federation of State, County, and Municipal Employees (AFSCME)**, was the voice for American public employees. When Wurf took over leadership of the AFSCME in 1964, the union had approximately 200,000 members. Under Wurf, the union grew to represent over a million public workers. The son of Sigmund Wurf, a textile jobber, and Lena (Tanenbaum) Wurf, Jerry (as he preferred to be known) moved from the Bronx to Brooklyn with his mother and her new husband following his father's death. In Brooklyn's James Madison High School, Wurf was challenged by his high school English teacher to avoid a failing grade by improving his communication skills. Wurf became involved in local political groups, which gave him an opportunity to develop his public speaking. He became active in the Young People's Socialist League (YPSL), which he later described as "the most important thing in my life" at the time. It was to the YPSL that Wurf ascribed his "moderate" radicalism, which he likened to that of his hero, **Eugene Debs**. Wurf particularly admired Debs's determination to never become "a zealot and [never to be] taken in by the **communists**." He praised Debs for remaining "an American man."

Wurf enrolled in New York University and eventually obtained a bachelor of arts degree, completing his studies in night school due to family financial circumstances. Following graduation, Wurf obtained a food-service job in a Brooklyn cafeteria. Prompted by unfavorable working conditions, he organized his fellow workers into Local 448 of the Food Checkers and Cashiers Union of the **Hotel and Restaurant Employees**. Wurf was so effective that the Yiddish-speaking owners referred to him as "Malach Hamoves" (the Angel of Death).

Young Wurf's effectiveness as an organizer drew the attention of Arnold S. Zander, whose AFSCME had grown from a single-state employees' union in Madison, Wisconsin, in 1932, to an **American Federation of Labor (AFL)**–chartered union. Zander hired Wurf in 1947 to organize an AFL competitor to the **Congress of Industrial Organizations (CIO)** Transport Workers' Union. When Wurf failed at this task, Zander assigned him to beef up AFSCME's New York City affiliate. Wurf was assisted by Mayor Robert Wagner's 1954 executive order recognizing city workers' rights to unionize. This pressured Park Commissioner Robert Moses, the planning guru of modern New York City, to consent grudgingly to a representation election. By 1958, New York City public workers had gained equality with their organized counterparts in the private sector, and District Council 37 elected Jerry Wurf as executive director in the following year.

Jerry Wurf. © George Meany Memorial Archives.

In 1962, Wurf challenged his mentor, Arnold Zander, for the AFSCME presidency. Zander had invested union funds heavily in pricey housing developments while his union lagged in pay and benefit increases. Although he failed in 1962, by 1964, Wurf succeeded in dislodging Zander. Wurf sold off the housing developments, sold the union's national-headquarters building in Washington, D.C., and restructured the union leadership to fight off competitors and position the AFSCME for efficiency and growth. As president, Wurf discovered that the Central Intelligence Agency (CIA) had been using AFSCME's international connections with other unions to channel funds to anticommunist unionists in foreign countries. He terminated this arrangement and concentrated the union's efforts on bargaining gains for AFSCME members. In New York state, the AFSCME was instrumental in persuading the legislature to repeal the Condon-Wadlin Act, which required that striking public employees be dismissed.

With a significant African American membership, Wurf saw the importance of racial justice. Reverend Ralph Abernathy referred to him as a man "with a white skin but a black soul." On February 12, 1968, the largely African American members of the Memphis local walked off their jobs to protest racial discrimination. Twenty-two black sewer workers had been sent home without pay during a rainstorm, while white workers were allowed to remain on the job. Mass meetings, marches, and **boycotts** of white-owned businesses followed, with Wurf involved in strategic planning. Eventually he would be jailed for encouraging the work stoppage in violation of an injunction. On April 4, Reverend Martin Luther King, who had come to Memphis to support the strikers, was shot and killed. Shortly after Rev. King's assassination, city leaders acceded to union demands. Wurf compared the Memphis victory to classic labor battles of the past: **Homestead**; Hart, Schaffner, and Marx; and the General Motors Flint **sit-down strikes**.

During the 1970s, public employees, upset at their loss of purchasing power, flocked to the AFSCME, which briefly became the nation's fastest-growing union and the largest union in the AFL-CIO. In part this was a result of Wurf's active recruitment of women and African Americans, two groups often ignored by more traditional labor leaders. AFSCME's status assured that Wurf would be appointed to a vice presidency in the AFL-CIO, but his confrontational style and his open advocacy of positions counter to those supported by the AFL-CIO leadership would assure that his influence was less than would be expected from the leader of a large union. Wurf opposed American military involvement in Vietnam. He made President Richard Nixon's "enemies list," openly endorsed Senator George McGovern for the presidency of the United States in 1972, and he made no secret of his belief that AFL-CIO leadership had grown out of touch with ethnic minorities. The leadership, Wurf contended, was composed of elderly men, "products of an era and environment that is no longer," who had grown out of touch with their younger membership. Wurf feuded with AFL-CIO leadership over the formation of the Coalition of American Political Employees (CAPE), wherein Wurf allied with the **National Education Association**, an arch rival of the AFL-CIO's American Federation of Teachers (AFT). The AFT's **Albert Shanker** and Wurf were implacable enemies. Despite his differences with AFL-CIO leadership, Wurf publicly maintained his loyalty.

Wurf devoted his later years to national labor policy. He insisted on the importance of recognition by local government of the right of public employees to bargain collectively, while finding a way to avoid open confrontations between local government and public employees. Wurf saw the right of employees to **strike** or walk out as a fundamental right which could not be denied to a worker, yet he also saw that the exercise of that right by police officers, fire fighters, prison guards, and public-safety workers could create intolerable social chaos. Thus he argued strongly for compulsory **arbitration** which, he believed, should be extended to other public-sector employees. Jerry Wurf saw public-service workers as inherently conservative and reluctant to strike. As he once put it, "a guy whose been collecting garbage for twenty years is no militant but, when your employer is some elected official who wants to make a show of keeping down taxes and the worker is the guy who gets it in the neck, you do find him militant." During New York City's fiscal crisis of the 1970s, Wurf bitterly denounced demagogues who blamed the crisis on public employees. Wurf countered demagoguery with the fact that the average city employee at the time eked out a living on under $10,000 per year. Wurf argued for the creation of a leadership group of professional public managers who would bypass the political patronage system and bring efficiency and decent treatment to public employees. Under Wurf, the AFSCME became actively involved in public issues through its political office, Public Employees Organized to Promote Legislative Equality (PEOPLE), an organization not afraid to take outspoken positions on matters concerning public employees. Jerry Wurf died on December 10, 1981, survived by his wife of twenty-one years, Mildred (Kiefer), and their two children.

Suggested Reading: Joseph C. Goulden, *Jerry Wurf: Labor's Last Angry Man*, 1982.

James P. Hanlan

Y

Yablonski, Joseph A. (March 3, 1910–December 31, 1969). Joseph "Jock" Yablonski was a reform leader of the **United Mine Workers of America (UMWA)**. Yablonski was born in Pittsburgh, Pennsylvania, to a coal-mining family. His father died in the mines in 1933. At age fifteen, Yablonski entered the pits. He served in numerous UMWA posts from 1934 on, including a stint on the executive board from 1934 to 1942. He became president of Local 5 in 1958 and served until he was forced from office by UMWA national president W. A. "Tony" Boyle in 1966, when Yablonski supported reform candidates over Boyle and his cronies. By the mid-1960s, the UMWA had shed its former militancy in favor of a **business unionism** model. There were also allegations that union officials were corrupt and that the UMWA had ties to organized crime. Moreover, the gradual decline of the mining industry led to widespread **rank-and-file** discontent.

Yablonski allied himself with rank-and-file insurgents and announced his intention to challenge Boyle for the presidency. He was backed by consumer activist Ralph Nader and Washington, D.C., attorney Joseph Rauh, the vice chair of Americans for Democratic Action. He was also popular among the rank and file for his work with Labor's Non-Partisan League, and his efforts in getting the state of Pennsylvania to grant **workman's compensation** to **black-lung**-disease (pneumoconiosis) sufferers. Boyle was also unpopular because of his poor public relations handling of a 1968 mine disaster in which seventy-eight miners died, and he stood accused of embezzlement, questionable loans, and illegal campaign practices.

Boyle nonetheless defeated Yablonski. On December 31, 1969—just twenty-two days after the UMWA election—Yablonski, his wife, and a daughter were murdered in their Clarksville, Pennsylvania home. The crime received worldwide publicity, and suspicion centered on Boyle. Miners for Union Democracy, a rank-and-file movement, removed Boyle from the presidency in 1972 and elected Arnold Miller (1923–85), a former Yablonski supporter, in his stead. Boyle and several other officials were convicted of making illegal political contributions with union **pension** funds, and in 1974 Boyle was charged and convicted of Yablonski's murder. He died in prison in 1985. The UMWA—led by Rauh, Arnold Miller, Ed Sadlowski, Jerry Tucker, Yablonski's son, and others—carried on Yablonski's legacy and purged the UMWA of many of its abuses.

Suggested Readings: Joseph Finley, *The Corrupt Kingdom*, 1972; Elizabeth Levy, *Struggle and Lose, Struggle and Win*, 1987; Arthur Lewis, *Murder by Contract*, 1975.

Don Binkowski

Yellow-Dog Contract. The yellow-dog contract was an agreement signed by workers as a condition of employment in which they promised not to join a union during their term of employment with the company. In some cases, workers also had to sign affidavits that they had not previously belonged to a union. The term yellow-dog derives from a colloquial expression meaning an unworthy individual and is emblematic of the contempt in which unions and most workers held such **contracts**. The first known printed use of the term in a labor context is 1902, but it was probably used earlier than this.

Yellow-dog contracts were common in **company towns**, especially in coal-mining regions. Workers were threatened with firing and eviction from company housing for doing anything contrary to company policy. By the 1890s, widespread abuse led fifteen states to outlaw the use of yellow-dog contracts. However, such bans did little to deter the practice. Yellow-dog contracts were a centerpiece of the **National Civic Federation**'s 1903 **open-shop** drive, and they also factored prominently in so-called **American Plan** schemes in the 1920s, in which employers reinforced propaganda about the virtues of individual bargaining and self-reliance with yellow-dog contracts. A combination of the 1932 **Norris-La Guardia Act** and the 1935 **National Labor Relations Act** finally ended most uses of these contracts, although many workers in the 1980s complained that management imposed verbal forms of yellow-dog contracts.

Suggested Readings: Foster Rhea Dulles and Melvyn Dubofsky, *Labor in America*, 1993; Daniel Ernst, "The Yellow Dog Contract and Liberal Reform," *Labor History* vol. 30, no. 2 (1989); Joel Seidman, *The Yellow-Dog Contract*, 1932.

Robert E. Weir

Yeshiva Decision. *See National Labor Relations Board v. Yeshiva University*.

Appendix: Labor Documents

1. American Federation of Labor-Congress of Industrial Organizations (AFL-CIO) Constitution: Preamble and Article II

The ***American Federation of Labor*** *and the* ***Congress of Industrial Organizations*** *merged in 1955 to create a labor federation of 15.5 million members. Its joint constitution is an elaborate document that lays out its objects and principles, as well as the duties of officers, procedural details of operating the AFL-CIO bureaucracy, collecting per capita taxes, settling disputes, and defining the relationship of affiliates to the federation.*

Critics of the merger claim that the AFL-CIO is a bureaucratic ***business union*** *that is inattentive to* ***rank-and-file*** *members and lacks the militancy to affect meaningful social and economic change. As the document below reveals, however, in principle the AFL-CIO is committed to equity, democracy, and improving the lives of working men and women. While it lacks the defiant spirit of the* ***Industrial Workers of the World****'s Preamble or the utopian goals of the* ***Knights of Labor****'s statement of principles, the AFL-CIO's constitution most certainly outlines a version of a just society. Quoted below are the preamble and Article II of the constitution, "Objects and Principles."*

PREAMBLE

The American Federation of Labor and Congress of Industrial Organizations is an expression of the hopes and aspirations of the working people of America. We resolve to fulfill the yearning of the human spirit for liberty, justice and community; to advance individual and associational freedom; to vanquish oppression, privation and cruelty in all their forms; and to join with all persons, of whatever nationality or faith, who cherish the cause of democracy and the call of solidarity, to grace the planet with these achievements.

We dedicate ourselves to improving the lives of working families, bringing fairness and dignity to the workplace and securing social equity in the Nation. We will prevail by building a strong, free and democratic labor movement.

We will organize workers into unions allied by common purposes and mutual reliance. We will recruit generations of organizers, amass resources to sustain their efforts and inspire workers to achieve dignity and security through organization and collective bargaining. We will generate broad understanding of the necessity of organizing among our members, our leaders and all unorganized workers.

We will give political voice to workers in the Nation. We will fight for an agenda for working families at all levels of government. We will assemble a broad progressive coalition for social and economic justice. We will create a political force within the labor movement that will speak forcefully and persuasively on the public issues that affect our lives.

We will enable workers to shape a changing global economy. We will speak for working people in the international marketplace, in the industries in which we are employed, and in the firms where we work. We will expand the role of unions to securing worker influence in all the decisions that affect our working lives, from capital investment to the quality of products and services to how work itself is organized.

We will establish unions as active forces in our communities. We will make the voices of working families heard in our neighborhoods. We will create vibrant state, local and community labor councils. We will strengthen the ties of labor with our allies. We will speak out effectively and creatively on behalf of all working Americans. . . .

ARTICLE II: OBJECTS AND PRINCIPLES

The objects and principles of this Federation are:

1. To aid workers in securing improved wages, hours and working conditions with due regard for the autonomy, integrity and jurisdiction of affiliated unions.
2. To aid and assist affiliated unions in extending the benefits of mutual assistance and collective bargaining to workers and to promote the organization of the unorganized into unions of their own choosing for their mutual aid, protection and advancement, giving recognition to the principle that both craft and industrial unions are appropriate, equal and necessary as methods of union organization.
3. To affiliate national and international unions with this Federation and to establish such unions; to form organizing committees and directly affiliated local unions and to secure their affiliation to appropriate national and international unions affiliated with or chartered by the Federation; to establish, assist and promote state and local central bodies composed of local unions of all affiliated organizations and directly affiliated local unions; to establish and assist trade departments composed of affiliated national and international unions and organizing committees.
4. To encourage all workers without regard to race, creed, color, sex, national origin, religion, age, disability or sexual orientation to share equally in the full benefits of union organization.
5. To secure legislation which will safeguard and promote the principle of free collective bargaining, the rights of workers, farmers and consumers, and the security and welfare of all the people and to oppose legislation inimical to these objectives.
6. To protect and strengthen our democratic institutions, to secure full recognition and enjoyment of the rights and liberties to which we are justly entitled, and to preserve and perpetuate the cherished traditions of our democracy.
7. To give constructive aid in promoting the cause of peace and freedom in the world and to aid, assist and cooperate with free and democratic labor movements throughout the world.

8. To preserve and maintain the integrity of each affiliated union in the organization to the end that each affiliate shall respect the established bargaining relationships of every other affiliate and that each affiliate shall refrain from raiding the established bargaining relationship of any other affiliate and, at the same time, to encourage the elimination of conflicting and duplicating organizations and jurisdictions through the process of voluntary agreement or voluntary merger in consultation with the appropriate officials of the Federation, to preserve, subject to the foregoing, the organizing jurisdiction of each affiliate.
9. To aid and encourage the sale and use of union made goods and union services through the use of the union label and other symbols; to promote the labor press and other means of furthering the education of the labor movement.
10. To protect the labor movement from any and all corrupt influences and from the undermining efforts of authoritarianism, totalitarianism, terrorism and all other forces that suppress individual liberties and freedom of association and oppose the basic principles of our democracy and of free and democratic unionism.
11. To safeguard the democratic character of the labor movement and to protect the autonomy of each affiliated national and international union.
12. While preserving the independence of the labor movement from political control, to encourage workers to register and vote, to exercise their full rights and responsibilities of citizenship, and to perform their rightful part in the political life of the local, state and national communities.

Source: AFL-CIO Constitution.

2. Anthracite Coal Strike of 1902: Response to a *New York Times* Letter by Mine Owners Spokesman George Baer

The ***Anthracite Coal Strike of 1902*** *became a classic confrontation between capital and labor. Eventually, President Theodore Roosevelt intervened to avoid the hardships that a winter without coal would bring to many Americans. The settlement that resulted exemplified what Roosevelt would call the "Square Deal" with mine owners, mineworkers, and the general public all gaining in the process and avoiding social and political upheaval. In the midst of the* ***strike****, George Baer, spokesman for the mine owners, responded to a letter in the New York Times and asserted what amounted to the divine right of capital. Baer's uncompromising stance, his assertion that God himself was on the side of the owners, and his defense of the rights of the wealthy proved unpalatable to the general public.*

WILKES BARRE, PA, Aug. 20, 1902—W. F. Clark, a photographer of this city, recently addressed a letter to President Baer of the Philadelphia and Reading

Railroad Company, appealing to him as a Christian to settle the miners' strike. The writer said if Christ were taken more into our business affairs there would be less trouble in the world, and that if Mr. Baer granted the strikers a slight concession they would gladly return to work and the President of the Philadelphia and Reading would have the blessing of God and the respect of the nation.

President Baer replied as follows:

> I see that you are evidently biased in your religious views in favor of the right of the working man to control a business in which he has no other interest than to secure fair wages for the work he does. I beg of you not to be discouraged. The rights and interests of the laboring man will be protected and cared for, not by the labor agitator, but by the Christian men to whom God in His infinite wisdom has given the control of the property interests of the country. Pray earnestly that the right may triumph, always remembering that the Lord God Omnipotent still reigns and that His reign is one of law and order, and not of violence and crime.

Source: The New York Times, August 21, 1902.

---

3. Black Workers after the Knights of Labor: July 1918 Article from *The Messenger*

The decline of the **Knights of Labor** *in the 1890s did not bode well for African American laborers. Although the* **American Federation of Labor (AFL)** *was founded in 1886, many of its constituent* **craft unions** *refused to accept black members. By the early twentieth century, some black leaders openly called upon black workers to* **scab** *upon white strikers to punish them for their racism. During the Progressive Era, cooler heads prevailed, and both black leaders and AFL officials at least broached the subject of organizing African Americans. But, except for a few select unions like the* **United Mine Workers**, *the AFL remained largely closed to African Americans well into the 1930s. On July 1, 1918, the following article appeared in the important African American journal* The Messenger. *Published in Harlem in New York City and associated with* **A. Philip Randolph**, *the future leader of the* **Brotherhood of Sleeping Car Porters**, *the article is both a plea for cooperation and a warning to white unionists.*

As workers, black and white, we all have one common interest, viz., the getting of more wages, shorter hours and better working conditions.

Black and white workers should combine for no other reason than that for which individual workers should combine, viz., to increase their bargaining power, which will enable them to get their demands.

Second, the history of the labor movement in America proves that the employing class recognizes no race lines. They will exploit a white man as readily as a black man. They will exploit women as readily as men. They will even go to the extent of coining the labor, blood and suffering of children into dollars. The introduction of women and children into the factories proves that capitalists are only concerned with profits and that they will exploit any race or class in order to make profits, whether they be black or white men, black or white women, or black or white children.

Third, it is apparent that every Negro worker or non-union man is a potential scab upon white union men and black union men.

Fourth, self-interest is the only principle upon which individual or groups will act if they are sane. Thus, it is idle and vain to hope or expect Negro workers out of work and who receive less wages when at work then white workers, to refuse to scab upon white workers when an opportunity presents itself.

Men will always seek to improve their condition. When colored workers, as scabs, accept the wages against which white workers strike, they (the Negro workers) have definitely improved their conditions.

That is the only reason why colored workers scab upon white workers or why non-union men scab upon white union men.

A scab who is ignorant of his class interest does not realize that it is necessary to sacrifice a temporary gain in order to secure a greater future gain which can only be secured through collective action.

Every member which is a part of the industrial machinery must be organized, if labor would win its demands. Organized labor cannot afford to ignore any labor factor of production which organized capital does not ignore.

Fifth, if the employers can keep the white and black dogs, on account of race prejudice, fighting over a bone; the yellow capitalist dog will get away with the bone—the bone, to which we refer, is profits. No union man's standard of living is safe as long as there is one man or woman who may be used as a scab.

Source: Philip Foner and Ronald Lewis, eds., *Black Workers: A Documentary History from Colonial Times to the Present* (Philadelphia: Temple University Press, 1989), pp. 354–55.

4. "Bread and Roses": Poem by James Oppenheim—1912

James Oppenheim (1882–1932) was inspired to write his poem, "Bread and Roses," by some of the ***Lawrence textile strikers*** *of 1912, who carried a banner reading "we want bread and roses too." Workers in Lawrence had walked off the job in response to pay cuts instituted by the American Woolen Company; the wool trust was the city's predominant employer. The poem was set to music by Caroline Kohlsaat and came to represent the goals of the women strikers: a life wherein both the necessities and the beauties of the world could be enjoyed by all. The Lawrence Textile Strike is thus sometimes known as the "bread and roses" strike.*

As we come marching, marching in the beauty of the day,
A million darkened kitchens, a thousand mill lofts gray,

Are touched with all the radiance that a sudden sun discloses,
For the people hear us singing: "Bread and roses! Bread and roses!"

As we come marching, marching, we battle too for men,
For they are women's children, and we mother them again.
Our lives shall not be sweated from birth until life closes;
Hearts starve as well as bodies; give us bread, but give us roses!

As we come marching, marching, unnumbered women dead
Go crying through our singing their ancient cry for bread.
Small art and love and beauty their drudging spirits knew.
Yes, it is bread we fight for—but we fight for roses, too!

As we come marching, marching, we bring the greater days.
The rising of the women means the rising of the race.
No more the drudge and idler—ten that toil where one reposes,
But a sharing of life's glories: Bread and roses! Bread and roses!

Source: Joyce L. Kornbluh, ed., *Rebel Voices: An I.W.W. Anthology* (Ann Arbor: University of Michigan Press, 1964), 195–96.

---

5. Cesar Chavez: "The Mexican-American and the Church"

Cesar Chavez** (1927–93) was an important voice for agricultural workers, especially Chicanos and other Latinos. Until his death, Chavez was the leading spokesperson for the* ***United Farm Workers of America (UFW)*, a union that sprang to public consciousness during the* ***grape boycott*** *of 1965 to 1970. One of the things that made Chavez effective was his deep understanding of the Chicano community in which he grew up. He was a fervent follower of the Roman Catholic religion, and was aware of the moral and political sway it held among Chicanos. Whenever he could, Chavez fostered ties between his union and his church. The following piece was written in 1968, during a fast Chavez held to pressure California growers into recognizing the UFW.*

THE MEXICAN-AMERICAN AND THE CHURCH

The place to begin is with our own experience with the Church in the strike which has gone on for thirty-one months in Delano. . . . [I]n Delano the church has been involved with the poor in a unique way which should stand as a symbol to other communities. . . . [W]hen we refer to the Church we should define the word a little. We mean the whole Church, the Church as an ecumenical body spread around the world, and not just its particular form in a parish in a local community. The Church we are talking about is a tremendously powerful institution in our society, and in the world. That Church is one form of the Presence of God on Earth, and . . . is a powerful moral and spiritual force which cannot be ignored by any movement. Furthermore, it is an organization with tremendous wealth. Since the Church is to be servant to the poor, it is our fault if that wealth is not channeled to help the poor in our world. In a small way we have been able, in the Delano strike, to work together with the Church . . . to bring some of its moral and economic power to bear on those who want to maintain the status quo, keeping farm workers in virtual enslavement. . . .

Some years ago . . . some of us . . . began to realize the powerful effect which the Church can have on the conscience of the opposition. In scattered instances, in San Jose, Sacramento, Oakland, Los Angeles and other places, priests would speak out loudly and clearly against specific instances of oppression, and in some cases, stand with the people who were being hurt. Furthermore, a small group of priests . . . began to pinpoint attention on the terrible situation of the farm workers in our state. At about that same time, we began to run into the California Migrant Ministry in the camps and field. They were about the only ones there, and a lot of us were very suspicious, since we were Catholics and they were Protestants.

However, they had developed a very clear conception of the Church. It was called to serve, to be at the mercy of the poor, and not to try to use them. After a while this made a lot of sense to us, and we began to find ourselves working side by side with them. In fact, it forced us to raise the question why OUR Church was not doing the same. We would ask, "Why do the Protestants come out here and help the people, demand nothing, and give all their time to serving farm workers, while our own parish priests stay in their churches, where only a few people come, and usually feel uncomfortable?" It was not until some of us moved to Delano and began working to build the National Farm Workers Association that we really saw how far removed from the people the parish Church was. . . . [W]e could not get any help at all from the priests of Delano. When the strike began, they told us we could not even use the Church's auditorium for . . . meetings. The farm workers' money helped build that auditorium! But the Protestants were there again, in the form of the California Migrant Ministry, and they began to help in little ways. . . .

[W]hen the strike started in 1965, most of our "friends" forsook us for a while. . . . But the California Migrant Ministry held a meeting with its staff and decided that the strike was a matter of life or death for farm workers everywhere, and that even if it meant the end of the Migrant Ministry they would turn over their resources to the strikers. The political pressure on the Protestant Churches was tremendous and the Migrant Ministry lost a lot of money. But they stuck it out, and they began to point the way to the rest of the Church. In fact, when 30 of the strikers were arrested for shouting "Huelga" [strike], 11 ministers went to jail with them. . . . Then the workers began to raise the question: "Why ministers? Why not priests? . . . " [S]lowly the pressure of the people grew . . . until finally we have in Delano a priest . . . who is there to help minister to the needs of farm workers.

Finally, our own Catholic Church has decided to recognize that we have our own peculiar needs, just as the growers have theirs. But outside of the local diocese, the pressure built up on growers to negotiate was tremendous. Though we were not allowed to have our own priest, the power of the ecumenical body of the Church was tremendous. The work of the Church, for example, in the Schenley, Di Giorgio, Perelly-Minetti strikes was fantastic. They applied pressure—and they mediated. When poor people get involved in a long conflict, such as a strike, or a civil rights drive, and the pressure increases each day, there is a deep need for spiritual advice. Without it we see families crumble, leadership weaken, and hard workers grow tired. And in such a situation the spiritual advice must be given by a friend, not by the opposition. What sense does it make to go to Mass on Sunday and reach out for spiritual help, and instead get sermons about the wickedness of your cause? That only drives one to question and to despair. The growers in Delano have their spiritual problems . . . we do not deny that. They have every right to have priests and ministers who serve their needs. BUT WE HAVE DIFFERENT NEEDS, AND SO WE NEEDED A FRIENDLY SPIRITUAL GUIDE. . . .

But the opposition raises a tremendous howl about this. They don't want us to have our spiritual advisors, friendly to our needs. Why is this? Why indeed except that THERE IS TREMENDOUS SPIRITUAL AND ECONOMIC POWER IN THE CHURCH. The rich know it, and for that reason they choose to keep it from the people. The leadership of the Mexican-American Community must admit that we have fallen far short in our task of helping provide spiritual guidance for our people. . . . For example, the Catholic Charities agencies of the Catholic Church has millions of dollars earmarked for the poor. But often the money is spent for food baskets for the needy instead of for effective action to eradicate the causes of poverty. The men and women who administer this money sincerely want to help their brothers. It should be our duty to help direct the attention to the basic needs of the Mexican-Americans in our society . . . needs which cannot be satisfied with baskets of food, but rather with effective organizing at the grass roots level.

Therefore, I am calling for Mexican-American groups to stop ignoring this source of power. It is not just our right to appeal to the Church to use its power effectively for the poor, it is our duty to do so. . . . Furthermore, we should be prepared to come to the defense of that priest, rabbi, minister, or layman of the Church, who out of commitment to truth and justice gets into a tight place with his pastor or bishop. It behooves us to stand with that man and . . . see to it that his rights of conscience are respected and that no bishop, pastor or other higher body takes that God-given, human right away. Finally, in a nutshell, what do we want the Church to do? . . . We ask for its presence with us, beside us, as Christ among us. We ask the Church to sacrifice with the people for social change, for justice, and for love of brother. We don't ask for words. We ask for deeds. We don't ask for paternalism. We ask for servanthood.

Source: TM/© 2003 the Cesar E. Chavez Foundation. www.chavezfoundation.org.

6. Coalition of Labor Union Women: Mission Statement

Since 1974, the **Coalition of Labor Union Women (CLUW)** *has fought to make certain that union women receive fair treatment and opportunities within the very organizations that are designed to liberate them. The CLUW formed after many decades in which male chauvinism was standard operating procedure for unions. Like millions of women in the culture at large, union women were inspired by the revitalization of the feminist movement in the 1960s. The CLUW's mission statement is a brief but poignant summary of the organization's aims. It also encapsulates the movement's broader concerns.*

The Coalition of Labor Union Women is America's only national organization for union women. Formed in 1974, CLUW is a nonpartisan organization within the union movement. The primary mission of CLUW is to unify all union women in a viable organization to determine our common problems and concerns and to develop action programs within the framework of our unions to deal effectively with our objectives. At its founding convention in Chicago, Illinois, CLUW adopted four basic goals of action: to promote affirmative action in the workplace; to strengthen the role of women in unions; to organize the unorganized women; and to increase the involvement of women in the political and legislative process. These goals continue to be the cornerstone of CLUW's activities as members speak out for equal pay, child and elder care benefits, job security, safe workplaces, affordable health care, contraceptive equity, and protection from sexual harassment and violence at work. . . .

Source: "Coalition of Labor Union Women," www.cluw.org.

7. Colored National Labor Union

The **Colored National Labor Union (CNLU)** *was largely the brainchild of African American ship caulker Isaac Myers. Myers convened a December 1860 meeting in his hometown of Baltimore to consider questions relating to black laborers. He did so mindful of the fact that the newly formed* **National Labor Union (NLU)** *was divided over the question of whether or not to admit black members, given that numerous affiliated unions barred African Americans. The issue of contract and coolie labor was a central concern for the early NLU. Myers may well have added this as a subtle appeal to white NLU leaders to recognize that white and black workers shared common interests and concerns. The CNLU and the NLU made overtures to each other, but differences ultimately undid a fragile alliance, and neither organization survived the Panic of 1873. Below is a call for a national convention of "Colored Men of the United States," which was published in* The Christian Recorder *on September 18, 1869. (Note: The seem-*

ingly random capitalization of words was common in eighteenth- and nineteenth-century documents and was done to call attention to key points.)

FELLOW CITIZENS:—At a State Labor Convention of the Colored Men of Maryland, held July 20, 1869, it was unanimously resolved a that a National Convention be called . . . to consider:

1st. The Present Status of Colored Labor in the United States and its Relationship to American Industry.

2d. To adopt such rules and devise such means as will systematically and effectively organize all the departments of said labor, and make it the more productive in its new Political relationship to Capital, and consolidate the Colored Workingmen of the several States to act in co-operation with our White Fellow-Workingmen . . . who are opposed to Distinction in the Apprenticeship Laws on account of Color. . . .

3d. To consider the question of the importation of Contract Coolie Labor, and to petition the Congress for the adoption of such Laws as will prevent its being a system of Slavery.

4th. And to adopt such other means as will best advance the interests of the Colored Mechanics and Workingmen of the whole country.

Fellow-Citizens: You cannot place too great an estimate upon the important objects this Convention is called upon to consider. . . . In the greater portion of the United States, Colored Men are excluded from the workshops on account of their *color*.

The laboring man in a large portion of Southern States, by a systematic understanding prevailing there, is unjustly deprived of the price of his labor, and in localities far removed from the Courts of Justice is forced to endure wrongs and oppressions worse than Slavery.

By falsely representing the laborers of the South, certain *interested* writers and journals are striving to bring Contract Chinese or Coolie Labor into popular favor there, thus forcing American laborers to work at Coolie wages or starve. . . .

Delegates will be admitted without regard to race or color. . . . It is hoped that all who feel an interest in the welfare and elevation of our race will take an active part in making the Convention a grand success. . . .

Source: Philip Foner and Ronald Lewis, eds., *Black Workers: A Documentary History from Colonial Times to the Present* (Philadelphia: Temple University, 1989), pp. 163–64.

8. Communist Manifesto (1848)

Historians have debated the question of why American workers have been historically less committed to ***socialist*** *and* ***communist*** *ideals than those in other indus-*

trialized nations. The reasons for this are complex, but the very question often misleads. While it is true that independent socialist or labor parties have often struggled in the United States, it does not mean that workers had no interest in such movements. From the 1870s through the red scare following World War I, consideration of Marxist ideals was among the options that American workers considered. Very often, communist organizers exerted great influence on labor organizations, even when their actual numbers were few. (This is especially the case inside the early ***Congress of Industrial Organizations****.) For whatever faults they possessed, communists also played key roles in agitating for social change, were instrumental during the* ***Popular Front****, and did much to publicize basic inequities in American society.*

The Communist Manifesto was published by Karl Marx and Friedrich Engels in 1848. It made its way to the United States through immigrants, then through the work of the First International Working Men's Association (1864), which in 1872, moved its headquarters to New York City. Socialist and communist influence waxed and waned, but legions of native-born and immigrant workers had at least passing knowledge of the manifesto and its central thesis: "The history of all hitherto existing society is the history of class struggles." This is also true of the document's stirring conclusion, quoted below. Its final line is a rallying cry for workers everywhere.

When, in the course of development, class distinctions have disappeared, and all production has been concentrated in the hands of a vast association of the whole nation, the public power will lose its political character. Political power, properly so called, is merely the organized power of one class for oppressing another. If the proletariat during its contest with the bourgeoisie is compelled by the force of circumstances to organize itself as a class, if, by means of a revolution, it makes itself the ruling class, and, as such, sweeps away by force the old conditions of production, then it will, along with these conditions, have swept away the conditions for the existence of class antagonisms and of classes generally, and will thereby have abolished its own supremacy as a class.

In the place of the old bourgeois society, with its classes and class antagonisms, we shall have an association in which the free development of each is the condition for the free development of all.

. . . the Communists everywhere support every revolutionary movement against the existing social and political order of things.

In all these movements they bring to the front . . . the property question, no matter what its degree of development at the time.

Finally, they labor everywhere for the union and agreement of the democratic parties of all countries.

The communists disdain to conceal their views and aims. They openly declare that their ends can be obtained only by the forcible overthrow of all existing social conditions. Let the ruling classes tremble at a Communistic revolution. The proletarians have nothing to lose but their chains. They have a world to win.

WORKINGMEN OF ALL COUNTRIES, UNITE!

9. Comparable Worth: 1986 Minnesota Study by Sara Evans and Barbara Nelson

One of the more controversial struggles of recent years has been the battle over comparable worth. The 1963 **Equal Pay Act** *made it illegal, in most circumstances, to pay differing* **wage** *rates to employees doing the same job, if they have equal* **seniority**. *Women and minorities often found, however, that some employers sought to preserve traditional privileges—usually those of white males—by fudging on job classifications. For example, a woman doing filing and typing might be classified as a "secretary," while a man doing the same duties might be labeled an "executive assistant." Another way to perpetuate traditional discriminatory patterns is to reassign job duties so that, technically, two workers are doing different tasks when, in actuality, they are of comparable levels of expertise and difficulty. Comparable worth addresses such inequity by reclassifying work and pegging pay rates according to the skill required to produce it. To date, comparable-worth laws remain mostly local and state efforts.*

The excerpt below comes from a 1986 study done in Minnesota by Sara Evans and Barbara Nelson. It lays out the problem and offers a justification for considering comparable worth.

Wendy Robinson worked as an intro level secretary at the University of Minnesota at a time some years ago when there was a severe shortage of clerical workers. Interested in other opportunities, she would wander by the employment bulletin board in the basement of Morrill Hall to look at the jobs posted there. In the section labelled "clericals" there were "scads" of jobs, each of which had a lengthy description including requirements from three to five years of post-high-school education or experience, typing skills, shorthand, excellent command of grammar, and basic writing skills. The pay rate for such jobs, like her own, was $756 per month. One day she glanced over at the section of the bulletin marked "technical," where there was only one job posted. "Custodian," it read, "job requirement: eighth grade education, the ability to read and write, no experience." The starting salary, however, was $200 a month more than Wendy was making. . . .

Comparable worth or pay equity as it is often called, is the concept of providing equal pay for different jobs of equal value (i.e., jobs with similar scores along measures of skill, effort, responsibility, and working conditions). . . .

This type of analysis also takes into account race and ethnicity, looking to see if jobs held disproportionately by racial or ethnic minorities are paid less than equivalently valued jobs held primarily by whites. What is important to remember about comparable worth is that *only* equivalently evaluated jobs within a specific workplace are compared. Clerk typist salaries are not compared to doctors' salaries, and clerk typists working for the state of Minnesota are not compared with clerk typists working elsewhere. Comparable worth is an *internal* wage policy.

Why do most male jobs like delivery van drivers consistently get better pay than mostly female jobs like clerk typists? Among full time workers, why do white women make 64 cents, black women make 58 cents, Hispanic women make 54 cents, Black men make 74 cents, and Hispanic men make 71 cents, compared to every dollar made by white men? There are no easy answers. . . .

The problem of low wages for women and minorities is indeed broad and systematic. Opponents of public policies addressing wage rates cite the market system as the best mechanism for adjusting wages. Proponents point out that until the early 1960s it was perfectly legal and customary to pay women and men, and whites and minorities differently for exactly the same work, and market or no market that is precisely what was done. When women entered the teaching profession and factory work in the nineteenth century wages dropped. Employers argued that men had to support families and that women's income was secondary. The primacy of women's responsibilities for home and family meant that few considered them seriously as wage earners.

Not only did women and minorities receive lower pay, however. In addition they generally found jobs in separate sectors of the economy, jobs specifically for women or minorities. This was true in the 1820s when young white women entered newly opened textile mills, in the 1880s when white women dominated teaching in public schools, in the 1920s when they flocked into the new pink-collar ghetto of clerical work, and it is still true today.

Source: Sara Evans and Barbara Nelson "Comparable Worth in Minnesota: Implementing an Innovative Wage Policy," *Northwest Report* (Fall 1986): 18–21. Reprinted with permission.

---

10. Direct Action and Sabotage: Excerpt from May 1912 Article by Frank Bohn in *Solidarity*

Throughout the history of the labor movement, American labor leaders have quarreled over the use of violence to obtain their objectives, with some on the extreme left arguing that it is justifiable to use force against an oppressive state. The vast majority of leaders rejected violence, however, and asserted that such tactics only robbed unions of needed public support and/or justified harsh crackdowns on all labor movements, including those not engaged in illegal activities. Most of the violence associated with organized labor in the United States was done to, not by, workers.

Those who criticized violence as a tactic had a point. Enemies of organized labor played upon various fears to break unions, often employing illegal methods of their own to do so. Few unions suffered as much repression as the **Industrial Workers of the World (IWW)***. Its own fiery concepts often came back to haunt it, especially the ideas of* **direct action** *and sabotage. IWW opponents claimed that the first idea stood for revolutionary violence and the second for wanton destruction of private property. Although a few hotheads occasionally expressed such views, the IWW's official position on these matters was quite different. In the passage below, IWW member Frank Bohn—who was also a committed* **socialist***—explains what most early-twentieth-century workers meant by the terms. These definitions originally appeared in the May 18, 1912, issue of the IWW journal* Solidarity.

Direct Action: . . . By direct action is meant any action taken by workers directly at the point of production with a view to bettering their conditions. The organization of any labor union whatever is direct action. Sending the shop committee to demand of the boss a change of shop rules is direct action. To oppose direct action is to oppose labor unionism as a whole with all its activities. In this sense, the term has been used by those who made use of it down to the time of the late controversy. It was the misuse of this expression by the comrades who oppose class-labor unionism which has caused so much uneasiness in the Socialist Party. When we come to the question as to what direct action shall be taken and when and how—that is for the organization on the job to determine. For the Socialist Party to try to lay down rules for the conduct of unions or one union in this matter would be as ridiculous as for the Socialist Party to seek to determine what the workers shall eat for breakfast. It is the business of the Socialist Party to organize and conduct political education activity. . . .

Sabotage:—Sabotage means "strike and stay in the shop." Striking workers thus are enabled to draw pay and keep out scabs while fighting capitalists. Sabotage does not necessarily mean destruction of machinery or other property, although that method has always been indulged in and will continue to be used as long as there is a class struggle. More often it is used to advantage in a quieter way. Excessive limitation of output is sabotage. So is any obstruction of the regular conduct of the industry. Ancient Hebrews in Egypt practiced sabotage when they spoiled bricks. Slaves in the South practiced it regularly by putting stone and dirt in their bags of cotton to make them weigh heavier. An old cotton mill weaver in Massachusetts once told me that when baseball was first played, the boys in his mill stuck a bobbin in the running gear of the water wheel and so tied up the shop on Saturday afternoon that they could go and see the ballgame. . . . When the workers face a specific situation, they will very likely continue to do as their interests and intelligence dictate.

Source: Joyce Kornbluh, ed., *Rebel Voices: An I.W.W. Anthology* (Ann Arbor: University of Michigan Press, 1968), pp. 52–53.

---

11. Dodge Revolutionary Union Movement (D.R.U.M.): Excerpt of February 1971 Article in *Inner-City Voice*

African American workers had long lobbied and pressured white-dominated unions to recognize black workers as equal partners. By the mid-1960s, patience was growing thin both within the labor movement and in society at large. Many black activists associated with the civil-rights movement were attracted to the rising wave of militancy as embodied in organizations like the Black Panthers and the post-1965 Student Non-Violent Coordinating Committee. It was only a matter of time until militants espousing "black power" made their presence known in organized labor. In May 1968, the

***Dodge Revolutionary Union Movement (D.R.U.M.)** was born, a radical black-labor caucus within the **United Auto Workers**. D.R.U.M. spawned numerous like-minded groups. The passage below appeared in Inner-City Voice, D.R.U.M.'s official newspaper in the greater Detroit area, in February 1971.*

Groups like D.R.U.M. engendered great fear with their fiery rhetoric. Like many groups emerging in the late 1960s, D.R.U.M.'s words were far more radical than its actions. In the end, one of the major accomplishments of militant groups was shaking up entrenched leaders and calcified organizations. Organized labor did not accede to D.R.U.M.'s most radical demands, but most unions began paying closer attention to African American concerns because of it.

Amidst the miserable conditions of a people whose legitimate struggle had for over 400 years been stifled by the forces of oppression rose the murmur of D.R.U.M. beats. D.R.U.M. beats could be heard in the wildcat strikes, and union elections at Dodge Main. . . . D.R.U.M. beats rapidly permeated to other plants; such as Eldon Gear and Axle, and Ford Rouge. As far away as Mahway, New Jersey (United Black Brothers) and Cambridge, Massachusetts (Polaroid Workers Revolutionary movements) similar beats could be heard.

The increased militancy on the part of black workers found both the bureaucratic unions and management unprepared. But, with great resilience on the part of these reactionary elements, they were able to a certain degree impede the tangible development of these black workers' movements, in 1970, toward the end of a two day union election held in Detroit at the U.A.W., workers who had served as voting challengers were forcibly removed from the union hall by union officials and the local police with three voting booths left open. As a result of this violation of election procedure the U.A.W. functionaries were able to maintain their strangle hold on the local.

Now the D.R.U.M. beats are sounding the tune of International Black Appeal. The International Black Appeal is a charitable fund apparatus, which is attempting to address itself to the problems of black, non-white, and poor white workers. It has five major areas of concern: (1) Emergency food and Health Centers; This component speaks firstly to the severe nature of hunger and incorrect diets of the black and poor people. . . . In addition, and equally important, we seek the immediate construction of medical neighborhood clinics which will provide immediate emergency relief. This would also identify and assist in developing drug centers to alleviate the problem as much as possible. (2) Labor strike [sic] and deals with the problems of black and poor workers' families who because of circumstances many times beyond their control, find the worker of the family is fired, laid off, or becomes severely ill. We want to address ourselves to the families of these needy workers and assist the worker in combating his problems (i.e. stamping out racism in plants, better work conditions, safety conditions, etc.). Families of the black and poor feel these problems in an economic and social order that's overflowing with racism and class preferences. (3) Legal Defense services: Black and poor people are the greatest victims of racism and unequal justice under the law. Here again, the problems of families are affected many times by the loss of the bread winner, inadequate or non-existent money for bail, equally little money for food, lawyers, etc. It is within this realm that the fund wishes to address itself. (4) Welfare system: Here the fund shall address itself to groups of organizations that attempt to make the welfare system and its agencies more responsive and cognizant to the needs of the black and poor communities. (5) Housing and Recreation: This field of endeavor is crucial to the black and poor people's areas. Many problems occur because of the inadequacy or lack of both these facilities. The fund shall seek out organizations to involve itself in combating these problems.

Albeit the I.B.A. is still in its initial stages, however black workers from many of the Detroit area plants have given it their full support. Already many of these workers have spent invaluable time working for I.B.A. . . . It is incumbent upon black and poor people to take an interest in the development of a program, which like no other program in the history of America is geared to operate in their interest. Black workers, especially, must make resolute their determination to insure that in 1971 D.R.U.M. BEATS WILL BE HEARD.

Source: "Drum Beats Will Be Heard," *Inner-City Voice* 3 (February 1971): 3. Reprinted with permission.

---

12. Edward Bellamy: Excerpts from *Looking Backward* (1888)

Few novels have had as much impact on society as Edward Bellamy's Looking Backward. *Some accounts claim that, among nineteenth-century works of fiction, only* Uncle Tom's Cabin *and* Ben-Hur *sold more copies.*

Edward Bellamy (1850–98) was a lifelong social reformer who was working as a newspaper journalist for the Springfield Union, near his home in Chicopee Falls, Massachusetts, at the time his novel was published in 1888. Looking Backward *was an overnight success. It follows the fate of Julian West, an insomniac Boston Brahmin, who is put under hypnosis in 1887 and awakens in the year 2000. By then, the strife-torn Boston of his youth has been supplanted by an egalitarian utopia devoid of class strife. The book is essentially an extended lecture delivered by West's benevolent caretaker, Dr. Leete, who painstakingly explains how the utopia came to pass. (An appended Victorian romance enhanced the book's popularity.) The book resonated with Gilded Age audiences for its searing indictment of class conflict and deteriorating social conditions, and proved as popular among middle-class as among working-class readers. Within one year of the book's release,* **Bellamyite Nationalist** *clubs sprung up around the nation, all of which were devoted to bringing Bellamy's fictive utopia into a working reality.*

Key to the utopia was the reorganization of labor. All productive, service, and distributive enterprises were controlled by the state, and all citizens were compelled to serve in the "Industrial Army" from ages twenty-one to forty-five. In the first passage below, Bellamy discusses how industry and commerce came to be rethought. In the second, he lays out the organization of the Industrial Army. In both cases, the speaker is Dr. Leete, and Julian West asks the questions.

Early in the last [nineteenth] century the evolution was completed by the final consolidation of the entire capital of the nation. The industry and commerce of the country, ceasing to be conducted by a set of irresponsible corporations and syndicates of private persons at their caprice and for their profit, were entrusted to a single syndicate representing the people, to be conducted in the common interest for the common profit. The nation, that is to say, organized as the one great business corporation in which all other corporations were absorbed; it became the one capitalist in the place of all other capitalists, the sole employer, the final monopoly in which all previous and lesser monopolies were swallowed up, a monopoly in the profits and economics of which all citizens shared. The epoch of trusts had ended in The Great Trust. In a word, the people of the United States concluded to assume the conduct of their own business, just as one hundred-odd years before they had assumed the conduct of their own government, organizing now for industrial purposes on precisely the same grounds that they had then organized for political purposes. . . .

Organization of labor under one direction was the complete solution of what was, in your day and under your system, just regarded as the insoluble labor problem. When the nation become the sole employer all the citizens, by virtue of their citizenship, became employees, to be distributed according to the needs of industry. . . .

The people were already accustomed to idea that the obligation of every citizen not physically disabled, to contribute his military services to the defense of the nation was equal and absolute. That it was equally the duty of every citizen to contribute his quota of industrial or intellectual services to the maintenance of the nation was equally evident, thought it was not until the nation became the employer of labor that citizens were able to render this sort of service with any pretence either of universality or equity. No organization of labor was possible when the employing power was divided among hundreds or thousands of individuals and corporations. . . .

It is regarded as so absolutely natural and reasonable that the idea of its being compulsory has ceased to be thought of. He would be thought to be a incredibly contemptible person who should need compulsion in such a case. . . .

"Is the term of service in this industrial army for life?" Oh, no; it both begins late and ends earlier than the average working period in your day. Your workshops were filled with children and old men but we hold the period of youth sacred to education, and the period of maturity, when the physical forces begin to flag, equally sacred to ease and agreeable relaxation. The period of industrial service is twenty-four years beginning at the close of the course of education at twenty-one and terminating at forty-five. After forty-five, while discharged from labor the citizen remains liable to special calls in case of emergencies. . . .

The fifteenth day of October of every year is what we call Muster Day, because those who have reached the age of twenty-one are then mustered into the industrial service, and at the same time those who, after twenty-four years' service, have reached the age of forty-five are honorably mustered out.

Source: Edward Bellamy, *Looking Backward* (New York: Signet, 1960), pp. 53–54, 57–58.

---

13. Eight-Hour Association: 1886 Appeal for Reduction in Working Hours

The quest for shorter working hours has long been a mainstay of the labor movement. In the early nineteenth century, factory workers customarily toiled twelve or more hours per day. By the Civil War, many workplaces had reduced the workday to ten hours, though longer days continued to prevail in many places. Post–Civil War leaders like ***Ira Steward*** *began to press Congress to legislate an eight-hour day and a veritable* ***eight-hour movement*** *emerged across the United States. The following document comes from the Eight-Hour Association, a Boston-based organization with a national presence, which was supported by various trade unions and the* ***Knights of Labor****. Note that part of its appeal rests on opportunities for workers to improve themselves morally and intellectually. This is a clever appropriation of popular middle-class self-improvement schemes.*

This particular appeal appeared in ***John Swinton****'s paper and was a prelude to the events that culminated in the* ***Haymarket Square bombing*** *in Chicago.*

The Eight-Hour Association asks for a reduction of all daily toil from ten hours to eight, for the reason that such reduction of time will give opportunity for two more men to work for every eight now employed. In other words, the work now performed by eight men will require ten men to achieve the same result. This will be twenty more men employed for every eighty, thus giving immediate, and for some years, constant labor to all who are willing and able to work.

That every one shall have steady employment at good wages, working eight hours daily, it is necessary that all agree and unite in this movement. In order for each workman to prosper it is essential that all other workmen prosper; because all people support each other by exchanging each others' production and services. Therefore everybody who has commodities or services for sale is interested in having everybody else have a sufficient income from his own earnings to make a mutual exchange. United action in this effort means not only strength but prosperity for all.

The advocates of eight hours for a day's labor advise all workers to take for this number of hours an eight hour price, allowing the law of supply and demand to regulate wages in the future. We fully believe that while merchants, manufacturers and all employers will be benefited, the wages for laborers will soon be higher than ever heretofore, for the following reasons: A reduction of one fifth of laboring time for all that work will make a reduction of one-fifth of all kinds of products in the near future, which will make proportionate scarcity. With scarcity will come advance in prices for every commodity, giving merchants and manufacturers a fair profit, and wage workers an advance in wages. Ere long, all being employed, the production will be as great as now, but, all earning wages, the consumption and demand will be greater than now, so that prices and wages will still continue better than at present.

Eight hours, instead of ten, means a gain of two hours each day—more than one day each week—*seventy-eight days a year!*—a time sufficient to enable every unlettered person to learn to read and write; time in which every foreigner can learn to speak the English language and familiarize himself with his political duty as an American citizen. The extra time thus gained in the year will afford every workingman not only a sufficient recreation, but opportunity to attend the State and county fairs, the National Exposition, and make a visit to the childhood home, with time to spare for a journey to Europe.

This appeal is in the interest of capital as well as labor. The plain facts are that the strikes, lockouts, business failures, general business depression throughout the world, overflowing prisons and poorhouses, are the result of the producing power of the country being far in excess of the practical ability to consume. We make, raise and produce more than we can readily eat, wear, or dispose of. This results, first, in a falling of prices; then a lowering of wages, succeeded by strikes and resistance of wage workers, and a final discharge of workmen into idleness. Then, as men are unable to buy, there is a great underconsumption, goods piling up on one side, while great want and destitution exist on the other. To remedy this, productive power, temporarily, must be lessened. To do this by destroying machinery is barbarous. It is wiser far to accomplish this result, and benefit all mankind, by lessening the hours in which machines and men labor in the work of production. . . .

The advantage of eight hours to the laboring classes will be: (1st) employment; (2d) steady employment; (3d) better wages; (4th) relief from anxiety that comes from idleness and poverty; (5th) an opportunity to lay aside the means for the purchase of a home; (6th) opportunity to see and get acquainted with the family by daylight; (7th) more time for intellectual improvement; (8th) a chance for outdoor recreation on the secular day, without being compelled to take Sunday for that purpose; (9th) the ability to obtain respectable dress and make a good appearance, whereby encouragement is given to attend church and social gatherings, resulting in intellectual, moral and spiritual improvement. . . .

To fully lay this matter before the people, through literature, discussion, lecture, sermon and study, we recommend Saturday, April 24, 1886, as a general holiday for the laboring classes, preparatory to inaugurating the Eight-Hour Movement seven days afterwards, on the first day of May.

In this effort we fervently invoke the aid of the press, the clergy, legislators, teachers, employers, and all persons in authority. Give us employment for the idle masses who are struggling for bread; give us a chance to send pauper and criminal back to shop, and field, and factory, where they may get an honest living; give us back again health and bloom for the sunken eyed, starving sewing-woman; give us homes for working people, and a chance to earn them; give us an honest opportunity for every human being to possess the reasonable comforts of life—GIVE US EIGHT HOURS!

Source: Paul Boller and Ronald Story, *A More Perfect Union: Documents in U.S. History*, vol. 2 (1992), pp. 45–48.

---

14. Emma Goldman: Excerpts from Her Autobiography

Few women have ever made middle-class citizens as nervous as ***Emma Goldman*** *(1869–1940). Goldman was born in Lithuania and immigrated to the United States when she was seventeen. She began attending* ***socialist*** *meetings while working as a factory worker in Rochester, New York. By the late 1880s, Goldman converted to* ***anarchism****. She saw the state as an oppressive force and advocated its violent overthrow. She was a dramatic and dynamic speaker who forcefully put forth anarchist precepts from any platform to which she gained access. A worldwide spate of anarchist bombings and assassinations from the 1880s on only added to the fears that Goldman engendered. In 1892, her lover, Alexander Berkman, attempted to murder Homestead Steel manager Henry Clay Frick. Goldman was assumed to have been involved, but there was no evidence linking her to Berkman's attempt. Likewise, prosecutors unsuccessfully sought to connect Goldman to President William McKinley's assassination in 1901. Goldman was deported in 1919 because of her opposition to the United States' entry into World War I.*

In the first passage below, Goldman articulates her intense dislike of governmental authority. It is excerpted from a public speech Goldman made in New York's Union Square, during a severe economic depression that began in 1893. The second excerpt reveals Goldman's take on the question of patriotism. Goldman was an internationalist who felt that shared social class was the true bond between peoples, not artificially constructed national identities. The latter she viewed as vehicles of social control emanating from an oppressive state. Both passages come from the first book of her two-volume autobiography, a rambling affair that is often more episodic than chronological, but which is filled with Goldman's passionate views on individualism, love, social conditions, and politics.

(Note: The reference to Cardinal Manning in the first passage is to Henry Edward Manning [1808–92], an English convert to Catholicism. He won renown for helping settle an 1889 London dockworkers' strike.)

"Men and women," I begin amidst sudden silence, "do you not realize that the State is the worst enemy you have? It is a machine that crushes you in order to sustain the ruling class, your masters. Like naïve children you put your trust in your political leaders. You make it possible for them to creep into your confidence, only to have them betray you to the first bidder. But even where there is no direct betrayal, the labour politicians make common cause with your enemies to keep you in leash, to prevent your direct action. The State is the pillar of capitalism, and it is ridiculous to expect any redress from it. Do you not see the stupidity of asking relief from Albany with immense wealth within a stone's throw from here? Fifth Avenue is laid in gold, every mansion is a citadel of money and power. Yet there you stand, a giant, starved and fettered, shorn of his strength. Cardinal Manning long ago proclaimed that 'necessity knows no law' and that 'the starving man has a right to share of his neighbour's bread.' Cardinal Manning was an ecclesiastic steeped in the traditions of the Church, which has always been on the side of the rich against the poor. But he had some humanity, and he knew that hunger is a compelling force. You, too, will have to learn that you have a right to share your neighbour's bread. Your neighbours—they have not only stolen your bread, but they are sapping your blood. They will go on robbing you, your children, and your children's children, unless you wake up, unless you become daring enough to demand your rights. Well, then, demonstrate before the palaces of the rich; demand work. If they do not give you work, demand bread. If they deny you both, take bread. It is your sacred right!"

Uproarious applause, wild and deafening, broke the stillness like a sudden storm. The sea of hands eagerly stretching out towards me seemed like the wings of white birds fluttering. . . .

[W]hat is patriotism? Is it the love of one's birthplace, the place of childhood recollections and hopes, dreams and aspirations? Is it the place where, in childlike naïveté, we used to watch the passing clouds and wonder why we, too, could not float so swiftly? The place where we used to count the milliard glittering stars, terror stricken lest each one an eye should be, piercing the very depths of our little souls? Is it the place where we would listen to the music of the birds and long to have wings to fly, even as they, to distant lands? Or the place where we would sit at Mother's knee, enraptured by tales of great deeds and conquests? In short, is it love for the spot, every inch representing dear and precious recollections of a happy, joyous, and playful childhood?

If that were patriotism, few American men of today could be called upon to be patriotic, since the place of play has been turned into factory, mill, or mine, while the deafening sounds of machinery have replaced the music of the birds. Nor can we hear any longer the tales of great deeds, for the stories our mothers tell today are but those of sorrow, tears, and grief.

What, then, is patriotism? "Patriotism, sir, is the last resort of scoundrels," said Dr. Johnson. Leo Tolstoy, the greatest anti-patriot of our times, defined patriotism as the principle that justifies the training of wholesale murderers; a trade that requires better equipment for the exercise of man killing than the making of such necessities as shoes, clothing, and houses; a trade that guarantees better returns and greater glory than that of the honest workingman.

Source: Emma Goldman *Living My Life, Volume One* (New York: Dover, 1970; reprint of 1931 original), pp. 122–23, 428–29.

15. Eugene V. Debs: Excerpts from His Statement Upon Sentencing for Violation of the Espionage Act, 1918

Eugene V. Debs *(1855–1926) came to national prominence with the* ***Pullman Strike*** *of 1894, which resulted in Debs's first imprisonment, for violating a court injunction. In the years after Pullman, Debs was active in* ***socialist*** *politics and ran for the presidency of the United States five times. In 1918, at the height of popular agitation to support World War I, Debs was arrested for making an antiwar speech in Canton, Ohio, in violation of the Espionage Act. Debs was tried, found guilty, and sentenced to serve ten consecutive one-year terms in the Atlanta federal penitentiary. When asked if he had anything to say to the court, Debs delivered this statement, in which he affirmed his ideals, expressed his belief in the need for social change, and insisted that a reorganized social order would eventually come about. During his imprisonment, Debs ran for the presidency again in 1920 and garnered almost a million popular votes. He was pardoned after the war by President Warren G. Harding.*

Your honor, years ago I recognized my kinship with all living beings, and I made up my mind that I was not one bit better than the meanest on earth. I said then, and I say now, that while there is a lower class, I am in it, while there is a criminal element, I am of it, and while there is a soul in prison, I am not free.

I listened to all that was said in this court in support and justification of this prosecution, but my mind remains unchanged. I look upon the Espionage Law as a despotic enactment in flagrant conflict with democratic principles and with the spirit of free institutions. . . .

Your Honor, I have stated in this court that I am opposed to the social system in which we live; that I believe in a fundamental change—but if possible by peaceable and orderly means. . . .

Standing here this morning, I recall my boyhood. At fourteen I went to work in a railroad shop; at sixteen I was firing a freight engine on a railroad. I remember all the hardships and privations of that earlier day, and from that time until now my heart has been with the working class. I could have been in Congress long ago. I have preferred to go to prison. . . .

I am thinking this morning of the men in the mills and factories; of the men in the mines and on the railroads. I am thinking of the women who for a paltry wage are compelled to work out their barren lives; of the little children who in this system are robbed of their childhood and in their tender years are seized in the remorseless grasp of Mammon and forced into the industrial dungeons, there to feed the monster machines while they themselves are being starved and stunted, body and soul. I see them dwarfed and diseased and their little lives broken and blasted because in this high noon of our twentieth-century Christian civilization money is still so much more important than the flesh and blood of childhood. In very truth gold is god today and rules with pitiless sway in the affairs of men.

In this country, the most favored beneath the bending skies—we have vast areas of the richest and most fertile soil, material resources in inexhaustible abundance, the most marvelous productive machinery on earth, and millions of eager workers ready to apply their labor to that machinery to produce an abundance for every man, woman, and child—and if there are still vast numbers of our people who are the victims of poverty and whose lives are an unceasing struggle all the way from youth to old age, until at last death comes to their rescue and stills their aching hearts and lulls these hapless victims to dreamless sleep, it is not the fault of the Almighty: it cannot be charged to nature, but it is due entirely to the outgrown social system in which we live, that ought to be abolished not only in the interest of the toiling masses but in the higher interest of all humanity. . . .

I believe, Your Honor, in common with all Socialists, that this nation ought to own and control its own industries. I believe, as all Socialists do, that all things that are jointly needed and used ought to be jointly owned—that industry, the basis of our social life, instead of being the private property of the few and operated for their enrichment, ought to be the common property of all, democratically administered in the interest of all. . . .

I am opposing a social order in which it is possible for one man who does absolutely nothing that is useful to amass a fortune of hundreds of millions of dollars, while millions of men and women who work all the days of their lives secure barely enough for a wretched existence.

This order of things cannot always endure. I have registered my protest against it. I recognize the feebleness of my effort, but fortunately I am not alone. There are multiplied thousands of others who, like myself, have come to realize that before we may truly enjoy the blessings of civilized life, we must reorganize society upon a Mutual and co-operative basis; and to this end we have organized a great economic and political movement that spreads over the face of all the earth.

There are today upwards of sixty millions of Socialists, loyal, devoted adherents to this cause, regardless of nationality, race, creed, color, or sex. They are all making common cause. They are spreading with tireless energy the propaganda of the new social order. They are waiting, watching, and working hopefully through all the hours of the day and the night. They are still in a minority. But they have learned how to be patient and to bide their time. They feel—they know, indeed—that the time is coming, in spite of all opposition, all persecution, when this emancipating gospel will spread among all the peoples, and when this minority will become the triumphant majority and, sweeping into power, inaugurate the greatest social and economic change in history.

In that day we shall have the universal commonwealth—the harmonious co-operation of every nation with every other nation on earth. . . .

Source: Eugene V. Debs, *Writings and Speeches* (New York: Hermitage Press, 1948).

16. Excluding Black Workers: 1902 Letter in *Locomotive Firemen's Magazine* and 1929 Article by Elmer Anderson Carter in *Opportunity*

Although labor unions have often been at the forefront of progressive change in the United States, they have had their share of blind spots as well. One of the worst of these has been race, especially as it pertains to African American workers. Many trade unions forbade black members well into the twentieth century, and some black leaders claim there are still prejudice barriers to overcome. Only a handful of organizations—most notably the **Knights of Labor***, the* **United Mine Workers of America***, and the* **Industrial Workers of the World***—have consistently good records relating to black laborers, and there were plenty of ugly, racist incidents within even those organizations. The excerpts below highlight some of the challenges faced by black workers.*

The first letter appeared in a 1902 issue of the Locomotive Firemen's Magazine *and is in response to an appeal to accept black members, from a New Yorker named George Peters. It is important to realize that the response was typical and that the Firemen were no worse than many other trade unions, despite the fact that the rebuttal comes from a Southerner. Racism was pervasive, not regional.*

The second article contains Elmer Anderson Carter's blistering 1929 condemnation of the racial policies of the **American Federation of Labor***. It appeared in* Opportunity *on November 7, 1929. Many of the same charges were echoed by* **A. Philip Randolph** *in a 1961 report to the American Federation of Labor-Congress of Industrial Organizations. Although the executive council refuted his charges, they resonated among many black workers.*

RESPONSE TO GEORGE H. PETERS

I have just read an article . . . entitled "The Negro and Organized Labor in the South." The brother's motives may be all right, but his article will receive a cup of very cold water in the South.

The Negro can organize on his own responsibility if he likes, but he can never affiliate with southern organizations of any kind. The firemen of the South have a great work to do . . . without crossing the color line and reaching out to Mr. "Burr Head," to assist him to a place of safety and security. . . .

What has the Negro done to merit recognition by the Firemen? The brother from New York says the Negro will accept his inferiority to the white man . . . but all southern men would laugh at the brother's ignorance of the Negro . . . for if he is given a foot, he tries to take a block. In many, many cases, he is thick headed and non-progressive, and when he goes to school for a couple of years he begins to think he knows it all, and it only makes a worthless fool of him. The southern man . . . draw(s) the line when it comes to taking him into our worthy order. . . .

Member of 522
Shreveport, LA

THE A.F.L. AND THE NEGRO

It has often been asserted that black workers have been slow in accepting the doctrines and methods of organized labor. . . . This apparent indifference of the black worker . . . has served to draw the fire of various officials of the American

Federation of Labor who, when accused of apathy to the fate of Negro labor, have replied . . . that the Negro worker was unorganizable. . . .

The recent convention of the American Federation of Labor . . . lacked much of being able to convince observers that it is the pillar of flame . . . to lead the black worker, or for that matter the white worker, out of the wilderness. Out of the thirty million workers in America less than three million are enrolled in the American Federation. . . .

Only in those occupations, generally semi-skilled or unskilled, which attract large numbers of Negroes, such as longshoremen, hod-carriers, common building laborers, or those in which Negroes enjoy a comparative monopoly, such as dining-car porters; or those in which Negro competition is able to cope . . . with the competition of white workers, as in the coal mining industry . . . has American organized labor made any real effort to enlist the black worker. . . . There are approximately 100,000 Negro workers who are affiliated with some form of labor organization, a remarkable number when one considers that the Negro not only is outside the pale of the skilled craft organizations, but also is compelled . . . to face the opposition of white labor, organized and unorganized, to gain a foothold in industry.

It is true that the American Federation of Labor has issued several lofty pronouncements to the effect that no discrimination because of race or color should govern admission to unions. It is also true that only eleven unions . . . specifically deny Negroes membership. But . . . even when racial prejudice does not operate . . . to keep Negroes put, craft limitations and restrictions achieve the same result. . . .

[T]here will be but little hope for the black worker in the American Federation of Labor as long as it is the so-called "aristocracy of labor," as long as it remains structurally a craft organization. . . .

Source: Philip Foner and Ronald Lewis, eds., *Black Workers: A Documentary History from Colonial Times to the Present* (Philadelphia: Temple University, 1989), pp. 255–56, 409–10.

---

17. Fair Wages: Excerpt from John L. Lewis's *The Miners' Fight for American Standards* (1925)

One of the clearest statements ever uttered on ***wages*** *was by* **John L. Lewis**, *who headed the* **United Mine Workers of America (UMWA)** *from 1920 to 1960 and was a founder of the* **Congress of Industrial Organizations** *and served as its president from 1935 to 1940. Before Lewis was such a well-known national figure, he penned* The Miners' Fight for American Standards *in 1925. The book's title is deliberate and strategic; Lewis wanted to show that what the UMWA wanted was in keeping with American values and aspirations. In the wake of the post–World War I crackdown on radicals, to say nothing of bloody capital/labor clashes involving coal miners in places like*

***Matewan** and **Blair Mountain**, Lewis insisted that miners were loyal Americans seeking only a fair deal.* Miners' Fight *is, above all, a defense of prudent unionism. Lewis locates the desire for higher wages within the very logic of **capitalism**.*

> Primarily the United Mine Workers of America insists upon the maintenance of the wage standards, guaranteed by the existing contractual relations in the industry, in the interests of its own membership. It is acting in that respect exactly as any other individual, organization, or corporation would do under like circumstances. The theory of our system of free enterprise is that the ultimate prosperity of all is best assured by the utmost endeavor of each to better his own condition. Trade unionism is an integral part of the existing system of industry first called by its critics capitalism. The word once used in reproach has in these times been adopted with pride by the advocates and defenders of the system, as was the case in regard to great religious sects and political parties, which adopted as badges of honor names first hurled at them as epithets.
>
> Distrust and hostility toward the business system wane as it is becoming better understood how the general prosperity and individual and family welfare of modern peoples had been increased by the use of capital in production to multiply the productive power of man's labor, whether of hand or brain. Trade unionism is a phenomenon of capitalism quite similar to the cooperation. One is essentially a pooling of labor for purposes of common action in production and in sales. The other is a pooling of capital for exactly the same purposes. The economic aims of both are identical—gain. . . .

Source: John L. Lewis, *The Miners' Fight for American Standards* (Indianapolis: Bell Publishing Company, 1925), pp. 40–41.

---

18. Flint Sit-Down Strike: Excerpt of 1976 Interview of Genora Johnson Dollinger

*One of the seminal events in American labor history was the 1936–37 **sit-down strike** against General Motors (GM) in Flint, Michigan. Most analysts credit success at Flint as establishing the **United Auto Workers (UAW)** as a legitimate bargaining agent in the automotive industry. Still others claim that this strike virtually transformed the **Congress of Industrial Organizations** from a fledgling federation into a powerful rival to the established **American Federation of Labor**. For forty-four days, workers barricaded themselves inside the Chevrolet Number 1 and Fisher Body Number 2 buildings, key plants in GM's production. One estimate claims that 112,000 of the company's 150,000 employees were affected by the sit-down strike.*

The story of Flint usually centers on the men who stayed inside the factory, but they could not have held out were it not for the massive logistical and material support of the Women's Emergency Brigade. Women also placed their bodies and lives on the line in support of the strike. A key moment came on January 11, 1937, when GM tried to forcibly evict the sit-down strikers. First they cut off heat and power to Fisher Num-

ber 2, despite the sixteen-degree weather, then police rushed the plant. They were rebuffed by a fusillade of auto parts from occupying workers. As Victor Reuther, Roy Reuther, and Bob Travis arrived on the scene with a UAW sound truck, Genora Johnson took the microphone and exhorted the women of Flint to stand up for their husbands, boyfriends, and brothers. As the women surged, Flint police retreated, and the Battle of the Running Bulls ended in victory for the union. (Note: The term bull is a slang reference to police officers.)

In 1976, Genora Johnson Dollinger related the story to historian Sherna Gluck. This passage comes from Gluck's interview.

> [W]e had the water hoses from the plant, and the hinges. . . . Those hinges were kind of heavy hinges. You know, the old car-door hinge was a different thing. And they got the big boxloads of them and they got them down to look so they could fire them from downstairs, and they were upstairs on the roof firing them, too. . . .
>
> There was no hand-to-hand combat. [The police] . . . had rifle shot and buckshot. There was firebombs and those tear gas canisters. And we would run out and grab [those]—the men were much faster at that, and . . . they were better pitchers. . . . They'd get tear gas canisters and hurl them back. And the firebombs, they usually got those . . . but the timing on those was very important. . . .
>
> So anyway, the sound car was down there, and we had Victor Reuther as the primary speaker. And then he would pull up other men, making their appeals, and this went on and on. It never dawned on me . . . to speak. In the first place, this was primarily a man's operation, and I'm down there helping out, although I never thought too much about men and women when we were right in the heart of a battle. . . . I'd never made any kind of a public speech over a microphone, and it—until [Victor Reuther] came back and told us. He said, "Well, we may have lost the battle. The war is not lost, but we may have lost this battle." And he gave us the idea that we had to prepare people for . . . this little defeat. And I said to him then, I said, "Well, Victor, why don't I speak over the . . . loudspeaker? . . . " And he says, "Well, we've got nothing to lose." He had great confidence . . . in women. . . . So that's when I got up to take the mike. And, again, there, you lose yourself. You go beyond yourself and think of the cause. And I was able to make my voice really ring out on that one because I knew that [sound system] battery was going down. We only had a few moments left. And so, that's when I appealed to the women of Flint. I bypassed everybody else . . . and went right to the women and told them what was happening. And that's when I said, "There are women down here, mothers of children," and I made it sound plural, because I knew that here was this gallantry that's always present in the hearts of men and other women that are going to come down and stand by women in such a situation. So that's when I said, "There are women down here, mothers of children, and I beg of you to come down here and stand with your husband, your loved ones . . . your brothers, and even your sweethearts," because we had a lot of couples . . . and I'd get their girlfriends.
>
> And when I made that appeal, it was a strange thing. It was dark, too. But I could almost hear a hush. . . . I could hear a hush over that crowd the minute a woman's voice went over. It was startling, you know. All night long, they didn't know there was even a woman down there.

And as that happened, I thought I saw . . . car lights. Whatever it was in this darkness, we could see the action going on up [at Fisher Number 2]. . . . [M]aybe they were factory headlights or spotlights on us or . . . police lights. But I saw a first woman struggling, and I noticed that she had started to come down, and a cop grabbed her by the coat and she went right out of that coat. And this was in freezing weather. . . . There was ice on the . . . pavement and everything. And she just kept right on coming. And as soon as that happened, other women broke through, and again we had that situation where cops didn't want to fire into backs of women. And once they did that, the men came, naturally, and that was the end of the battle.

Source: Interview conducted by Sherna Gluck. © Feminist History Research Project, 1976. http://historymatters.gmu.edu/d/136/.

19. Forcing the Hand of the Fair Employment Practices Committee: Excerpt from November 1942 Article in *Survey Graphic* Magazine

As World War II loomed, African Americans found themselves in a precarious situation. Most of American society, North and South, was still deeply in the throes of Jim Crow systems that segregated whites and blacks. Good-paying jobs existed in the burgeoning defense industry, but most employers refused to hire black workers (often at the insistence of white labor unions). If work could be secured, it was often in jobs considered too degrading for white workers. The mobilization of large numbers of white workers—the armed forces remained segregated until after World War II—made it apparent that black labor would play an important part in America's defense efforts. ***A. Philip Randolph*** *seized upon the situation. Randolph put out a call for African Americans to march upon Washington, D.C., on July 1, 1941, to protest job and social discrimination. The prospect of tens of thousands of black citizens marching on the nation's Capitol at the same time efforts were afoot to counter fascism abroad forced the hand of President Franklin Roosevelt. In exchange for Randolph's agreement to call off the march, President Roosevelt issued Executive Order 8802, which created the* ***Fair Employment Practices Committee (FEPC)****, which mandated that all federal agencies, contractors, and job-training programs were to be free of religious or racial discrimination.*

The FEPC was an important first step, but hardly the panacea that cured racial discrimination. Randolph cagily kept the threat of a march on Washington alive, though most historians now believe that he was bluffing about the alleged numbers of African American marchers he could muster. Randolph nonetheless used his threat to keep demands for black equality alive. The piece from Randolph excerpted below appeared in the November 1942 issue of Survey Graphic *magazine.*

Though I have found no Negroes who want to see the United Nations lose this war, I have found many who, before the war ends, want to see the stuffing knocked out of white supremacy and of empire over subject peoples. American Negroes, involved as we are in the general issues of the conflict, are confronted not with a choice but with the challenge both to win democracy for ourselves at home and to help win the war for democracy the world over.

There is no escape from the horns of this dilemma. There ought not to be escape. For if the war for democracy is not won abroad, the fight for democracy cannot be won at home. If this war cannot be won for the white peoples, it will not be won for the darker races.

Controversially, if freedom and equality are not vouchsafed for the peoples of color, the war for democracy will not be won. Unless this double-barreled thesis is accepted and applied, the darker races will never whole-heartedly fight for the victory of the United Nations. That is why those familiar with the thinking of the American Negro have sensed his lack of enthusiasm, whether among the educated or uneducated, rich or poor, professional or non-professional, religious or secular, rural or urban, north, south, east or west. . . .

What are the reasons for this state of mind? The answer is: discrimination, segregation, Jim Crow. Witness the navy, the army, the air corps; and also government services at Washington. In many parts of the South, Negroes in Uncle Sam's uniform are being put upon, mobbed, sometimes even shot down by civilian and military police, and on occasion lynched. Vested political interests in race prejudice are so deeply entrenched that to them winning the war against Hitler is secondary to preventing Negroes from winning democracy for themselves. This is worth many divisions to Hitler and Hirohito. While labor, business, and farm are subjected to ceilings and floors and not allowed to carry on as usual, these interests trade in the dangerous business of race hate as usual.

When the defense program began and billions of taxpayers' money were appropriated for guns, ships, tanks, and bombs, Negroes presented themselves for work only to be given the cold shoulder. North as well as the South, and despite their qualifications, Negroes were denied skilled employment. Not until their wrath and indignation took the form of a proposed protest march on Washington, scheduled for July 1, 1941, did things begin to move in the form of defense jobs for Negroes. The march was postponed by the timely issuance (June 24, 1941) of the famous Executive Order No. 8802 by President Roosevelt. But this order and the President's Committee on Fair Public Practice, established there under, have as yet only scratched the surface by way of eliminating discriminations on account of race or color in war industry. Both management and labor unions in too many places in too many ways are still drawing the color line. . . .

PROGRAM OF THE MARCH ON WASHINGTON MOVEMENT

1. We demand, in the interest of national unity, the abrogation of every law which makes a distinction in treatment between citizens based on religion, creed, color, or national origin. This means an end to Jim Crow in education, in housing, in transportation and in every other social, economic, and political privilege; and especially, we demand, in the capital of the nation, an end to all segregation in public places and in public institutions.

2. We demand legislation to enforce the Fifth and Fourteenth Amendments guaranteeing that no person shall be deprived of life, liberty or property without due process of law, so that the full weight of the national government may be used for the protection of life and thereby may end the disgrace of lynching.
3. We demand the enforcement of the Fourteenth and Fifteenth Amendments and the enactment of the Pepper Poll Tax bill so that all barriers in the exercise of the suffrage are eliminated.
4. We demand the abolition of segregation and discrimination in the army, navy, marine corps, air corps, and all other branches of national defense.
5. We demand an end to discrimination in jobs and job training. Further, we demand that the F.E.P.C. be made a permanent administrative agency of the U.S. Government and that it be given power to enforce its decisions based on its findings.
6. We demand that federal funds be withheld from any agency which practices discrimination in the use of such funds.
7. We demand colored and minority group representation on all administrative agencies so that these groups may have recognition of their democratic right to participate in formulating policies.
8. We demand representation for the colored and minority racial groups on all missions, political and technical, which will be sent to the peace conference so that the interests of all people everywhere may be fully recognized and justly provided for in the post-war settlement.

Source: Philip Foner and Ronald Lewis, eds., *Black Workers: A Documentary History from Colonial Times to the Present* (Philadelphia: Temple University Press, 1989), pp. 527–30.

---

20. Forty Years in a Steel Mill: Studs Terkel Interviews Steelworker Steve Dubi

In 1972, Studs Terkel interviewed more than eighty Americans engaged in a wide variety of jobs about their work. Terkel called the resulting work a book about violence, both to body and to spirit. For many workers, he found the workday to be a struggle by the "walking wounded." Here Terkel talks with veteran Chicago steelworker Steve Dubi about his forty years in the steel mill. Dubi's discouragement is obvious, as is his pride in seeing his sons steer clear of work in the steel mills.

We're in Pullman, an industrial neighborhood on the far South Side of Chicago. It is a one-family dwelling, much like all the others on the block. He has lived in this area all his life. "I was born in the shadow of them steel mills." He has worked as an inspector at the South Works of U.S. Steel for forty years.

"I was hired in '29 as a water boy. I was sixteen. I had to be seventeen, but in those days they overlooked a little thing here, a little thing there. I worked for a year. Then came the Crash. I was rehired in June '33 and I've been inspecting ever since. I'm ready for retirement. But the home we live in isn't paid for yet. The car I'm driving isn't paid for yet. Nothing to show for forty years of work."

His wife is a licensed practical nurse who "works with geriatrics." They have two sons. Robert, a Vietnam war veteran, is married. He's in the field of sales. Their other son, Father Leonard Dubi, is one of the city's most renowned activist priests. As a passionate spokesman for the blue-collar community in which his parish is located, he has on numerous occasions challenged some of the city's most powerful men and institutions.

During the visit, as his weariness is evident, his wife joins the conversation.

When we were kids we thought the steel mill was it. We'd see the men comin' out, all dirty, black. The only thing white was the goggles over their eyes. We thought they were it, strong men. We just couldn't wait to get in there. When we finally did get in, we were sorry. (Chuckles.) It wasn't what it was cut out to be.

You're on your feet all day, on concrete. They lay the steel out on the skids. It's like a long horse, and they lay the steel across. You get your flashlight and you walk over it and you chalk it and mark the defect. You look for the defect in the steel. You watch the tolerances for lengths and thickness and what not. You have a chipper or a grinder to smooth it out. If it comes within the tolerance the customer allows, it's all right. If it goes too deep, you scrap the bar or recut it. When we broke in, the older men showed us what defects to look for. A crack in the bar is called a seam. Some would be wide open where you couldn't miss 'em. Some were real tight and you would have to look close. It's hard on the eyes. Oh, your eyes do get tired. I put some drops in my eyes.

I'm getting up in the age now where I can't take it any more. In my younger days I used to work eight hours, go out and play a doubleheader of softball, go out and drink a shot, and sleep it off (laughs), and go back to work in the morning. And not feel too much pain. (Sighs.) But now I can't take it any more. I'd like to retire. I think I've worked hard enough and long enough, but I still can't see my way out. I don't know if I'll make it. I got sore legs and a sore back, sore arms, arthritis, bursitis, and every other thing is catching up on me. (Laughs.)

Everyone looks forward to retirement, but there's a lot of 'em not makin' it. That's all they talk about is retirement. Where are you gonna go? What are you gonna do? And the poor soul never makes it. A lot of 'em, they're countin' the months instead of the years—and pass away. A lot of my friends are passed away already.

I can take it any time I want, but I won't be fifty-nine until December. I don't get on social security until I'm sixty-two. Why, that'll be another three years. I don't want to go just yet, but maybe I won't be able to take it any more. It's gettin' tougher. I'm not like a machine. Well, a machine wears out too sometimes.

And they're forcin' more work on ya. It's knockin' off men, makin' cutbacks here and there to save money. They've knocked off an awful lot of jobs. With the foreign imports of steel they're losin' money. That's what they say. I suppose in order to make a profit they have to cut somewhere. But I told 'em "After forty years of work, why do you take a man away from me? You're gonna force me into retirement." All of us were real angry. But there's nothin' we can do about it. What can I do? Quit?

I try not to take this home with me. I don't tell her nothin' about it. It'll cause her to worry. There's nothin' I can do about it. About four o'clock I'll sit down here and watch TV, maybe get my dinner on a TV table and I watch the finish of the ball game or the finish of a good movie. I'll sit back here and work the crossword puzzle and read the sports news and I fall asleep. (Laughs.)

I had to ask [for] this coming Sunday off because I'm going to a golf outing. Otherwise I'd have had to work from three to eleven. They're working us twelve days in a row. When I'm workin' on the day shift I'll work Monday through Saturday, seven to three. The following week I'll be lined up on the three to eleven shift. It's a forty-hour week, but it's always twelve days in a row.

If they're in a slack time, they go down to one shift. You can't make any long-range plan. When we bought this house fourteen years ago, the real estate man wanted to sell me a lot more expensive house. I said no. With the job I have I don't know if I'll be workin' three, four months from now. We might go out on strike. We may go down to four days a week. Been like this all these years.

I got nothin' to show for it. I live in a home the bank has a mortgage on. (Laughs.) I own a car the finance people have the title to. (Laughs.) I don't know where they got the idea that we make so much. The lowest class payin' job there, he's makin' two dollars an hour if he's makin' that much. It starts with jobs class-1 and then they go up to class-35. But no one knows who that one is. Probably the superintendent. So they put all these class jobs together, divide it by the number of people workin' there, and you come up with a fabulous amount. But it's the big bosses who are makin' all the big money and the little guys are makin' the little money. You hear these politicians give themselves a thousand-dollar raise, and they scream when the steelworker asks for fifty cents an hour raise.

You pack your lunch, or you buy it at the vending machine. We used to have a canteen in there, but they cut that out. The vending machine is lousy. It hurts a man when he'll put his quarter or thirty-five cents in there for a can of vegetable soup and it takes the coin but don't kick anything out. There's no one there to open the machine and give him his quarter back or a can of food. (Laughs.) A lotta machines are broken that way. Every day it occurs.

You're not regarded. You're just a number out there. Just like a prisoner. When you report off you tell 'em your badge number. A lotta people don't know your name. They know you by your badge number. My number is 44–065. When your work sheet is sent in your name isn't put down, just your number. At the main office they don't know who 44–065 is. They don't know if he's black, white, or Indian. They just know he's 44–065.

Of course, there are accidents. They're movin' a lot of steel—a lot of crane movement and transfer buggy movement and switchin' and trucks. And there's machinery that straightens the bars and turning lathes. Always movement. You eat the dust and dirt and take all the different things that go with it. How you gonna grind a defect out of a bar without creating dust? How you can scarf the billet without makin' smoke? When a man takes off sick, he's got a chest cold, how do you know what he's got? A lot of people died, they just had a heart attack. Who knows what they die of?

We have to slog our way through dirt and smog and rain and slush to get to our place of work. From the mill gate to where I work is about a fifteen-, twenty-minute walk. In-between that you have puddles. We don't have a nice walkway with an overhead ramp. We don't have a shuttle bus. If it's raining, you walk through the rain. If it's snowin' or blowin', you're buckin' that snow and the wind. In the wintertime that wind is comin' off that lake, it's whippin' right into your face.

That place is not inside a building. It's just under a roof. There's no protection against the winds. They won't even plug up the holes to keep the draft off you. Even the snow comes through and falls on you while you're workin'. The roof is so leaky they should furnish you with umbrellas.

His wife murmurs: "He's sick all the time."

The union squawks about it, but if the steel mill don't fix it, what are you gonna do? The washrooms are in terrible shape. But when they get around to fixin' 'em, there's five hundred men usin' one bowl to sit on. The union's helped a great deal, but the steel mill is slow in comin' across with things like they should.

If I retire right now, I would make $350 a month. There's a woman across the street got a half a dozen kids and no husband, and she's probably gettin' five hundred dollars a month from ADC. She gets more money than I would right now after workin' for forty years. If I retire now, my insurance is dropped. I belong to this Blue Cross-Blue Shield insurance now. If I go on a pension, I would get dropped automatically. The day you retire, that's the day it's out.

I told my sons, "If you ever wind up in that steel mill like me, I'm gonna hit you right over your head. Don't be foolish. Go get yourself a schooling. Stay out of the steel mill or you'll wind up the same way I did." Forty years of hard work and what have I got to show for it? Nothing. I can't even speak proper. When you're a steelworker (laughs), you don't get to speak the same language that you would do if you meet people in a bank or a business office.

When I was going to school I really loved mechanical drawing. I really excelled in it in high school. I was gettin' good marks. But my dad died. Well, most of the children had saloon keepers and grocery store keepers, they had dads workin', and they were able to buy things. I felt embarrassed because I couldn't buy the proper paper. I would use the other side of someone else's discarded paper. I did love mechanical drawing and I was good at it. Well, I had to get a job. . . ."

I was hopin' Leonard would be a doctor. When he entered the seminary, I thought: Gee, what caused him to go in there? When he was an Andy Frain usher he was assigned to Holy Name and he got acquainted with a lot of priests there. A lot of the ushers were at the seminary. They probably influenced him. He's happy, so I'm happy for him. At first I wasn't sure he was gonna stay, 'cause he loved life too much. He loved everything, people and animals. (Muses) Maybe that's why he became a priest . . . (Trails off.)

In the past, it was strictly parish. They come out once a year to bless the house and shake the hand. But now, with the younger set, things have changed. All the priests are goin' without their collars and doin' a lot of things that the old-time priest would never think of doin'. I don't think they were allowed to.

Henrietta Dubi reflects: "I'll never forget those women, my neighbors, they were sittin' out on the porch and they couldn't understand why I'm grievin' that Leonard went into the seminary. They said, 'Oh, it's such an honor.' I said, 'Yes, but it's gonna be a hard life.' No freedom, no privileges. We could only see him once a month. I figured he was in prison. One day I said to him, 'Leonard, are you happy?' He said, 'I can't begin to tell you how happy I am. Please don't ask again. I chose this life and this is the life I'm going to lead.' When he was havin' his senior prom, I should have known then. Everything he was buying was black. It never dawned on me. The first time I seen Skid Row in my life was when my son took me down there. He said, 'I want to save people like this.' In a kidding way I said, 'These people are beyond saving.' He said, 'As long as there's breath in 'em, they can be saved.' I was sad and depressed when he first went in. I couldn't understand why. Now I'm very proud of him. I wish there were more like him to speak out, but some are afraid. We pray for him all the time."

Sometimes I worry about him. He takes on the real big shots. He might buck the wrong person. They've been shooting Presidents and senators. He could be shot at too—if he says the wrong thing or gets the wrong man angry. When you're foolin' around with a politician, why you got troubles. But he's for the people, he wants 'em to have a square deal. And I'm glad. If the people don't like what he's sayin', why that's too bad.

You know the big joke? When Len was an Andy Frain usher, he used to seat Mayor Daley in his box at Comiskey Park. Ten years later he's fightin' him on the Crosstown Expressway business and the county assessor's office. (Laughs.) When we first started visiting Leonard at the seminary we weren't even allowed to bring him a newspaper. He wasn't allowed to have a radio. It was so strict at that time. What amazes me now, I turn on the TV and I see him arguin' with the mayor. (Laughs.) Or the county assessor and them politicians. It's so different, it's fantastic.

When he started on this pollution against the steel mills, I told Leonard everybody knows the steel mill is polluting. How can you make steel without polluting? I'm not gonna bite the hand that feeds me. They been doing it for a hundred years. It could be cut down a great deal, I suppose, if they wanted—which they are trying to do. They're putting in a lot of new buildings. I don't know what they are, but they claim it's for ecology. Who knows?

This pollution business. He helped them people on the West Side where he lived. When we used to go to visit him it seemed you are going into a valley. It seemed you hit a fog bank. We learned later it was smog from the Edison plants. And he cleared it up. So we're for him one hundred percent. But this fightin' with the mayor and the aldermen, that scares me. (Laughs.)

Mrs. Dubi interjects: "When I see him on television, I run. There might be a nut in the audience who'll shoot."

She's scared. We're real proud of him. All my friends cut clippings out of the newspaper and bring 'em to me and they'll say, "Hey, I heard Leonard on the radio on my way to work." They'll tell me they're all for him. My sister was tellin' us the other day that her doctor was speakin' of a young priest who was doin' so much for the people in the neighborhood. She said, "That's my nephew." He said, "Gee, he's wonderful."

You know what I told him to start on next? He's fightin' for lower taxes, which is all right. And better livin' conditions, which is all right. And this road that he's against, it's all right. Like he said, they're gonna demolish a lotta homes, a lotta people are gonna be put out. So the next thing I want him to do is lower this age of retirement, social security to about sixty, so I can get out of the mill sooner. If they lowered the age to about sixty, maybe they'd get a year or two benefit out of the pension before they die.

Hard workin' never killed a man, they say. I say workin' in the steel mill is not like workin' in an air-conditioned office, where politicians and bankers sit on their fannies. Where you have to eat all that dust and smoke, you can't work hard and live a long life. You shouldn't be made to work till sixty-two or sixty-five to reap any benefit. We're paying social security, and most of us will never realize a penny from it. That's why they should give it to him at a younger age to let him enjoy a few years of the life he ruined workin' in the factory. I told him. "Leonard, you get to work on that next." (Laughs.)

Yeah, we're proud of Len. At least he's doin' somethin'. What have I done in my forty years of work? I led a useless life. Here I am almost sixty years old and I don't have anything to show for it. At least he's doing something for his people. I worked all my life and helped no one. What I'm happy about is that them two boys took my advice and stayed out of the steel mill. (Laughs.) We're a couple of dummies. We worked all our lives and we have nothing.

MRS. DUBI: You know what we have? We got two million dollars in our children. Even in this angered world, both these kids turned out good, right? So we're still winners. (To him) Even though we don't have the cash, Father, we don't have nothin' to retire with we still got two million dollars.

You gotta show it to me.

MRS. DUBI: You see him on TV, don't you?

No thanks to me. I had nothin' to do with makin' him what he is. I told you I am nothing. After forty years of workin' at the steel mill, I am just a number. I think I've been a pretty good worker. That job was just right for me. I had a minimum amount of education and a job using a micrometer and just a steel tape and your eyes—that's a job that was just made for me. But they don't appreciate it. They don't care. Bob worked in the mill a few months during a school vacation. He said, "I don't know how you done it all these years. I could never do it." I said, "I been tellin' you all your life never get into that mill." (Laughs.)

---

21. Founding of the American Federation of Labor (AFL): Excerpts from the AFL Call to Action (1886)

The largest labor federation of the late nineteenth century was the ***Knights of Labor****. The Knights, however, organized workers irrespective of their skill level, trade, race, ethnicity (except for Chinese), or gender. Its local assemblies often mixed workers from various walks of life. Some* ***craft unionists*** *disagreed with the Knights' catholic approach to organizing and felt that true solidarity could only be obtained among workers sharing the same skilled trades. Moreover, some resented what they perceived* *as the Knights of Labor's interference in matters pertaining to the trades. The Knights had many trade assemblies, but by the 1880s, it and national trade unions often found themselves embroiled in bitter battles over* **jurisdiction**, **strikes**—*which the Knights opposed—and numerous other tactics and issues. The Knights had an especially tumultuous relationship with the Cigar Makers International Union and two of its leaders,* **Adolph Strasser** *and* **Samuel Gompers**.

In May 1886, a "peace" conference between the Knights and trades unions ended acrimoniously, with the Knights of Labor claiming it was the only true repository of labor solidarity, while craft unions passed resolutions demanding that the Knights of Labor confine itself to unorganized and unskilled workers and leave all craft workers to their respective national and international unions. In December 1886, craft unionists met to transform a moribund craft federation, the Federation of Organized Trades and Labor Unions. It became the **American Federation of Labor (AFL)**. *The AFL's call to action is excerpted below.*

The time has now arrived to draw the bonds of unity much closer together between all the trades unions of America. We need an annual Trades Congress that shall have for its object:

1. The formation of trades unions and the encouragement of the trades union movement in America.
2. The organization of trades assemblies, trades councils or central labor unions in every city in America and the further encouragement of such bodies.
3. The founding of state trades assemblies or state labor congresses to influence state legislation in the interest of the working masses.
4. The establishment of national and international trades unions based upon the strict recognition of the autonomy of each trade, and the promotion and advancement of such bodies.
5. An American Federation of Alliance of all national and international trades unions to aid and assist each other and furthermore to secure national legislation in the interest of the working people and influence public opinion by peaceful and legal methods in favor of organized labor.
6. To aid and encourage the labor press of America and to disseminate tracts and literature on the labor movement. . . .
7. . . . Whereas the Knights of Labor have persistently attempted to undermine and disrupt the well-established trades unions [, have] organized and encouraged men who have proven untrue to their trade, false to the obligation of their union, embezzlers of moneys and expelled by many of the unions and conspiring to pull down the trades unions. . . .

Resolved: That we condemn the acts above recited and call upon all workingmen to join the unions of their respective trades and urge the formation of national and international unions and the centralization of all under one head, the American Federation of Labor.

Source: Norman Ware, *The Labor Movement in the United States 1860–1895: A Study in Democracy* (1929; reprint; Gloucester: Peter Smith, 1959), pp. 294–97.

22. Gilded Age Social Conditions: Testimony before the U.S. Senate Committee upon the Relations between Labor and Capital (1883)

The period from roughly the end of the Civil War to the turn of the twentieth century is often dubbed the "Gilded Age" by historians taking their lead from an eponymous 1873 novel by Mark Twain and Charles Dudley Warner. Although the decades following the Civil War saw the maturing of America's industrial revolution, a massive expansion of production, and the making of fabulous fortunes, it was marked also by a widening gap between rich and poor, labor strife, and deteriorating social relations. The underlying dross beneath the gilding was revealed to all during the traumatic railroad strikes that made up the ***Great Labor Uprising*** *of 1877. Moreover, though the economy grew, its pace was quite unstable, with periods of boom followed by equally dramatic depressions. The early 1880s saw one such economic downturn. In 1883, the United States Senate convened a Committee upon the Relations between Labor and Capital to investigate social and economic conditions. A parade of witnesses—industrialists, clerics, labor leaders, economists, financiers, health-care workers, and ordinary workers—offered testimony before the committee, which was chaired by Senator Henry W. Blair of New Hampshire.*

Two pieces of testimony are excerpted below. The first comes from Conrad Carl, a New York City tailor, who was questioned by Senators Blair and James L. Pugh of Alabama. The second comes from Dr. Timothy D. Stow, who shared his experiences of being a physician in the textile city of Fall River, Massachusetts.

TESTIMONY OF CONRAD CARL

Conrad Carl: During the time I have been here the tailoring business is altered in three different ways. Before we had sewing machines we worked piecework with our wives, and very often our children. We had no trouble then with our neighbors, nor with the landlord, because it was a very still business, very quiet; but in 1854 or 1855, and later, the sewing machine was invented and introduced, and it stitched very nicely, nicer than the tailor could do; and the bosses said: "We want you to use the sewing machine; you have to buy one." Many of the tailors had a few dollars in the bank, and they took the money and bought machines. Many others had no money, but must help themselves; so they brought their stitching, the coat or vest, to the other tailors who had sewing machines, and paid them a few cents for the stitching. Later, when the money was given out for the work, we found out that we could earn no more than we could without the machine; but the money for the machine was gone now, and we found that the machine was only for the profit of the bosses; that they got their work quicker, and it was done nicer. . . . The machine makes too much noise in the place, and the neighbors want to sleep, and we have to stop sewing earlier; so we have to work faster. We work now in excitement—in a hurry. It is hunting; it is not work at all; it is a hunt.

Senator Pugh: You turn out two or three times as much work per day now as you did in prior times before the war?—A. Yes, sir; two or three times as much; and we have to do it, because the wages are two-thirds lower than they were five or ten years back. . . .

Senator Blair: What proportion of them are women and what proportion men, according to your best judgment?—A. I guess there are many more women then men.

Q. The pay of women is the same as the pay of the men for the same quantity of work, I suppose?—A. Yes; in cases where a manufacturer—that is, a middleman—gets work from the shop and brings it into his store and employs hands to make it, women get paid by the piece also. If the manufacturer gets $.25 for a piece, he pays for the machine work on that piece so many cents to the finisher, and so many to the button-sewer—so much to each one—and what remains is to pay his rent and to pay for the machinery.

Q. What is your knowledge as to the amount that workers of that class are able to save from their wages?—A. I don't know any one that does save except those manufacturers.

Q. As a class, then, the workers save nothing?—A. No.

Q. What sort of house-room do they have? What is the character, in general, of the food and clothing which they are able to purchase with what they can make by their labor?—A. They live in tenement houses four or five stories high, and have two or three rooms.

Q. What is the character of their clothing?—A. They buy the clothing that they make—the cheapest of it.

Q. What about the character of food that they are able to provide for themselves?—A. Food? They have no time to eat dinner. They have a sandwich in the middle of the day, and in the evening when they go away from work it is the same, and they drink lager or anything they can get.

Q. They are kept busy all the time and have but little opportunity for rest?—A. Yes

Q. What is the state of feeling between the employers and their employees in that business? How do you workingmen feel towards the people who employ you and pay you?—A. Well, I must say the workingmen are discouraged. If I speak with them they go back and don't like to speak much about the business and the pay. They fear that if they say how it is they will get sent out of the shop. They hate the bosses and the foremen more than the bosses, and that feeling is deep.

Q. Why do they feel so towards the foremen?—A. They know that they do a wrong onto them; they know that.

Q. Do not the foremen act under the instruction of the bosses?—A. Well, it seems so.

Q. Could not the boss correct the wrong that the foreman does, if it is a wrong?—A. Well, when we complain that the foreman is so and so, the boss says, "Oh, I have nothing to do with it; I don't know; go to the foreman; it is the foreman's business." Then when we go to the foreman he says, "Oh, I can't pay more; these are my rules; if you don't like it, go to the boss."

Q. And when you do go to the boss he sends you back to the foreman?—A. Yes; he says, "I have nothing to do with this; that is my foreman's business; go to him." Therefore the workmen hate them both. . . .

Sen. Pugh: Then you are testifying here under the apprehension of punishment for what you have stated?—A. Well, I have no fear for anyone, you know, and if you think it is better that I say it, I do so.

Q. What is your feeling of restraint in testifying? What injury would you be subjected to for telling the truth? Would the workingmen in your business testify under a fear of being punished by their employers for telling the truth?—A. Yes. It is nothing but fear. . . .

Sen. Blair: Have you any objection to giving us the names of some of the bosses and foremen that you know, who control a large number of laborers of the class to which you belong? This committee desires to obtain such information as you can give in regard to the condition of the engaged trade, and if there is any attempt to punish you for giving such information I think you can find protection from the country, or from some source. We cannot compel you to give the information but we desire you to state, if you will, the names of some of the bosses and foremen, so that if they do not think proper to come here and speak for themselves the country will understand that you have told us the truth.—A. Now, sir, if I lose my work who can give me another work? I am an old man now, you know, and the young ones, they get work and they say, "He is an old man; what can he do? . . . "

TESTIMONY OF DR. TIMOTHY STOW

Sen. Blair: You are a physician?—A. Yes.

Q. You live at Fall River?—A. Yes.

Q. Won't you state how you happen to appear before the committee, what your object is in coming here, and at whose request you come; and then give us the benefit of any observations you choose to lay before us?—A. Mr. Robert Howard, of our city, called on me yesterday, and desired me to appear here today before your committee to give whatever testimony I could relating particularly to the physical and mental and perhaps the moral condition of the operatives and laboring classes of Fall River. I have made no notes, and I hardly know what your plan is; but I would as soon answer questions as to make any detailed statement.

Sen. Blair: We want to find out how the working people of Fall River are living and doing. You can tell us that in the way in which one gentleman would talk to another, the one understanding the subject and the other not understanding it. Just tell us the condition of the operatives there, in your own way, bearing in mind that we would rather have it without premeditation than as a prepared statement.

Stow: I have been in Fall River about eleven years. . . . As a physician and surgeon, of course, I have been brought into contact with all classes of people there, particularly the laboring classes, the operatives of the city. . . .

As a class they are dwarfed physically. Of course there are exceptions to that; some notable ones. On looking over their condition and weighing it as carefully as I have been able to, I have come to the conclusion that the character and quality of the labor which they have been doing in times past, and most of them from childhood up, has been and is such as to bring this condition upon them slowly and steadily.

They are dwarfed, in my estimation, sir, as the majority of men and women who are brought up in factories must be dwarfed under the present industrial system; because by their long hours of indoor labor and their hard work they are cut off from the benefit of breathing fresh air, and from the sights that surround a workman outside a mill. Being shut up all day long in noise and in the high temperature of these mills, they become physically weak.

Then, most of them are obliged to live from hand to mouth, or, at least, they do not have sufficient food to nourish them as they need to be nourished. Those things, together with the fact that they have to limit their clothing supply—this constant strain upon the operative—all tend to make him on the one hand uneasy and restless, or on the other hand to produce discouragement and recklessness. They make him careless in regard to his own condition. All those things combined tend to produce what we have in Fall River.

Now, first, as to the moral condition of the operatives of Fall River. I think so far as crime is concerned we have quite as little crime there as in any city of its size. We have a population rising on 50,000. There is a disposition at times, and under certain pressure, for some operatives to violate the law, to pilfer, or something of that kind, and I think it grows out of not what is called "pure cussedness," but a desire to relieve some physical want. For instance, a man wants a coat and has not the means of earning it, and he is out of employment, and being pinched with cold, and with no prospect of getting employment, or of getting a coat by honest means, he steals one. Or perhaps he steals food on the same principle.

But so far as crime is concerned, we have comparatively little. But what I do say, and what has been on my mind ever since I came to Fall River, with reference to operatives there, is the peculiar impress they seem to bear, a sort of dejected, tired, worn-out, discouraged appearance, growing out of the bad influences of long hours of labor, the close confinement of the mills, the din of the machinery, their exclusion from social intercourse, except at night.

And I think we can look for a solution of the problem which the country at large is endeavoring to solve—that with reference to the intemperate habits of the laboring classes and the operatives—in those facts that I have mentioned.

I have questioned many thoughtful men and women in regard to that I have said, "Why is it that at night particularly you frequent the dramshops? Why is it that by day you drink; that you store enough even for the day in your houses?" The answer is, "Well, doctor, I tell you the fact is this, there is a sense of fatigue over us which we do not know how to overcome, and which we must overcome for the time being if we are to have any social qualities of an evening, and we can't do it without taking something which will bridge over the time and make us equal to the emergency of the evening or the occasion. . . ." But I have said, "How does this make you feel? You say you have been feeling fatigued in the evening and discouraged; that your future does not look bright; how do you feel when you get the liquor?" "Why," he will say, "it covers that all up; we lose all thought of that, and for the time being we feel well." And so they go on from day to day, and from night to night.

Now, after all, I do not know of many drunkards in Fall River, but this is true: the operative spends his five, ten, or fifteen, or twenty-five cents a night for liquor, and it is so much lost money to him, and yet he feels impelled to it, because he does not know how otherwise to adapt himself to the circumstances of the evening. . . .

Now, it is invariably the testimony of the more intelligent men and women in answer to the question, "Why do you persist in drinking?" "It makes us feel better; we are relieved of the ennui of life; we are relieved of mental depression for the time being, and after the evening's social engagements are over we get home and go to bed, and think nothing of it, and the next day resume our day's work." And so it goes on from day to day.

Now there are other things which hinge upon low wages and long hours of labor to demoralize the operative. For instance, his food. I think it is safe to say that the great mass of operatives there are forced to buy the cheapest food. They go to the meat stores and purchase joints, which, of course, made up into soup, generally makes good food, but it does not do to have soup all the time. Then they purchase the cheapest vegetables and endeavor to make the money go as far as it possibly will to supply their wants. But all that produces this condition: they lack that sort of nutrition which is essential to an increase of fiber and flesh, and to maintain that elasticity which they ought to have for the performance of a fair amount of labor. I think if the food of the operatives could be increased it would be better.

Q. You mean increased in quantity, quality, or both?—A. I mean both.

Q. You mean that they do not have enough to eat?—A. Many of them do not, they are limited in amount. I have occasion almost every day to see the manner in which the average operative has his table spread, and certainly it seems to me eminently proper that if it be within the scope of human legislation, or within the scope of the religion which men and women profess, to alleviate the condition of the laboring classes who are our producers, it should be done. . . .

Source: John Garraty, ed., *Labor and Capital in the Gilded Age: Testimony taken by the Senate Committee upon the Relations between Labor and Capital—1883* (Boston: Little, Brown, and Company, 1968), pp. 20–22, 30–33.

---

23. Grape Boycott: September 1965 Memo of Cesar Chavez

*The **grape boycott** from 1965 through 1970 was one of the most successful uses of the **boycott** tactic in U.S. labor history and a seminal event in transforming the **Agricultural Workers Organizing Committee** (AWOC) into the **United Farm Workers of America**. It was so successful that the **strike** that accompanied it is sometimes overlooked. Filipino and Chicano workers struck for humane working conditions and a living **wage**. **Cesar Chavez** and others were able to turn the strike into a nationwide boycott of California table grapes and wines. The following memo from Chavez was written on September 16, 1965, to rally support and boost the morale of workers in the Delano, California, region, the epicenter of the ongoing strike. His evocation of the Rev. Martin Luther King, Jr., was deliberate and genuine; Chavez knew and admired Rev. King. Soon the phrases "Viva La Causa" (Cause) and "Viva La Huelga" (Struggle) could be seen on banners, badges, and rally posters across the United States.*

"WE SHALL OVERCOME"

In a 400 square mile area halfway between Selma and Weedpatch, California, a general strike of farm workers has been going on for six weeks. The Filipinos, under AWOC, began the strike for a $1.40 per hour guarantee and a union contract. They were joined by the independent Farm Workers Association which has a membership of several thousand Mexican-Americans.

Filipino, Mexican-American and Puerto Rican workers have been manning picket lines daily for 41 days in a totally non-violent manner. Ranchers in the area, which include DiGiorgio Fruit, Schenley, and many independent growers, did not take the strike seriously at first. By the second or third week, however, they began taking another look—and striking back. Mechanized agriculture began picketing the pickets—spraying them with sulfur, running tractors by them to create dust storms, building barricades of farm machinery so that scabs could not see the pickets. These actions not only increased the determination of the strikers, but convinced some of the scabs that the ranchers were, in fact, less than human. Scabs quit work and the strike grew.

The growers hired security guards for $43 a day. They began driving their Thunderbirds, equipped with police dogs and rifles, up and down the roads. The people made more picket signs, drew in their belts, and kept marching. Production was down 30% and the growers began looking for more and more scabs. They went to Fresno and Bakersfield and Los Angeles to find them. They didn't tell the workers that they would be scab crews. The pickets followed them into every town and formed ad hoc strike committees to prevent scabbing. They succeeded in these towns. Within two weeks, only one bus, with half a dozen winos, escorted by a pearl gray Cadillac, drove into the strike zone.

A new plan was formed. The ranchers would advertise in South Texas and old Mexico. They bring these workers in buses and the workers are held in debt to the rancher before they even arrive in town. We have a new and more difficult task ahead of us with these scabs.

As our strike has grown, workers have matured and now know why and how to fight for their rights. As the strike has grown into a movement for justice by the lowest paid workers in America, friends of farm workers have begun to rally in support of LA CAUSA. Civil rights, church, student and union groups help with food and money.

We believe that this is the beginning of a significant drive to achieve equal rights for agricultural workers. In order to enlist your full support and to explain our work to you, I would like to bring some of our pickets and meet with you.

VIVA LA CAUSA Y
VIVA LA HUELGA

Cesar Estrada Chavez
General Director,
National Farm Workers Association

Source: TM/© 2003 the Cesar E. Chavez Foundation. www.chavezfoundation.org.

24. Immigrant Workers: Excerpt from a December 1881 Article by Elizabeth Buffum Chase in the *Labor Standard*

Between 1870 and 1910, more than twenty-one million immigrants poured into the United States. Many of them became the very bone and sinew of the economic expansion of post–Civil War America. Although many immigrants bettered their lives, it was usually difficult for the first generation. They were not only subject to intense nativist discrimination at the hands of those native-born groups who feared them, but also frequently found themselves toiling in some of the Gilded Age's worst sweatshops, factories, and mills.

The passage below was written by Elizabeth Buffum Chase, a suffragist, labor advocate, social reformer, and former abolitionist. It originally appeared in December 1881 in the Labor Standard*, a working-class newspaper published in Fall River, Massachusetts. Fall River was dotted with numerous textile and shoe mills and owed its explosive late-nineteenth-century population growth to the influx of immigrant workers. Chase was rare among Gilded Age writers in that she posited that poverty was linked to social conditions rather than individual failings or ethnic characteristics. Here she defends the dignity of Irish, French Canadian, and Catholic immigrants.*

Thus it is a fact, that a very large number of women and girls, from ten years old to forty or fifty are employed in the cotton and woolen mills of the northern and middle states of this country mostly in New England. It is, therefore, a subject of great concern as to what is their actual condition, and, what are the duties of other women toward them. Many of those born in England, Ireland, and Canada cannot read or write; and of those who have had a chance in our public schools most of them have gone to work so early that their schooling has been of the most rudimentary character, and is easily forgotten. They are excluded from the society of their own sex and outside of the factory by a variety of barriers—chief of which are their foreign birth or extraction, *their poverty*, their want of education, and the necessity that they should always be at work. [Emphasis in original] Two other causes also contribute to this large exclusion. These people are mostly Catholic in their religion, and this excludes them from Protestant companionship, and the other is, the growing tendency in our civilization toward class distinction.

Many of the operatives live a floating life. Unsettled from their native homes, the older members of the families never become truly nationalized anywhere; and the children grow up with the idea that they are an alien people. So, trifling circumstances and the hope of improving their condition lead them to move about, and this they continue unthrifty and poor; and whatever unfortunate results follow, they all bear with most hardship upon the women. On the contrary, those who remain in one place, if they cultivate habits of industry and sobriety, do constantly improve their circumstances and become more and more assimilated to the native inhabitants. But, with rare exceptions, they have brought with them the inherited improvidence, which comes from many generations in hopeless poverty under old world oppression.

Source: Labor Standard, December 10, 1881. Reprinted in Irwin Yellowitz, ed., *The Position of the Worker in American Society, 1865–1896* (Englewood Cliffs, N.J.: Prentice Hall, 1969), pp. 69–70.

25. Indentured Servant Contract (1627)

English colonists to the Americas often came under the illusion that Native Americans would willingly work for them. When persuasion and coercion of Native Americans proved unworkable, the colonies endured a labor crisis. To alleviate this, planters and investors turned to Great Britain's indigenous poor. Enclosure movements, industrialization, and increased agricultural yields conspired to create a large unemployed and underemployed group known as "sturdy beggars," who were deemed surplus labor within Great Britain. Thousands of these individuals were so poor they could not pay passage to the colonies. In exchange for transportation to the New World and basic sustenance, individuals agreed to work for their sponsor for a given number of years, customarily four to seven. In Virginia and elsewhere, individuals who completed their indentures were given land allotments, called headrights, to sustain themselves in the future. In the early days of Virginia, very few lived to collect their headrights, with death rates of over 50 percent per year typical into the mid-1620s. Most indentured servants died from a combination of malnutrition and overwork. By the time Richard Lowther arrived in 1627, tobacco had begun to rescue the colony financially and the death rate was dropping, but the indentured servant's lot was still a hard one.

Indentured servitude is an old European practice that was simply transplanted to the New World. The word indenture is an Anglicized version of the French dent, meaning tooth. Some contracts were written twice on a sheet of paper and then jaggedly torn apart in a toothlike pattern. The validity of the contract could be verified by matching the halves. The document below is typical of indenture contracts in seventeenth-century Virginia, although its language and spelling have been edited to make it more readable.

THIS WRITING INDENTED made the Last day of July . . . 1627 And in the Third year of the reign of our Sovereign Lord Charles by the Grace of God king of England Scotland France and Ireland Defender of the faith &c. between Richard Lowther of Broome in the Parish of Southwell [i.e., Southill] in the County of Bedford brewer of the one party and Edward Hurd Citizen and Iron monger of London of the other party witnesses that the said Richard Lowther . . . hired himself and . . . does Covenant and agree and bind himself to be remain and Continue the Covenant servant of him the said Edward Hurd his heirs and assigns to be by him or them sent and transported unto the Country and land of Virginia, in the parts beyond the Seas & to be by him or them employed upon his plantation there, for and during the space of Four years to begin at the feast day of St. Michael . . . now next coming during which said term the said Richard Lowther shall and will truly employ and endeavor himself to the utmost of his power knowledge and skill to do and perform true and faithful service unto the said Edward Hurd his heirs and assigns in for and concerning all such Labor and business as he or they shall think good to use and employ him the said Richard Lowther in, And shall and will be tractable and obedient as a good and a faithful servant ought to be in all such things as shall be Commanded him by the said Edward Hurd his heirs or assigns in Virginia aforesaid or elsewhere during the said term. IN CONSIDERATION whereof the said Edward Hurd for himself his executors administrators or assigns and for every of them do covenant promise and grant to and with the said Richard Lowther his heirs executors administrators and assigns . . . that . . . Edward Hurd his heirs executors administrators and assigns shall and will (at his and their own charges) not only transport and furnish out the said Richard Lowther to and for Virginia aforesaid and there find provide and allow unto him sufficient meat drink apparel and other necessaries for his livelihood and maintenance during the said term But also at the expiration of the said term shall and will grant assign and allot unto him the said Richard Lowther the quantity of Fifty acres of Land in Virginia aforesaid to hold to him his heirs and assigns for ever as in such Cases usual without fraud or Coven. . . .

Source: "Indentured Servant Contract." Virtual Jamestown. http://etext.lib.virginia.edu/etcbin/jamestown-browsemod?id=J1046.

26. An Insider's View of the Fair Employment Practices Committee: An Interview with Earl B. Dickerson

Born in Mississippi, Earl B. Dickerson (1891–1986) moved to Chicago at the age of fifteen. After obtaining a law degree from the University of Chicago, Dickerson rose to leadership of the country's largest African American–owned law firm, becoming known as "the dean of Chicago's black lawyers." Dickerson was active in Chicago and national politics, argued successfully before the Supreme Court for an end to restrictive real-estate covenants, and served on the **Fair Employment Practices Committee (FEPC)** *from 1941 to 1943. Established in wartime by President Franklin D. Roosevelt, the FEPC continued until 1946 when, against the recommendation of President Harry Truman, the Senate terminated the program. In this selection from the 1980s, Dickerson tells Studs Terkel about his experiences on the FEPC.*

Around 1940, '41, the war industries were set in motion: Lockheed, Boeing, all the rest. If this was a war to see that democracy prevails, preparations should involve all our people equally. Since blacks had been to a large extent excluded, A. Philip Randolph and Walter White planned a march on Washington. I knew both men intimately. To prevent this from happening, Mr. Roosevelt put forth Executive Order 8802. This set up the Fair Employment Practices Committee. I was one of the first named.

Because I was the only lawyer in this group, I was always sent out in advance of any hearing. With some investigators, I prepared the cases for the committee when it met.

One of the first hearings was here in Chicago at City Hall. It was a wonderful three days, examining these people from industry. I remember some fellow from LaGrange. It was one of these General Motors subsidiaries. We had him on the stand: "How many Negroes do you employ?" He replied, "One."

I distinctly remember the hearings in Los Angeles. I had gone out a week before the hearings with a couple of investigators. Lockheed had employed some twenty thousand people in the war effort. No Negroes. Not until the morning of the hearings did they employ any. I asked the head of personnel, "Are you familiar with the contents of Executive Order 8802?" He said yes. I said, "Do you have any Negroes in your employ?" He said yes. "How many do you have?" He said nine. I said, "In what department?" He said, "In the custodial department." That meant they were sweeping floors. (Wryly) Well, that was a beginning.

Another company, there were no black bricklayers. The reason given: one or two couldn't work alongside whites. They'd have to get enough to work one side of the building. Since they couldn't find that many, they'd employ none.

I distinctly remember the hearings in Birmingham. One of my colleagues on the committee, a southern newspaper publisher, called me on the phone a few days before the scheduled hearings: "Earl, perhaps you shouldn't go down there. There have been all sorts of threats." I said, "I want you to read Executive Order 8802 again. It says, 'the jurisdiction of this committee shall be in all states and territories of the United States.'" I had it before me. "The question I ask you now is, 'Is Birmingham within the jurisdiction of the United States?'" He said yes. I said, "That being the case, I'll be there."

When I got off the plane at Birmingham to walk to the terminal, a man about six feet four, a tall Caucasian, came to me and said, "Are you Mr. Earl B. Dickerson?" I said yes. He said, "I'm the United States marshal in this district and I have been requested by the Justice Department to protect you during your trip here." In those days, blacks couldn't stay in hotels in Birmingham. So he would come and pick me up each of those three days. And in the federal court, where the hearings were held, he stood beside me the whole three days.

There was another black fellow on the committee. He was very black and I'm sort of brown. The newspapers came out and described us as the black and brown babies from Chicago. That was around 1942.

You must remember Roosevelt had to be pushed. I had no personal relationship with President Roosevelt until he issued Executive Order 8802. It was June 25, 1941.

We had hearings in Washington, D.C., from time to time. The streetcar system did not employ blacks as motormen or conductors. This was during the war, and every day there were ads in the papers advertising for people to apply for jobs as motormen and conductors. The civil rights people there told blacks to apply for these jobs. They had no luck. We set a date for the hearings on this. I was the acting chairman at the time and prepared the case. It was in all the newspapers.

Just the day before the hearing, I got a call from a fellow named McIntyre. He was Roosevelt's secretary. He said, "We understand you are having hearings tomorrow. President Roosevelt has asked me to request that you postpone the hearings until some later date." I said that all the newspapers not only here but throughout the United States know about these hearings tomorrow. We have prepared the case, a noted lawyer from New York has come in, and it will be at Dumbarton Oaks. I said, "I can't go out to the public and postpone this case unless Mr. Roosevelt himself would tell me."

This was about one o'clock in the afternoon. He called me right back. "At two-thirty this afternoon, the President will meet with you in the White House." When I walked in the White House, Mrs. Mary McLeod Bethune was sitting just outside his office. She was the most influential black around, very close to Mrs. Roosevelt. I think Mrs. Roosevelt was one of the sparkplugs behind Executive Order 8802. After she hugged me, Mrs. Bethune said, "The President asked that I be in on this conversation."

Well, the President simply told me he wanted permission to defer the hearings. I said, "I'm just wondering why it is, Mr. President. He said, "I want it delayed until I return." I said, "Very well, Mr. President." Of course, the next morning we read about Mr. Roosevelt having flown to Yalta to meet with Churchill and Stalin.

Soon after this, Attorney General Francis Biddle came up with a proposal to reorganize the commission. All the members were reappointed except me. It was one of my major disappointments in life. I knew it was because I had been so aggressive. I had been the leader of all the agitation that went on in the committee.

What did they give as the reason?

They didn't have to, did they? Oh, they had hearings, but not the kind of aggressive ones I'd been pushing. Nobody ever criticized me. I was in all the newspapers throughout the country.

Roosevelt wanted to go slow. I was taking 'em too fast. When you talk about him, he was not unlike any other Caucasian in that position. The blacks had never challenged authority like that before, except for individuals. Here was a collective attack on the practices of the American people.

Do you know that my work on that committee has affected my life? Years later, when Governor Kerner appointed me as one of the first members of the Illinois Fair Employment Practices Committee, I had to be confirmed by the state senate. This fellow Broyles was chairman of the Illinois Un-American Activities Committee. On the day of the hearings, on the wall of that room, they had my files posted. My membership in the Soviet-American Friendship Committee, my membership in the National Lawyers' Guild—and all my activities on the Fair Employment Practices Committee. The fifteen Republicans voted no, the thirteen Democrats voted yes. I was not confirmed.

It was in World War Two—because it was so clear, it was against Hitler—that the blacks began to measure the rights they had as against the rights that the whites were given. Now I tell you, this measuring will never end. Not until they have the rights the others have.

Source: Reprinted by permission of Donadio & Olson, Inc. Copyright © 1974 by Studs Terkel.

---

27. Knights of Labor: Preamble and Platform to Their Constitution (1891)

The largest and most successful labor federation of the nineteenth century was the Noble and Holy Order of the **Knights of Labor (KOL)**. *The KOL was founded in 1869 and enjoyed its greatest strength in the mid-1880s, growing to perhaps as many as one million members by 1886. It quickly contracted from that plateau due to lost* **strikes**, *battles with rival unions, and internal dissension. Mostly, though, it faded due to the fierce counter assault of organized capital. The KOL was not a trade union battling just for improved wages, shorter hours, and better working conditions. As the preamble to its constitution shows, the KOL advocated revamping society along quite different lines than those which came to pass. The KOL's* reform unionism *produced a backlash in which some of the late nineteenth century's richest and most powerful corporate magnates decided to crush the organization at any cost*

The following document lays out the KOL's vision for reforming American society. The preamble and the first nine platform items were adopted in 1878, when the group held its first national convention. Additional agenda items were added after 1884. This document is a mature version of the platform from 1891. Comparing the KOL's goals with those of the **American Federation of Labor**, *which supplanted the Knights, suggests that the latter organization survived, in part, because its objectives* *meshed better with the capitalist forces that subdued the Knights. Some elements of the KOL platform remain progressive (and unrealized) to the present day.*

(Note: The five asterisks below stand for the Noble and Holy Order of the Knights of Labor. When the preamble was written, the KOL operated in total secrecy and even the organization's name was hidden from public view.)

The recent alarming development and aggression of aggregated wealth, which, unless checked, will invariably lead to the pauperization and hopeless degradation of the toiling masses, render it imperative, if we desire to enjoy the blessings of life, that a check should be placed upon its power and upon unjust accumulation, and a system adopted which will secure to the laborer the fruits of his toil; and as this much desired object can only be accomplished by the thorough unification of labor, and the united effort of those who obey the divine injunction that "In the sweat of thy brow shalt thou eat bread," we have formed the * * * * * with a view of securing the organization and direction, by co-operative effort, of the power of the industrial classes; and we submit to the world the object sought to be accomplished by our organization, calling upon all who believe in securing "the greatest good to the greatest number" to aid and assist us-

I. To bring within the folds of organization every department of productive industry, making knowledge a standpoint for action, and industrial and moral worth, not wealth, the true standard of individual and national greatness.

II. To secure to the toilers a proper share of the wealth that they create; more of the leisure that rightfully belongs to them; more societary advantages; more of the benefits, privileges, and emoluments of the world, all those rights and privileges necessary to make them capable of enjoying, appreciating, defending, and perpetuating the blessings of good government.

III. To arrive at the true condition of the producing masses in their educational, moral, and financial condition, by demanding from the various governments the establishment of bureaus of labor statistics.

IV. The establishment of co-operative institutions, productive and distributive.

V. The reserving of the public lands—the heritage of the people—for the actual settler; not another acre for railroads or speculators.

VI. The abrogation of all laws that do not bear equally upon capital and labor, the removal of unjust technicalities, delays, and discriminations in the administration of justice, and the adopting of measures providing for the health and safety of those engaged in mining, manufacturing, or building pursuits.

VII. The enactment of laws to compel chartered corporations to pay their employees weekly, in full, for the labor of the preceding week, in the lawful money of the country.

VIII. The enactment of laws giving mechanics and laborers a first lien on their work for their full wages.

X. The abolishment of the contract system on national, state, and municipal work.

X. The substitution of arbitration for strikes, whenever and wherever employers and employees are willing to meet on equitable grounds.

XI. The prohibition of the employment of children in workshops, mines, and factories before attaining their fifteenth year.

XII. To abolish the system of letting out by contract labor of convicts in our prisons and reformatory institutions.

XIII. To secure for both sexes equal pay for equal work.

XIV. The reduction of the hours of labor to eight per day, so that the laborers may have more time for social enjoyment and intellectual improvement, and be enabled to reap the advantages conferred by the labor-saving machinery which their brains have created.

XV. To prevail upon governments to establish a purely national circulating medium, based upon the faith and resources of the nation, and issued directly to the people, without the intervention of any system of banking corporations, which money shall be a legal tender in payment of all debts, public or private.

Source: Journal of the Knights of Labor, June 4, 1891. (Nearly every edition of this paper printed the above document.)

---

28. The Lawrence Strike, 1912: Excerpt from the Autobiography of Big Bill Haywood

William D. (Big Bill) Haywood *(1869–1928) led the* ***Wobblies (Industrial Workers of the World)*** *at the height of their most turbulent years. Haywood was known for his stirring rhetoric. Following the arrest of Joe Ettor and Arturro Giovanitti, Haywood personally took over leadership of the Lawrence* ***strike****. In his autobiography, Haywood gave the following account of the IWW's one great eastern victory: the* ***Lawrence, Massachusetts, textile strike*** *of 1912. In 1918, Haywood was convicted of violating the Espionage Act during World War I. He eventually fled the country and died in exile.*

I pointed out that although the I.W.W. would not affiliate with any political party, this action did not make them anti-political; that I was as much a Socialist as any other member of the Socialist Party. I remember that after the meeting, Hubert Harrison, a colored man, said to me that while Douglas had won the debate, Lincoln had carried the country. I took this to mean that Hillquit had won the debate, but the workers of the nation were with me.

This meeting was attended by many leading members of the I.W.W. Ettor, Giovanitti, Gurley Flynn, and Jim Thompson were there. Ettor had just received a telegram from the Italians of Lawrence, Massachusetts, asking him to come there, as there was going to be a strike of the textile workers. Ettor left for Lawrence at once and in a few days I got a telegram from him asking me to come and help him with the strike.

When I got to Lawrence, Ettor had the situation well in hand. There was a General Strike Committee organized, composed of one or more members from every mill or large department of the mills that were on strike.

The legislature of Massachusetts had passed a law reducing the hours of labor in the textile industry from fifty-six to fifty-four a week. The cotton and woolen companies announced that when this law went into effect wages would be reduced in proportion. The workers declared that wages were already lower than they should be. The average weekly wage was eight dollars and seventy-six cents, the women getting an average of only seven dollars and forty-two cents. This was the average for all workers, including the skilled. The average for the workers who conducted this strike was six dollars a week. These wages were only for time at work; there were no vacations, and all the holidays were deducted from the weekly pay. It was impossible to bring up families on such wages. The workers went on strike.

It was a strike against all the mills, and every worker, except a few of the most skilled, took part in the struggle. The strikers demanded a fifty-four hour week, a fifteen per cent increase in pay, double pay for overtime, abolition of all bonus or premium systems, and no discrimination against workers for activities during the strike.

The Lawrence strike grew, until by the latter part of January, 1912, there were twenty-five thousand workers taking part in it. They were of about twenty-eight different nationalities and spoke forty-five different dialects. The entire textile industry of Lawrence and vicinity was closed down tight.

On my arrival in Lawrence a reception committee met me, composed of ten or fifteen thousand strikers. A parade was formed as we marched to the common, as the public park of every New England town is called. This, the *Lawrence Tribune* said, was the greatest demonstration ever accorded a visitor to Lawrence. On the common I spoke to the strikers.

I spoke many times to the strikers, and left Lawrence to go out and raise funds and create sympathy for the strike, until on February second, Ettor and Giovanitti were arrested under a framed-up charge of murder. Anna LaPiza, an Italian girl striker, had been killed by a policeman, but the charge was laid against the leaders of the strike. I returned at once to Lawrence and became chairman of the strike committee, which was composed of fifty-six members. Back of these were another fifty-six members ready to take the places of the strike committee if any arrests were made.

A writer in the *Outlook*, a conservative weekly which reported the strike, said

> Haywood does not want unions of weavers, unions of spinners, unions of loomfixers, unions of woolsorters, but he wants one comprehensive union of all textile workers, which in time will take over the textile factories, as the steelworkers will take over the steel mills and the railway workers the railways. Haywood interprets the class conflict literally as a war which is always on, which becomes daily more bitter and uncompromising, which can end only with the conquest of capitalistic society by proletarians or wage workers, organized industry by industry.
>
> Haywood places no trust in trade agreements, which, according to his theory, lead merely to social peace and "put the workers to sleep." Let the employer lock out his men when he pleases, and let the workmen strike when they please. He is opposed to arbitration, conciliation, compromise; to sliding scales, profit sharing, welfare work; to everything, in short, which may weaken the revolutionary force of workers. He does not ask for the closed shop or the official recognition of the union, for he has no intention of recognizing the employer. What he desires is not a treaty or industrial peace between the two high contracting parties, but merely the creation of a proletarian impulse which will eventually revolutionize society. Haywood is a man who believes in men, not as you and I believe in them, but fervently, uncompromisingly, with an obstinate faith in the universal goodwill and constancy of the workers worthy of a great religious leader. That is what makes him supremely dangerous.

To the Legislative Committee which came to Lawrence I showed pay envelopes of the workers—six dollars and ninety-nine cents, five dollars and forty-five cents, six-thirty, and so on. I showed them, printed on the envelope marked five forty-five, advice about saving money, and the advertisement of the local bank. Five forty-five for a week's work—and advice about saving thrown in free! This was adding insult to injury indeed! The old man who had given me this particular envelope was an old-time employee of the mill, who should have been pensioned long before, after a life-time in the mill. Instead he had been reduced and reduced as he grew less active, until he was plugging along as a wool-sorter on five dollars and forty-five cents a week.

I knew the investigation would result in nothing; but it was good publicity.

After the arrest of Ettor and Giovanitti a demand was made for their release on bail. These men had been charged with being ascessories to the death of Anna LaPiza, although nineteen witnesses had seen Policeman Beloit murder the girl. Ettor and Giovanitti were refused bail and held in jail for seven months.

Elizabeth Gurley Flynn, the leading woman organizer of the I.W.W., gave splendid service at Lawrence, speaking to the strikers, and also at meetings outside the strike district, raising money for the relief fund and for the defense of prisoners.

We were sending the children of strikers to sympathizers in other cities, to be cared for during the strike. Some of the groups of children were large and attracted a good deal of attention and sympathy. One day when a group was to be sent away, the militia formed a cordon around the depot and the police attempted to prevent the children getting on the train. When one of these big burleys would lay his hand on a child, of course it would scream, and its mother would fly to the rescue of her captive young. There was a turmoil in the station between the policemen and the fighting women. They stopped the children leaving this day, but they never attempted it a second time.

One morning on the picket line a Syrian boy, who belonged to the strikers fife and drum corps, was stabbed in the back with a bayonet. He died soon after being taken to the hospital.

Not only the local police force was used against the strikers, but police from other cities, the state police, and the state militia had been called in. These organized forces used the mills as their barracks.

The women strikers were as active and efficient as the men, and fought as well. One cold morning, after the strikers had been drenched on the bridge with the firehose of the mills, the women caught a policeman in the middle of the bridge and stripped off his uniform, pants and all. They were about to throw him in the icy river, when other policemen rushed in and saved him from the chilly ducking.

We appealed to Congressman Victor Berger for an investigation of the Lawrence strike, and through this Socialist congressman's efforts, a hearing was arranged before the Rules Committee of the House, in Washington, D.C. When we got news of this, the General Strike Committee decided to send sixteen witnesses to Washington, all boys and girls under sixteen years of age. One of them was a little girl whose hair had been caught in a machine and her scalp torn from her head. These child workers from the mills were able to picture their working conditions and their home life, and we felt convinced of their ability to explain why they and twenty-five thousand others were striking in the textile center of Lawrence and adjacent towns. Margaret Sanger, who afterward became famous for her campaigns for birth control, went with the children to Washington.

On the day of their arrival there, the boys and girls appeared before the Rules Committee. Samuel Gompers was present presumably in the interests of the A. F. of L. He was called as a witness, and condemned the strike and its leaders. Suddenly a childish voice rang out:

"You old son-of-a-bitch! You're telling a god-damned lie!"

It was a Polish boy who had interrupted Gompers. The chairman of the Committee rapped vigorously with his gavel and, looking sternly at the boy, said

"Young man, that sort of language will not be tolerated here. Do not attempt it again!"

"It's the only kind of language I know," answered the boy, "and I'm not a-goin' to let that guy lie about us and get away with it!"

This incident is not reported in Gompers' *Seventy Years of Life and Labor.*

A newspaper reporter at the hearing remarked that "here was presented the old and the new of the labor movement."

When the committee in Lawrence heard that Gompers was taking part in the hearing, they decided to send me down to Washington to help the children who were representing the strikers, if they should need help. But the children had told everything about conditions in the mills, even to being compelled to buy drinking water.

The arranging of this hearing was not the only time that Victor Berger had responded to requests of the I.W.W. On a previous occasion I had appealed to him, when Federal Judge Hanford of Seattle had denied men citizenship because they belonged to the I.W.W. Hanford lost his job as a result of Berger's investigation.

The newspapers had a staff of reporters in Lawrence to cover the strike. Many of them were of the usual type; one told me that he was the man who had concocted the scheme for my arrest in Yakima, in order to test the anti-cigarette law and to make a good story that he could sell.

Gertrude Marvin was reporting for the *Boston American*. She came to me for an interview and got it. When the story was finished, she thought she had something good for her paper, but the managing editor remarked, as he threw it in the wastebasket

"That big two-fisted thug has put it all over you!"

Miss Marvin resigned and went to work for the I.W.W. in Lawrence, doing publicity work for the strike. Later she was engaged by the United Press to assist Marlen Pew. The stories these two sent out about the strike were so thoroughly appreciated by the papers subscribing to the United Press that these papers sent hundreds of letters from all over the country commending the stories. I saw these letters posted up all over the walls of the United Press' New York office.

The managing editor of the *Boston American* finally came to Lawrence and asked Gertrude Marvin to arrange an interview with me. After a long talk with me, he told her that he knew that he had made a mistake in throwing away that story.

I was speaking one night to a meeting made up almost entirely of Polish workers, when two Italian women came into the hall and were brought to the platform. The younger of the two said to me, "To-morrow morning man no go on picket line. All man, boy stay home, sleep. Only woman, girl on picket line to-morrow morning. Soldier and policeman no beat woman, girl. You see—" turning to her companion, she said, "I got big belly, she too got big belly. Policeman no beat us. I want to speak to all woman here."

I presented her to the assembled strikers and told them what she had said to me. Then she spoke herself, in plaintive voice reciting her message, and all agreed that next morning no men or boys should be on the picket line.

The women were out in full force, many of them pregnant mothers. Horrible to relate, the little Italian woman who had organized the women pickets, and another woman, Bertha Crouse, were so terribly beaten by the police that they gave premature birth to their babies and nearly died themselves.

Later a gang of gunmen was brought in. One night they went to the room of Jim Thompson, I.W.W. organizer and prominent figure in the steel strike. When he opened the door the crowd pushed in. Several shots were fired, but Thompson, a big man, was able to force his way out of the room, and ran naked to an adjoining harness shop. He had severe contusions on the head, but no other injuries. A stranger's gun and hat were found in his room, but there was no effort made by the Lawrence police to discover the culprits; they probably knew who they were.

Besides the mass picket line every day, there were many parades. One day sympathizers from Boston joined with the strikers in parade, carrying a banner inscribed

> "Arise! Slaves of the World! No God! No Master!"
> "One for all and all for one!"

This was answered by a parade called by the mill owners, which included some of the priests and ministers, the business men, and most of the public school children, although their parents were strikers. Across the principal street a banner was stretched, reading

> "For God and Country!"
> "The stars and stripes forever!"
> "The red flag never!"

A protest against the I.W.W., its principles and methods! A mad wave of patriotism came over the business element, and for a time they all wore little American flags in their buttonholes to the great satisfaction of the flag-manufacturers.

The mill owners were becoming desperate, and they resorted to the trick of planting dynamite where it would be found and charged to the strikers. But being on the alert, the workers discovered that the dynamite had been planted by the coroner of the county. This coroner, tool of the textile trust, was arrested, convicted, and fined five hundred dollars. Later a high official of the American Woolen Company committed suicide. It was rumored that he, too, had had something to do with the planted dynamite.

There were many hundreds of workers arrested during the strike. The United States Commissioner of Labor, in his report on the strike, cites three hundred and fifty-five arrests, but this makes no mention of the many hundreds thrown into jail and held for a time, and then released without a hearing or record. A man by the name of Caruso had been arrested later, on the same charge as Ettor and Giovanitti.

The United Textile Workers which belonged to the A. F. of L., and the Loom Fixers, most of them having no work on account of the strike, decided to go on strike themselves. They started a relief fund and sent out appeals. It has always been my opinion that most of the money, clothes and other supplies that they gathered in were intended by the donors for the great mass of the strikers. These skilled workers received the same proportional increase in pay, in the settlement, notwithstanding the fact that they had been scabbing during the early part of the strike, and grafting during the later.

The I.W.W. was active in every textile center that we could reach. The blaze in Lawrence had spread, and when the strike was settled, two hundred and fifty thousand other textile workers received a small increase in wages.

The strike committee had its last meeting after a sub-committee had gone to Boston and made a settlement with William Wood of the American Woolen Company. The report of the sub-committee was received with long cheers. The strike was off, if the settlement should prove satisfactory to the majority of the workers of all the mills involved, and there was no reason to suppose they would not be satisfied. I appealed to the committee and the strikers that filled the hall, to hold their union together, as there would be a time when they would have to strike again, if Ettor and Giovanitti were not released from prison. I helped twenty-three members of the strike committee to climb up on the platform. They were all of different nationalities, and we sang the *International* in as many different tongues as were represented on the strike committee.

When the strike was settled, early in March, it was a sweeping victory for the workers. Hours of labor were reduced, wages were increased from five to twenty per cent, with increased compensation for overtime, and there was to be no discrimination against any person who had taken part in the strike. The strike had been a magnificent demonstration of solidarity, and of what solidarity can do for the workers.

Jim Thompson, Grover Perry, Gurley Flynn, Bill Trautmann, and other I.W.W. organizers, including myself, went on the road to raise funds for the approaching murder trial of Ettor, Giovanitti, and Caruso.

Source: William D. Haywood, *The Autobiography of Big Bill Haywood* (New York: International Publishers, 1929), 246–53.

29. Life in Lowell, Massachusetts: Boarding House and Factory Rules for the Hamilton Manufacturing Company (1848)

Textiles were the first American industry to experiment with mass-production techniques. The most famous nineteenth-century industrial city was Lowell, Massachusetts. By 1836, Lowell was one of the largest industrial cities in the world, with twenty mills employing nearly 7,000 workers. Lowell was also a **company town** *with most of the businesses, boarding houses, and infrastructure owned by a consortium known as the Boston Associates. The vast majority of Lowell's workforce was young women, especially those drawn from New England farms. Although economically depressed*

New England farmers certainly welcomed the income that their daughters could earn in Lowell, they also sought assurances that mill operators would safeguard their daughters' morality. What evolved in Lowell—and in many other nineteenth-century workplaces—was a form of **paternalism** *that blended prevailing moral and gender constructs with employer desires to create a pliant and disciplined workforce.*

The first document illustrates moral concerns, while the second is more authoritarian.

BOARDING HOUSE RULES OF THE HAMILTON MANUFACTURING COMPANY: 1848

The tenants of the boarding-houses are not to board, or permit any part of their houses to be occupied by any person, except those in the employ of the company, without special permission.

They will be considered answerable for any improper conduct in their houses, and are not to permit their boarders to have company at unreasonable hours.

The doors must be closed at ten o'clock in the evening, and no person admitted after that time, without some reasonable excuse.

The keepers of the boarding-houses must give an account of the number, names and employment of their boarders, when required, and report the names of such as are guilty of any improper conduct, or are not in the regular habit of attending public worship.

The buildings, and yards about them, must be kept clean and in good order; and if they are injured, other-wise than from ordinary use, all necessary repairs will be made, and charged to the occupant.

The sidewalks, also, in front of the houses, must be kept clean, and free from snow, which must be removed from them immediately after it has ceased falling; if neglected, it will be removed by the company at the expense of the tenant.

It is desirable that the families of those who live in the houses, as well as the boarders, who have not had the . . . pox, should be vaccinated, which will be done at the expense of the company, for such as wish it.

Some suitable chamber in the house must be reserved, and appropriated for the use of the sick, so that others may not be under the necessity of sleeping in the same room.

JOHN AVERY, Agent.

FACTORY RULES FOR THE HAMILTON MANUFACTURING COMPANY: 1848

The overseers are to be always in their rooms at the starting of the mill, and not absent unnecessarily during working hours. They are to see that all those employed in their rooms, are in their places in due season, and keep a correct account of their time and work. They may grant leave of absence to those employed under them, when they have spare hands to supply their places, and not otherwise, except in cases of absolute necessity.

All persons in the employ of the Hamilton Manufacturing Company, are to observe the regulations of the room where they are employed. They are not to be absent from their work without the consent of the over-seer, except in cases of sickness, and then they are to send him word of the cause of their absence.

They are to board in one of the houses of the company and give information at the counting room, where they board, when they begin, or, whenever they change their boarding place; and are to observe the regulations of their boarding-house.

Those intending to leave the employment of the company, are to give at least two weeks' notice thereof to their overseer.

All persons entering into the employment of the company, are considered as engaged for twelve months, and those who leave sooner, or do not comply with all these regulations, will not be entitled to a regular discharge.

The company will not employ any one who is habitually absent from public worship on the Sabbath, or known to be guilty of immorality.

A physician will attend once in every month at the counting-room, to vaccinate all who may need it, free of expense.

Any one who shall take from the mills or the yard, any yarn, cloth or other article belonging to the company, will be considered guilty of stealing and be liable to prosecution.

Payment will be made monthly, including board and wages. The accounts will be made up to the last Saturday but one in every month, and paid in the course of the following week.

These regulations are considered part of the contract, with which all persons entering into the employment of the Hamilton Manufacturing Company, engage to comply.

JOHN AVERY, Agent.

Source: Illinois Labor History Society, http://www.kentlaw.edu/ilhs/lowell.html.

---

30. Molly Maguires: Excerpts from an 1894 Article by Cleveland Moffet in *McClure's Magazine*

The case of the **Molly Maguires** *is one of the more perplexing ones facing students of American labor history. Nineteen men were eventually hanged for involvement in what was supposedly a clandestine Irish and Irish American terrorist organization responsible for disorder and murders in coal mining regions of northeast Pennsylvania between 1870 and 1876. It has never been definitively proven that such an organiza-*

tion actually existed. Most of the testimony that condemned alleged Mollies came from **Pinkerton** *agent James McParland, who supposedly infiltrated the Molly Maguires.*

Critics of the verdict claim that the organization was a fiction invented by coal and railroad barons as an excuse for crushing a legitimate trade-union movement that threatened to loosen the autocratic grip of mine owners, who kept workers toiling in **company towns** *as impoverished chattel. They also point out that McParland was exposed as a pathological liar in a twentieth-century case involving the Western Federation of Miners, in which* **William Haywood** *and others were acquitted.*

The passage below recounts McParland's exploits on behalf of the Pinkertons. It was written by acclaimed journalist Cleveland Moffett for McClure's Magazine, a publication popular among the Gilded-Age middle class.

Some twenty years ago five counties in eastern Pennsylvania were dominated, terrorized, by a secret organization, thousands strong, whose special purpose was to rob, burn, pillage, and kill. Find on the map that marvelous mineral country, as large as Delaware, which lies between the Blue Mountains on the south and the arm of the Susquehanna on the north, and there you will see what was the home of these banded outlaws, the merciless Molly Maguires. . . .

The origin and development of the Molly Maguires will always present a hard problem to the social philosopher, who will, perhaps, find some subtle relation between crime and coal. One understands the act of an ordinary murderer who kills from greed, or fear, or hatred; but the Molly Maguires killed men and women with whom they had had no dealings, against whom they had no personal grievances, and from whose death they had nothing to gain, except, perhaps, the price of a few rounds of whiskey. They committed murders by the score, stupidly, brutally. . . . The men who decreed these monstrous crimes did so for the most trivial reasons—a reduction in wages, a personal dislike, some imagined grievance of a friend. These were sufficient to call forth an order to burn a house where women and children were sleeping, to shoot down in cold blood an employer or fellow workman, to lie in wait for an officer of the law and club him to death. In . . . trial of one of them, Mr. Franklin B. Gowen described the reign of these ready murderers as a time "when men retired to their homes at eight or nine o'clock in the evening and no one ventured beyond the precincts of his own door; when every man engaged in any enterprise of magnitude, or connected with industrial pursuits, left his home in the morning with his hand upon his pistol, unknowing whether he would again return alive; when the very foundations of society were being overturned."

In vain the officials of the Philadelphia and Reading and Lehigh Valley Railroads . . . offered thousands of dollars in rewards for the apprehension of the criminals. In vain Archbishop Wood, of Philadelphia fought the Molly Maguires with the whole power of the Catholic Church. . . . In vain, reputable citizens in almost every town, formed and armed committees of vigilantes who were to take the law into their own hands, inasmuch as the forces of the law were paralyzed. All was of no avail; public offices remained in the hands of ruffians; the same fierce crimes persisted; people were assaulted, robbed, and murdered with increasing frequency. . . .

In 1873, Mr. Franklin B. Gowen, then President of the Philadelphia and Reading Railroad, took counsel with Allan Pinkerton in regard to the matter. "It was owing to Mr. Gowen," says Mr. Robert A. Pinkerton in a recent letter, "that the Molly Maguire organization was broken up. . . ." [I]n order to protect its interests, and its employees, and the managers and superintendents of the mines . . . [Gowen] consulted Mr. Allan Pinkerton. "I have the very man for you," said Allan Pinkerton . . . James McParland.

A few weeks after the interview between Mr. Gowen and Mr. Pinkerton, James McParland was announced to have sailed for Europe on an important mission. Only two men in the country knew that he had really set out for the terrorized region, with instructions to run down these Molly Maguire bandits. . . . After some weeks of reconnoitering on foot through the coal regions, the young detective arrived in Pottsville, where he established himself in a boarding-house kept by a Mrs. O'Regan. There he met a man named Jennings, who volunteered to show him the sights of the city that same night. Passing a noisy drinking-place called the Sheridan House, McKenna, for that was McParland's assumed name, proposed going in. Jennings warned him as he valued his life never to cross the threshold of that place. "It's kept by Pat Dormer," he said, "the big body-master of the Molly Maguires. . . ."

[McKenna slowly ingratiated himself with Dormer, then moved to Shenandoah, where he met "Muff" Lawler, the Molly Maguires body-master for that region, whose life he saved in a barroom dispute.] . . . [H]e made the acquaintance of most of the prominent Mollys, including Jack Kehoe, of Girardville, and "Yellow Jack" Donahue, both of whom were afterwards hanged on his testimony. Everywhere he found that his reputation had preceded him, and he was received by all the Mollys with the respect which ruffians never fail to pay men whom they regard as greater ruffians than themselves. At each new stopping place he came into possession of new secrets touching crimes of the order already committed, and others that were planning, all of which he reported day by day to Allan Pinkerton. . . .

He learned that the number of Molly Maguires in the five counties had been much exaggerated in the popular mind, through fear, and that there were not really more than three or four thousand active members of the organization, whereas it had been reported through the State that there were ten times that many. McKenna saw, however, that it was impossible to exaggerate the desperate character of these men. He found that each county was governed by a "county delegate," his territory being divided into districts, or "patches," each under a "body-master" or chief officer, who gave out the signs and pass-words to trusted members, and ordered the execution of crimes that had been decided upon. In nearly every case the body-master was the keeper of a saloon near one of the shafts, slopes, or drifts. . . . If any superintendent dared to refuse the request of a body-master to hire or discharge any man, with or without reason, that superintendent's life was as good as forfeited. "Bosses" were in the same way constrained to give Mollys the best jobs—that is, the easiest—and in case of their failure to do so they were promptly made an example of with clubs or revolvers. Before killing a superintendent or a colliery "boss," the body-master would usually serve him with a "coffin notice," a roughly written warning, bearing crudely drawn knives and revolvers, and a large coffin in the center. Woe to the man who allowed such a notice to go unheeded! In nearly every instance he was shot or clubbed to death within a few days by unknown assailants. . . .

Early in July, 1875, while McKenna was still in Shenandoah, acting as a body-master, a shocking murder was committed by Molly Maguires at the town of Tamaqua . . . the east. The victim was Franklin B. Yost, a policeman, and a man who had served honorably in the civil war, and a most peaceful and worthy citizen. Hurrying to the scene of the crime, McKenna addressed himself to "Powder Keg" Carrigan, the body-master of that patch. . . .

McKenna was not long in learning that "Powder Keg" himself was the man at whose instigation the murder had been committed. Carrigan explained to him that they had killed the wrong man, his grievance having been not against Yost, but against another policeman, Bernard McCarron, who had aroused "Powder Keg's" enmity years before by frequently arresting him for disorderly conduct. Carrigan nursed the memory of this treatment, and when he had became a body-master at once proceeded to arrange for the killing of McCarron. Having applied to Alexander Campbell, the body-master of Landsford, Carbon County . . . for two men to do a "clean job," he brought the men to a retired spot on McCarron's beat. Later in the night, when a policeman passed by, the two men shot him, according to orders, and then started for their homes. But on that night McCarron had exchanged beats with Yost, who accordingly came to a violent death, although neither the Mollys nor anyone else in the region had any but kind feelings toward him. Carrigan showed McKenna the revolver, a weapon of thirty-two caliber, with which the policeman had been killed, and explained that it had been borrowed from a Molly named Roarity by the two men, Hugh McGehan and James Doyle, who with others had done the murder. McGehan was the man who fired the fatal shot. McKenna secured the names of every man concerned in the crime, and ultimately, on his evidence, it was punished by the hanging, in Pottsville, of Hugh McGehan, Thomas Duffy, James Roarity, James Carl, and James Doyle.

. . . Following closely upon the murder of Yost, there came in August, 1875, a "Bloody Saturday," as it was called by the Mollys, when they killed on that one day, Thomas Guyther, a justice of the peace, at Gerardville, and, at Shenandoah, Gomer James, the same whose life had been saved a few weeks before by McKenna's intervention. James was a desperado himself, having some time before, while drunk, shot down an Irishman named Cosgrove, and this offense the Mollys had sworn to avenge. . . . The Shenandoah firemen were giving a banquet in a public hall, and Gomer James was serving as bartender. A little before midnight, when the gaiety was at its height, Thomas Hurler left his mother, who was sitting on a bench near the bar, and going up to James ordered a glass of beer. James served him promptly, whereupon Hurley threw down a nickel, and lifting the glass in his left hand, pretended to drain it. but he held a pistol, ready cocked, in the right-hand pocket of his sack coat, and while the glass was at his lips, he pulled the trigger. Then, quite unconcerned, he finished his beer, and affected to join in a search for the murderer. . . .

. . . Toward the end of 1875, the strain under which McParland had been working for eighteen months began to tell upon him and he appealed to Allan Pinkerton to be allowed to strike the final blow. . . . Allan Pinkerton and his assistants . . . concluded that the evidence McParland had secured was sufficient, and steps were forthwith taken to close in on the murderers. McParland had still, however; many dangers to face; first from fellow members of the order who were beginning to believe he had played them false, and then from outraged citizens, who regarded him as a monster of crime whose unceremonious killing would be a service to the State. One night, in Tamaqua, bands of armed men searched for him from house to house until morning, and would certainly have discovered and lynched him, had he not, by pretending to fall into a drunken sleep, succeeded in remaining all night in the house of a respectable citizen who was not suspected of harboring him. . . .

Jack Kehoe, the county delegate whose influence in the order was very great, was now busily reporting his suspicion that "James McKenna" was a detective. To meet this danger McParland boldly went straight to Kehoe, accused him of treachery and demanded an immediate investigation. As county delegate, Kehoe instructed McKenna, who was at that time county secretary, to write notices to all the body-masters in the county to meet at Shenandoah at a given date, to conduct the investigation. He was writing the notices in a room over Kehoe's saloon, where Mrs. Kehoe was sewing, when Kehoe came in suddenly with a glass of soda for his wife, and a hot whiskey for McKenna. Having placed the two glasses on the table, he left the room. . . . As soon as he had gone, Mrs. Kehoe, who was a good woman at heart, and devoted to McKenna, took up the hot whiskey, threw it into the stove, and then burst into tears. . . . It is certain that the whiskey was poisoned. A second attempt to poison McKenna was made the day before his trial at Shenandoah. He was lifting the drugged glass to his lips when an instinctive suspicion moved him to set it down.

On the day of the trial Jack Kehoe did not appear. He was expecting that there would be no trial; for he had engaged sixteen men to murder McKenna, and had even advanced several of them twenty-five dollars each for the service.

McKenna's life was probably saved by the personal devotion of a Molly Maguire named Frank McAndrew, who told him of the plot to kill him, and swore to stand true to him. . . . By McAndrew's aid he stole away and returned to Philadelphia, where he was warmly welcomed by Allan Pinkerton and the president of the Philadelphia and Reading Railroad, Mr. Gowen. . . . And here the services of McParland (alias McKenna) as a detective in the Molly Maguire cases ended; but he had still a most important service to render as a witness. . . .

. . . [O]n May 6, 1876 a number of arrests were made, [and] the trials that followed were highly dramatic. Held as they were at the very center of the lawless district, there was more or less danger that persons engaged in them would themselves suffer the fraternity's vengeance. The result of the trials—which is to say the result of McParland's dangerous investigations and subsequent testimony—was the complete extermination of the order of Molly Maguires. A score or more of the desperadoes were condemned to longer or shorter terms in the penitentiary. Nineteen were hanged. Among the latter was Jack Kehoe, who had been among the first to suspect McParland of being a detective, and had expended all his power and ingenuity to get him killed and well out of the way.

Source: Cleveland Moffett, "The Overthrow of the Molly Maguires," *McClure's Magazine*, 1894; Ohio State University, Department of History, http://www.history.ohio-state.edu/projects/coal/MollyMaguire/mollymaguires.htm.

31. National Labor Relations (Wagner) Act (1935)

The National Labor Relations Act (Wagner-Connery Act) established the right of workers to organize unions of their own choosing, free from employer coercion, and established the obligation of employers to recognize such unions and bargain in good faith with them. Senator Robert Wagner (D-N.Y.) drew upon his experience as chairman of the National Labor Board, established under the ***National Industrial Recovery Act****, to draft this legislation. The* ***National Labor Relations Act*** *(NLRA) established a National Labor Relations Board to oversee the rights and obligations of employees and employers as established under the act. Additionally, the NLRA defined unfair labor practices on the part of employers. In 1937, the Supreme Court upheld this legislation, and it has remained the foundation of American labor law to the present day.*

FINDINGS AND POLICY

Sec. I. The denial by employers of the right of employees to organize and the refusal by employers to accept the procedure of collective bargaining lead to strikes and other forms of industrial strife or unrest, which have the intent or the necessary effect of burdening or obstructing commerce by (a) impairing the efficiency, safety, or operation of the instrumentalities of commerce; (b) occurring in the current of commerce; (c) materially affecting, restraining, or controlling the flow of raw materials or manufactured or processed goods from or into the channels of commerce, or the prices of such materials or goods in commerce; or (d) using diminution of employment and wages in such volume as substantially to impair or disrupt the market for goods flowing from or into the channels of commerce.

The inequality of bargaining power between employees who do not possess full freedom of association or actual liberty of contract, and employers who are organized in the corporate or other forms of ownership association substantially burdens and affects the flow of commerce, and tends to aggravate recurrent business depressions, by depressing wage rates and the purchasing power of wage earners in industry and by preventing the stabilization of competitive wage rates and working conditions within and between industries.

Experience has proved that protection by law of the right of employees to organize and bargain collectively safeguards commerce from injury, impairment, or interruption, and promotes the flow of commerce by removing certain recognized sources of industrial strife and unrest, by encouraging practices fundamental to the friendly adjustment of industrial disputes arising out of differences as to wages, hours, or other working conditions, and by restoring equality of bargaining power between employers and employees.

It is hereby declared to be the policy of the United States to eliminate the causes of certain substantial obstructions to the free flow of commerce and to mitigate and eliminate these obstructions when they have occurred by encouraging the practice and procedure of collective bargaining and by protecting the exercise by workers of full freedom of association, self-organization, and designation of representatives of their own choosing, for the purpose of negotiating the terms and conditions of their employment. . . .

NATIONAL LABOR RELATIONS BOARD

Sec. 3. (a) There is hereby created a board, to be known as the "National Labor Relations Board," which shall be composed of three members, who shall be appointed by the President, by and with the advice and consent of the Senate. One of the original members shall be appointed for a term of one year, one for a term of three years, and one for a term of five years, but their successors shall be appointed for terms of five years each, except that any individual chosen to fill a vacancy shall be appointed only for the unexpired term of the member whom he shall succeed. The President shall designate one member to serve as chairman of the Board. Any member of the Board may be removed by the President, upon notice and hearing, for neglect of duty or malfeasance in office, but for no other cause. . . .

Sec. 4. (a) Each member of the Board shall receive a salary of $10,000 a year, shall be eligible for reappointment, and shall not engage in any other business, vocation, or employment. . . . The Board may establish or utilize such regional, local, or other agencies, and utilize such voluntary and uncompensated services, as may from time to time be needed. . . .

Sec. 6. (a) The Board shall have authority from time to time to make, amend, and rescind such rules and regulations as may be necessary to carry out the provisions of this Act. Such rules and regulations shall be effective upon publication in the manner which the Board shall prescribe.

RIGHTS OF EMPLOYEES

Sec. 7. Employees shall have the right of self-organization, to form, join, or assist labor organizations, to bargain collectively through representatives of their own choosing, and to engage in concerted activities, for the purpose of collective bargaining or other mutual aid or protection.

Sec. 8. It shall be an unfair labor practice for an employer

(1) To interfere with, restrain, or coerce employees in the exercise of the rights guaranteed in section 7.

(2) To dominate or interfere with the formation or administration of any labor organization or contribute financial or other support to it: *Provided*, That subject to rules and regulations made and published by the Board pursuant to section 6 (a), an employer shall not be prohibited from permitting employees to confer with him during working hours without loss of time or pay.

(3) By discrimination in regard to hire or tenure of employment or any term or condition of employment to encourage or discourage membership in any labor organization: *Provided,* That nothing in this Act, or in the National Industrial Recovery Act (U.S. C., Supp. VII, title 15, secs. 701–712), as amended from time to time, or in any code or agreement approved or prescribed thereunder, or in any other statute of the United States, shall preclude an employer from making an agreement with a labor organization (not established, maintained, or assisted by any action defined in this Act as an unfair labor practice) to require as a condition of employment membership therein, if such labor organization is the representative of the employees as provided in section 9 (a), in the appropriate collective bargaining unit covered by such agreement when made.

(4) To discharge or otherwise discriminate against an employee because he has filed charges or given testimony under this Act.

(5) To refuse to bargain collectively with the representatives of his employees, subject to the provisions of Section 9 (a).

REPRESENTATIVES AND ELECTIONS

Sec. 9. (a) Representatives designated or elected for the purposes of collective bargaining by the majority of the employees in a unit appropriate for such purposes, shall be the exclusive representatives of all the employees in such unit for the purposes of collective bargaining in respect to rates of pay, wages, hours of employment, or other conditions of employment: *Provided,* That any individual employee or a group of employees shall have the right at any time to present grievances to their employer.

(b) The Board shall decide in each case whether, in order to insure to employees the full benefit of their right to self-organization and to collective bargaining, and otherwise to effectuate the policies of this Act, the unit appropriate for the purposes of collective bargaining shall be the employer unit, craft unit, plant unit, or subdivision thereof.

(c) Whenever a question affecting commerce arises concerning the representation of employees, the Board may investigate such controversy and certify to the parties, in writing, the name or names of the representatives that have been designated or selected. In any such investigation, the Board shall provide for an appropriate hearing upon due notice, either in conjunction with a proceeding under section 10 or otherwise, and may take a secret ballot of employees, or utilize any other suitable method to ascertain such representatives.

(d) Whenever an order of the Board made pursuant to section 10 (c) is based in whole or in part upon facts certified following an investigation pursuant to subsection (c) of this section, and there is a petition for the movement or review of such order, such certification and the record of such investigation shall be included in the transcript of the entire record required to be filed under subsections 10 (e) or 10 (f), and thereupon the decree of the court enforcing, modifying, or setting aside in whole or in part the order of the Board shall be made and entered upon the pleadings, testimony, and proceedings set forth in such transcript.

PREVENTION OF UNFAIR LABOR PRACTICES

Sec. 10. (a) The Board is empowered, as hereinafter provided, to prevent any person from engaging in any unfair labor practice (listed in section 8) affecting commerce. This power shall be exclusive, and shall not be affected by any other means of adjustment or prevention that has been or may be established by agreement, code, law, or otherwise.

(b) Whenever it is charged that any person has engaged in or is engaging in any such unfair labor practice, the Board, or any agent or agency designated by the Board for such purposes, shall have power to issue and cause to be served upon such person a complaint stating the charges in that respect, and containing a notice of hearing before the Board or a member thereof, or before a designated agent or agency, at a place therein fixed, not less than five days after the serving of said complaint. Any such complaint may be amended by the member, agent, or agency conducting the hearing or the Board in its discretion at any time prior to the issuance of an order based thereon. The person so complained of shall have the right to file an answer to the original or amended complaint and to appear in person or otherwise and give testimony at the place and time fixed in the complaint. In the discretion of the member, agent or agency conducting the hearing of the Board, any other person may be allowed to intervene in the said proceeding and to present testimony. In any such proceeding the rules of evidence prevailing in courts of law or equity shall not be controlling.

(c) The testimony taken by such member, agent or agency or the Board shall be reduced to writing and filed with the Board. Thereafter, in its discretion, the Board upon notice may take further testimony or hear argument. If upon all the testimony taken the Board shall be of the opinion that any person named in the complaint has engaged in or is engaging in any such unfair labor practice, then the Board shall state its findings of fact and shall issue and cause to be served on such person an order requiring such person to cease and desist from such unfair labor practice, and to take such affirmative action, including reinstatement of employees with or without back pay, as will effectuate the policies of this Act. Such order may further require such person to make reports from time to time showing the extent to which it has complied with the order. If upon all the testimony taken the Board shall be of the opinion that no person named in the complaint has engaged in or is engaging in any such unfair labor practice, then the Board shall state its findings of fact and shall issue an order dismissing the said complaint. . . .

(e) The Board shall have power to petition any circuit court of appeals of the United States, or if all the circuit courts of appeals to which application may be made are in vacation, any district court of the United States, within any circuit or district, respectively, wherein the unfair labor practice in question occurred or wherein such person resides or transacts business, for the enforcement of such order and for appropriate temporary relief or restraining order, and shall certify and file in the court a transcript of the entire record in the proceeding, including the pleadings and testimony upon which such order was entered and the findings and order of the Board. Upon such filing, the court shall cause notice thereof to be served upon such person, and thereupon shall have jurisdiction of the proceeding and of the question determined therein, and shall have power to grant such temporary relief or restraining order as it deems just and proper, and to make and enter upon the pleadings, testimony, and proceedings set forth in such transcript a decree enforcing, modifying, and enforcing as so modified, or setting aside in whole or in part the order of the Board. . . .

Source: U.S. Statutes at Large, vol. XLIX.

---

32. Persecution of the Industrial Workers of the World: "Big Bill" Haywood's Description of the 1919 Murder of Wesley Everest

The ***Industrial Workers of the World (IWW)*** *was one of the most colorful and overtly radical labor organizations to appear on American soil. Because the IWW openly espoused the destruction of the* ***wage*** *system, it engendered great opposition. For most of its most active period—roughly 1907 to 1919—the IWW's own revolutionary rhetoric contributed to the ferocity with which organized capital sought to silence the group. Fears of revolution and sabotage were used by IWW enemies to justify crackdowns of dubious legality. For all the IWW's fiery words, far more violence was done to IWW members than by them. Persecutions of IWW members intensified once the United States entered World War I. The IWW viewed the war as a capitalist struggle and many of its leaders encouraged workers to avoid taking part in it. Official raids took place, and quasi-legal vigilante actions proliferated.*

One of the worst of the latter took place in Centralia, Washington, in 1919, where the American Legion and local citizens, encouraged by timber barons, targeted IWW organizers and took it upon themselves to destroy the town's IWW labor hall. That raid led to the lynching of Wesley Everest. Everest is one of the three most-famed martyrs of the early IWW, and joined a pantheon also occupied by Frank Little, who was killed by a Montana mob in 1917, and songwriter ***Joe Hill****, who was executed for murder in 1915. The story of Everest's martyrdom is told by famed IWW organizer* ***William "Big Bill" Haywood****.*

On November 11th, 1919, a parade of American Legion men and assorted patriots was held. At the meeting to "deal with the I.W.W." . . . a secret plot was concocted among the Lumber Trust leaders to mob the I.W.W. Hall, leading the paraders into the attack.

At the moment agreed upon, the leaders cried out upon signal from a man on horseback, "Let's go-o-o! At 'em boys!" and the door of the hall was smashed in, some entering, when a rain of bullets came from within, halting the attack and leaving two attackers dead and several wounded. Some of the mob carried ropes, evidently ready to lynch the union men. . . .

But the hall was surrounded and the attackers gained entrance in force, seizing the few workers there, with the exception of one man, Wesley Everest. Leaving the hall by the rear door he broke through the mob and made for the river, rifle bullets of his prepared assassins zipping around him. With the ammunition, he stopped to reload, reached the river and tried to ford it. Failing because of its depth, he came back to shore and shouted his readiness to surrender to any constituted authority.

The mob paid no attention and came on, firing as they came, until Everest saw there was no hope of ceasing the fight and resumed with firing. This halted the mob but one man came on, armed and firing. With his last cartridge Everest shot this fellow, Dale Hubbard, nephew of the chief conspirator. Everest was seized by the mob.

On the way to the jail he was beaten, kicked and cursed. With a rifle-butt his front teeth were knocked out. A rope was thrown round his neck, but with characteristic defiance he told them, "You haven't got the guts to lynch a man in the daytime."

Night came. Maimed and bleeding in a cell next to his fellow workers, lay Everest. At a late hour the lights of the city suddenly were extinguished. The jail door was smashed. No one tried to stop the lynchers. Staggering erect, Everest said to the other prisoners: "Tell the boys I died for my class."

A brief struggle. Many blows. A sound of dragging. The purring of high-powered cars. Again the lights came on. The autos reached the bridge over the Chehalis River. A rope was tied to the steel framework and Everest with a noose around his neck was brutally kicked from the bridge. After a pause he was hauled up, and it being found that he had some life left, a longer rope was used and the brutal process repeated. Again hauled up, the ghouls again flung the body over. An auto headlight was trained on the body disclosing that some sadist, more degenerate than the rest, had ripped Everest's sexual organs almost loose from his body with some sharp instrument during the auto trip to the bridge.

Finally, after riddling the body with bullets, it was cut loose and let fall in the river later to be found, a sodden, ghastly thing, taken back to the jail where it was placed in view of Everest's friends there in prison and at last buried in an unmarked grave.

Source: William Haywood, *The Autobiography of Big Bill Haywood* (1929; reprint New York: International Publishers, 1966), pp. 355–56.

33. Principles of Scientific Management: Excerpt from Frederick Winslow Taylor's *Shop Management*, 1911

Frederick Winslow Taylor (1856–1915) was known as the "father" of scientific management. Taylor utilized time-motion studies to analyze the work process. Using incentive pay, Taylor aimed to coordinate human efforts with the maximum efficiency of production. Taylor's system of work measurement, work design, and production control transformed the nature of American industrial production. Taylor believed that the key to higher ***wages*** *and higher profits, simultaneously, was to increase productivity. With increased wages, hence increased worker satisfaction, it was believed that the incentive to join unions would be lessened.* **Taylorism**, *as Taylor's "brand" of scientific management came to be known, achieved great popularity in the first two decades of the twentieth century. In this 1911 publication, Taylor explains his system.*

INTRODUCTION

President Roosevelt, in his address to the Governors at the White House, prophetically remarked that "The conservation of our national resources is only preliminary to the larger question of national efficiency."

The whole country at once recognized the importance of conserving our material resources and a large movement has been started which will be effective in accomplishing this object. As yet, however, we have but vaguely appreciated the importance of "the larger question of increasing our national efficiency."

We can see our forests vanishing, our water-powers going to waste, our soil being carried by floods into the sea; and the end of our coal and our iron is in sight. But our larger wastes of human effort, which go on every day through such of our acts as are blundering, ill-directed, or inefficient, and which Mr. Roosevelt refers to as a lack of "national efficiency," are less visible, less tangible, and are but vaguely appreciated.

We can see and feel the waste of material things. Awkward, inefficient, or ill-directed movements of men, however, leave nothing visible or tangible behind them. Their appreciation calls for an act of memory, an effort of the imagination. And for this reason, even though our daily loss from this source is greater than from our waste of material things, the one has stirred us deeply, while the other has moved us but little.

As yet there has been no public agitation for "greater national efficiency," no meetings have been called to consider how this is to be brought about. And still there are signs that the need for greater efficiency is widely felt.

The search for better, for more competent men, from the presidents of our great companies down to our household servants, was never more vigorous than it is now. And more than ever before is the demand for competent men in excess of the supply.

What we are all looking for, however, is the ready-made, competent man; the man whom some one else has trained. It is only when we fully realize that our duty, as well as our opportunity, lies in systematically cooperating to train and to make this competent man, instead of in hunting for a man whom some one else has trained, that we shall be on the road to national efficiency.

In the past the prevailing idea has been well expressed in the saying that "Captains of industry are born, not made" and the theory has been that if one could get the right man, methods could be safely left to him. In the future it will be appreciated that our leaders must be trained right as well as born right, and that no great man can (with the old system of personal management) hope to compete with a number of ordinary men who have been properly organized so as efficiently to cooperate.

In the past the man has been first; in the future the system must be first. This in no sense, however, implies that great men are not needed. On the contrary, the first object of any good system must be that of developing first-class men; and under systematic management the best man rises to the top more certainly and more rapidly than ever before.

This paper has been written:

First. To point out, through a series of simple illustrations, the great loss which the whole country is suffering through inefficiency in almost all of our daily acts.

Second. To try to convince the reader that the remedy for this inefficiency lies in systematic management, rather than in searching for some unusual or extraordinary man.

Third. To prove that the best management is a true science, resting upon clearly defined laws, rules, and principles, as a foundation. And further to show that the fundamental principles of scientific management are applicable to all kinds of human activities, from our simplest individual acts to the work of our great corporations, which call for the most elaborate cooperation. And, briefly, through a series of illustrations, to convince the reader that whenever these principles are correctly applied, results must follow which are truly astounding.

This paper was originally prepared for presentation to The American Society of Mechanical Engineers. The illustrations chosen are such as, it is believed, will especially appeal to engineers and to managers of industrial and manufacturing establishments, and also quite as much to all of the men who are working in these establishments. It is hoped, however, that it will be clear to other readers that the same principles can be applied with equal force to all social activities: to the management of our homes; the management of our farms; the management of the business of our tradesmen, large and small; of our churches, our philanthropic institutions, our universities, and our governmental departments.

CHAPTER I: FUNDAMENTALS OF SCIENTIFIC MANAGEMENT

The principal object of management should be to secure the maximum prosperity for the employer, coupled with the maximum prosperity for each employee. The words "maximum prosperity" are used, in their broad sense, to mean not only large dividends for the company or owner, but the development of every branch of the business to its highest state of excellence, so that the prosperity may be permanent.

In the same way maximum prosperity for each employee means not only higher wages than are usually received by men of his class, but, of more importance still, it also means the development of each man to his state of maximum efficiency, so that he may be able to do, generally speaking, the highest grade of work for which his natural abilities fit him, and it further means giving him, when possible, this class of work to do.

It would seem to be so self-evident that maximum prosperity for the employer, coupled with maximum prosperity for the employee, ought to be the two leading objects of management, that even to state this fact should be unnecessary. And yet there is no question that, throughout the industrial world, a large part of the organization of employers, as well as employees, is for war rather than for peace, and that perhaps the majority on either side do not believe that it is possible so to arrange their mutual relations that their interests become identical.

The majority of these men believe that the fundamental interests of employees and employers are necessarily antagonistic. Scientific management, on the contrary, has for its very foundation the firm conviction that the true interests of the two are one and the same; that prosperity for the employer cannot exist through a long term of years unless it is accompanied by prosperity for the employee, and vice versa; and that it is possible to give the workman what he most wants high wages and the employer what he wants a low labor cost—for his manufactures.

It is hoped that some at least of those who do not sympathize with each of these objects may be led to modify their views; that some employers, whose attitude toward their workmen has been that of trying to get the largest amount of work out of them for the smallest possible wages, may be led to see that a more liberal policy toward their men will pay them better; and that some of those workmen who begrudge a fair and even a large profit to their employers, and who feel that all of the fruits of their labor should belong to them, and that those for whom they work and the capital invested in the business are entitled to little or nothing, may be led to modify these views.

No one can be found who will deny that in the case of any single individual the greatest prosperity can exist only when that individual has reached his highest state of efficiency; that is, when he is turning out his largest daily output. The truth of this fact is also perfectly clear in the case of two men working together.

To illustrate: if you and your workman have become so skillful that you and he together are making two pairs of shoes in a day, while your competitor and his workman are making only one pair, it is clear that after selling your two pairs of shoes you can pay your workman much higher wages than your competitor who produces only one pair of shoes is able to pay his man, and that there will still be enough money left over for you to have a larger profit than your competitor.

In the case of a more complicated manufacturing establishment, it should also be perfectly clear that the greatest permanent prosperity for the workman, coupled with the greatest prosperity for the employer, can be brought about only when the work of the establishment is done with the smallest combined expenditure of human effort, plus nature's resources, plus the cost for the use of capital in the shape of machines, buildings, etc. Or, to state the same thing in a different way: that the greatest prosperity can exist only as the result of the greatest possible productivity of the men and machines of the establishment that is, when each man and each machine are turning out the largest possible output; because unless your men and your machines are daily turning out more work than others around you, it is clear that competition will prevent your paying higher wages to your workmen than are paid to those of your competitor. And what is true as to the possibility of paying high wages in the case of two companies competing close beside one another is also true as to whole districts of the country and even as to nations which are in competition. In a word, that maximum prosperity can exist only as the result of maximum productivity. Later in this paper illustrations will be given of several companies which are earning large dividends and at the same time paying from 30 per cent to 100 per cent higher wages to their men than are paid to similar men immediately around them, and with whose employers they are in competition. These illustrations will cover different types of work, from the most elementary to the most complicated. If the above reasoning is correct, it follows that the most important object of both the workmen and the management should be the training and development of each individual in the establishment, so that he can do (at his fastest pace and with the maximum of efficiency) the highest class of work for which his natural abilities fit him.

These principles appear to be so self-evident that many men may think it almost childish to state them. Let us, however, turn to the facts, as they actually exist in this country and in England. The English and American peoples are the greatest sportsmen in the world. Whenever an American workman plays baseball, or an English workman plays cricket, it is safe to say that he strains every nerve to secure victory for his side. He does his very best to make the largest possible number of runs. The universal sentiment is so strong that any man who fails to give out all there is in him in sport is branded as a "quitter," and treated with contempt by those who are around him. When the same workman returns to work on the following day, instead of using every effort to turn out the largest possible amount of work, in a majority of the cases this man deliberately plans to do as little as he safely can—to turn out far less work than he is well able to do—in many instances to do not more than one-third to one-half of a proper day's work. And in fact if he were to do his best to turn out his largest possible day's work, he would be abused by his fellow-workers for so doing, even more than if he had proved himself a "quitter" in sport. Under working, that is, deliberately working slowly so as to avoid doing a full day's work, "soldiering," as it is called in this country, "hanging it out," as it is called in England, "ca' cannie," as it is called in Scotland, is almost universal in industrial establishments, and prevails also to a large extent in the building trades; and the writer asserts without fear of contradiction that this constitutes the greatest evil with which the working-people of both England and America are now afflicted. It will be shown later in this paper that doing away with slow working and "soldiering" in all its forms and so arranging the relations between employer and employee that each workman will work to his very best advantage and at his best speed, accompanied by the intimate cooperation with the management and the help (which the workman should receive) from the management, would result on the average in nearly doubling the output of each man and each machine. What other reforms, among those which are being discussed by these two nations, could do as much toward promoting prosperity, toward the diminution of poverty, and the alleviation of suffering? America and England have been recently agitated over such subjects as the tariff, the control of the large corporations on the one hand, and of hereditary power on the other hand, and over various more or less socialistic proposals for taxation, etc. On these subjects both peoples have been profoundly stirred, and yet hardly a voice has been raised to call attention to this vastly greater and more important subject of "soldiering," which directly and powerfully affects the wages, the prosperity, and the life of almost every working-man, and also quite as much the prosperity of every industrial establishment in the nation.

The elimination of "soldiering" and of the several causes of slow working would so lower the cost of production that both our home and foreign markets would be greatly enlarged, and we could compete on more than even terms with our rivals. It would remove one of the fundamental causes for dull times, for lack of employment, and for poverty, and therefore would have a more permanent and far-reaching effect upon these misfortunes than any of the curative remedies that are now being used to soften their consequences. It would insure higher wages and make shorter working hours and better working and home conditions possible.

Why is it, then, in the face of the self-evident fact that maximum prosperity can exist only as the result of the determined effort of each workman to turn out each day his largest possible day's work, that the great majority of our men are deliberately doing just the opposite, and that even when the men have the best of intentions their work is in most cases far from efficient? There are three causes for this condition, which may be briefly summarized as:

First. The fallacy, which has from time immemorial been almost universal among workmen, that a material increase in the output of each man or each machine in the trade would result in the end in throwing a large number of men out of work.

Second. The defective systems of management which are in common use, and which make it necessary for each workman to soldier, or work slowly, in order that he may protect his own best interests.

Third. The inefficient rule-of-thumb methods, which are still almost universal in all trades and in practicing which our workmen waste a large part of their effort.

This paper will attempt to show the enormous gains which would result from the substitution by our workmen of scientific for rule-of-thumb methods.

To explain a little more fully these three causes:

First. The great majority of workmen still believe that if they were to work at their best speed they would be doing a great injustice to the whole trade by throwing a lot of men out of work, and yet the history of the development of each trade shows that each improvement, whether it be the invention of a new machine or the introduction of a better method, which results in increasing the productive capacity of the men in the trade and cheapening the costs, instead of throwing men out of work make in the end work for more men.

The cheapening of any article in common use almost immediately results in a largely increased demand for that article. Take the case of shoes, for instance. The introduction of machinery for doing every element of the work which was formerly done by hand has resulted in making shoes at a fraction of their former labor cost, and in selling them so cheap that now almost every man, woman, and child in the working-classes buys one or two pairs of shoes per year, and wears shoes all the time, whereas formerly each workman bought perhaps one pair of shoes every five years, and went barefoot most of the time, wearing shoes only as a luxury or as a matter of the sternest necessity. In spite of the enormously increased output of shoes per workman, which has come with shoe machinery, the demand for shoes has so increased that there are relatively more men working in the shoe industry now than ever before.

The workmen in almost every trade have before them an object lesson of this kind, and yet, because they are ignorant of the history of their own trade even, they still firmly believe, as their fathers did before them, that it is against their best interests for each man to turn out each day as much work as possible.

Under this fallacious idea a large proportion of the workmen of both countries each day deliberately work slowly so as to curtail the output. Almost every labor union has made, or is contemplating making, rules which have for their object curtailing the output of their members, and those men who have the greatest influence with the working-people, the labor leaders as well as many people with philanthropic feelings who are helping them, are daily spreading this fallacy and at the same time telling them that they are overworked. A great deal has been and is being constantly said about "sweat-shop" work and conditions. The writer has great sympathy with those who are overworked, but on the whole a greater sympathy for those who are under paid. For every individual, however, who is overworked, there are a hundred who intentionally underwork—greatly underwork—every day of their lives, and who for this reason deliberately aid in establishing those conditions which in the end inevitably result in low wages. And yet hardly a single voice is being raised in an endeavor to correct this evil.

As engineers and managers, we are more intimately acquainted with these facts than any other class in the community, and are therefore best fitted to lead in a movement to combat this fallacious idea by educating not only the workmen but the whole of the country as to the true facts. And yet we are practically doing nothing in this direction, and are leaving this field entirely in the hands of the labor agitators (many of whom are misinformed and mis-guided), and of sentimentalists who are ignorant as to actual working conditions.

Second. As to the second cause for soldiering—the relations which exist between employers and employees under almost all of the systems of management which are in common use—it is impossible in a few words to make it clear to one not familiar with this problem why it is that the ignorance of employers as to the proper time in which work of various kinds should be done makes it for the interest of the workman to "soldier."

The writer therefore quotes herewith from a paper read before The American Society of Mechanical Engineers in June, 1903, entitled "Shop Management," which it is hoped will explain fully this cause for soldiering:

> This loafing or soldiering proceeds from two causes. First, from the natural instinct and tendency of men to take it easy, which may be called natural soldiering. Second, from more intricate second thought and reasoning caused by their relations with other men, which may be called systematic soldiering. There is no question that the tendency of the average man (in all walks of life) is toward working at a slow, easy gait, and that it is only after a good deal of thought and observation on his part or as a result of example, conscience, or external pressure that he takes a more rapid pace. There are, of course, men of unusual energy, vitality, and ambition who naturally choose the fastest gait, who set up their own standards, and who work hard, even though it may be against their best interests. But these few uncommon men only serve by forming a contrast to emphasize the tendency of the average. This common tendency to "take it easy" is greatly increased by bringing a number of men together on similar work and at a uniform standard rate of pay by the day.
>
> Under this plan the better men gradually but surely slow down their gait to that of the poorest and least efficient. When a naturally energetic man works for a few days beside a lazy one, the logic of the situation is unanswerable. "Why should I work hard when that lazy fellow gets the same pay that I do and does only half as much work?"
>
> A careful time study of men working under these conditions will disclose facts which are ludicrous as well as pitiable.
>
> To illustrate: The writer has timed a naturally energetic workman who, while going and coming from work, would walk at a speed of from three to four miles per hour, and not infrequently trot home after a day's work. On arriving at his work he would immediately slow down to a speed of about one mile an hour. When, for example, wheeling a loaded wheelbarrow, he would go at a good fast

pace even uphill in order to be as short a time as possible under load, and immediately on the return walk slow down to a mile an hour, improving every opportunity for delay short of actually sitting down. In order to be sure not to do more than his lazy neighbor, he would actually tire himself in his effort to go slow.

These men were working under a foreman of good reputation and highly thought of by his employer, who, when his attention was called to this state of things, answered: "Well, I can keep them from sitting down, but the devil can't make them get a move on while they are at work."

The natural laziness of men is serious, but by far the greatest evil from which both workmen and employers are suffering is the systematic soldiering which is almost universal under all of the ordinary schemes of management and which results from a careful study on the part of the workmen of what will promote their best interests.

The writer was much interested recently in hearing one small but experienced golf caddy boy of twelve explaining to a green caddy, who had shown special energy and interest, the necessity of going slow and lagging behind his man when he came up to the ball, showing him that since they were paid by the hour, the faster they went the less money they got, and finally telling him that if he went too fast the other boys would give him a licking.

This represents a type of systematic soldiering which is not, however, very serious, since it is done with the knowledge of the employer, who can quite easily break it up if he wishes.

The greater part of the systematic soldiering, however, is done by the men with the deliberate object of keeping their employers ignorant of how fast work can be done.

So universal is soldiering for this purpose that hardly a competent workman can be found in a large establishment, whether he works by the day or on piece work, contract work, or under any of the ordinary systems, who does not devote a considerable part of his time to studying just how slow he can work and still convince his employer that he is going at a good pace.

The causes for this are, briefly, that practically all employers determine upon a maximum sum which they feel it is right for each of their classes of employees to earn per day, whether their men work by the day or piece.

Each workman soon finds out about what this figure is for his particular case, and he also realizes that when his employer is convinced that a man is capable of doing more work than he has done, he will find sooner or later some way of compelling him to do it with little or no increase of pay.

Employers derive their knowledge of how much of a given class of work can be done in a day from either their own experience, which has frequently grown hazy with age, from casual and unsystematic observation of their men, or at best from records which are kept, showing the quickest time in which each job has been done. In many cases the employer will feel almost certain that a given job can be done faster than it has been, but he rarely cares to take the drastic measures necessary to force men to do it in the quickest time, unless he has an actual record proving conclusively how fast the work can be done.

It evidently becomes for each man's interest, then, to see that no job is done faster than it has been in the past. The younger and less experienced men are taught this by their elders, and all possible persuasion and social pressure is brought to bear upon the greedy and selfish men to keep them from making new records which result in temporarily increasing their wages, while all those who come after them are made to work harder for the same old pay.

Under the best day work of the ordinary type, when accurate records are kept of the amount of work done by each man and of his efficiency, and when each man's wages are raised as he improves, and those who fail to rise to a certain standard are discharged and a fresh supply of carefully selected men are given work in their places, both the natural loafing and systematic soldiering can be largely broken up. This can only be done, however, when the men are thoroughly convinced that there is no intention of establishing piece work even in the remote future, and it is next to impossible to make men believe this when the work is of such a nature that they believe piece work to be practicable. In most cases their fear of making a record which will be used as a basis for piece work will cause them to soldier as much as they dare.

It is, however, under piece work that the art of systematic soldiering is thoroughly developed; after a workman has had the price per piece of the work he is doing lowered two or three times as a result of his having worked harder and increased his output, he is likely entirely to lose sight of his employer's side of the case and become imbued with a grim determination to have no more cuts if soldiering can prevent it. Unfortunately for the character of the workman, soldiering involves a deliberate attempt to mislead and deceive his employer, and thus upright and straightforward workmen are compelled to become more or less hypocritical. The employer is soon looked upon as an antagonist, if not an enemy, and the mutual confidence which should exist between a leader and his men, the enthusiasm, the feeling that they are all working for the same end and will share in the results is entirely lacking.

The feeling of antagonism under the ordinary piece-work system becomes in many cases so marked on the part of the men that any proposition made by their employers, however reasonable, is looked upon with suspicion, and soldiering becomes such a fixed habit that men will frequently take pains to restrict the product of machines which they are running when even a large increase in output would involve no more work on their part.

Third. As to the third cause for slow work, considerable space will later in this paper be devoted to illustrating the great gain, both to employers and employees, which results from the substitution of scientific for rule-of-thumb methods in even the smallest details of the work of every trade. The enormous saving of time and therefore increase in the output which it is possible to effect through eliminating unnecessary motions and substituting fast for slow and inefficient motions for the men working in any of our trades can be fully realized only after one has personally seen the improvement which results from a thorough motion and time study, made by a competent man.

To explain briefly: owing to the fact that the workmen in all of our trades have been taught the details of their work by observation of those immediately around them, there are many different ways in common use for doing the same thing, perhaps forty, fifty, or a hundred ways of doing each act in each trade, and for the same reason there is a great variety in the implements used for each class of work. Now, among the various methods and implements used in each element of each trade there is always one method and one implement which is quicker and better than any of the rest. And this one best method and best implement can only be discovered or developed through a scientific study and analysis of all of the methods and implements in use, together with accurate, minute, motion and time study. This involves the gradual substitution of science for rule of thumb throughout the mechanic arts.

This paper will show that the underlying philosophy of all of the old systems of management in common use makes it imperative that each workman shall be left with the final responsibility for doing his job practically as he thinks best, with comparatively little help and advice from the management. And it will also show that because of this isolation of workmen, it is in most cases impossible for the men working under these systems to do their work in accordance with the rules and laws of a science or art, even where one exists.

The writer asserts as a general principle (and he proposes to give illustrations tending to prove the fact later in this paper) that in almost all of the mechanic arts the science which underlies each act of each workman is so great and amounts to so much that the workman who is best suited to actually doing the work is incapable of fully understanding this science, without the guidance and help of those who are working with him or over him, either through lack of education or through insufficient mental capacity. In order that the work may be done in accordance with scientific laws, it is necessary that there shall be a far more equal division of the responsibility between the management and the workmen than exists under any of the ordinary types of management. Those in the management whose duty it is to develop this science should also guide and help the workman in working under it, and should assume a much larger share of the responsibility for results than under usual conditions is assumed by the management.

The body of this paper will make it clear that, to work according to scientific laws, the management must take over and perform much of the work which is now left to the men; almost every act of the workman should be preceded by one or more preparatory acts of the management which enable him to do his work better and quicker than he otherwise could. And each man should daily be taught by and receive the most friendly help from those who are over him, instead of being, at the one extreme, driven or coerced by his bosses, and at the other left to his own unaided devices.

This close, intimate, personal cooperation between the management and the men is of the essence of modern scientific or task management.

It will be shown by a series of practical illustrations that, through this friendly cooperation, namely, through sharing equally in every day's burden, all of the great obstacles (above described) to obtaining the maximum output for each man and each machine in the establishment are swept away. The 30 per cent to 100 per cent increase in wages which the workmen are able to earn beyond what they receive under the old type of management, coupled with the daily intimate shoulder to shoulder contact with the management, entirely removes all cause for soldiering. And in a few years, under this system, the workmen have before them the object lesson of seeing that a great increase in the output per man results in giving employment to more men, instead of throwing men out of work, thus completely eradicating the fallacy that a larger output for each man will throw other men out of work.

It is the writer's judgment, then, that while much can be done and should be done by writing and talking toward educating not only workmen, but all classes in the community, as to the importance of obtaining the maximum output of each man and each machine, it is only through the adoption of modern scientific management that this great problem can be finally solved. Probably most of the readers of this paper will say that all of this is mere theory. On the contrary, the theory, or philosophy, of scientific management is just beginning to be understood, whereas the management itself has been a gradual evolution, extending over a period of nearly thirty years. And during this time the employees of one company after another, including a large range and diversity of industries, have gradually changed from the ordinary to the scientific type of management. At least 50,000 workmen in the United States are now employed under this system; and they are receiving from 30 per cent to 100 per cent higher wages daily than are paid to men of similar caliber with whom they are surrounded, while the companies employing them are more prosperous than ever before. In these companies the output, per man and per machine, has on an average been doubled. During all these years there has never been a single strike among the men working under this system. In place of the suspicious watchfulness and the more or less open warfare which characterizes the ordinary types of management, there is universally friendly cooperation between the management and the men.

Several papers have been written, describing the expedients which have been adopted and the details which have been developed under scientific management and the steps to be taken in changing from the ordinary to the scientific type. But unfortunately most of the readers of these papers have mistaken the mechanism for the true essence. Scientific management fundamentally consists of certain broad general principles, a certain philosophy, which can be applied in many ways, and a description of what any one man or men may believe to be the best mechanism for applying these general principles should in no way be confused with the principles themselves.

It is not here claimed that any single panacea exists for all of the troubles of the working-people or of employers. As long as some people are born lazy or inefficient, and others are born greedy and brutal, as long as vice and crime are with us, just so long will a certain amount of poverty, misery, and unhappiness be with us also. No system of management, no single expedient within the control of any man or any set of men can insure continuous prosperity to either workmen or employers. Prosperity depends upon so many factors entirely beyond the control of any one set of men, any state, or even any one country, that certain periods will inevitably come when both sides must suffer, more or less. It is claimed, however, that under scientific management the intermediate periods will be far more prosperous, far happier, and more free from discord and dissension. And also, that the periods will be fewer, shorter and the suffering less. And this will be particularly true in any one town, any one section of the country, or any one state which first substitutes the principles of scientific management for the rule of thumb.

That these principles are certain to come into general use practically throughout the civilized world, sooner or later, the writer is profoundly convinced, and the sooner they come the better for all the people.

Source: Frederick Winslow Taylor, *Shop Management* (New York: Harper & Brothers, 1911).

---

34. Excerpts from Henry George's *Progress and Poverty* (1879)

It would be nearly impossible to exaggerate the impact that **Henry George** *had on the thinking of late-nineteenth-century workers and reformers. The 1879 publication of* Progress and Poverty *caused an overnight sensation. In it, George rejects the popular Malthusianism and* **Social Darwinism** *of his day that posited that poverty was the result of a natural struggle for resources in which the fittest rose to the top of the economic heap. George attacked Malthusian assumptions at their core and demonstrated that the causes of poverty were rooted in unfair advantages in the way that tax policies, rents, and social improvements were allocated. In particular, George felt that social improvements and a steep decline in the availability of land had led to steep increases in the value of the latter. George targeted land speculators and others holding "idle" lands and argued that the state should abolish all taxes except for a "single tax" on unimproved land, which would be used by the state for all its needs, including alleviating poverty. Unimproved land would be taxed at its full value, thereby discouraging speculation, making more land available, and encouraging development that would benefit all of society.*

George's theories are rooted in agrarian ideals and, like most panaceas, were criticized for being overly simplistic or impractical. Millions of people around the world disagreed and formed single-tax associations. Whatever one thinks of George's theories, he deserves credit for exposing the illogic of Social Darwinism. The popularity of his views may also help explain why imported ideas—like **socialism**, *communism, and* **anarchism**—*held relatively less sway in the United States than they did elsewhere.*

In the two passages below, George lays out "The True Remedy" to society's problems, then explains "How Equal Rights to the Land May Be Asserted and Secured." [All emphasis in original]

We have traced the unequal distribution of wealth which is the curse and menace of modern civilization to the institution of private property in land. We have seen that so long as this institution exists no increase in productive power can permanently benefit the masses but, on the contrary, must tend still further to depress their condition. We have examined all the remedies, short of the abolition of private property in land . . . and have found them all inefficacious or impracticable.

There is but one way to remove an evil—and that is, to remove its cause. Poverty deepens as wealth increases, and wages are forced down while productive power grows, because land which is the source of all wealth and the field of all labor, is monopolized. To extirpate poverty, to make wages what justice commands they should be . . . we must therefore substitute for the individual ownership of land a common ownership. . . . *We must make land common property*. . . .

But a question of method remains. How shall we do it? . . .

I do not propose either to purchase or confiscate private property in land. The first would be unjust; the second needless. Let the individuals who now hold it still retain . . . possession of what they are pleased to call *their* land. Let them continue to call it *their* land. Let them buy and sell, and bequeath and devise it. . . . *It is not necessary to confiscate land; it is only necessary to confiscate rent*. . . .

What I, therefore, propose, as the simple yet sovereign remedy, which will raise wages, increase the earnings of capital, extirpate pauperism, abolish poverty, give remunerative employment to whomever wishes it, afford free scope to human powers, lessen crime, elevate morals . . . purify government, and carry civilization to yet nobler heights, is—*to appropriate rent by taxation*. . . .

Now, insomuch as the taxation of rent, of land values, must necessarily be increased just as we abolish other taxes, we may put forth the proposition into practical form by proposing—

To abolish all taxation save that upon land values. . . .

Source: Henry George, *Progress and Poverty: An Inquiry Into the Cause of Industrial Depressions and of Increase of Want with Increase of Wealth* (New York: Walter J. Black, 1942 reprint), pp. 274, 338, 340–41.

35. Pullman, Illinois, a Company Town: Excerpt from U.S. Strike Commission Report on the Chicago Strikes of June and July 1894

The Pullman ***boycott*** *of 1894 was one of the most famed clashes of* ***capital*** *and labor in American labor history. The violence associated with it, the wholesale abuse of injunctions, and the dramatic leadership of* ***Eugene Debs*** *notwithstanding, the boycott and* ***strike*** *shocked many Americans because Pullman, Illinois, was considered by many to be a model town. It was built by George Pullman, whose initial goal was to build a workers' town to surround the factories wherein his railroad sleeper and bag-*

gage cars were produced. Pullman's artificial lake, its grand hotel, its leafy boulevards, and its neat houses attracted tourists and some hailed him as a social reformer.

But, Pullman quickly betrayed the underlying illogic of ***company towns****. As a corporate-owned enterprise, Pullman was part of the same for-profit system as the ever-looming factories in its midst. Rents, utilities, store prices, and rail service were more expensive than those in nearby Chicago, and many workers also resented the degree of social and cultural control demanded by the moralistic Pullman. Like most company towns, Pullman unraveled due to economic pressures. The Panic of 1893 exacerbated an already tense situation.* ***Wage*** *cuts were bad enough, but increased rents and other costs within the Pullman-owned town pushed many workers to desperation. In 1895, a special government commission on Pullman rents issued a critical report of how the town of Pullman operated. It is excerpted below:*

> If we exclude the aesthetic and sanitary features at Pullman, the rents there are from twenty to twenty-five per cent higher than rents in Chicago or surrounding towns for similar accommodations. The aesthetic features are admired by visitors, but have little money value to employees, especially when they lack bread. The company aims to secure six per cent upon the cost of its tenements, which cost includes a proportionate share for paving, sewerage, water, parks, etc. It claims now to receive less than four per cent. . . . The company makes all repairs and heretofore has not compelled tenants to pay for them. Under the printed leases, however, which tenants must sign, they agree to pay for all repairs which are either necessary (ordinary wear and damages by the elements not excepted) or which the company *chooses* to make.
>
> The company's claim that the workmen need not hire its tenements and can live elsewhere if they choose is not entirely tenable. The fear of losing work keeps them in Pullman as long as there are tenements unoccupied, because the company is supposed, as a matter of business, to give preference to its tenants when work is slack. The employees, believing that a tenant at Pullman has this advantage, naturally feel some compulsion to rent at Pullman, and thus to stand well with management. Exceptional and necessary workmen do not share this feeling to the same extent and are more free to hire or own homes elsewhere. While reducing wages the company made no reduction in rents. Its position is that the two matters are distinct, and that none of the reasons urged as justifying wage reduction by it as an employer can be considered by the company as a landlord.
>
> The company claims that it is simply legitimate business to use its position and resources to hire in the labor market as cheaply as possible and at the same time to keep rents up regardless of what wages are paid to its tenants or what similar tenements rent for elsewhere; to avail itself to the full extent of business depression and completion in reducing wages, and to disregard these same conditions as to rents. No valid reason is assigned for this position except simply that the company has the power and the legal right to do it.

Source: U.S. Strike Commission, *Report on the Chicago Strikes of June–July, 1894* (U.S. Government Printing Office, 1895), xxxv–xxxvi. Reprinted in Leon Litwack, *The American Labor Movement* (Englewood Cliffs, N.J.: Prentice-Hall, 1962), pp. 20–21.

36. Pullman Strike: Another Excerpt from the U.S. Strike Commission Report

The U.S. Strike Commission reported on the Pullman Strike to the House of Representatives in 1894. The Pullman Strike was prompted by George Pullman's repeated reductions in ***wages*** *of his workers, while he simultaneously refused to cut fees charged to those workers who rented their homes in his* ***company town****. The Pullman Strike brought* ***Eugene V. Debs****, leader of the* ***American Railway Union****, to national prominence. It also set unfortunate precedents for the use of injunctions in labor disputes, as well as for the employment of federal troops. Troops were sent to Chicago by President Grover Cleveland at the urging of his Attorney General Richard Olney, formerly an attorney associated with the railway operators.*

Mr. President and Brothers of the American Railway Union: We struck at Pullman because we were without hope. We joined the American Railway Union because it gave us a glimmer of hope. Twenty thousand souls, men, women, and little ones, have their eyes turned toward this convention today, straining eagerly through dark despondency for a glimmer of the heaven-sent message you alone can give us on this earth.

In stating to this body our grievances it is hard to tell where to begin. You all must know that the proximate cause of our strike was the discharge of two members of our grievance committee the day after George M. Pullman, himself, and Thomas H. Wickes, his second vice-president, had guaranteed them absolute immunity. The more remote causes are still imminent. Five reductions in wages, in work, and in conditions of employment swept through the shops at Pullman between May and December, 1893. The last was the most severe, amounting to nearly thirty per cent, and our rents had not fallen. We owed Pullman $70,000 when we struck May 11. We owe him twice as much today. He does not evict us for two reasons: One, the force of popular sentiment and public opinion; the other because he hopes to starve us out, to break the back of the American Railway Union, and to deduct from our miserable wages when we are forced to return to him the last dollar we owe him for the occupancy of his houses.

Rents all over the city in every quarter of its vast extent have fallen, in some cases to one-half. Residences, compared with which ours are hovels, can be had a few miles away at the price we have been contributing to make a millionaire a billionaire. What we pay $15 for in Pullman is leased for $8 in Roseland; and remember that just as no man or woman of our 4,000 toilers has ever felt the friendly pressure of George M. Pullman's hand, so no man or woman of us all has ever owned or can ever hope to own one inch of George M. Pullman's land. Why, even the very streets are his. His ground has never been platted of record, and today he may debar any man who has acquiring rights as his tenant from walking in his highways. And those streets; do you know what he has named them? He says after the four great inventors in methods of transportation. And do you know what their names are? Why, Fulton, Stephenson, Watt, and Pullman.

Water which Pullman buys from the city at 8 cents a thousand gallons he retails to us at 500 per cent advance and claims he is losing $400 a month on it. Gas which sells at 75 cents per thousand feet in Hyde Park, just north of us, he sells for $2.25. When we went to tell him our grievances he said we were all his "children."

Pullman, both the man and the town, is an ulcer on the body politic. He owns the houses, the schoolhouses, and churches of God in the town he gave his once humble name. The revenue he derives from these, the wages he pays out with one hand—the Pullman Palace Car Company, he takes back with the other—the Pullman Land Association. He is able by this to bid under any contract car shop in this country. His competitors in business, to meet this, must reduce the wages of their men. This gives him the excuse to reduce ours to conform to the market. His business rivals must in turn scale down; so must he. And thus the merry war—the dance of skeletons bathed in human tears—goes on, and it will go on, brothers, forever, unless you, the American Railway Union, stop it; end it; crush it out.

Source: U.S. Congress, House of Representatives, U.S. Strike Commission, *Report on the Chicago Strike* (Washington: U.S. Government Printing Office, 1895).

---

37. Real-Life Rosie the Riveter: Excerpt of Augusta Clawson's Experiences as a World War II Shipyard Worker

World War II abruptly ended the Great Depression. Almost overnight, the labor surplus disappeared and demand for female labor skyrocketed, as men joined the military. Before the war, women made up about 25 percent of the workforce; by 1945, they were around 38 percent. In raw numbers, the number of working women jumped from around fourteen million in 1940, to more than twenty million by early 1945. Women not only worked in larger numbers, they also entered skilled occupations once closed to them, such as welding, precision-parts grinding, and riveting. The famed "Rosie the Riveter" campaign was part of an overall government and industry program to encourage women to tackle what was before considered "men's work."

Millions of women heeded the call and, in many locales, surpassed the output in divisions once reserved for male workers. Although postwar propaganda and mass firings either convinced or coerced women to surrender their jobs to returning male veterans, real-life Rosie the Riveters altered the American labor force. Short-term drops in female employment quickly reversed and women reentered the job market in ever-

increasing numbers, albeit usually not in the skilled, high-paying jobs they held during World War II.

Breaking male preserves during the war was more than just learning a craft; it also involved significant shifts in self-perception, confidence, and values. Again, many of these persisted long after women left the defense plants. Augusta Clawson left a government job to work in a shipyard in Oregon during the war. Some of her experiences are recounted below.

I, who hate heights, climbed stair after stair after stair till I thought I must be close to the sun. I stopped in the top deck. I who, hate confined spaces, went through narrow corridors, stumbling my way over rubber coated leads—dozens of them, scores of them, even hundreds of them. I went into a room about four feet by ten where two shipfitters, a shipfitter's helper, a chipper, and I all worked. I welded in the poop deck lying on the floor while another welder spattered sparks from the ceiling and chippers like giant woodpeckers shattered our eardrums. I, who've taken welding, and have sat at a bench welding flat and vertical plates, was told to weld braces along a baseboard below a door opening. On these a heavy steel door was braced while it was hung to a fine degree of accuracy. I welded more braces along the side, and along the top. I did overhead welding, horizontal, flat, vertical. I welded around curved hinges which were placed so close to the side wall that I had to bend my rod in a curve to get it in. I made some good welds and some frightful ones. But now a door in the poop deck of an oil tanker is hanging, four feet by six of solid steel, by my welds. Pretty exciting! . . .

I talked with Joanne, a very attractive brunette who had previously been a waitress in Atlantic City. She came West when her husband came for a job. She, like the other waitresses, preferred welding because you "don't have to take so much from the public. . . ."

I had a good taste of summer today, and I am convinced that it is going to take backbone for welders to stick to their jobs through the summer months. It is harder on them than on any of the other workers—their leathers are so hot and heavy, they get more of the fumes, and their hoods become instruments of torture. There were times today when I'd have to stop in the middle of a tack and push my hood back just to get a breath of fresh air. It grows unbearably hot under the hood, my glasses fog and blur my vision, and the only thing to do is to stop. . . .

Yet the job confirmed my strong conviction—I have stated it before—what exhausts the woman welder is not the work, nor the heat, nor the demands upon physical strength. It is the apprehension that arises from inadequate skill and consequent lack of confidence; and this can be overcome by the right kind of training. I've mastered tacking now, so that no kind bothers me. I know I can do it if my machine is correctly set, and I have learned enough of the vagaries of machines to be able to set them. And so, in spite of the discomforts of climbing, heavy equipment, and heat, I enjoyed the work today because I could do it. . . .

Source: From *Shipyard Diary of a Woman Welder* by Augusta Clawson, illustrated by Boris Givotovsky, copyright 1944 by Penguin Books Inc. Used by permission of Viking Penguin, a division of Penguin Group (USA) Inc.

38. *Rerum Novarum*: Excerpts from Bull Issued by Pope Leo XIII in 1891

Rerum Novarum *was a landmark papal encyclical issued by Leo XIII in 1891 that paved the way for Roman Catholic workers to join labor unions without fear of reprisal from their spiritual confessors. The Catholic Church had troubled relations with organized labor in the period immediately following the Civil War. Many unions operated in secrecy and/or required workers to swear oaths the church found objectionable. Moreover, the* **Molly Maguire** *agitations of the 1870s involved large numbers of Irish Catholics, a public relations nightmare for a church that was already distrusted by nativists and other bigots. The Holy See also disapproved of most of the radical economic and political theories of the day. Catholic workers nonetheless joined unions, and some were forced out of the church. The spectacular rise of the* **Knights of Labor** *altered matters considerably, with officials like James Cardinal Gibbons warning the Vatican that forcing workers to choose between union and church imperiled the latter.*

The modern reader will no doubt notice the extreme caution of Leo XIII's language. That said, Rerum Novarum *marks a dramatic change in direction. Subsequent encyclicals, like* Quadragesimo Anno *(1931) and* Laborem Exercens *(1981) have further clarified church doctrines on labor.*

RIGHTS AND DUTIES OF CAPITAL AND LABOR

That the spirit of revolutionary change, which has long been disturbing the nations of the world, should have passed beyond the sphere of politics and made its influence felt in the cognate sphere of practical economics is not surprising. The elements of the conflict now raging are unmistakable, in the vast expansion of industrial pursuits and the marvelous discoveries of science; in the changed relations between masters and workmen; in the enormous fortunes of some few individuals, and the utter poverty of the masses; the increased self reliance and closer mutual combination of the working classes; as also, finally, in the prevailing moral degeneracy. The momentous gravity of the state of things now obtaining fills every mind with painful apprehension; wise men are discussing it. . . .

2. . . . The discussion is not easy, nor is it void of danger. It is no easy matter to define the relative rights and mutual duties of the rich and of the poor, of capital and of labor. . . .
3. In any case we clearly see . . . that some opportune remedy must be found quickly for the misery and wretchedness pressing so unjustly on the majority of the working class. . . . [B]y degrees it has come to pass that working men have been surrendered, isolated and helpless, to the hardheartedness of employers and the greed of unchecked competition. The mischief has been

increased by rapacious usury, which, although more than once condemned by the Church, is nevertheless . . . still practiced by covetous and grasping men. To this must be added that the hiring of labor and the conduct of trade are concentrated in the hands of comparatively few; so that a small number of very rich men have been able to lay upon the teeming masses of the laboring poor a yoke little better than that of slavery itself.

4. To remedy these wrongs the socialists, working on the poor man's envy of the rich, are striving to do away with private property, and contend that individual possessions should become the common property of all, to be administered by the State or by municipal bodies. . . . But their contentions are so clearly powerless to end the controversy that were they carried into effect the working man himself would be among the first to suffer. They are, moreover, emphatically unjust. . . .

5. . . . when a man engages in remunerative labor, the impelling reason and motive of his work is to obtain property, and thereafter to hold it as his very own. . . . Socialists, therefore, by endeavoring to transfer the possessions of individuals to the community at large, strike at the interests of every wage earner, since they would deprive him of the liberty of disposing of his wages, and thereby of all hope and possibility of increasing his resources and of bettering his condition in life. . . .

15. . . . The door would be thrown open to envy, to mutual invective, and to discord; the sources of wealth themselves would run dry, for no one would have any interest in exerting his talents or his industry; and that ideal equality about which they entertain pleasant dreams would be in reality the leveling down of all to a like condition of misery and degradation. Hence, it is clear that the main tenet of socialism, community of goods, must be utterly rejected. . . . The first and most fundamental principle, therefore, if one would undertake to alleviate the condition of the masses, must be the inviolability of private property. . . .

20. Of these duties, the following bind the proletarian and the worker: fully and faithfully to perform the work which has been freely and equitably agreed upon; never to injure the property, nor to outrage the person, of an employer; never to resort to violence in defending their own cause, nor to engage in riot or disorder; and to have nothing to do with men of evil principles, who work upon the people with artful promises of great results, and excite foolish hopes which usually end in useless regrets and grievous loss. The following duties bind the wealthy owner and the employer: not to look upon their work people as their bondsmen, but to respect in every man his dignity as a person ennobled by Christian character. They are reminded that, according to natural reason and Christian philosophy, working for gain is creditable, not shameful, to a man, since it enables him to earn an honorable livelihood; but to misuse men as though they were things in the pursuit of gain, or to value them solely for their physical powers—that is truly shameful and inhuman. . . . Furthermore, the employer must never tax his work people beyond their strength, or employ them in work unsuited to their sex and age. His great and principal duty is to give every one what is just. . . . To defraud any

one of wages that are his due is a great crime which cries to the avenging anger of Heaven. . . . Lastly, the rich must religiously refrain from cutting down the workmen's earnings, whether by force, by fraud, or by usurious dealing. . . .

39. When work people have recourse to a strike and become voluntarily idle, it is frequently because the hours of labor are too long, or the work too hard, or because they consider their wages insufficient. The grave inconvenience of this . . . should be obviated by public remedial measures; for such paralyzing of labor not only affects the masters and their work people . . . but is extremely injurious to trade and to the general interests of the public; moreover, on such occasions, violence and disorder are generally not far distant. . . . The laws should forestall and prevent such troubles from arising. . . .

40. The working man, too, has interests in which he should be protected by the State; and first of all, there are the interests of his soul. . . . No man may with impunity outrage that human dignity which God Himself treats with great reverence, nor stand in the way of that higher life which is the preparation of the eternal life of heaven. . . .

41. From this follows the obligation of the cessation from work and labor on Sundays and certain holy days. . . .

42. If we turn not to things external and material, the first thing of all to secure is to save unfortunate working people from the cruelty of men of greed, who use human beings as mere instruments for money-making. . . . Daily labor, therefore, should be so regulated as not to be protracted over longer hours than strength admits. . . . In all agreements between masters and work people there is always the condition expressed or understood that there should be allowed proper rest for soul and body. . . .

45. Let the working man and the employer make free agreements, and in particular let them agree freely as to the wages; nevertheless, there underlies a dictate of natural justice more imperious and ancient than any bargain between man and man, namely, that wages ought not to be insufficient to support a frugal and well-behaved wage-earner. If through necessity or fear of a worse evil the workman accept harder conditions because an employer or contractor will afford him no better, he is made the victim of force and injustice. . . .

48. In the last place, employers and workmen may of themselves effect much, in the matter We are treating, by means of such associations and organizations as afford opportune aid to those who are in distress, and which draw the two classes more closely together. . . .

49. The most important of all are workingmen's unions. . . .

58. . . . The offices and charges of the society should be apportioned for the good of the society itself . . . It is most important that office bearers be appointed with due prudence and discretion, and each one's charge carefully mapped out, in order that no members may suffer harm. The common funds must be administered with strict honesty. . . . Among the several purposes of a society, one should be to try to arrange for a continuous supply of work at all

> times and seasons; as well as to create a fund out of which the members may be effectually helped in their needs, not only in the cases of accident, but also in sickness, old age, and distress. . . .

Given at St. Peter's in Rome, the fifteenth day of May, 1891, the fourteenth year of Our pontificate.

LEO XIII

---

39. Social Darwinism: Excerpt from Rev. Henry Ward Beecher's "Bread-and-Water" Sermon (1877)

Railroad ***strikes*** *associated with the* ***Great Labor Uprising*** *of 1877 badly frightened middle-class Americans not yet recovered from the Civil War, which had ended a scant dozen years earlier. The violence, property destruction, and loss of life led some nervous bourgeois members of society to fear a revolution was brewing, perhaps on a scale of that of the 1871 Paris Commune. Most middle-class publications and public figures spoke out against the strike. A few, like the Rev. Henry Ward Beecher, articulated views associated with* ***Social Darwinism****, a philosophy that attempted to explain the unequal distribution of wealth through a social application of Charles Darwin's biological theories of natural selection.*

At the height of tension during the summer of 1877, the Rev. Beecher took to his pulpit in New York's Plymouth Church and delivered what became known as the "bread-and-water" sermon. Beecher was among the era's best-known Protestant ministers. He was the son of a famed family of preachers, and the brother of Catherine Beecher and Harriet Beecher-Stowe. The Rev. Beecher may well have been using some poorly considered levity to try to break the solemn fear-induced mood, but his remarks were published in the New York Times *and circulated broadly. These remarks became shorthand for workers wishing to express their contempt for middle-class hypocrisy, and they made Beecher one of the Gilded Age's most reviled figures among the working class. They embody the ultimate logic of unbridled Social Darwinian thought.*

(Note: The Times *reported that laughter accompanied many of Beecher's comments.)*

What right had the workmen, the members of those great organizations, to say to any one, "You shall not work for wages which we refuse." They had a perfect right to say to employers, "We shall not work for you," but they had no right to tyrannize over their fellowmen. They had put themselves in an attitude of tyrannical opposition to all law and order and they could not be defended. The necessities of the great railroad companies demanded that there should be reduction of wages. There must be continual shrinkage until things come back to the gold standard, and wages, as well as greenbacks, provisions and property, must share in it. It was true that $1 a day was not enough to support a man and five children, if a man would insist on smoking and drinking beer. Was not a dollar a day enough to buy bread? Water costs nothing. Men cannot live by bread alone, it is true; but the man who cannot live on bread and water is not fit to live. When a man is educated away from the power of self-denial, he is falsely educated. A family may live on good bread and water in the morning, water and bread at midday, and good water and bread at night. Such may be called the bread of affliction, but it was fit that man should eat of the bread of affliction. Thousands would be very glad of a dollar a day, and it added to the sin of the men on strike for them to turn and say to those men, "You can do so, but you shall not." There might be special cases of hardships, but the great laws of political economy could not be set at defiance.

Source: The New York Times, 23 July 1877.

---

40. "Solidarity Forever": Ralph Chaplin's American Labor Anthem (1915)

"Solidarity Forever" is the de facto official anthem of the American labor movement. It was penned by Ralph Chaplin (1887–1961), a member of the **Industrial Workers of the World (IWW)**, *in 1915. Chaplin claimed the inspiration came to him while he was editing a labor journal during a Kanawha Valley, West Virginia, coal* **strike**, *although he did not write out the lyrics until he was living in Chicago. Like many labor songwriters, Chaplin chose an already familiar tune, "John Brown's Body," which by then had been appropriated for an even-more-famed song, "The Battle Hymn of the Republic."*

"Solidarity Forever" appeared in the IWW journal, Solidarity, in January 1915, and became an immediate favorite of American workers. Although its writer was a radical IWW member and that organization was brutally suppressed during and after World War I, by the 1920s it carried less ideological baggage than two alternatives popular in the international labor movement, "The Marseillaise," and "The Internationale." Chaplin's song became standard fare even among conservative craft unionists in the **American Federation of Labor**, *many of whom sang it oblivious of its IWW origins. It remains the best-known labor song in the United States.*

When the union's inspiration through the workers' blood shall run,
There can be no power greater anywhere beneath the sun;
Yet what force on earth is weaker than the feeble strength of one,
But the union makes us strong.

CHORUS:

Solidarity forever,
Solidarity forever,

Solidarity forever,
For the union makes us strong.

Is there aught we hold in common with the greedy parasite,
Who would lash us into serfdom and would crush us with his might?
Is there anything left for us but to organize and fight?
For the union makes us strong.

It is we who plowed the prairies; built the cities where they trade;
Dug the mines and built the workshops, endless miles of railroad laid;
Now we stand outcast and starving midst the wonders we have made;
But the union makes us strong.

All the world that's owned by idle drones is ours and ours alone.
We have laid the wide foundations; built it skyward stone by stone.
It is ours, not to slave in, but to master and to own.
While the union makes us strong.

They have taken untold millions that they never toiled to earn,
But without our brain and muscle not a single wheel can turn.
We can break their haughty power, gain our freedom when we learn
That the union makes us strong.

In our hands is placed a power greater than their hoarded gold,
Greater than the might of armies, magnified a thousand-fold.
We can bring to birth a new world from the ashes of the old
For the union makes us strong.

---

41. Steel Workers: Excerpt from John Fitch's *The Steel Workers,* 1910

John Fitch was a student of John R. Commons, the pioneering labor historian. Fitch spent over a year, in 1907 and 1908, interviewing and observing steel workers in Pittsburgh, where 80,000 workers were employed by the steel companies that dominated every aspect of community life. The result of Fitch's work was The Steel Workers *(1910), one of the six volumes of the famous Pittsburgh Survey (1909–14), an attempt to carefully document life in an American industrial city from a social science perspective. In the selection reproduced here, Fitch observes the importance of the saloons in the lives of workers and the way in which the steel companies promoted the interests of the saloons.*

Thus it was that my residence in the mill towns brought it home to me that three institutions organized to promote enjoyment and progress are not, in these communities, exerting their proper influence. As was shown in an earlier chapter, the schedule of hours does not permit the home and the library to fulfill their natural functions. We have now seen how lethargy within and pressure without are tending to nullify or misdirect the influence of the church.

But this does not mean that the workingmen in the mill towns have no opportunity whatever for pleasure or society. It is only the moral and intellectual forces that are insulated. Young men who work in the mills cannot have their spirits utterly dampened by a long working day, and they often take trouble to dress for an evening's entertainment or to meet their friends socially. This does not last long, for youth itself is not long-lived in the steel mills; but whether young or old, men cannot thus easily be deprived of the social instinct. It is essential that they should meet together somehow and somewhere in fellowship and in relaxation from their work. The saloon and the lodge remain as the social centers for the steel workers.*

There are other reasons, to be sure, than the desire to mingle with one's fellows, for the popularity of the saloon; drinking is traditional among iron and steel workers. But there is no doubt that the craving for companionship is one of the strongest reasons for its hold upon a community of workingmen. The nature of mill work is such as to make the saloon habit one of the most natural ones in the world. Practically every man is affected by the heat even if he does not have a "hot job." The whole atmosphere is such as to induce perspiration and enhance thirst. All the workers drink water in great quantities as long as they are in the mill. Sometimes a man drinks too much, so that he leaves at the end of a day's work feeling half nauseated. Such a man steps into a saloon for a glass of something to set his stomach right. Or if a man does not overdrink during the day, he is still chronically thirsty, and it is to satisfy a real longing for drink that he stops for his beer. The dust of the mills, too, that the men have been breathing for twelve hours, sends another quota to their beer or whiskey to clear out their throats. Then comes the largest contingent of all, the men wearied with the heat and the work, some almost overcome and dragging their feet. These feel the necessity of a stimulant, and they get it day after day, regardless of the waste of physical and nervous energy involved in keeping themselves keyed up to their work by an artificial aid. I do not think I am far wrong when I say that a large majority of steel workers sincerely believe that the regular use of alcoholic drinks is essential to keep them from breaking down. It is seldom a pleasure-seeking crowd that fills the saloons after the whistle has blown at the end of a turn. The men line up at the bar, each one taking one drink and paying for it himself. The first line of men put down their glasses and leave, and the bar is filled again with a second group. There are very few who take more than one drink on coming from the mill.

There is more conviviality on Saturday nights and after pay days than on an ordinary midweek night. Then is the time the men relax; then the treating is done. The saloon becomes a social center and the men find the fellowship that they crave. It is a following of the line of least resistance that makes the saloon supplant all better forms of social life. A man does not need to change his clothing and get a shave before he is made welcome here. He may come covered with the grime of the mill and not feel out of place. In slack times, when the mills are not running, the saloon becomes a regular meeting place, and men go there primarily for companionship, the drinking becoming secondary. Ordinarily one does not see very much drunkenness. The men want to be fit for work the next day. On the eve of a holiday some will go too far, but these are most likely to be the unskilled workmen. The only men whom I found in a state of intoxication when I looked for them at their homes were blast furnace men—men who had been working for months without a holiday or a Sunday. The men I refer to had had a brief holiday and they spent it in the only way they knew. The better class of steel workers, who view their fellows with a sympathetic eye, explain the holiday intoxication of a certain element in the industry as a logical result of steady work and the long day. After weeks and months of work, twelve hours a day, and no holidays, a man gets far behind in his accumulation of the pleasure that he feels to be his due. When a holiday comes it is all too short to collect the overdue bill; pleasure of a concentrated sort must be sought in order to make up for lost time.

As a result of all these cumulative promptings, the saloons take more of the steel worker's money than do many of the legitimate business interests of the mill towns. During 1907 there were 30 saloons in Duquesne, a mill town of 10,000 or 12,000 population. I was told in 1908, by one who was in a position to know, that the leading saloonkeeper in this borough drew from the bank, regularly, every two weeks, just before pay day, between $200 and $300 to be used as change in anticipation of the bills of large denomination that would be handed over the bar. Braddock, where the Edgar Thomson steel works are located, had in 1907, 65 saloons. Braddock and North Braddock together had a population of about 25,000. I was told that a considerably larger sum was required for change on pay days here than in Duquesne, the average to each saloon being $500, making over $30,000 in all. I cannot vouch for the truth of this statement—it was a report which reached me indirectly and may be only an expression of some one's opinion and not based on facts. But information in regard to the situation in McKeesport in 1906 came to me through such channels that there can be little doubt as to its accuracy. McKeesport had about 40,000 people in 1906, and 69 saloons. On the Thursdays preceding the semi-monthly pay days, which fall on Fridays and Saturdays, the three leading saloonkeepers of the city were accustomed to draw from their bank accounts from $1200 to $1500 each in dollar bills and small denominations, to be used as change. Other saloonkeepers drew varying amounts, and the totals thus drawn each fortnight footed up to $60,000. On the Mondays after pay days the saloonkeepers usually deposited double the amount drawn. These periodic leaps in deposits never failed to coincide with pay days, and the inevitable conclusion is that about $60,000 of the steel workers' wages were regularly expended in the saloons within the two days. If this seems overdrawn, let me cite the case of George Holloway, who was blacklisted in 1901 after leading a strike in the Wood plant of the American Sheet and Tin Plate

Company in McKeesport. With what was generally understood to be borrowed funds—for Holloway was left almost penniless by the strike—he started a saloon in McKeesport. I saw and talked with him in the fall of 1907, and he told me that in 1905, four years from the time of entering business, he had sold out. He has established a son in a saloon in the west, and with the rest of his family he is now living in McKeesport on the income of his investments, a retired capitalist.

The liquor situation in an American town bears a very direct relation to the political life. This is true in these boroughs. In earlier chapters we have seen how the steel companies deny the employees the right to organize in unions. In spite of this, the situation is not hopeless so long as the workingman is secure in his possession of the ballot. It is commonly understood that the United States Steel Corporation is the dominant force in politics in the mill towns, except in McKeesport, where authority seems to be divided with the brewing interests.**

Repeatedly I was told that workmen have been discharged at Duquesne for refusing to vote the way the company wished. I was told by one employee that he had been called into the office of his superintendent and remonstrated with working against the company ticket, and an indirect threat was made of discharge. I was told by men of unimpeachable standing in Braddock, who were not steel works employees, that in the spring of 1908, preceding the May primaries, men were induced to vote for the candidates favored by the Corporation by promises of a resumption in industry if the right men were nominated. But the most damaging testimony that I received regarding the interference of the Steel Corporation in politics came from a source clearly authoritative.

For obvious reasons I cannot give my informant's name. "A short time before the primaries of May, 1908," he said, "orders came from the New York office of the United States Steel Corporation, to the general superintendent of the Edgar Thomson plant at Braddock, directing him to order the department superintendents to line up their employees for the Penrose candidates for the legislature. The general superintendent called a meeting of the department superintendents and delivered the orders. This created considerable dismay, for local option was an issue in the primaries and the Penrose candidates were opposed to local option. Some of the superintendents were already prominently identified with the local option party and had been assisting in organizing the campaign. How they could with honor or self-respect abandon the issue at this point was not clear to the officials. But the answer to the objections was clear and to the point. They were told that their first duties were to the Corporation. They must, accordingly, break any or all promises and work for Penrose, because the United States Steel Corporation needed him in the Senate."

After this information had come to me, I received other corroborative testimony. I had a talk with a man who had been prominent in the local option campaign previous to the primaries of 1908 at Braddock. I wrote down what he said, and after he had read my manuscript he indorsed every word. His statement was as follows:

> The most damnable feature of the whole campaign was the attitude of the United States Steel Corporation. There is not such a perfect political organization in the country as the steel trust. They aim to control the politics of every borough and town where their works are located, and usually they do control. They plan their campaigns far in advance; they are laying their wires now to control the borough council three years ahead. You ought to see the way they line up their men at the polls and vote them by thousands. What does a secret ballot amount to? In every ward in this borough the steel works employees are in the majority. There are two or three foremen in nearly every ward, and it is up to them to round up the vote. If there are not enough foremen in a ward, they send them over from the next ward to help out. Naturalized foreigners can be handled easily, but so can men of three and four generations of American blood. These men have been so long dominated by the Corporation that they dare not disobey. They have a sort of superstitious feeling that somehow the boss will know if they vote wrong. And the workingmen are not the only ones that can be managed. Before the May primaries we perfected an organization in this borough to fight for local option. Several of the foremen and assistant superintendents in the mills were among our most active workers. Some of them helped in the speaking campaign. One day an order came that the thing must stop. The United States Steel Corporation needs to have Boies Penrose in the Senate, and the political life of Penrose is bound up with the liquor interests of the state. So a blow to liquor is a blow to Penrose, and the steel trust cannot have that. So the superintendents and foremen were ordered to line up their men for Penrose and the saloon. One young man who had been speaking in the campaign refused to stop, and he was called into the office and plainly told that he must either quit local option or quit the mills. That was not unusual though. The bread and butter argument is always used. As a result, the local optionists were badly broken up. The speaking campaign practically stopped and men whom we had counted on and who had been with us, actually turned around and made a show at least of opposing local option. Then the company gave it out that if the Penrose candidates to the legislature were nominated, the mill would be likely to resume operations, and the men who had been idle half or two-thirds of the time since October, clutched at that half promise like drowning men.

It is probably unnecessary to add that Penrose carried Allegheny County.

*For description of the fraternal orders see *Homestead: The Households of a Mill Town*, by Margaret F. Byington.

**In McKeesport, during the strike of 1901, when the threat was made that the Dewees Wood plant would be dismantled on account of the alleged hostility of the people of the town, the mayor issued a statement in which he charged that the property of the Steel Corporation in this city was assessed at 40 per cent of its market value, while the houses of the citizens were assessed at 70 per cent. (*Outlook*, August 17, 1901, p. 889.)

Source: John A. Fitch, *The Steelworkers* (New York: Russell Sage Foundation, 1910).

42. Stella Nowicki: Interview with a Meatpacking Plant Worker, 1973

In 1973, Alice and Staughton Lynd conducted a series of interviews with rank-and-file workers, not union leaders, but Midwestern men and women who worked on the job and were active in organizing unions, some in the 1930s and some in the post–World War II period. Stella Nowicki moved to Chicago from the family farm in 1933 and worked in the cook room at the Armour meatpacking plant. Here she tells of the excitement of her involvement in the **Congress of Industrial Organizations (CIO)** *during the height of its power and through the purge of the radicals after the war.*

The union mushroomed; it spread. The union had a certain vitality about it that was just tremendous. We had many problems but they were all problems of growth. We tried to make sure that there were both Negroes and whites as officers, stewards, etc., in all the locals. There were people vying for jobs—they wanted to be leaders of this union. It was a marvelous time.

For a long time I fought dishonesty within my local. There were some guys who would pocket the dues money. I would debate them on the union floor. Many times I was the only female there.

The women felt the union was a man's thing because once they got through the day's work they had another job. When they got home they had to take care of their one to fifteen children and the meals and the house and all the rest, and the men went to the tavern and to the meetings and to the racetrack and so forth. The fellows were competing for positions and the women didn't feel that that was their role. They were brainwashed into thinking that this union was for men.

The union didn't encourage women to come to meetings. They didn't actually want to take up the problems that the women had. I did what I could to get the women to come to the meetings but very few came—only when there was a strike. I tried to make the meetings more interesting than just a bunch of guys talking all evening.

We organized women's groups, young women's groups. They liked to dance and I loved to dance so we went dancing together and I talked to them about the union. The women were interested after a while when they saw that the union could actually win things for them, bread and butter things.

We talked about nurseries. In World War II we finally did get some because women were needed in greater quantities than ever before in the factories. But the unions had so many things they had to work for—the shorter work day, improved conditions—so many things that they couldn't worry about these things in relation to women.

Later on, during the war, there was one department where I got the women but couldn't get the guys in. They hung out in the tavern and so I went there and started talking with them. I didn't like beer, but I'd drink ginger ale and told them to show me how to play pool. I learned to play pool and I got the men into the union. I did what they did. I went into the taverns. I became a bowler and I joined the league. The only thing I didn't do is rejoin the Catholic Church.

I was on the grievance committee and I was on the Swift nationwide negotiating team. Before I left, there were a whole number of job evaluations. It was one of the things we fought for on the wage policy committees. I remember talking with Helstein (president of UPWA) in the national office one day and saying that I thought there should be a study made of jobs, especially for women, because I didn't see that a job had a sex. He said that it was a very interesting idea and that maybe I could do something about it. But I wasn't equipped to go into research, nor did I have the time even if I were. Later on they set up a Women's Department and did it.

There were only so many things that we could do and there were so many big things, we couldn't handle everything. You'd have to have socialism.

About socialism, you didn't talk about socialism per se. You talked about issues and saw how people reacted. You talked about how one could attain these things. The only time I ever heard anyone from the union talk about socialism outside of the small meetings was the head of another CIO local, a Scotsman. After negotiations and they didn't get all they wanted, the guys were turning down the contract. He said, "Look, you bunch of bastards, you're not going to get all of this stuff, not until you have socialism." That's the way he put it to them and I thought it was great. "This is a limited contract under capitalism." I think the workers got the message. It all depends what your relationship is to the people you are talking with.

If you are an honest leader, recognized and supported by the workers, you could raise and talk about issues. You couldn't talk about socialism and what it meant in an abstract sense. You had to talk about it in terms of what it would mean for that person. We learned that you can't manipulate people but that you really had to be concerned with the interests and needs of the people. However, you also had to have a platform—a projection of where you were going.

At certain times we felt that the union wasn't enough. We worked in the stockyards with blacks but when we came home, we went to lily-white neighborhoods and the blacks went to their ghetto. How were we going to bridge that? There was unemployment and people were being laid off. There were many young people who didn't get jobs. There was no concern on the part of anyone, the city fathers, the church, the union and others, about the needs of young people and places to play. What are unemployed young people going to do? There were a bunch of young people—I was twenty-four or so—and we felt that our needs were not being met by the union.

The Yards YCL group got together and talked about getting more playgrounds for baseball, basketball and so forth. One of the things that we felt we should do was fight to get blacks into professional baseball. I remember being part of the delegation that went to see Fitzpatrick, who was chairman of the

Central Labor Council, about labor exerting its influence to get blacks on organized professional baseball teams. It was one of the initial things our union did.

We tried to show the community that the union was concerned about the welfare of the young people. We raised the problems of youth; we raised the problems of women; we raised the problem of inequality. We tried through the National Youth Act to get some funds to set up facilities for young people in the community. We had to find ways to attract youth and women and keep all these people within the union.

We asked the union to back us up in calling a community conference to set up a council, a Back of the Yards Youth Council, which would be concerned about these kinds of things in the community. The union said OK. They gave us their blessings. We went ahead and we did it. Actually there were three of us young women who did it.

We had a successful conference. The place wasn't big enough, it was such a turn-out—young people from about 18 to about 25 from the neighborhood.

The man who really organized some massive youth activities was Bishop Shiel. I think he was the first major churchman to recognize the CIO. The first time this bishop of the Catholic Church accepted to come to a CIO meeting, it was historic.

Remember that the CIO didn't have bargaining rights in the different plants yet. This was 1938, '39, '40. We were in the organizational stage and there was tremendous ferment. There were strikes. There were beatings. There were people being fired and laid off and there were test cases in the NLRB [National Labor Relations Board]. There was picketing going on.

The AFL was opposing it. During the early organizing meetings they sent goons with guns to threaten individuals to scare them so they would not organize. Twice they shot at Herb March.

But you had this sense that people were ready come hell or high water to get together, to protect each other, and come into the union. It did happen that people were fired but when people were fired the whole department just closed down. People refused to work until this person was put back. They had this feeling of solidarity, this sense, because they knew that if the company could get by with doing it to one they could do it to another, maybe me.

By the 1940s, we had meetings on every issue where we would call on the workers to come out. The union would come around with their sound truck and everybody would come to the CIO corners in the Yards. The butchers would all come out with their boots and their bloody white smocks. Thousands and thousands of people would show up for meetings right there in the middle of the stockyards at noontime. Even people who were not in the union would come out.

There would be an issue a day, just about. The Armour Plant, Local 347, would have meetings on Wednesday. Friday was payday so it was sacrosanct and there were no meetings. Tuesday was our day. Wilson's on Thursday. Then for some overall issue we'd have everybody come out. There would be so many people coming that the companies would protest to the union—we had half hour lunch breaks and we would stay out for an hour. The companies never did a thing about it because the turnout was that tremendous and massive.

The union leadership would be negotiating within a particular plant on a grievance and the agreement was that if they hadn't received word that the matter was settled by a certain time, the department would walk out. The beef kill at Armour's stopped so many times! They were the best organized and most militant. (These were blacks, by the way.) And if this department went down, the whole plant went down. The kill floors were the key floors. This was true all over. The beef kill was the most important because more beef was killed; then the hog kill, then the sheep.

We participated in all sorts of things beyond just our own industry.

At that time there were no black bus drivers. Bus and streetcar driver jobs were considered very good-paying jobs and our union promoted the idea of having blacks work as streetcar and bus conductors.

The contract and recognition were the thing that everybody wanted. Armour's was the plant with the greatest concentration of people and the union came to be recognized there in 1941. Wilson went before our plant did. Swift's had to have two elections and it was the toughest. We won there during the war, I think in '42. We didn't have the militancy in the Swift plant that we did elsewhere. The Swift Company bought off many guys. Later on we found out that some of the white leaders were paid agents because they testified before the House Committee on Un-American Activities on a lot of us. They were stool pigeons.

I worked in the yards during the war because I thought that it was my patriotic duty. It was part of the thinking of everybody within unions that you just couldn't quit. We even tried to get people to produce more in our zeal to support the war effort. Besides, I had all this seniority and all this history. Then I got frozen on the job. There was a job freeze because white workers were leaving the industry to go to higher-paid jobs in defense plants.

No-strike was part of the deal. The men in the union felt that the company was making all kinds of money on the war and the workers weren't. During that time there were slow-ups and workers who didn't join the union were ostracized. Grievances were hung up without being settled or turned down because the company knew we couldn't do anything. We knew that the company took advantage of the war in a whole number of situations.

I left packing in 1945. With recognition and with the war ending, certain changes took place within the union itself and within the union officialdom. Soon after, a whole group of radical CIO unions were kicked out of the CIO and the McCarthy period set in. I think this ended that era. It was a privilege and a wonderful experience to participate in the excitement of those times.

Source: Alice and Staughton Lynd, eds., *Rank and File: Personal Histories by Working-Class Organizers* (Boston: Beacon Press, 1974).

43. Strikes: Excerpts from Samuel Gompers's Testimony before a U.S. House Committee upon the Relations between Labor and Capital (1899)

Strikes have long been the hallmark of clashes between capital and labor. To leaders like ***Samuel Gompers*** *of the* ***American Federation of Labor (AFL)****, the right to withhold labor was the primary weapon that workers could use in their struggle to obtain higher* ***wages****, shorter working hours, and better conditions. The AFL actively defended the right to* ***strike****, unlike earlier labor federations like the* ***National Labor Union*** *and the* ***Knights of Labor****, whose leaders felt strikes should only be undertaken as a last resort, and only if strict conditions prevailed that made success likely. (See Document Number 46,* ***Terence V. Powderly****, on strikes.)*

The passage below excerpts Gompers's 1899 testimony before a House of Representatives committee on capital-labor relations. In it, he defends strikes.

The working people find that improvements in the methods of production and distribution are constantly being made, and unless they occasionally strike, or have the power to enter upon a strike the improvements will all go to the employer and all the injuries to the employees. A strike is an effort on the part of the workers to obtain some of the improvements that have occurred resultant from the bygone and present genius of our intelligence, of our mental progress. We are producing wealth today at a greater ratio than ever in the history of mankind and a strike on the part of workers is, first against deterioration in their condition, and, second, to be participants in some of the improvements. Strikes are caused from various reasons. The employer desires to reduce wages and lengthen hours of labor, while the desire on the part of the employees is to obtain shorter hours of labor and better wages, and better surroundings. Strikes establish or maintain the rights of the unionism; that is, to establish and maintain the organization by which the rights if the workers can be the better protected and advanced against the little forms of oppression, sometimes economical, sometimes political—the effort on the part of employers to influence and intimidate workmen's political preferences; strikes against victimization; activity in the cause of the workers against the blacklist. . . .

It required 40,000 people in the city of New York in my own trade [cigar making] in 1877 to demonstrate to the employers that we had the right to be heard in our own defense of our trade, and an opportunity to be heard in our own interests. It cost the miners of the country, in 1897, sixteen weeks of suffering to secure a national conference and a national agreement. It cost the railroad brotherhoods long months of suffering, many of them sacrificing their positions, in the railroad strike of 1877, and in the Chicago, Burlington, and Quincy strike, of the same year, to secure from the employers the right to be heard through committees, their representatives—that is, their committee of the organization to secure these rights. Workmen have had to stand the brunt of the suffering. The American

Republic was not established without some suffering, without some sacrifice, and no tangible right has yet been achieved in the interest of the people unless it has been secured by the sacrifices and persistency. After a while we become a little more tolerant to each other and recognize all have rights; get around the table and chaff each other and recognize that they were not so reasonable in the beginning. Now we propose to meet and discuss our interests, and if we can not agree we propose in a more reasonable way to conduct our contests, each to decide how to hold out and bring the other one to terms. . . . A strike on the part of the workmen is to close production and compel better terms and more rights to be acceded to the producers. The economic results of strikes to workers have been advantageous. Without strikes their rights would not have been considered. It is not that workmen or organized labor desires the strike, but it will tenaciously hold the right to strike. We recognize that peaceful industry is necessary to successful civilized life, but the right to strike and the preparation to strike is the greatest preventative to strikes. If the workmen were to make up their minds tomorrow that they would under no circumstances strike, the employers would do all the striking for them in the way of lesser wages and longer hours of labor.

Source: Testimony of Samuel Gompers, November 29, 1899, U.S. Congress, House, *Report of the Industrial Commission on the Relations and Conditions of Capital and Labor Employed in Manufactures and General Business* (Washington: U.S. Government Printing Office, 1901), VII pp. 605–9. Reprinted in Leon Litwack, *The American Labor Movement* (Englewood Cliffs, N.J.: Prentice-Hall, 1962), pp. 34–35.

---

44. Sweatshops: Excerpt from Louis Levine's Description of Turn-of-the-Century Abuses in Garment-Industry Sweatshops

The battle to regulate ***sweatshops*** *is one of the oldest and most enduring struggles facing American organized labor. The term first appeared in the United States in the 1860s, though complaints resonated long before. For most of the eighteenth and nineteenth centuries, there were few regulations governing the safety and sanitary conditions under which laborers toiled, and the very definition of what constituted a "sweatshop" was open to broad interpretation. In general, a sweatshop was an inordinately cramped and unhealthy workplace in which laborers toiled long hours at monotonous jobs for very low pay. These workplaces often appeared in run-down buildings with poor ventilation and light. Frequently, they were also dangerous, as driven home during such horrible episodes as the 1911* ***Triangle factory fire****. The garment industry was marked by some of the worst sweatshop abuses, as is revealed in the passage below from Louis Levine, the official historian for the early* ***International Ladies' Garment Workers' Union****. Cigarmakers and assembly workers also complained of sweatshop conditions.*

Although laws regulate current practices and the classic sweatshop has receded from public consciousness, many labor advocates charge that sweatshops are still alive, especially in large cities where immigrant labor—much of it undocumented or illegal—

continues to toil in the sort of Dickensian conditions described by Levine. This excerpt comes originally from Louis Levine's The Women Garment Workers *(New York: B. W. Hebsch, 1924).*

The three main features of the sweat-shop have been described as unsanitary conditions, excessively long hours, and extremely low wages. The shops were generally located in tenement houses. As a rule, one of the rooms of the flat in which the contractor lived was used as a working place. Sometimes work would be carried on all over the place in the bedroom as well as in the kitchen. Even under the best conditions this would have made for living and working in grime and dirt. But the conditions were not of the best. . . . Investigations showed that about one out of every three persons whose living quarters were examined "slept in unventilated rooms without windows." One can imagine what happened when these "homes" were also turned into shops and became home and workshop at the same time.

A writer who made a valiant fight against the evils of the tenement house and of the sweat-shop, gives a graphic description of the district in New York City where the sweat-shops were situated.

. . . "Take the Second Avenue Elevated," he writes, "and ride up half a mile through the sweaters' district. Every open window of the big tenements, that stand like a continuous brick wall on both sides of the way, give you a glimpse of one of these shops as the train speeds by. Men and women bending over their machines or ironing clothes at the window, half-naked. . . . The road is like a big gangway through an endless workroom where vast multitudes are forever labouring [sic]. Morning, noon, night, it makes no difference; the scene is always the same." Not only insides of the tenements were turned into work places. "It is not unusual," reported the New York State factory inspector, "when the weather permits to see the balconies of the fire escapes occupied by from two to four busy workmen. The halls and roofs are also utilized for workshop purposes very frequently." The same factory inspector describes one of the many sweatshops which he visited. This particular one, which was typical of others, was that "of a cloakmaker, who used one room for his shop, while the other three rooms were supposed to be used for domestic purposes only, his family consisting of his wife and seven children. In the room adjoining the shop, used as the kitchen, there was a red-hot stove, two tables, a clothes rack, and several piles of goods. A woman was making bread on a table upon which there was a baby's stocking, scraps of cloth, several old tin cans, and a small pile of unfinished garments. In the next room was an old woman with a diseased face walking the floor with a crying child in her arms."

In the "outside" shops, the working hours were eighty-four per week. But besides "regular" hours, there was "overtime" in both the "inside" and "outside" shops, and in addition many of the workers "took material home and worked until two and three o'clock in the morning." It was quite common to work fifteen and sixteen hours a day, from five in the morning to nine at night, and in the busy season many frequently worked all night. "If you look into the streets any morning," wrote an investigator of conditions in New York City, "at four o'clock you will see them full of people going to work. They rouse themselves at three o'clock and are often at their machines at four. The latest is sure to be there by five. The general time is five o'clock all year round in good times, winter and summer, and if the boss will give them gaslight, some will go even earlier than three o'clock." Old-timers in the industry are fond of telling to-day about the over-zealous workers of those days, cloak pressers and operators, who saved time and rent by sleeping on "bundles" in the shop between working. It was a current saying that one could always do with a little more work by "borrowing a couple hours from the following days." No wonder the industry, and especially the cloak making trade, early acquired the sad distinction of being the "worst-driven trade in the matter of hours in the season."

Source: Rosalyn Baxandall and Linda Gordon, eds., *America's Working Women: A Documentary History 1600 to the Present* (New York: W. W. Norton, 1995), pp. 91–93.

---

45. Taft-Hartley Labor Relations Act (1947)

Among labor union members and advocates, the 1947 ***Taft-Hartley Act*** *is the single most unpopular piece of labor legislation ever passed in the United States. Its passage was hailed by supporters as a needed corrective to the* ***National Labor Relations Act (NLRA)*** *and defended as restoring balance to relations between capital and labor. Critics claim it so tilted the balance in favor of employers as to negate vast sections of the NLRA.*

Passage of the bill took place as Republicans regained control of Congress in 1946, after many years of backbench sniping against Franklin Roosevelt's New Deal policies. It is named for Ohio Senator Robert Taft and New Jersey Representative Fred Hartley, the Republicans who coauthored the bill. President Harry Truman vetoed the Taft-Hartley Act, but Congress overrode that veto. Unions have repeatedly lobbied for its repeal, as yet to no avail. The excerpts below outline some of the act's key provisions, including controversial passages outlining ***unfair labor practices*** *on the part of unions, the requirement that union officials sign anticommunist affidavits, the outlawing of secondary* ***boycotts****, mandated "cooling-off" periods, forbidding* ***strikes*** *among government employees, and curtailing union political action committees.*

Section 7. Employees shall have the right to self-organization, to form, join, or assist labor organizations, to bargain collectively through representatives of their own choosing, and to engage in other concerted activities for the purpose of collective bargaining or other mutual aid or protection, and shall also have the right to refrain from any or all of such activities except to the extent that such right may be affected by an agreement requiring membership in a labor organization as a condition of employment. . . .

Section 8. (a) It shall be an unfair labor practice for an employer—

(1) to interfere with, restrain, or coerce employees in the exercise of the rights guaranteed in section 7;
(2) to dominate or interfere with the formation or administration of any labor organization or contribute financial or other support to it. . . .
(3) by discrimination in regard to hire or tenure of employment or any term or condition of employment to encourage or discourage membership in any labor organization. . . .
(4) to discharge or otherwise discriminate against an employee because he has filed charges or given testimony under this Act;
(5) to refuse to bargain collectively with the representatives of his employees. . . .

It shall be an unfair labor practice for a labor organization or its agents—

(1) to restrain or coerce employees in the exercise of the rights guaranteed in section 7: Provided (A)That this paragraph shall not impair the right of a labor organization to prescribe its own rules with respect to the acquisition or retention of membership therein- or (B) an employer in the selection of his representatives for the purposes of collective bargaining or the adjustment of grievances;
(2) to cause or attempt to cause an employer to discriminate against an employee . . . or to discriminate against an employee with respect to whom membership in such organization has been denied or terminated on some ground other than his failure to tender the periodic dues and the initiation fees uniformly required as a condition of acquiring or retaining membership;
(3) to refuse to bargain collectively with an employer. . . .
(4) to engage in, or to induce or encourage the employees of any employer to engage in, a strike or a concerted refusal in the course of their employment to use, manufacture, process, transport, or otherwise handle or work on any goods, articles, materials, or commodities or to perform any services, where an object thereof is: (A) forcing or requiring any employer or self-employed person to join any labor or employer organization or any employer or other person to cease using, selling, handling, transporting, or otherwise dealing in the products of any other producer, processor, or manufacturer, or to cease doing business with any other person; (B) forcing or requiring any other employer to recognize or bargain with a labor organization as the representative of his employees unless such labor organization has been certified as the representative of such employees . . . (C) forcing or requiring any employer to recognize or bargain with a particular labor organization as the representative of his employees if another labor organization has been certified as the representative of such employees . . . (D) forcing or requiring any employer to assign particular work to employees in a particular labor organization or in a particular trade, craft, or class rather than to employees in another labor

organization or in another trade, craft, or class, unless such employer is failing to conform to an order or certification of the Board determining the bargaining representative for employees performing such work. . . .

(5) to require of employees covered by an agreement . . . as a condition precedent to becoming a member of such organization, of a fee in an amount which the Board finds excessive or discriminatory under all the circumstances. In making such a finding, the Board shall consider, among other relevant factors, the practices and customs of labor organizations in the particular industry, and the wages currently paid to the employees affected; and

(6) to cause or attempt to cause an employer to pay or deliver or agree to pay or deliver any money or other thing of value, in the nature of an exaction, for services which are not performed or not to be performed. . . .

The expressing of any views, argument, or opinion, or the dissemination thereof, whether in written, printed, graphic, or visual form, shall not constitute or be evidence of an unfair labor practice under any of the provisions of this Act, if such expression contains no threat of reprisal or force or promise of benefit. . . .

That where there is in effect a collective-bargaining contract covering employees in an industry affecting commerce, the duty to bargain collectively shall also mean that no party to such contract shall terminate or modify such contract, unless the party desiring such termination or modification—(1) serves a written notice upon the other party to the contract of the proposed termination or modification sixty days prior to the expiration date thereof, or in the event such contract contains no expiration date, sixty days prior to the time it is proposed to make such termination or modification; (2) offers to meet and confer with the other party for the purpose of negotiating a new contract . . . (3) notifies the Federal Mediation and Conciliation Service within thirty days after such notice of the existence of a dispute, and simultaneously . . . notifies any State or Territorial agency established to mediate and conciliate disputes . . . and (4) continues in full force and effect without resorting to strike or lockout, all the terms and conditions of the existing contract for a period of sixty days after such notice is given or until the expiration date of such contract, whichever occurs later. . . .

No investigation shall be made by the Board of any question affecting commerce concerning the representation of employees, raised by a labor organization . . . shall be entertained, and no complaint shall be issued pursuant to a charge made by a labor organization . . . unless there is on file with the Board an affidavit executed contemporaneously or within the preceding twelvemonth period by each officer of such labor organization and the officers of any national or international labor organization of which it is an affiliate or constituent unit that he is not a member of the Communist Party or affiliated with such party, and that he does not believe in, and is not a member of or supports any organization that believes in or teaches, the overthrow of the United States Government by force or by any illegal or unconstitutional methods. The provisions of section 35 A of the Criminal Code shall be applicable in respect to such affidavits. . . .

Section 301. . . . (b) Any labor organization which represents employees in an . . . industry affecting commerce . . . whose activities affect commerce . . . shall be bound by the acts of its agents. Any such labor organization may sue or be sued as an entity and in behalf of the employees whom it represents in the courts of the United States. Any money judgment against a labor organization in a district court of the United States shall be enforceable only against the organization as an entity and against its assets, and shall not be enforceable against any individual member or his assets. . . .

Section 303: (a) It shall be unlawful, for the purposes of this section . . . in an industry or activity affecting commerce, for; any labor organization to engage in, or to encourage the employees of any employer to engage in, a strike or a concerted refusal in the course of their employment to use, manufacture, process, transport, or otherwise handle or work on any goods, articles, materials, or commodities or to perform any services, where an object thereof is (1) forcing or requiring any employer or self-employed person to join any labor or employer organization or . . . to cease using selling, handling, transporting, or otherwise dealing in the products of any other producer, processor or manufacturer, or to cease doing business with any other person; (2) forcing . . . any other employer to recognize or bargain with a labor organization as the representative of his employees unless such labor organization has been certified as the representative of such employees . . . (3) forcing . . . any employer to recognize or bargain with a particular labor organization as the representative of his employees if another labor organization has been certified as the representative of such employees . . . (4) forcing . . . any employer to assign particular work to employees in a particular labor organization or in a particular trade, craft or class rather than to employees in another labor organization or in another trade, craft, or class unless such employer is failing to conform to an order of certification of the National Labor Relations Board. . . .

Section 305: It shall be unlawful for any individual employed by the United States or any agency thereof including wholly owned Government corporations to participate in any strike. Any individual employed by the United States or by any such agency who strikes shall be discharged immediately from employment, and shall forfeit his civil service status, if any, and shall not be eligible for re-employment for three years by the United States or any such agency. . . .

Section 313: It is unlawful for any national rank, or any corporation organized by authority of any law of Congress, to make a contribution or expenditure in connection with any election to any political office, or in connection with any primary election or political convention or caucus held to select candidates for any political office, or for any corporation whatever, or any labor organization to make a contribution or expenditure in connection with any election at which Presidential and Vice Presidential electors or a Senator or Representative in or a Delegate or Resident Commissioner to Congress are to be voted for, or in connection with any primary election or political convention or caucus held to select candidates for any of foregoing offices, or for any candidate, political committee, or other person to accept or receive any contribution prohibited by this section.

Source: "MultiEducator, Inc.," http://www.multied.com/documents/Tafthartley.html.

---

46. Terence V. Powderly: Excerpts from His Autobiography

Terence Powderly *(1849–1924) led the* ***Knights of Labor (KOL)*** *from 1879 to the end of 1893. He presided over the KOL's dramatic rise in the 1880s and its equally precipitous decline after 1888. In many respects, he was the first American labor leader to attract widespread national attention. At the height of his fame—roughly 1885 to 1890—Powderly's opinion on numerous matters was sought by journalists, clerics, politicians, and social reformers. He was a complex man, prone both to acts of admirable selflessness and self-seeking pettiness. Powderly seldom disappointed those seeking his opinion. By the mid-1880s, Powderly was so well known that his very name rallied some Gilded Age workers and repulsed others. His was such a strong personality that some workers and scholars mistakenly identified Powderly as synonymous with the KOL, though he himself was always careful to differentiate personal views from "official" statements on behalf of the Knights.*

In the passages below, Powderly explains the Knights of Labor's policies on ***strikes*** *and why both he and the Knights were against them. In other passages, he gives a powerful indictment of Gilded Age churches and explains why working people often distrusted them.*

It never was the intention of those who founded and built up the Knights of Labor to resort to the strike as first aid in the settlement of differences between employer and employed. Don't forget that the founders were all trade unionists who had seen the futility of ill-advised, hastily begun strikes. . . .

The public has been educated to believe that labor leaders . . . just glory in and fatten on strikes. Prior to my first election as G[eneral] Master Workman I declared my position on the strike question and stated I would never favor a strike until I became convinced:

First: That the cause was just.

Second: That every reasonable means had been resorted to to avert the strike.

Third: That the chances of winning were at least as good as the prospect of losing.

Fourth: That the means of defraying the expenses of the strike and assisting those in need were in the treasury or in sight of it.

. . . Our membership knew that I regarded the strike as a system of warfare, and that if I should be expected to make war the law should be complied with and the sinews of war provided prior to declaring war.

Whenever a strike was forced upon us, as it frequently was, the case would differ from one in which we, as an organization, declared a strike. . . . Not once did I, during my fourteen years' incumbency of the office of General Master Workman, order a strike. . . .

The world has been educated by a not overscrupulous press to believe that every "labor leader" . . . revels in strikes, and goes out of his way to order strikes. The reverse is true. I do not know . . . a labor officer who did not view the strike with gravest apprehension. Nothing can injure the conscientious officer . . . any more than to lose a strike unless it is to win one. If he loses he is sure to be charged with selling out, if he wins he'll be expected to keep on striking—and winning. . . .

While I never ordered a strike, I was directly responsible for the settlement of four hundred and eight cases of dispute between employer and employed . . . and was instrumental in the adjustment of some seven hundred other differences between workmen and employers. . . .

Precious lives were lost in strikes; homes were wrecked, and children deprived of education through strikes, millions of dollars were lost to labor through them, and in the main this great waste and loss could have been avoided. I could never rid my mind of the idea that in these avoidable strikes we were injuring posterity. . . .

Conditions change so rapidly that what we strike for and win this year may not be worth having next year. . . . Today's loss can seldom be replaced by tomorrow's gain.

Too many ministers today regard their calling as a profession or a trade to make a living by and not as a mission from on high . . . Churchianity, which largely supplanted Christianity and is often mistaken for it, has not stayed the hand of an individual trader, a national commercialist, or international murderer whose greed prompted him to reach out for the market of neighbor and enemy and gather in all that could be gained. . . .

The great power that came to Christianity through the teachings of Jesus Christ has been largely frittered away through the practice of Churchianity. . . . I can find little or no evidence to prove that the ordained teacher and preacher of Christianity has attempted to walk directly in the footsteps of the crucified One in driving the waterer of stocks, the gambler of life's necessities, the despoiler of children, the exploiter of labor, or the grabber of profits from the temple wherein the products of industry are exchanged.

Source: From *The Path I Trod: The Autobiography of Terence V. Powderly* by Harry Carman, Henry David and Paul Gutherie.

47. Textile Workers: Excerpt of Testimony before the U.S. Senate by John Hill, 1885

In the mid-1880s, at the height of the Gilded Age, when clashes between labor and capital seemed inevitable, the United States Senate held hearings on labor relations. The testimony of John Hill, a representative of a Georgia textile manufacturer, explained the natural advantages of the southern climate and defended the southern use of ***child labor*** *in the textile mills. Hill's 1885 comparison of southern workers with the immigrant workers of the Amoskeag Mills in Manchester, New Hampshire, suggests that southern workers were happy with child labor, long hours, and an inferior system of public education and that relations between the races were harmonious—at least in the workplace.*

Now as to the efficiency of labor in the two sections. The Southern operative is native born, while the average Northern operative is not. They have got more Canadian operatives in Manchester, N. H., than they have natives. Now, as it is a well-known fact to all who have studied the subject, the elements of mind, the general mental make-up and intelligence of the native American exceeds by far the average of like qualities in the lower classes of foreigners, the classes who immigrate into this country to work in mills. So in the same proportion are you likely to find the comparative intelligence of the Northern and the Southern operatives, the Southern being native and the Northern being a foreigner. There is more endurance in the constitution in a cold climate than in a warm one, and our advantage becomes a disadvantage in this respect, where it is a question of hard, heavy labor. Natural laws would therefore indicate that for heavy labor the Northern operative would be superior to the Southern, but while this is true, it is also true that a warm climate develops the human system earlier, and makes the action of both mind and body quicker than in a cold climate. The natives of warm climates are more impulsive, quicker to learn, and quicker in action, though not so enduring. This climate advances the period of manhood or womanhood fully a year and a half over the average climate of New England, so far as development is concerned. A man or a woman here in Columbus is as far advanced in physical development at fifteen years of age as a like person would be in Lowell at sixteen and a half years of age.

Now, for cotton manufacturing, capacity to endure hard labor is not a material point, because the labor is not hard. The motions required are quick rather than laborious, except in certain departments. In weaving there is probably about as much of one kind as the other, and, of course, weaving is a very important department. It may be stated as a general fact, therefore, that in this regard the advantages in the South are at least equal to those in the North.

In the matter of education the native American of the North averages superior to the native of the South, owing to the fact that for many years, covering the lives of all the operatives now in the mills of the North, the free-school system has been universal there, and the necessity of education has been generally and fully appreciated. In the South, while a free-school system does exist in this State, yet it is not so far advanced as the free-school system in New England; not so liberal; not so easy to be availed of. It furnishes less school accommodation in proportion to population, and there is less disposition on the part of the people to patronize it, and, generally speaking, owing to the very limited time it has been in existence, the advantages of our free school system here have not been reaped by our people to an extent that will at all compare with the benefits that the New England system has conferred upon the people there.

But again, as compared with foreign help, the probabilities are that even in the matter of education our Southern operatives have the advantage. In Alabama, South Carolina, and other States, where no attention has been paid to the free-school system, the operatives have not had the advantages that they have in Georgia.

The hours of labor in cotton manufacture in the Eagle and Phoenix mills average eleven per day, but in many mills they average twelve per day. In New England, in some of the States, the law prescribes ten hours as a day's work. That is so in Massachusetts, but not in New Hampshire. . . .

I might state that all mill operatives having to do with the process of cotton manufacturing involving quick perception and manipulation are white. In portions of the work, where it is only a question of muscle, and where intelligence is not a necessity, the laborers employed are either black or white, the preference, where it comes to a matter of mere muscle, being given to the colored laborer. I refer now to rolling a bale of cotton in, tearing it open, tumbling around boxes and bales, and such heavy work. It has been found, and is a fact patent to all who have studied the question, that the employment of colored labor in the finer processes of manufacturing is a question which is mooted only by those who know nothing about it. . . . It may be regarded as a fact about which those who understand the question can have no dispute, that it will be many years before the present condition of things can be changed. There are places to which each of these labor elements is specially adapted. The supply of both races is about equal to the demand, and there is an opportunity for support and for fair and reasonable prosperity open to one race as well as to the other.

There is a good feeling existing between the employers and the employed, both white and black, in the South, which is not equaled in any other section of this country, or in Europe either. There are no strikes here, no rebellions of the laborers, no disposition on the part of labor to combine against capital, and no disposition on the part of capital to oppress labor. Everything is in harmony, and a state of harmony and of prosperity in this respect exists which is to be found in no other place in the civilized world to the same extent as in the cotton States of the South. That is caused by the fact that there is a liberality upon the part of the employers which dispenses justice to the employed willingly and cheerfully, and without compulsion. This fact is recognized by the employees, and where there is justice between capital and labor, and no oppression, there is, of course, no necessity for collisions, strikes, or animosities. . . .

Now, I will make another statement which will probably be interesting to people who do not live here. The cotton States of the South are the only portion of the United States where whites and blacks work together upon the same work at the same pay and under the same regulations, the only part of this country where the two races will work side by side, justice being rendered to each, and the laborers of both races working in harmony and in unison, without rebellion and with mutual goodwill. I employed on mill No. 3 from fifty to seventy-five brick masons, and probably from fifteen to twenty rock masons. The men of both races were mixed, working side by side, black and white. They were paid equal wages, and there was perfect harmony between them and equal proficiency except in cases where special acquirements were necessary on special work, and, in one instance, for considerable length of time, a state of facts existed that could not exist in any other country in the world, viz, that the entire lot of laborers were superintended by a colored man. You can't see anything like that in New England, can you? But what I say of the harmonious relations between the laborers of the two races has particular reference to Georgia, and other States where the races have not been antagonized by violent political agitations in the past. . . .

I have been simply calling attention to the fact that we can do here what you cannot do there; that is, we can work the two races together on the same work in harmony, and I say again that you could not do that in the mines of Pennsylvania, in the rolling mills of Pittsburgh, in the manufacturing establishments of New York, or upon the buildings of New York, Boston, or Chicago. You could not find or get up in any of those places the same harmonious feeling which exists here between the races to-day.

The CHAIRMAN. Then it is not really the race question at all. It is simply this: that such a large part of your working population is colored that if you should undertake to exclude them from your labor market there would be nobody to do the work, and therefore, there being sufficient employment for both races, they work quietly alongside of each other, neither feeling that it is necessary to compete with the other for employment.

The WITNESS. Well, always, both before the war and since the war, there has been a better feeling between the two races here than at the North. The question of race, the question of the color of a man's face, does not arise at all in reference to this kind of labor, but in the North it does come in, and the consequence is that you find it impossible there to work the two races together harmoniously as we do here. I simply state this as a fact not generally known by parties at the North who have not investigated it. . . .

It is only in the proper place that the two races can come together harmoniously. They don't come together in the dining-room, they don't come together in society, but there is a place where they can come together harmoniously, and that is right down on this basis where it is a question of labor, and where the common sentiment of the people is that the two races are equal. So far as regards this question of such labor as can earn 60 or 70 cents a day, there is perfect equality between white and black labor here in the South. But that does not mean at all social equality. It has nothing to do with politics or with social equality or anything of the kind. It means just 75 cents a day for a day's work, whether the laborer is white or black, or $2.50 a day for a black mason, and $2.50 for a white mason. We have two blacksmiths at work at the Eagle and Phoenix mill, one of them being white and the other black, and they are on an equality in wages and in work. One of them is a very intelligent white man and the other is a very intelligent colored man. The question of equality does not come up with reference to those two men at all. They are both just blacksmiths working at $2.50 a day each, and drawing that amount of wages at the end of the week, and that is all there is to it. We do not mix the races in the machine shop. It is done only where there seems to be a certain suitableness in it. We do it on our rock walls and our brick walls, and among our carpenters, and we pay each one at the same rate for equal work.

Q. And give neither race the preference in selecting the men to be employed?

A. If I want a man to do certain things I want a colored man every time, while, on the other hand, if I want a man to do certain other things, I want a white man. I don't know that it hinges on the question of the whiteness or blackness of the man's skin; it hinges rather on the adaptability of the man to do the particular work that is required.

Q. Now, what have you to say to us in regard to child labor in factories?

A. Well, the child labor question is different here from what it is in the North, for sundry reasons. In the first place, it is a lamentable fact that parents here do not recognize the necessity of education to the extent that they do in the North. In the North all the people, including all the laboring classes, think it a duty to have their children educated, and the facilities which the free-school system gives them for that purpose are very largely used. Perhaps the laws of the Northern States regulate the matter somewhat; but laws are second to facts, and if the sentiment of the people did not justify such laws they would not be made. Then, too, a law that would be good in that regard in Massachusetts would not be good for anything in Alabama. You must adapt your laws to the State and conditions of society. Suppose you should pass a law in Alabama that, up to a certain age, children should not work because they must go to school, it wouldn't be good for anything; for the reason that, in the first place, even if they did not work, they would not go to school, because the parents would not want to send them, and also because if they did there are no schools to which they could send them generally. Again, on the other hand, that is not true of Georgia. Of course, I am now speaking only of the average. There are many people here who would be very apt and anxious to educate their children, and who would be very glad to send them to school. There are many who do send their children to school wherever they have the opportunity, but there are many others who do not; from want of thrift, or from the fact which does not exist elsewhere

> in this country, that the devastation produced by the war has swept away the material prosperity of the people and probably set them back fifty years in that respect, and as a consequence they are unable to educate their children as they would wish. For these reasons, and also because of the fact generally admitted, that economy is not one of the strongest points of the Southern people, there are a great many parents who would be glad to send their children to school, but who have not the opportunity or the means, being compelled to keep the children employed in procuring the necessaries of life.

In regard to the small children, more especially those in our spinning room, they are worth all they are paid, and the fact is that the wages they earn are a necessity for the support of the families from which the children come; so that if they were turned out there would be suffering upon the part of those families for want of that income. We do not really employ those children as a matter of preference, but as a matter of necessity. When a family comes here and a portion of them go to work in the mill they are sure to make application for employment for all their children who are of sufficient age to go to work in the mill, and they persist in those applications until those children are employed.

> Q. At what ages are the children employed?
>
> A. About ten years, I believe, is the youngest age at which we employ them.
>
> Q. What do children of ten years and upward do?
>
> A. They do this very light work, attending the spinning and winding machinery—very light work. There is no work that those children do that is sufficiently arduous to over-tax them or to interfere with their health or development. Their work is all light, and the only thing that can tax them is perhaps the hours of labor. . . .

Source: Report of the Committee of the Senate upon the Relation between Labor and Capital, 48th Congress, 4 (1885).

---

48. "There Is Power in a Union": A Song by Joe Hill, 1913

Joseph Hillstrom (1879–1915) is the best known of the **Wobbly** *songwriters. Known as* **Joe Hill**, *born as Joel Emmanuel Haggland, the Swedish immigrant was executed by firing squad in Utah after being convicted of murdering a store keeper. Hill joined the* **Industrial Workers of the World (IWW)** *in 1910 and, over the next five years, captured and articulated the meaning of the Wobbly cause in his songs, which, he argued were far more effective in promoting the union's cause than were pamphlets or posters, since the song would be repeated many times over. Hill set his lyrics to popular tunes of hymns, as he does in this selection.*

There Is Power in a Union
By Joe Hill
(Tune: "There Is Power in the Blood")

Would you have freedom from wage slavery,
Then join in the grand Industrial band;
Would you from mis'ry and hunger be free,
Then come! Do your share, like a man.

Chorus:

There is pow'r, there is pow'r
In a band of workingmen,
When they stand hand in hand,
That's a pow'r, that's a pow'r
That must rule in every land—
One Industrial Union Grand.

Would you have mansions of gold in the sky,
And live in a shack, way in the back?
Would you have wings up in heaven to fly,
And starve here with rags on your back?

If you've had "nuff" of "the blood of the lamb,"
Then join in the grand Industrial band;
If, for a change, you would have eggs and ham,
Then come, do your share, like a man.

If you like sluggers to beat off your head,
Then don't organize, all unions despise,
If you want nothing before you are dead,
Shake hands with your boss and look wise.

Come, all ye workers, from every land,
Come, join in the grand Industrial band,
Then we our share of this earth shall demand.
Come on! Do your share, like a man.

Source: I.W.W. Songs (Chicago: I.W.W. Publishing Bureau, 1916).

---

49. Thomas Geoghegan: Excerpt from *Which Side Are You On?*, 1991

Thomas Geoghegan, in the course of practicing labor law, represented workers at Wisconsin Steel. Here he gives an account of his efforts to recoup some of the pension funds due to his clients after the sale of Wisconsin Steel by International Harvester.

Geoghegan writes in the context of the decline of labor unions following the election of Ronald Reagan to the presidency and the emergence of a national climate of opinion that looked distrustfully upon unions.

For seven years (1981–88), I represented 2,500 former employees of Wisconsin Steel. We sued International Harvester, their former employer, for the benefits they lost when Harvester sold the mill to a tiny, undercapitalized company that quickly went bankrupt.

Wisconsin Steel was the first of the big Chicago mills to crash, and the crash was the most dramatic, because here, unlike most mills, the workers were cheated of their shutdown benefits. Even with the payments from the PBGC [Pension Benefit Guarantee Corporation], the workers still lost nearly $45 million. By 1988, if the interest on this money was added up, they had lost nearly $90 million. The benefits they lost, among others, include severance pay, supplemental unemployment benefits pay, extended vacation pay, "special payment," health insurance (for retirees). They even lost two weeks of wages because the paychecks bounced without warning when the mill suddenly closed in March, 1980.

But worst of all, 500 or so of them lost their pension benefits, often up to 60 percent, especially the "Rule of 65" pensions, which were the special shutdown benefits that went into effect only if the mill closed.

So not only did the workers lose their jobs; that would have been bad enough. But they also lost the $45 million, which was their "deindustrialization" money. The closing of Wisconsin Steel was, in many ways, like an earthquake. The first shock was that the mill closed. The second shock, like an aftershock, was that they would not get this money either. The money that would have cushioned the blow, that would have given them time to think, figure out what to do next, hold on to the car or the home a little longer: it was not much money, really, but it was enough, just enough, to make people lose their balance. Some of them could never get their balance back.

I spent all the Reagan years on this one case. It was endless. I felt like I was in prison. I used to think of that line from Richard II: "I wasted time, and now doth time waste me." I came to hate "deindustrialization." The mill had closed, but it seemed as if the litigation would never end, and I might have to clean up after this mill forever. I felt as the men must have felt: I was always living in the year 1980. I could not seem to leave 1980.

I wanted to move, go to New York, do anything else, but people told me, "You can't, you're stuck here," and they were right. I was stuck here. I was trapped in a way, just as the people in the neighborhood were trapped, trapped in homes they could not sell, like victims of an earthquake. Nobody was moving, nobody was going away. I was a labor lawyer, like it or not, until this damn case was done.

Here is how the case started:

> In 1977, Harvester had owned Wisconsin Steel for seventy-five years, and the mill made the specially hardened steel for the trucks and machinery that Har-

vester manufactured. Gradually, Harvester had let the mill run down, and sometime in the mid-seventies, it began looking for a buyer. But no one in the business wanted to buy Wisconsin Steel. Not only was it run down, but there was an even bigger problem: the pension fund was short $65 million.

Wisconsin Steel, in short, was unsalable. Yet Harvester did not want to close it either. If it did so, it would owe the whole $65 million in pensions, plus another $20 million in special shutdown benefits, like severance pay. It almost seemed as if Harvester was trapped into keeping the mill open. Nor was Harvester the only steel company in the 1980s to have this problem. A union lawyer once told me, "The only reason half the steel mills in this country are still going is that they can't afford to pay the pensions." It was the revenge of the weak on the strong. "Shut us down, Mr. Employer, and you die, too."

So Harvester tried to close the mill indirectly. It transferred title to a dummy corporation. Then, when this corporate shell went bankrupt, Harvester could say, "Too bad, they're not our pensions now." But Harvester had to have an accomplice. It found one in a small engineering company, Envirodyne, Inc., which knew nothing about steel. Envirodyne was not much of a company, just two yuppies in a garage. But Envirodyne did not want to have to pay the pensions either. So Envirodyne transferred title to a subsidiary it created, EDC Holding Company. Then EDC transferred title to a subsidiary it created, WSC Corporation. One corporate shell came after another. It was like a game of Chinese boxes, and when you got to the last box, nothing was in it. Nobody would be paying the pensions.

Under our law, a subsidiary can go bankrupt and normally the parent company will not be liable for its debts. So when EDC or WSC went bankrupt, Harvester and even Envirodyne could say they owed nothing. Indeed, Harvester was not even the parent. But Harvester was the biggest creditor and held on through mortgages to everything of value. That was the malign beauty of it all, which I spent seven grudging years admiring. Harvester had dumped all the pension liabilities but kept control of all the assets. It could keep running the mill as if it still owned it. Envirodyne could conduct its little engineering experiments. And the workers, who may have been there twenty or thirty years, would lose their pensions, health insurance, severance pay, etc. Dumb, stupid organized labor would take the fall.

The deal was so mean, so vile, that even the investment bankers gagged. Lehman Brothers, the investment banking firm handling the sale, went to Harvester and objected on simple moral grounds. Peter Peterson, the president of Lehman, came out to a Harvester board meeting to express his distaste. He talked about the "appearance" and the "reality" of the transaction. He was ignored, but he made a record, at least, and it does show a certain honor: sometimes, even on Wall Street, someone may write a memo to the file.

Harvester kept the mill going for a decent interval (two years). Then, on March 28, 1980, with no warning to the workers, Harvester pulled the plug. It foreclosed on the mortgage, and the mill went down the drain. In minutes, WSC was in bankruptcy.

Everybody was stunned. They thought, "How could anything be wrong?"

Right before the mill closed, production almost cruelly began to go up. People were getting more overtime than ever. They were like old ladies, on their deathbeds, rougeing up their cheeks.

But no, it was something else: they never knew they were about to die, it was a total shock. They say people who die sudden, violent deaths are most likely to become ghosts and haunt the earth. On March 28, 1980, all the workers died a sudden, violent death, no time to say goodbye.

Men were obsessed with "the last day." Even seven years later, as we prepared for trial, they could not talk about anything else. Dozens of times, I asked potential witnesses, "Now what did you lose as a result of the closing of the mill?" And they answered with non sequiturs, their little stories about "the last day."

Mr. J. said, for example, "I'm walking off the shift, and my foreman comes over and says, 'Don't come back.'

"I said, 'What?'

"He said, 'Don't come back. It's over.'

"I said, 'What? What?'"

Another man said he was asleep, and someone phoned and woke him from a dream and said, "Don't come in, it's gone."

These stories might go on for fifteen, twenty minutes, just pointless stories. As witnesses, they worried me. They did not seem to care about the loss of pensions, etc. It was that phone call saying, "Don't come back." I was afraid that, as witnesses, they would talk about nothing else, and the jury would think, "What's the big deal about the last day?"

But maybe it was the day he died. The last day a man could remember himself as middle-class. The rest of his life began happening to someone else.

Over the years, I drove down to South Chicago to talk to the workers. I saw the neighborhood around Wisconsin Steel change. At first, in '81, '82, it was simply dead. By '85, it was beyond dead, and much more skeletal-looking: old tires, hubcaps, rusted human bones. Once, in the seventies, I used to dine in Slavic splendor at places like the Golden Shell. But nothing was that good now. Now I went hungry. Or I would drive twenty blocks north to the U of C and eat tunaburgers with biologists.

In the old days, driving down here, I used to see a sign: "Welcome to the Tenth Ward, Edward R. Vrdolyak, Alderman." Now I see a sign about a clinic for male impotence. This is how you know now you have entered the Tenth Ward.

Even the geography has begun to change. Now there is a whole mountain range of chemical waste rising to the south along I-80. What was once the Midwest has begun to look like the Adirondacks. There is even talk of ski lodges. Steelworkers from sex clinics could run the lifts.

When the mill crashed, so did the Union. Same week. Nobody ever saw it again.

It had never been much of a union anyway, just a small independent, not affiliated with the Steelworkers or the AFL-CIO. It did not even have a real labor lawyer: just Edward R. Vrdolyak (or ERV), the alderman, who wanted the worker-comp cases. ERV had a little office, and Tony Roque, the Union president, was an employee. Roque was an investigator or "runner," who brought in the injured men. Under Vrdolyak, the Union became a big, grinding worker-comp. machine, spitting out missing fingers, broken bones, all of it money in Eddie's pocket.

When the mill went down, ERV closed down the Union and walked away. He's got nothing against labor law. But there is no money in it, see? The money is in worker comp.

Poor Roque, the president, was in over his head. He was just a working guy, no genius, trying to figure out a Wall Street deal, with no one to help him, not even his boss, Vrdolyak. Even a good labor lawyer might not have been much help.

When Roque complained, Harvester handed him a sheet of paper. It said this document was a guarantee of the pensions. Roque signed it. Didn't really grasp it. In fact, the paper guaranteed just a tiny sliver of the pensions. By signing it, Roque unwittingly released Harvester from everything else: $65 million in pensions, $20 million in shutdown benefits.

Despite the shell, some lawyers at Harvester had thought the company could still be liable for the pensions. But now there was Roque's waiver. Harvester was delighted, amazed, that the Union could be so dumb.

When the mill went down, Tony Roque fled. Nobody saw him. He unlisted his phone number. People said he was in the hospital. Or he was dead. He was like a pilot who crashes a plane and 600 people die, the bodies lying all over South Chicago.

It was a mess.

Source: Thomas Geoghegan, *Which Side Are You On?: Trying to be for Labor When It's Flat on Its Back* (New York: Farrar, Strauss, Giroux: 1991).

---

50. Triangle Fire: Excerpts from the March 1911 *New York Times* Account of the Fire and from an April 1911 Speech by Rose Schneiderman

The ***Triangle Factory Fire of 1911*** *was not America's worst industrial accident, but it nonetheless captured the public imagination. Partly this was because it coincided with Progressive Era reform efforts to improve working conditions. The fire also served to underscore the dangers of* ***sweatshop*** *production against which labor unions had long warned. But a big part of Triangle's lurid appeal was also rooted in sexism. Prevailing views of women as fair, frail, and vulnerable enhanced the public's horror over the tragedy, as did graphic newspaper accounts like the one that appeared in the* New York Times *on March 26, 1911.*

The Triangle Fire came on the heels of the ***Uprising of the 20,000*** *and the two did much to bolster the recruitment efforts of the* ***International Ladies' Garment Workers' Union (ILGWU)****. The second document excerpts a famed speech from ILGWU organizer* ***Rose Schneiderman****, which she published in* The Survey *on April 8, 1911.*

New York Times, March 26, 1911

Three stories of a ten-floor building at the corner of Greene Street and Washington Place were burned yesterday, and while the fire was going on 141 young men and women at least 125 of them mere girls were burned to death or killed by jumping to the pavement below. . . .

Most of the victims were suffocated or burned to death within the building, but some who fought their way to the windows and leaped met death as surely, but perhaps more quickly, on the pavements below. . . .

The victims who are now lying at the Morgue waiting for some one to identify them by a tooth or the remains of a burned shoe were mostly girls from 16 to 23 years of age. They were employed at making shirtwaists by the Triangle Waist Company, the principal owners of which are Isaac Harris and Max Blanck. Most of them could barely speak English. Many of them came from Brooklyn. Almost all were the main support of their hard-working families. . . .

A heap of corpses lay on the sidewalk for more than an hour. The firemen were too busy dealing with the fire to pay any attention to people whom they supposed beyond their aid. When the excitement had subsided to such an extent that some of the firemen and policemen could pay attention to this mass of the supposedly dead they found about half way down in the pack a girl who was still breathing. She died two minutes after she was found. . . .

At 4:40 o'clock, nearly five hours after the employees in the rest of the building had gone home, the fire broke out. The one little fire escape in the interior was resorted to by many of the doomed victims. Some of them escaped by running down the stairs, but in a moment or two this avenue was cut off by flame. The girls rushed to the windows and looked down at Greene Street, 100 feet below them. Then one poor, little creature jumped. There was a plate glass protection over part of the sidewalk, but she crashed through it, wrecking it and breaking her body into a thousand pieces. Then they all began to drop. The crowd yelled "Don't jump!" but it was jump or be burned the proof of which is found in the fact that fifty burned bodies were taken from the ninth floor alone. They jumped, they crashed through broken glass, they crushed themselves to death on the sidewalk. . . .

[Fire] Chief Croker said it was an outrage. He spoke bitterly of the way in which the Manufacturers' Association had called a meeting in Wall Street to take measures against his proposal for enforcing better methods of protection for employees in cases of fire.

Four alarms were rung in fifteen minutes. The first five girls who jumped did so before the first engine could respond. . . . Thirty bodies clogged the elevator shaft. These dead were all girls. They had made their rush there blindly when they discovered that there was no chance to get out by the fire escape. Then they found that the elevator was as hopeless as anything else, and they fell there in their tracks and died.

The Triangle Waist Company employed about 600 women and less than 100 men. One of the saddest features of the thing is the fact that they had almost finished for the day. In five minutes more, if the fire had started then, probably not a life would have been lost.

How the fire started no one knows. On the three upper floors of the building were 600 employees of the waist company, 500 of whom were girls. The victims mostly Italians, Russians, Hungarians, and Germans were girls and men who had been employed by the firm of Harris & Blanck, owners of the Triangle Waist Company, after the strike in which the Jewish girls, formerly employed, had been become unionized and had demanded better working conditions. The building had experienced four recent fires and had been reported by the Fire Department to the Building Department as unsafe in account of the insufficiency of its exits.

The building itself was of the most modern construction and classed as fireproof. What burned so quickly and disastrously for the victims were shirtwaists, hanging on lines above tiers of workers, sewing machines placed so closely together that there was hardly aisle room for the girls between them, and shirtwaist trimmings and cuttings which littered the floors above the eighth and ninth stories.

Girls had begun leaping from the eighth story windows before firemen arrived. The firemen had trouble bringing their apparatus into position because of the bodies which strewed the pavement and sidewalks. While more bodies crashed down among them, they worked with desperation to run their ladders into position and to spread firenets. . . .

Thousands of people who had crushed in from Broadway and Washington Square and were screaming with horror at what they saw watched closely the work with the firenet. Three other girls who had leaped for it a moment after the first one, struck it on top of her, and all four rolled out and lay still upon the pavement.

Five girls who stood together at a window close [to] the Greene Street corner held their place while a fire ladder was worked toward them, but which stopped at its full length two stories lower down. They leaped together, clinging to each other, with fire streaming back from their hair and dresses. They struck a glass sidewalk cover and [into] the basement. There was no time to aid them. With water pouring in upon them from a dozen hose nozzles the bodies lay for two hours where they struck, as did the many others who leaped to their deaths. . . .

Source: "The Triangle Factory Fire," www.ilr.cornell.edu/trianglefire/texts/newspaper/nyt_032611_5.html.

"WE HAVE FOUND YOU WANTING"—ROSE SCHNEIDERMAN

I would be a traitor to these poor burned bodies if I came here to talk good fellowship. We have tried you good people of the public and we have found you wanting. The old Inquisition had its rack and its thumbscrews and its instruments of torture with iron teeth. We know what these things are today; the iron teeth are our necessities, the thumbscrews are the high-powered and swift machinery close to which we must work, and the rack is here in the firetrap structures that will destroy us the minute they catch on fire.

This is not the first time girls have been burned alive in the city. Every week I must learn of the untimely death of one of my sister workers. Every year thousands of us are maimed. The life of men and women is so cheap and property is so sacred. There are so many of us for one job it matters little if 146 of us are burned to death.

We have tried you citizens . . . you have a couple of dollars for the sorrowing mothers, brothers and sisters by way of a charity gift. But every time the workers come out in the only way they know to protest against conditions which are unbearable the strong hand of the law is allowed to press down heavily upon us. Public officials have only words of warning to us—warning that we must be intensely peaceable, and they have the workhouse just back of all their warnings. The strong hand of the law beats us back, when we rise, into the conditions that make life unbearable.

I can't talk fellowship to you who are gathered here. Too much blood has been spilled. I know from my experience it is up to the working people to save themselves. The only way they can save themselves is by a strong working-class movement.

Source: Rosalyn Baxandall and Linda Gordon, eds., *America's Working Women: A Documentary History* (New York: W. W. Norton, 1995), pp. 176–77.

---

51. Voluntarism: Excerpts from Samuel Gompers's Autobiography (1925)

American workers have often been ambivalent about the role of the State. Some workers have looked to government to alleviate injustice, legislate decent working conditions, eliminate class-based privilege, and otherwise level the playing field between employees and employers. Still others have feared the power of government, arguing that government is too often an arm of organized capital and is more likely to be a repressive agent than a progressive one.

The early ***American Federation of Labor (AFL)*** *fell into the latter category. AFL President* ***Samuel Gompers*** *embraced a labor version of laissez-faire in that he felt that capital and labor needed to resolve their disputes independent of government intervention. In Gompers's view, State intervention was dangerous on many levels, not the least of which was its tendency to undo what workers managed to win through their own efforts. But Gompers also feared benevolent government action, arguing that it weakened the labor movement by making workers beholden to the government rather than relying on their own organized might. (Some argue that those fears came to pass under the New Deal.)*

Gompers and the AFL endorsed a rather elusive concept known as **voluntarism**. *They saw both trade unions and political parties as noncoercive bodies that individuals could choose to join, or not. Thus, just as the AFL could not compel individual unions to join the federation or interfere in its personal affairs, neither should the State juxtapose itself between employees and employers. Gompers explains below:*

> The methods and agencies for progress in the economic world must be evolved out of economic experience and life. It is a serious mistake to confuse the two fields or to carry the problems of one into the other. Trade unions or voluntary associations of wage-earners constitute one of the essential agencies for establishing procedure of control. The development of large-scale production, the increasing authority of science in determining processes, and the more recent investigations of management for the purpose of making it truly scientific, together with the marked tendency toward trade associations, are to me a most gratifying exemplification of my thought that discernment of the essential difference between the economic and the political clarifies the problem of progress.
>
> Several times the plain question has been put to me by members of the Senate Committee on Judiciary: "Mr. Gompers, what can we do to allay the causes of strikes that bring discomfort and financial suffering to all alike?" I have had to answer, "Nothing." My answer has been interpreted as advocating a policy of drift. Quite the contrary to my real thought. Foremost in my mind is to tell the politicians to keep their hands off and thus preserve voluntary institutions and opportunity for individual and group initiative and leave the way open to deal with problems as the experience and facts of industry shall indicate. I have, with equal emphasis, opposed submitting determination of industrial policies to courts. But it is difficult for lawyers to understand that the most important human justice comes through other agencies than the political.

Source: Nick Salvatore, ed., *Seventy Years of Life and Labor: An Autobiography of Samuel Gompers* (1925; reprint Ithaca: ILR Press, 1984), pp. 134–35.

---

52. Women in the American Federation of Labor: Excerpt from Writings of Edward O'Donnell

Women have always worked, but men have not always felt comfortable with that fact. For much of the nineteenth century, a Victorian ideal prevailed that held that male **wage** *earners should be paid a* **family wage** *sufficient for them to provide for wives and children. This was only partially linked to the notion of a just wage; it also connected to the Victorian notion that the home was a woman's proper sphere, and that her natural realm of expertise and talent centered on the home and domestic duty.*

Social and economic reality clashed with hegemonic Victorian ideals. Millions of workingmen could not provide for their families adequately, forcing wives, sons, and daughters into the workplace. There, they often encountered hostility from the very organizations that sought to defend workers: labor unions. Although many unions organized women, quite a few labor advocates complained—not entirely without justification—that the presence of women in the workplace undermined wages for men and threatened the very concept of the family wage. In their view, employers hired women (and children) at reduced rates as a way of curtailing union demands for higher wages.

Skilled craftsmen were among the most vocal in their opposition to women workers, and numerous unions affiliated with the early **American Federation of Labor (AFL)** *excluded women from membership. The views of Edward O'Donnell, of Boston's Central Labor Union, are typical of AFL attitudes about women in the pre-1920 period, though such views persisted well into the 1970s in some trades. Even today, some women complain they are not yet full partners in the labor union movement. This excerpt comes originally from Edward O'Donnell's "Women as Bread Winners—The Error of the Age," an article that appeared in October 1897 in the* American Federationist, *the official journal of the AFL.*

The invasion of the crafts by women has been developing for years amid irritation and injury to the workman. The right of the woman to win honest bread is accorded on all the sides, but with craftsmen it is an open question whether this manifestation is of a healthy social growth or not.

The rapid displacement of men by women in the factory and workshop has to be met sooner or later, and the question is forcing itself upon the leaders and thinkers among the labor organizations of the land.

Is it a pleasing indication of progress to see the father, the brother and the son displaced as the bread winner by the mother, sister and daughter?

Is not this revolutionary backslide, which certainly modernizes the present wage system in vogue, a menace to prosperity—a foe to our civilized pretensions? . . .

The growing demand for female labor is not founded upon philanthropy, as those who encourage it would have sentimentalists believe; it does not spring from the milk of human kindness. It is an insidious assault upon the home; it is the knife of the assassin, aimed at the family circle—the divine injunction. It debars the man through financial embarrassment from family responsibility, and physically, mentally and socially excludes the woman equally from nature's dearest impulse. Is this the demand of civilized progress; is it the desire of Christian dogma? . . .

The wholesale employment of women in the various handicrafts must gradually unsex them, as it most assuredly is demoralizing them, or stripping them of that modest demeanor that lends itself to the charm to their kind, while it numerically strengthens the multitudinous army of loafers, paupers, tramps and policemen, for no man who desires honest employment, and can secure it, cares to throw his life away upon such a wretched occupation as the latter.

The employment of women in the mechanical departments is encouraged because of its cheapness and easy manipulation, regardless of the consequent perils; and for no other reason. The generous sentiment enveloping this inducement is of criminal design, since it comes from a thirst to build riches upon the dismemberment of the family or the hearthstone cruelly dishonored. . . .

But somebody will say, would you have women pursue lives of shame rather than work? Certainly not; it is to the alarming introduction of women into the mechanical industries, hitherto enjoyed by the sterner sex, at a wage uncommandable by them, that leads so many into that deplorable pursuit. . . .

Source: Rosalyn Baxandall and Linda Gordon, eds., *America's Working Women: A Documentary History 1600 to the Present* (New York: W. W. Norton, 1995), pp. 162–64.

---

53. Women on the Breadlines During the Depression: An Account Published by Meridel Le Sueur in *New Masses*, 1932

Meridel Le Sueur (1900–96) was the daughter of **socialist***-feminist parents, Marion Wharton and Alfred Le Sueur. She grew up in the Midwest amongst populist farmers and* **Industrial Workers of the World (IWW)** *activists. Le Sueur moved to the East Coast where she lived briefly with* **Emma Goldman** *and was friendly with John Reed and Edna St. Vincent Millay. She published her first article in 1927 and thereafter wrote numerous pieces on labor struggles; women's issues; and the plight of Native Americans, rural peoples, and the poor during the depression. With the women's movement of the 1970s, many of Le Sueur's works were given new life—several were published for the first time or reprinted. Below she gives an account of unemployed women in Minneapolis during the Great Depression. She continued writing progressive literature until close to her death, in St. Paul at age ninety-six. This account originally appeared in* New Masses *in 1932.*

I am sitting in the city free employment bureau. It's the woman's section. We have been sitting here now for four hours. We sit here every day, waiting for a job. There are no jobs. Most of us have had no breakfast. Some have had scant rations for over a year. Hunger makes a human being lapse into a state of lethargy, especially city hunger. Is there any place else in the world where a human being is supposed to go hungry amidst plenty without an outcry, without protest, where only the boldest steal or kill for bread, and the timid crawl the streets, hunger like the beak of a terrible bird at the vitals?

We sit looking at the floor. No one dares think of the coming winter. There are only a few more days of summer. Everyone is anxious to get work to lay up something for that long siege of bitter cold. But there is no work. Sitting in the room we all know it. That is why we don't talk much. We look at the floor dreading to see that knowledge in each other's eyes. There is a kind of humiliation in it. We look away from each other. We look at the floor. It's too terrible to see this animal terror in each other's eyes.

So we sit hour after hour, day after day, waiting for a job to come in. There are many women for a single job. A thin sharp woman sits inside the wire cage looking at the book. For four hours we have watched her looking at that book. She has a hard little eye. In the small bare room there are half a dozen women sitting on the benches waiting. Many come and go. Our faces are all familiar to each other, for we wait here everyday.

This is a domestic employment bureau. Most of the women who come here are middle aged, some have families, some raised their families and are now alone, some have men who are out of work. Hard times and the man leaves to hunt for work. He doesn't find it. He drifts on. The woman probably doesn't hear from him for a long time. She expects it. She isn't surprised. She struggles alone to feed the many mouths. Sometimes she gets help from the charities. If she's clever she can get herself a good living from the charities, if she's naturally a lick spittle, naturally a little docile and cunning. If she's proud then she starves silently, leaving her children to find work, coming home after a day's searching to wrestle with her house, her children.

Some such story is written on the faces of all these women. There are young girls too, fresh from the country. Some are made brazen too soon by the city. There is a great exodus of girls from the farms into the city now.

Thousands of farms have been vacated completely in Minnesota. The girls are trying to get work. The prettier ones can get jobs in the stores when there are any, or waiting on tables but these jobs are only for the attractive and the adroit, the others, the real peasants have a more difficult time. . . .

It's one of the great mysteries of the city where women go when they are out of work and hungry. There are not many women in the bread line. There are no flop houses for women as there are for men, where a bed can be had for a quarter or less. You don't see women lying on the floor at the mission in the free flops. They obviously don't sleep in the jungle or under newspapers in the park. There is no law I suppose against their being in these places but the fact is they rarely are.

Yet there must be as many women out of jobs in cities and suffering extreme poverty as there are men. What happens to them? Where do they go? Try to get into the Y.W.[C.A.] without any money or looking down at heel. Charities take care of very few and only those that are called "deserving." The lone girl is under suspicion by the virgin women who dispense charity.

I've lived in cities for many months broke, without help, too timid to get in bread lines. I've known many women to live like this until they simply faint on the street from privations, without saying a word to anyone. A woman will shut herself up in a room until it is taken away from her, and eat a cracker a day and be as quiet as a mouse so there are no social statistics concerning her.

I don't know why it is, but a woman will do this unless she has dependents, will go for weeks, verging on starvation, crawling in some hole, going through the streets ashamed, sitting in libraries, parks, going for days without speaking to a living soul like some exiled beast, keeping the runs mended in her stockings, shut up in terror in her own misery, until she becomes too super sensitive and timid to even ask for a job.

Bernice says even strange men she has met in the park have sometimes, that is in better days, given her a loan to pay her room rent. She has always paid them back.

In the afternoon the young girls, to forget the hunger and the deathly torture and fear of being jobless, try and pick up a man to take them to a ten cent show. They never go to more expensive ones, but they can always find a man willing to spend a dime to have the company of a girl for the afternoon.

Sometimes a girl facing the night without shelter will approach a man for lodging. A woman always asks a man for help. Rarely another woman. I have known girls to sleep in men's rooms for the night, on a pallet without molestation, and given breakfast in the morning.

It's no wonder these young girls refuse to marry, refuse to rear children. They are like certain savage tribes, who, when they have been conquered refuse to breed.

Not one of them but looks forward to starvation, for the coming winter. We are in a jungle and know it. We are beaten, entrapped. There is no way out. Even if there were a job, even if that thin acrid woman came and gave everyone in the room a job for a few days, a few hours, at thirty cents an hour, this would all be repeated tomorrow, the next day and the next.

Not one of these women but knows, that despite years of labour there is only starvation, humiliation in front of them. . . .

So we sit in this room like cattle, waiting for a non-existent job, willing to work to the farthest atom of energy, unable to work, unable to get food and lodging, unable to bear children; here we must sit in this shame looking at the floor, worse than beasts at a slaughter.

It is appalling to think that these women sitting so listless in the room may work as hard as it is possible for a human being to work, may labour night and day, like Mrs. Gray wash street cars from midnight to dawn and offices in the early evening, scrubbing for fourteen and fifteen hours a day, sleeping only five hours or so, doing this their whole lives, and never earn one day of security, having always before them the pit of the future. The endless labour, the bending back, the water soaked hands, earning never more than a week's wages, never having in their hands more life than that.

It's not the suffering, not birth, death, love that the young reject, but the suffering of endless labour without a dream, eating the spare bread in bitterness, a slave without the security of a slave.

Source: Meridel Le Sueur, *New Masses*, 1932.

---

54. Yellow-Dog Contract (1904)

As more and more workers banded together in unions, fearful employers sought a variety of methods to deter organization. One of the most infamous of these was the ***yellow-***

***dog contract**, an agreement in which a worker swore not to join a labor union as a condition of employment. Although the term was not common until after 1902, the practice was common in the nineteenth century. The 1932 **Norris-LaGuardia Act** and the 1935 **National Labor Relations Act** abolished the practice, though many workers continue to complain that unwritten de facto yellow-dog contracts persist. The example below comes from a 1904 document required of Colorado miners seeking employment in the Cripple Creek region. It was usually accompanied by a housing lease agreement that reinforced the antiunion bias of the contract. The Colorado coalfield struggles convulsed the region from the 1890s through World War I. Although this document specifically mentions the Western Federation of Miners, its force was applied equally to other organizations, including the **American Federation of Labor**.*

Mine No.______ Office No.______
APPLICATION FOR WORK
______Mine.
______ 190_.
Name, ______ ______.
Age, ____. Married? _____. Nationality, _____.
Residence, _____.
Occupation, _____.
Where last employed? _____.
For how long? _____.
In what capacity? _____.
Did you quit voluntarily, or were you discharged? _____.
If discharged, for what reason? _____.
How much experience have you had as _____? _____.
Where employed before coming to Cripple Creek district? _____.
Are you a member of the Western Federation of Miners? _____.
Have you ever been a member of the Western Federation of Miners? _____.
If so, when did you sever your connection with same? _____.
Do you belong to any labor organization; and if so, what? _____.
References: _____ _____.

__________,
Applicant.
Remarks: _____

Source: U.S. Congress, *A Report on Labor Disturbances in Colorado from 1880 to 1904, Inclusive* (1905), pp. 278–80.

55. Yellow-Dog Contract in the Coal Industry (1917)

The "yellow-dog contract" came to be so known because the popular saying was that it was so vile that no decent human being would even require an old yellow dog to sign such an agreement. The yellow-dog contract required workers, as a condition of employment, to agree not to join a union. The contract reproduced here was used by the Hitchman Coal and Coke Company. The majority of the Supreme Court, in Hitchman Coal and Coke v. Mitchell, *found the use of such contracts to be permissible under the Constitution.*

I am employed by and work for the Hitchman Coal & Coke Company with the express understanding that I am not a member of the United Mine Workers of America, and will not become so while an employee of the Hitchman Coal & Coke Company; that the Hitchman Coal & Coke Company is run non-union and agrees with me that it will run non-union while I am in its employ. If at any time I am employed by the Hitchman Coal & Coke Company I want to become connected with the United Mine Workers of America, or any affiliated organization, I agree to withdraw from the employment of said company, and agree that while I am in the employ of that company I will not make any efforts amongst its employees to bring about the unionizing of that mine against the company's wish. I have either read the above or heard the same read.

Source: Hitchman Coal and Coke Company v. Mitchell, 245 U.S. 229 (1917).

Bibliography

Compiling a bibliography of useful labor history books and sources is akin to trying to dam the ocean. Each year more superb works appear, and no one should construe the following list as definitive. These are mere starting points for deeper research. The books listed below are useful for the categories under which they appear. The editors in no way endorse *any* of these works in any sort of *best of* spirit. There are (literally) hundreds of stellar works that did not make it into the bibliography. The journal *Labor History* compiles a yearly list of titles published in the field of American history; we encourage researchers to consult the *Labor History* archive.

In keeping with the spirit of these volumes, we have largely avoided works on specialized topics. Readers are encouraged to see individual entries for suggestions on specialized topics. Our omission extends to individual trade unions. For the most part, we have listed works that deal with labor federations, but not individual unions. Many individual unions have histories that are easily located in databases. An excellent, though dated, guide to individual unions is Gary Fink, ed., *Labor Unions*, Westport, Conn.: Greenwood Press, 1977.

GENERAL SURVEYS

There are many fine labor-history-survey texts. Among the most thorough is Philip S. Foner's multivolume History of the American Labor Movement, *New York: International Publishers. Foner (1910–1994) was the preeminent labor historian of the twentieth century, and his survey encompasses nine volumes, all of which are now available in inexpensive paperback editions. Other good survey texts include the following:*

Babson, Steve. *The Unfinished Struggle: Turning Points in American Labor: 1877 to the Present*. New York: Rowman & Littlefield, 1999.

Brecher, Jeremy. *Strike!* Cambridge, Mass.: South End Press, 1997.

Dulles, Foster Rhea. *Labor in America: A History*. 6th ed. New York: Harlan Davidson, 1999.

Filipelli, Ronald. *Labor in the USA: A History*. New York: Alfred Knopf, 1984.

Green, James R. *The World of the Worker: Labor in Twentieth Century America*. New York: Hill and Wang, 1980.

Laurie, Bruce. *Artisans into Workers: Labor in Nineteenth-Century America*. New York: Hill and Wang, 1989.

Lens, Sidney. *The Labor Wars: From the Molly Maguires to the Sitdowns*. Garden City: Anchor Books, 1974.

Lichtenstein, Nelson. *State of the Union: A Century of American Labor*. Princeton, N.J.: Princeton University Press, 2002.

Meltzer, Milton. *Bread and Roses: The Struggle of American Labor 1865–1915*. New York: Mentor, 1967.

Rayback, Joseph G. *A History of American Labor*. New York: Free Press, 1966.

Zieger, Robert H. *American Workers: American Unions*. Baltimore: Johns Hopkins, 1994.

COLONIAL AMERICAN LABOR

Colonial labor is perhaps the least-studied aspect of American labor. Nonetheless, several very fine titles are available. Volume 1 of Philip Foner's History of the American Labor Movement *is a useful survey. Other good titles include the following:*

Applebaum, Herbert. *Colonial Americans at Work*. Lanham, Md.: University Press of America, 1996.

Innes, Stephen, ed., *Work and Labor in Early America*. Chapel Hill: University of North Carolina Press, 1988.

Jernegan, Marcus W. *Laboring and Dependent Classes in Colonial America, 1607–1783*. Westport, Conn.: Greenwood Press, 1980.

Morgan, Kenneth. *Slavery and Servitude in Colonial North America: A Short History*. New York: New York University Press, 2001.

EARLY REPUBLICAN AND ANTEBELLUM LABOR

We consciously chose not to list titles dealing with slavery, simply because said titles are too voluminous. More has been written about slavery than almost any other subject. Scholars researching slavery and slave work patterns would need to narrow their search parameters beyond those that make sense for us to list. We have included more general works on African American labor as a separate subsection.

Boydston, Jeanne. *Home and Work: Housework, Wages, and the Ideology of Labor in the Early Republic*. New York: Oxford Press, 1994.

Clark, Christopher. *The Roots of Rural Capitalism: Western Massachusetts, 1780–1860*. Ithaca, N.Y.: Cornell University Press, 1995.

Dawley, Alan. *Class and Community: The Industrial Revolution in Lynn*. Cambridge, Mass.: Harvard University Press, 1976.

Dublin, Thomas. *Women at Work: The Transformation of Work and Community in Lowell, Massachusetts, 1826–1860*. New York: Columbia University Press, 1979.
Glen, Robert. *Urban Workers in the Early Industrial Revolution*. New York: St. Martin's, 1984.
Hahn, Steven, and Jonathan Prude, eds. *The Countryside in the Age of Capitalist Transformation*. Chapel Hill: University of North Carolina Press, 1985.
Laurie, Bruce. *Working People of Philadelphia, 1800–1850*. Philadelphia: Temple University Press, 1980.
Pessen, Edward. *Most Uncommon Jacksonians: The Radical Leaders of the Early Labor Movement*. Albany: State University of New York Press, 1967.
Rock, Howard R., ed. *The New York City Artisan, 1789–1825: A Documentary History*. Albany: State University of New York Press, 1989.
Schultz, Ronald. *The Republic of Labor: Philadelphia Artisans and the Politics of Class, 1720–1840*. New York: Oxford Press, 1993.
Ware, Norman. *The Industrial Worker, 1840–1860*. 1924. Reprint, Chicago: Ivan R. Dee, 1990.
Wilentz, Sean. *Chants Democratic: New York City and the Rise of the American Working Class, 1788–1850*. New York: Oxford Press, 1984.

AMERICAN LABOR FROM THE CIVIL WAR TO 1900

Avrich, Paul. *The Haymarket Tragedy*. Princeton, N.J.: Princeton University Press, 1984.
Brundage, David. *The Making of Western Labor Radicalism: Denver's Organized Workers, 1878–1905*. Urbana: University of Illinois Press, 1994.
Fink, Leon. *Workingmen's Democracy: The Knights of Labor and American Politics*. Urbana: University of Illinois Press, 1983.
Foner, Philip. *The Great Labor Uprising of 1877*. New York: Monad Press, 1977.
Grob, Gerald. *Workers and Utopia: A Study of Ideological Conflict in the American Labor Movement, 1865–1900*. New York: Quadrangle Books, 1961.
Gutman, Herbert. *Power and Culture: Essays on the American Working Class*. New York: Pantheon, 1987.
———. *Work, Culture, and Society in Industrializing Society*. New York: Alfred A. Knopf, 1976.
Messer-Kruse, Timothy. *The Yankee International: Marxism and the American Reform Tradition*. Chapel Hill: University of North Carolina Press, 1998.
Montgomery, David. *Beyond Equality: Labor and the Radical Republicans 1862–1872*. Urbana: University of Illinois, 1981.
———. *Citizen Worker: The Experience of Workers in the United States with Democracy and the Free Market during the Nineteenth Century*. Cambridge: Cambridge University Press, 1993.
———. *Workers' Control in America*. Cambridge: Cambridge University Press, 1984.
Nelson, Bruce. *Beyond the Martyrs: A Social History of Chicago's Anarchists, 1870–1900*. New Brunswick, N.J.: Rutgers University Press, 1988.
Oestreicher, Richard. *Solidarity and Fragmentation: Working People and Class Consciousness in Detroit, 1875–1900*. Urbana: University of Illinois Press, 1986.
Rosenzweig, Roy. *Eight Hours for What We Will: Workers and Leisure in an Industrial City, 1870–1920*. Cambridge: Cambridge University Press, 1983.

Schneirov, Richard. *Labor and Urban Politics: Class Conflict and the Origins of Modern Liberalism in Chicago, 1864–97*. Urbana: University of Illinois Press, 1998.

Schneirov, Richard, Shelton Stromquist, and Nick Salvatore, eds., *The Pullman Strike and the Crisis of the 1890s*. Urbana: University of Illinois Press, 1999.

Stromquist, Shelton. *A Generation of Boomers: The Pattern of Railroad Labor Conflict in Nineteenth-Century America*. Urbana: University of Illinois Press, 1987.

Voss, Kim. *The Making of American Exceptionalism: The Knights of Labor and Class Formation in the Nineteenth Century*. Ithaca, N.Y.: Cornell University Press, 1993.

Ware, Norman. *The Labor Movement in the United States, 1860–1895: A Study in Democracy*. 1929. Reprint. Gloucester, Mass.: Peter Smith, 1959.

Weir, Robert E. *Beyond Labor's Veil: The Culture of the Knights of Labor*. University Park: Pennsylvania State University Press, 1996.

———. *Knights Unhorsed: Internal Conflict in a Gilded Age Social Movement*. Detroit: Wayne State University Press, 2000.

AMERICAN LABOR FROM 1900 TO 1929

Barrett, James R. *Work and Community in the Jungle: Chicago's Packinghouse Workers, 1894–1922*. Urbana: University of Illinois Press, 1987.

Bernstein, Irving. *The Lean Years: A History of the American Worker, 1920–1933*. Boston: Houghton Mifflin, 1960.

Brandes, Stuart. *American Welfare Capitalism, 1880–1940*. Chicago: University of Chicago Press, 1976.

Brody, David. *Labor in Crisis: The Steel Strike of 1919*. Urbana: University of Illinois Press, 1987.

———. *Steelworkers in America: The Non-Union Era*. Cambridge, Mass.: Harvard University Press, 1960.

Dubofsky, Melvyn. *Industrialism and the American Worker, 1865–1920*. 3rd ed. Arlington Heights, Ill.: AHM Publishing, 1996.

———. *We Shall Be All: A History of the Industrial Workers of the World*. Urbana: University of Illinois Press, 1988.

Ginger, Ray. *The Bending Cross: A Biography of Eugene Victor Debs*. New Brunswick: Rutgers University Press, 1949.

Goldberg, David. *A Tale of Three Cities: Labor Organization in Paterson, Passaic, and Lawrence, 1916–1921*. New Brunswick: Rutgers University Press, 1989.

Haydu, Jeffrey. *Making American Industry Safe for Democracy: Comparative Perspectives on the State and Employee Representation in the Era of World War I*. Urbana: University of Illinois Press, 1997.

Jacoby, Sanford. *Employing Bureaucracy: Managers, Unions, and the Transformation of Work in American Industry, 1900–1945*. New York: Columbia University Press, 1985.

Kazin, Michael. *Barons of Labor: The San Francisco Building Trades and Union Power in the Progressive Era*. Urbana: University of Illinois Press, 1987.

Keyssar, Alexander. *Out of Work: The First Century of Unemployment in Massachusetts*. New York: Cambridge University Press, 1986.

Lynd, Robert, and Helen Lynd. *Middletown: A Study in Contemporary American Culture*. New York: Harcourt Brace, 1929.

McCartin, Joseph. *Labor's Great War: The Struggle for Industrial Democracy and the Origins of Modern American Labor Relations, 1912–1921*. Chapel Hill: University of North Carolina Press, 1997.

Morris, James O. *Conflict Within the AFL: A Study of Craft versus Industrial Unionism, 1901–1938*. Ithaca: Cornell University Press, 1958.

Nelson, Daniel. *Frederick W. Taylor and Scientific Management*. Madison: University of Wisconsin Press, 1980.

———. *Managers and Workers: The Origins of the New Factory System in the United States, 1880–1920*. Madison: University of Wisconsin Press, 1975.

Russell, Francis. *A City in Terror: 1919, The Boston Police Strike*. New York: Viking Press, 1975.

Zieger, Robert. *Republicans and Labor, 1919–1929*. Lexington: University of Kentucky Press, 1969.

Zunz, Olivier. *The Changing Face of Inequality: Urbanization, Industrial Development, and Immigration in Detroit, 1880–1920*. Chicago: University of Chicago Press, 1983.

AMERICAN LABOR, THE DEPRESSION, THE NEW DEAL, AND WORLD WAR II

Alinsky, Saul. *John L. Lewis: An Unauthorized Biography*. New York: Putnam, 1949.

Atleson, James B. *Labor and the Wartime State: Labor Relations and Law During World War II*. Urbana: University of Illinois Press, 1998.

Auerbach, Jerold S. *Labor and Liberty: The LaFollette Committee and the New Deal*. Indianapolis: Bobbs-Merrill, 1966.

Bakke, E.W. *The Unemployed Worker: A Study of the Task of Making a Living Without a Job*. New Haven, Conn.: Yale University Press, 1940.

Bernstein, Irving. *A Caring Society: the New Deal, the Workers, and the Great Depression: A History of the American Worker, 1933–1941*. Boston: Houghton Mifflin, 1985.

———. *Turbulent Years: A History of the American Worker, 1933–1941*. Boston: Houghton Mifflin, 1969.

Cohen, Lizabeth. *Making a New Deal: Industrial Workers in Chicago, 1919–1939*. New York: Cambridge University Press, 1990.

Dubofsky, Melvin, and Warren Van Tine. *John L. Lewis: A Biography*. Ann Arbor: University of Michigan Press, 1969.

Fine, Sidney. *The Automobile Under the Blue Eagle: Labor, Management, and the Automobile Manufacturing Code*. Ann Arbor: University of Michigan Press, 1963.

———. *Sit-Down: The General Motors Strike of 1936–1937*. Ann Arbor: University of Michigan Press, 1969.

Friedlander, Peter. *The Emergence of a UAW Local, 1936–1939*. Pittsburgh: University of Pittsburgh Press, 1975.

Galenson, Walter. *The CIO Challenge to the AFL: A History of the American Labor Movement, 1935–1941*. Cambridge, Mass.: Harvard University Press, 1960.

Gerstle, Gary. *Working-Class Americanism: The Politics of Labor in a Textile City, 1914–1960*. New York: Cambridge University Press, 1989.

Gross, James A. *The Making of the National Labor Relations Board*. Albany: SUNY Press, 1974.

Hodges, James A. *New Deal Labor Policy and the Southern Cotton Textile Industry, 1933–1941*. Knoxville: University of Tennessee Press, 1986.

Horowitz, Roger. *"Negro and White, Unite and Fight": A Social History of Industrial Unionism in Meatpacking, 1930–1990*. Urbana: University of Illinois Press, 1997.

Leab, Daniel J. *A Union of Individuals: The Formation of the American Newspaper Guild, 1933–1936*. New York: Columbia University Press, 1970.

Lens, Sidney. *The Labor Wars: From the Molly Maguires to the Sitdowns*. Garden City: Doubleday, 1973.

Lichtenstein, Nelson. *Labor's War at Home: The CIO in World War II*. New York: Cambridge University Press, 1982.

Lynd, Robert, and Helen Lynd. *Middletown in Transition*. New York: Harcourt Brace, 1937.

Meier, August, and Elliott Rudwick. *Black Detroit and the Rise of the UAW*. New York: Oxford University Press, 1979.

Mortimer, Wyndham. *Organize!: My Life as a Union Man*. Boston: Beacon Press, 1971.

Nelson, Bruce. *Workers on the Waterfront: Seamen, Longshoremen, and Unionism in the 1930s*. Urbana: University of Illinois Press, 1988.

Plotke, David. *Building a Democratic Political Order: Reshaping American Liberalism in the 1930s and 1940s*. New York: Cambridge University Press, 1996.

Schatz, Ronald W. *The Electrical Workers: A History of Labor at General Electric and Westinghouse, 1923–1960*. Urbana: University of Illinois Press, 1983.

Zieger, Robert. *The CIO, 1935–1955*. Chapel Hill: University of North Carolina Press, 1995.

AMERICAN LABOR FROM 1945 TO 1980

Aronowitz, Stanley. *False Promises: The Making of American Working-Class Consciousness*. New York: McGraw Hill, 1973.

Berger, Bennett. *Working-Class Suburb: A Study of Autoworkers in Suburbia*. Berkeley: University of California Press, 1960.

Boyle, Kevin. *The UAW and the Heyday of American Liberalism, 1945–1968*. Ithaca: Cornell University Press, 1995.

Cochran, Bert. *Labor and Communism: The Conflict that Shaped American Unions*. Princeton: Princeton University Press, 1977.

Filipelli, Ronald L., and Mark D. McColloch. *Cold War in the Working Class: The Rise and Decline of the United Electrical Workers*. Albany: SUNY Press, 1995.

Fine, Sidney. *"Without Blare of Trumpets": Walter Drew, the National Erectors' Association, and the Open Shop Movement, 1903–1957*. Ann Arbor: University of Michigan Press, 1995.

Jacoby, Sanford. *Modern Manors: Welfare Capitalism Since the New Deal*. Princeton, N.J.: Princeton University Press, 1997.

Keeran, Roger. *The Communist Party and the Autoworkers Unions*. Bloomington: Indiana University Press, 1980.

Kornblum, William. *Blue-Collar Community*. Chicago: University of Chicago Press, 1974.

Levenstein, Harvey. *Communism, Anticommunism, and the CIO*. Westport: Greenwood Press, 1981.

Lichtenstein, Nelson. *State of the Union: A Century of American Labor.* Princeton, N.J.: Princeton University Press, 2002.

Meister, Dick, and Anne Loftis. *A Long Time Coming: The Struggle to Unionize America's Farm Workers.* New York: Macmillan, 1977.

Montgomery, David. *Workers' Control in America: Studies in the History of Work, Technology, and Labor Struggles.* Cambridge: Cambridge University Press, 1979.

Taft, Philip. *Organizing Dixie: Alabama Workers in the Industrial Era.* Westport: Greenwood Press, 1981.

Terkel, Studs. *Working.* New York: Pantheon Books, 1974.

AMERICAN LABOR 1980 TO THE PRESENT

Bensman, David, and Roberta Lynch. *Rusted Dreams: Hard Times in a Steel Community.* New York: McGraw-Hill, 1987.

Fink, Leon, and Brian Greenberg. *Upheaval in the Quiet Zone: A History of the Hospital Workers' Union, Local 1199.* Urbana: University of Illinois Press, 1989.

Geoghegan, Thomas. *Which Side Are You On?: Trying to Be For Labor When It's Flat on Its Back.* New York: Farrar, Strauss, Giroux, 1992.

Goldfield, Michael. *The Decline of Organized Labor in the United States.* Chicago: University of Chicago Press, 1987.

Gross, James. *Broken Promise: The Subversion of United States Labor Relations Policy, 1947–1995.* Philadelphia: Temple University Press, 1995.

Milkman, Ruth. *Farewell to the Factory: Auto Workers in the Late Twentieth Century.* Berkeley: University of California Press, 1997.

Moody, Kim. *An Injury to All: The Decline of American Unionism.* New York: Verso, 1988.

———. *Workers in a Lean World.* New York: Verso, 1997.

Parker, Mike, and Jane Slaughter. *Choosing Sides: Unions and the Team Concept.* Boston: South End Press, 1988.

Rosenblum, Jonathan D. *Copper Crucible: How the Arizona Miners' Strike of 1983 Recast Labor-Management Relations in America.* Ithaca: ILR Press, 1995.

Rosner, David. *Deadly Dust: Silicosis and the Politics of Occupational Disease in Twentieth-Century America.* Princeton, N.J.: Princeton University Press, 1991.

Sellers, Christopher C. *Hazards of the Job: From Industrial Disease to Environmental Health Science.* Chapel Hill: University of North Carolina Press, 1997.

Sugrue, Thomas J. *The Origins of the Urban Crisis: Race and Inequality in Postwar Detroit.* Princeton, N.J.: Princeton University Press, 1996.

Weiler, Paul C. *Governing the Workplace: The Future of Labor and Employment Law.* Cambridge, Mass.: Harvard University Press, 1990.

AFRICAN AMERICAN LABOR AND RACE

Arneson, Eric. *Brotherhoods of Color: Black Railroad Workers and the Struggle for Equality.* Cambridge, Mass.: Harvard University Press, 2001.

Asher, Robert, and Charles Stephenson, eds. *Labor Divided: Labor and Ethnicity in United States Labor Struggles, 1835–1960.* Albany: State University of New York Press, 1990.

Foner, Philip. *Organized Labor and the Black Worker, 1619–1973*. New York: Praeger Books, 1974.

Foner, Philip, and Ronald L. Lewis, eds. *Black Workers: A Documentary History From Colonial Times to the Present*. Philadelphia: Temple University Press, 1989.

Harris, William. *The Harder We Run: Black Workers Since the Civil War*. New York: Oxford Press, 1982.

———. *Keeping the Faith: A. Philip Randolph, Milton P. Webster, and the Brotherhood of Pullman Car Porters, 1925–1937*. Urbana: University of Illinois Press, 1997.

Hill, Herbert. "The Problem of Race in American Labor History." *Reviews in American History* 24 (1996): 189–208.

Honey, Michael K. *Southern Labor and Black Civil Rights: Organizing Memphis Workers*. Urbana: University of Illinois Press, 1993.

Letwin, Daniel. *The Challenge of Interracial Unionism: Alabama Coal Miners, 1878–1921*. Chapel Hill: University of North Carolina Press, 1998.

Mason, Patrick L., ed., *African Americans, Labor, and Society: Organizing for a New Agenda*. Detroit: Wayne State University Press, 2000.

Nelson, Bruce. *Divided We Stand: American Workers and the Struggle for Black Equality*. Princeton, N.J.: Princeton University Press, 2000.

Rachleff, Peter. *Black Labor in Richmond, 1865–1890*. Urbana: University of Illinois Press, 1989.

Roediger, David. *The Wages of Whiteness: Race and the Making of the American Working Class*. London: Verso, 1991.

Santino, Jack. *Miles of Smiles, Years of Struggle: Stories of Black Pullman Porters*. Urbana: University of Illinois Press, 1991.

Stromquist, Shelton, and Marvin Bergman, eds. *Unionizing the Jungles: Labor and Community in the Twentieth Century Meatpacking Industry*. Iowa City: University of Iowa Press, 1997.

ETHNICITY AND LABOR

Bodnar, John. *Immigration and Industrialization: Ethnicity in an American Milltown*. Pittsburgh: University of Pittsburgh Press, 1977.

———, et al. *Lives of Their Own: Blacks, Italians, and Poles in Pittsburgh, 1900–1960*. Urbana: University of Illinois Press, 1982.

Buhle, Paul, and Dan Georgakas, eds. *The Immigrant Left in the United States*. Albany: SUNY Press, 1996.

Chan, Sucheng. *This Bittersweet Soil: The Chinese in California Agriculture*. Berkeley: University of California Press, 1986.

Deutsch, Sarah. *No Separate Refuge: Culture, Class, and Gender on an Anglo-Hispanic Frontier in the American Southwest, 1880–1940*. New York: Oxford University Press, 1987.

Foley, Neil. *The White Scourge: Mexicans, Blacks, and Poor Whites in Texas Cotton Culture*. Berkeley: University of California Press, 1997.

Friday, Chris. *Organizing Asian American Labor: The Pacific Coast Salmon Industry, 1870–1942*. Philadelphia: Temple University Press, 1994.

Greene, Victor. *The Slavic Community on Strike: Immigrant Labor in Pennsylvania Anthracite*. South Bend: University of Notre Dame Press, 1968.

Griffen, Clyde, and Sally Griffen. *Natives and Newcomers: The Ordering of Opportunity in Mid-Nineteenth Century Pittsburgh*. Cambridge: Harvard University Press, 1978.

Guerin-Gonzalez, Camille. *Mexican Workers and American Dreams: Immigration, Repatriation, and California Farm Labor, 1900–1939*. New Brunswick: Rutgers University Press, 1994.

Haveven, Tamara. *Family Time and Industrial Time: The Relationship Between Family and Work in a New England Industrial Community*. New York: Cambridge University Press, 1982.

Ichioka, Yuji. *The Issei: The World of First-Generation Japanese Immigrants, 1885–1924*. Berkeley: University of California Press, 1988.

Kessner, Thomas. *The Golden Door: Italian and Jewish Immigrant Mobility in New York City, 1880–1915*. New York: Oxford University Press, 1977.

Korman, Gerd. *Industrialization, Immigrants and Americanizers: The View from Milwaukee*. Madison: State Historical Society of Wisconsin, 1967.

Morawska, Ewa T. *For Bread with Butter: The Life-Worlds of East Central Europeans in Johnstown, Pennsylvania, 1890–1940*. New York: Cambridge University Press, 1985.

Weber, Devra. *Dark Sweat, White Gold: California Farm Workers, Cotton, and the New Deal*. Berkeley: University of California Press, 1994.

GENDER AND LABOR

Baron, Ava. *Work Engendered: Toward a New History of American Labor*. Ithaca, N.Y.: Cornell University Press, 1991.

Baxandall, Rosalyn, and Linda Gordon, eds. *America's Working Women: A Documentary History 1600 to the Present*. New York: W. W. Norton, 1995.

Benson, Susan Porter. *Counter Cultures: Saleswomen, Managers, and Customers in American Department Stores, 1890–1940*. Urbana: University of Illinois Press, 1986.

Blewett, Mary H. *Men, Women, and Work: Class, Gender, and Protest in the New England Shoe Industry, 1780–1910*. Urbana: University of Illinois Press, 1990.

Buhle, Mari Jo. *Women and American Socialism 1870–1920*. Urbana: University of Illinois Press, 1983.

Foner, Philip S. *Women and the American Labor Movement: From the First Trade Unions to the Present*. New York: Free Press, 1982.

Gabin, Nancy. *Feminism and the Labor Movement: Women and the United Auto Workers, 1935–1975*. Ithaca, N.Y.: Cornell University Press, 1990.

Glenn, Susan A. *Daughters of the Shetl: Life and Labor in the Immigrant Generation*. Ithaca, N.Y.: Cornell University Press, 1990.

Groneman, Carol, and Mary Beth Norton. *"To Toil the Livelong Day": America's Women at Work, 1780–1980*. Ithaca, N.Y.: Cornell University Press, 1987.

Jones, Jaqueline. *Labor of Love, Labor of Sorrow: Black Women, Work and Family, from Slavery to the Present*. New York: Vintage Books, 1985.

Kesler-Harris, Alice. *Out to Work: A History of Wage-Earning Women in the United States*. Oxford: Oxford University Press, 1982.

Milkman, Ruth. *Women, Work, and Protest: A Century of U.S. Women's Labor History*. London: Routledge, 1987.

Strasser, Susan. *Never Done: A History of American Housework.* New York: Pantheon, 1982.

LAW, LABOR, AND THE STATE

Carrell, Michael R., and Christina Heavrin. *Labor Relations and Collective Bargaining: Cases, Practices, and Law.* Upper Saddle River, N.J.: Pearson Education, 2000.

Cihon, Patrick J., and James O. Castanega. *Employment and Labor Law.* Mason, Ohio: South-Western Publishing, 2001.

Dubofsky, Melvyn. *The State and Labor in Modern America.* Chapel Hill: University of North Carolina Press, 1994.

Feldpacker, Bruce. *Labor Guide to Labor Law.* Upper Saddle River, N.J.: Pearson Education, 1999.

Fick, Barbara J. *The American Bar Association Guide to Workplace Law: Everything You Need to Know about Your Rights as an Employee or Employer.* New York: Random House, 1997.

Sack, Steven M. *The Employee Rights Handbook.* New York: Warner, 2000.

Sexton, Patricia Cayo. *The War on Labor and the Left: Understanding America's Unique Conservatism.* Boulder, Colo.: Westview Press, 1991.

LEADERS OF LABOR

The single best source with which to begin a search on any American labor leader is Gary M. Fink, ed., Biographical Dictionary of American Labor Leaders, *Westport, Conn.: Greenwood Press, 1974. There are also fifteen insightful profiles in Melvyn Dubofsky and Warren Van Tine, eds.,* Labor Leaders in America, *Urbana: University of Illinois Press, 1987. Profiles of prominent radicals often appear in Mari Jo Buhle, Paul Buhle, and Dan Georgakas,* Encyclopedia of the American Left, *Urbana: University of Illinois Press, 1992. Below are biographies and autobiographies of some of the individuals who appear in these volumes.*

Anderson, Jervis A. A. *Philip Randolph: A Biographical Portrait.* Berkeley: University of California Press, 1990.

Atkinson, Linda. *Mother Jones: The Most Dangerous Woman in America.* New York: Crown, 1978.

Barnard, John. *Walter Reuther and the Rise of the Auto Workers.* Boston: Little, Brown, and Company, 1982.

Buhle, Paul. *Taking Care of Business: Samuel Gompers, George Meany, Lane Kirkland, and the Tragedy of American Labor.* New York: Monthly Review, 1999.

Camp, Helen. *Iron in Her Soul: Elizabeth Gurley Flynn and the American Left.* Pullman: Washington State University Press, 1995.

Ferris, Susan, Ricardo Sandoval, and Diana Hembree. *The Fight in the Fields: Cesar Chavez and the Farmworkers Movement.* New York: Harcourt, 1998.

Foner, Philip S., ed. *The Autobiographies of the Haymarket Martyrs.* New York: Monad, 1983.

Garrison, Dee. *Mary Heaton Vorse: The Life of an American Insurgent.* Philadelphia: Temple University Press, 1989.

Goldman, Emma. *Living My Life*. 2 vols. 1931. Reprint, New York: Dover, 1970.

Haywood, William. *The Autobiography of Big Bill Haywood*. 1929. Reprint, New York: International, 1966.

Jones, Mary. *The Autobiography of Mother Jones*. 1925. Reprint, Chicago: Charles Kerr Publishing, 1980.

Kaufman, Stuart, ed. *The Samuel Gompers Papers*. Vols. 1–9. Urbana: University of Illinois Press, 1986–.

Lichtenstein, Nelson. *Walter Reuther: The Most Dangerous Man in Detroit*. Urbana: University of Illinois Press, 1995.

Livesay, Harold. *Samuel Gompers and Organized Labor in America*. Boston: Little, Brown, and Company, 1978.

Phelan, Craig. *Grand Master Workman: Terence Powderly and the Knights of Labor*. Westport, Conn.: Greenwood Press, 2000.

———. *William Green: Biography of a Labor Leader*. Albany: State University of New York Press, 1989.

Powderly, Terence. *The Path I Trod: The Autobiography of Terence V. Powderly*. New York: Columbia University Press, 1940.

Reuther, Victor. *The Brothers Reuther and the Story of the UAW: A Memoir*. Boston: Houghton Mifflin, 1976.

Salvatore, Nick. *Eugene Debs: Citizen and Socialist*. Urbana: University of Illinois Press, 1982.

———, ed. *Seventy Years of Life and Labor: An Autobiography of Samuel Gompers*. Ithaca, N.Y.: Cornell University Press, 1984.

Seretan, L. Gene. *Daniel DeLeon: The Odyssey of an American Marxist*. Cambridge, Mass.: Harvard University Press, 1979.

Shulman, Alix Kates. *Red Emma Speaks: Selected Writings and Speeches by Emma Goldman*. New York: Random House, 1972.

Smith, Gibbs. *Joe Hill*. Salt Lake City: Peregrine Smith, 1984.

Wathen, Cindy, ed. *Remembering Cesar: The Legacy of Cesar Chavez*. Sanger, Calif.: Quill Driver Books, 2000.

Zipser, Arthur. *Workingclass Giant*. New York: International Publishers, 1981.

MEDIA, MUSIC, THE ARTS, AND LABOR

Boris, Eileen. *Art and Labor: Ruskin, Morris, and the Craftsman Ideal in America*. Philadelphia: Temple University Press, 1986.

Denisoff, R. Serge. *Great Day Coming: Folk Music and the American Left*. Baltimore: Penguin Books, 1973.

Foner, Philip S. *American Labor Songs of the 19th Century*. Urbana: University of Illinois Press, 1975.

Foner, Philip S., and Reinhard Schultz. *The Other America: Art and Labour [sic] in the United States*. West Nyack, N.Y.: Journeyman Press, 1985.

Godfried, Nathan. *WCFL: Chicago's Voice of Labor 1926–78*. Urbana: University of Illinois Press, 1997.

Greenway, John. *American Folksongs of Protest*. Philadelphia: University of Pennsylvania Press, 1953.

Halker, Clark D. *For Democracy, Workers, and God: Labor Song-Poems and Labor Protest, 1865–95*. Urbana: University of Illinois Press, 1991.

Lieberman, Robbie. "My *Song Is My Weapon": People's Songs, American Communism, and the Politics of Culture, 1930–50*. Urbana: University of Illinois Press, 1989.
O'Neill, William. *Echoes of Revolt: The Masses 1911–1917*. Chicago: Ivan Dee, 1966.
Ross, Steven J. *Working-Class Hollywood: Silent Film and the Shaping of Class in America*. Princeton, N.J.: Princeton University Press, 1998.
Schnapper, M. B. *American Labor: A Pictorial Social History*. Washington, D.C.: Public Affairs Press, 1972.
Seeger, Pete, and Bob Reiser. *Carry It On!: A History in Song and Picture of America's Working Men and Women*. New York: Simon and Schuster, 1985.
Stead, Peter. *Film and the Working Class: The Feature Film in British and American Society*. London: Routledge, 1991.

USEFUL LABOR WEB SITES

American Federation of Labor-Congress of Industrial Organizations (AFL-CIO) Labor History, www.aflcio.org.
American Federation of State, County and Municipal Employees (AFSCME) African American Labor History, www.afscme.org/about/aframlink.htm.
American Federation of State, County and Municipal Employees (AFSCME) Women's Labor History, www.afscme.org/otherlnk/whlinks.htm.
Child Labor Photographs of Lewis W. Hine, 1908–1912, www.boondocksnet.com/gallery/nclc/.
H-Net Bibliography of Comparative Labor History, www.h-net.msu.edu/~labor/threads/thrclhb.html.
Illinois Labor History Society, www.kentlaw.edu/ilhs.
Labor History Manuscripts in the Library of Congress, www.loc.gov/rr/mss/laborlc.html.
Mark Lause, American Labor History: An Online Study Guide, www.geocities.com/CollegePark/Quad/6460/AmLabHist/.
Organization of American Historians' Labor Bibliography, www/oah.org/pubs/magazine/labor/labor-bib.html.
Reference Source List Prepared by Andrew H. Lee, Tamiment Librarian, www.nyu.edu/library/bobst/research/tam/resources.
University of Illinois, Urbana-Champaign, Labor in Illinois, http:www.ilir.uiuc/edu/lii/.
U.S. Department of Labor, www.dol.gov/asp/programs/history/main.htm.
Wisconsin Labor History Society, www.wisconsinlaborhistory.org.

Index

Page numbers in bold indicate main discussion of entry.

List of Contributors

Carolyn Anderson
University of Rhode Island

Michael Bailey
University of Rhode Island

Lisa Barber
Bay Path College

Jaime Barnes
University of Rhode Island

John P. Beck
Michigan State University

Jon Bekken
Editor, *Industrial Worker*

Michele Bernier
Bay Path College

Don Binkowski
National Coalition of Independent Scholars

Mike Bonislawski
Boston College

Kevin Boyle
Ohio State University

Susan Roth Breitzer
University of Iowa

John W. Budd
University of Minnesota

Linnea Goodwin Burwood
State University of New York at Delhi

Stephen Burwood
State University of New York at Geneseo

Amanda Busjit
University of Rhode Island

Victor Caron
University of Rhode Island

John Cashman
Boston College

Bruce Cohen
Worcester State College

Cheryl Conley
Bay Path College

Alex Corlu
State University of New York at Binghamton

Yasmin Correa
Bay Path College

Evan Daniel
United Federation of Teachers

Howard Davis
University of Rhode Island

Dennis A. Deslippe
Australian National University

Timothy Draper
Waubonsee Community College

Babette Faehmel
University of Massachusetts at Amherst

Kenneth Ferus
University of Rhode Island

Pete Gingras
University of Rhode Island

Pauline Gladstone
Bay Path College

Tom Glynn
Rutgers University Libraries

Janet Greenlees
University of Exeter

James P. Hanlan
Worcester Polytechnic Institute

Simon Holzapfel
University of Massachusetts at Amherst

Walter Hourahan
University of Rhode Island

Shalynn Hunt
Bay Path College

Elizabeth Jozwiak
University of Wisconsin-Rock County

Leslie Juntunen
Bay Path College

Andrew E. Kersten
University of Wisconsin at Green Bay

Frank Koscielski
Wayne State University

Albert V. Lannon
Laney College

Penny Lewis
City University of New York

Erik Loomis
University of New Mexico

John F. Lyons
Joliet Junior College

Mark Marianek
University of Missouri

Dinah Mayo
University of Massachusetts at Amherst

Cornelia McAndrew
University of Rhode Island

Joseph A. McCartin
Georgetown University

Jeff McFadden
State University of New York at Binghamton

John McKerley
University of Iowa

Danielle McMullen
University of Rhode Island

Stephen Micelli
University of Toledo

Jay Miller
Wayne State University

Scott Molloy
University of Rhode Island

R. David Myers
The College of Santa Fe

Mitchell Newton-Matza
University of St. Francis

Mark Noon
Bloomsburg University

Kathleen Banks Nutter
Smith College

Chad Pearson
State University of New York at Albany

Sara Pleva
Bay Path College

Cristina Prochilo
National Trust for Historic Preservation

Margaret Raucher
Wayne State University

Jonathan Rees
University of Southern Colorado

Jim Riordan
University of Massachusetts at Amherst

Joseph F. Rodgers
University of Rhode Island

Maria Ruotolo
Bay Path College

Robert D. Sampson
University of Illinois at Urbana-Champaign

Patricia Shackleton
Michigan State University

Ralph Shaffer
California State University at Pomona

Robert Shaffer
Shippensburg University

Susan Sherwood
San Francisco State University

Anthony Silva
National Coalition of Independent Scholars

Edward Slavishak
University of North Carolina at Chapel Hill

T. Jason Soderstrum
Iowa State University

Joseph Turrini
Catholic University of America

Teri Voight
Bay Path College

Carl Weinberg
North Georgia College and State University

Emily Harrison Weir
Mount Holyoke College

Robert E. Weir
Bay Path College

Lisa J. Wells
Memorial University of Newfoundland

John Whitmer
Simpson College

James Wolfinger
Northwestern University

About the Editors

ROBERT E. WEIR is Associate Professor of History and Liberal Studies at Bay Path College. A 2001 Senior Fulbright Scholar, Weir is the author of *Knights Unhorsed: Internal Conflict in a Gilded Age Social Movement* and *Beyond Labor's Veil: the Culture of the Knights of Labor.*

JAMES P. HANLAN is Associate Professor of History and Secretary of the Faculty of Humanities and Arts at Worcester Polytechnic Institute. He is the author of *The Working Population of Manchester, New Hampshire, 1840–1866.*